PURCHASING AND MATERIALS MANAGEMENT

PURCHASING AND MATERIALS MANAGEMENT

MICHIEL R. LEENDERS, PMAC Fellow

Professor and Chairman, Operations Management
School of Business Administration
University of Western Ontario

HAROLD E. FEARON, C.P.M.

Professor and Chairman
Department of Management
Arizona State University

WILBUR B. ENGLAND, C.P.M.

Sebastian S. Kresge Professor of Marketing Emeritus
Graduate School of Business Administration
Harvard University

1980   Seventh edition

RICHARD D. IRWIN, INC.   Homewood, Illinois   60430

Earlier editions of this book were published under the titles
Procurement: Principles and Cases and *Modern Procurement
Management: Principles and Cases.*

© RICHARD D. IRWIN, INC., 1948, 1952, 1957, 1962, 1970, 1975, and 1980

ISBN 0-256-02374-3
Library of Congress Catalog Card No. 79–91639

Printed in the United States of America

4 5 6 7 8 9 0 MP 7 6 5 4 3 2

PREFACE

Business conditions during the last decade placed as much, if not more, strain and pressure on the purchasing/materials management function as has occurred at any time in the 20th century. Critical material shortages, two-digit inflation, and arbitrary actions by governments seriously interfered with the orderly operation of business and the economy.

Many managers became painfully aware of the shortcomings of the operations of their purchasing/materials management functions. Past indifference to proper placement of the function in the organization structure and failure to staff with highly competent professional buyers have proved to be costly oversights.

The objective behind the writing of earlier editions of this book initiated by the late Professor Howard T. Lewis in the 1930s, 40s, and early 50s was to provide carefully researched text materials about the organization and operation of the procurement function, along with cases detailing actual business experiences in procurement operations. This objective was continued from the middle 1950s to the middle 1970s by Wilbur B. England and is further strengthened in this seventh edition by the work of coauthor Harold E. Fearon.

The primary emphasis continues on the acquisition of materials, parts, equipment, and services for further manufacture or end use in the organization rather than purchasing for resale. The authors are fully satisfied that the materials area will continue to provide exciting management career opportunities for those who are able to bring imagination and aggressiveness to bear on the continuing challenges of marrying evolving needs with a capricious market.

New chapters in this edition cover transportation and public purchasing, both areas of growing interest. Major text revisions have been made in every chapter to reflect the changes which have occurred in the purchasing materials management function since 1975. Every effort has been made to condense the material, and make the readings simpler and more enjoyable. This shorter text also reflects our growing concern with energy and material shortages, inflation, and the continuing need to consider ethical, social, and environmental concerns. Review and discussion questions have been added at the end of every chapter to assist readers in self-evaluation, and to provide a starting point for class review. A number of very short cases and exercises have been substituted for the traditional longer cases. Thus, in every chapter there is at least one very short case or exercise followed by some a little longer, and a bit more complex. In total, there are about two dozen new cases and exercises in this book, all of which have been researched and written within the past two years. The case problems are copyrighted by the President and Fellows of Harvard College and The University of Western Ontario and are used with their respective permissions.

The evaluation and feedback from educators who use this text and cases has always been a valuable guide in revisions. For this edition the authors would like to acknowledge the thoughtful comments by Robert B. Monczka and Richard L. Shell, and all teachers of the Principles of Buying course.

Gratitude is also expressed to Lawrence E. Fouraker of the Harvard Business School; to C. B. Johnson of the School of Business Administration, The University of Western Ontario; and to Glenn D. Overman, of the College of Business Administration, Arizona State University, for assistance and understanding support.

Relevant cases based on actual situations are not possible without the wholehearted cooperation of many managers. We are grateful for their help and cooperation, as well as the assistance of many of our colleagues, past and present.

The burden of the secretarial work has been borne by Peggy J. Bateman, Lucy Tom, Evelyn Gaskell, and Chris Gibson, and we are indebted to them for the dedicated manner in which they carried out this responsibility.

We also appreciate the forbearance of our families who were willing to play the role of "book widows and orphans."

As is customary, the blame for any errors or shortcomings is the responsibility of the authors.

March 1980   Michiel R. Leenders
                                                             Harold E. Fearon
                                                             Wilbur B. England

CONTENTS

Definition of need—function. Suitability. Reliability. Quality. Decision on "best buy." Importance of service in determining quality. Responsibility for determining quality. Responsibility of purchasing personnel. Purchase analysis section. Description of quality. Description by brand. Description by specification. Specification by physical or chemical characteristics. Specification by material and method of manufacture. Sources of specification data. Standard specifications. Standardization and simplification. Specification by performance. Specification to meet government legal requirements. Description by engineering drawing. Miscellaneous methods of description. Combination of methods of description. Metric conversion. Control of quality—inspection and testing: *Inspection of purchased items. What is reasonable inspection? Specification of inspection method. Quality control department. Inspection at the seller's premises. The quality capability survey. Commercial testing labs and services. Inspection methods. Process quality control. Output inspection—100 percent inspection and sampling. Operating characteristic curves. Sequential sampling. Computer programs. Responsibility for adjustments and returns. Importance of inspection records. Zero defects programs.*

Quantity considerations. Forecasting. Forecasting techniques. Product explosion and requirement accumulation. ABC analysis. Definition of inventory policy. Inventories: Their functions, forms, and control. Why do inventories exist? What functions do inventories provide? Inventory forms. Inventory function and form framework. Transit inventories. Cycle inventories. Buffer inventories. Anticipation inventories. Spare parts inventory. Decoupling inventory. Implications for the control of inventories. The price-discount problem. Inventory models. Use of integrated data processing systems. Stores. Materials requirements planning (MRP). Conclusion.

Introduction. The supplier selection decision. Necessity for supplier goodwill. Qualifications of a good supplier. Sources of information about suppliers. Supplier evaluation—existing and potential sources. Vendor rating and evaluation. Evaluation of potential sources. Financial evaluation. Management evaluation. Concentration of purchases with one source. Purchase through manufacturer or distributor. Geographical location of sources. Reciprocity. Attitude toward gratuities. Joint purchasing with supplier. Purchasing for company personnel. Social, political, and environmental concerns. Supplier development: *The need for supplier development. The supplier development*

PURCHASING AND MATERIALS MANAGEMENT IN THE DECADE OF THE 1980s

 Effective management of materials and purchasing can contribute significantly to the success of most modern organizations. This text will explore the nature of this contribution and the management requirements for effective and efficient performance. The acquisition of materials, supplies, services, and equipment—of the right qualities, in the right quantities, at the right prices, at the right time, and on a continuing basis—long has occupied the attention of many managers in both the public and private sectors. The rapidly changing supply scene, with cycles of abundance and shortages, varying prices, lead times, and availabilities, provides a continuing challenge to those organizations wishing to obtain a maximum contribution from this area.

Prior to World War I, most firms regarded the purchasing function primarily as a clerical activity. However, during the time periods of World War I and World War II, the success of a firm was not dependent on what it could sell, since the market was almost unlimited. Instead, the ability to obtain from vendors the raw materials, supplies, and services needed to keep the factories and mines operating was the key determinant of organizational success. Attention was given to the organization, policies, and procedures of the purchasing function, and it emerged as a recognized managerial activity. During the 1950s and 1960s, purchasing continued to gain stature as the techniques for performing the function became more refined and as the supply of people trained and competent to make sound purchasing decisions increased. Many companies elevated the chief purchasing officer to top management status, with titles such as Vice President of Purchasing, Director of Materials, or Vice President of Purchasing and Supply.

As the decade of the 70s opened, organizations faced two vexing problems: an international shortage of almost all the basic raw materials needed to support operations, and a rate of price increases far above the norm since the end of World War II. The Middle East oil embargo during the summer of 1973 intensified both the shortages and the price escalation. These developments put the spotlight directly on purchasing departments, for their performance in obtaining needed items from vendors at realistic prices spelled the difference between suc-

1

cess or failure. This emphasized again to top management the crucial role played by purchasing. As we move into the decade of the 1980s, it has become clear that organizations must have a capable, efficient purchasing and materials function. Additionally, the purchasing department should play a key role in combatting inflation by resisting unwarranted price hikes.

Growing management interest through necessity and improved insight into the opportunities in the materials area has resulted in a variety of organizational concepts. Terms like purchasing, procurement, supply, material, materials management, and logistics are used almost interchangeably. No agreement exists on the definition of each of these terms, and managers in public and private institutions may have identical responsibilities but substantially different titles. The following definitions may be helpful in sorting out the more common understanding of the various terms.

In general usage, the term *purchasing* describes the process of buying: learning of the need, locating and selecting a supplier, negotiating price and other pertinent terms, and following up to ensure delivery. *Procurement* is a somewhat broader term, and includes purchasing, stores, traffic, receiving, incoming inspection, and salvage.

Supply is often used in North America by industrial concerns to cover the stores function of internally consumed items like stationery and office supplies. In the United Kingdom and Europe the term supply has a broader meaning to include at least purchasing, stores, and receiving. In the governmental sector, supply also has this broader interpretation. In Canada, for example, the Department of Supply and Services is responsible for procurement in the federal government. *Material* has a military or governmental connotation and often includes the same functions as those identified under materials management.

An organization which has adopted the materials management organizational concept will have a single manager responsible for the planning, organizing, motivating, and controlling of all those activities principally concerned with the flow of materials into an organization. Materials management views material flows as a system. Another way to look at materials management is to indicate its major activities:

1. Anticipating material requirements.
2. Sourcing and obtaining materials.
3. Introducing materials into the organization.
4. Monitoring the status of materials as a current asset.

The specific functions which might be included under the materials manager are material planning and control, production scheduling, material and purchasing research, purchasing, incoming traffic, inventory control, receiving, incoming quality control, stores, in-plant materials movement, and scrap and surplus disposal. Not all 11 functions are necessarily included; the ones often excluded are production scheduling, in-plant materials movement, and incoming quality control.

Adoption of the materials management concept largely grew out of problems in the airframe industry during World War II. Production of an aircraft requires a large number of individual items, many of which are quite sophisticated and must meet stringent quality standards, procured from thousands of vendors located over a wide geographic area. Each item is vital to the total functioning of the end product. The objectives of materials management are to solve materials problems from a total company viewpoint (optimize) by *coordinating* performance of the various materials functions; providing a *communications* network; and *controlling* materials flow. As the computer was introduced into organizations, this provided a further reason to adopt materials management, for the materials functions have many common data needs and can share a common data base.

Logistics has its origin near the year 1670, when a new staff structure proposed for the French army included the position of "Marechal General des Logis," who was responsible for supply, transportation, selecting camps, and adjusting marches.[1] Although logistics long has been a military term, its application to nonmilitary management occurred primarily in the 1960s and included: "the optimum co-ordination of the inbound raw material movements, raw material storage, work in process handling, and of the outbound packaging, warehousing of finished products, and movements of finished products to the customer."[2] Although the logistics concept is attractive from a theoretical point of view, encompassing the complete systems approach, two major problems of implementation still exist: first is the ability of a logistics manager to handle a job with this scope, crossing so many traditional lines of organizational authority and responsibility, and second is the current state of computer software systems.[3] This text will cover primarily those functions normally included in the purchasing and materials management definitions. The activities usually included in physical distribution management, such as determining finished goods inventory levels, finished goods warehouse locations, and levels of inventory; outbound transportation; packaging; and customer repair parts, warranty, and installation service, will receive no special coverage. Our main concern is the inflow of goods and services, rather than the outflow. Even within the materials management area, greater emphasis will be placed on areas like source selection and determining the price to be paid than on inventory control and traffic.

What is currently feasible or desirable in one organization may not be applicable in another, for sound reasons. The relative importance of the area compared to the other prime functions of the organization will be a major determinant of the management attention it will receive. How to assess the materials needs of a particular organization in context is one of the purposes of this book. Cases are provided to illustrate a variety of situations and to give practice in resolving managerial problems.

---

[1] J. D. Little, *The Military Staff, Its History and Development*, 3d ed. (Harrisburg, Pa.: Stackpole Co., 1961), pp. 48–49.

[2] E. G. Plowman, *Elements of Business Logistics* (Stanford, Calif.: Stanford Graduate School of Business, 1964).

[3] H. E. Fearon, "Materials Management: A Synthesis and Current View," *Journal of Purchasing* 9 (February 1973): 28–47.

SIGNIFICANCE OF MATERIAL DOLLARS

U.S. manufacturing firms purchased materials totaling $681 billion in 1976. Capital expenditures amounted to another $40 billion. By 1985 these figures probably will have doubled. The magnitude of these figures emphasizes the importance to the U.S. economy of performing the purchasing function in the most effective manner possible.

Purchasing is the largest single dollar control area with which most managements must deal. Obviously, the percent of the sales or income dollar which is paid out to vendors will vary greatly from industry to industry. For example, in a + hospital, airline, or bank, purchasing dollars as a percent of operating income will be less than 20 percent, since these industries are labor, rather than material, intensive. But in the manufacturing sector, material dollars typically account for well over half of the sales dollar. When an automobile producer sells a new car to a dealer for $6,000, it already has spent over $3,000 (over 50 percent) to buy the steel, tires, glass, paint, fabric, aluminum, copper, and electronic components necessary to build that car. When a soft drink producer sells $1,000 of packaged beverage to the supermarket, it already has paid to vendors close to $750 for the liquid sugar, carbonation, flavoring, bottles, caps, and cardboard containers necessary to make the end product.

Table 1–1, using data collected by the U.S. Bureau of the Census for their *Annual Survey of Manufacturers,* presents aggregate purchase/sales data for the entire U.S. manufacturing sector, broken down by type of industry. These figures show that in the average manufacturing firm, materials account for 57 percent of the sales dollar; if expenditures for capital equipment are included, this percentage goes up to 61 percent. This is about one-and-a-half times the remaining 39 percent available to pay salaries, wages, other operating expenses, taxes, and dividends. The material/sales ratio varies dramatically among industries. For example, in standard industrial classification 38, "Instruments and Related Products" it is only 36 percent, but this industry includes firms making items such as the autopilot used on large commercial aircraft, which requires a high percentage of engineering, quality control, and direct assembly labor. On the other hand, in SIC 20, "Food and Kindred Products," it is 71 percent. This industry includes commercial bread bakeries and beverage producers, whose production process is material intensive and requires a minimum amount of labor cost due to use of highly mechanized/automated manufacturing processes. Table 1–1 shows that the average material/sales ratio in manufacturing has moved up from 53 percent to 57 percent in 1976, as manufacturing processes have become more material, and less labor, intensive. Any function of the firm which accounts for the use of over half of the firm's receipts certainly deserves a great deal of managerial attention!

Decision making in the materials management context

One of the challenging aspects of the materials management function to its practitioners is the variety and nature of the decisions encountered. Should we make or buy? Must we inventory materials and how much? What price shall we pay? Where shall we place this order? What should the order size be? When will we require the material? Which alternative looks best as an approach to this problem? Which transportation route should we use? Should we make a long- or a short-term contract? Should we cancel? How do we dispose of surplus material? Who will form the negotiation team and what shall its strategy be? How do we protect ourselves for the future? Shall we change operating systems? Should we wait or act now? In view of the trade-offs what is the best decision? What stance do we take regarding our customers who wish to supply us? Do we standardize? Is systems contracting worthwhile here? Decisions like these will have a major impact on the organization. What makes the decisions exciting is that they are almost always made in a context of uncertainty.

Advances in management science in recent decades have substantially enlarged the number of ways in which materials decisions can be analyzed. The basic supplier selection decision is a classical decision tree model as shown in Figure 1–1. This is a choice between alternatives under uncertainty. In this example, the uncertainty relates to our own demand: we are not sure if it will be high, medium, or low. The outcome is concerned with both price and ability to supply. Does the decision maker wish to trade a higher price against supply assurance under all circumstances? That it is difficult to quantify all consequences reinforces the need for sound judgment in key decisions. It also means that the decision maker's perception of the risk involved may in itself be a key variable. Thus, the opportunity is provided to blend managerial judgment, gained through experience and training, with the appropriate decision concepts and techniques.

THE DIFFERENCES BETWEEN COMMERCIAL AND CONSUMER ACQUISITION

Purchasing is a difficult function to understand because almost everyone is familiar with another version, that of personal buying. It is easy for one to presume a familiarity or expertise with the acquisition function for this reason. A consumer point of view is characterized by a shopping basket philosophy. It assumes a retail type of marketing operation where there are many suppliers of relatively common items. Every customer buys on a current need basis and also is the final consumer of the product or service acquired. Some price variation may occur from supplier to supplier depending on what marketing strategy the supplier chooses to follow. The consumer has the freedom to choose the nature and quality of items required and to choose the appropriate supplier. With few exceptions the individual consumer has no power to influence the price, the method of marketing, or the manufacturer chosen by the supplier's management. The individual consumer's total business is a very small portion of the supplier's total sales.

Commercial materials management presents a totally different picture. The needs of most organizations are often specialized and the volumes of purchase tend to be large. The number of potential sources may be small and there may be

Table 1-1
Cost of materials—Value of industry shipments ratios for manufacturing firms, 1976

Standard industrial code	Industry	Cost of materials (millions)*	Capital expenditures, new (millions)†	Total material and capital expenditures (millions)	Value of industry shipments (millions)‡	Material-sales ratio	Total purchase-sales ratio
20	Food and kindred products	128,618	3,817	132,435	180,930	71	73
21	Tobacco products	4,659	130	4,789	8,786	53	55
22	Textile mill products	22,194	1,087	23,281	36,389	61	64
23	Apparel and related products ...	18,150	423	18,573	34,758	52	53
24	Lumber and wood products	18,121	1,232	19,353	31,239	58	62
25	Furniture and fixtures	6,946	295	7,241	14,232	49	51
26	Paper and allied products ...: ..	27,877	3,010	30,887	48,218	58	64
27	Printing and publishing	15,288	1,261	16,549	42,838	36	39
28	Chemicals and allied products ...	53,725	7,122	60,847	104,139	52	58
29	Petroleum and coal products	69,392	2,837	72,229	82,347	84	88
30	Rubber and plastics products	15,885	1,317	17,202	31,765	50	54
31	Leather and leather products	3,691	89	3,780	7,176	51	53
32	Stone, clay, glass products	14,056	1,504	15,560	30,635	46	51
33	Primary metal industries	59,932	4,179	64,111	93,002	64	69

34	Fabricated metal products	38,720	2,223	40,943	77,507	50	53
35	Machinery, except electric	48,648	3,428	52,076	105,525	46	49
36	Electric, electronic equipment	32,831	2,240	35,071	73,867	44	47
37	Transportation equipment	85,892	3,131	89,023	141,026	61	63
38	Instruments and related products	8,989	783	9,772	25,030	36	39
39	Miscellaneous manufacturing	7,580	561	8,141	16,286	47	50
	All operating manufacturing establishments						
	1971	356,016	20,940	379,418	670,970	53	57
	1972	407,395	24,073	431,468	756,467	54	57
	1973	478,279	26,976	505,255	875,245	55	58
	1974	581,580	35,546	617,126	1,017,873	57	61
	1975	597,327	37,262	634,589	1,039,377	57	61
	1976	681,194	40,670	721,864	1,185,695	57	61

*Refers to direct charges actually paid or payable for items consumed or put into production during the year, including freight charges and other direct charges incurred by the establishment in acquiring these materials. It excludes the cost of services used, such as advertising, insurance, telephone, etc., and research, developmental, and consulting services of other establishments. It also excludes materials, machinery, and equipment used in plant expansion or capitalized repairs which are chargeable to fixed assets accounts.

†Includes funds spent for permanent additions and major alterations to plant as well as new machinery and equipment purchases chargeable to a fixed asset account.

‡The received or receivable net selling values, f.o.b. plant, after discounts and allowances, and excluding freight charges and excise taxes.

Source: U.S. Bureau of the Census, *Annual Survey of Manufacturers: 1976* (Washington, D.C.: U.S. Government Printing Office, 1977), General Statistics for Industry Groups, p. 4 and Appendix.

Figure 1–1
Simplified one stage decision tree showing a supplier selection decision

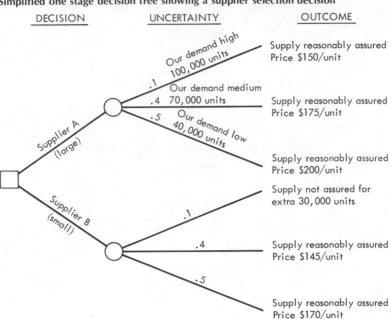

DECISION   UNCERTAINTY   OUTCOME

Our demand high 100,000 units
.1
Supply reasonably assured
Price $150/unit

Our demand medium
.4 70,000 units
Supply reasonably assured
Price $175/unit

.5 Our demand low 40,000 units
Supply reasonably assured
Price $200/unit

Supplier A (large)

Supplier B (small)

.1
Supply not assured for extra 30,000 units

.4
Supply reasonably assured
Price $145/unit

.5
Supply reasonably assured
Price $170/unit

few customers in the total market. Many organizations acting as buyers are larger than their suppliers and may play a multiplicity of roles with respect to their sources. Because large sums of money are involved, suppliers have a large stake in an individual customer and frequently will resort to many kinds of strategies to secure the wanted business. In such an environment, the right to award or with-hold business represents real power. Special expertise is required to assure proper satisfaction of needs on the one hand and the appropriate systems and procedures on the other to assure a continually effective and acceptable performance.

Suppliers spend large sums annually to find ways and means of persuading their customers to buy. Purchasing strength needs to be pitted against this marketing strength to assure that the buying organization's needs of the future are adequately met. The materials function needs to be staffed with people who can counterbalance this marketing force. It is not sufficient in this environment to be only reactionary to outside pressures from suppliers. Foresight and a long-range planning outlook is vital so that future needs can be recognized and met on a planned basis.

CONTRIBUTION OF THE PURCHASING/MATERIALS MANAGEMENT FUNCTION

Performance of the materials function can be viewed in two contexts: trouble avoidance and opportunistic. The trouble avoidance context is the most familiar.

Many people inside the organization are inconvenienced to varying degrees when the materials function does not meet with minimum expectations. Improper quality, wrong quantities, and late delivery may make life miserable for the ultimate user of the product or service. This is so basic and apparent that "no complaints" is assumed to be an indicator of good materials performance. The difficulty is that some users never expect anything more and hence may not receive anything more.

The second context is that of potential contribution to organizational objectives. At least eight major areas of potential contribution are possible: profit leverage, return on assets, information source, effect on efficiency, effect on competitive position, image, training provided, and management strategy and social policy.

Profit-leverage effect

If, through better purchasing, a firm saves $100,000 in the amounts paid to vendors for needed materials supplies and services, that $100,000 savings goes directly to the bottom line (before tax) account on its profit and loss statement. If that same firm sells an additional $100,000 of product, the contribution to profit, assuming a 5 percent before tax profit margin, would be only $5,000. Purchase dollars are high-powered dollars!

Perhaps an example, using a hypothetical manufacturer, would help:

```
Gross Sales . . . . . . . . . . . . . . . . . . . . . . . . . . . . . . . . . . . . . . . . . . . . . . . . . . . . . . . . . . . . . . . . . . .$1,000,000
Purchases (assuming purchases account for 50 percent of the sales dollar) . . . . . . .   500,000
Profit (assuming a before-tax profit margin of 5 percent) . . . . . . . . . . . . . . . . . . . . .    50,000
```

Now, assume this firm were able to reduce its overall purchase cost by 10 percent through better management of the function. This would be a $50,000 additional contribution to before-tax profits. To increase before-tax profits by $50,000 solely through increased sales would require an additional $1,000,000, or a doubling, of sales.

This is not to suggest that it would be easy to reduce overall purchase costs by 10 percent. In a firm which has given major attention to the purchasing function over the years it would be difficult, and perhaps impossible, to do. But, in a firm which has neglected purchasing, it would be a realistic objective. Because of the profit-leverage effect of purchasing, large savings are possible relative to the effort that would be needed to increase sales by the much larger percentage necessary to generate the same effect on the P & L statement. Since, in many firms, sales already has received much more attention, purchasing may be the last untapped "profit producer."

Return-on-assets effect

Firms are increasingly-more interested in return on assets (ROA) as a measure of performance. Figure 1-2 shows the standard ROA model, using the same figures as in the previous example, and assuming, realistically, that inventory

Figure 1–2
Return on assets factors

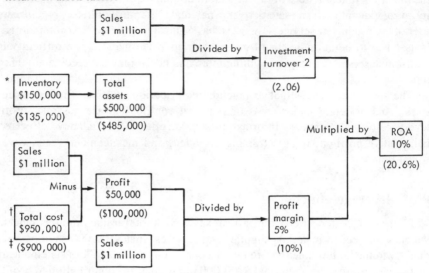

*Inventory is approximately 30 percent of total assets.
†Purchases account for half of total sales, or $500,000.
‡(Figures in parentheses assume a 10 percent reduction in purchase costs.)

accounts for 30 percent of total assets. If purchase costs were reduced by 10 percent, that would effect a 10 percent reduction in the inventory asset base. The numbers in the boxes show the initial figures used in arriving at the 10 percent ROA performance. The numbers below each box are the figures resulting from a 10 percent overall purchase price reduction, and the end product is a new ROA of 20.6 percent. This is a highly-feasible objective for many firms.

Information source

The contacts of the purchasing function in the marketplace provide a logical source of information for various functions within the organization. Primary examples include information about prices, availability of goods, new sources of supply, new products, and new technology, all of interest to many other parts of the organization. New marketing techniques used by suppliers may be of interest to the marketing group. News about major investments, mergers, international political and economic developments, pending bankruptcies, major promotions and appointments, and current and potential customers may be relevant to marketing, finance, research, and top management. New systems of distribution, payment, and materials management may affect the logistics function. Purchasing's unique position vis-a-vis the marketplace should provide a comprehensive listening post.

Effect on efficiency

The effectiveness with which the purchasing function is performed will show up in other operating results. While the firm's accounting system may not be sophisticated enough to identify poor efficiency as having been caused by poor purchase decisions, that very often is the case. If purchasing selects a vendor who fails to deliver raw materials or parts which measure up to the agreed-upon quality standards, this may result in a higher scrap rate or costly rework, requiring excessive direct labor expenditures. If the vendor does not meet the agreed-upon delivery schedule, this may require a costly rescheduling of production, decreasing overall production efficiency, or in the worst case it will result in a shutdown of the production line—and fixed costs continue even though there is no output.

Effect on competitive position

A firm cannot be competitive unless it can deliver end products or services to its customers when they are wanted and at a price the customer feels is fair. If purchasing doesn't do its job, the firm will not have the required materials when needed and at a price needed to keep end-product costs under control.

Some years ago, one of the major automobile producers decided to buy all its auto glass from one firm (a single source). Some months into the supply agreement, it became evident that the forthcoming labor-contract negotiations might result in a deadlock and a long strike. To protect themselves, the auto company built up a 90-day glass stockpile, even though the inventory carrying costs were high and they had problems of finding the physical storage facilities for that much glass. They were right; there was a strike in the glass industry, but the union struck only the glass firm supplying that auto producer. The strike lasted 118 days and the auto producer had to shut down their production lines for over a month.

The auto producer had a large net financial loss that year, since that sales loss dropped them below their break-even point. The president explained to the stockholders that the glass strike cost them the sale of about 100,000 cars (a month's sales). Auto customers evidently were not willing to wait until the strike ended, and they went "across the street" and bought a car made by a competitor. The dealer can tell a customer, "Here's the car. Bring it back in a month and we'll put the hubcaps on for you," and he'll make the sale. But it's difficult to convince the customer to take the car now and bring it back later for the windshield! Actually, they probably lost closer to 500,000 future auto sales, because if a customer bought another maker's car, and liked the different make, this person probably went back to the new dealer for future purchases.

Effect on image

The actions of the purchasing department influence directly the public relations and image of a company. If actual and potential vendors are not treated in a businesslike manner, they will form a poor opinion of the entire organization and will communicate this to other firms. This poor image will adversely affect the purchaser's ability to get new business and to find new and better vendors. Public confidence can be boosted by evidence of a sound policy and fair implementation.

Training ground

The purchasing area is also an excellent training ground for new managers. The needs of the organization may be quickly grasped. Exposure to the pressure of decision making under uncertainty with potentially serious consequences allows for evaluation of the individual's ability and willingness to take risk and assume responsibility. Contacts with many people at various levels and a variety of functions may assist the individual in charting a career plan and will also be of value as the manager moves up the organization. Many organizations find it useful to include the purchasing area as part of a formal job rotation system for high potential employees.

Organizational strategy and social policy

The materials function also can be used as a tool of organizational strategy and social policy. Does management wish to introduce and stimulate competition? Does it favor geographical representation, minority interest, and environmental and social concerns? For example, are domestic sources preferred? Will resources be spent on assisting minority suppliers? As part of an overall organization strategy, the materials function can contribute a great deal. Assurance of supply of vital materials or services in a time of general shortages can be a major competitive advantage. Similarly, access to a better quality or a lower priced product or service may represent a substantial gain. These strategic positions in the marketplace may be gained through active exploration of international and domestic markets, technology, innovative management systems, and the imaginative use of corporate resources in the materials area. Vertical integration and its companion decision of make or buy are ever present considerations in the management of materials.

The potential contribution to strategy is obvious. Achievement depends on both top executive awareness of this potential and the ability to marshall corporate resources to this end. At the same time, it is the responsibility of those charged with the management of the materials function to seek strategic opportunities in the environment and to draw top executive attention to them. This requires a thorough familiarity with organizational objectives, strategy, and long-term plans and the ability to influence these in the light of new information.

This is briefly a capsule of the potential contributions of the function. It does not just happen, however. In some organizations the materials function is not management's prime concern. Continued lack of management interest and commitment can defeat the objectives of competent purchasing performance, causing a weak link in the total chain. The experience of many companies has shown that a relatively small amount of time and effort in the materials area will provide a substantial return on investment. This is an opportunity which should be brought to the attention of the key decision makers.

An effective materials function can and must be highly responsive to the users' needs in terms of quality, quantity, price, and delivery. It also can contribute to policy objectives as well as the overall public image of the organization. Those in the materials function cannot accomplish this without assistance and cooperation from suppliers, users, and others involved in the total process.

Progressive managers have recognized these potential contributions of the materials area and have taken the necessary steps to assure results. The most important single step in successful organizations has been the elevation to top executive status of the purchasing/materials manager. This, coupled with high-caliber staff and the appropriate authority and responsibility, has resulted in an exciting and fruitful realization of the potential of the materials function.

QUESTIONS FOR REVIEW AND DISCUSSION

1. "In the long term, the success of any organization depends on its ability to create and maintain a customer." Do you agree? What does this have to do with purchasing and materials management?
2. Differentiate between purchasing, procurement, materials management, and logistics.
3. What is the profit-leverage effect of purchasing? Is it the same in all organizations?
4. How does purchasing and materials management affect return on assets (ROA)? In what specific ways could you improve ROA through purchasing/materials management?
5. How has the purchasing function evolved over the last 80 years? What factors have influenced this evolution? How will it change over the next decade?
6. "Purchasing is not profit making; instead, it is profit taking since it spends organizational resources." Do you agree?

CASE 1-1
THE TRAGA BANK

The Traga Bank, a large Western financial institution, was well-known for its active promotional efforts to attract consumer deposits. The bank provided standard personalized consumer checks free of charge, a substantial printing order, totaling about $4,000,000 per year. Betty Small was a purchasing agent in charge of all printing for Traga, and reported directly to the director of purchasing.

It had been Betty's decision to split the printing of checks equally among two suppliers. During the last three years both suppliers had provided quick and quality service, a vital concern of the bank. Almost all checks were mailed directly to the consumer's home or business address by the suppliers. Because of the importance of check printing, Betty had requested a special cost analysis study a year ago, with the cooperation of both suppliers. The conclusion of this study had been that both suppliers were receiving an adequate profit margin, were efficient and cost conscious, and that the price structure was fair.

Two weeks ago, Betty received an unsolicited, unofficial quotation from a third printing supplier, Killoran Inc. at a price 10 percent below that of the current sources. Betty believed that Killoran was underbidding to gain part of the check printing business. This in turn would give Killoran access to Traga's customers' names. Betty suspected tht Killoran might then try to pursue these customers more actively than the current two suppliers to sell special "scenic checks" which customers paid for themselves.

Betty was not sure how she should react and wondered what action to take now.

CASE 1–2
JEAN PRINCE, LTD.

Jean Prince, Ltd., was an integrated producer of canned vegetables. Most vegetables were contracted by the company with local farmers. The company did most of its harvesting with its own equipment. Purchases accounted for an important part of the product cost and were decentralized.

The president, Mr. Lemay, looked after can purchases. He was also responsible for the purchases of cardboard and sugar. The sales manager bought the labels; and the production manager, an agronomist, negotiated the vegetable contracts with farmers and also bought the seeds, fertilizers, and all other factory and agricultural materials.

Mr. Lemay wondered if this delegation of purchases made sense and if it might be possible to improve the total supply situation.

Company background

Jean Prince, Ltd., was founded in 1929 by Mr. J. Prince, a northern Vermont farmer. In 1964 Mr. Prince sold his enterprise to a large financial organization for the sum of $4.5 million. Mr. Lemay, president of the company since 1964, bought the enterprise in 1978. Jean Prince, Ltd., was one of Vermont's largest canneries with sales amounting to $10 million in 1979.

The company produced many kinds of canned vegetables. Beans accounted for more than 50 percent of its sales. According to Mr. Lemay, the

Exhibit 1
Organization chart

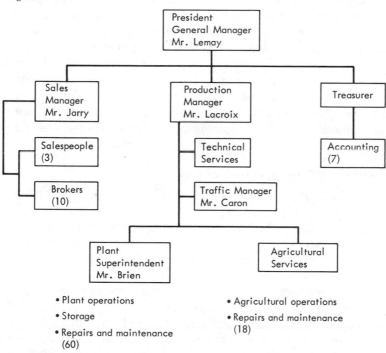

keys to the success of his enterprise were the first-rate quality of its products and a competitive pricing strategy.

Production facilities were located 35 miles north of Burlington. Headquarters, including the sales and accounting departments, were in Burlington (see Exhibit 1 for the organization chart). The seasonal nature of the company's activities was reflected in the variation of the number of employees: from 100 during the winter season up to 450 in summer time. The company cultivated about 20 percent of its vegetables on rented lands; the balance was contracted with approximately 600 local farmers. In April, farmers sowed their fields with seeds supplied by Jean Prince, Ltd. Crops depended heavily on the farming conditions; for example, 1,000 acres could produce from 20,000 to 80,000 cases[1] of peas. The canning operations started at the end of June with peas and finished in late September or early October with carrots, potatoes, and beets. Seasonal employees were recruited among students and people normally on welfare. Total employee turnover reached 1,200 people during the summer. The short harvesting season necessitated intensive use of equipment and almost no machinery servicing. Approximately 80 people, mainly supervisory staff during the sum-

---

[1]One case contains 24 cans of 19 ounces each.

mer, stayed during the off-season and most of them were committed to the maintenance and reconditioning of agricultural and factory equipment.

The president said that sales had not been satisfactory because of poor crops in 1978 and 1979. However, prices had increased, and Jean Prince's profits had improved. In 1980 Mr. Lemay expected to exceed the $11 million sales forecast. The profitability of the company during the past years had not been sufficient to pay dividends, finance inventories, and maintain adequate cash flows. Therefore, Mr. Lemay had to rely heavily on bank loans to meet his financial obligations. "The canning industry is capital intensive," he explained, "with equipment working only a few weeks a year. Stock turnover is only about one and inventory costs are very high."

Production purchasing activities

Raw materials and packaging supplies accounted for more than 70 percent of the product cost (Exhibit 2 is a list of main purchases and their approximate value for 1979). Mr. Lemay explained that the highly seasonal nature of the business forced him to keep the number of permanent employees to a minimum. The company had no purchasing department nor any standard purchasing procedures. As there was no requisition form, internal purchasing communications were mostly verbal and done on a day-to-day basis during the canning period. The president was involved in strategic decisions concerning certain purchases. The production manager, Mr. Lacroix, was responsible mainly for determination of quantities, supplier choice, and price negotiations for purchases not looked after by the president or the sales manager, Mr. Jarry. Mr. Caron, traffic manager, prepared the purchase orders and did the expediting during the summer season. The plant superintendent, Mr. Brien, was responsible for controlling inventories of materials according to minimum and maximum stock policies. Foremen sent daily inventory reports of the main materials to the superintendent who communicated his needs to Mr. Caron. Mr. Lacroix signed almost every purchase order.

Exhibit 2
List of main purchases for 1979

Products	Approximate annual value (in $1,000)
Cans	$2,418
Vegetables	1,357
Seeds	624
Sugar	366
Spare parts	264
Cartons	216
Labels	158
Fuel	66
Starch	53
Fertilizers	46

Cans. Cans had always been a major purchase. For the past 30 years, the company had bought cans exclusively from American Can Company. The president explained that Jean Prince, Ltd., was tied to this supplier as it had been renting canning machinery from American Can since the founding of the enterprise. This machinery was worth $450,000 in 1979. Mr. Lemay said the purchasing process of cans was very simple, almost automatic year after year. He did not sign a contract. Mr. Lacroix established required quantities for each size of can for the complete season. These quantities were based on the sales manager's forecasts. Mr. Lacroix had given the responsibility for the day-to-day purchasing releases to Mr. Caron. The main decision Mr. Lemay had to make was to determine which quantity should be bought in the pre-season. American Can offered an important discount on cans delivered before June. The company had traditionally taken delivery of almost half of its total can requirements in advance to take advantage of this discount.

Vegetables. Contract negotiations for vegetables were made in early spring and usually took a few days. Mr. Lacroix, agronomist by profession, was in charge of these negotiations. He dealt with 12 local or regional producers' representatives and their president. Mr. Lacroix proposed tariffs for each kind of vegetable. These tariffs were based on the real cost per acre for each type of culture. The company experimental farm provided these cost data. Mr. Lacroix added what he considered a reasonable profit and submitted tariffs to the negotiation committee. Producers' representatives insisted that Mr. Lemay be present at these negotiations. Contracts were written only after an oral agreement was reached. Then, a Jean Prince representative visited each of the 600 producers to sign individual contracts. Jean Prince, Ltd., sowed on rented lands what producers did not want to grow on their lands.

Other purchases related to agricultural operations. Seeds had to be bought one year in advance. Mr. Lacroix thought negotiation for this purchase was not possible. The cost of seeds had risen 40 percent from 1978 to 1979. Mr. Lacroix expected prices to double in 1980. He dealt with two main suppliers and three secondary ones. Producers were required to buy their seeds from Jean Prince who sold the seeds to them at cost price.

Fertilizers and pesticides were also important items. Normally, Mr. Lacroix tried to obtain quotations from suppliers. However, in 1979 suppliers would not commit themselves for any price. Mr. Lacroix recommended to Mr. Caron what share of purchases to give to each supplier.

Other purchases related to the canning operations. Sugar was a highly speculative item mainly used in the canning of corn and peas, and the president felt he had to assume personally the risk associated with this purchase. Mr. Lemay's role was to determine when to buy and from whom. Normally, a contract was signed for the complete season with a provision made in case of a contract surplus at the end of the canning period. For the coming season, he was still unsure whether he should sign a contract or buy at market prices.

Mr. Lemay was also involved in the purchasing of corrugated cartons. He said that finding packaging at this time was as difficult as finding raw materials and that successful purchases depended on the company's relationship with its suppliers. Mr. Lemay tried to keep three carton suppliers: two sharing in equal parts the bulk of the cardboard requirements and the third as a watch-dog.

Mr. Lacroix looked after the other factory purchases like salt, starch, glue, and the like. Most of these items were purchased only once a year. He said that normally these purchases were quite easy to handle.

The president had delegated responsibility for labels purchases to the sales manager. Mr. Jarry determined quantities based on his sales forecasts, asked for quotations, and gave his recommendations to Mr. Lemay for final approval. The sales manager usually dealt with two suppliers. He ordered labels only once a year. The purchase order had to be sent at least four months in advance because of the long lead time. The traffic manager looked after label delivery instructions during the canning season.

Mr. Lemay believed the present production purchasing system was running smoothly considering available resources. However, he was concerned about the off-season purchasing activities.

Non-production purchasing activities

Jean Prince, Ltd., had $2.3 million (book value) worth of fixed assets. Mobile equipment included over 375 vehicles: trucks, fork lifts, tractors, plows, harrows, seeders, watering machines, and harvesters of all kinds. Mr. Lemay estimated that each piece of agricultural equipment did in one season the normal work of a machine in five seasons. In the factory, salt and sugar had corrosive effects on the canning equipment. All machinery had to be completely overhauled at the end of the canning season. The plant superintendent inspected the equipment with machinists and estimated the repairs to be done on each piece. Estimation of required spare parts was made visually by the machinists, keeping in mind past repairs or considering weather conditions when the machinery had been working. The objective of these estimates was to produce a list of all necessary spare parts and to establish the amount of labor for the following year's budget. Agriculture and factory expenses were reflected on two different budgets. One machinist's team was assigned to the factory maintenance and the other to agricultural equipment reconditioning. However, this task division was flexible, and all maintenance personnel reported to the plant superintendent. Mr. Caron sent spare parts orders to the different dealers and suppliers as soon as the list of required spare parts was ready. Lead time could be several months. Every year, Jean Prince, Ltd., spent between $225,000 to $300,000 on spare parts.

During the winter the plant superintendent, Mr. Brien, helped by his best machinists, planned the general execution of the maintenance activities and submitted a weekly program to Mr. Lacroix. However, a day-to-day control of labor and materials used was not practiced. The repair and maintenance operations were spread throughout the plant as there was no specific repair shop. There was no central store; parts and supplies were kept in about six little stockrooms. There was no control over incoming and outgoing materials and parts. Inventory included approximately $90,000 worth of used and new parts. Any machinist could help himself in any of these open stock corners. No one had ever attempted to determine how much pilferage took place, but Mr. Lacroix estimated pilferage at 10 percent of the small items in inventory. The superintendent tried to keep in stock the majority of standard parts, but Mr. Lacroix was aware that quantities kept in inventory were not necessarily optimal. Machinists made oral requisitions to their foreman, and Mr. Lacroix signed every purchase order written by Mr. Caron, the traffic manager.

The president was conscious of the weak control in this part of the operation. He suspected there were many excess parts in stock and that many had been poorly purchased. He wanted to know the reconditioning costs per machine. In 1978 he found out by accident that the cost of reconditioning five tractors purchased in 1960 exceeded the cost of buying new ones. He was wondering if it would be profitable to have a buyer/storekeeper in charge of the management of spare parts. In addition, this person could control incoming and outgoing materials and keep files on each asset (covering labor data, list of spare parts purchased, and the like). Mr. Lemay realized that the creation of this job could provide an opportunity to centralize all purchases and, therefore, to unburden Mr. Caron during the canning season.

Mr. Lacroix was aware that a central store would be required; however, presently there was no space available for this purpose. Another problem he anticipated concerned the status of this buyer/storekeeper. He thought he would have to pay him at a mechanic's rate but did not know how the union would react and accept this new job.

CASE 1–3
LARIC CORPORATION INC.

Early in January, Mr. C. Moran, controller of A. G. Furniture realized that he had accepted a substantial challenge in assuming the vice presidency of Laric Corporation. It was a new organization composed of ten small to medium furniture manufacturers located in Quebec, Canada. The corporation's principal objective was the pooling of its members' purchases in order to get better prices.

By January, only certain types of purchases had gone through Laric. Some of its members had not yet used Laric's services, as their own prices were equal to if not better than Laric's. In a market context of shortages and rising prices, Mr. Moran found it difficult to fulfill Laric's objectives.

Furniture industry

The Canadian furniture industry had broken the $1.5 billion sales mark last year. Quebec manufacturers accounted for about 40 percent of this volume and Ontario about 45 percent.

The industry was experiencing a boom period which was expected to continue through the current year but the industry was still beset by several problems. The Quebec industry was of high quality but still essentially conventional. In spite of major efforts in design modernization, it had not completed its evolution from a craft to a manufacturing process. It was facing problems in lumber procurement, technology, marketing, and labor. There were also difficulties with the rising prices of materials, slow deliveries, and the need to carry high inventories. Costs had escalated, and for the last six months shortages were found in metal products and hardware, upholstery fabrics, and fuel oil. The immediate future of the industry was clouded by the shortage and price of lumber. For example, hardwood had more than doubled in price in the past 12 months.

Laric's history

The original idea behind Laric had been conceived on a golf course after a game between Mr. B. Roy, president of Roy Furniture, an important manufacturer in the industry, and Mr. P. Labelle, promoter of a successful purchasing group in the furniture retailing area. They asked Mr. Dupre, a local lawyer, to join them and incorporated Laric. The first directors were Mr. Roy, president, Mr. Labelle, vice president, and Mr. Dupre, secretary. They decided that the best way to approach prospective members would be the offering of a purchasing service for imported raw materials. To this end, they retained the services of an importer. As this man knew nothing about the industry, no concrete results were obtained. Nevertheless, they used the first year and a half to recruit seven members. Then Mr. Moran, controller of A. G. Furniture, and Mr. Larue, president of Kay Furniture, whose companies were among the larger members of Laric, took the initiative to get Laric off the ground. They both became directors, increasing the total to five, each one holding 20 shares of the corporation. The following month, the directors hired a competent purchasing agent, Mr. Proulx, to become the first full-time employee of the organization. (See Exhibit 1 for the organization chart.)

Laric's members

Laric totaled ten members. Most of them were small family enterprises. Total combined sales for Laric's members for the previous year amounted to $22 million and purchases to approximately $8 million. For the current year an 18 percent sales increase was expected (see Exhibit 2 for data on each of the members). Anxious to ensure profitable operations, the board of directors chose its members carefully. Potential members were screened on the basis of their financial situation and willingness to cooperate.

Exhibit 1
Organization chart

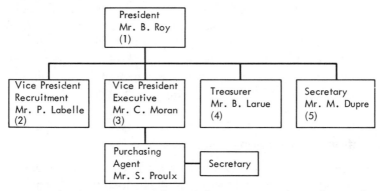

(1) President, Roy Furniture, Ltd., (2) Marketing Promoter of several companies, (3) Controller, A. G. Furniture, Ltd., (4) President, Kay Furniture, Ltd., (5) Lawyer.

Exhibit 2
Data on members

Members*	Production (materials)	Sales for 1974 ($ million)	Raw materials / sales percent	Distance from Laric (miles)	Current buying done by (decision maker)
Roy Furniture, Ltd. . . .	Bedroom, dining room (exotic veneers)	4.50	34	45	Buyer (president)
A. G. Furniture, Ltd. . .	Bedroom, dining-room (hardwood and exotic veneers)	6.00	34	25	Purchasing agent
Kay Furniture, Ltd. . . .	Bedroom, dining-room (hardwood and exotic veneers)	4.50	34	0	Buyer (president)
Rempal, Ltd.	Bedroom (printed)	2.50	34	105	Production manager (president)
Suprem, Ltd.	Upholstered furniture	1.50	30	3	Buyer (general manager)
Bert Furniture, Ltd. . . .	Bedroom (hardwood)	1.00	43	65	Buyer (president)
Touchette, Ltd.	Kitchen, dining-room (hardwood, plywood, formica, arborite)	1.00	48	280	Vice president
St. Jac, Ltd.	Bedroom (printed)	1.75	34	150	Buyer (general manager)
Paradis, Inc.	Dining-room, living-room, and bedroom (hardwood, plastic)	.75	36	80	Treasurer
Brossard, Ltd.	Bookcase, tables (particle board)	2.50	50	75	Vice president

*Names have been disguised.

The contract binding a member to Laric stipulated a corporation remuneration of 3 percent of the cost of the goods purchased through Laric. In addition, an entrance fee of $3,000 was charged to cover the research done on a new member and to guarantee the member's seriousness. Members were not obliged to purchase through Laric. It was still not clear to Laric's management what percentage of member's purchases would be channeled through Laric. An estimate of 40 percent was assumed reasonable if Laric could get a well-organized service going.

Organization and functions

No director received direct payment for his services; consequently, most of the daily work was executed by Mr. Proulx, the purchasing agent. He and his secretary were the only two full-time employees.

After a contract was signed with a new member, Mr. Proulx had to make a detailed survey of the member's needs and means, involving transportation, receiving, stockroom, and production facilities, in addition to the financial and other management policies and procedures.

He had to obtain, or sometimes develop, forecasts for the production material requirements. He also inquired about the maximum and minimum levels of inventory the member wanted to keep in stock for its various commodities. Lastly, he tried to ascertain at what price the member would no longer be interested in dealing through Laric.

After he had surveyed the needs of every member, Mr. Proulx made a summary of the items common to all in order to find the potential amount of purchases for the group. Then quotations were sought. Mr. Proulx looked after all negotiations with suppliers. After he had obtained what he considered an acceptable price, he checked to see which members wished to take advantage of the offer. He sent copies of quotations to members by mail and received the same copy back with comments if a member wished to pursue the offer. He also telephoned members to inform them of a buying opportunity and to check whether they were interested. He was in touch by telephone with each member at least once a week, whether the member was currently using his services or not.

The purchase order form used by Laric was a standard three-copy document on which the Laric name was stamped. The first copy was sent to the supplier, and the two others were kept in Laric's files for alphabetical and numerical reference. Mr. Proulx did not consider the present form to be the best vehicle possible but used it in the short term for simplicity and economy. Goods purchased through Laric were invoiced and sent directly to the member. Mr. Proulx received a copy of the supplier's invoice and charged 3 percent of its amount to the member. An exception was lumber on which the commission was fixed at $6.00 for 1,000 board feet for all species. Laric had experienced some difficulties in getting suppliers to send a copy of the invoice back to Laric. Although the purchase order had a stamp requesting confirmation by return mail and a copy of the invoice, suppliers frequently ignored this. Consequently, Mr. Proulx had prepared a standard form letter, to accompany each purchase order, requesting invoice copies so that members could be properly charged.

Laric's long-term prospects

Mr. Moran explained the purpose and prospects for Laric. "The small companies in grouping themselves," Mr. Moran said, "are able to get hospital prices instead of pharmacy prices on their raw materials. That way they can have at least the same advantages as our biggest members. This can mean, in certain cases, more than a 20 percent discount."

Laric continued to seek new members, and it was expected that, in the long run, at least 20 members might belong. Mr. Moran and Mr. Proulx were well aware that future growth was heavily dependent on the ability to offer worthwhile services. As a first step, therefore, Mr. Proulx's current performance was a vital indicator to current and prospective members.

In addition to the possibility of getting better prices, the corporation attempted to sell its members on the idea of a better purchasing service. Only one member could afford a real purchasing agent. Mr. Proulx offered more security of supply in raw materials, an increase in the number of sources, a potential inventory reduction, and the opportunity to relieve the members from the procedural tasks.

In the long run, Mr. Moran considered the possibility of offering financial or legal consulting services. The board of directors was well endowed for this purpose, having as secretary a lawyer, specialist in labor relations, and two others were experienced financiers. The corporation might eventually provide the services of a designer or an industrial engineer. Most of the members did not need full-time employees in these fields. Mr. Moran also foresaw the possibility of future mergers.

In the short term, he expected that Laric would receive and pay all supplier's bills itself. Mr. Proulx thought this would provide an opportunity for additional income, as the corporation could take advantage of cash discounts. He said: "Presently about 80 percent of the raw materials suppliers are allowing cash discounts but nine of our ten members are not taking them." Goods could eventually be delivered to Laric which would then need stockroom, receiving, and shipping facilities and also its own trucks. Mr. Proulx was aware that direct payment of suppliers' bills and central receiving could not be done without: (1) a stronger financial position at Laric; (2) a well-established purchasing system; and (3) at least twice as many members.

Laric's first purchases

Until January, 75 percent of Laric's purchases on behalf of its members had been of particle board. The remaining purchases had been primarily of species of lumber which were in short supply like walnut, elm, and ash. A few types of veneers, plywood, screws, and standard hardware had also been bought. Almost all purchases had been made from wholesalers with the exception of a few items like sandpaper and screws, which had been bought directly from manufacturers. Exhibit 3 shows the dollar volume of purchases and commissions from those members who used the corporation since August, last year.

Laric's problems

In January, one of the main problems the corporation faced was the difficulty of obtaining interesting discounts. Because of rising demand and growing scarcities, almost all raw materials were in a seller's market. For example, 12 months previously, the price of particle board or "rip" was $95 for 1,000 board feet; by November, it was about $195, and it was expected to reach $210 by February.

Price at the Time of Shipment (PTS) stamps on confirmations of orders were becoming a current practice. Few suppliers could guarantee the price at delivery time. Two years earlier, it had been possible to confirm prices for materials to be delivered 12 months later.

Laric had to obtain at least a 5 percent discount in order to guarantee a justification for the member to adhere to the group. This discount was reduced to only 2 percent after the commission of 3 percent to Laric was deducted. Obtaining good discounts ran into the major problem of recognition by suppliers as an important buying group. Wholesalers were reluctant to cooperate with Laric, an eventual competitor, afraid that Laric would go directly to the mills. Their salesmen were afraid to lose their commission as Laric would become a house account. In the present market, many manufacturers were protecting their wholesalers and were actively discouraging distribution channel bypasses.

Attracting profitable new members into Laric was becoming increasingly difficult. The philosophy of the corporation was quite new in the industry. Many of the companies approached found the idea good on paper but were not convinced of its practicability.

The situation of the larger members in Laric was troublesome. A. G. Furniture, for example, of which Mr. Moran was the controller, had bought nothing yet through the corporation. It was the largest member with purchases amounting to $2 million. As it had enough volume, it was able to get the same prices as Laric. In the long run, if Laric met its growth objectives, it could become interesting for A. G. Furniture. Recently A. G. Furniture had attempted to bring pressure on Laric, asking for compensation since it was because of its participation in the group that the others could get better prices. It had suggested that Laric's 3 percent charge should be dropped for A. G. Furniture. Mr. Proulx could not determine exactly why certain other members had not used Laric's services to date. His best information was that they apparently thought they could do as well or better on their own.

Exhibit 3
Purchases—Commissions

Last year	Brossard		Touchette		Bert		Kay		Rempal		St. Jac		Total	
	P	C	P	C	P	C	P	C	P	C	P	C	P	C
August	—	—	662	21	—	70	—	—			—	—	662	21
September	—	—	9,783	135	2,339	201	—	200			—	—	12,122	205
October	—	—	—	—	6,661		8,575				2,517	292	17,753	693
							15,566*	467*					24,251*	727*
November	8,871	265	156	4	5,310*	159*	6,325	111	3,375*	101*	3,206	96	18,558	476
											58,620*	1,759*	58,620*	1,759*
December	10,129	304	292	9	248	7	—	236			15,059	452	25,728	772
Paid	136	4	10,601	161	9,000	271	10,479				9,797	292	40,013	964
To be received	3,848	115	180	5	248	7	—	—			7,223	217	11,499	344
Orders not delivered	15,016	450	112	3	5,310	159	19,987	542	3,375	101	62,382	2,090	106,182	3,345
Total $	19,000	569	10,893	169	14,558	437	30,466	778	3,375	101	79,402	2,599	157,694	4,653

*Blanket orders.
Note: P—Purchases, C—Commissions.

Mr. Moran hoped that Laric's financial picture in the current year would show a break-even operation. He estimated that annual purchases of $1.5 million with a 3 percent commission would be enough to meet current expenses. He realized that break-even operation would not be acceptable to the directors in the longer run. Further financing would be required if Laric was to expand its range of services. Where such funds would come from was not clear to him yet.

Mr. Moran was convinced that if Laric Corporation reached a certain degree of maturity, it would be profitable for both its shareholders and its members. With Laric's present resources and problems, he was wondering what measures should be adopted to get through this difficult period.

OBJECTIVES AND ORGANIZATION FOR EFFECTIVE PURCHASING AND MATERIALS MANAGEMENT

Every organization in both the public and private sector is in varying degree dependent on materials and services supplied by other organizations. Even the smallest office needs space, heat, light, power, communication and office equipment, furniture, stationery, and miscellaneous supplies to carry on its functions. No organization is self sufficient. Purchasing is, therefore, one of the basic, common functions of every organization. Organizing the materials function to obtain the appropriate contribution to objectives is one of the challenges of management.

OBJECTIVES OF PURCHASING/MATERIALS MANAGEMENT ✕

The standard statement of the overall objectives of the purchasing function is that it should obtain the *right materials* (meeting quality requirements), in the *right quantity,* for delivery at the *right time* and *right place,* from the *right source* (a vendor who is reliable and will meet its commitments in a timely fashion), with the *right service* (both before and after the sale), and at the *right price.* The purchasing decision-maker might be likened to a juggler, attempting to keep several balls in the air at the same time, for the purchaser must achieve several goals simultaneously—the seven *rights* previously listed. It is not efficient to buy at the lowest price, if the goods delivered are unsatisfactory from a quality/performance standpoint, or if they arrive two weeks behind schedule, causing a shutdown of a production line. On the other hand, the *right* price may be a much-higher-than-normal price if the item in question is an emergency requirement on which the buyer cannot afford the luxury of adhering to the normal lead time. The purchasing decision-maker attempts to balance out the often-conflicting objectives and makes trade-offs to obtain the optimum mix of these seven *rights.*

A more specific statement of the overall goals of purchasing would include the following nine items:

1. *Provide an uninterrupted flow of materials, supplies, and services required to operate the organization.* Stock outs of raw materials and production parts would shut down an operation and be extremely costly in terms of lost

production, escalation of operating costs due to fixed costs, and inability to satisfy delivery promises to customers. For example, (1) an automobile producer cannot complete the car without the purchased tires; (2) an airline cannot keep its planes flying on schedule without purchased fuel; and (3) a hospital cannot perform surgery without purchased IV (intraveneous) solutions.

2. *Keep inventory investment and loss at a minimum.* One way to assure an uninterrupted material flow is to keep large inventory banks. But inventory assets require use of capital which cannot be invested elsewhere; the cost of carrying inventory may be 20 to 36 percent of value per year. If purchasing can support operations with an inventory investment of $10 million instead of $20 million, at an annual inventory carrying cost of 30 percent, the $10 million reduction in inventory represents a saving of $3 million.

3. *Maintain adequate quality standards.* To produce the desired product or service, a certain quality level is required for each material input; otherwise the end product or service will not meet expectations or will result in higher-than-acceptable production costs. For example, if carbon paper supplied to secretarial personnel is of poor quality, two things will result: the appearance of the end typed product will not be satisfactory and much typing will have to be redone.

4. *Find or develop competent vendors.* In the final analysis, the success of the purchasing department depends on its skill in locating or developing vendors, analyzing vendor capabilities, and then selecting the appropriate vendor. Only if the final selection results in vendors who are both responsive and responsible will the firm obtain the items it needs at the lowest ultimate cost. For example, if the purchase of a complex computer system is made from a vendor who later goes out of business and is not able to perform the long-term maintenance, modification, and updating of the system, the initial favorable price turns out to be a very high price, due to the vendor's inability to make good on the original commitment.

5. *Standardize, where possible, the items bought.* The best item possible, from an overall company viewpoint, for the intended application should be bought. If purchasing can buy a quantity of one item to do the job that two or three different items previously did, the organization may gain efficiency advantages through a lower initial price resulting from a quantity discount, lower total inventory investment without lowering service levels, reduced costs of personnel training and maintenance costs in the use of equipment, and increased competition among suppliers.

6. *Purchase required items and services at lowest ultimate price.* The purchase activity in the typical organization consumes the largest share of that organization's dollar resources. In addition, the profit-leverage effect of the purchasing activity, as discussed in the previous chapter, can be very significant. While the term "price buyer" has a derogatory connotation, suggesting that the only factor purchasing considers is price, the purchasing department should strive to obtain needed items and services at the lowest-possible price, assuming that the quality, delivery, and service requirements also are satisfied.

7. *Maintain the organization's competitive position.* An organization will be competitive only if it can control costs in order to protect profit margins. Purchase costs are the largest single element in the operation of many organizations. Additionally, product design and manufacturing methods changes are needed to keep pace with changing technology and production environments; the purchasing department can supply information to product design and manufacturing engineering on new products available and what changes are occurring and are likely to occur in production technology. Finally, the purchasing department is responsible for assuring the smooth flow of materials necessary to enable the production of products and provision of services as required to meet delivery commitments to customers; in the long run, the success of any organization is dependent on its ability to create and maintain a customer.

8. *Achieve harmonious, productive working relationships with other departments within the organization.* Purchasing actions cannot be effectively accomplished solely by the efforts of the purchasing department; cooperation with other departments and individuals within the firm is vital to success. For example, the using departments and production control must provide information on material requirements in a timely fashion if purchasing is to have the lead time needed to locate competent vendors and make advantageous purchase agreements. Engineering and production must be willing to consider the possible economic advantages of using substitute materials and different vendors. Purchasing must work closely with quality control in determining inspection procedures for incoming materials, in communicating to vendors the changes needed in the event that quality problems are found, and assisting in evaluating the performance of current vendors. Accounting must pay vendors in a timely fashion, to take advantage of quantity discounts and maintain good long-term vendor relations. If there is a problem with the flow of information from purchasing, receiving, or incoming inspection which is necessary for making payment to vendors, it is purchasing's responsibility to correct the problem for the vendor does not deal directly with accounting, receiving, or incoming inspection. Instead, the vendor deals with purchasing and expects to be paid on schedule.

9. *Accomplish the purchasing objectives at the lowest possible level of administrative costs.* It takes resources to operate the purchasing department: salaries, telephone and postage expense, supplies, travel costs, and accompanying overhead. If purchasing procedures are not efficient, purchasing administrative cost will be excessive. The objectives of purchasing should be achieved as efficiently and economically as possible, which requires that the purchasing manager continually review the operation to assure that it is cost effective. If the firm is not realizing its purchasing objectives due to inadequate analysis and planning, perhaps additional personnel are needed. But the firm should be continually alert to improvements possible in purchasing methods, procedures and techniques. Perhaps unneeded steps in processing purchasing paperwork could be eliminated; perhaps the computer could be used to make the storage and recall of necessary data more efficient.

ORGANIZATION FOR PURCHASING/MATERIALS MANAGEMENT

A large number of ideas regarding proper organization have been advanced over many years. That this is a continuing process is underlined by Chandler, who identifies four evolutionary stages in organizational growth:

1. Initial expansion and accumulation of resources.
2. Rationalization of the use of resources.
3. Expansion into new lines and markets to ensure continuing use of resources.
4. Development of new structures to allow continuing mobilization of resources to meet changes in both short-run and long-run demands and trends in markets.[1]

The process of building effective organizations involves innumerable activities, but none are more important at the outset than the relationship between strategies, structures, and delegation. Strategies, once devised, must be carried out in some structural framework; and no matter what organizational design is chosen, delegation takes place within it. Whether the organization structure is based on building blocks, information flows, or people-oriented concepts is immaterial; what really matters is that work must be assigned and executed in accordance with strategic plans and organizational goals. It follows logically that organizational planning and delegation procedures are important segments of the integration of strategic goals and organizational designs.[2]

What makes the task of organizing the materials function particularly difficult is that not only corporate strategy and internal needs have to be considered but the outside world as well. Both the purchasing and traffic functions have daily contact with the marketplace and have to be responsive to market developments. If suppliers place high emphasis on marketing and staff the area with well-qualified, aggressive, and imaginative personnel with high status, buying organizations must find a suitable way to counterbalance this outside force.

Models of buying behavior

How these organizational ideas and concepts currently are shaping managerial thinking is outlined by Feldman and Cardozo, who perceive three models of buying behavior.[3]

> During the last decade, a virtual revolution has occurred in industrial buying. In an increasing number of companies, purchasing (exchanging money for goods) has become procurement (total responsibility for acquiring goods). Where the purchasing agent formerly influenced primarily routine repurchases of standard supplies, he now frequently exercises considerable influence not only in the routine purchase of highly important material but also in the decision to adopt entirely new products

---

[1] A. E. Chandler, Jr., *Strategy and Structure* (Cambridge, Mass.: M.I.T. Press, 1972).

[2] John G. Hutchinson, *Management Strategy and Tactics* (New York: Holt, Rinehart and Winston, Inc., 1971), p. 205.

[3] W. Feldman and R. Cardozo, "The 'Industrial' Revolution and Models of Buyer Behavior," *Journal of Purchasing* 5, no. 4 (November 1969): 77–88.

and processes. In many firms the purchasing "agent" has become a "manager," responsible for managing all phases of the supplier-buyer relationship. In short, the procurement department has taken over functions which formerly were performed by company departments other than purchasing.

To an increasing extent, procurement departments are headed by professional executives, rather than senior clerks whose role resembled that of foremen. These executives act more as administrators than as buyers and frequently are members of top company management.

The industrial buying process has changed much more rapidly than the literature on industrial buying would indicate. A major reason for this gap between current practice and ways of thinking about industrial buying is that these "ways of thinking," or "models," in general have not been clearly spelled out. Consequently, it has been impossible to appraise their usefulness or to update them.

The classical or simplistic model. This title seems appropriate for this oldest and crudest conception of industrial buying behavior. In this model, the buyer's job is to act as a clerk who receives requisitions from "management" and catalogs from suppliers. His sole duty is to buy what is specified, at the lowest price per unit.

The underlying assumptions of this model closely resemble classical economic buying motives under conditions of pure competition. The buyer is regarded as completely rational and adequately, if not fully, informed about available alternatives.

To sell this "honest clerk," marketers presumably need only a complete catalog and the lowest price. But many marketers and analysts recognized that this "honest clerk" has a greedy, self-serving brother whose goal is not to minimize expense to the firm but instead is to maximize personal gain. The marketing strategy adopted for this man stresses social activities between salesman and buyer and other personal side benefits to the purchasing agent.

The neoclassical model. The typical current conception of industrial buying behavior well could be called a much extended and modified version of the classical model. The inputs which the purchasing agent receives are not only routine requisitions but also more complex requisitions which allow and require him to exercise greater discretion. The neoclassical purchasing agent performs cost and value analyses in addition to seeing that routine purchases are made. His objective is to minimize total cost for the firm. Since shutting down an automated production line may be quite costly, the purchasing agent may choose a supplier for the ability to meet delivery schedules rather than lowest price per unit.

The neoclassical model extends the "rational" portion of the simplistic model. In addition, some versions of the neoclassical model add specific provisions for "emotional" factors. This more recent neoclassical model could be stated as an equation:

Industrial Buying
= f (Economic Rationality + Correction for Emotional Factors)

A new approach. As a first step in overcoming the limitations of earlier models, a "consumeristic" model is proposed. While it shares earlier models' emphasis on rationality, the consumeristic model also provides a framework for understanding "emotional," "social," and other "nonrational" behavior. Figure 2–1 presents an outline comparison of all three models.

Figure 2–1
Comparative analysis of models of industrial buying

Purchasing process	Classical (simplistic) model	Neoclassical model	Consumeristic model
Inputs to buyers	From suppliers: Supplier catalogs and salesmen	From suppliers: Catalogs, salesmen, advertising	From suppliers: Information sought by purchaser from periodicals, catalogs, advertising material, salesmen
	From management: Requisitions for specific items	From management: Complex requisitions allowing discretion	From management: Requisitions of all types, many of which will have been discussed with and initiated by purchasing
Buyer's activities	Clerical only	Initiates supplier contact; performs cost and value analyses, plus clerical functions	Contacts suppliers and other departments within the firm; has several roles: Buyer, manager, and perhaps member of top management team
Purchasing strategy	Objective: Minimize cost to firm (or maximize personal gain)	Objective: Minimize total cost and obtain emotional satisfactions from supplier relationships	Objective: Solve wide variety of purchasing and management problems within acceptable levels of risk and resource expenditure; strategies vary by firm, situation, and individual buyer

Appropriate marketing strategy			
Market segmentation..........	Product and/or use, geography	Product and/or use, geography	Product and/or use, geography, purchasing strategies (which vary by firm and purchasing problem)
Communications:			
Selling	Stress low price (or personal benefits)	Negotiate terms in addition to price; enhance buyer's status	Provide detailed information on supplier capability and offerings
Advertising	Not applicable	Provide information on supplier capability; build favorable supplier image	Provide varying amounts and types of information on supplier capability
Other...........	Large and complete catalog	Catalog of capabilities, not just items	Catalog, stressing capabilities more than specific items
Price	Lowest possible or competitive	Offer lowest total cost, not necessarily lowest item price	Buyer's sensitivity to item price and total cost varies by product, firm, and individual
Follow-up service	None except, in some cases, social activities	Follow-up service part of contract or provided as customary practice; some "status enhancement" may be necessary	Service specified in contract or provided as customary practice; varies by market segment

Source: W. Feldman and R. Cardozo, "The 'Industrial' Revolution and Models of Buyer Behavior," *Journal of Purchasing* 5, no. 4 (November 1969): 82–83.

An overview of the model. The consumeristic model defines the purchaser as a manager rather than a purchasing agent. His job is problem solving, not simply buying. To solve problems, purchasing managers employ a variety of strategies designed to solve particular problems within acceptable limits of risk and resource allocation. Because this problem-solving activity occurs in a social context, it requires both analytical skills and skill in interpersonal relations.

The consumeristic model suggests that industrial markets may usefully be segmented on the basis of purchasing strategies. The model implies that salesmen, advertising, price, and service may have quite specific uses as marketing tools, which vary according to the segment (defined by purchasing strategy) of the industrial market to be reached.

This interesting definition of three models of buyer behavior shows the evolutionary nature of the materials function. Decisions about the reporting level, functionalization, and degree of decentralization will determine the real effectiveness of the function.

Centralization versus decentralization

If a firm approaches purchasing on a *decentralized* basis, individual department managers will handle their own purchasing. The advantage to this approach is that the user knows departmental needs better than anyone else. Also, it may be faster, since when a department needs something, the manager simply picks up the phone and orders it.

However, the advantages of *centralized purchasing* are so great in comparison with decentralized purchasing that almost all but the smallest of firms are centralized. In centralized purchasing, a separate individual or department is established and given authority to make all (except, perhaps, the very unusual buy, such as a new company aircraft) purchases. The advantages to be gained from centralized purchasing are:

1. It is easier to standardize the items bought if purchasing decisions go through one central control point.

2. It cuts down on administrative duplication. Instead of each department head writing a separate PO for lightbulbs, the purchasing department writes only one PO for the firm's total requirement.

3. By combining requirements from several departments, purchasing can go to a vendor and discuss an order quantity that is large enough to really get the vendor's interest. This is called "clout," and often the purchasing department can persuade the vendor to give concessions, such as faster delivery or a quantity discount. There also may be freight savings, because shipment now can be made in carload quantities.

4. In periods of materials shortage, one department does not compete with another department for the available supply and by this action drive up the price.

5. It is administratively more efficient for vendors, since they need not call on several people within the company. Instead, they "make their pitch" to the purchasing manager.

6. It provides better control over purchase commitments. Since a large percent of a firm's cash outflow goes for material purchases, a central control point is needed to monitor the aggregate commitment amount at any specific point in time. Also, purchasing decisions about placement of orders with vendors are sensitive in that the opportunity for kickbacks and bribery is great if POs are issued to unscrupulous vendors. It is easier to prevent such illegal/unethical practices if all decisions on the flow of purchase commitments go through one central "funnel," for the spotlight can be focused on the purchasing department instead of attempting to monitor purchase decisions that are scattered throughout the various departments of the firm.

7. It enables the development of specialization and expertise in purchasing decisions and is a better use of time. If a department head acts as the purchasing agent, the time spent on purchasing probably better could be used in managing the department. Additionally, the department manager will not spend enough time in purchasing to develop any real expertise. A full-time buyer, who can devote undivided attention to purchasing, will rapidly develop expert knowledge of purchasing techniques, sources of supply, available and new materials and manufacturing processes, markets, and prices. This *development of expertise is the primary reason why almost all firms have gone to centralization of the purchasing function.*

If the contention that purchasing is a major function holds, then it must be recognized in its organization structure. There can be no more justification for investing the authority to make purchases in a dozen or more individuals in a company than there is for diffusing the responsibility for production or sales or finance among a similar number of persons. The manager's responsibilities may be divided and apportioned among subofficials and departments, but the functional responsibility and authority of any department head should be definitely recognized. Moreover, functionalization implies that all the responsibilities reasonably involved in the purchasing function must be given to the purchasing officer as a major official. It is not sufficient to make the purchasing officer's sole responsibility the placing of orders as a matter of clerical routine. There should be a clear and definite understanding of the officer's responsibilities and authority. The purchasing officer must be given adequate assistance and must have the backing of executive management.

The difficulty, of course, is in determining exactly what are the purchasing officer's responsibilities and in defining the officer's authority. Certain duties are, for example, to interview all salespeople before they call on other members of the company personnel, to see that the goods purchased conform with the requirements or specifications, to select the source from which the purchase is to be made, to conduct all intermediate negotiations between the vendor and the buyer, and to consummate the purchase by actually placing the order. Additional responsibilities and duties may depend very largely upon circumstances. The essential principle is that there are certain universally recognized duties pertinent to this function and that these duties should be definitely placed in a separate department coordinate in status with the other major departments of business.

Where purchasing is organized under a competent director and where full cooperation with other departments is enjoyed, definite advantages may and do follow. Responsibility is placed on officials who have the interest and the skill to do the work properly and whose primary concern is in the performance of this special task. It aids in fixing responsibility and in measuring the consequences of any given purchasing policy. It permits setting up uniform policies for vendor relationships. It facilitates prescribing procedures, records and routine, and also expedites inspection and approval of materials and payment. It encourages market analysis, study of price trends, and analysis of vendors' production costs, with the result that purchases are made under the most favorable conditions and at the most favorable times. It promotes economy by consolidating requirements and by setting up material standards for inventories. Through searching for substitute materials and materials exactly suited to the requirements demanded, it encourages cost reduction without impairing the quality of the product.

SPECIALIZATION WITHIN THE PURCHASING FUNCTION ◆

Within the purchasing department itself, the overall purchasing function often is organized on the basis of further specialization and the development of expertise which results from specialization. Obviously, in a small firm, where there is a one-person purchasing department, no specialization is possible and the one person must be a "jack of all trades"—a difficult assignment. But in the larger purchasing organization, the usual functional breakout identifies the four specialized activities shown in Figure 2–2.

1. *Buying and negotiation.* These personnel locate potential vendors, analyze vendor capabilities, select vendors, and determine prices, terms, and con-

Figure 2–2
Organization structure of a typical large purchasing department

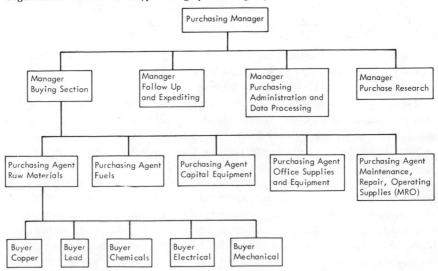

ditions of the agreements made with vendors. This activity normally is further specialized by type of commodity to be purchased; i.e., raw materials (which may be further specialized); fuels, capital equipment; office equipment and supplies; and maintenance, repair, and operating (MRO) supplies. Figure 2–3 presents typical job descriptions for a buyer and an expediter.

A variation of this is project buying, where the specialization of buying and negotiation is based upon specific end products or projects, because of the supposed advantage of the buyer concentrating on and becoming intimately familiar with all aspects of the project from beginning to end. At the completion of the project, the buyer then would be reassigned to another project. Project buying might be used in the purchasing organization of a large general contractor, where each construction job and the purchasing for that job is set up with its own self-contained, temporary organization.

2. *Follow up and expediting.* This group takes the purchase agreement and keeps track of how the vendor is doing in meeting its delivery and quality commitments, so as to avoid any disruptive surprises. If problems develop, this group pressures and assists the vendor to resolve them. (See Figure 2–3.)

3. *Administration.* This group handles the physical preparation and routing of the formal purchase documents, keeps the necessary data required to operate the department, and prepares those periodic reports needed by top management and materials personnel. Operation of the integrated materials computer data system, if in use, will be handled by these personnel.

4. *Purchase research.* This individual or group works on special projects relating to the collection, classification, and analysis of data needed to make better purchasing decisions. Studies on use of alternate materials, price and supply forecasts, analysis of what it should cost an efficient vendor to produce and deliver an item, or studies to develop a more effective system of rating vendor performance are the types of special studies done.

PURCHASING PREROGATIVES

The purchasing department must have four key prerogatives, if it is to meet the objectives of good purchasing:

1. *Right to select the vendor.* Purchasing should be the expert in knowing who has the capability to produce needed items and how to analyze vendor reliability. If someone else selects the vendor, purchasing then is in a sole source situation and can do little to bargain for an advantageous purchase agreement.

2. *Right to use whichever pricing method is appropriate and to determine the price and terms of the agreement.* This is one of the main expertise areas of purchasing; it must have room to maneuver if it is to achieve lowest ultimate price.

3. *Right to question the specifications.* Purchasing often can suggest substitute or alternate items which will do the same job and it has the responsibility of bringing these items to the attention of the requisitioner. The final decision on accepting a substitute is made by the user.

4. *Right to control all contacts with potential vendors.* Communication with potential vendors must flow through purchasing. If users contact vendors directly, this encourages "back door selling," in which a potential vendor will influence the specifications so that it will be in a sole source situation. Or the requisitioner will make commitments to vendors which prevent purchasing from arriving at agreements that will give the buying firm the lowest ultimate price. If vendor technical personnel need to talk directly with engineering or operating personnel in the buyer's firm, purchasing will arrange for such discussions and monitor their outcome.

The above-discussed purchasing prerogatives should be established as matters of company policy, approved by the chief executive officer.

Figure 2–3

BUYER JOB DESCRIPTION

Job summary

Responsible for meeting general purchasing needs in an assigned area of commodities and services, including requisition review, order placement, and follow-up.

Dimensions

Volume of annual purchases—2.0 MM.

Nature and scope of position

This position reports to a Purchasing Manager along with other exempt Associate and Senior buyers and Sub-Contract administrators.

The job depends upon effective working relationships with supervisory and nonsupervisory employees in Engineering, Production Control, Accounting, and other functional areas within the Division.

External contacts are normally with vendor's salesmen and sales engineers related to the assigned commodities and services. The travel involved includes trips to vendors to survey facilities, to expedite delinquent deliveries and individually or in conjunction with a Purchasing Manager to conduct price negotiations at vendor facilities.

This position originates meetings in conjunction with the Purchasing Manager between our company and vendor management to resolve problems and to build good working relationships. As directed, the incumbent may also coordinate vendor presentations on new products, processes or capability to internal personnel.

The Buyer may give work direction and guidance to an Assistant Buyer and/or Expediter who helps expedite purchase of assigned commodities and services.

This position normally requires a B.S. degree in Business Administration, Engineering or its equivalent in experience plus two years of purchasing experience in a related industry.

The principal challenge of this position is to insure that vendors in assigned commodities meet the established delivery date at the lowest possible price consistent with required quality.

The position has the authority to resolve all problems associated with satisfying and fulfilling standard purchase requests in assigned commodities and services. The incumbent is also authorized to commit the Division up to $4,000 on any one purchase contract on his or her own judgement, subject to the Purchasing Procedures and controls as outlined in the purchasing manual, and to negotiate contracts in excess of this amount, subject to countersignature by higher authority in the Department.

The position refers problems in pricing agreement for review and approval, vendor relationship problems, and problems on delivery and quality to his or her supervisor, the Purchasing Manager.

Figure 2–3 (*continued*)

EXPEDITER JOB DESCRIPTION

Job summary

Under general supervision monitors, reports, and takes authorized corrective action to coordinate the timely delivery of purchased parts and materials. May provide general administrative support to the Purchasing Department as required.

Minimum qualification

Educational: Must be able to communicate verbally and in writing and possess basic arithmetic skills normally associated with high school training.

Experience: Two years in production control, material control, or equivalent combination of training and closely related administrative experience.

Special qualifications:

Must be capable of:
  –exercising initiative, common sense, and ability to interpret data
  –maintaining effective internal and external working relationships
  –establishing and maintaining purchasing records
  –recognizing and identifying errors or inconsistencies and requesting contingency plans.
Must have knowledge of:
  –basic electronic terms.
Must have an understanding of:
  –production cycle
  –basic human relations in the art of motivation
  –purchasing cycle.

Significant duties

1. Contacts vendor by telephone, letter, or wire and/or responds to inquiries from vendors regarding delivery status of purchased material or company supplied materials and specifications.
2. Identifies actual or potential delivery or documentation problems, and takes authorized corrective action or refers to higher authority.
3. Obtains and maintains records on specifications, delivery status, and vendor performance and presents higher authority with timely reports on status.
4. Maintains contacts with user departments and responds to inquiries on delivery status.
5. Performs other duties of a similar or related nature.

Reporting and relations with other departments

The executive to whom the purchasing manager reports gives a good indication of the status of purchasing and the degree to which it is emphasized within the organization. If the chief purchasing officer has vice presidential status and reports to the CEO, this indicates that purchasing has been recognized as a top management function.

However, in many firms, purchasing reports to the executive immediately in charge of the manufacturing function, since the major share of purchasing activity is directed at buying items needed to support production. In other firms, purchasing might report to an administrative support vice president due to purchasing's role in providing service to all functional areas of the organization. Or purchasing may report to the chief financial officer, based on its immediate impact on cash flows and the large number of dollars tied up in inventory. In a heavily engineering-oriented firm, the reporting relationship might be to the chief of engineering, to get closer communication and coordination on product specification and quality control matters. Figure 2–4 presents the results of a study of 500 purchasing managers who were asked to indicate to whom they report.[4]

Figure 2–4
Who's purchasing's immediate boss?

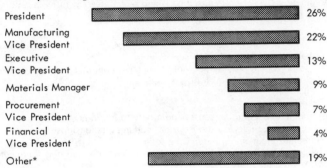

President	26%
Manufacturing Vice President	22%
Executive Vice President	13%
Materials Manager	9%
Procurement Vice President	7%
Financial Vice President	4%
Other*	19%

*Includes administrative services managers, general managers, etc.

A similar survey of 350 nationally recognized leaders of purchasing made by one of the editors of the *Purchasing Handbook* shows the following distribution of reporting levels and size of companies (Table 2–1).[5]

Table 2–1
To whom purchasing reports, based on company size

	Under $5 million, percent	$5 to $50 million, percent	Over $50 million, percent	Total percent
President	56.1	30.8	19.0	34.7
Vice president	15.8	20.5	41.3	25.4
Executive vice president	5.3	10.2	27.6	13.9
General manager	8.8	13.0	1.7	8.3
Treasurer (or secretary and treasurer)	1.7	5.1	—	2.6
Others	12.3	20.4	10.4	15.1

The factors which influence the level at which the purchasing function is placed in the organization structure cover a broad spectrum. Among the major ones are:

1. The amount of purchased material and outside services costs as a percentage of either total costs or total income of the organization. A high ratio emphasizes the importance of effective performance of the purchasing function.

2. The nature of the products or services acquired. The acquisition of com-

[4] "To Whom Purchasing Reports." Reproduced by permission from *Purchasing,* 9 December, 1971: 59.

[5] George W. Aljian, ed., *Purchasing Handbook,* 3d ed. (New York: McGraw-Hill Book Co., 1973), pp. 2–6. Reproduced with permission of McGraw-Hill Book Co.

plex components or extensive use of subcontracting represents a difficult purchasing problem.

3.   The conditions in the marketplace for those products and services of vital importance to the organization.

4.   The talent available for assignment.

5.   The problems and opportunities present in the purchasing area to achieve organizational objectives.

The important consideration in determining to whom purchasing will report relates to where it will be most effective in realizing the organization's objectives. Certainly, purchasing should be at a level high enough that it can be "heard," and that the purchasing aspects of key managerial decisions will receive proper consideration.

Purchasing must have a close working relationship with several other areas of the firm. It depends on production to supply realistic plans so that purchases can be made within normal vendor lead times to obtain best ultimate value. It depends on engineering to evaluate the cost advantages of using alternate materials. It depends on marketing for long-term market plans, so that realistic material-supply strategies can be developed. It depends on accounting to pay invoices in a timely fashion to take advantage of cash discounts and maintain good vendor relationships. In addition, if organized as separate departments and not a responsibility of purchasing, close cooperation is needed between receiving, stores, inventory control, traffic, and scrap disposal, since they all impact on the ability of purchasing to do an effective job.

This is not a one-way street. The other functions within the firm have a right to expect that their material needs will be met in a timely and cost-effective manner. Also, they expect to get reliable and timely information, as needed, from purchasing.

✗ Purchasing in the multi-plant organization

A variation of centralized purchasing often is present in the multi-plant organization. Here the firm operates several different producing divisions which often make different products requiring a different mix of purchased items. The firm often uses a profit-center management motivation and control technique in which the division manager is given total responsibility for running the division, acts as president of an independent firm, and is judged by profits made by the division. Since material purchases are the largest single controllable cost of running the division and have a direct effect on its efficiency and competitive position, the profit-center division manager insists on having direct authority over purchasing. It would be difficult to hold the division manager responsible for results without having decision-making power over the major expenditure area. This has led firms to adopt decentralized-centralized purchasing in which the purchasing function is centralized on a division or plant basis but decentralized on a corporate basis. Often there is a corporate purchasing organization which operates in a staff capacity, and assists the division purchasing departments in those tasks which are more effectively handled on a corporate basis: (1) establishment of policies, procedures, and controls, (2) recruiting and training of personnel, (3) coordinating the purchase of common-use items in which more "clout" is needed, and (4) auditing purchasing performance. Figure 2–5 presents a simplified organization chart for a firm organized on a profit-center basis.

To what extent the purchasing function should follow this trend is an interesting question. Today so many organizations are spread geographically and have a variety of products and services to offer through subunits that centralized purchasing may not be compatible with the general corporate philosophy. This raises questions such as:

1.   Should there be a headquarters purchasing organization and what should be its role?

2.   Should a headquarters purchasing organization buy the major raw materials for several or all of the divisions?

3.   Where one division uses products manufactured by another division, should the using division be required to buy from the making division when an outside supplier can supply proper quality at a substantially lower price?

4.   How far should the organization's chief purchasing officer go in evaluating the performance of a divisional purchasing executive?

Obviously, there are no readymade answers to such decisions—much depends on the abilities and personalities of the executives in such an organization.

Insofar as divisions or geographically dispersed units are uniform in terms of common needs and services and deal with the same suppliers, centralized purchasing may well make sense. It is important, however, that the purchasing function fits reasonably with organizational policies regarding divisionalized responsibilities. Obviously, the greater the geographical spread and the greater the divergence in organizational needs, the stronger the argument for purchasing decentralization to distinct subunits becomes.

Figure 2–5
Multi-division organization structure for purchasing

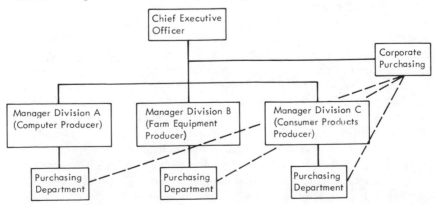

Purchasing problems in conglomerate organizations

Conglomerate types of organizations are usually large groupings of companies which have been acquired by a parent organization. In many instances, there is no direct relationship among the types of industries represented by the acquired companies, although there may be an underlying relationship centering on an area of science or technology. Because of the diversity of the member companies of a conglomerate corporation and in many cases the large size of each member company, the problems of developing any meaningful concept of corporate purchasing are immense.

Any solution to the problem must be developed over long time periods to have any chance for success. Some conglomerate companies have found that one way to start to develop sound purchasing policies and coordination among the member companies is to have a small headquarters group of highly competent purchasing executives who are available to act as consultants on purchasing problems when called on by the appropriate division executives. Needless to say, the success of the consultants will depend as much on their abilities in the human relations field as their competence in the purchasing function.

Several problems are associated with complete functional decentralization without a corporate headquarters group. Where the decentralized units are small in size, they may become so involved in operating matters that the impetus for change and planning is overlooked. Status of such decentralized units also may be relatively low, with the resulting problems of quality of personnel and identification of supply opportunities. No subunit may be large enough to justify functional expertise in areas such as customs, traffic, warehousing, inventory management, purchasing, research, materials handling, and value analysis. Corporate benefits may be lost, because of a low level of performance and lack of coordination in each of these areas. Even in those organizations where the individual units are large enough in size that the above problems are not serious, they may compete with one another in the marketplace for the same suppliers or materials without knowing it.

ORGANIZATION FOR MATERIALS MANAGEMENT

The rationale of materials management may be better comprehended through understanding of the growth of a small firm through three separate stages. These stages are complete integration, evolution of independent functions, and reintegration of related activities.

Complete integration

When an organization initially is established, almost all functions are performed by the chief executive (often the owner) or by a few key individuals who make up the management team. For example, the purchasing function might be performed by the chief executive who also handles the scheduling of production and watches inventory levels closely so that there will be no problem of coordination or control. This system works reasonably well, for the evidence shows that the materials-type functions (e.g., purchasing, inventory control, stores, and traffic) typically are grouped together and assigned to one person.

Evolution of independent functions

As the firm's business increases and additional personnel are added to the organization, it becomes evident that certain advantages would accrue if individual functions, such as purchasing, stores, traffic, production scheduling, inventory control, and quality control were separated and made full-time managerial assignments. The primary advantage, assuming the workload is sufficient to justify a full-time job assignment, is that of occupational specialization. The purchasing agent and later on the buyers that are added to the purchasing department (using that function as an example) become professional specialists. They bring to their function an expertise available only when an individual can devote all energies solely to one job. But with the emergence of these independent functions a problem of coordination develops.

The organizational assignment of individual functions to other major activities normally will be done on a "most use" criterion. Thus, purchasing might be assigned to the operations or production manager, since the major dollars are spent for raw materials; traffic might be assigned to the sales manager, since he would be responsible for delivery of finished items to customers. The "critical relationship" is a second criterion which might be used to assign certain functions. For example, inventory control might be assigned to finance, in view of the dollar investment involved. Other functions might be assigned on an "executive interest" basis. For example, the value analysis/engineering function might be assigned to engineering, since the engineering manager may be the one who has promoted and pushed this activity. The point is that the responsibility for different, but interrelated, functions becomes widely dispersed throughout the organization structure, creating very real problems of coordination and communication which prevent the organization from effectively and efficiently achieving its overall goals.

Reintegration of related activities

Eventually it becomes clear that substantial advantages, through the reduction of communication and coordination problems, could be obtained by bringing together again, under one responsible individual, all those functions which clearly are interrelated. This reintegration of interrelated materials functions is the basis of the materials management concept.[6]

If an organization adopted a "full-blown" materials management concept, following the principle of homogeneous assignment, the organizational structure might appear as in Figure 2–6.

---

[6]Harold E. Fearon, "Materials Management: A Synthesis and Current View," *Journal of Purchasing* 9, no. 1 (February 1973): 35–36.

The single-manager materials concept overcomes the shortcomings of the conventional organization, in which the various materials functions are organizationally splintered, by recognizing (1) that materials decisions are additive and not independent of actions elsewhere, (2) the self-interest and potentially conflicting objectives of the individual materials functions, and (3) the need to concentrate authority and responsibility for materials decisions to avoid "buck passing." Materials management in a formal organization sense is not needed in the small organization, for there the chief executive (normally the owner) makes all the materials decisions and can provide the needed coordination and control.

Functions included in materials management

1. *Material planning and control.* This is the aggregate planning of material requirements to meet the broad, overall production plan. It is concerned with the approximate quantities of the key and critical purchased materials needed to produce the approximate quantities of end products needed in specific time periods (probably by weeks). If problems in obtaining needed quantities are apparent, the aggregate production plan must be adjusted.

2. *Production scheduling.* The production scheduling manager plays an important part in establishing the total production schedule. Working with information inputs which either estimate future demands for a company's products or are based on the receipt of actual orders or are a combination of both, production control develops the specific time and quantity schedules for parts and materials and amounts needed to facilitate the production schedule.

Production scheduling is concerned with numbers of units to be produced, the

Figure 2–6
Organization structure for materials management

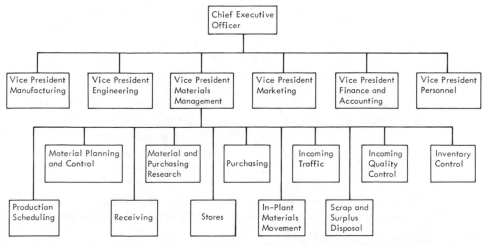

time intervals over which production will occur, and the availability of materials and machines to produce the number of units specified within the scheduled time constraints.

Once the number of units to be produced within a specified time period is determined, production scheduling is in a position to figure detailed requirements for parts and materials, both purchased and manufactured, by using bills of materials and specifications supplied by engineering. Companies with integrated data processing systems which have incorporated bills of material and specification requirements within the system can determine material requirements for any production schedule with great rapidity. Materials requirements planning (MRP) fits in well with the materials management concept.

A good production scheduling department should provide for follow-up activities to make certain that its schedules are met. If records are kept of materials in various stages of fabrication, it is helpful in limiting losses from spoilage, pilferage, or obsolescence and in maximizing turnover.

3. *Receiving.* The receiving department is responsible for the physical handling of incoming shipments, the identification of such material, the verification of quantities, the preparation of reports, and the routing of the material to the place of use or storage. In some organizations, the responsibilities for the packaging of finished products for shipment, the stenciling or labeling of the shipping instructions on the shipping containers, and the delivery to the carrier also are included.

4. *Materials and purchasing research.* This function is concerned with the collection, classification, and analysis of data necessary to find alternate materials; forecasts of supply, demand, and price of major purchased commodities; analysis of vendor costs and capabilities; and devising new and more effective methods for processing the paperwork necessary to operate the materials system.

5. *Stores.* This function physically controls and maintains all inventory items. Appropriate physical safeguards must be established to protect items from damage, unnecessary obsolescence due to poor stock rotation procedures, and theft. Records must be maintained which enable immediate location of items.

6. *Purchasing.* The purchasing department has the responsibility of buying the kinds and quantities of materials authorized by the requisitions issued by production scheduling, inventory control, engineering, maintenance, and any other department or function requiring materials. Where the purchasing department has the right and the duty to advise, question, and even to challenge other departments on matters of material specification and selection, a dynamic value is added to the operation of the purchasing function and the firm.

The basic activities of purchasing can be grouped as follows:

a. Checking the specifications of materials which are requisitioned in an endeavor to standardize where possible and to buy the materials which are the best values for the purposes intended.

b. Selecting the best available sources of supply, negotiating the terms of purchase, including delivery and performance, and preparing the proper purchase orders. Maintaining the necessary records to provide historical data on price trends, vendor performance, and the like.

c. Follow-up to ensure on-time delivery and receipt of the proper quality and quantity.

d. Acting as the company's "G2" or intelligence unit in the marketplace, constantly searching for new and more effective suppliers and new materials and products with the objective of reducing costs or improving the company's product.

e. Supervising or conducting all contacts between suppliers and all other company departments on all matters relating to the purchase of materials.

7. *In-plant materials movement.* This includes all those activities involved in moving materials from their point of receipt or storage to the point of usage. This involves the physical handling and transportation of materials from their storage area to the point where they will be employed; issuance of material to using departments; maintenance of records necessary to transfer accountability from the materials function to the user; and provision of information which will enable preparation of useful accounting reports. The "kitting" of parts for the production floor would be performed in this activity.

8. *Traffic.* Transportation costs have had an increasing influence on material costs in recent years. Also, types of transportation have had a major influence on inventory policy, e.g., the use of air freight and air express has reduced size of inventory stocks for certain items. There are two basic traffic activities:

a. Traffic control involves the selection of carriers, documentation of shipments, study of carrier services and rates, tracing shipments, audit and approval for payment of carrier charges, and the evaluation of carrier performance.

b. Traffic analysis is concerned with assessing the total cost of transportation, including loading and unloading, methods of packaging, transit time, and thefts and other losses, and with developing techniques for reducing overall transportation costs.

9. *The disposal of scrap and surplus.* Traditionally this has been a function included with the responsibilities of purchasing. Aside from the desire to obtain good value for disposals, two major additional concerns stem from protection of the environment and shortages of critical materials.

10. *Quality control.* Quality control continues to be a difficult function to place in many organizations. The responsibility for inspection of incoming raw materials and supplier's operations places it directly with materials management.

11. *Inventory control.* The inventory control function is responsible for keeping detailed records of parts and materials used in the production process. Records of parts and materials on order are maintained and periodic physical inventories are taken to verify or adjust the records. Material requirements determined by production control are checked against the inventory records before requisitions detailing needs are sent to the purchasing department.

In addition to the control of production inventories, there is need to control the nonproduction materials such as expendable tools, office supplies, and maintenance, repair, and operating supplies. The specific control methods include:

a. Maintenance of records of items on hand, on order, and total usage. Establishment of controls to minimize losses from spoilage and theft and to prevent stock-outs or duplication.

b. Handling the physical stocks of MRO (maintenance, repair, and operating supplies) items to be issued as needed for operations or maintenance.

c. Issuing requisitions to the purchasing department when stocks reach the reorder point or special needs arise.

Both production and nonproduction parts, materials, and supplies can be controlled through one inventory control department, or they can be organized into two separate departments.

PURCHASING IN THE MATERIALS MANAGEMENT CONTEXT

What happens to the purchasing function when it becomes part of a materials management concept in an organization? Will it lose status? Will the former purchasing manager become the new materials manager? These interesting questions were raised by G. J. Zenz in a research study involving almost 300 companies.

A survey of the functions included under the materials management umbrella showed purchasing to be the most frequently included function (Table 2–2).

Table 2-2
Functions included under materials management

Function	Percent of firms including under materials management
Purchasing	68
Production control	61
Inventory control	51
Traffic (including shipping)	49
Stores	29
Schedules (and planning)	26
Receiving	16
Warehousing	10
Distribution	6
Customer service	6
Other	10

Source: *Journal of Purchasing*, 4, no. 2 (May 1968): 41. Reproduced with permission of the *Journal of Purchasing and Materials Management*, National Association of Purchasing Management, Inc., 11 Park Place, New York, N.Y. 10007.

Respondents from firms utilizing materials management showed that 60 percent thought purchasing's status would be unchanged, 24 percent expected an increase, and 16 percent a decrease. It may be that in those organizations in which purchasing has relatively low internal status at the time of materials management introduction, the renewed management awareness may result in substantial improvement. It has traditionally been argued that the purchasing manager should be a prime candidate for the position of materials manager. The research showed that 29 percent of the materials managers came from the purchasing function, 33 percent from production control, and 38 percent from areas normally considered outside the materials management area. Apparently the growing sophistication of management concepts and techniques, including the use of the behavioral sciences as well as mathematical and EDP concepts in many of the materials management functions, puts a premium on managerial skills, as opposed to knowledge of a specific functional area.[7]

QUESTIONS FOR REVIEW AND DISCUSSION

1. What are the specialized functions within purchasing? Is this idea used in a very small organization? How?
2. Why do almost all organizations use centralized purchasing? How might a large, multi-plant organization set up their purchasing function?
3. Where should the purchasing function report in the organization structure?
4. What interactions and information flows are needed between purchasing and the other functional areas of an organization?
5. Discuss the specific objectives of purchasing and materials management. Relate these to (1) a company producing washing machines, (2) a large, fast food restaurant chain, and (3) a hospital.
6. What is materials management; how is it used; and why is it used?
7. What prerogatives must purchasing have, if it is to be truly effective? What will happen if purchasing does not have these "rights"?

CASE 2–1
LOCKHURST RAILWAY COMPANY

Mr. Alex Jones, vice president of purchasing at Lockhurst Railway, faced the following decision. His chief purchasing agent, John Shipley, had received an offer of employment with another railway, at an increase in salary of $8,000 per year. John was well liked by all employees but was perhaps not quite as efficient as Mr. Jones would like him to be. Mr. Jones was, therefore, considering hiring Jim Martin, a materials manager in the transportation industry on the West Coast. Jim was well known for his technical ability, and Mr. Jones expected he could make improvements which might result in substantial savings. On the other hand, Jim had an abrasive personality, and he might antagonize supervisors and employees to such an extent that operations could deteriorate so that severe losses might occur. Should

---

[7]Gary J. Zenz, "Materials Management: Threat to Purchasing," *Journal of Purchasing* 4, no. 2 (May 1968): 39–45.

this happen, Mr. Jones would have no choice but to fire Jim and try to find someone else. Jim Martin would have to be paid $12,000 more than Shipley's current salary.

The last alternative was to let John go and replace him by his current subordinate, Don Mix. Don would require some further training and experience, but Mr. Jones thought that in a year or so Don could be just as effective as John Shipley. Don Mix would undoubtedly be happy to accept this promotion and would start at a salary of $4,000 below John Shipley's present level.

CASE 2–2
✗ THOMAS MANUFACTURING COMPANY

"Delivery of our 412 casting is critical. Production just cannot be stopped for this casting, every time you have a minor pattern problem," said Mr. Litt, engineer for Thomas Manufacturing.

"I'm not interested in running rejects," answered Mr. James of A & B Foundry. "I cannot overextend my time on these castings when other jobs are waiting."

"If you can't cast them properly and on time, I'll just have to take our pattern to another foundry that can," retorted Mr. Litt.

"Go ahead! It's all yours. I have other jobs with fewer headaches," replied Mr. James.

Mr. Litt returned to Thomas Manufacturing with the 412 casting pattern.[1] He remembered that Mr. Dunn, vice president of manufacturing for Thomas, (see Exhibit 1) had obtained a quote on his casting from Dawson, another gray-iron foundry, several months before. It seemed that Dawson had the necessary capabilities to handle this casting.

To Mr. Litt's surprise, Mr. Dunn was not entirely happy to find the 412 pattern back in the plant. Mr. Dunn contacted Dawson foundry who said that they could not accept the job because of a major, six-month facilities conversion. Locating another supplier would be difficult. Most foundries would only undertake complex casting if a number of orders for simple casting were placed at the same time.

Mr. Dunn knew that gray-iron foundry capacity was tight. In general, foundries were specializing or closing down. Mr. Dunn had gathered some data on the gray-iron industry located within a 500-mile radius of his plant (see Exhibit 2), which highlighted the problems his company was facing. There were three gray-iron foundries located within 60 miles of Thomas Manufacturing. Thomas had dealt with one foundry until that supplier suf-

---

[1]A pattern is used in making molds in which the gray iron is formed. The mold after cooling is broken off leaving the desired casting.

Exhibit 1

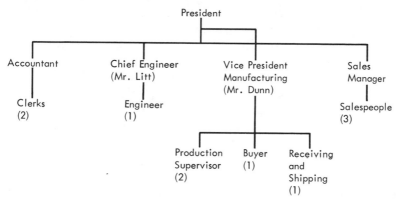

Exhibit 2
Foundry data for area with a 500-mile radius at the Thomas plant

a. Shipments of manufactured goods		
Gray iron (commercial castings)	Quantity	Value
Previous year	280,000 tons	$65,000,000
Current year	243,000 tons	$54,000,000

b. Number of establishments

									Current year
140	133	131	134	137	134	134	128	126	116

Ten-year history

fered a 12-month strike. Thomas then moved most of its casting needs to A & B Foundry, but Mr. Dunn had given the occasional order to Dawson and requested quotes quite regularly from them. In the last four years all had gone well with A & B Foundry. He had planned to share his business with both foundries. A & B was comparable to Dawson on price and had done an excellent job until now.

A telephone call back to A & B Foundry indicated to Mr. Dunn that Mr. James was adamant in his refusal to take the pattern back.

Thomas Manufacturing Company was a portable generator manufacturer with sales above the $6 million level. Thomas employed approximately 160 people in a fairly modern plant. Many of its small portable generators were sold to clients all over North America.

The 412 casting

The 412 casting was part of the most popular "middle-of-the-line" generator. The casting weighed 70 pounds, cost approximately $60.00—

and its pattern was worth $8,000. A run normally consisted of 100 castings, and Thomas usually received 100 castings every month. The 412 represented about 15 percent of Thomas's casting needs.

Normal lead time was at least eight weeks. When the supply problem arose, Thomas held six weeks inventory.

Mr. Litt, an expert in pattern work, explained that the pattern was tricky, but, once the difficulties were ironed out and the job set up, a hand molder could pour 50 castings in two days without any problems.

CASE 2–3
CASSON KNITWEAR, LTD.

Mr. Downe president of Casson Knitwear, Ltd., was concerned about the purchasing operation in his firm. He had added the responsibility for purchasing to the plant manager's duties when the purchasing agent left the organization in 1978. The president thought the plant manager, who was also in charge of production and personnel, might be too busy to give proper attention to all of his tasks. In the spring of 1979, Mr. Downe knew that some action should be taken, but he was unsure about his best alternative.

Company background

Casson Knitwear, Ltd., was founded in 1939 as a family-owned concern. In 1964 Mr. Casson sold his enterprise to a powerful financial organization. Subsequently, a new management was brought in, and in 1972 Mr. Robert Downe was appointed president. With sales of approximately $7 million the company was among the larger in the clothing industry. "This industry is a very tough one," Mr. Downe said, "where one must react very quickly to unpredictable fashion trends." In the spring of 1979 stylists were giving the final touch to the 1980 spring collection.

Total number of employees varied from 250 at the end of September to 400 in the spring because of the seasonal character of the operations. The president said it was becoming more and more difficult to find suitable employees in the small town where the factory was located. He also said he tried as much as possible to involve each manager in the decision-making process. The factory, the warehouse, and the accounting department were situated about 100 miles east of the fashion center in which the president's office and the sales and styling departments were located (see Exhibit 1 for the organization chart).

Until 1967 Casson Knitwear produced only stockings. Then, the company started diversifying into all kinds of single knitted sportswear articles to the extent that, in 1979 the stocking line represented no more than 30 percent of

Exhibit 1
Organization chart

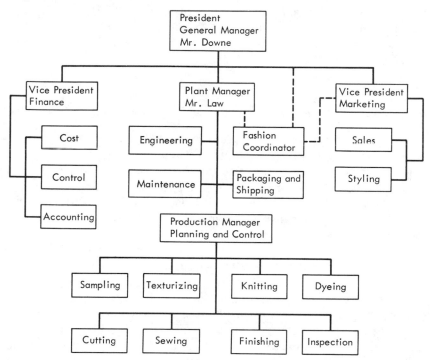

total sales. The sportswear line included over 450 different styles of clothes (shorts, bathing suits, pants, etc.) for the spring collection and around 200 in the fall. Taking into account all sizes and colors for each style, the company produced over 15,000 different types of garments. Between 65 percent and 70 percent of its sales volume was realized from January to June. Mr. Downe said he wanted to reduce the seasonal character of the operations by enlarging his fall collection. He also wished to decrease the number of styles because of the administrative difficulties of managing such a wide variety.

Casson Knitwear sold its products at low or budget prices and under private labels mainly through chain and discount stores like Woolco, Woolworth, and Zellers. Promotion activities were confined to volume discounts. Major efforts had been made to sell through department stores, but the company seemed to be closely associated with a low-price type of distribution. "Department store distribution would have permitted us to increase our prices by one third," commented Mr. Downe. "Unfortunately, our attempt has been fruitless up to now, and I rather believe that it is impossible to make Cadillacs in a Ford plant."

Since 1969, sales followed a downward trend. Imports from Hong Kong, Taiwan, and other countries had severely affected Casson's sales. However,

Mr. Downe expected 1980 to be a better year which would provide an opportunity to reverse this trend. He anticipated 1980 sales to reach $9 million. Despite net losses incurred in the last two years, Mr. Downe believed the financial situation of his firm was acceptable.

He thought the company generated sufficient cash flows; its main shareholder was in a strong financial position; its bank credit line was good and its financial structure satisfactory.

Production activities

Casson Knitwear's operations were integrated, i.e., the company produced its own fabrics for all its garments. It manufactured about 80 kinds of fabric, in seven or eight colors, changing every six months. First, filaments (mainly synthetics) were textured to give the material its stretchability; second, yarn was knitted to form cloth; third, the yarn was dyed. Then, clothes were cut and sewn. Finally, the sewn articles went through the finishing operations and inspection.

"In this type of business, the purchasing function is closely related to the sales and styling departments," noted Mr. Downe. To prepare a new collection, the stylists first met with the supervisors of the knitting and dyeing departments to decide on a range of colors and choice of fabrics for the season in question. Availability of raw materials was considered at this point. The marketing vice president had the last word in this selection. Fabrics were developed in the factory while stylists designed their new models. Once fabrics were produced, seamstresses made two samples of each model: one for the showroom and the other for the factory. Detailed production specifications, like fabric number, description, and name of supplier for each material included in the garment, were attached to the factory sample. The collection was presented to management and salesmen who were sent right away to prospect the market and to get orders. Simultaneously, production activities were started. Basic clothes offering less risk were produced at first. The production manager, the marketing vice president, and the fashion coordinator established production forecasts for each garment. Subsequently, in the factory the production manager, with the help of the different department supervisors, calculated quantities required for each kind of material. At the beginning of a season, production forecasts were readjusted once a week for each of the 450 styles, depending on market reaction and acceptance of the new collection.

Purchasing activities

The plant manager, Mr. Law, was in charge of the purchasing activities in addition to his production and personnel responsibilities. The purchasing agent had left the organization the previous year and had not been replaced partly for economy reasons and partly because Mr. Law had not been able to find a knowledgeable person with sufficient purchasing background.

Purchases consisted mainly of nylon filaments, yarns (polyester, nylon, cotton, and wool), dye stuffs, accessories (sewing threads, buttons, zippers, elastics, etc.), labels, packaging, machinery spare parts, etc. (See Exhibit 2 for the approximate value of each type of purchase for 1978).

Every purchase order passed through Mr. Law's hands. Requisitions came from each of the production departments. However, there were no requisitions for large volume orders, like filaments, directly handled by the production manager. Mr. Law negotiated all prices, searched for suppliers if they were not already specified, and looked after all other kinds of communication involved in purchasing. A secretary typed the purchase orders, but Mr. Law personally checked each order before it was sent out.

Casson Knitwear purchased nylon filaments exclusively from Du Pont, without a contract, on a quota system because of the shortages in the nylon industry. However, Mr. Law said this dependence could be reduced because he could still buy nylon in its yarn form. He purchased the other types of yarn from 12 different suppliers. However, 80 percent of these purchases were made with Du Pont and one other supplier. Mr. Law also tried to buy on the free market, but he was often hampered by the difficulties of controlling the quality or making adaptability tests. "You never know the possible dyeing implications of yarn coming from a different supplier," he explained. However, the plant manager noted that large volume items were in general the easiest to purchase.

Exhibit 2
Main purchases and their
approximative value for 1978
($000s)

Filaments (nylon)	$ 520
Yarns:	
Polyester	520
Nylon	160
Cotton	220
Wool	90
Dye stuffs	150
Accessories:	
Threads	70
Buttons	60
Zippers	60
Elastics	160
Trimmings	90
Other	70
Labels	60
Packaging	80
Machinery spare parts	80
Miscellaneous	90
Total purchases	$2,480

Dye stuff involved over 140 different products. Problems of color matching tied the company with certain suppliers. In that specialized area Mr. Law relied mainly on the dyeing department supervisor.

According to the plant manager, most purchasing problems originated from small purchases like buttons, trimmings, and other accessories. These purchases were made on a weekly basis after the production program was established by the production manager. Mr. Law thought that buttons and zippers, for example, could be bought three or four times per season, but he had no time to study the total corporate requirements for these materials with a view towards grouping these orders. These repetitive purchases involved a lot of work because there was a large number of suppliers, and, therefore, he had to ask for several quotes. Mr. Law thought labels purchases were really a nuisance. Prices varied considerably with volume. In addition, marginal suppliers could price their products as much as 50 percent below the others. However, they were less reliable and could offer poor quality products. The government required a label indicating the fabric content of each garment, which should resist at least ten washings, and should not vary from more than 5 percent of the real fabric content. Mr. Law said he was forced to buy in large quantities to avoid excessive prices. "Demands in our industry are great," he added, "if you think that customers can choose any style, in any quantity, within a short delivery period."

Staffing options

The plant manager confessed that his purchasing responsibilities were the most time-consuming of all his duties. He found that the purchasing function required detailed knowledge of textile materials and technology. Presently, he was engrossed in labor contract negotiations and did not even have time to delegate some purchasing responsibilities to his subordinates. He wished he could get an assistant who could be used full time on purchasing activities. He knew it was almost impossible to hire an experienced person because of the diversity and complexity of the company's operations and also because of the failure of his attempts to replace the previous purchasing agent. Therefore, he wondered if he should get a younger person that he could train himself.

The president, on the other hand, considered decentralization of all purchasing activities. Mr. Downe thought that Mr. Law could delegate the purchasing responsibilities to the main users of the different materials. Thus, the supervisor of the knitting department could look after filaments and yarns purchases. Responsibilities for dye stuffs could be given to the dyeing department's supervisor and labels and cardboard to the supervisor of the packaging and shipping department after consultation with the sales department. One of the stylists could purchase buttons, zippers, and other accessories. Mr. Downe was aware that Mr. Law's load was quite heavy and that with the present raw materials market conditions efficient purchasing management had never been more desirable.

CASE 2–4
MICHIGAN PHARMACEUTICALS, LTD.

One afternoon in September, Mr. James Wilson, assistant purchasing manager of Michigan Pharmaceuticals Ltd. (M.P., Ltd.), was discussing the purchase of packaging materials and contract filling of tablet samples with a supplier's representative. When the details of the packaging purchase order were finalized, Mr. Wilson told the salesman, Mr. Fred Brown, of Christie Paper Box Company, that he would send him the purchase order for the packaging components and 25 percent of the contract filling. Mr. Brown replied that Mr. Peter O'Toole, of the marketing department, had promised him 100 percent of the contract filling. "This is the first I've heard of that," snapped Mr. Wilson. "It's not marketing's responsibility," he continued, controlling his temper, "to decide what percentages of contract filling a particular supplier will get. Purchasing arranges the contract filling with the suppliers that can give the best quality, delivery, and price."

Mr. Brown, an experienced salesman, remained unperturbed. He replied that he had always dealt with both marketing and purchasing and that sometimes purchasing was not involved at all in the projects. He said that in this case where both marketing and purchasing were involved that he was just keeping purchasing informed of what marketing wanted. Mr. Wilson closed the interview by politely telling the salesman that he would have to clear up the situation between the two company departments. He told Mr. Brown he would let him know how much of the contract packaging he would be getting.

Mr. Wilson, his immediate superior, Mr. Rose, and a senior buyer made up the total purchasing staff (see Exhibit 1). One of Mr. Wilson's responsibilities was to handle the purchase of the marketing department's requirements. He also acted as liaison between the department and the production planning, manufacturing, and packaging departments. In recent weeks Mr. Wilson was finding the job more and more frustrating.

The company carried an extensive line of prescription and nonprescription items which were manufactured in Michigan. M.P., Ltd., had 10,000 drugstore customers plus hospital and government accounts. Annual sales of close to $20 million were handled by 50 sales representatives from coast to coast. Although the nonprescription items, known as over-the-counter (O.T.C.) products, were promoted directly to the drug stores, most business was generated by convincing the doctors to prescribe M.P., Ltd., products for their patients. No selling or advertising was directed at the consumer.

The basic idea was that the M.P., Ltd., salesmen would give samples to a doctor after getting a verbal promise to prescribe. These samples would be used to start the patient on an M.P., Ltd., product, and the doctor would write a prescription for the patient to pick up at the drugstore. With a large number of similar products on the market, it was a difficult marketing prob-

Exhibit 1
Organization chart

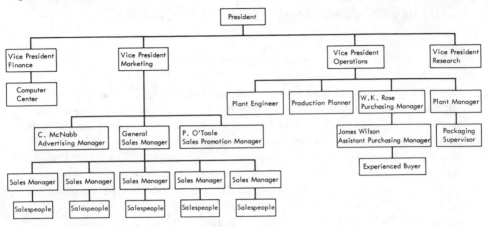

lem to keep M.P., Ltd.'s brand name in the doctor's mind, days or weeks after the salesman's visit. To help solve this problem, salesmen asked the doctors to sign forms requesting additional samples at spaced intervals.

The marketing department had been recently reorganized, and the two new men, Mr. P. O'Toole, sales promotion manager, and Mr. C. McNabb, advertising manager, were understandably anxious to do a good job. Both had made a lot of progress in working with Mr. Brown of Christie, standardizing the samples to be used for sales promotion and advertising mailings. Essentially, both samples were now the same, the only difference was the advertising sample was enclosed in an outer mailer to be posted to the doctor.

The package contract under discussion totaled $22,000 or one half of 1 percent of Christie's annual sales of $4 million. In the past, Christie had sold $20,000 worth of materials annually to M.P., Ltd. Mr. Brown had designed an attractive new style of sample. Basically, it was a folded card holding strips of tablets which could be pushed through one at a time, as required by the patient. This one idea was to be used in the near future to sample several other tablet products. Mr. Brown had developed the idea for marketing, expecting that he would get both the printing and contract filling.

Although M.P., Ltd., did 90 percent of their manufacturing and packaging, they did not have the equipment to strip or heat seal the strip into the folded cards. When goods came in from a contract packager, such as Christie, they were held in inventory until required by marketing.

While Mr. O'Toole and Mr. McNabb had been able to work well together, they were having their difficulties in getting the cooperation of other departments involved. Frequent instances of sample mailings being late or salesmen samples being out of stock continued to plague the success of their program. Delays had been caused by late ordering of components from outside suppliers, shortages of tablets, and computer mailing lists being incorrectly printed. In their attempts to remedy the situation, the marketing men had trampled on a few toes. During attempts to investigate the causes for these delays, the vice president of operations discovered that there were usually good reasons offered by the departments involved.

Purchasing, production, and the computer center pointed out that they could not drop their usual work "everytime marketing wanted something in a rush." The feeling expressed by the production planner was typical of most department supervisors. He commented, "It's fine to get out the samples but rather pointless if we are running out of trade size in the meantime. Some of those unusual sample carton constructions slow us up 50 percent."

While it was part of Mr. Wilson's job to coordinate marketing's sample requirements, he was not making much progress. His attempts to get each department to cooperate met with the usual arguments that marketing was only one department and had to wait its turn. Mr. O'Toole and Mr. McNabb at times grew impatient with Mr. Wilson's efforts, and they started to go directly to each department supervisor.

Mr. Wilson felt that the action taken by Mr. O'Toole in telling the supplier how much contract filling business he would get was the last straw. With this in mind he went to see his immediate superior, Mr. Rose, to try to get a policy statement on the matter. He wanted to know where the line was drawn between purchasing and marketing's responsibility in matters dealing with company suppliers.

Mr. Rose explained that, because marketing promotion expenditure totaled $4.2 million or 21 percent of sales, M.P., Ltd., as most other companies in the industry, faced similar purchasing marketing problems.

If marketing was responsible for their budgets, they had the right to spend $1 each for 10,000 items, or if they wanted they could buy 5,000 items at $2 each and still stay within their budget. It was a marketing decision whether they were getting better results from the $1 or $2 item. For these items purchasing merely typed a purchase order to confirm the deal already made by marketing with the supplier. This policy applied to nonproduction items, such as calendars, letter openers, diet sheets, patient history cards for doctors, or displays and posters for drugstores. In contrast, production and inventory purchases had last year reached 20 percent of sales dollars.

However, he pointed out that final selection of sources for any purchased items which had to be packaged by the plant had always been the responsibility of the purchasing department. In this particular case there was still a significant inventory of old style samples in the building, which marketing had not considered when they promised Mr. Brown 100 percent of the contract filling. Mr. Wilson felt that placing all the contract filling right away would build up the stock of samples unnecessarily. Besides this, he had negotiated a much better price from another reliable supplier and felt that he would give the balance of 75 percent to them.

Marketing, Mr. Rose explained, was only charged for samples as they were shipped to salesmen or mailed out to doctors. Therefore, marketing was not too concerned about inventory levels as long as there were no shortages. Packaging components and bulk products held in inventory were not segregated from trade sizes in the warehouse or in accounting records. Only the finished samples were given a special account number so that the marketing budgets could be debited as the samples were sent out.

Mr. Rose suggested that a marketing-purchasing meeting be held so that each department could state its case. The main points brought up were as follows:

Marketing—Mr. O'Toole and Mr. McNabb

1. Samples were the keystone to the marketing program. M.P., Ltd., could not afford the delays which were depriving salesmen and doctors from receiving adequate supplies on time.
2. It was necessary to operate within their budgets, and therefore they should have a say in selecting suppliers.
3. Continual foul-ups had delayed marketing objectives because of the inability of purchasing, production-planning, packaging, and the computer center departments to meet deadlines set by marketing.
4. Since Mr. Brown had done so much development work to design the new sample, he was entitled to the printing as well as the contract filling business if his prices were reasonable.

Purchasing—Mr. Rose and Mr. Wilson

1. It was agreed that samples were very important but not at the expense of trade size production and general efficiency of the plant.
2. Marketing budgets were one thing, but all departments had budgets and one department could not be favored over another. Purchasing did not deny marketing a say in supplier selection, but the final selection had to be made by purchasing.
3. Why were there foul-ups? Did marketing allow these departments sufficient lead time? Did they familiarize other departments with their plans early in their development? Were these deadlines reasonable in light of other departments' schedules?
4. Purchasing had a corporate responsibility to see that the greatest possible value was received for each dollar spent. How did we know prices were reasonable without getting other quotations?

If Christie got the initial orders for the new sample program, how much of their price per M was actually the cost of their idea? If someone else quoted lower, what premium was marketing prepared to pay the originator of the idea?

Before these last questions could be answered by marketing, the meeting had to be adjourned because of a shortage of time. Before parting, all those involved felt that some progress had been made but that they still had a long way to go.

PROCEDURES, COMPUTERIZATION, AND INFORMATION FLOWS

3

The materials management area requires a wide range of standard operating procedures to deal with the normal daily tasks. The large volume of items, the large dollar volume involved, the need for an audit trail, the severe consequences of unsatisfactory performance, and the potential contribution to effective corporate operations inherent in the function are five major reasons for developing a sound system. The acquisition process is closely tied to almost all other functions included in an organization and also to the external environment, creating a need for complete information systems. The introduction of electronic data processing has had a substantial impact on the acquisition process and its management. Considerable management skill is required to assure continuing effectiveness.

STEPS OF THE PURCHASING SYSTEM

Only a simple statement of the broad outlines of any system of sound purchasing procedure will be presented.

The essential steps of purchasing procedure are as follows:

1. Ascertainment of need.
2. Accurate statement of the character and amount of the article or commodity desired.
3. Selection of possible sources of supply.
4. Analysis of alternatives and the placing of the order.
5. Follow-up on the order.
6. Receipt and inspection of the goods.
7. Checking of the invoice and payment of the supplier.
8. Maintenance of records.

Ascertainment of need

Any purchase originates with the recognition of a definite need by someone in the organization. The person responsible for a particular activity should know what the individual requirements of the unit are: what, how much, and when it is needed. This may result in a material requisition on the stores department. Occasionally, such requirements may be met by the transfer of surplus stock from another department. Sooner or later, of course, the purchase of new supplies will become necessary. Some purchase requisitions originate within the production or using department. Requests for office equipment of all sorts might come from the office manager or from the controller of the company. Some requests may come from the sales or advertising departments or from research laboratories. Frequently, special forms will indicate the source of requisitions; where this is not the case, distinctive code numbers for each department may be used. A typical requisition is shown in Figure 3–1.

It is, of course, also the responsibility of the purchasing department to help anticipate the needs of using departments. It is part of the purchasing manager's work to urge not only that the requirements of other departments be as nearly standard in character as possible and that a minimum of special or unusual orders be placed, but also that requirements be anticipated far enough in advance to prevent an excessive number of "rush" orders. Also, since the purchasing department is in touch with price trends and general market conditions, the placing of forward orders may be essential to protect against shortage of supply or increased prices. This means that purchasing should supply using departments with the normal lead time, and any major changes, for all standard purchased items.

Figure 3–1
Purchasing requisition
(8½ × 5½ in.)

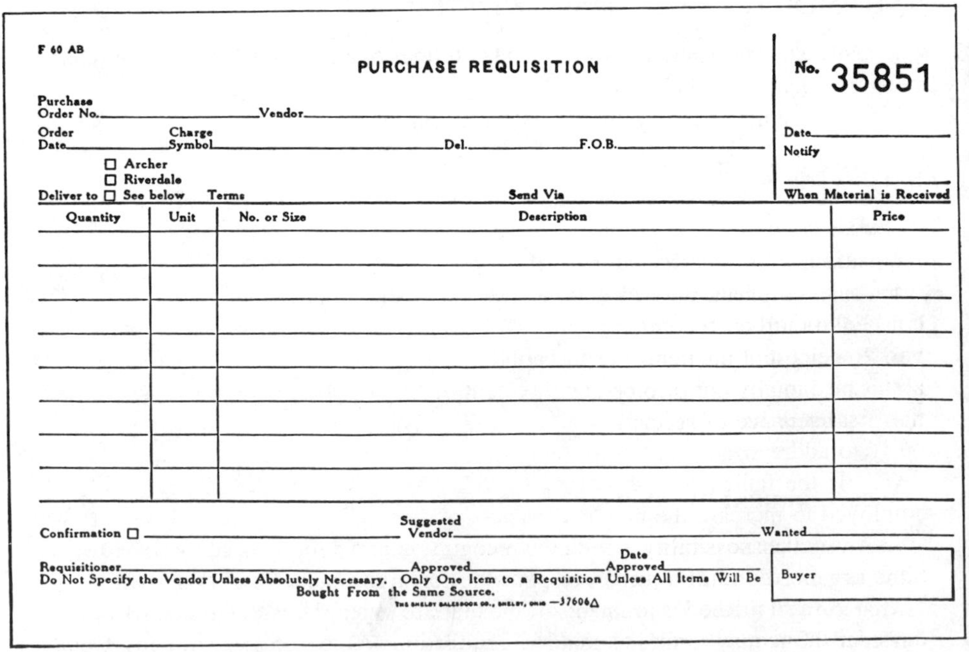
F 60 AB

PURCHASE REQUISITION

No. 35851

Purchase Order No. ____ Vendor ____

Order Date ____ Charge Symbol ____ Del. ____ F.O.B. ____

Date ____

Notify ____

☐ Archer
☐ Riverdale
Deliver to ☐ See below Terms ____ Send Via ____ When Material is Received

Quantity	Unit	No. or Size	Description	Price

Confirmation ☐ ____ Suggested Vendor ____ Wanted ____

Requisitioner ____ Approved ____ Date Approved ____

Buyer

Do Not Specify the Vendor Unless Absolutely Necessary. Only One Item to a Requisition Unless All Items Will Be Bought From the Same Source.

THE SHELBY SALESBOOK CO., SHELBY, OHIO —37606△

✗ Emergency and rush orders

Frequently an excessively large number of requisitions will be received marked "rush." Rush orders cannot always be avoided; emergencies do arise which justify their use. Sudden changes in style or design and unexpected changes in market conditions may upset a most carefully planned material schedule. Breakdowns seemingly are inevitable, with an accompanying demand for parts or material which it would be quite unreasonable to carry in stock regularly.

There are, however, so-called rush orders that cannot be justified on any basis. They consist of those requisitions which arise because of (a) faulty inventory control, (b) poor production planning or budgeting, (c) an apparent lack of confidence in the ability of the purchasing department to get material to the plant by the proper time, and (d) the sheer habit of marking the requests "rush." Whatever the cause, such orders are costly. This higher cost is due in part to the greater chance of error when the work is done under pressure. Rush orders also place an added burden on the seller, and this burden must directly or indirectly find its way into the price paid by the buyer.

What can be done to reduce the seriousness of this problem? For an excessive number of rush orders that are not actually emergency orders, the solution is a matter of education in the proper purchasing procedure. In one company, for example, a ruling has been made that when a "rush" requisition is sent to the purchasing department, the department issuing such an order has to explain to the general superintendent the reason for the emergency, and secure approval. Furthermore, even if the requisition is approved by the superintendent, the extra costs, so far as they can be determined, are charged to the department ordering the material. The result has been a marked reduction in the number of such orders.

✗ Small orders

Small orders are a continuing matter of concern in every organization. Most requisitions follow Pareto's Law, which says that about 70 percent of all requisitions only amount to about 10 percent of the total dollar volume. One important consideration then becomes the cost of the system set up to handle small orders versus the cost of the items themselves. Since the lack of a small item may create a nuisance totally out of proportion to its dollar value, assured supply is usually the first objective to be met. A number of approaches need to be used continuously to address the small order question. A few examples are:

1. If the fault lies with the using department, perhaps persuasion may be employed to increase the number of standardized items requested.

2. Another possibility is for the purchasing department to hold small requisitions as received until a justifiable total, in dollars, has been accumulated.

3. A third method is to establish a requisition calendar, setting aside specific days for the requisitioning of specific supplies, so that all requests for a given

item are received on the same day. As an aid to the storeskeeper, the calendar also may be so arranged that practically all the supplies secured from any specific type of vendor are requisitioned on the same day.

4.   Still another method of procedure is to make use of the "stockless buying" or "systems contracting"[1] concept. This concept has been used most widely in the purchase of MRO (maintenance, repair, and operating supply) items. (See explanation later in this chapter.)

Blank check purchase order

This method for combatting the small-order problem often is referred to as the "Kaiser Purchase Order Draft" system. Some years ago when the Kaiser Aluminum and Chemical Corporation analyzed their purchasing paperwork, they found that 75 percent of their purchase orders had a face value of $200 or less but accounted in total for only 5 percent of total purchase dollars; further, 92 percent of their PO's were for a face value of $1000 or less but accounted for only 6 percent of total purchase dollars. To handle these small orders, they devised the blank check buying procedure.

The blank-check PO is a special form, in which the vendor is sent a check along with the PO (Figure 3–2). When the merchandise is shipped, the vendor enters the amount due on the check and cashes it. This system has certain built-in safeguards: the check can be deposited only to the vendor's account; it must be presented for deposit within 60 days; and the check clearly is marked "not good for an amount over $1,000." The risk to the buyer is small under these restrictions and it cuts down paperwork on those low-dollar purchases. The procedure has other major advantages: it saves postage; the buyer can negotiate a larger cash discount in return for instant payment; and it requires complete shipment (no back orders allowed) which cuts down on the number of receiving reports, inventory entries, and payments. The vendor has a real incentive to ship the order complete, since payment is immediate for items shipped.

Accurate description of desired commodity

No purchaser can be expected to buy without knowing exactly what the using departments want. For this reason, it is essential to have an accurate description of the need, the article, the commodity, or the service which is requested.

The purchaser should question a specification if it appears that the organization might be served better through a modification. An obvious case is the one where market shortages exist in the commodity requested and a substitute is the only reasonable alternative. Since future market conditions play such a vital role, it makes sense to have a high degree of interaction between the purchasing and specifying groups in the early stages of need definition. At best, an inaccurate description may result in some loss of time; at worst it may have serious financial

---

[1]Systems contracting is a term registered by the Carborundum Company.

consequences and cause disruption of supply, hard feelings internally, and loss of supplier respect and trust.

Since the purchasing department is the last one to see the specification before it is sent on to the supplier, the need for a final check here is clear. Such a check is not possible if purchasing department personnel have no familiarity with the product or service requested. Any questions regarding the accuracy of the requisition should be referred back to the requisitioner and should not be settled unilaterally in the purchasing department.

There should be substantial uniformity in the use of terms to describe desired articles. The importance of proper nomenclature as a means of avoiding misunderstanding cannot be overemphasized. The most effective way to secure this uniformity is to maintain in the purchasing office a file listing the articles usually purchased. Such files may be kept in various ways. Some organizations have found it worthwhile to maintain a general catalog, which lists all the items used, and a stores catalog, which contains a list of all of the items carried in stock. Such catalogs may be kept in loose-leaf form or in a card index. Provided that such catalogs are adequately planned and properly maintained, they tend to promote the uniformity in description. They also tend to reduce the number of odd sizes or grades of articles requisitioned, and they facilitate accounting and stores procedures. Unless such catalogs or their equivalent are properly planned, maintained, and actually used, they are confusing and expensive beyond any benefits which could be derived from them.

A requisition should provide space for the following information from the requisitioner:

1. Date.
2. Number (identification).
3. Originating department.
4. Account to be charged.
5. Complete description of material desired and quantity.
6. Shipping instructions including date material is wanted.
7. Signature of person(s) authorized to issue requisition.

Flow of the purchase requisition

At a minimum, at least two copies of the requisition should be made: one to be retained by the issuer and one to be forwarded to the purchasing department. It is a common practice to allow only one item to appear on any one purchase requisition, particularly on standard items. In the case of some special items, such as plumbing fittings not regularly carried in stock, several items may be covered by one requisition, provided they are likely to be purchased from one vendor and for delivery at the same time. This simplifies record keeping, since specific items are secured from various suppliers, call for different delivery dates, and require separate purchase orders and different treatment.

It is important for the purchasing department definitely to have established

Figure 3–2
Blank-check form

FUND	DEPT.	DIV.	C C	W O	ACCT. NO.

MARICOPA COUNTY ARIZONA

CASH PURCHASE ORDER This number MUST appear on ALL documents.	C.P.O. No. X 00057

DATE

CONTRACT NO.

CASH PURCHASE ORDER
MARICOPA COUNTY
DEPARTMENT OF MATERIALS MANAGEMENT
MATERIALS MANAGEMENT CENTER, 320 W. LINCOLN
PHOENIX, ARIZONA 85003

DELIVERY INSTRUCTIONS

SEE ATTACHED INSTRUCTIONS

V
E
N
D
O
R

SHIP
TO

ON OR
BEFORE

I T M	CATALOG NO. REQ/ITEM NO.	D E S C R I P T I O N	QUANTITY AND UNIT OF ISSUE	UNIT PRICE	EXTENDED PRICE

I M P O R T A N T

TO AVOID INVOICING, THE VENDOR MUST ITEMIZE THIS SALE IN THE SPACE PROVIDED BELOW. ▼

ALL DISCREPANCIES MUST BE RECONCILED WITH THE DEPARTMENT OF MATERIALS MANAGEMENT BEFORE THIS ORDER IS FILLED. PLEASE CALL—
(602) · 262-3244

LESS CASH DISCOUNT		%	—
ON $	TAX	%	+
BUYER		TOTAL	

NEW 6-78 20-05-11

91-170
1221

▼ **VENDOR MUST COMPLETE THIS SECTION** ▼

ITM	QUANTITY	UNIT PRICE	AMOUNT
INVOICE #	CASH DISCOUNT ____ %		—
	TAX ____ %		+
		TOTAL	

TREASURER OF MARICOPA COUNTY
PHOENIX, ARIZONA
CASH PURCHASE ORDER

	WARRANT & CLAIM NO. X 00057

FUND	VOID 90 DAYS AFTER	DATE	AMOUNT $

NOT VALID FOR MORE THAN $500.00

PAY
TO THE
ORDER
OF

DRAWN BY MARICOPA COUNTY BOARD OF SUPERVISORS

MATERIALS MANAGEMENT DEPARTMENT AUTHORIZED SIGNATURE	CONTROLLER'S DEPARTMENT AUTHORIZED SIGNATURE

⑆90000057⑆ ⑈122101706⑈ 212 001⑉000212⑈

Figure 3-2 (*continued*)

DO NOT BACK ORDER

— N O T I C E —

This purchase order utilizes a recent development in purchasing procedures. You will be pleased to note that a warrant is attached so that you can receive immediate payment for this order for an amount LESS THAN $500.00.

As soon as you have shipped the order and calculated the amount due you you need only to do the following:

(1)   Complete the detail of the invoice section of the warrant and fill in the amount due you on the face of the warrant. Be sure you allow applicable cash discount.

(2)   Detach the warrant, endorse it, and deposit it in your bank.

(3)   This order has been issued pursuant to a quotation and your warrant entries must conform hereto. Please fill in one shipment--- do not backorder.

(4)   If you are unable to ship within 20 days, please advise the appropriate Buyer at once.

(5)   All discrepancies must be reconciled with the Department of Materials Management before this order is filled. Please call (602) 262-3244.

We feel certain that you will be pleased to receive immediate payment upon shipment. We both will gain through your careful attention to the details of processing this order.

SHIP COMPLETE TO ADDRESS SHOWN IN SHIP TO BLOCK

who has the power to requisition. Under no circumstances should the purchasing department accept requisitions from anyone other than those specifically authorized. This is just as important as it is for all sales personnel to know definitely that a requisition is not an order.

All requisitions should be checked carefully before any action is taken. The requested quantity should be based upon anticipated needs and should be compared to economical purchasing quantities. The delivery date requested should allow for sufficient time to secure quotations and samples, if necessary, and to execute the purchase order and obtain delivery. If insufficient time is allowed, or the date would involve additional expense, this should be brought to the attention of the requisitioner immediately.

The procedure for handling requisitions upon receipt in the purchase office is of sufficient importance to warrant citing an example:

Upon receipt of the requisitions in the purchasing office, after being time-stamped, all requisitions are turned over to the order typist or clerk, who has the specification cards and who will attach the proper specification card to each individual requisition. The requisitions then are turned over to the buyer, who will mark all contract items, placing on the requisition the word "contract," the name of the firm with which the order is to be placed, the price, terms, the f.o.b. point, the total value, and the payment date, for the controller's information. The requisitions then will be turned back to the order typist, who will type the order, after which it will be carefully checked with the specification card, the price, terms, etc., before the order is finally mailed to the vendor.

When items are not covered by contract, request for quotations will be sent out on standard inquiry blanks provided for this purpose. Where quotations are to be requested, a list of the names of potential vendors will be written on the back of the requisitions. The requisitions then will be turned over to the typist, who will make out standard inquiry forms and turn them over to the buyer, who will check and sign before mailing.

When the quotations are received from the various vendors, they will be entered on the quotation sheet by the clerk and then turned over to the buyer, who will determine the vendor with whom the business is to be placed. The buyer then initials the requisition and turns it over to the order typist who will type the order.

Use of the traveling requisition

In the search to reduce operating expenses, some companies have found it desirable to use the so-called traveling requisition for recurring requirements of materials and standard parts. The traveling requisition is a cardboard form used when a particular item must be purchased frequently for a given department. The traveler contains a complete description of the item, and is sent to purchasing when a resupply of the item is needed by the user, indicating quantity and date needed. Purchasing writes the PO, enters data on vendor, price, and PO number on the traveler, and sends it back to the requisitioner, who puts the card in the files until a subsequent resupply is needed. As many as 24 to 36 purchases can be triggered by this traveler card. Use of the traveler eliminates the recopying of routine description data and substitutes for 24 to 36 individual purchase requisitions, saving paperwork and clerical time. It also provides a complete, cumulative purchase history and use record on one form.

One side of the card provides for the following information:
Across the top of the card:

1. Part number or description of item or material to be covered and where it is used.
2. Maximum stock; ordering point; and minimum stock.

Lower portion of the card:

1. At the left, an "Ordered" section provides for the date; purchase order number; date required; the department for which the requisition is placed; the quantity required; and a space for an authorized signature of approval.
2. On the right, a "Received" section provides for recording the date; purchase order number; quantity; and the cost of the ordered item when received.

The reverse side of the card provides for the purchase order description of the item and part number, if any; a list of approved vendors, including the cash discount terms and f.o.b. point for each; and columns to show which vendor received the order, the purchase order number, the quantity, required date, unit price, and a place for the name of the buyer and date.

When parts or material covered by the traveling requisition are being ordered, the inventory control clerk inserts the date, the date required, the name of the department for which the request is made, and the quantity, and obtains an authorized signature prior to sending the requisition to the purchasing department. After selecting the vendor, the buyer fills in the vendor's code number, quantity, required date, unit price, and his or her name and date, and returns the card to the inventory control department after the PO is prepared.

Use of the bill of materials requisition

A second variation is the bill of material (B/M). It is used by firms who make a standard, manufactured item over a relatively-long period of time, as a quick way of notifying purchasing of production needs. A B/M for a toaster made by an appliance manufacturer would list the total number or quantity, including an appropriate scrap allowance, of parts or material to make one end unit. Production scheduling then merely notifies purchasing that it has scheduled 18,000 of that model into production next month. Purchasing then will "explode" the B/M (normally by a computerized system) by multiplying through by 18,000 to determine the *total* quantity of material needed to meet next month's production schedule. Comparison of these numbers with quantities in inventory will give purchasing the "open to buy" figures. Use of the B/M system is a means of simplifying the requisitioning process where a large number of frequently-needed line items is involved.

Stockless buying or systems contracting[2]

This technique is relatively new and has been used most frequently in buying stationery and office supplies, repetitive items, and maintenance and repair materials, and operating supplies (MRO). This latter class of purchases is characterized by many different types of items, all of comparatively low value and needed immediately when any kind of a plant or equipment failure occurs. The technique is built around a blanket-type contract which is developed in great detail regarding approximate quantities to be used in specified time periods, prices, provisions for adjusting prices, procedures to be followed in picking up requisitions daily and making delivery within 24 hours, simplified billing procedures, and a complete catalog of all items covered by the contract.

Generally the inventory of all items covered by a contract is stored by the supplier, thus eliminating the buyer's investment in inventory and space. Requisitions for items covered by the contract go directly to the supplier and are not processed by the purchasing department. The requisition is used by the supplier to pull stock, to pack, to invoice, and as a delivery slip. The streamlined procedure reduces paper handling costs for the buyer and the seller and has been a help in solving the small-order problem.

Some organizations use a Data Phone system in systems contracting which requires a data transmission terminal in the purchasing department. The buyer simply inserts a pre-punched card for each item needed and indicates the quantity required, which is transmitted electronically to the vendor's computer, which types out the purchase order, at the previously-agreed-upon contract price for each item.

Systems contracting has become popular in nonmanufacturing organizations as well. It is no longer confined to MRO items and may well include a number of high-dollar volume commodities. The shortening of the time span from requisition to delivery has resulted in substantial inventory reductions and greater organizational willingness to go along with the supply system. The amount of "red tape" has become minimal. Since the user normally provides a good estimate of requirements and compensates the supplier in case the forecast is not good, the supplier risks little in inventory investment. The degree of cooperation and information exchange required between buyer and seller in a systems contract often results in a much warmer relationship than normally exhibited in a traditional arms-length trading situation.

Selection of possible sources of supply

Supplier selection constitutes an important part of the purchasing function, and involves the location of qualified sources of supply and making a satisfactory agreement as to delivery and price of the desired material. Among the basic

---

[2]For a full description see American Management Association, *Systems Contracting,* Management Bulletin 63, New York, 1965; and Ralph A. Bolton, *Systems Contracting* (New York: American Management Association, 1966).

records in a well-organized purchasing office should be:

1. a record of outstanding contracts against which orders are placed as required.
2. a commodity classification of items purchased.
3. a record of vendors.

With many commodities which are in constant use by an organization, particularly those for which there is an open and free market on which quotations can be obtained at practically any hour of the day, no problem is involved. Bids are often called for, however, on merchandise of common use, such as stationery. A typical bid form is illustrated by Figure 3–3.

Analysis of bids; placing order

Analysis of the quotes and the selection of the vendor lead to the placing of an order. Since analysis of bids and the selection of the vendor are matters of judgment, it is necessary only to indicate here that they are logical steps in purchasing. A form is used by many firms to assist in making an analysis of the propos-

Figure 3–3
Quotation request

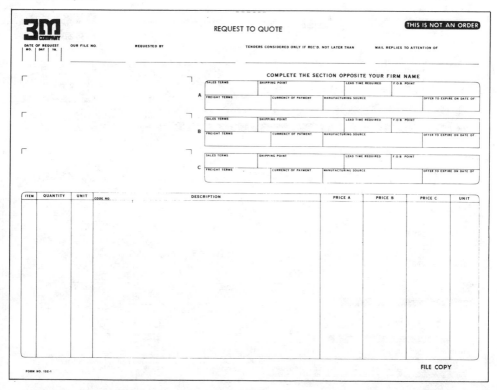

als, but there is no uniformity of practice. Purchase orders at times may be placed without securing any quotations.

The placing of an order usually involves the use of a purchase order (see Figure 3–4) unless it becomes necessary to use the vendor's sales agreement instead, or if a stockless buying contract is used. Failure to use proper contract form may result in serious legal complications. Furthermore, the transaction may not be properly recorded. Therefore, even where an order is placed by telephone, a written order should follow for purposes of confirmation. At times, when emergency conditions arise it may be expedient to send a truck to pick up parts without first going through the usual procedure of requisition and purchase order. But in no instance—unless it be for minor purchases from petty cash—should materials be bought without a written order of some sort.

All companies have purchase order forms; in practice, however, all purchases are not governed by the conditions stipulated on the purchase order but rather are governed by the sales agreement submitted by the seller. A comparison of the sales agreements and the purchase order forms may be interesting. Since every company naturally seeks to protect itself as completely as possible, responsibilities which the purchase order form assigns to the source of supply are, in the

Figure 3–4
Purchase order

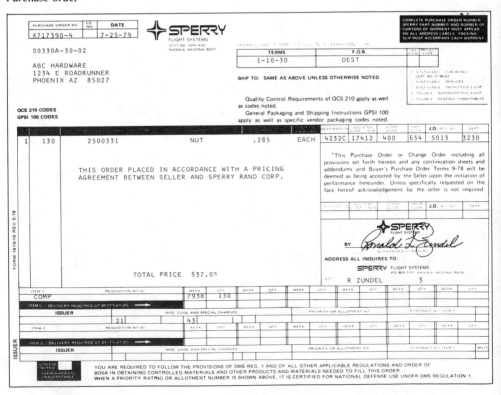

sales agreement, often transferred to the buyer. Naturally, a company is anxious to use its own sales agreement when selling its products and its own purchase order form when buying.

Some purchasing officers assert that they will not make any purchase except on their own order form. If the seller strenuously objects to any of the conditions contained in the order form and can present good reasons for the modification of such provisions, a compromise is effected. In a strong sellers' market, however, it may be difficult to adhere to this rule. Also, some suppliers refuse to sell except when the buyer signs their sales order form. If there is no alternative source, as, for example, when an electrical company holds a patent on an article, the value of which is so outstanding that no substitute is acceptable, then the purchasing officer has no choice in the matter. But ordinarily the choice as to which document shall actually be used depends somewhat upon the comparative strength of the two parties, the character of the commodity being purchased, the complexity of the transaction, and the strategy used in securing or placing the order.

A good deal of confusion seems to prevail on this whole matter. A purchasing agent may freely sign a salesman's order form (which, though it may bind the purchaser, legally is not likely to be binding upon the vendor until later confirmed by his home office) and then send a purchase order to the vendor, expecting it to govern. Or a purchasing agent, subsequent to the mailing of a purchase order, may receive in reply not an acceptance but a sales order, which really is a counteroffer, and not an acceptance.

However, in the case of low-dollar-value POs, having a legally-binding agreement may not be of great importance, for the likelihood of subsequent legal action is very low.

Form of the purchase order ✗

Purchase order forms vary tremendously as to format and routing through the organization. The movement to secure a standard purchase order form has not gained much headway.

The essential requirements on any satisfactory purchase order form are: the serial number, date of issue, the name and address of the firm receiving the order, quantity and description of the items ordered, date of delivery required, shipping directions, price, terms of payment, and conditions governing the order.

These conditions governing the relations between the buyer and the seller are extremely important and the question of what should and what should not be included is subject to a good deal of discussion. What actually appears on the purchase order form of any individual company is usually the result of experience. The items included in the conditions might:

1. Contain provisions to guard the buyer from damage suits caused by infringement.
2. Contain provisions concerning prices, such as, "If the price is not stated on

this order, material must not be billed at a price higher than last paid without notice to us and our acceptance thereof.''

3. Contain clauses stating that no charges will be allowed for boxing, crating, or drayage.
4. Contain stipulations stating that the acceptance of the materials is contingent upon inspection and quality.
5. Require in case of rejection that the seller receive a new order from the buyer before replacement is made.
6. Mention rejection because of quality.
7. Provide for cancellation of the order if deliveries are not received on the date specified in the order and agreed to by the seller.
8. Contain conditions stating that the buyer refuses to accept drafts drawn against him.
9. Have some mention of quantity, presumably relating to overshipments or undershipments of the quantities called for. The explanation of this provision is probably to be found in the fact that in certain industries it is hard to control definitely the amount obtained from a production run, and in such instances overruns and underruns are usually accepted within certain limits.
10. Provide for matters of special interest to the companies issuing the forms, governing such matters as arbitration, and the disposition of tools required in making parts.

Individual companies differ widely both in the number of copies of a purchase order issued and in the method of handling these copies. In a typical example, the distribution may be as follows: The original is sent to the supplier, sometimes accompanied by a duplicate copy to be returned by the vendor as an acceptance. One copy is sent to the stores or other requisitioning department to serve as notice that the order has been placed, to give an opportunity to check it against the corresponding requisition, and, if necessary, to furnish a purchase order number which is entered on the copy of the requisition held by stores. Two copies may be retained by the purchasing department for its own use. One copy is sent to the accounting department. Sometimes a copy is sent to the receiving department (particularly if receiving and stores are organizationally separate) where it may be filed alphabetically by vendor until the goods arrive.

All the copies of the purchase order, though essentially identical and all typed at one operation, are by no means identical in form. For instance, the vendor's acceptance copy may contain an acceptance statement not reproduced on any of the other copies. Only the receiving department's copy may provide for entering the receiving data. The purchasing department copies may provide space for data regarding delivery promise, invoices, and shipments. Pricing information is often eliminated from the receiving copy.

As might be expected, purchase orders are filed in various ways. The really important thing is to be able to locate the documents any time they are wanted. So far as possible, too, all papers relating to a particular purchase order should be attached to one copy or, if necessary to file some elsewhere, cross-referenced so they can be found quickly. Nothing reflects more unfavorably on a purchasing department than to have inquiries made by users, production, stores, engineering, or accounting personnel concerning information answerable only from the purchase order and to find the purchasing personnel cannot answer the questions promptly and authoritatively.

One method of filing the purchase orders, where two are kept, is to file one numerically by purchase order number, and to file the second, together with the accompanying requisition and correspondence, alphabetically by vendor's name.

Still another procedure is to file one alphabetically by vendor, and the second copy in a tickler file under the date the acceptance copy should be received from the vendor. In case acceptance is not received according to the time due, this fact is noted on this copy of the purchase order, follow-up is instituted in an effort to get the acceptance, and the purchase order is moved ahead to a second "acceptance date." When the order is finally accepted, the tickler copy is again moved, this time being filed under the date either by which final follow-up is desirable or by which the shipment is due.

Giving or sending a purchase order does not constitute a contract until it has been accepted. The usual form of acceptance requested is that of an "acknowledgement" sent by the vendor to the purchasing department. Just what does constitute mutual consent and the acceptance of an offer is primarily a legal question. Generalizations concerning the acceptance of offers, as any lawyer will indicate, are likely to be only generalizations with many exceptions.

One further reason for insisting upon securing an acceptance of the purchase order is that, quite aside from any question of law, unless the order is accepted, the buyer can only assume that delivery will be made by the requested date. When delivery dates are uncertain, definite information in advance is most important if the buyer is to plan operations effectively.

Blanket and open-end orders ✕

The cost of issuing and handling purchase orders may be reduced when conditions permit the use of blanket or open-end orders. A blanket order usually covers a variety of items. An open-end order allows for addition of items and/or extension of time. MRO items and production line requirements used in volume and purchased repetitively over a period of months may be bought in this manner.

All terms and conditions involving the purchase of estimated quantities over a period are negotiated and incorporated in the original order. Subsequently, releases of specific quantities are made against the order. In some instances, it is possible to tie the preparation of the releases into the production scheduling procedures and forward them to the purchasing department for transmission to the vendor. It is not unusual for an open-end order to remain in effect for a year, or until changes in design, material specification, or conditions affecting price or delivery make new negotiations desirable or necessary. Figure 3–5 shows a form used to authorize release of materials on a blanket order.

Figure 3–5
Blanket order release

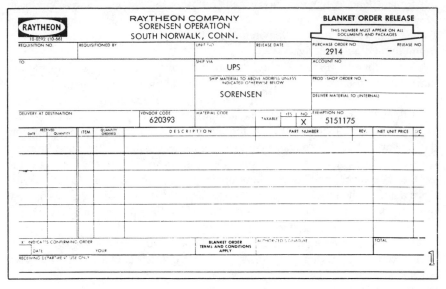

Follow-up and expediting

After a PO has been issued to a vendor, the buyer may wish to follow up and/or expedite the order. At the time the order is issued, an appropriate follow-up date is indicated. In some firms, purchasing has full-time follow-up and expediting personnel.

Follow-up is the routine "tracking" of an order to assure that the vendor will be able to meet delivery promises. If problems, e.g., quality or delivery, are developing, the buyer needs to know this as soon as possible, so that appropriate action can be taken. Follow-up, which requires frequent inquiries of the vendor on progress and possibly a visit to the vendor's facility, will be done only on large-dollar and/or long-leadtime buys. Figure 3–6 shows one follow-up form.

Expediting is the application of pressure on vendors to get them either to meet the original delivery promise or to deliver ahead of schedule. It may involve the threat of order cancellation or withdrawal of future business if the vendor cannot meet the agreement. Expediting should be necessary on only a small percentage of the PO's issued, for if the buyer has done a good job of analyzing vendor capabilities, only reliable vendors—ones who will perform according to the purchase agreement—will be selected. And if the firm has done an adequate job of planning its material requirements, it should not need to ask a vendor to move up the delivery date except in unusual situations. Of course, in times of scarcity such as the early 1970s, the expediting activity assumes greater importance.

Conditions do exist, with both the supplier and the buyer, which warrant definite provision for some kind of follow-up and expediting system. Though a

Figure 3–6
Follow-up on order   (8½ × 11 in.)

Purchasing Department

Date_____

We are trying to conserve your time
as well as ours by using this form. It is sent
you in duplicate to enable you to use one copy
for a REPLY and keep the other for your files.

Gentlemen:
   This is an IMPORTANT REQUEST for INFORMATION concerning
   SHIPMENTS against our

Order No._____   Dated_____   Please answer items checked.

SHIPMENTS			
1. When will you ship?			
2. In what quantity will you ship?			
3. Did you ship on date shown on order? How?			
4. Can you advance promised shipping date?			
5. Why did you not ship as promised?			
6. Make your delivery promise more specific.			
7. Please start tracer on shipment made.			
8. Release shipments as shown under remarks.			
9. Give us forwarding reference so we can trace.		Date shipped	
		From	
		Consignee	
		Car initials and number	
		Waybill reference	
		Carding Points	
		Remarks	
10. When will you ship balance of order?			
11. Advise present status of order and when you expect to complete.			

REMARKS

_____

_____

Mail Reply to   Yours truly,

_____

_____

general policy should be established for the entire purchasing department, the immediate responsibility for expediting is likely to rest upon the buyer who placed the order, on the ground that this buyer knows the individuals to be contacted in the vendor firm and is therefore able to get more personal and prompt attention, while at the same time (and this is most important) preserving friendly relations.

ⅹ Receipt and inspection of goods

The proper receipt of materials and other items is of vital importance. The great majority of firms have, as a result of experience, centralized all receiving under one department, the chief exceptions being those large companies with multiple plants. Receiving is so closely related to purchasing that, in probably 70 percent of the cases, the receiving department is directly or indirectly responsible to the purchasing department.

The arrival of the goods always involves one additional step, and sometimes two. All incoming shipments must be checked by the receiving department. In practice, receiving is not always provided with a copy of the purchase order. This way the check by receiving against the goods on receipt is a completely independent one, commonly reported on a "materials received" form and transmitted to the stores division. This report (Figure 3–7) gives the vendor's name, the order number, and the quantity received. Three or four copies of this report are commonly made; one is sent to the purchasing department to close its files; one to the stores department; one to the accounts payable department to be checked against the invoice; and sometimes one also is sent to the traffic department.

Aside from checking the quantity of goods received, there is the problem of inspection. Inspection for quality is handled differently by various concerns. Some merchandise is not inspected for quality at all; some is inspected only by sampling; and some is checked by the laboratory. A concern may have a quality control department which determines how much and how frequently and in what manner inspection shall be made. Following inspection, it may be necessary to return some of the material to the supplier. The problem of inspection is discussed in more detail in Chapter 4.

In checking the goods received, it sometimes will appear that shortages exist either because material has been lost en route or because it was short-shipped. Occasionally, too, there is evidence that the shipment has been tampered with or that the shipment has been damaged in transit. In all such cases, full reports are called for, going to both the traffic department and the purchasing department.

ⅹ Clearing the invoices

Invoices usually arrive before the goods, except on local deliveries, in which case they arrive almost simultaneously with them. Since the invoice constitutes a definite claim against the buyer, it needs to be handled with great care. Invoices are commonly requested in duplicate. In addition, it is not uncommon to find

Figure 3-7
Materials received record

121 D-F110

WHITE—Accts. Payable
CANARY—Receiving Dept. ,
PINK—Stores Dept.
BLUE—Purch. Dept.

№ 833602

RECEIVING SLIP

RECEIVING DEPT.   Date_____19____

Received for_____

Shipped by_____

P. O._____Req._____Dept._____

Rolls	Bundles	Boxes	Crates	Pkgs.	Drums	Reels	Bbls.

Via_____   Charges_____   Pro._____   Date_____

Car No._____   Seals_____

Our Weight_____

Carrier's Weight_____

Pack. Slip No._____

Case Nos._____

Delivered to_____

For { Weights and Chgs. / Bal. of Shipment } See

R. S. No._____

Card No._____

Charges Carried $_____

Invoice No._____Date_____

Amount_____Date Passed_____

Passed by_____ As Checked_____

For balance of shipment see R. S._____

Complete File R. S._____Auditor

Z Order No._____

Mat'l._____
Billed—CONTRA
          NO CHARGE_____

such statements as "invoices must show our order number and itemized price for each article invoiced."

Procedure relating to invoice clearance is not uniform. In fact, there is difference of opinion on whether the checking and approval of the invoice is a function of the purchasing department or of the accounting department. Clearly, the invoice must be checked and audited. Many concerns maintain that since the work is accounting in character, the accounting department should do it. In such companies, verification of delivery is given by the receiving department; inspection verifies quality; and prices, terms, and extensions are checked in the accounting department. For this purpose a copy of each purchase order is filed in the accounting department. The arguments for this procedure are that such checking is essentially an accounting function; that it relieves the purchasing department of the performance of a task not essential to purchasing; and that it concentrates all the accounting work in a single office. This practice constitutes a safeguard against dishonesty in the purchase or receipt of goods that might lead to some irregularities in billing. On the other hand, sending the invoices to the accounting department for checking and auditing complicates the procedure, results in an additional administrative cost, and tends to slow down the clearing of the transaction. Occasional "spot-checking" may remove any temptation toward collusion between buyer and vendor.

The prime reason for having invoices checked in the purchasing department is that this is where the original agreement was made. If discrepancies exist, immediate purchasing action can be taken.

Where the invoice is normally handled by the accounting department, the following procedure is typical:

1.   All invoices are mailed in duplicate by the vendor directly to the accounting department, where they are promptly time-stamped. The accounting department checks all invoices and certifies them for payment, except where the purchase order and the invoice differ.

2.   Invoices at variance with the purchase order on price, terms, or other features are referred to the purchasing department for approval.

If any of the necessary information is not on the invoice or if the information does not agree with the purchase order, the invoice is returned to the vendor for correction. Ordinarily, the buyer insists that, in computing discounts, the allowable period dates from the receipt of the corrected invoice, and not from the date originally received.

In every instance of cancellation of a purchase order involving the payment of cancellation charges, the accounting department requires from the purchasing department a "change notice" referring to the order and defining the payment to be made before passing an invoice for such payment. The director of purchases must approve cancellation charges if the amount is over a specified figure.

In cases where purchasing does the invoice checking, the following procedure applies: after being checked and adjusted for any necessary corrections, the original invoice is forwarded to the accounting department to be held until the purchasing department authorizes its payment. The duplicate invoice is retained by the purchasing department until the receiving department notifies it of the receipt of the materials. As soon as the purchasing department obtains this notification in the form of a receiving report, it checks that report against the invoice. If the receiving report and invoice agree, the purchasing office keeps both documents until it receives assurance from inspection that the goods are acceptable. The purchasing department then forwards its duplicate copy of the invoice and the report from the receiving department to the accounting department, where the original copy of the invoice is already on file.

The purchasing department will check the receiving report in cases where the receiving department has made a blind check of the goods received, without reference to the original purchase order. In companies which follow a practice of having the receiving department compare the merchandise received with the purchase order, the purchasing department does not check the receiving report; upon receipt of this report and of a favorable report from the inspection division, it simply sends the receiving report with the invoice to the accounting department as authorization for payment.

Sometimes suppliers are negligent about invoicing goods shipped, and it may be necessary to request the invoice to complete the transaction. On the other hand, payment of an invoice prior to the receipt of material is often requested. The question then is: When invoices do provide for cash discounts, do you pay the invoice within the discount period, even though the material may not actually have been received, or do you withhold payment until the material arrives, even at the risk of losing cash discounts?

The arguments for withholding payment of the invoice until after the goods have arrived are as follows:

1. Frequently the invoice does not reach the buyer until late in the discount period and, on occasion, may even arrive after it. This situation arises through a failure on the part of the vendor (a) to mail the invoice promptly, especially where due allowance is not made for the Saturdays, Sundays, or holidays which elapse between the dating of the invoice and the processing and mailing of it, and (b) where the vendor is, in terms of "mailing time," several days away from the buyer.

2. It is unsound buying practice to pay for anything until an opportunity has been given for inspection. The transaction has not, in fact, been completed until the material or part has actually been accepted, and payment prior to this time is premature. In fact, legally, the title to the goods may not have passed to the buyer until acceptance of them.

3. In any event, the common practice of dating invoices as of the date of shipment should be amended to provide that the discount period runs from receipt of the invoice or the goods.

The arguments in favor of passing the invoice for payment without awaiting the arrival, inspection, and acceptance of the material are several:

1. The financial consideration may be substantial.

2. Failure to take the cash discounts as a matter of course reflects unfavorably on the credit standing of the buyer.

3.   When purchasing from reputable vendors, mutually satisfactory adjustments arising out of unsatisfactory material will easily be made, even though the
invoice has been paid.

Obviously, the problem of payment to take cash discounts before material
actually is received can be solved if purchasing is successful in negotiating cash
discount terms "from receipt of invoice or material, whichever occurs later."

Maintenance of records

After having gone through the steps described, all that remains for the disposal of any order is to complete the records of the purchasing department. This
operation involves little more than assembling and filing the purchasing department's copies of the documents relating to the order and transferring to ap-
propiate records the information the department may wish to keep. The former is
largely a routine matter. The latter involves judgment as to what records are to be
kept and also for how long.

Most companies differentiate between the various forms and records as to
their importance. For example, a purchase order constitutes evidence of a contract with an outside party and as such may well be retained much longer than the
requisition, which is an internal memorandum.

Importance of a procedure and policy manual

Carefully prepared, detailed statements of organization, of duties of the various personnel, and of procedures and filing systems (including illustrative forms,
fully explained) are of value not only to the senior members of the department but
even more so to newcomers. A manual is almost an essential for a well-con-
ceived in-company training program for junior members. Furthermore, it adds an
element of flexibility in facilitating the transfer of personnel from one job to
another in case of vacation, illness, or the temporary overburdening of a particular segment of the organization. Finally, the manual is useful in explaining
to those not in the department what and how things are done.

Some managers feel that because their departments are not so large as those in
bigger companies, there is no special need for a manual. They feel that everyone
knows all that would commonly be put in a manual anyway and that hence there
is no need for writing it all down. This argument overlooks the benefits gained in
the actual task of preparing the manual.

The preparation of a manual is a time-consuming and somewhat tedious task,
to be sure, but one well worth the cost. It is well to bear in mind that unless the
work is carefully planned and well done, is accurate, and is reasonably complete,
it might almost as well not be done at all. Careful advance planning of the coverage, emphasis, and arrangement is essential, to include a clear definition of the
purposes sought in issuing the manual and the uses to which it is to be put, for
both of these have bearing on its length, form, and content.

Very early in the project, the preparer must decide whether the manual is to cover only policy or is to include also a description of the organization and the procedure, and if the latter, in how much detail. A collection of manuals now in use should be the starting point. Fortunately, excellent sample manuals that will serve as guides can be obtained from any number of companies.

When the general outlines have been determined, the actual writing may be undertaken. This work need not be done all at one time but section by section as the opportunity presents itself. It also is well to have the work thoroughly discussed and carefully checked, not only by those within the department itself but by those outside, such as engineering and production personnel, whose operations are directly affected. When a section is completed, that portion may provide the basis for a department discussion forum, not only for the sake of spotting errors and suggesting modifications before the material is actually reproduced but also to ensure that everyone understands its contents. This should be done prior to issue. When reproduced, a loose-leaf form generally may be found preferable, to allow for easy revision. Another worthwhile step is to have the president of the company write a short foreword, endorsing the policy and practices of the department and defining its authority.

While many subjects might be covered in the manual, some of the more common are: authority to requisition, competitive bidding, approved vendors, vendor contacts and commitments, authority to question specifications, purchases for employees, gifts, blanket purchase orders, confidential data, rush orders, vendor relations, lead times, determination of quantity to buy, over and short allowance procedure, local purchases, capital equipment, personal service purchases, repair service purchases, authority to select vendors, confirming orders, unpriced purchase orders, documentation for purchase decisions, invoice clearance and payment, invoice discrepancies, freight bills, change orders, samples, returned materials, disposal of scrap and surplus, determination of price paid, small order procedures, salesperson interviews, and reporting of data.

Use of data processing in purchasing

Up to this point, the discussion and the analysis of the procedures needed and used in performing the purchasing function have been based on the use of traditional office equipment and clerical methods. Within the past 25 years, however, we have witnessed a remarkable development of data processing equipment use in aiding the recording, analysis, and reporting of information in the operation of complex business systems, scientific research, and the military.

When data processing equipment is installed to assist in performing the purchasing function, the essential steps of good purchasing remain much the same as those of the manual methods. The change occurs only in the way the essential steps are performed. When it is economically feasible to introduce data processing equipment, four basic benefits are obtained:

1. The mechanized handling of procedures reduces clerical manual effort to a minimum.

2. Information from records becomes available almost instantly.
3. Control over operations is improved, not only by the timely availability of the information for sound decision making but also by the flexibility afforded by the ease of handling vast quantities of detail, thus providing new tools for the buyer and manager.
4. Operating performance is improved by the availability of information and the improved control of operations.

At the beginning of this chapter, the essential steps of purchasing were listed. Here we will consider briefly how integrated data processing equipment and procedures apply to each step.

1. *Ascertainment of need.* When used properly, computers can be of great assistance in analyzing information pertaining to past usage, markets, economic factors, prices, and expected usage, to the end that forecasts can be made with promptness and improved accuracy. Computers can assist in translating forecasts into estimates of requirements and of the required materials, quantities, and delivery dates.

2. *Accurate statement of the character and amount of article or commodity desired.* The responsibility for developing an accurate statement or specification for the article or the commodity used in the firm normally rests with the engineering or the using department. After determination, the specification can be made readily available for use by data processing equipment by recording the specification on cards, tape, disc, or any of the various devices for storing information.

The quantities of the items required to be purchased are determined after obtaining the breakdown of the information mentioned in step 1 and exploding the bill of materials to determine the effect of existing inventories and open orders on the specific requirements. The requisition for specific requirements can be fed into the computer for an economical purchasing quantity analysis to consider such things as acquisition costs (including costs of placing an order, quantity discounts, transportation costs, and the like) against inventory carrying costs.

3. *Selection of possible sources of supply.* As the requisition is processed by the computer, information regarding suppliers, previously stored in the memory device of the computer, can provide lists of vendors and their past prices and record of performance.

4. *Analysis of alternatives and placement of order.* While it is possible to analyze vendors' proposals by programming them into a computer, it is probably not practical to do so except in situations in which there are many variable factors present, such as quantity discounts, transportation allowances, multiple plants to be supplied, and numerous suppliers scattered geographically. Usually, human judgment is used in making the final selection of the vendor. Once the final selection is made, the computer can produce the purchase order automatically.

5. *Follow-up the order.* When the purchase order is placed, an order status record is created. This record is kept up to date by recording the receipts of the ordered material, the invoices, the change orders, and the expediting data, thus providing the current status of each open order. This record becomes the basic

file for the invoice and receiving audit, the follow-up and expediting procedures, and some of the management and operations reports.

6. *Receipt and inspection of the goods.* Receiving and inspection reports can be fed into the order status record as received and used in auditing the invoice, in keeping inventory records, and in compiling quality reports.

7. *Checking the invoice.* When invoices are received, the computer matches the invoices to the purchase orders, and the computer can be programmed to audit price, quantity, extension, discounts if any, routing, and transportation terms. Where everything is in order, a check for the proper payment can be written automatically and held for the payment due date.

8. *Completion of the record.* Closed orders are usually carried in the order status record for a period to allow adequate time for any rejections or adjustments. Data on vendor performance and price and commodity history files can be maintained in the computer and produced on demand.

Figure 3–8 shows a simple flow chart of an automated purchasing system.

There are a larger number of potential uses to which the computer may be put and a number of research studies have attempted to determine the nature of current application. The first question deals with what is being done. Second, what are the implications of using computer-based systems?

Figure 3–8
Simplified flow chart of an automated purchasing system

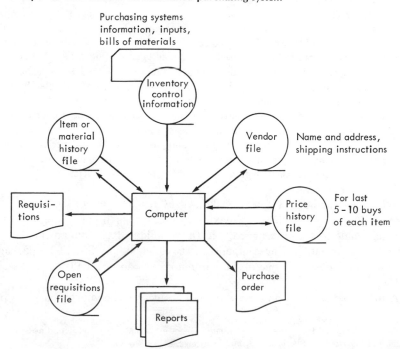

Computerized operating and reporting systems

A study by D. L. Moore and H. E. Fearon looked at the status of well-developed computer operating systems, and concluded:

> This study was done to determine how the computer is being used to aid purchasing in two specific application areas; (1) computer operating systems, and (2) computer management-reporting systems. With the background information from a number of articles which have been written on what several companies have done in computer applications principally during the decade of the 1960s, 15 firms or divisions of a larger firm were selected as a survey group to determine specifically how the computer currently is being used. These operations, geographically located in all parts of the United States, were selected on the basis of their having a sophisticated purchasing organization and sophisticated computer systems.
>
> Based on the interviews in these 15 operations, it was concluded that purchasing can benefit substantially from use of the computer. Major organizations processing tens of thousands of orders involving thousands of suppliers and items could not administer the purchasing function competitively without computer assistance. For the manufacturing firm that produces high-technology, complex products with significant amounts of purchased material content, computer assistance cannot be considered a luxury. It is a necessity.
>
> Each of the 15 firms has utilized computer technology to automate the data handling in most large-volume, repetitive situations. Accuracy and timeliness have been enhanced. The visibility of expenditures and the supplier base have been improved. Progressive organizations have third-generation computers and utilize the latest on-line communication devices. Purchasing management has been able to improve its planning, staffing, and controlling ability. Computers have been programmed to prepare reports which forecast beyond the order release period, allowing management to expand its planning horizon. Computers have been adopted for the measurement of work-loads, which has facilitated staffing decisions. Exception reporting techniques and comparison of actual results with predetermined goals are commonplace and provide opportunities for better management control. The orderliness, rapidity, and accuracy of the current computer applications have enabled purchasing management to achieve many of its objectives to a degree which would have been impractical, if not impossible, ten years ago.
>
> The major area of computer application is in the purchasing operating systems area. This area is a "natural" for the computer, since it involves principally the rapid and accurate manipulation and feedback of repetitive data.[3]

Tables 3–1 and 3–2 summarize the survey results. One of the key conclusions of this study was that, for maximum success, such purchasing computer systems should be "user designed," to fit the unique data requirements of each particular organization. Those organizations which simply installed a packaged program purchased from one of the computer companies usually were dissatisfied with the results.

A major development in the 1980s will be increased computer usage in pur-

---

[3] D. L. Moore and H. E. Fearon, "Computer Operating and Management Reporting Systems in Purchasing," *Journal of Purchasing* 9, no. 3 (August 1973): 38–39.

Table 3-1
Organization and system characteristics

Characteristics	Case 1	Case 2	Case 3	Case 4	Case 5	Case 6	Case 7	Case 8	Case 9	Case 10	Case 11	Case 12	Case 13	Case 14	Case 15
1. Number of different items purchased annually	10,000	20,000	25,000	10,000	122,000	25,000	25,000	30,000	(1)	50,000	31,000	16,000	(1)	90,000	(2)
2. Annual sales	$100-200 Mill	$50-100 Mill	$100-200 Mill	$40 Mill	$700 Mill	$70 Mill	$1,000 Mill +	$300 Mill (3)	(1)	$300 Mill	$200 Mill (3)	$200 Mill	$1,300 Mill	$500-1,000 Mill	$200 Mill (3)
3. Annual value of purchased materials and services	$45 Mill	$23 Mill	$71 Mill	$9 Mill	$155 Mill	$25 Mill	$500 Mill +	$100 Mill (3)	(1)	$120 Mill	$70 Mill	$80 Mill	$700 Mill	$230,000	$80 Mill
4. Number of personnel in purchasing organization	46	24	92	20	28	35	95	60	(1)	300	125	60	800	600	50
5. Annual computer system operating cost	$50,000	(2)	(2)	$70,000 (3)	$100,000 (3)	$120,000	$100,000 +	$300,000 (3)	(1)	$80,000	$200,000 (3)	$300,000 (3)	(1)	$3,000,000	(2)
6. Purchase orders issued annually	25,000	40,000	30,000	20,000	60,000	50,000	(2)	70,000	(1)	$100,000	50,000 (3)	40,000	(1)	60,000	(2)
7. System design responsibility in purchasing															
In materials	•						•	•					•		
In other organizational units		•	•	•	•	•			•	•	•	•		•	•
8. Purchasing within a materials management organization?	Yes	Yes	No	No	No	Yes	No	No	(1)	Yes	Yes	No	No	Yes	Yes
9. System installation date	1966	1960	1960	1969	1967	1965	1965	1960	1970	1967	1968	1972	1965-1970	1960	(1)
10. Primary file updating method batch	•	•	•		•	•	•	•	•	•		•	•	•	•
Online				•							•				
11. Online enquiry capability		•	•	•		•			•		•	•			•

(1) Not applicable
(2) Not available
(3) Estimated

Source: D. L. Moore and H. E. Fearon, "Computer Operating and Management Reporting Systems in Purchasing," *Journal of Purchasing* 9, no. 3 (August 1973): 25.

Table 3–2
Research findings—utilization of computer operating systems

Computer applications found in purchasing	Case 1	Case 2	Case 3	Case 4	Case 5	Case 6	Case 7	Case 8	Case 9	Case 10	Case 11	Case 12	Case 13	Case 14	Case 15
1. Receiving status systems	*	*	*	*	*	*	*	*	*	*	*	*	*	*	
2. Schedule control and expediting systems	*	*	*	*	*	*	*	*	*	*	*	*	*	*	
3. Open purchase order status systems	*	*	*	*	*	*		*	*	*	*	*	*		
4. Commodity expenditure profile systems	*	*	*			*	*	*	*	*		*	*	*	
5. Vendor expenditure profile systems	*	*	*			*	*	*	*	*		*	*	*	
6. Price and source history systems	*			*		*		*	*	*		*	*		*
7. Material requisition status systems	*					*	*	*	*		*	*	*		
8. Supplier delivery rating systems		*		*		*	*	*	*					*	*
9. Department and buyer workload measurement systems	*		*			*				*			*	*	
10. Supplier quality rating systems		*		*		*	*	*	*						
11. Forecasting systems			*		*	*	*					*			
12. Analysis of degree of competition systems		*								*			*		
13. Invoice exception systems					*		*	*	*						
14. Material price analysis systems						*							*		
15. Long-term contract status systems	*					*									
16. Subcontract management status systems														*	*

Source: D. L. Moore and H. E. Fearon, "Computer Operating and Management Reporting Systems in Purchasing," *Journal of Purchasing* 9, no. 3 (August 1973): 27.

chasing due to the mini- and micro-computer availability. With miniaturization and advancing technology, complete computer systems now are available in the $20,000 to 50,000 range. This puts computerization in reach of almost all but the smallest of organizations.

Implications of computer usage

Another study, by Wilson and Mathews,[4] tried to determine the effects of DP introduction on the purchasing function, and concluded there were three major implications for purchasing:

1. *Increased productivity.*

First, and foremost, improved purchasing information systems are creating a new class of purchasing people whose responsibilities are to structure and analyze purchasing problems. As routine tasks are taken over by the computer, it was anticipated that the purchasing manager's time, or a larger share of his time, would be devoted to increased use of creative decision-making techniques and problem solving. This trend is occurring slowly. Our data indicate that productivity, in terms of increased workload of the purchasing manager, has been tremendous. In other words, while we expected to find more time being spent in the creative aspects of decision making, it appears that the net result has been the more efficient use of time in much the same type of activities as before. In some instances, the productivity of a purchasing department was doubled through the use of a computer. While the computer does not replace the buyer, it does reduce the clerical support necessary to operate the department.

2. *Buying environment.*

A second area of change involves the structure of the buying environment. Our data showed that companies which had become involved in DP purchasing actually were using fewer suppliers than previously. A close analysis indicated that they were concentrating orders with fewer suppliers. The search of potential sources appeared to increase, but larger orders were placed with fewer vendors. The computer permits multiplant companies to accumulate their corporate purchasing requirements by item or commodity. It appears that the computer will stimulate systems or contract purchasing.

These forces also tend to increase the role of the corporate or staff purchasing group, since the development and maintenance costs of computer systems legislate against each plant unit independently developing its own system. These high costs encourage central coordination of computer activities to develop compatibility between the computer systems of the different corporate units.

3. *Effect on people.*

A third area of major importance is the effect of DP on the people currently in purchasing. The buyer's role is one of increased frustration. Instead of handling routine tasks, he now is confronted constantly with a new crisis or a problem from

---

[4]D. T. Wilson and H. L. Mathews, "Impact of Management Information Systems Upon Purchasing Decision Making," *Journal of Purchasing* 7, no. 1 (February 1971): 53–54.

the management by exception system that the computer necessitates. Our data indicate that it is very disturbing for a buyer to view his personal relations with the
marketing, production control, and production people as a constant series of problems. In other words, with the computer system, the buyer interacts with production or production control people only when a problem has arisen. It takes time for
all parties to recognize the change in their interaction pattern and to adjust.

INFORMATION SYSTEMS

Purchasing procedures are established basically to process inputs of information from outside the purchasing function and to produce outputs of information
needed by other functions and institutions outside the purchasing function. Few
business functions have the breadth of contacts both within the firm and with the
external environment that the well-operated purchasing function has.

Internal information flows to purchasing

Every functional activity within the firm generates information to, and/or requires information from the purchasing system. Figure 3–9 diagrams the information flows to purchasing. The information sent to purchasing breaks down into
the following two major categories.

1. Statements of needs for materials and services obtained from inside the firm.
2. Requests for information available within purchasing or obtainable from outside the firm.

A brief description of the information flows charted in Figure 3–9 follows.

Planning.   This function provides purchasing with information important in
obtaining the long-term future requirements of the firm for facilities, materials,
and outside services. Competent planning is of special importance in preparing
for future construction needs and for raw materials in tight or diminishing supply.

Sales forecasting.   Well-developed sales forecasts are one of the most helpful tools available to purchasing in planning strategies. Business operations usually achieve the greatest degree of operating efficiency when orderly planning
permits orderly acquisition and scheduling of requirements. When purchasing
has adequate advance notice of kinds of materials likely to be required and approximate quantities, it is in a favorable position to obtain the optimum balance
between the conditions in the marketplace and the needs of the firm.

Budgeting and financial control.   The information provided by the budgeting function helps in coordinating the information from planning and sales forecasting and brings into focus any constraints imposed by the financial control
function. Such constraints may apply to the operating expenses of the purchasing
system as well as to the possibilities of following other than a buy-as-required
inventory policy.

Accounting.   The accounting function supplies information on payments to
suppliers, cost studies for make-or-buy decisions, and comparison of actual expenditures to budget.

Figure 3-9
Internal information flows to purchasing

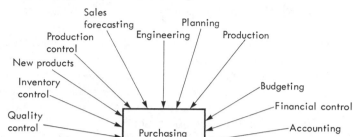

Legal. Since the purchasing function is the major activity authorized to commit the firm to contracts for materials and outside services, the legal function provides information regarding contracts and procedures.

Engineering. The basic responsibility of engineering is to provide information on what types of materials are needed and the specification of the qualities needed. The acknowledged right of purchasing to challenge specifications usually promotes more effective operation of the function for the benefit of the firm.

Production and production control. The production function frequently provides information on the quality requirements for materials. The production control and scheduling function provides information on what materials are needed and in what quantities for a given time period covered by a production cycle. Properly compiled, such information provides a useful tool in planning purchasing operations.

Inventory control. This function provides basic information on what needs to be purchased or ordered at any given time. The use of economic order quantities will be determined by the inventory policy which governs the investment in inventory at any given period. An inventory policy may be influenced by the financial resources of the firm, future plans, current market conditions, and lead time in the purchase of materials.

Quality control and receiving. Both of these functions provide information which determines if the suppliers have furnished materials of the quality and quantity specified. Such information is essential to the proper performance of the purchasing function.

New products. The importance of new products development to the success of a company has increased greatly in recent years. Unless information about new product development reaches purchasing at the inception of the project, the full contribution possible from purchasing will seldom be realized.

External information flows to purchasing

The efficiently operated purchasing department is one of the firm's major contact points with the external world and as such is a receiving point for a flow of information from sources outside the firm. Much of this information is essential to the operation of the firm. Figure 3–10 shows the nature of the information. A brief explanation of each of the major types of information coming from external sources follows:

General market conditions.   Competent purchasing executives and buyers become specialists on general market and business conditions. Suppliers' salesmen, purchasing trade publications, various National Association of Purchasing Management publications and services, and local purchasing association meetings and publications provide a constant stream of information about prices, supply and demand factors, and competitors' actions.

Sources of supply.   Suppliers' salesmen, advertising media of all types, special promotions, exhibits at trade shows and conventions, and credit and financial reports provide information initiated by vendors and aimed at their customers and potential customers.

Suppliers' capacity, suppliers' production rates, and labor conditions in the suppliers' plants and industries.   Information flows on these factors are of great importance in determining inventory policy and assuring continuity of production.

Prices and discounts, customs, sales and use taxes.   Information of any nature regarding prices is important to the effective functioning of purchasing. Much of the price information is obtained directly from suppliers or salesmen representing potential suppliers. The services of consultants specializing in economic trends are frequently useful in determining price trends, particularly of commodities. Both the customs and tax fields are rapidly changing, requiring continuous monitoring.

Transportation availability and rates.   The types, availability, and rates of transportation services have had an increasingly important bearing on the cost of materials within recent years. Whether problems involving transportation are the direct responsibility of a traffic department is not the critical point. It is how the information which is of importance in its effect on costs of material is used by purchasing.

New product and product information.   The great emphasis on creating new products has placed a heavy burden on the purchasing function. Purchasing must

Figure 3–10
External information flows to purchasing

process the information about products received from the outside in such a way that the appropriate function within the firm will be alerted to any product information, whether it be new or old, which can be useful in improving effectiveness, reducing costs, or aiding in developing new products for the firm.

Internal information flows from purchasing to the organization

There are very few functions of a business which are not concerned to some degree with the information which flows or can be generated from purchasing. Figure 3–11 diagrams the major types of information which flow from purchasing to the organization:

General management. Purchasing personnel have daily contact with a wide spectrum of the marketplace, and if properly qualified by education, ability, and experience, are in an advantageous position to collect up-to-the-minute information about current market and business conditions. These data, when correlated and refined, can provide top management with information valuable in the operation of the company.

Engineering. The engineering function requires much information from the marketplace. While there are situations which warrant the engineers making their own direct contacts with suppliers in order to obtain product and/or price information or place orders, such situations should be the exception. Competent purchasing specialists can provide more effective service by better sourcing and negotiation of lower prices than an engineer whose special competence is concerned with an engineering specialty.

Product development. Product development departments, regardless of whether they are part of the engineering or the marketing functions, benefit from new materials information and price information which the purchasing function

Figure 3–11
Internal information flows from purchasing

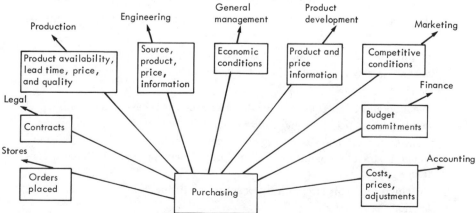

can provide from its contact in the marketplace. A purchasing function which recognizes its obligation to maximize information flow to new product activities performs a valuable service.

Marketing. The purchasing department is a target for the sales and promotion plans of many different suppliers from many industries. Perceptive purchasing personnel can frequently provide information on new types of selling campaigns which have value to the marketing function of their own·firm.

Production. The production function depends on purchasing for information about materials, material availability, material delivery lead times, material substitutes, and help in locating sources of supply for production equipment. Production also can be aided by purchasing with information about maintenance, repair, and operating supply items.

Legal. The purchasing department furnishes the legal department with all the information needed for drawing contracts for all types of materials purchased under a blanket contract or a stockless buying arrangement.

Finance and accounting. Purchasing is in a position to provide the finance and accounting functions with information basic to budget development and administration and determining cash requirements. Material and transportation costs and trends in costs, need for forward buying because of possible shortages resulting from greater demand, or anticipated interruption of supply such as happens during a major strike are some of the kinds of information purchasing provides to aid in planning financial operations.

Stores. The formulation of an inventory policy for a store's department is dependent on information concerning lead times and availability of materials, price trends, and substitute materials. The purchasing department is the best source of such information.

QUESTIONS FOR REVIEW AND DISCUSSION

1. In a company not now using the computer in purchasing, where would you start and what would you need to do to develop an integrated computer purchasing/materials management system?
2. What approaches, other than the standard purchasing procedure, might be used to minimize the small order problem?
3. Outline and discuss the steps involved in a sound purchasing procedure.
4. Where, and how, should invoices be cleared for payment within an organization?
5. What should be the information flows between purchasing and (1) internal organizational activities and (2) external activities?
6. What contribution to purchasing efficiency might be effected through the use of (1) the traveling requisition, (2) the bill of material, and (3) systems contracting?
7. In which areas of purchasing procedure might the computer profitably be applied?

8. How do follow-up and expediting procedures differ?
9. What items should be covered in a policy manual? Write a proposed policy statement for three of the items.
10. Are "rush orders" ever justified? When? How should they be handled?

CASE 3–1
VANIER UNIVERSITY

In August, Mr. Emery, newly appointed executive assistant to the vice president of administration and finance of Vanier University, assumed the responsibility for the purchasing department. Previously, it had been under the comptroller's authority. In discussions with purchasing personnel, Mr. Emery found out that the receiving processes on the campus were a source of annoyance. For example, lost orders, missing goods, and delays seemed to occur frequently.

University background

Vanier University was a large, well-known Louisiana university. Like most universities, it expanded rapidly in the 60s and early 70s; currently it included over 200 administrative and academic departments. More than 14,000 full-time students were registered in its faculties. Vanier's total budget amounted to approximately $95 million a year.

Five access roads led to the 500-acre campus site which included over 50 buildings. Each building could be considered as a receiving center for the university's various requirements. More than half of the buildings had special delivery facilities like unloading docks.

Purchases

The nature of purchases was very broad and varied from mice to computer equipment. The purchasing department grouped products and services in 83 different classes of expenses. Thirty-nine classes of these 83 had annual expenditures of $75,000 and over (see Exhibit 1). Forty-nine percent of all classes used 94 percent of the total dollars recorded. During the last year, 32,000 purchase orders were issued on 4,000 account numbers. Records from purchasing's Annual Activity Report indicated a total of $25.1 million spent with 9,345 different suppliers. This amount did not include $5.7 million for three types of goods purchased independently: books for the libraries, food for the cafeterias, and supplies to be resold by the bookstore.

Exhibit 1
Selected list of product classes by supplier for last year

Product class	Class title	Suppliers	Purchase orders	Average $ per each supplier	Average $ per each purchase order
A045	Decor	33	163	$3338	$ 676
A060*	Electrical supplies & equipment ..	100	604	970	161
A070*	Heating	100	390	5798	149
A080*	Plumbing	57	128	428	191
A090	Clean supplies & equipment	112	757	1507	223
A100	Contracts.....................	—	(Range too Wide)		—
A110	Construction	1	1	—	—
C020	Furniture	116	687	6826	1153
C030	Class supplies & equipment	32	112	5146	1470
D010	Lab chemicals	252	1987	646	82
D020	Lab glass	93	651	891	127
D030	Lab supplies	1281	5401	495	118
D035	Lab electronics.................	112	495	764	173
D040	Scientific equipment	441	1088	3192	1294
D070	Surgical supplies & equipment ...	105	476	1888	417
D100	Scientific maintenance	161	451	551	197
D120	Physical education	95	225	840	355
E010	A/V supplies & equipment	406	1175	770	266
E030	Photo supplies	137	894	686	105
H010*	Computers	103	292	7198	2539
H020	Business supplies & equipment ...	66	470	6347	891
H030	Business maintenance...........	51	734	1508	105
H040*	Copier supplies & equipment	38	181	2704	568
H050	Printing maintenance	31	102	3567	1084
K020	Forms	29	144	3831	771
K030	Printing	79	331	3374	805
K040	Printing M & S	78	549	3276	465
K050	Books	1276	3879	97	32
K060	Journals	1126	2080	78	42
K080	Stationery	173	1178	972	143
M020	Staff—temporary	40	202	757	150
M025*	Professional fees	97	158	1310	804
M030	Travel expenses	93	522	1811	323
M040*	Telephone & telegraph	—	(No Range)		—
M050	Entertainment	72	210	2085	715
M060*	Miscellaneous	303	601	672	339
M085	Insurance	7	15	12295	5737
M090*	Taxes—property................	—	(No Range)		—
M130*	Dues, memberships	219	298	306	225

*Extraordinary high value, monopoly, or public service suppliers have been extracted from these classes to reduce distortion.

Responsibility and authority

Each department at Vanier had its own budget for capital and current expenditures. Over the years a variety of operating policies and procedures had evolved, many of which were not in written form. The purchasing department was no exception in this respect. Regarding its role, the university's standard administration manual said: "The Board of Governors established the policy that all purchasing for the university be centralized for the sake of economy, budgeting control, and accounting" and "direct ordering from supplier by any department or person is not permitted and the University will not accept responsibility for goods so ordered." These statements were not fully accepted by many departments, and it was not unusual for individual professors, secretaries, technicians, or administrators to establish supplier contacts and make commitments without purchasing's knowledge or involvement.

For example, this spring, Mr. Thompson, one of the assistant purchasing agents, received an order requesting confirmation for the purchase of a $280 piece of photographic equipment. He quickly found out that the price for the same product from the same catalog of the same company was $220. The 21 percent saving was never realized as the head of the requesting department politely told Mr. Thompson to mind his own business with the justification that he could spend the department's own money in his own ways.

Another incident involved printing and Mr. David, another assistant purchasing agent. Without reference to purchasing, the assistant dean of one of the faculties contacted a printing supplier and obtained a verbal quotation to perform an important printing job. He instructed the supplier to proceed and issued a requisition based on the original verbal quotation. No competitive quotation was sought. The supplier was advised to send the invoice to the faculty. Unexpected changes occurred which increased the costs of the job, raising the actual price 75 percent higher than the estimated one. Mr. David's first indication of this transaction appeared when he received a requisition with the invoice attached and a request for help from the assistant dean.

Mr. Emery suspected that examples like these were common in the whole university. He also knew that certain departments were taking full advantages of the purchasing services, while others seemed to accomplish a reasonably conscientious buying job, even though they by-passed purchasing or used it only for confirmation and paper work.

Purchasing department

As of this August, the purchasing department reported directly to Mr. Emery, the executive assistant of the vice president of administration and finance. Mr. Martin, purchasing agent, was helped by four assistants specializing in different areas. Their principal functions were to place orders within authorized budget allowances, to secure quotations on goods and services required, to coordinate the purchases of commonly used items, to negotiate with suppliers, to interview sales representatives, and to maintain records of quotations and purchases. The total purchasing department staff amounted to 14 people (see Exhibit 2).

Exhibit 2

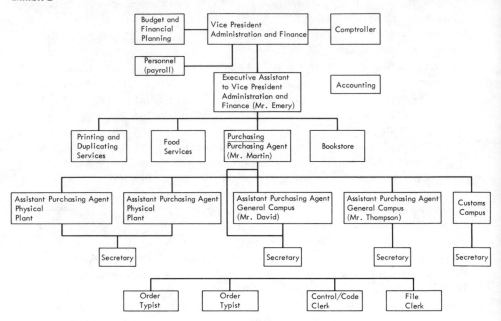

Purchasing had completed several years ago a changeover to computerized operations to produce purchase orders and to gather statistical information.

Normal procedure. When university personnel requested goods, the following normal steps took place:

1. A department secretary prepared a purchase requisition and sent it by campus mail to purchasing.
2. In purchasing, the code clerk verified the account number validity, checked if sufficient funds were available in the budget allotment of the requisitioning department, and passed the requisition to Mr. Martin (or one of his assistants).
3. Mr. Martin completed delivery, shipping, and terms details; he entered commitment amount and follow-up date; he checked for tax exemptions as applicable and initialed the requisition.
4. An order typist produced a purchase order from the requisition.
5. A secretary checked the order and passed it to Mr. Martin for approval.
6. Mr. Martin returned the signed order to the secretary for mailing.
7. Finally, the file clerk distributed copies of the order to the accounts payable section, the requisitioning department, and the purchasing files.

The vendor subsequently delivered the goods to the requisitioning department. Then someone in this department was asked to sign the shipping documents. Purchasing did not receive any notification of a shipment's arrival. Each department was responsible for the receiving and inspection of its own goods.

Mr. Martin estimated that the campus received more than 150 deliveries a day. No data were available on the frequency of deliveries per receiving center, per day, or per year.

Emergency procedure. In case of an emergency, a department could order directly from a supplier. The requisitioner then called purchasing, giving the account number and the purchasing requisition number. Purchasing scanned the account and assigned a purchase order number if there were sufficient funds in the free balance. A "confirmation" stamp identified this purchase requisition.

During the previous period, 30 percent of all requirements processed were marked confirmation; 16 percent of all requisitions handled were the result of requests by departments via telephone for purchase order numbers.

Standing orders. A department could establish a standing purchase order with a supplier where the user department expected to secure multiple deliveries of various repetitive items or services over the year from the same supplier. Once a standing order was made out, the user department normally dealt directly with the supplier, provided the requests did not exceed the terms and conditions set out in the standing order. To initiate a standing order the requesting department had to complete the normal requisition form with mention of time and total dollar limits.

Systems contracting. Ten years ago, Mr. Martin introduced the use of systems contract purchasing; for the current period, systems contracting represented less than 1 percent of total purchases. It was confined to electrical, plumbing, and fasteners requirements.

Receiving problems

In October, Mr. Emery initiated an inquirty into the newly renovated Central Administration Building to study the need for a centralized mailing, shipping, and receiving center in this building. It included 18 administrative departments. Excerpts from this inquiry were self-explanatory:

> Stuff gets all over.
> We have to bring dozens of boxes up, and we don't think this should be our job.
> Hard to know if we've got everything.
> Material can be here for two or three days, and we don't even know it's here.
> Delivery men are wandering all over looking for someone to sign.
> Delivery men can't find the room numbers of departments.

In discussion with Mr. Martin and his assistants, Mr. Emery learned that these findings could be a revealing sample of the receiving situation throughout the campus.

With budget cuts, limited personnel, and physical building limitations, many departments had not placed someone in charge of the reception of goods. Therefore, no formal inspection was done. Purchasing's only involvement in the receiving process came when Mr. Martin or one of his assistants received calls to handle the problems caused by loss or damage. On occasion the shipper or the supplier dismissed any responsibility, arguing that materials had been delivered a week previously and that damage must have occurred afterwards. When a shipment was lost, purchasing had to reorder it, and it was quite possible that the university had to pay twice. Sometimes, when a follow-up order was delivered, it was found that the original need no longer existed.

Shippers were required to obtain a signature on their bill of lading. Delivery men often had difficulties finding someone willing to sign for a shipment. As a result, technicians, maintenance employees, and even students were approached by truckers. Sometimes a driver would get so frustrated that he dropped the goods off without a signature.

Even in those buildings where someone was placed in charge of receiving, truckers were often confused by the lack of signs and inconsistency of room numbers (e.g., Room 248 beside Room 232 and 234).

Because of the university's receiving arrangements, all kinds of situations could happen. For example, in September, a problem cropped up with the university directories. According to the supplier, the directories had been shipped; but nobody could find them. Finally, someone discovered that the garbage men had picked them up and that directories were missing throughout the campus. The university was obliged to reprint the order.

Sometimes it could take a long time to find out who owned parcels. A new receiver had been assigned at the physical plant department. In a dusty corner of the stockroom, he discovered two shipments from a year earlier. The receiver called Mr. Thompson, the assistant agent, who checked all requests of the previous year and wrote to the supplier. But he had not been able to trace or identify the requisition. It was possible that a department had paid for it. Nobody knew.

The purchasing department had no record to indicate the frequency and the dollar value these incidents represented. Mr. Martin had no idea of how they related to total purchases, as most of the time each department found it easier to take care of its own problems. He estimated that such incidents might happen at least once a week in each receiving center. Nevertheless, he had never found out about an official claim from any supplier related to the receiving situation.

Mr. Emery was puzzled about improving the receiving situation as no proof existed that these unidentified but surely significant costs would be reduced if the receiving processes were changed. He wondered what steps could be undertaken to address this issue.

CASE 3-2
× BARBER BUILDING SUPPLIES

In July, 1979, Mr. Bill Hope was hired as general manager of Barber Building Supplies. During his first few months on the job he became very concerned about a number of problems in the organization, including the way purchasing functioned. Mr. Diamond, president and owner of Barber wanted to retire in a few years and wished to groom Bill Hope as his successor. He had given the new general manager free rein to do as he pleased. "You prove to me that you can handle this business, and it will be yours," he said. Bill Hope was a graduate of a well-known school of business administration. He was 34 years old and had several years retailing and marketing experience.

Company background

In November, 1979, Barber was celebrating its fifth year of operation. The company had grown from a small lumber yard to a combined retail lumber, building suppliers, and home care center with annual sales of $1.6 million. In addition, the company had in 1978 invested $65,000 in the construction and equipping of a plant producing prefabricated trusses, a combination of wooden beams arranged in a group of triangles. The beams formed a rigid framework and were used in house construction for supporting the roof. This operation now yielded $150,000 per year in additional sales.

Of the company's sales, 50 percent were to contractors in the form of rough lumber and associated construction materials. The remaining 50 percent were retail sales in the home center product line, including hardware, flooring materials, carpeting, lamps, ceiling fixtures, decorative wall paneling, room dividers and gardening utensils.

Barber employed 27 people in November, 1979, down from 39 in July. Bill Hope in the first few months weeded out what he called "fat in the system." He said: "When I arrived here, most people spent the day standing around looking at each other. Most of them had been with Barber from the start. I asked lots of questions for which there were no answers. Some quit because of the pressure; others, I fired. We still have too many people." (See Exhibit 1 for the current organization chart.)

The retail building supply business

The retail building supply business in North America was undergoing rapid change. Bill Hope said: "According to a market study, Americans spend over $25 billion a year on their homes—building rumpus rooms, refinishing basements, and just puttering around. But instead of spending most

Exhibit 1
Organization chart

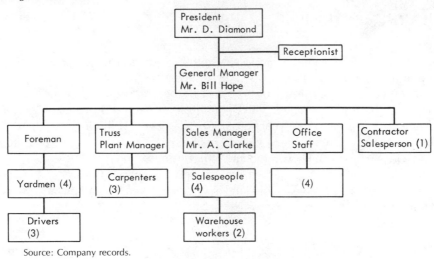

Source: Company records.

of it in the retail lumber yards, as we used to, more Americans now take their do-it-yourself business to retail home centers. The growing market has attracted such concerns as K-Mart, Sears, and other large firms into the home care center business. Consequently, we are competing with large organizations with sophisticated mass merchandising techniques. These people have tremendous purchasing power which we smaller dealers don't enjoy. It seems to be an industry-wide trend for suppliers to try and take advantage of the lack of sophistication of the little guys—cute tricks like short shipping, double-invoicing, and the like. It's getting tougher to be in the business all the time."

Purchasing at Barber

In the 1978–79 fiscal year, sales totaled $1.6 million; purchases were $1 million and profit after tax was $28,000. Mr. Diamond said: "Because the industry is so price sensitive, and because mark-ups tend to be so low, purchasing is an essential ingredient of success in this business." Bill Hope added: "Lumber yards have always been based on sound purchasing. However, many times we worry so much about how much it costs us to put it on the shelf and about how many hot deals we get that we lose sight of the fact that we have to sell it. Because of the price sensitivity of the consumer and the apparent inability (at least at this point in time) to forecast customer demand with any reliability or accuracy, purchasing and inventory control can be key factors in generating profits for this company."

When Bill Hope arrived in July, 1979, he found the purchasing system strange. In his own words: "Anybody and everybody was purchasing, from the salesmen to the yard men and truck drivers. A person who wanted something simply picked up a purchase order, filled it in, and had it processed through one of the secretaries. Or worse yet, anybody could phone a supplier and not bother with a purchase order at all."

The purchasing situation will be described under the following heads:

1. Ascertainment of need.
2. Selection of source of supply.
3. The purchase order.
4. Follow-up.
5. Receiving and payment.
6. Problems in purchasing.

1. Ascertainment of need. The order procedure at Barber was informal and unstructured. In the absence of a defined inventory control system, the primary method of determining need was by periodic visual check. The check of items in stock on the shelves of the sales floor was carried out by the sales manager, Mr. Clarke, and to some extent by his sales staff. There were no prescribed inspection cycles (one per week, one per month, etc.). The salespeople normally noticed low stocks after the sale of a particular item. At this point, they completed a "Low Stock Card" and forwarded it to Mr. Clarke. Depending on the urgency of demand for the item and the dollar value, these cards were accumulated by Mr. Clarke until:

1. A company representative visited Barber (there were normally eight calls by various salespeople per week); or
2. Sufficient quantity was generated to qualify for the prepaid shipping terms granted by supplying companies (normally a 200-pound minimum).

It was not unusual to run low of certain supplies unexpectedly, either in the truss plant or the sales floor. Then anyone could phone a supplier and ask for immediate delivery of the item in question. Mr. Clarke and Mr. Diamond had jointly looked after most of the lumber purchases and the acquisition of new lines. Mr. Diamond had traditionally been responsible for most capital investment and carload purchases. Mr. Clarke usually purchased for all 2,500 items carried on sales floor shelves.

2. Selection of source of supply. The source of supply was determined by the class of item desired. Lumber was purchased primarily from brokers who periodically contacted Barber. If an urgent need existed for lumber to augment low stocks or to meet a large customer order, Mr. Diamond or Mr. Clarke would contact a number of brokers to obtain lumber. This process took up to a day for one carload. Lead time for delivery of shipments varied from three to four days if the car was on the rails, up to 16 weeks or longer on hard-to-get items.

In many cases, the purchase process was initiated by brokers who had lumber on hand for disposal. In this case, Barber management had to make an extremely fast analysis of stock on hand, demand (turnover), price trends, and the offered price. Often Mr. Diamond or Mr. Clarke had five minutes or less to make a purchase decision, particularly if the broker was calling from the West Coast and substantial long distance charges were involved. If, based on their analysis, the shipment was deemed to be a good deal, the purchase was made. Mr. Diamond estimated that most of their lumber business was carried out with ten brokers.

Most of the estimated 2,500 items displayed on the sales floor shelves were purchased from some 50 wholesaler and factory representatives. These representatives visited Barber at various intervals to take orders and to maintain and service their respective product displays. Three of the major wholesalers' representatives visited twice weekly. It had been Mr. Diamond's stated management policy that cordial relations be established and maintained with sales representatives.

For specialty items not normally carried by Barber, the sales department maintained a large collection of dealers' and manufacturers' catalogs for ordering references and prices. Mr. Clarke stated that very little "shopping" was done when purchasing most items. He placed a premium on supplier service and reliability and felt that these factors more than offset the small price savings he might realize through "shopping." The president, Mr. Diamond, also placed a premium on supplier service.

3.   Purchase order.   Over 70 percent of Barber's purchasing was carried out by telephone. The remaining orders were placed directly with salespeople calling on the firm. A purchase order was prepared by the receptionist or one of the three women on the office staff. Because of the telephone ordering procedure, no copy of the purchase order was sent to the supplier. The prime purpose for purchase order preparation was to provide information for the cost book. This book, kept manually, contained a record of all purchases and was used by Mr. Diamond and Mr. Clarke to determine prices in advance of delivery. When the occasion warranted, new price lists were prepared by the receptionist for use by the salespeople. When landed cost could not be determined at the time the purchase order was prepared, a pricing decision would be delayed until the supplier's invoice arrived.

One copy of the purchase order was filed on a spindle file in the sales area for reference by sales personnel. The second copy was filed numerically in a purchasing file.

4.   Follow-up.   There was no formal follow-up system to ensure on-time delivery of an order. When a "tickler file" of purchase orders arranged by due date was suggested as a possible method by one of the salespeople, Mr. Clarke said that such a system had been tried elsewhere and that experience has shown that such a system required the full-time attention of one of his salespeople. Mr. Clarke said that his people were able to remember large orders and to initiate follow-up action on these orders when the due date drew near.

5.   Receiving and payment.   There were two principal receiving areas at

Barber, the warehouse in the lumberyard where rail cars and large truckloads of lumber were received, and the small area at the back of the store for materials for the sales floor shelves and displays.

The yard foreman was charged with receiving lumber shipments, checking for quantity, and for informing Mr. Diamond, Mr. Clarke, or the office manager of any shortages, damage, or other discrepancies between the shipment and the shipping slip.

Shipments arriving at the rear of the store were checked in a similar fashion by the receiver. He, in turn, advised Mr. Clarke of any discrepancies between the shipment and the shipping slip.

If there were discrepancies between the shipping slip and the shipment received, Mr. Clarke noted the discrepancy and attached an information slip to the package. He also notified the supplier involved in order to obtain a credit note for the difference. Normally, no problems were involved in obtaining credit notes if the company involved was a regular Barber supplier.

When the supplier's invoice arrived, the bookkeeper looked after payment, making sure that cash discounts were taken. Approximately 600 invoices were processed a month, and the bookkeeper attempted to even out the work, avoiding a backlog.

Purchasing problems

The present purchasing system seemed to work well according to Mr. Diamond. It had served the organization during five years of substantial growth and was simple with a minimum of red tape and paperwork. Suppliers were generally reliable, and good relations existed with sales representatives and brokers.

Mr. Hope did not share this view and had a number of points of concern. Under the present system a number of orders were placed for which no purchase order was prepared. Thus, no record existed, creating the risk that a second order for the same item might be placed or that a supplier might send goods which had not been ordered. Moreover, anyone could initiate a purchase order, leading to confusion in responsibilities.

Purchase orders were not checked against invoices, because Mr. Clarke considered this a waste of time. Mr. Hope had recently spent several weeks at home at night and on weekends going over purchase orders and invoices placed during the first six months of 1979. He found that discrepancies in shipments, prices, shipping terms and double invoicing had cost Barber at least $50,000 during this period.

A recent incident with a lumber broker had placed in question the telephone ordering procedure. Barber had not received a carload of lumber containing 54,000 board feet ordered from a broker, because the $25,000 order had not been confirmed in writing. The load had been sold in advance of receipt, and Mr. Hope estimated it had cost Barber an additional $5,000 to secure an alternate supply at an inflated price in a hurry. Customer goodwill had also suffered from this incident because delivery was still a week late. Rapidly increasing prices, lengthening lead times, and shortages in the marketplace created further worries for Mr. Hope. He was not sure how much time he could spend personally on the purchasing function, because of the other duties of his position. He was not satisfied that the area was running smoothly and wanted improvements but was not sure where and how to begin.

CASE 3–3
VICTORIA HOSPITAL

In November, 1979, Mr. Don Palmer, director of management services, received a request to study and recommend improvements to the Victoria Hospital purchasing department functions. After completing the study of existing methods, he was considering ways in which the operations might be streamlined. Given the hospital's operating needs in relation to budget increase restrictions, Mr. Palmer presumed that any cost-reducing steps would be considered favorably by the administration. However, he also knew that service levels would have to be maintained or improved and that only limited amounts of funds could be allocated for any alterations he might recommend.

Background

The purchasing department was one of the nine service functions under the control of the director of hospital services. This department was responsible for:

1. Purchasing all hospital supplies (capital and noncapital).
2. Receiving, storage and distribution of supplies.
3. Maintenance of inventory control over all capital and noncapital stock items.
4. The billing of requisitions and recording any cost revisions.
5. Maintenance of forms control (designing and revising printed forms).
6. Printing services.

Purchasing was responsible for the supply of about $1,100,000 of capital supplies and $10–12 million of noncapital supplies during 1978. Inventory records were kept for 8,000 to 10,000 individual items and about 120,000 requisitions were processed during 1978. Forms control and printing represented about 12 percent of the work of this department. Although the total level of services provided by Victoria Hospital had been rising steadily and total hospital employees had increased from 2,000 to 2650 since 1974, purchasing and stores had operated with the same work force.

Organization

The department was under the direct supervision and control of Ms. Sally Loucks, purchasing agent in the organization shown in Exhibit 1. The four main functions were considered by Mr. Palmer to be purchasing, receiving, storing and issuing, and controlling. Since the forms control function had no effect on purchasing procedures, he did not take it into consideration in the study. The purchasing agent was responsible for 25 people in these four main functions.

Purchasing responsibilities were divided as follows:

1. Purchasing agent—capital equipment, blanket laboratory orders.
2. Assistant purchasing agent—operating room orders, special telephone orders.
3. Buyer—food, stationery, maintenance supplies.

The stores were considered as two sections—wholesale and retail—though there was no physical isolation of the two types of stock. Wholesale activities included receiving all supplies and maintenance of adequate stock levels. The stock control clerks kept the wholesale inventory records up-to-date by posting orders, receipts, and issues. The retail stores received regular issues from wholesale and was responsible for distribution throughout the hospital. There were no inventory records for retail stores—requisitions filled could be balanced against issues from wholesale.

Requisitions normally would be filled from retail stock. If there was none of a particular item in "retail," the storesperson would issue it from "wholesale" and stamp the requisition accordingly. "Wholesale" requisitions were sent to the stock control clerks for recording. However, under that system, Don Palmer pointed out that it was very easy for a storesperson to issue some item from wholesale without stamping the requisition.

Another potential error source was that of routine transfers from wholesale to retail. Stores personnel recorded issues in a book that was sent wholesale to retail. Storespersons recorded issues in a book that was sent to stock control daily. Transfers could be made without being recorded. Don felt these factors would explain many of the frequent discrepancies between stock control records and actual stock. There were two counts during the year that revealed a total of approximately $200,000 in wholesale shortages. With no evidence of theft, the most reasonable explanation Ms. Loucks could provide was that stores personnel likely depleted wholesale stocks to fill requisitions without noting the issue information for stock control and accounting.

Requisition procedures

There were two methods for wards and departments to requisition supplies from stores.

A. Traveling requisitions. Traveling requisitions were used by the

Exhibit 1
Purchasing department organization chart, November 1979

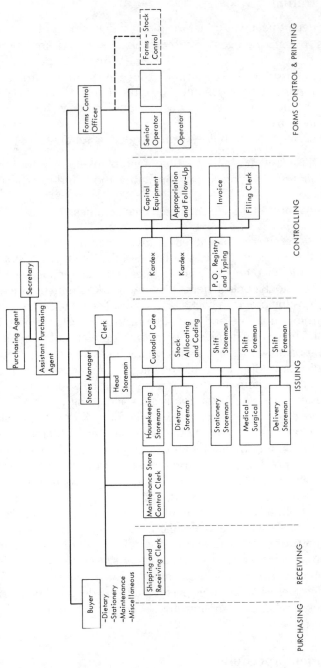

wards to request recurring items such as stationery, daily food supplies for ward kitchens, cutlery and crockery, and medical and surgical supplies. These requisitions were kept in book form and completed by the requisitioner using the appropriate catalog number and goods descriptions. The requesting department would send the requisition to stores to have the order filled and the goods delivered.

Filling and delivering the daily food orders and the weekly stationery orders was particularly time-consuming for the stores. Don Palmer also found wards frequently would submit a supplementary food order, in addition to their daily traveling requisition, for food stuffs they had either omitted on the original order or had not ordered in sufficient quantity.

At the end of the month each ward or department was issued a new 25-page traveling requisition for the next month as they returned the filled ones to the purchasing office for costing. Costing was a time-consuming process as not all traveling requisition books were submitted on the date requested, and it was often necessary to obtain the books from the ward and then tally and price the entries. The list was then sent to accounts payable.

The traveling requisition procedure had been introduced by Ms. Loucks, as a temporary fact-finding document, since no suitable catalog existed. The system had become permanent.

B. Stores requisitions. (See Exhibit 2) To obtain items other than those specified on the traveling requisition, a requesting department first had to complete four copies of a stores requisition.

That department would retain one copy and forward three to stores for action. Each requisition was date-stamped on receipt and directed for action appropriate to stock or nonstock items.

1. In stock items. These would be filled directly from retail or wholesale stores, with the supplies and third copy of the requisition being sent to the requesting department. If issued from "retail," the first copy would be stamped to indicate this and then sent directly to the filing clerk.

After "wholesale" issues had been made, copies one and two of the requisition were sent to the appropriate stock control clerk. She would check for accuracy and completeness, enter the prices of items on copy one, control stamp and sign that copy, and forward it to the filing clerk for filing under the appropriate account number. Stock control retained copy two of the requisition.

At the beginning of each month, the filing clerk would send the previous month's completed requisitions to accounts payable. There each requisition would be checked for account and subaccounts number accuracy. Errors or omissions were frequently made, and accounts payable would return the forms to stock control or stores. When assured of the accuracy, the charges would be posted against the appropriate account.

2. Not in stock items. Requisitions were routed to the stock control office. Stock control passed the stores requisitions to the person responsible for purchase order preparation. The secretary would type purchase orders to

Exhibit 2
Stores requisition flow diagram

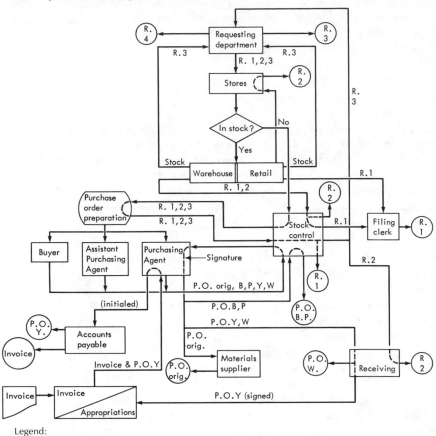

Legend:
R.1—Requisition, Copy 1.
P.O.B.—Purchase Order, Copy Blue.

be handled by the purchasing agent, while the purchase order registry clerk would type purchase orders for the assistant purchasing agent and the buyer.

Purchase orders were passed to the appropriate stock control clerk to enter the order on the inventory control card. After entry, she would stamp and initial the purchase orders. Subsequently, all purchase orders were recorded in a register (which contained the date of the order, the supplying company, the purchase order number, and the originating department) and then were passed to the purchasing agent for signature.

Purchase orders were prepared in five copies. After being signed, the copies were separated and distributed as follows:

a. White original—to supplier.
b. Blue and pink copies—filed together in a bin in the stock control office.
c. Yellow and white copies—to receiving.

When stock control received its copies, the purchase order number and date would be entered on the stores requisition, and the third copy of the requisition would be sent to the requesting department. Reasons for returning a copy to the departments were: (a) it notified them that their request had been received and actioned, (b) and if they had queries to direct to purchasing, they had available the purchase order number (there were many queries). The second requisition copy was sent to receiving to be held with the yellow and white purchase order copies. Stock control held the first requisition copy on separate file for use in the event of a query from any requesting department. These requisition copies would be destroyed periodically.

Receiving functions

Receiving maintained a book record of all purchase orders as outgoing copies arrived. Photocopies were made and held for the 40 percent of all purchase orders that were likely to be back orders or partial shipments.

Part of the book record was the date on which an order was completely received, and the packing slip(s) and purchase order tallied. Receiving filed the complete order packing slip and the white purchase order copy together. The yellow copy would be signed by the stores manager and sent to the invoice clerk. The goods would be sent to the requesting department or placed in stores and a purchase order copy would be sent to stock control for recording.

Receiving handled an incomplete, or partial, shipment in much the same way. However, only a photocopy of the purchase order, indicating quantity received, was forwarded to invoicing, stock control, and the requesting department for direct deliveries. The purchase order record would be kept open until all items had been received.

Follow-ups were also a receiving responsibility. The purchase order registry was checked on a regular basis for orders outstanding one month or more (regardless of the promised delivery date). The clerk would first check the white purchase order copies of any such orders to see if partial deliveries had been received. If no partial orders had been received, she would complete a follow-up form to be signed by the stores manager. The details would be entered in a back-order ledger and a copy forwarded to the supplier to expedite the order. When a reply was received from a supplier, the receiving clerk would check to see if the order had been completed in the meantime and close the record if it had. If the order was not yet complete, further follow-up action might be taken.

Invoicing, appropriations and accounts payable

The invoicing clerk held the purchase order pending the invoice receipt. When the invoice arrived, it would be verified, the extensions would be checked, and invoice and purchase order copies would be sent to the appropriations clerk. She would check the invoice against the original requisition, verify the accuracy of tax charges, and sign and return copies of the purchase order and invoice to the invoice clerk. The appropriations clerk would next update the purchase order ledger and pass the documents to the purchasing agent. She would initial the documents and forward them to accounts payable.

Accounts payable processed all complete and incomplète order receipts as invoiced. Each would be checked for accuracy, correct appropriation, discounts where applicable, and the purchasing agent's initials. A machine remittance would then be made and checked against the invoice before being passed to the accountant for final approval and payment.

Exchanges, miscellaneous, and books

If a department wished to return goods that were "unsatisfactory" (for any reason), the department called or wrote a memo to the purchasing department. Purchasing would check with the supplier to determine the best method of return. Then purchasing would complete a "Return Goods Memorandum" and send it and the goods to shipping for packaging and shipment. The goods would then be returned to the supplier for an exchange or credit. Separate ledgers were kept for exchange items and for credit items. An exchange required only a record on its completion and a receipt for goods when forwarded to the requesting department. Any credits received had to be posted to the requesting department's account and to accounts payable. Don Palmer found that the procedures tended to be time-consuming but caused few problems except when goods returned for exchange and replacement items were not of equal value—an infrequent occurrence. (It was later determined that accounting did not always post credits or returns to accounts).

The miscellaneous returns could cause many difficulties. Shipping maintained a ledger for miscellaneous returns such as furniture sent for recovering. Such goods were sent out with the purchase order attached. Don Palmer found that miscellaneous items often were returned and the purchase order processed without the completion being noted in the shipping ledger.

Another problem area was the receipt of books. If the original supplier was out of stock, he would frequently refer the order to another supplier, and, when the shipment was received, the packing slip would refer to an unknown supplier who could not be matched with a purchase order. Even more frequently departments would order books direct from the publisher, and, when they were received, much time would be spent by receiving trying to find first a purchase order and then the original requisitioner.

Expanding the study

Mr. Palmer had been assigned the task of examining and improving the information flows in the purchasing and accounting system. However, he found it impossible to do this without examining the work environment. Touring the facilities in the stores building left him with the impression that the operation was crowded and likely inefficient. Don Palmer, therefore, felt a work study might indicate some potential for change. Accordingly, a work sample was taken over a period of five days between 6:30 A.M. and 4:00 P.M. The sampling did not cover the stores manager, receiving, stationery storespersons and the night and weekend shifts. The results of Mr. Palmer's work sampling are shown in Exhibit 3.

The sampling indicated that storespersons were engaged in productive activities 70.9 percent of the time. This included 1.6 percent of supervisory time. Don Palmer suggested, "The small percentage of supervisory time (due largely to the illness of the supervisor during the time study) could be the reason for the level of productivity. More supervision could bring about higher productivity." Counting delivery of pharmacy supplies, 20.4 percent of the storespersons' productive time (81 man-hours in the sample period) was used portering or delivering stocks.

Mr. Palmer continued, "The assignment of specific responsibilities to supervisors and the development of job descriptions for all could bring about better supervision and greater productivity. The sampling indicated about 115 nonproductive hours which amounts to almost three persons."

Record keeping functions

The purpose of stock control was to ensure the maintenance of adequate bulk or wholesale supplies. However, the stock control system at Victoria Hospital exhibited many discrepancies between stock and records for which exact causes could not be defined. Don Palmer thought the problem could be due to over-control (or overly complex control). There were eight books for recording transfers from wholesale to retail stores—three for medical/surgical suppies, two for dietary, one for housekeeping, one for paper, and one for stationery. When making transfers from wholesale to retail, the storeman had to ensure details were entered in the appropriate book. Records also had to be kept separately when stores requisition forms were filled direct from wholesale rather than retail stores.

The record keeping was complicated because transfers of stock from wholesale to retail normally occurred daily. The retail stores were not stocked to any standard daily levels either, so extra transfers could be needed for any item at any time. Don Palmer wondered what effects this compounding of transfers could have on the accuracy of records. He also wondered if it might be better to stock retail stores to a standard level of items based on weekly consumption. He did not feel that adequate space was available in retail to accommodate the inventory that would be required, however.

The records kept and procedures for purchasing stock also varied. Don Palmer found that some orders were made through purchase orders, others

Exhibit 3
Activity sampling study—central stores

Total number of work hours sampled:
7	Storespersons × 8.5 hours per day × 5 days =	297.5 hours
1	Storespersons × 8.5 hours per day × 3 days =	25.5 hours
1	Storespersons × 8.5 hours per day × 4 days =	34.0 hours
2	Storespersons × 4.0 hours per day × 5 days =	40.0 hours

Total   397.0 hours

Element description	Percent of observation	Work hours
Major element breakdown:		
Nonproductive elements	29.1	115.5
Productive elements (indirect)	8.1	32.2
Productive elements (direct)	62.8	249.3
Totals	100.0	397.0
Detailed element breakdown:		
Nonproductive elements		
Personal	1.4	5.5
Break and/or lunch period	14.7	58.4
Idle	9.4	37.3
Away from work place	3.6	14.3
Totals	29.1	115.5
Productive elements (indirect):		
Give or receive instructions		
Given by supervisors	1.6	6.4
Received by stores	1.8	7.1
Talk to salespersons	0.3	1.2
Walk empty handed	1.2	4.8
Operate photocopier	0.4	1.6
Talk to supervisor	0.1	0.4
Receive or make telephone call	0.9	3.6
Routine clean-up of work area	1.8	7.1
Totals	8.1	32.2
Productive elements (direct):		
Prepare pharmacy supplies	2.6	10.3
Deliver pharmacy supplies	1.2	4.8
Price pharmacy supplies	0.7	2.8
Prepare medical and surgical supply orders	10.4	41.3
Prepare dietary supply orders	2.6	10.3
Prepare housekeeping supply orders	0.5	2.0
Porter	19.2	76.2
Stock returned items from floors	0.7	2.8
Stock wholesale supplies	4.9	19.5
Stock retail supplies	3.0	11.9
Stock dietary supplies to refrigerator	1.5	5.9
Serve at issuing window	3.1	12.3
Code cases and/or individual items	1.2	4.8
Unpack cartons and check contents against packing slip	2.4	9.5
Miscellaneous paper work	2.9	11.5
Receive	1.8	7.1
Obtain supplies from supply houses	0.3	1.2
Package items for repair or return to supplier	0.4	1.6
Load and/or operate conveyor	1.0	4.0
Prepare stock orders	1.5	5.9
Assemble travelling requisition books	0.9	3.6
Totals	62.8	249.3

by stock requirement sheets, and still others by telephone (blanket orders). The paper work also varied. Purchase orders were kept as described previously. The stores requisition was used for telephoning blanket contract orders. And when a stock card indicated replenishment was needed, a stock requirement sheet would be made up to place an order.

QUALITY AND INSPECTION

4

The first step in any acquisition is to determine what is needed. This is followed by a decision on the quality of the material or item required and the control and measurement of this quality.

Definition of need—function

The term "need" is still a nebulous one. Every item to be purchased must perform a function. It must perform certain tasks. If it does not perform the function intended, the purchase may be a totally useless one and a waste of time, money, and effort. Similarly, quantity and price needs exist which are discussed in later chapters.

The function need requires some clarification. We seldom bother to think of the basic function the item must perform. We tend to speak of "a box" instead of "something to package this in;" "a bolt" instead of "something that fastens." We think of a steak, instead of something to eat; a bed, instead of something to sleep in; and a house, instead of a place to live. Note, that even when we issue an engineering drawing for a part, we really just say to a supplier, "Make this." And presumably, in our wisdom we have already made the decision that if the supplier makes the part as specified, it will perform the intended function. Seldom in our purchases do we dwell on this basic function aspect.

Why make an issue of this? It seems so simple and basic as to be hardly worth mentioning. But, actually, this is the heart of a sound purchasing system. Here lie the clues for improving the profitability of purchasing operations. A few simple examples will illustrate what is meant. A casual bypassing of the function need frequently results in improper specification. For example, a hose will be too short, a lining will shrink, a bolt shear, a motor burn out, a paint peel, a machine vibrate, a vessel burst, a part won't fit, an insurance policy won't cover, and a host of other troubles of this sort arise. Many of these troubles will result from underestimating the function required or from negligence, error, or oversight, because certain functional needs have been forgotten or overlooked. We all laugh when we hear the story about the fellow who built the speedboat in the basement but couldn't get it out of the door. Yet, every day many people make this kind of mistake, perhaps not as glaring, or obvious, but often just as painful.

The answer to this problem, one will say, is to buy quality. As long as you buy good quality material you can't go wrong. Quality is really part of our function need. If the item is not of sufficient quality to perform the task required of it, it does not fulfill our function. Moreover, quality can be a cloak for various inadequacies. Buying the best quality, high alloy ½" screws will not help if ⅝"

116

screws were needed in the first place. Buying high alloy screws when plain carbon mild steel ones will do is also going to increase costs unnecessarily.

If we define our basic functional need as a self-tapping or sheet metal screw, instead of a need to fasten together two sheets of metal of certain physical and chemical characteristics, we miss the first basic step in purchasing. We also miss the opportunity to invesitage such alternatives as bolts, rivets, and spot welds, to name just a few. Frequently, and perhaps understandably, the tendency is to forget about the basic function need and to purchase something that will do the job for better or worse. This may become a dangerous guessing game that can lead to much trouble and cost a lot of extra money.

It is proper to emphasize here that in almost all industrial organizations the final responsibility for specifications lies with engineering. In public organizations the writing of specifications frequently is the responsibility of the purchasing department. This specification is the basis which all suppliers use to prepare their bids.

Suitability

There is no such thing as quality divorced from an intended use. "Suitability" is more accurate.

The relationship between technical quality, on the one hand, and cost, on the other, is subject to a good deal of misunderstanding. Some persons believe there are just two classes of goods in the market: one purchased on the basis of quality and another which is sold entirely on price. This conception is not sound. In every transaction, questions of price and quality are interrelated. The purchases made solely on a quality basis and with absolutely no reference to the price involved are so few both in number and in value as to make them practically negligible. On the other hand, goods in the so-called price class must have certain attributes of value or they could not command any price at all. The most that can be said, therefore, is that in some cases high quality is not as important as in other cases, and in some cases low-price merchandise is just as satisfactory to the buyer as high-price merchandise.

Reliability

In an effort to describe quality by a number, the engineering profession has developed the concept of reliability: the mathematical probability that a product will function for a stipulated period of time. Originally, calculations like this were used in complex military electronic systems, but their use has spread into almost all types of products. The design of components in harmony with this concept allows for pre-determination of service calls at the design stage of equipment and, hence, the need for training of repair personnel and the size of spare parts inventory prior to actual manufacture. Complex military equipment is notoriously expensive to maintain with annual maintenance costs ranging from 60 percent to 1,000 percent of initial purchase cost.

Complexity is the enemy of reliability because of the multiplicative effect of probabilities of failure of components.

> Consider a piece of equipment in which all parts have a reliability of 99.99 percent. If there are 100 parts, the overall reliability is reckoned to be 99 percent; 1,000 parts, 90 percent; 3,000 parts, 75 percent; 10,000 parts, 36.8 percent. The Telstar communication satellite has more than 10,000 electronic parts.
>
> Such calculations are not entirely realistic, for they depend on two assumptions: first, that the failure of a single component causes failure of the whole system and, second, that failure of one component does not hasten or delay the failure of another. But designers often take pains to compensate for the partial or complete failure of some critical components, so that the whole equipment is not put out of action. In many instances the second assumption is nullified by the fact that the failure of one component changes the environment so greatly—e.g., by overheating—that nearby parts are likely to be affected.
>
> The only way to get an entirely accurate reliability figure for a system is to build a number of the systems and test them until they fail. Unfortunately, in practice, the engineer can seldom do enough testing to get a figure that he can trust. It may be economically out of the question to fire off dozens of missiles or burn out many large radar receivers just to make a reliability prediction.[1]

The distribution of failures is normally considered to be exponential, with failures occurring randomly. This facilitates calculations by making the reliabilities of the components additive. Testing is also more flexible because of the time-numbers trade-off. The same inference may be drawn from 20 parts tested for 50 hours as for 500 parts tested for 2 hours. Exceptions like the Weibull distribution (which accounts for the aging effect) and the bath tub curve (which recognizes the high probability of early failure, a period of steady state and a higher probability of failure near the end of the useful life) can also be handled, but they require more complex mathematical treatment.

From a procurement standpoint it is useful to recognize the varying reliabilities of components and products acquired. Penalties or premiums may be assessed for variation from design standard depending on the expected reliability impact.

Quality

"Quality" is a combination of characteristics, not merely one. The specific combination finally decided on is almost always a compromise, since the particular aspect of quality to be stressed in any individual case depends largely upon circumstances. In some instances the primary consideration is reliability; questions of immediate cost or facility of installation or the ease of making repairs are all secondary. In other instances the lifetime of the item of supply is not so important; efficiency in operation becomes more significant. Certain electrical supplies suggest themselves as illustrations. While a long life is desired, it is

---

[1]G. A. W. Boehm. "Reliability Engineering," *Fortune Magazine*, April 1963, pp. 7–8.

more important that the materials always function during such life as they may have, than that they last indefinitely. Assuming dependability in operation and a reasonable degree of durability, the ease and simplicity of operation may become the determining factor. For instance, it is well known that the mechanism of the modern typewriter makes it dependable under all ordinary usages but that it is not essential for a typewriter to last indefinitely. Given these two factors more or less standardized among various types of machines, the determining factor is the ease with which the machine can be operated. What constitutes a satisfactory quality, therefore, depends largely on what a person is seeking in particular goods.

Perhaps an illustration will be helpful:

> Paper towels come under the classification of bibulous papers, which are characterized by absorptiveness, loose formation, and softness. Blotting paper is a well-known example of a paper in this group. Towel and blotting papers are similar in their absorptive requirements, but the former must possess much greater strength than blotting papers. Unlike the latter they must be comparatively thin to have the required flexibility and yet must possess much greater strength than blotting paper so that they will not break under the severe conditions of usage. A good grade of paper toweling has two or three times the strength of blotting paper of the same fiber composition. In evaluating paper towels, therefore, the main consideration, in addition to absorptiveness and softness, is the strength. It is difficult to secure such a combination of desirable properties in the same sheet of paper.[2]

Decision on "best buy"

The decision on what to buy involves more than balancing various technical considerations. The most desirable technical quality or suitability for a given use, once determined, is not necessarily the desirable quality to buy. The distinction is between "technical" quality, which is strictly and entirely a matter of dimension, design, chemical, or physical properties, and the like, and the more inclusive concept of "economic" quality. Economic quality assumes, of necessity, a certain minimum measure of suitability but considers cost and procurability as well.

If the cost is so high as to be prohibitive, one must get along with an item somewhat less suitable. Or if, at whatever cost or however procurable, the only available suppliers of the technically perfect item lack adequate productive capacity or financial and other assurance of continued business existence, then, too, one must give way to something else. Obviously, too, frequent reappraisals are necessary, although a workable balance between technical and economic quality has been established. If copper rises from $0.70 a pound to $1.00 or more, its relationship to aluminum may change.

The decision on what constitutes the best buy for any particular need is as much conditioned by procurement considerations as by technical quality. "Best

---

[2]Bourdon W. Scribner and Russell W. Carr, *Standard for Paper Towels*. Circular C407 of the National Bureau of Standards.

quality'' and ''best buy'' are one and the same. It should be clear that neither the engineer, the user or the production man, on the one hand, nor the purchasing officer, on the other, is qualified to reach a sound decision on the best buy unless they work closely together. The ability and willingness of all parties concerned to view the trade-offs in perspective will significantly influence the final decisions reached.

Importance of service in determining quality

Surely, with many items the service the vendor performs in connection with these items is quite as important as any attribute of the product itself. Many goods bought require no service; standard basic raw materials passing into manufacture are usually in this class. Many machines are so simple in construction that any ordinary mechanic can make repairs. At the other extreme are machines so complicated and delicate in adjustment that the manufacturer believes satisfactory performance of the machines can be warranted only if trained employees service them. One reason why the International Business Machines Corporation and the United Shoe Machinery Corporation originally had a policy of leasing many of their machines instead of selling them outright is that these companies wished to control the servicing of machines. Service may include: installation, training, inspection, repair, advice, as well as a willingness to make satisfactory adjustments for misunderstandings or clerical errors. Some purchasing agents even include the supplier's willingness to change orders on short notice and to be particularly responsive to unusual requests as part of their evaluation of the service provided. To cover some types of service, vendors issue guarantees, covering periods of varying length. The value of such guarantees rests less upon the technical wording of the statement itself than upon the goodwill and reliability of the seller.

Many vendors specifically include the cost of service in the selling price. Others absorb it themselves, charging no more than competitors and relying for the sale upon the superior service. One of the difficult tasks of a buyer is to get only as much of this service factor as is really needed without paying for the excessive service the vendor may be obliged to render to some other purchaser. In many instances, of course, the servicing department of a manufacturing concern is maintained as a separate organization. The availability of service is an important consideration for the buyer in securing the proper quality at the outset.

Responsibility for determining quality

It is generally accepted that the final verdict on technical suitability for a particular use should rest with the using department. Thus, questions on the quality of office supplies and equipment may be settled by the office manager; the quality of advertising material by the advertising department; maintenance supplies by the maintenance department; and operating supplies by the production department.

The ultimate responsibility for the quality of manufactured items should rest primarily with the engineering department charged with design and standards involving raw or semiprocessed materials and component parts. Basically, the immediate decision is an engineering-production decision. The person responsible for converting primary materials or semimanufactured articles into the finished product is the person who should have the authority to determine what is to be required. It is the purchasing agent's task to keep the cost of material down to the lowest point consistent with the standard quality required in the completed product. Purchasing's right to audit, question, and suggest must be recognized if this task is to be successful.

Purchasing fails to live up to its responsibility unless it insists that technical quality factors be considered and unless it passes on, to those immediately responsible for quality, suggestions of importance that may come as a result of its normal activities. The procurement officer is in a key position to present the latest information from the marketplace which may permit modifications in design, more flexibility in specifications, or changes in manufacturing methods which will reduce the cost of materials without detracting from their performance. Unless the engineer and the production executive are willing to consider such information in attempting to determine the "best buy," the full benefits of effective operation of the procurement function are lost to the firm.

Responsibility of purchasing personnel

The trend toward securing full and active cooperation between the engineering, using, and procurement departments places a heavy responsibility upon purchasing personnel, for unless they are well qualified to make real contributions toward determining the best buy, their suggestions are not likely to be considered seriously.

There are several ways this responsibility can be met. All of them seek to ensure that buyers, regardless of the particular items they buy, or the uses to which the items are put, know as much as possible about the products they purchase. Of course, an adequate technical knowledge of maintenance, repair, operating, and other supplies is much more easily acquired than that for highly technical products, particularly those still in the developmental stage. The amount and character of the technical background required of a qualified buyer will therefore depend upon the nature of the commodities purchased. Likewise, the number of engineering qualified buyers in a department will vary from one type of company to another. This needs to be kept in mind by the reader evaluating the following alternatives.

The purchasing department may seek to increase the ability of its buyers to be of service in selecting the best quality in various ways:

1. Select only persons with engineering training to fill buyers' jobs. It is argued that an engineer has an advantage over a nontechnical person in buying because the basic engineering training and experience have given a thorough knowledge of materials, manufacturing methods, and inspection procedures.

Thus equipped, the engineer commands the respect of those in the engineering and production departments and is able to "talk the language" of the designer and vendor.

There appears to be a trend toward employing engineers as buyers, although few purchasing departments are entirely so staffed, and many seriously question the necessity or desirability.

2. *Employ one or more engineers in the purchasing department to serve in a staff capacity as advisors to the various buyers in cases in which their advice and help are useful and to serve in a liaison capacity between the purchasing and engineering departments.* This procedure can be helpful. Its value may be limited by the great variety of engineering problems with which they may be called to deal. It does not ensure that the buyer is qualified to know when and how best to use the services of these advisors.

3. *A third alternative is to transfer physically some of the purchasing personnel to the engineering department, where they are assigned desks adjacent to the engineers working on the same class of items as those in which the buyer is interested.* The reverse of this procedure is also followed at times, in which engineers (in some cases on a part-time basis) are assigned to purchasing departments for the purpose of furthering coordination between the two departments. Both these alternatives have obvious limitations, but they are steps in the right direction.

4. *Without making any changes in organization or personnel, buyers, assistant buyers, and others are encouraged to take advantage of night courses in blueprint reading, design, machine tool operations, cost accounting, engineering, materials, and similar studies.* Supervised plant visitations, films, and organized reading also may be used to advantage. Many executives feel this type of training is for most purposes entirely adequate, particularly when employees are brought into the purchasing department after plant experience. They feel that much of the work in the usual engineering school is of no special value to a buyer. They think that an alert, serious, conscientious person can gain an adequate background in those aspects of engineering and production necessary for satisfactory purchasing performance, particularly where a spirit of cooperation prevails.

Purchase analysis section

A development further emphasizing the effort to equip the purchasing department to deal more adequately with these technical problems is creating a purchase analysis[3] section within the department. The basic aim of purchase analysis is to determine what constitutes good value to assist in negotiations. In this respect there is nothing new about the idea. What is new is the increased emphasis placed on purchase analysis using a separate group of purchase analysts to coordinate this particular activity into an organized program. They work con-

---

[3]Other terms in common use include: value analysis, value engineering, and purchase research.

stantly in close cooperation with the engineering and production units of their own company and with vendors to determine designs, processes, and materials resulting in optimal value. These analysts are part of the purchasing department and are trained materials men and experienced engineers. In such companies as the Ford Motor Company, General Electric Company, and others, they evaluate each product or component, piece by piece. They are concerned primarily with two questions: is its usefulness proportionate to its cost, and is a new or lower cost equivalent material or process available?

It should be emphasized that final responsibility for applying purchase analysis rests with the buyer. What an analyst seeks to do is to combine information on products, manufacturing methods, costs, prices, and markets, furnishing skilled advisory service to the buyer, who in turn coordinates the whole pricing operations and negotiates with vendors. (See also purchasing research and value analysis in Chapter 15.)

Description of quality

In any company it is not sufficient for the using department merely to know what quality is desired; that quality must be capable of reasonably accurate description. In no other way can the using department be assured of getting exactly what it wants. Although the responsibility for defining the quality needed usually rests with the using department in the first instance, the purchasing department has a very direct and immediate responsibility in checking the description given. The purchasing department should not, of course, be allowed to exercise its authority arbitrarily or to alter the description and change the quality or the character of the item being procured. It should, however, have the authority to insist that the description be sufficiently accurate and detailed to be perfectly clear to the supplier with whom the purchasing department must place the order. The purchasing officer has the direct responsibility of calling the attention of the using department to the added expense resulting when the description calls for an article not standard and likely to be more expensive for that reason.

The description of an item may take any one of a variety of forms or, indeed, may be a combination of several different forms. For our discussion, therefore, "description" will mean any one of the various methods by which a buyer undertakes to convey to a seller a clear, accurate picture of the required item. The term "specification" will be used in the narrower and commonly accepted sense of referring to one particular form of description.

The methods of description ordinarily used may be listed as follows and will be discussed in order:

1. By brand.
2. By specification:
    a. Description of physical or chemical characteristics;
    b. Material and method of manufacture;
    c. Performance.

3. By engineering drawing.
4. By miscellaneous methods, such as:
   a. Market grade;
   b. Sample.
5. By a combination of two or more of the above.

Description by brand ⚡

There are two questions of major importance in connection with the use of branded items. One relates to the desirability of using this type of description and the other to the problem of selecting the particular brand. Both these questions call for some detailed consideration.

Description by brand or trade name indicates a reliance upon the integrity and the reputation of the supplier. It assumes that the supplier is anxious to preserve the goodwill attached to a trade name and is capable of doing so. Furthermore, when a given supply is purchased by brand and is satisfactory in the use for which it was intended, the purchaser has every right to expect that any additional purchases bearing the same brand name will correspond exactly to the quality first obtained. The brand name is put upon an article to identify its origin. The manufacturer uses a brand name so that any goodwill cultivated among satisfied customers may rebound to his benefit and profit and not to that of the distributor or of some other person. To protect this goodwill, however, is is essential that consistent quality be provided. Failure to maintain a consistent quality results in loss of confidence in the article by the users and, consequently, in ill will rather than goodwill.

There are certain circumstances under which description by brand may be not only desirable but also necessary:

a. When, either because the manufacturing process is secret or because the item is covered by a patent, specifications cannot be laid down.
b. When specifications cannot be laid down with sufficient accuracy by the buyer because the vendor's manufacturing process calls for a high degree of that intangible labor quality sometimes called "workmanship" or "skill," which cannot be defined exactly.
c. When the quantity bought is so small as to make the setting of specifications by the buyer unduly costly.
d. When, because of the expense involved or for some similar reason, testing by the buyer is impractical.
e. When the item is a fabricated part so effectively advertised by the maker as to create a real preference for the article in which it is incorporated.
f. When users often develop very real, even if unfounded, prejudices in favor of certain branded items, a bias the purchasing officer may find almost impossible to overcome.

On the other hand, there are some definite objections to purchasing branded items, most of them turning on cost. Although the price may often be quite in line with the prices charged by other vendors for similarly branded items, the whole price level may be so high as to cause the buyer to seek unbranded substitutes or even, after analysis, to set its own specifications. There are many articles on the market which, in spite of all the advertising, have no brand discrimination at all. Thus, the purchaser may just as well prefer using trisodium phosphate at 14 cents per pound as a branded cleaning compound costing 20 to 24 cents per pound.

A further argument, frequently encountered, against using brands is that undue dependence on them tends to restrict the number of potential suppliers and deprives the buyer of the possible advantage of a lower price or even of improvements brought out by competitors through research and invention.

If a purchase is to be made on the basis of brand, how is one to select the particular brand to buy? The buyer is, of course, confronted by many questions, of which quality, although primary, is but one. Testing provides an answer.

Testing. Testing products may be necessary before a commitment is made to purchase. The original selection of a given item may be based either upon a specific test or a preliminary trial. Once selected, it may or may not be subjected to periodic comparative tests. These tests are, in most instances, brought to the attention of the buyer by sales personnel, although the purchasing officer may initiate an inquiry.

When salespeople offer samples for testing, the general rule apparently followed by purchasers is to accept only samples which have some chance to be used. Buyers generally are more likely to accept samples than to reject them, since they are always on the lookout for items that may prove superior to those in current use. For various reasons, however, care has to be exercised. For one thing, the samples cost the seller something, and the buyer will not wish to raise false hopes on the part of the salesperson. Sometimes, too, the buyer lacks adequate facilities for testing and testing may be costly to the buyer.

To meet these objections, some companies insist on paying for all samples accepted for testing, partly because they believe that a more representative sample is obtained when it is purchased through the ordinary trade channels and partly because the buyer is less likely to feel under any obligation to the seller. Some companies pay for the sample when the value is substantial; some follow the rule of allowing whoever initiates the test to pay for the item tested; some pay for it only when the outcome of the test is satisfactory. The general rule is for sellers to pay for samples on the theory that, if they really want the business and have confidence in their products, they will be willing to bear the expense.

Use and laboratory tests. The type of test given also varies, depending upon such factors as the attitude of the buyer toward the value of specific types of tests, the type of item in question, its comparative importance to the company, and the buyer's facilities for testing. At times a use test alone is considered sufficient, as with paint and typewriter ribbons. One advantage of a use test is that the item can be tested for the particular purpose for which it is intended and under the particular conditions in which it will be used. The risk that failure may be costly or interrupt performance or production is, however, present. At other times a laboratory test alone is thought adequate and may be conducted by a commercial testing laboratory. Frequently, a preliminary laboratory test is given to determine whether or not a use test is worthwhile.

The actual procedure, in accordance with which samples are handled, need not be outlined here. It is important that full and complete records concerning each individual sample accepted should be made out and filed. These records should include not only the type of test but the conditions under which it was given, the results, and any representations made about it by the seller. It is sound practice to discuss the results of such tests with supplier representatives so that they know their samples have received a fair evaluation.

Description by specification X

Description of desired material on a basis of specifications constitutes one of the best known of all methods employed. A lot of time and effort has been expended in making it possible for purchasing officers to buy on a specification basis. Closely related to these endeavors is the effort toward standardization of product specifications and reduction in the number of types, sizes, and so on, of the products accepted as standard.

Traditional advantages in buying on specifications include:

1. Adequate specifications are evidence that thought and careful study have been given to the need for which the material is intended and to the particular characteristics of the material demanded to satisfy this need.
2. Specifications constitute a standard for measuring and checking materials as supplied, preventing delay and waste that would occur with improper materials.
3. They are of definite value to the large consumer wishing to purchase identical material from a number of different sources of supply, either because no one manufacturer possesses the productive capacity to meet all the buyer's requirements or because the buyer considers it good policy. To ensure identity of materials secured, adequate specifications are almost indispensable.
4. Purchase on a basis of specification tends toward ensuring more equitable competition. This is why governmental agencies place such a premium on specification writing. In securing bids from various suppliers, a buyer must be sure that the suppliers are quoting for exactly the same material or service.
5. When the buyer specifies performance, the seller will be responsible for performance.

While there are certain distinct advantages in buying on specification, using specifications does not constitute a panacea for all difficulties involving quality. The limitations involved in using specifications fall into seven classes:

1. There are many items for which it is practically impossible to draw adequate specifications.
2. Although a saving may sometimes be realized in the long run, the use of specifications adds to the immediate cost. If, therefore, the article desired is one

not purchased in large quantities and does not need to conform particularly to any definite standards, it is frequently inadvisable to incur the additional expense. Buyers, when sending specifications for a special item, request the vendor to quote on the basis of the specifications and at the same time to indicate whether or not a standard article closely approaching the one specified is available and, if so, to quote a price on the standard article, indicating how it differs from the specifications submitted.

3.   Compared with purchase by brand, the immediate cost is also increased by the necessity of testing to insure that the specifications have been met.

4.   One of the difficulties arising from the use of specifications come from carelessness in drawing them when they are likely to give the purchaser a false sense of security.

5.   At the opposite extreme is setting up specifications so elaborate and so detailed as to defeat their own purpose. Unduly elaborate specifications sometimes result in discouraging possible suppliers from placing bids in response to inquiries.

6.   Unless the specifications are of the performance type, the responsibility for the adaptability of the item to the use intended rests wholly on the buyer, provided only that the item conforms to the description submitted.

7.   The minimum specifications set up by the buyer are likely to be the maximum furnished by the supplier.

If after weighing these advantages and disadvantages, the buyer decides to purchase on a specification basis, four major choices are available: specification by physical or chemical characteristics, by material or method of manufacture, by standards, or by performance.

Specification by physical or chemical characteristics

Specification by physical or chemical characteristics provides definitions of the properties of the materials the purchaser desires. They represent an effort to state in measurable terms those properties deemed necessary for satisfactory use at the least cost consistent with quality. They often include information on methods of test and disposition of material in case of failure to meet requirements. Most buyers use it to some extent for such items as oil, paint, and cotton gray goods, although this usage varies widely from company to company.

Specification by material and method of manufacture

The second type of specification includes those prescribing both the material and method of manufacture. Outside of some governmental purchases, such as those of the armed forces, this method is used when special requirements exist and when the buyer is willing to assume the responsibility for results. Many organizations are not in this position, and as a result, comparatively little use is made of this form of specification.

It is with particular reference to the two methods of specification just considered that most of the well-known "standard" specifications apply. Some attention, therefore, may well be given to the matter of sources of specifications before considering other methods of quality description.

✗ Sources of specification data

Speaking broadly, there are three major sources from which specifications may be derived: (1) individual standards set up by the buyer; (2) standards established by certain private agencies—either other users, suppliers, or technical societies; and (3) governmental standards.

Individual standards require extensive consultation between users, engineering, purchasing, quality control, suppliers, marketing, and, possibly, ultimate consumers. This means the task is likely to be arduous and expensive.

A buyer needs to be quite sure not only that it is best to acquire a given item on the basis we are now considering but also that there is no standard specification available serving this purpose equally well. A common procedure is for the buying company to formulate its own specifications on the basis of the foundation laid down by the governmental or technical societies. To make doubly sure that no serious errors have been made, some companies mail out copies of all tentative specifications, even in cases where changes are mere revisions of old forms, to several outstanding manufacturers in the industry to get the advantage of their comments and suggestions before final adoption.

✗ Standard specifications

If an organization wishes to buy on a specification basis, yet hesitates to undertake to originate its own, it may resort to one of the so-called standard specifications. These have been developed as a result of a great deal of experience and study by both governmental and nongovernmental agencies, and substantial effort has been expended in promoting them. They may be applied to raw or semimanufactured products, to component parts, or to the composition of material. The well-known SAE steels, for instance, are a series of alloy steels of specified composition and known properties, carefully defined, and identified by individual numbers.

When they can be used, standard specifications have certain definite advantages. For one, they are widely known and commonly recognized. This makes them readily available to every buyer. Furthermore, this standard should have somewhat lower costs of manufacture. Finally, because they have grown out of the wide experience of producers and users, they should be adaptable to the requirements of a great many purchasers.

On the other hand there are certain disadvantages limiting the value of standard specifications. One of the most commonly urged objections is that just because they are standard, some of them are of necessity so broad as to be unsuited to the requirements of particular users. In some instances, too, certain so-called standard specifications have not been, as yet, sufficiently well accepted to warrant such designation.

Standard specifications have been developed by a number of nongovernmental engineering and technical groups. Among them may be mentioned the American Standards Association, the American Society for Testing Materials, the American Society of Mechanical Engineers, the American Institute of Electrical Engineers, the Society of Automotive Engineers, the American Institute of Mining and Metallurgical Engineers, the Underwriters Laboratories, the National Safety Council, the Canadian Engineering Standards Association, the American Institute of Scrap Iron and Steel, the National Electrical Manufacturers' Association, and many others.

While governmental agencies have cooperated closely with the above mentioned organizations, operations for compiling specifications have been conducted independently in developing standards for use in purchasing for the various governmental departments and agencies. The National Bureau of Standards in the U.S. Department of Commerce compiles commercial standards. The General Services Administration coordinates standards and federal specifications for the nonmilitary type of items used by two or more services. The Defense Department issues military (MIL) specifications for items involving all types of military equipment.

Standardization and simplification

No consideration of specifications would be complete without some reference to the efforts to standardize and simplify them. Some comments need to be made on this movement from a procurement angle, although no extended discussion is possible here.

In many discussions of this subject, these two terms are used as meaning much the same thing. Strictly speaking, they refer to two different ideas. "Standardization" means agreement upon definite sizes, design, quality, and the like. It is essentially a technical and engineering concept. "Simplification" refers to a reduction in the number of sizes, designs, and so forth. It is a selective and commercial problem, an attempt to determine the most important sizes, for instance, of a product and to concentrate production on these wherever possible. Simplification may be applied to articles already standardized as to design or size, or it may be applied as a step preliminary to standardization.

There are several sales aspects to the simplification-standardization movement. To the extent that standardization occurs, the salesperson is compelled to stress not diversity in production as much as better product or service at the same price or of the same product at a lower price. It is just at this same point that a problem is created. If the product the buyer is purchasing is itself a completed product consumed in its finished form, then some reasonable measure of diversity in suppliers' offerings may well be desirable to get as large a degree of suitability for a particular use as possible. As N. F. Harriman has so aptly said in his *Standards and Standardization:* "Standardization is a useful servant but a bad master." That variations in completed products may have embodied a substantial measure of standardized components is no drawback to the buyer. Because it facilitates replacements, it becomes a positive advantage. The problem from a selling angle becomes one of how to secure all the advantages of technological improvement, of originality and advanced design, to have "something better" to sell, while at the same time securing the economies of production.

For the industrial product the answer to this dilemma is probably to be found in two different areas. The first is in the large measure of cooperation among the production, procurement, and sales divisions that we have stressed so continually.

A second part of the answer is to be found in stressing not standardization and simplification in the end product but the component parts. By so doing, the production economies are combined with individuality of end product. So, too, can be obtained the procurement advantages of low initial cost, lower required inventory, and diversity in selection of source.

Specification by performance

Performance specification is a method employed to considerable extent, partly because it throws the responsibility for a satisfactory product back to the seller. Performance specification is results and use oriented, leaving the supplier with the decisions on how to make the most suitable product. This enables the supplier to take advantage of the latest technological developments and to substitute anything that exceeds the minimum performance required.

The satisfactory use of a performance specification, of course, is absolutely dependent upon securing the right kind of supplier. There are also some buyers who may resort to such specifications as an alibi for not going to the trouble of getting an exact method of description or of locating more satisfactory sources. Finally, particularly because of the difficulty of comparing quotations, the price paid may prove rather high.

Specification to meet government legal requirements

Recent federal legislation concerning employee health and safety and consumer product safety requires increased vigilance on the part of purchasing personnel to be sure that products purchased meet the government requirements. The Occupational Safety and Health Administration (known as OSHA) of the U.S. Department of Labor has broad powers to investigate and control everything from noise levels to sanitary facilities in places of employment. The Consumer Product Safety Act gives broad regulatory power to a commission to safeguard consumers against unsafe products. Purchasing people have the responsibility to make sure that the products they buy meet the requirements of the legislation. Severe penalties both criminal and civil can be placed on violators of the regulations.

Description by engineering drawing

Description by a blueprint or dimension sheet is very common and may be used in connection with some form of descriptive text. It is particularly applicable to the purchase of machine parts, forgings, castings, and punchings. It is an expensive method of description not only because of the cost of preparing the print itself but also because it is likely to be used to describe an item which is quite special as far as the vendor is concerned and, hence, expensive to manufacture. However, it is probably the most accurate of all forms of description and is particularly adapted to purchasing those items requiring a high degree of manufacturing perfection and close tolerances.

Miscellaneous methods of description

Description by market grades.   Purchase on the basis of market grades is confined to certain primary materials. Wheat and cotton[4] have already been referred to in this connection; lumber, butter, and other commodities will suggest themselves. Purchase by grade is for some purposes entirely satisfactory. Its value depends upon the accuracy with which grading is done and the ability to ascertain the grade of the material by inspection. Setting up a definite series of grades sufficiently numerous to cover all major and perhaps minor divisions and the common acceptance of these grades by the trade are, of course, essential. The grading, furthermore, must be done by those in whose ability and honesty the purchaser has confidence. It may be noted that even for wheat and cotton, however, grading may be entirely satisfactory to one class of buyer and not satisfactory to another class. The differences between the upper and the lower limits of the recognized grades of wheat are such as to make possible delivery of wheat not at all suited to the user's requirements. It is for this reason that millers buy only by sample or after physical examination of the wheat. Another difficulty arises in cases in which cotton is bought on the cotton exchange permitting delivery of various grades of cotton and adjustment of payment on a basis of the commercial differences in price between the grades delivered. Although this method may be satisfactory for a cotton merchant, it will not serve a cotton manufacturer.

Description by sample.   Still another method of description is by submission of a sample of the item desired. Almost all purchasing officers use this method from time to time but ordinarily—there are some exceptions—for a minor percentage of their purchases and then more or less because no other method is possible.

Good examples are: items requiring visual acceptance, e.g., wood grain, color, appearance, etc.

Combination of methods of description

A company frequently uses a combination of two or more of the methods of description already discussed. The exact combination found most satisfactory for

---

[4]For agricultural raw materials, such as wheat and cotton, the grades are established by the U.S. Department of Agriculture. These include all food and feed products, the standards and grades for which have been established in accordance with the Federal Food and Drugs Act, the Grain Standards Act, and other laws enacted by Congress. As will be noted later, establishing grades acceptable to the trade is essential to the successful operation of a commodity exchange.

an individual organization will depend, of course, upon the type of item needed by the organization and the importance of quality in its purchases. There is no one best method applicable to any single product, nor is there for any particular organization a best method of procedure. The objective of all description is to secure the right quality at the best price that can be secured.

Metric conversion

North America is currently engaged in a major planning program to convert to the metric system of measurement. Plans call for industry-wide changes in stages and a high degree of participation and consultation between companies and government. The International System of Units or "SI" in abbreviated form has the advantage of simplicity and universality. It is expected that the conversion will be largely accomplished over the next ten years. Since the conversion of industries and individual organizations is expected to follow voluntary lines, metric conversion committees of national associations are expected to play a major role. The National Association of Purchasing Management recommends that every corporation form a metric conversion committee to plan for orderly internal change. The materials manager and purchasing manager are obvious candidates to be members of or head such a committee.

CONTROL OF QUALITY—INSPECTION AND TESTING

Inspection and testing may be done at two different stages in the acquisition process. Before a commitment is made to a supplier, it may be necessary to test samples to see if they are adequate for the purpose intended. Similarly, comparison testing may be done to determine which product is better from several different sources. After a purchase commitment has been made, inspection is required to assure that the items delivered conform to the original description.

Inspection of purchased items

Just as the purpose of adequate description is to convey to the vendor a clear idea of the item being purchased, so the purpose of inspection is to assure the buyer that the supplier has delivered an item which corresponds to the description furnished. Regardless of how reliable the purchaser may have found the seller to be in the past and regardless of the care with which a manufacturer may inspect a product before shipping it, mistakes and errors of various sorts do occur. No such body of past experience exists when new suppliers are being tried, and their products must be watched with particular care until they have proved themselves dependable. Unfortunately, too, production methods and skills, even of old suppliers, change from time to time; operators become careless; and occasionally a seller may even try to reduce production costs to the point where quality suffers. Thus, for a variety of reasons, it is poor policy for a buyer to neglect inspection methods or procedures. There is no point in spending time and money upon the development of satisfactory specifications unless adequate provision is made through inspection to see that these specifications are lived up to by vendors.

The type of inspection and the frequency and thoroughness with which it is conducted clearly vary with circumstances. In the last analysis, this problem resolves itself into a matter of comparative costs. How much must be spent to ensure compliance with specifications?

What is reasonable inspection?

What is reasonable inspection? No formula will give the answer. The importance of inspection is in proportion to the importance of the quality. Even a small quantity of a material in which quality is highly important may call for very rigid inspection, and permissible variations from standard may be very small. Generally speaking, when quantities are small and considerable variations of quality are permissible, inspection is of less importance than when the contrary conditions prevail. Merchandise which is bought by brand may call for occasional inspection to ensure consistency of quality, but it is more than likely that a check on the results obtained by the using department would be satisfactory for this purpose. Products bought on the basis of grades must be checked as to their compliance with the grade specified. The same rule applies to purchases made on a basis of samples. Products which are bought on a specification basis are usually sufficiently important to require rather close checking.

While it is true that on items of major equipment and, in some cases, on fabrication parts, a very careful and detailed inspection is called for on every item delivered, inspection based on a test of samples taken from the shipment should, in the main, prove adequate. In all cases, of course, where the purchaser has any reason to question the condition of an incoming shipment, inspection is necessary.

Specification of inspection method

In setting specifications, it is sometimes the practice to include the procedure for inspection and testing. This leaves the method of testing within the discretion of the buyer. Since methods may vary widely, they can be made unfair to the seller and be made grounds for rejection of merchandise almost at the whim of the purchaser. Specifying the inspection method is a protection to the buyer. The vendor cannot refuse to accept rejected goods on the ground that the type of inspection to which the goods would be subjected was not known or that the inspection was unduly rigid. Instructions which indicate merely that a specified number of samples of a shipment are to be tested may have little value unless it is made clear how these samples are to be chosen. For instance, if all the samples are taken from the top of a certain solution, the results are likely to be very different from what they would be if the samples were taken from the bottom. Similarly, samples chosen from the beginning of a run from a die are likely to be different from the one-thousandth or one-millionth sample from the same die.

In such a situation, not only the method of selecting the sample but also the statistical limits (as distinct from the so-called engineering limits) to be imposed should be indicated. Indeed, it may be well for a company doing a large amount of buying of items that require statistical methods in sampling to work out in some detail a standardized statement of procedure, perhaps even with some discussion of the theory and practice involved. Such a statement placed in the hands of a supplier might avoid considerable misunderstanding.

Quality control department

Up to this point we have assumed that the responsibility of a quality control group is narrowly confined to the technical task of submitting incoming material to certain definite tests in order to answer the one question: "Does this item comply with the description as defined in the purchase order?"

Actually, a number of duties other than straight testing of incoming material may be undertaken by the quality control group. Thus, it should assist in setting specifications, if for no other reason than to pass upon the company's ability to test for compliance with them. Clearly, it is useless to call for characteristics the presence or absence of which cannot be determined. Again, the quality group can initiate material studies. It can be called upon to pass on samples left by salespeople. Frequently it must investigate claims and errors, both as to incoming items and as to outgoing or finished products. It may pass upon material returned to stores to determine its suitability for reissue. Similarly, it may be called upon to examine salvage material and to make a recommendation as to its disposition. It may also assist in assessing the quality assurance programs in supplier's plants.

The structure and location of the quality control function constitutes a relevant problem of administration. In most cases, the work of inspection is performed by a separate department whose work may be divided into three main parts: the inspection of incoming materials, the inspection of materials in process of manufacture, and the inspection of the finished product. The assignment of this work to a separate department is supported partly on the ground that if the inspectors of materials in process and of the finished product report to the executive in charge of production, there may be occasions when inspection standards are relaxed in order to cover up defects in production.

If the inspectors of incoming materials were under the administration of the purchasing director, there might, on some occasions, be a tendency to relax inspection standards in order to pass materials which the purchasing director had procured because of a substantial reduction in price but which did not meet the quality standards specified.

Since the production department is frequently expected to discover defects in materials during the manufacturing process, the contention is often held that it should also have responsibility for the inspection of material before it enters the manufacturing process. However, the inspection of incoming materials by a purchasing department is not parallel to this. The test being made is not of the purchasing department's own work but rather of that of the vendors. It is true that an undue number of rejections may reflect upon the buyer's selection of a source, but no one is more interested in eliminating unreliable vendors than the purchasing officer. The only exceptions to this statement are those cases in which collusion or dishonesty exists or the purchasing officer is buying on a price basis.

The really important things to keep in mind are:

1. Inspection involves not only purchased material and parts but also work in process and finished goods.
2. Inspection at any stage is a technical problem of where, when, how much, and how to inspect. Also, it frequently requires the use of more or less technical equipment.
3. The importance of quality varies from industry to industry and from company to company.
4. Inspection should be remedial and preventive as well as negative. The constructive aspects of inspection are as important as that of testing.
5. Any organization for inspection involves intraplant administrative problems pertaining to personnel, cost control, and relations with various departments, such as stores and production units, records, and so forth.
6. The real purpose of all inspection is to get materials and parts of the sort needed. This cannot be attained in the long run without good vendor relations and a sound purchasing policy.

Inspection at the seller's premises

Occasionally, inspection is conducted by the buyer in the plant of the vendor. A great proportion of the procurements by the armed services are so inspected, for several reasons. The usual methods of inspection of the finished item may not be adequate. Latent defects not determinable may appear only after the purchaser has further processed the material or part. Again, the correction of defects, if attended to as soon as possible, avoids the additional costs of carrying the work on to completion, only to find the end result unacceptable. Furthermore, transportation charges incident to the return to the vendor of rejected material, especially on heavy material or that shipped long distances, can be avoided. On the other hand such inspection has two definite disadvantages. One is the heavy cost of maintaining such an inspection staff. The second is that the presence of inspectors in the plant may be strongly resented by the supplier.

A different kind of buyer inspection at the seller's premises takes place when selection, rather than production of a commodity, determines the quality and when price varies accordingly. Examples would include but are not limited to: veneer and saw logs, pulp wood, livestock, land, feed and mixed grains, used equipment, antiques, paintings, scrap, and professional contracts. Furthermore, on premise buyer inspection almost always applies in conventional auctions but almost never in the case of dutch auctions.

The quality capability survey

The increased emphasis on reliability brought on by space age technology has created the requirement that suppliers be evaluated prior to the placing of an order and that continuous subsequent monitoring take place. This "quality capability survey" has become especially widespread in the aerospace and military industries with a reported use in excess of 80 percent of all cases. It is interesting that despite widespread use of this technique, research findings show the survey's results to be statistically questionable.[5,6] This is unfortunate, because the ability to determine, a priori, whether one supplier has a better chance than another of meeting the desired quality standards is highly desirable. Since the principle is obviously attractive, the real question deals with our future ability to develop a better test instrument.

Commercial testing labs and services

The type of inspection required by a company may, in fact, be so complicated or so expensive that it cannot be performed satisfactorily in the company's own organization. In such cases some companies employ the services of commercial testing laboratories, particularly in connection with new processes or materials or for aid in the setting of specifications. The use of these agencies by manufacturers for any other purpose is limited; most companies do not use them at all and others only under unusual circumstances.

It is possible that the services of commercial testing laboratories are not used by some companies as much as they should be. Many of these laboratories are dependable. They employ capable staffs and own the most modern of photometric, X-ray, electrical, chemical, and physical testing equipment. Their charges are commonly not unreachable for manufacturers in a position to use them. Standard testing reports of commonly used items are available from several commercial testing laboratories. They are the commercial equivalent of consumer's reports and can be a valuable aid.

Inspection methods

Although it is not the purpose of this text to cover the choice of inspection methods extensively, it is proper to mention them briefly here in the recognition that procurement costs and performance may be significantly affected by this decision. The same inspection methods may be used by either the manufacturer or the purchaser. Since almost all output results from a manufacturing or transformation process of some sort, process quality control will be the first item discussed. This will be followed by screening and sampling which deal with items already produced. All quality control can be divided further into observations of attributes and variables. Attributes usually observed are whether the product is acceptable or not. For example, for an automobile assembly line, is the paint acceptable or not? In a hotel, have the rooms been properly cleaned or

---

[5]R. W. Olive, "The Quality Capability Survey: A Procurement Quality Management Control," *Journal of Purchasing* 5, no. 1 (February 1969): 5–22.

[6]R. W. Olive, "The Quality Capability Survey: Results, Reliability and Recommendations," *Journal of Purchasing* 5, no. 2 (May 1969): 15–42.

not? This type of yes or no inspection is usually based on the binominal distribution. The generating function for this distribution is:

$$P(r) = \frac{n!}{r!(n-r)!} P^r (1-p)^{n-r}\ ^7$$

where p is the probability that the event associated with r will occur on any single trial and n is the number of trials.

Observation by variables tries to determine by how much the sample varies from the specification or from other units. How many paint defects on this car? How many things are wrong with the way this hotel room has been cleaned? Observation by variables is usually based on the normal distribution.

Process quality control

In processes using repetitive operations, the quality control chart is often valuable. Management attempts to produce a satisfactory output population which can be measured by an acceptable mean and dispersion. The $\overline{X}$ chart is useful for charting the population mean and the $\overline{R}$ chart the dispersion.

One key decision in using the $\overline{X}$ and $\overline{R}$ charts involves the choice of upper and lower control limits. The tighter these limits are placed, the greater the probability of rejection and, hence, the larger the manufacturing cost will become. Normally, a plus or minus range of two to three standard errors of the mean is used. The desired population mean is drawn horizontally (or vertically) as the central line on the chart. See Figure 4–1.

Inspectors or operators make random checks of the variables to be controlled and plot the results on the graph. If the average of the samples fall within the limits of the control chart the process is allowed to continue. If the averages fall outside the control limits, the process is normally stopped, and action is taken to determine the cause for the shift so that corrections can be made. The control chart uses random sampling techniques and is well suited to most manufacturing operations of large output and where it is not necessary to screen every item produced. This raises the decision regarding inspection of output.

Output inspection—100 percent inspection and sampling

There are basically two major types of quality checks on output. One is to inspect every item produced. The other is to sample.

100 percent inspection or screening. It is traditionally held that 100 percent inspection, or screening, is the most desirable inspection method available. This is not true. Experience shows that 100 percent inspection seldom accomplishes a completely satisfactory job of separating the acceptable from the nonacceptable or measuring the variables properly. Actually, 200 percent or 300 percent inspection or even higher may have to be done to accomplish this objective. De-

---

[7] M. F. Spiegel, *Theory and Problems of Statistics* (New York: Schaum Publishing Co. 1961), p. 122.

Figure 4–1
Filler control chart, summary, and explanations

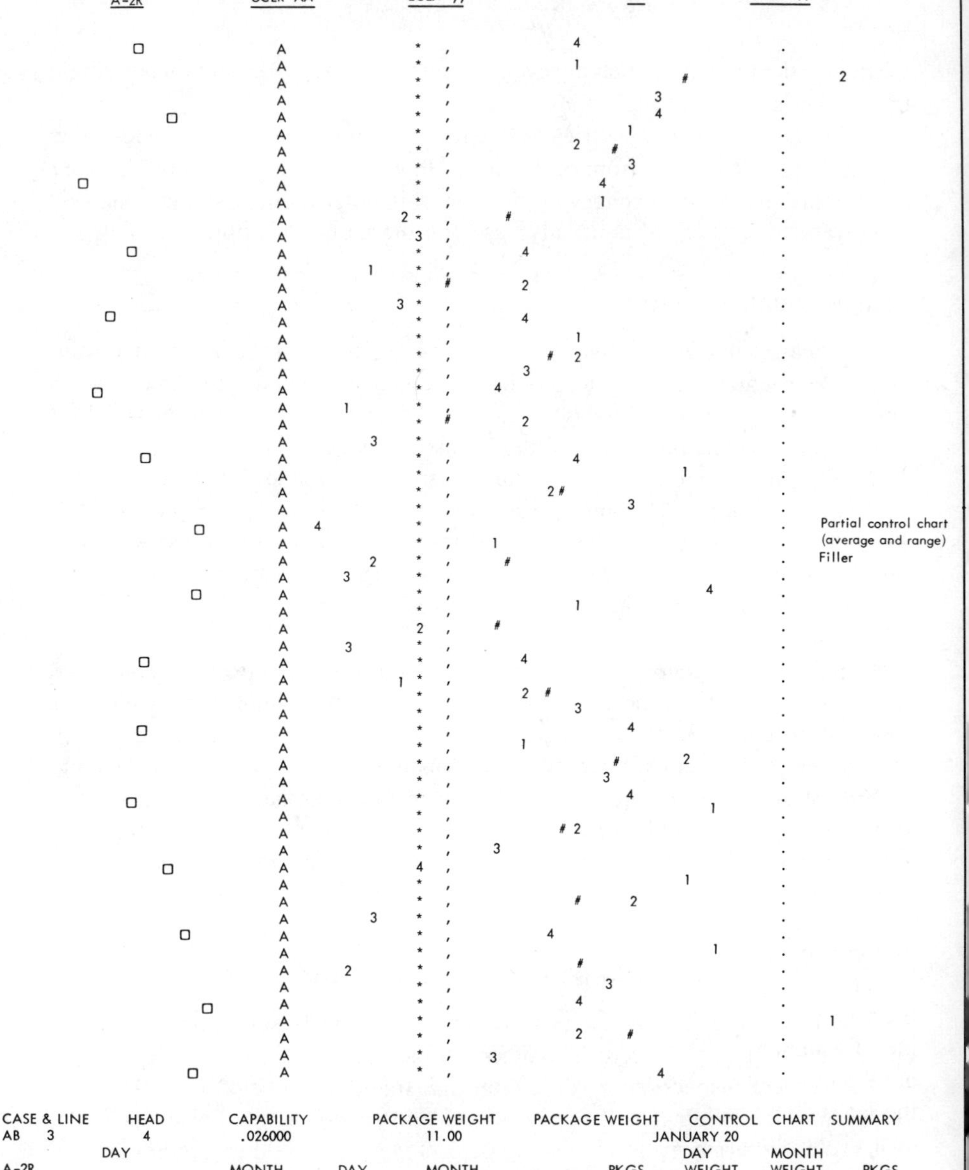

| A-2R | UCLR AA | LCLX ,, | X | UCLX .. |

Partial control chart
(average and range)
Filler

CASE & LINE	HEAD	CAPABILITY	PACKAGE WEIGHT		PACKAGE WEIGHT	CONTROL CHART SUMMARY		
AB 3	4	.026000	11.00			JANUARY 20		
	DAY						DAY	MONTH
A-2R		MONTH	DAY	MONTH		PKGS	WEIGHT	PKGS
STD DEV.		.037960	% VAR FROM CAPABIL.		LIGHT		4.90-	126
UCLR AA		.025255	100.00000	2.86538	% LIGHT			6.73
LCLX ..		.118560			TOTAL NA		75.06	1872
X 5% CTL		.003584			AV OVERWT		.04010	
UCLX ..		.041544			% OVERWT		.36455	
		.079504			TOTAL NR		23.70	1824

Figure 4-1 *(continued)*

Terminology:
A-$2R$—$(A_2\overline{R})$ where A_2 is a constant for a sample of 4 and $\overline{X}' \pm A_2\overline{R}$ gives the upper and lower control limits.
$UCLR$—(UCL_R) Upper control limit, range
$LCLX$—(LCL_X) Lower control limit, average
X 5% XTL—$(\overline{X}')_1$ point at which average is set to insure that 95 percent of packages will equal or exceed stated net weight (CTL—control limit)
$UCLX$—(UCL_X) Upper control limit, average
Capability—Capability of machine under control conditions
% Var. from capability—A percent by which the daily or month to date capability varies from the capability under control conditions
Package weight—Package weight (net) in ounces
Light—Number of packages under net weight
% LIght—Percent of packages under net weight
Total NA—Total sample size
Av overwt.—Total overweight divided by the total sample size (gives average weight over net weight)
% Overwt.—Average overweight divided by the package weight
Total NR—The Total NR figure is similar to the Total NA figure except that the computer rejects samples which have "gone wild." These are removed and the Total NR figure is used to calculate the standard deviation
Note: Figure 4–1 is a composite of two control charts. The two columns on the left refer to the range control chart while the remaining three columns represent the weight control chart. The symbols 1, 2, 3 and 4 on the weight control chart refer to the observation number and the sample average is designated by the symbol #.

pending on the severity of a mistake, an error of discarding a perfectly good part may be more acceptable than passing a faulty part. In some applications the use of such extreme testing may increase the cost of a part enormously. For example, a 5¢ part may well end up costing $3.00.

If the test is destructive, 100 percent testing is impractical. The cost of 100 percent testing is frequently high. The testing is seldom fully reliable, because of worker boredom or fatigue, or inadequate facilities or methods, and, therefore, it is not often used in high-volume situations.

Sampling. The alternative to inspection of every item produced is to sample. How a sample is taken will vary with the product and process. The purpose is always to attempt securing a sample that is representative of the total population being tested. Random sampling is one commonly used technique.

The method of taking a random sample will depend on the characteristics of the product to be inspected. If it is such that all products received in a shipment can be thoroughly mixed together, then the selection of a sample from any part of the total of the mixed products will represent a valid random sample. For example, if a shipment of 1,000 small castings of supposedly identical characteristics are thoroughly mixed together and a random sample of 50 castings is picked from the lot and inspected and 5 are found to be defective, it is probable that 10 percent of the shipment is defective.

If the product has characteristics which make it difficult or impractical to mix together thoroughly, consecutive numbers can be assigned to each product, and then, through the use of tables of random sampling numbers (of which there are several) or a standard computer program, a sample drawn by number is chosen for detailed inspection.

The general rule which the statisticians believe should be observed when drawing a random sample is: adopt a method of selection that will give every unit of the product to be inspected an equal chance of being drawn.

Operating characteristic curves

Operating characteristics (OC) curves are used to see how well a sampling plan distinguishes between acceptable and nonacceptable product. In procurement the purchaser has to determine what the probability is of accepting goods that do not meet the minimum level of quality specified. This is called the consumer's risk with a percentage β. There is a parallel risk α for the producer that work may be rejected at the plant when it is in reality acceptable. See Figure 4–2.

In the example shown, the purchaser and the producer must select a sampling plan which relates the desire for risk, accuracy, and inspection cost. Usually, as the number of samples is increased additional accuracy is obtained, but sampling cost is also increased. Theoretically, in the selection of any sampling plan the cost of sampling must be weighed against the losses that would be incurred if no sampling were done. It is unfortunate that the sampling cost is normally easier to determine than the losses arising from not sampling.

Sequential sampling

Sequential sampling may be used to reduce the number of items to be inspected in accept-reject decisions without loss of accuracy. It is based on the cumulative effect of information that every additional item in the sample adds as it is inspected. After each individual item's inspection three decisions are possible: to accept, to reject, or sample another item. A Wald[8] was one of the pioneers of sequential sampling development, and he estimated that using his plan the average sample size could be reduced to one half, as compared to a single sampling plan.

In a simple version of sequential sampling, often used by the military, 10 percent of the lot is inspected, and the whole lot is accepted if the sample is acceptable. If the sample is not acceptable, an additional 10 percent may be inspected if the decision to reject cannot be made on the basis of the first sample.

Computer programs

Many quality control computer programs are available in both real time, using remote terminals, and batch processing. They have resolved the tedium of extensive calculations and provide a range of applications not considered practical before EDP introduction. All computer manufacturers and many service companies maintain these programs for use by customers. Standard programs, for example, select sampling plan, calculate sample statistics and plot histograms,

---

[8] A. Wald, *Sequential Analysis* (New York: John Wiley & Sons, 1947).

Figure 4–2
Typical OC curve
(data showing probability of rejecting bad lots by the producer
with $a = .10$ and the probability of accepting bad lots by the
purchaser with $b = .10$)

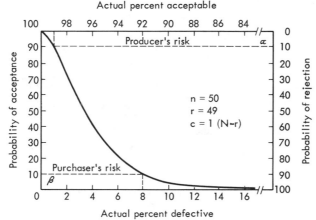

Source: R. B. Chase and N. J. Aquilano, *Production and Operations
Management,* (Homewood, Ill.: Richard D. Irwin, 1973), p. 156. © Richard
D. Irwin, Inc., 1973.

produce random selection of parts, plot OC curves, and determine confidence
limits.

Responsibility for adjustments and returns

Prompt negotiations for adjustments and returns made necessary by rejections
are a responsibility of the purchasing department, aided by the using, inspection,
or legal departments.

The actual decision as to what can or should be done with material that does
not meet specifications is both an engineering and a procurement question. It
can, of course, be simply rejected and either returned at the supplier's expense or
held for instructions as to its disposition. In either case the buyer must inform the
supplier whether the shipment is to be replaced with acceptable material or to
consider the contract canceled. Not infrequently, however, a material may be
used for some other than the originally intended purpose or substituted for some
other grade. It is also possible that some private readjustment is called for. A
third alternative is to rework the material, deducting from the purchase price the
cost of the additional processing involved. Finally, particularly in the case of
new types of equipment or new material to which the purchaser is not accus-
tomed, the vendor may send a technical representative to the buyer's organization in the hope that complete satisfaction may be provided.

A problem growing out of inspection is that of the allocation, between buyer and seller, of costs incurred in connection with rejected material. The following statement indicates the nature of the problem and the various practices in dealing with it:

The costs incurred on rejected materials may be divided into three major classes:

1. Transportation costs.
2. Cost of testing.
3. Contingent expense.

The practice of allocating these costs varies considerably with various purchasing departments. The practice is affected to some degree by the kind of material rejected, trade customs, the essential economies of the situation, the buyer's cost accounting procedure, and the positions of strength of each organization.

In practically all cases reported, transportation costs both to and from the rejection point are charged back to the supplier.

Very few companies report inspection or testing costs as items to be charged back to the supplier. Such costs are ordinarily borne by the buyer and are considered a part of purchasing or inspection costs.

In many cases contracts or trade customs provide definitely that the supplier will not be responsible for contingent expense, yet this is perhaps the greatest risk and the most costly item of all from the buyer's standpoint. Incoming materials which are not of proper quality may seriously interrupt production; their rejection may cause a shortage of supply which may result in delay or actual stoppage of production, extra handling, and other expense. Labor may be expended in good faith upon material later found to be unusable, and not only the material but the labor thus expended is a total loss to the buyer. It is, in general, however, not the practice of buyers to allocate such contingent costs to the vendor. Some buyers, however, insist upon agreements with their vendors to recover labor costs expended upon the material before discovery of its defective character.

Importance of inspection records

Complete and well-documented records of the results of the inspection of materials and products received from suppliers are an essential element of any formal method of evaluating suppliers. In companies where the nature of the products produced requires strict control of quality, it is of great importance to the proper performance of the procurement function to select suppliers who can deliver materials and products of the specified quality.

A supplier who submits the lowest bid but furnishes materials which fail in part to pass inspection for quality may actually be a high-cost supplier. Interruptions of production schedules caused by lack of material which meets quality standards can be very expensive. The time required of purchasing personnel to obtain replacement and other adjustments for materials which fail to pass quality inspection also adds to costs.

X Zero defects programs

Starting in the late 1950s, the U.S. Department of Defense encouraged many of its suppliers to install incentive programs aimed at defect prevention. These "Zero Defects Programs" had the objective to reduce to zero the rejection rates resulting from failure to meet quality standards. Benefits achieved from the successful operation of these programs included:

a. "On-time" delivery of products and materials which meet all quality specifications.
b. Lower costs because of less wasted materials.
c. Lower costs of inspection.

These motivational programs generally rely on moral suasion. PRIDE (Personal Responsibility in Daily Effort) and various other titles have been applied to these programs. It is useful to recognize that zero defects is usually not a process design possibility or a quality control system target. Machines are designed to operate within certain ranges, and all sampling plans are based on a certain percentage of consumer's risk and a probability of nonacceptable product. It is through the special care taken by operators, inspectors, and assemblers that better than design performance is obtained.

Purchasing managers have used the concept of "zero defects" in non-defense industries to encourage suppliers to provide defect-free materials and products.

QUESTIONS FOR REVIEW AND DISCUSSION

1. What makes a "best buy"?
2. What is the difference between function, quality, suitability, and reliability?
3. What are the common advantages and disadvantages of buying brand items?
4. Why might an inspector decide to sample and what should the objectives of sampling be?
5. What is the difference between standardization and simplification?
6. What recourse does a buyer have when a supplier delivers unsatisfactory goods?

CASE 4-1
X RANEK INC.

"Those WR93 castings you ordered from Roberts are no good, Marsha. They are all too short by a substantial margin, so I have no choice but to reject the whole batch. What do you want me to do with them?"

"Just hold on to them for awhile, Frank, till I find out what's going on here. I will get back to you shortly."

Marsha Dinsmore, buyer at Ranek Incorporated had just received the bad news from Frank Wild, head of quality assurance at Ranek regarding the 172 aluminum castings she had ordered for the first assembly run of the new PSW Model two weeks hence. She was not expecting any difficulties with this order, since she remembered buying the same castings for the earlier PSV Model. Marsha realized that a lack of castings could have a disastrous impact on the PSW assembly and introduction plans, for which extensive advance promotion had already begun. Therefore, she immediately tried to find out what went wrong with this order.

Engineering information

A few hours later Marsha found out that the $150 casting did not meet specifications as shown on the engineering drawing sent to the supplier. All previous deliveries of the same casting had been identical in defects. However, the chief engineer, John Vickers, had made some adjustments for the PSV Model which made it possible to use the castings as supplied. According to John Vickers it was not possible to make the same adjustments for the PSW Model, nor was it possible to fix up the defective castings.

The PSV model plans

Current plans for the PSV Model called for continued assembly until the PSW Model had taken over the complete market. No one was quite certain how many more PSVs might be made. Sales estimates ranged from a minimum of 100 over the next year to 500 over the next three years. It was unlikely that repairs of old PSV Models would require more than 10 castings per year for the next ten years.

Roberts Foundry

Mr. Steve Roberts, president and owner of Roberts Foundry, the supplier of the castings, claimed that the WR93 castings supplied were exactly the same as those of all earlier orders which had all been accepted by Ranek. He was very surprised to hear from Marsha that there were difficulties with the castings.

The normal lead time on aluminum castings with Roberts Foundry was about eight weeks. Marsha knew that Mr. Roberts was hungry for more business, even though his shop was very busy. He was currently working on a number of other Ranek orders. Roberts Foundry received about 40 percent of Ranek's $400,000 total aluminum casting business. Gaskell and Sons, a long-term reliable supplier, received the remaining 60 percent. The current lead time with Gaskell was about ten weeks.

After assembling this information Marsha wondered what action to take next.

CASE 4–2
SLAGKO AGGREGATE COMPANY

Mr. T. Bolton, director of purchasing for Slagko, was wondering whether he should set up a test trial to evaluate a proposal for tire chain nets for the company's six large slag loaders. The rubber tire loaders used in hot, sharp slag beds currently showed a disappointing tire life of 600 operating hours.

Company background

Slagko converted steel slag which was crushed, screened, and mixed with other aggregates to provide paving materials for use in the construction and building trade. Last year's sales had reached $85 million. The company was rapidly expanding in all areas of the construction trade. Recently the company's slag pit operation had moved from one to two shifts to increase production.

Slag association

Slagko was a member of the National Slag Association which met periodically to share information on equipment problems, maintenance and safety programs, tire damage and manufacturer's warranties.

Steel crawler tracks were exclusively used by all members in slag beds until 1963. A number of operators in that year began using rubber tire loaders because of their better maneuverability and greater output. Output with rubber tires was reported to have increased two- and three-fold per loader. Adoption by most association members was gradual, however, due to the substantial tire damage reported by the early trials. Tires costing $2,000 to $3,800 each were lasting from 5 minutes to 1,000 hours in the slag pit. Tire manufacturer's investigations of the problem could only offer a range of tire qualities and options such as extra heavy treads or steel belts as a solution. Further studies conducted for the Slag Association reported an increased safety hazard in the rubber tire loaders. Depending upon the terrain and movement of the loader, a tire when pierced would tilt the loader dangerously or tip it over. Guidelines were then established for traveling speed and speed of turning for loaders with rubber tires. Operators were warned of loader operations involving very uneven surfaces. Despite continued Slag Association concern over the safety issue and the high tire operating cost, equipment manufacturers and tire producers had not come up with any worthwhile solutions.

Slagko's present slag pit operation

Slagko operated six 61-ton rubber tire loaders on two shifts five days a week. The loaders, costing anywhere from $150,000 to $190,000 each were from six months to eight years old. Total operating costs were kept for each machine showing a cost from $26–$38 per operating hour. (See Exhibit 1.) Tire costs of $100,000 per year for each loader in the slag pit made a solution minimizing tire damage and costs very attractive. The critical problem in tire life was that sharp slag cut the tread or the vulnerable side wall. Slag material was also very hard and abrasive, compounding the problem. Average tire life on some loaders varied as much as 40 percent, depending upon the location in the slag pit that the loader was operating in. Tires costing $3,500 with steel belts had prolonged tire life by a multiple of two over less expensive tires costing $2,300. Nevertheless, Slagko's tire life with the $3,500 tires still varied between 600 and 700 operating hours.

Exhibit 1
Loader cost breakdown

The company kept a total maintenance record of costs for the life of each loader and used this to calculate the hourly operating cost for each loader. A computer record was kept for every machine. Actual and allocated costs were combined. For example, garage wages were actual wages paid out to date, but tire costs were allocated over the six company loaders on a monthly basis.

The following costs were for a loader which cost $180,000, was seven years old, and had operated for 31,200 hours. The other five loaders had operated from 3,000 to 35,000 hours.

Garage labor	$ 12,000
Parts	122,400
Outside repairs	27,600
Direct garage costs	67,200
Garage overhead	49,200
Total garage	$278,400
Gas, oil	38,400
Operating wages	170,400
Depreciation:	
Standard amount continued after end of estimated loader life	193,200
Tires (loader had been in slag pit for two years, five years in	
gravel operation)	213,600
Other	4,560
Total costs	$898,560
Cost per hour	$28.80

In most cases once a tire was damaged, it could not be repaired. Rear mounted tires where tire damage was less severe could be recapped. Front tire damage was nearly twice as much as rear tire damage. Presently, loaders were averaging 600 hours on front tires and 1,000 hours for rear tires.

Downtime, due to damaged tires, took one to two hours in the slag pit. The pit foreman would radio the maintenance shop which would send a new tire on a rim out to the site.

The chain net proposal

Mr. Bolton had always practiced an open-door policy to suppliers and had actively searched for ways to improve tire performance. A foreign sales representative from Europe contacted Mr. Bolton in regard to his company's tire chain nets, which it hoped to introduce and market in the United States. Recently a number of open pit mines in Europe had adopted the tire chain net idea. Loader maneuverability and output remained constant while tire wear and damage was significantly reduced. According to the sales representative, the tire chain nets also eliminated most unscheduled tire-related downtime and increased the operator's confidence, resulting in improved machine performance when working in sharp fragmented materials.

The chain net was a series of interlocking rings and links which covered the complete tire including the side walls. (See Exhibit 2.) The net would minimize overheating of the tires and add a margin of safety to the loader's operation. Tire wear under the chain was estimated at 10 percent per 1,000 operating hours. Each chain net for Slagko's heavy loaders would cost $5,084 and came with a reasonable supply of extra links and rings. A number of emergency links were also supplied that could be bolted quickly by the loader operator to prevent net tear and unnecessary tire exposure at a break point. After the loader's shift these emergency links could be properly replaced. A chain net for Slagko's loaders would last approximately 2,500 operating hours. The salesperson claimed chain tension, inspection, and replacement of broken links was estimated at one hour for every 40 operating hours for each net. Unscheduled maintenance was claimed to be no more than one hour for every 200 operating hours. Regular preventive maintenance was stressed as instrumental in good results from the chain nets. The salesperson supplied a sample calculation of the potential savings with the use of chain nets which looked very promising (See Exhibit 3.)

Mr. Bolton approached the tire department superintendent, Mr. Knight, and the slag pit foreman, Mr. Kitson, to obtain their views on the chain net proposal. Mr. Knight said that hard steel belted tires were cut with a 61-ton loader carrying a one-ton full shovel when moving in the pit. What difference would a chain net make? Either the tire of the net or both would have to be repaired. He thought maintenance of the net could be critical if tension slipped during operation or chain links broke. He saw his maintenance costs increasing significantly. Mr. Knight was also worried that a broken chain link might not be detected as easily as a damaged tire unless a periodic visual inspection was made. Undetected chain damage would cause unequal net stress and result in further chain link breaks plus tire damage.

Mr. Kitson's only concern was with the operation of the loaders in the pit. Would the operators, not fearing tire damage be less careful? Would chain breaks result in more pit downtime? Was the speed or operation of the loader restricted with the tire chain nets? As long as production could be increased or maintained, Mr. Kitson was in favor of the idea.

Conclusion

With so little to go on in making an evaluation of the chain nets, Mr. Bolton contemplated a test of the chain nets in the slag pit. He did not know

Exhibit 2

Loader with chain net mounted on front wheels.

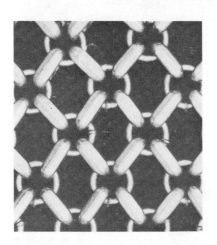

Ring & link
(actual size)

how many nets to buy, how long the trial run should be, what it would cost, or how the results should be interpreted. He also knew that it was up to him to suggest a reasonable test format since no one else at Slagko seemed particularly interested in following up the chain net idea.

Exhibit 3
Example of estimated owning and operating combined chain/tire cost in a typical open pit operation

1. Your machine was delivered new with four (4) L–5 extra deep tread tires, size 37.25–25 (36 ply), worth $4,000 each, including tax, on a replacement tire basis.
2. Recaps are worth $2,000 each.
3. In 6,000 hours machine operating time you have consumed eight new tires on the two front wheels (including the two original tires), 1,500 hour average tire life, with no recaps possible.
4. In 6,000 hours machine operating time you have consumed four new tires and two recaps on the two rear wheels (including the two original tires), 4,000 hour average tire life *including one recap,* before new tire replacement is necessary.
5. At 6,000 hours, front tires are ready for new tire replacement; rear tires are ready for recapping.

Front wheels:
8 new tires @ $4,000 = $32,000 (including two original tires)

Total front tire cost   = $32,000 (two front wheels)

Rear wheels:
4 new tires @ $4,000   = $16,000   (including two original tires)
2 recap tires @ $2,000 =   4,000

Total rear tire cost   = $20,000   (two rear wheels)

Hourly tire cost in 6,000 machine operating hours:
Two front wheels: $32,000 ÷ 6,000 hr. = $5.33/hr. (8 new tires)
Two rear wheels: 20,000 ÷ 6,000 hr. = $3.33/hr. (4 new tires and 2 recaps)

All four wheels: $52,000 ÷ 6,000 hr. = $8.66/hr. (12 new tires and 2 recaps)

---

6. The material the chain will work in is soft and low in abrasions. The material is sharply fragmented. Standard Service, Rock Super × 15, close mesh (4 × 4) Tire Protection Chain is selected for use.
7. The initial price for Erlau Rock Super × 15 is $5,084 each chain (U.S. Suggested List Price, Effective October 15).
8. Estimated average life of Rock Super × 15 in soft and low abrasive material is 6,500 hours.
9. Average cost of parts' consumption for 6,500 hours' service on a double shift, 2,000 hour work year basis ($16.00/mo. × 39 mos.) is $624.
10. Labor cost is figured as 4 hours/mo. × $6.00/hr (example only) × 39 months = $936.
11. Tire tread wear under the chain is figured as 65 percent tread wear (10%/1,000 hours' chain use). 65 percent of recap cost $2,000 = $1,300.
12. Freight is 2,487 lbs. (RX × 15, 37.25 –35 shipping weight) × $2.00/cwt. = $50.
13. Installation cost is $75.00 (average dealer cost each chain).

Exhibit 3 (*continued*)

New Erlau Rock Super × 15, size 37.25–35 ...	$5,084.00 each chain
Freight: 2,487 lbs. @ $2.00/cwt.	50.00 each chain
Dealer installation	75.00 each chain
Parts cost	624.00 each chain
Labor cost	936.00 each chain
Tire tread wear under the chain:	1,300.00 each tire
Total estimated owning and operating combined chain/tire cost	$8,069.00 each wheel

Hourly estimated O&O combined chain/tire cost each wheel:

Total estimated O&O chain/tire cost $8,069 ÷ 6,500 hrs. =	$1.24 each wheel
Two wheel chain/tire O&O cost = $2.48/hr. 2 wheels	
Four wheel chain/tire O&O cost = $4.96/hr. 4 wheels	

Comparisons with existing tire costs:
Using tire costs developed in the example and estimated O&O chain/tire costs, we have the following comparative example to prove, or disprove, economic justification for the use of Erlau Tire Protection Chain.

Two front wheels:

Existing unprotected tire cost   = $5.33/hr. (8 new tires)
Estimated chain/tire O&O cost = 2.48/hr. (2 chains/2 tires)

Estimated cost reduction by
  Erlau Chain   = $2.85/hr. (2 wheels)

Two rear wheels*:

Existing unprotected tire cost   = $3.33/hr. (4 new tires/2 recaps)
Estimated chain/tire O&O cost = 2.48/hr. (2 chains/2 tires)

Estimated cost reduction by
  Erlau Chain   = $ .85/hr. (2 wheels)

All four wheels:

Existing unprotected tire cost   = $8.66/hr. (12 new tires/2 recaps)
Estimated chain/tire cost   = 4.96/hr. (4 chain/4 tires)

Estimated cost reduction by
  Erlau Chain   = $3.70/hr. (4 wheels)

In 6,500 hours of anticipated average chain life, the total estimated tire-related operating cost reduction through the use of Erlau Tire Protection Chains, installed on all four wheels, would be $3.70/hr. × 6,500 = $24,050.

---

*Combined O&O chain/tire cost can be considered the same for front wheel and rear wheel installations.

CASE 4–3
NORTHWEST DIVISION

Alec Perrin, manager of corporate purchases for Northwest Division, had long been concerned about the engineering-purchasing relationship in Northwest Division. He had asked his assistant to prepare a set of suggestions on how the two functions might cooperate better in the future. His assistant, Ted MacDonald, had prepared a set of guidelines and had given these to Alec with the words: "If these rules can't fix it up, nothing can." Alec was not sure how he might assess the guidelines and what action to take subsequently.

Company background

Northwest Division was the agricultural and forest products branch of ATA Chemical Corporation, a large multinational concern with consolidated sales exceeding $1.7 billion. Northwest Division had annual sales exceeding $200 million and, like all divisions in ATACC, operated in a reasonably autonomous manner. Engineering had traditionally held a strong position at Northwest. The division had a reputation as a market leader in technological advances, new products, and high quality. (For organization chart see Exhibit 1.)

Engineering and purchasing

Annual purchases for Northwest exceeded $80 million and were growing rapidly. Alec Perrin had been manager for two years, having transferred from the forest products sales group to purchasing. The former manager of purchases had held the position for 37 years. He had not been successful in obtaining engineering cooperation. During his stay in forest products sales Alec Perrin had gained the impression that engineers preferred to bypass purchasing because they thought they could cut the red tape and do a better job.

As manager of purchases Mr. Perrin had spent the first two years becoming better acquainted with the job, looking after the most pressing crises, and building a stronger and more capable staff. The new group consisted primarily of university graduates in science, engineering, or business administration. About half had worked in other areas of Northwest Division prior to joining the new purchasing team. He found that his personnel resented the engineering bypass attitudes, and a number of incidents had occurred during the last two years convincing Alex Perrin that purchasing had a legitimate role to play in matters now apparently viewed as in the engineering domain.

The ability to influence specifications, early involvement in capital project planning, and awareness of engineering supplier contacts were three typical areas of major concern.

Exhibit 1
Organization chart

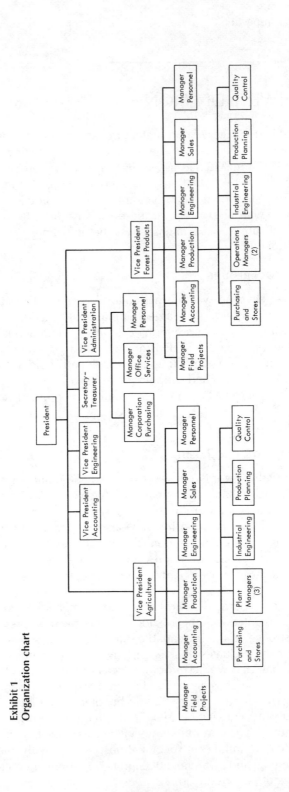

For example, in a recent incident a design engineer had specified an expensive alloy tank for an application where a standard stainless steel would have sufficed at savings of about $20,000. Despite the courteous attempts at questioning by the equipment buyer, an experienced engineer himself, the design engineer refused to discuss the matter saying: "My job is to design the equipment, yours is to buy what I tell you to get, where I want it and to look after the necessary paperwork. And if you don't like it that way, I'll be happy to look after the whole thing myself."

Purchasing was seldom aware of new capital projects until engineering sent the necessary details for the final purchase orders. Frequently, by that time there was considerable pressure to get the paperwork out quickly to avoid delaying the project. A recent purchase involving a $750,000 mixer unit was typical. Engineering handled all preliminary supplier contacts and price estimates without purchasing's knowledge. One of the design engineers involved had an automobile accident which delayed engineering planning about three months. When purchasing finally received instructions to purchase the mixer from a supplier chosen by engineering, a $100,000 premium had to be paid to assure on-time delivery, and there was no opportunity at all to search for alternate sources.

Alec Perrin was aware that the engineering group had traditionally made a significant contribution to Northwest because of its innovative role, strong expertise, and ability to maintain a high-quality consumer product. He, nevertheless, though that purchasing had its own contribution to make which could not be achieved with current engineering attitudes and practices.

After a particularly touchy deal in February, involving an engineering commitment to a supplier without the knowledge of purchasing, Alec Perrin had asked his assistant, Ted MacDonald, a recent business school graduate, to see what he could recommend. Ted immediately went to work. He talked with purchasing department personnel, supplier personnel, production people and engineers. He also contacted purchasing people in other ATACC divisions to see what they had done. He also did a library search of books and periodicals. His findings were summarized in the following set of guidelines.

Alec wished to review the guidelines carefully. He had a high regard for Ted MacDonald and knew that Ted expected action quickly. Nevertheless, he wanted to be absolutely sure he had a sound plan and approach before he committed himself.

GUIDELINES FOR ENGINEERING/PURCHASING RELATIONSHIP

1. Project planning and estimates

Collection of data and prices for project planning and preliminary estimating requires flexibility and cooperation between the engineering and the purchasing departments. Care should be taken to prevent individual suppliers from doing considerable work to supply initial estimates to us. Care should also be taken that specifications are not written to fit one supplier's product to the exclusion of other suppliers in the field.

All requests by engineering for commercial information from suppliers will be made through the purchasing department on form "Request for Information," copy attached. The proper use of this form will ensure that all of the data required for estimating and purchasing are obtained from the vendor.

2. Vendor contacts

Vendor contacts by the engineering department prior to the awarding of a contract or the placing of a purchase order require cooperation between the two groups. It is recognized that at times the engineering department will, of necessity, discuss preliminary information or technical aspects with a vendor. It is the responsibility of the engineering department to keep the purchasing department informed of the discussion and direct the vendor to send a copy of any pertinent correspondence to the purchasing department. The engineering department must not solicit bids from the representatives. If a quotation is required, a Request for Information should be filled out and the vendor's representative referred to the purchasing department.

After awarding of the contract, technical contacts may be made by engineering with a copy of any pertinent correspondence to purchasing. All commercial contacts must be made by the purchasing department with a copy of any pertinent correspondence to engineering. Assigned inspectors or expediters may contact the supplier in carrying out their respective responsibilities.

3. Bid lists

a. Bid lists for engineering consultants. The engineering department has the prime responsibility for the bid lists for engineering consultants after evaluating their personnel, facilities, and experience. If the project is particularly large or includes an arrangement for the consultant to do project purchasing, the purchasing department should be involved.

b. Bid lists for contractors. Preparation of bid lists for contractors is a joint responsibility of engineering and purchasing. Engineering should investigate technical ability, experience, and personnel. The purchasing department should investigate commercial standing, obtain financial data and suitability from past performance.

c. Bid lists for major equipment. Preparation of bid lists for major equipment is the joint responsibility of engineering and purchasing. Engineering will prepare detailed specifications of their requirements and provide purchasing with a list of suggested suppliers. Purchasing should take

Exhibit 2

REQUEST FOR INFORMATION

TO: Mr./Ms._____   FROM: _____
     Purchasing Department   Engineering Department

DATE:_____   SUBJECT:_____

                                      _____

                               Project_____W.O._____

Please obtain the following information on the subject item(s):

_____

_____

FOR ESTIMATING PURPOSES ☐   FOR PURCHASE ☐

Secure bids   ☐

Price   ☐

Shipping weight   ☐

Estimated freight   ☐

Taxes applicable   ☐

Duty (if imported)   ☐

Current delivery   ☐

Literature   ☐

Sample(s)   ☐

Arrange meeting with representative   ☐

List of recommended spare parts   ☐

Time required to supply approval drawings   ☐

Time required to supply certified drawings   ☐

Enclosed are_____ sets of specifications and/or drawings.

SUGGESTED VENDORS

_____   _____

_____   _____

_____   _____

INFORMATION/BIDS REQUIRED BY_____

ESTIMATED VALUE $_____

Copies to: Signature_____

this original list and endeavor to find or develop other sources of supply until an adequate number for competitive bidding is obtained. In the case of non-competitive or single supplier products, the engineering department must provide the purchasing department with the reason for handling in this manner. Purchasing may suggest that engineering rewrite specifications to enable them to obtain competitive bids.

   d.   Bid lists for minor equipment and construction supplies. The engineering department will prepare specifications for miscellaneous equipment and supplies. The preparation of the bid list is the prime responsibility of the purchasing department. Engineering department will comment, if necessary, on any particular item and supplier.

4.   Bid transmittal and comparison

Purchasing will prepare for Engineering a "Bid Transmittal and Comparison" and "Engineering Equipment Comparative Bid Sheet," forms attached. After complete technical analysis by engineering, the Bid Transmittal and Comparison form will be returned to purchasing—the bottom half completed, accompanied by an approved purchasing requisition. Engineering will make recommendations for preferred supplier and reason for same. Purchasing will negotiate the best commitment for the item or service.

5.   Supplier selection

Recommendation of the contractor, consultant, and supplier of major equipment and justification for the recommendations will be provided by the engineering department. The final decision on the contractor, consultant, or supplier is a joint responsibility of the two departments.

6.   Notification

The purchasing department will notify, in writing, the unsuccessful bidders on all major items and contracts.

7.   Specifications

Engineering specifications must be precise to prevent misunderstanding after the contract is let. In addition to details of buildings and equipment, items such as company's safety policies, work rules and restrictions, availability of utilities, and other items affecting contractor's cost should be included in the specifications. Care should be taken to see that items placed in the specifications conform with the requirements of standard Northwest Division documents such as contract forms, purchase orders, etc., to prevent undue costs due to ambiguity in specifications. Specifications should be reviewed by the plant management for the areas affected by the construction or installation. This is an engineering department responsibility.

Exhibit 3

Project:_____

Item No._____

360 Work Order:_____

BID TRANSMITTAL AND COMPARISON

TO: Engineering – Attention:

    Attached are Bids and Bid Comparisons covering

Buyer:_____

To be completed by Engineering

RECOMMENDATION FOR PURCHASE

TO: Purchasing – Attention

c.c.

    Attached is approved Requisition No.

    Recommended Vendor:

    Reason:

Engineer:_____

8. Contract preparation

It is the responsibility of the purchasing department to prepare the contracts. Contracts should include warranties, guarantees, payment schedules,
holdbacks, bonus/penalty clauses, etc. Purchasing department must consult
with engineering, legal department, etc., regarding their phases of the contract.

Exhibit 4

		ENGINEERING EQUIPMENT				
		COMPARATIVE BID SHEET				
					BIDDERS	
QTY.	ITEM					
	QUOTED PRICE					
	F.O.B.					
	TAXES					
	DUTY					
	ESTIMATED FREIGHT					
	TERMS					
	DELIVERED PRICE					
	DELIVERY					

COMMENTS:

PREPARED BY: DATE:

9.   Commitments

All commitments must take the form of a purchase order or purchase contract placed by the purchasing department. Field change orders may be committed in writing by the designated project engineer/manager. All additions or deletions including field changes must be confirmed by the purchasing department on a purchase order change notice.

10.   Noncompetitive purchasing policy

a.   Lowest cost, commensurate with quality and service, can only be achieved by competitive bidding from qualified suppliers. Vendors' qualifications and performance must be continually updated and new suppliers sought out and evaluated from three viewpoints: quality, price, and service, which includes meeting schedules. The purchasing organization and the engineering department share the evaluation requirements, with purchasing being responsible for permanent files.

b.   There are occasions when noncompetitive purchases must be made; for example, compressor parts, custom machine parts, instrument parts. However, ball bearings, seals, packing, gaskets, etc., do not normally fall in this category. Requisitions for noncompetitive materials must clearly identify the vendor's part number, vendor's serial or shop number, and Northwest's original purchase order number if needed by the vendor for identification purposes. The purchasing organization is authorized to make these purchases with normal approvals.

c.   Any purchase requisition originating in the engineering department limiting the purchase to one supplier, other than Statement (b) materials, will require the approval of the engineering manager if the purchase value exceeds $500. Multiple requisitions will not be used to circumvent this policy, and this aspect will be monitored by purchasing.

d.   The local purchasing manager will define the approval requirements for noncompetitive purchases less than $500. This may vary with locations in order to be compatible with the staffing at that location. The purchasing managers will also establish a maximum purchase value, whereby it costs more to obtain competitive prices than the potential saving of competitive bids.

11.   Contractor's performance report

The manager of engineering or a designated substitute will prepare a "Contractor's Performance Report" (attached) at the completion of the contract and forward to the local purchasing department. This department will make comments on commercial matters and forward a copy to the head office purchasing and engineering department.

12.   Equipment performance report

Due to the wide variety of equipment and applications it is not practical to have a standard single report. The local purchasing and engineering departments are responsible to report supplier and equipment performance in a similar fashion to contractor's performance. Such report would include all types of performance such as delivery, quality, service facilities, and costs of spare parts, etc.

Exhibit 5

CONTRACTOR'S PERFORMANCE REPORT	Contractor's Name
Product group and location	Contractor's representative

Project identification

Type of contract

☐ Lump sum ☐ Unit price ☐ Cost plus fixed fee ☐ Cost plus percentage fee

Contract amount	Final total payments	Reason for additional payments in excess of contract amount
$	$	

Contractor's claims for extras reasonable   Unreasonable number of petty extras submitted

   ☐YES   ☐ NO   ☐ YES   ☐ NO

Job progress – scheduled start	Scheduled completion	Actual start	Actual completion

Cause of delays (if any)

PERFORMANCE RATING	EXCELLENT	ADEQUATE	UNSATISFACTORY
Quality of subcontractors			
Scheduling and coordination			
Workers			
Labor relations			
Materials procurement and delivery			
Quality and supply of tools and equipment			
Cooperation with owner and/or owner's rep.			
Cooperation with other contractors			
Safety record			
Quality of field supervision			
General housekeeping of construction site			

Contractor recommended for future work   ☐ Yes   ☐ No (if no, give reason)

Submitted by	Date	Title

13. Expediting/inspection

The importance of expediting depends on the need for the particular item. Expediting of major or long-term items should be combined with inspection. It is usually necessary to inspect the fabrication or construction to assess properly accuracy of the vendor's delivery promise. On large projects, expediting and inspection may be a full-time job for a member of the project team. Outside inspectors and/or expediters may be hired for these projects by the project manager.

On all other items, expediting will be done by the purchasing department on an exception basis. These exceptions are in two classes:

a. When the time is late.
b. On a special request basis.

Request for expediting should accompany the purchase requisition to the purchasing department and indicate the minimum frequency of the expediting contacts.

Purchasing, with the approval of the engineering manager, may retain outside expediting/inspection services on major project items or on any items where delivery could affect the manufacturing operation. Purchasing should also notify the engineering manager when, in its opinion, expediting and inspection may be required.

14. Equipment delivery

Purchasing will endeavor in all cases to procure equipment when stated on requisition and will advise engineering prior to placing order if the requested delivery date is unattainable.

DETERMINATION AND CONTROL OF QUANTITY AND INVENTORIES

5

Quantity considerations

The decision of *how much* to require is the logical step following clarification of *what* is required. Quantity considerations involve some very tough issues in the materials area. "How much will we need in the future?" is a question that clearly implies forecasting. And the moment we move to a forecasting mode, the possibility of forecast error exists. At the moment of use, actual, not forecast, requirements are the relevant ones, and supply assurance of quantities actually required is a difficult objective to meet.

The first part of this chapter will provide traditional wisdom in inventory and scheduling management as applied to items of independent demand. For a manufacturer of bicycles, the consumer demand for bikes may be seen as independent. The internal requirements for bike components may be seen as dependent on management's decision on when and in what quantities to assemble finished bikes. Thus, dependent demand is addressed as part of the Materials Requirements Planning coverage at the end of the chapter.

In materials management, quantity considerations are a vital part of the total system and present a number of interesting tradeoffs.

The normal assumption behind quantity determination in procurement is that enough must be acquired to satisfy anticipated needs. In simple words: "Buy what you need." Unfortunately, it is not quite that simple. Part of the difficulty relates to the very large number of items acquired and another is lead time. Most items and services are not available instantaneously. Therefore, we have to commit ourselves before the item is actually used. If the lead time is long, this may well force us into forecasting future requirements. Price is another factor. Sometimes the quantity we need is not the quantity normally supplied nor the quantity at which the best price is possible. Inventory position also affects how much we should acquire. Transportation considerations may also have a bearing. General market conditions are another factor as are uncertainties in all these elements. Thus, our simple "buy what you need" model faces some complications. Let us see if we cannot unravel these in this chapter.

✕ Forecasting

Forecasting is very much a part of the materials management picture. Forecasts of usage, supply, market conditions, technology, or price are always necessary, whether they be implicit or explicit. How to plan to take care of the needs of the future is the problem. For usage estimates, where should the responsibility for forecasting lie? In addition, should the materials management group be allowed to second-guess sales, production, or user forecasts? In so far as forecasts are shared with suppliers, the interest of the procurement group is direct. Should the supplier be held responsible for performance to forecast or to actual requirements? A similar situation exists inside the organization. Should the procurement manager be held responsible for satisfying internal needs or internal forecasts? Since missed forecasts are quickly forgotten but substantial shortages or overages are long remembered, the above questions are largely rhetorical. In most manufacturing organizations the need for production materials and parts is usually derived from a sales forecast which is the responsibility of marketing. In service organizations and public agencies the materials function finds itself often in the position of having both to forecast and acquire.

The real problem with forecasts is their reliability. To what extent will actual requirements fall short of, or exceed, forecasted needs? In a chemical company the following forecast was made by the marketing group for a consumer product requiring the following purchase of a basic petrochemical commodity.

Year 1	70,000 barrels
Year 2	120,000 barrels
Year 3	190,000 barrels
Year 4	280,000 barrels
Year 5	390,000 barrels

The cost per barrel was close to $25.00 making this a significant purchase. Further discussions with the marketing group revealed that considerable uncertainty existed regarding this forecast. (See Figure 5–1).

It might be possible for demand to be as low as 70,000 barrels five years later, and it might be as high as 600,000 barrels. This spread between high and low estimates made the procurement plan far more difficult, because it had to be prepared recognizing the full range of possible outcomes. For example, a take-or-pay commitment for 100,000 barrels per year after the first year was obviously not acceptable because of the possibility that actual demand might be well below 100,000 barrels per year. Simultaneously, provisions had to be found for substantial increases in requirements should actual volume exceed forecast.

To a supplier a substantial variation from forecast may appear as a procurement ploy. Should actual demand fall below forecast, the supplier may suspect that the original forecast was an attempt to obtain a favorable price. If substantial increases beyond forecast are demanded, supplier's costs may well increase because of overtime, rush buying, and changed production schedules. There is a need to share forecast uncertainty information with suppliers so that their quota-

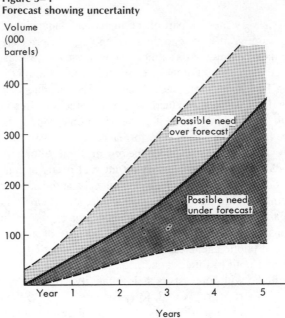

Figure 5–1
Forecast showing uncertainty

tions may take this into account. Such sharing is obviously impossible if buyers themselves are not aware of the uncertainty and its potential impact on the supplier.

Forecasting techniques

No matter where the forecasting is done in the organization, a number of techniques are available to assist in making better forecasts. They fall into two broad classes. The first presumes that past history is indicative of future expectations. By applying statistical techniques to known data, forecasts may be made. The second class includes activities such as marketing research, intention surveys of customers, consensus, correlation with economic indicators which are forecast separately, and salespeoples' reports. Often both classes are used in combination and reconciled with each other. At this time we will concern ourselves primarily with the first class, the statistical methods which may be used on past data.

Past usage data may be examined for six significant components which are: average period usage, seasonality, trend, cyclical aspects, and autocorrelation. Average usage is calculated by dividing the total usage by the number of periods. Seasonality shows regular changes which recur at certain times of the year. For example, heating oil usage is highly seasonal. Trend shows a general overall direction. For example, the trend in power consumption is up over many years. Cyclicality relates to variations caused by outside influences like the state of the economy, wars, and inflation rate but may also be of shorter duration and difficult to identify. Random variations, on the other hand, are those left over when seasonality, trend, and cycle have been accounted for. When there is no apparent reason for any deviation, the result may well be due to straight randomness. Lastly, autocorrelation describes the property whereby variation in usage in any one period is affected by the usage in the preceding periods. Power consumption tends to be highly autocorrelated as are many items normally carried in the supply category.

Forecasting techniques using past data include the moving average, regression analysis, and exponential smoothing. These are well documented in standard texts. Computer programs are readily available for all normal forecasting techniques and can be used by materials personnel to obtain better forecasts internally and to fix deviations which might affect contract terms.

Product explosion and requirement accumulation

The translation of sales or use forecasts into procurement plans requires identification of individual component or material needs and the accumulation of individual needs into total requirements for a specified time period.

Many manufacturers use product explosions to identify all components for a certain end product. For example, every automobile produced needs one steering wheel, five tires, and thousands of other parts. These requirements are normally listed on parts lists or bills of materials, and computerized files can be readily totaled with the necessary sales forecasts. Often, standardized components are common to a variety of end products requiring further combination to establish a total requirement.

For supplies and nonproduction materials the estimated requirements of organizational subunits need to be accumulated by materials management personnel.

It is exactly at this point that two major approaches in management treatment of quantity considerations exist. The traditional one has been to use statistical methods to identify demand and use inventories as a means of protection against differences between actual and forecast requirements. For independent demand and "non-lumpy" demand items, this approach is still viable and, with the exception of systems contracting, may well be the only reasonable one. For dependent items, the emergence of MRP has provided a strong alternative and this is covered at the end of this chapter.

ABC analysis X

The Pareto curve was named after its Italian originator, Alfredo Pareto. He observed the repetitive phenomenon that a small percentage of the total population controls most of the wealth, regardless of the country studied. This same principle holds in materials management and can be usefully applied to help us analyze and categorize decisions involving quantities. This applies to items purchased, as well as items carried in inventory, the total number of suppliers to the organization, and many other aspects. The two examples below show how it is applied to total purchases and a classification of inventory. We normally call the Pareto curve application: ABC analysis, resulting in three classes as follows:

Class	Percent of total items	Percent of total purchase dollars
A items	10	70–75
B items	10–20	10–15
C items	70–80	10–20

These percentages may vary somewhat from organization to organization, but the principle is particularly powerful in materials management, because it allows us to concentrate our efforts in the areas of the highest payoffs. For example, a manufacturing firm with a total dollar volume of purchases annually of $30.4 million had the following breakdown of purchases:

Number of items	Percent of total items	Annual dollar purchases	Percent total purchases
521	4.8	$15,400,000	50.7
574	5.3	6,200,000	20.4
1,023	9.4	3,600,000	11.8
1,145	10.5	2,300,000	7.6
3,754	34.0	1,800,000	5.9
3,906	36.0	1,100,000	3.6
10,923	100.0	$30,400,000	100.0

As can be seen, 10.1 percent of purchases (the A items) account for 71.1 percent of all the dollars spent. The following 19.9 percent of the number of items (the B category) accounts for 19.4 percent of the dollars, and 70.0 percent of the number of items (the C category) account for only 9.5 percent of the dollar value.

How can a purchasing manager use this information? Where would you assign your most skilled negotiators? Where would you put your value analysis and purchase research efforts? How would you allocate your own time?

Since annual purchase volume is a combination of usage volume and unit price, it is not sufficient to call A items high dollar value and C items low dollar value. Actually the following combinations are likely to result in the following classes.

A good starting point in developing an inventory system is to classify items into three groups: A, B, and C, on the basis of the number of dollars tied up annually for each item. (See Figure 5–2.)

In so far as dollar investment in inventory is concerned, it pays to spend far more managerial time and effort on A and B items than on C items. Since supply

Category		Dollar value/unit	volume/year
A	....	High	High
A	....	High	Medium
A	....	Medium	High
B	....	High	Low
B	....	Medium	Medium
B	....	Low	High
C	....	Medium	Low
C	....	Low	Medium
C	....	Low	Low

assurance is usually equally critical for all categories, it is common to carry sufficient inventories of C items to give a high service level, to create a minimum of paperwork, or to have stockless buying agreements, like systems contracting which provide a high service level. A items are particularly critical in terms of dollar investment and are, therefore, barring other considerations, normally carried in small quantities, ordered and reviewed frequently. B items fall between the A and C category and are well suited to a systematic approach with less frequent review than A items.

This discussion has centered on dollar impact alone, thus far. Certain C items may well require A type inventory care because of their special nature, perishability, or other considerations. For example, the flowers for the president's desk may require special attention.

Figure 5–2
A, B, C classification of inventory

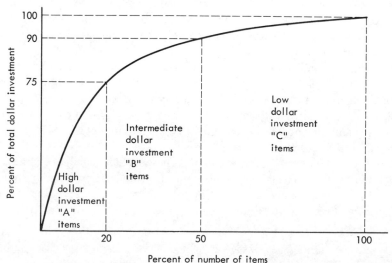

Definition of inventory policy

In most organizations the bulk of purchases are repetitive items which are normally carried in inventory. Thus, inventory policy has a tremendous bearing on the decision of how much to buy.

While it may be more practical to discuss inventory policy in terms of days' supply or of physical quantities, the question of what constitutes the proper inventory to carry resolves itself into a matter of dollars. "Too much" or "too little" or "badly balanced" inventories are all to be avoided because they "cost too much." They are expensive on many counts. "Too much" is "too much" because of undue carrying charges in the form of taxes, insurance, storage, obsolescence, and depreciation. They may be excessive because an undue proportion of the company's total working capital is invested in them. When material shortages exist, certain portions of the inventory may be too large, and capital may be frozen because other portions of the inventory cannot be maintained in proper amounts. On the other hand, "too little" is "too little" because of the costs of too frequent reordering, loss of quantity discounts, or higher transportation charges. Inventory may be too small in the face of probable price increases and subsequent higher material costs. It may be too low in view of likely shortages in the future, with a consequent costly "slowdown" resulting from delayed deliveries. In short, it is the costs that are ultimately significant.

But, however measured, what is the proper size of inventory? This, after all, is the crux of the matter. What is "too little" at one time can be very quickly "too much" in a subsequent period. When general business deteriorates, any particular manufacturer is likely to confront, like other businesspeople, reduced sales volume, lower production, and, therefore, markedly reduced material requirements. Moreover, such a condition is commonly accompanied by falling prices; hence, such quantitites of material as the manufacturer does require can be purchased more cheaply. These factors tend to reduce the size of forward commitments, to necessitate smaller stocks on hand, and to stress hand-to-mouth buying. Clearly, too, inventory purchased at higher prices remaining unused in stock or in uncancelable orders represents some loss, even though subsequently used. To any manufacturer, therefore, an inventory which was under one set of conditions too small—or even just right—under altered conditions might, perhaps within a matter of weeks, become excessive.

The costs associated with inventory. Since the decision to carry—or not to carry—inventory is largely an economic one, it is important to identify the associated costs. These include:

Carrying, holding or possession costs. These include handling charges, the cost of storage facilities and warehouse rentals, insurance, breakage, pilferage, taxes, obsolescence depreciation, and investment or opportunity costs. G. Aljian[1] presents the following detailed list:

---

[1] G. W. Aljian, ed., *Purchasing Handbook,* 3d ed. (New York: McGraw-Hill Book Co., 1973), pp. 11–14, 11–15.

Capital costs:
  Interest on money invested in inventory
  Interest on money invested in land and building to hold inventory
  Interest on money invested in inventory handling and control equipment
Storage space costs:
  Rent on building
  Taxes and insurance on building
  Depreciation on building
  Depreciation on warehouse installation
  Cost of maintenance and repairs
  Utility charges, including heat, light, and water
  Salaries of security and maintenance personnel
Inventory service costs:
  Taxes on inventory
  Labor costs in handling and maintaining stocks
  Clerical expense in keeping records
  Employee benefits for warehouse and administrative personnel
Handling-equipment costs:
  Taxes and insurance on equipment
  Depreciation on equipment
  Fuel expense
  Cost of maintenance and repairs
Inventory risk costs:
  Obsolescence of inventory
  Insurance on inventory
  Physical deterioration of inventory
  Losses from pilferage

Ordering or purchasing cost. These include the preparation costs for a purchase or production order. They include managerial clerical, material, and mailing costs and may be divided into line and header costs. Line cost refers to the computing cost per line item from a vendor. Header cost refers to the costs of identifying and placing an order with a vendor. In any purchase order where more than one item is acquired from one vendor, there should be several line costs and one header cost.

Set-up costs. For manufacturing, the set-up cost is often a significant consideration. It may include such learning curve related factors as early spoilage and low production rate until standard is reached as well as the more common considerations such as the set-up employee's cost, the machine downtime, the extra tool grinding, and the parts damaged during set-up.

Stock-out costs. These are the costs to the organization of not having the required parts or materials on hand when they are needed. They may include lost contribution on lost sales, both present and future, change-over costs necessitated by the shortage, substitution of less suitable or more expensive parts or materials, rescheduling costs and management, labor, and machine idle time. Occasionally, penalty costs may have to be paid, and often goodwill of users or customers may be affected.

The identification of the above costs suggests the difficulty of properly identifying and collecting at least some of them in real life situations. The relevant cost principle should hold, but often for one particular item some marginal or relevant costs may be meaningless. For example, the set-up employee is normally hired for a full work week, and one small set-up more or less may have no impact on what the set-up person is paid. An organization owns and operates its own warehouse and adding or removing a few individual items may have no effect on handling, depreciation, insurance costs, or taxes.

Stock-out costs present their own difficulties, because even at different times their impact may vary. In a seller's market an unsatisfied customer will not be lost as easily as in a buyer's market, and who will say what the cost of not satisfying this customer at this time will be in the long run? When a plant is operating well below capacity, changing over and set-up costs may not be as significant as when operating at capacity.

Two approaches may be used to address some of these difficulties. It is possible to trace and cumulate the individual costs attributable to individual items and use these for decision making. For example, what is the cost of issuing a purchase order for this item? Hopefully, such tracing would be applicable to a class or a number of different items and might, therefore, have broader applicability.

The second approach would be to forecast the impact of a major change in operations and predict the impact on various cost centers. For example, if for half of the C items we use systems contracting, what will the impact on the stores operation be? Or, if we introduce a new way of calculating order quantitites, order points, and safety stocks, what will be the impact of the larger or smaller number of orders on the purchasing group? Since most inventory models and theory is based on finding an optimal cost level, weighing carrying costs against ordering costs or stock-out costs, the quality and availability of cost data are relevant considerations.

Professor Robert Britney has developed an interesting framework for identifying and managing inventories. The authors gratefully acknowledge his contribution in the next section of this chapter, which is largely based on a paper presented by him.[2]

Inventories: Their functions, forms, and control

Of all the many aspects of business administration, few are more perplexing than inventories. Basically they are necessary for prompt customer service, and yet they always seem to be too high, too low, or of the wrong kind. When business activity slows down, the first economic move taken is management's edict to cut all inventories. As business picks up once more, a flurry of activity begins to rebuild inventory stocks on hand. This volatility contributes little to the enhancement of our understanding and control of inventories.

[2]R. R. Britney, "Inventories: Their Functions, Forms and Control." Paper presented to the Canadian Association for Production and Inventory Control, May 1971.

Although the economic order quantity (EOQ) was first introduced in 1915 by Harris, many companies today do not purchase or manufacture in EOQs. This model has not yet achieved the level of success of other management models such as critical path scheduling introduced as recently as 1957.

Inventories may be viewed in terms of the functions they provide and the forms in which they emerge. Within this framework, the potential role of "rules of thumb" and models such as "EOQ" can be assessed. Before doing this, one question should be considered: Why do inventories exist?

Why do inventories exist? ⬤✗ ✗

Inventories are important for many reasons; a few include:

1. Provide and maintain good customer service;
2. Smooth the flow of goods through the production process;
3. Provide protection against the uncertainties of supply and demand;
4. Obtain a reasonable utilization of equipment and manpower.

What we really mean is that the costs of not having inventories are usually greater than the costs of having them. They exist for this reason and for this reason alone.

Often these costs are difficult or impossible to obtain, and we simply may say that inventories are needed to do business. The implications here are that the costs associated with production inefficiencies, lost sales, and customer ill-will arising from not stocking inventories are perceived to be greater than the cost of maintaining stocks. If we are uncertain as to customer behavior, we then talk about the expected costs of inventories, combining probability estimates of customer demand with inventory costs.

This simple but effective definition of why inventories exist is intuitively reasonable and very useful. For example, the familiar EOQ formula can be derived directly from this definition.

Consider the situation where the yearly demand is R units, the cost purchase (or set-up) is S dollars, and the percentage annual cost of carrying inventory is K, and the purchase price (or cost) is C dollars per unit. We could look at a variety of lot sizes ranging from one unit lots up to large quantity lots. Let's assume that we know that a lot of some quantity Q is economical. Should we consider the next lot size larger by some small quantity q? The cost of not including q in the lot size will leave the number of orders required per year at R/Q with an annual purchase cost of $S(R)/Q$. If q is included the number of set-ups will fall to $(R)/(Q + q)$ with a cost of $S(R)/(Q + q)$ dollars. But the cost of having q will save $S(R)/Q - S(R)/(Q + q)$ dollars. The cost of having q in the lot size will increase the average level of inventory $q/2$, at an additional yearly carrying cost of approximately $KC(q)/2$. This will include q only if the cost of not having it is greater than the cost of having it. Further we would be indifferent when the costs are just equal. Equating these costs we obtain the equation:

$$S\,\frac{R}{Q} - S\,\frac{R}{Q+q} = KC\,\frac{q}{2}$$

Simplifying:

$$SR\,\frac{q}{Q(Q+q)} = KC\,\frac{q}{2}$$

Canceling q gives:

$$SR\,\frac{1}{Q(Q+q)} = \frac{KC}{2}$$

Rearranging:

$$Q^2 + Qq = \frac{2RS}{KC}$$

As q becomes rather small we consider the addition of an elemental quantity q only, then as q approaches a very small value so does Qq. This leaves: $Q^2 = 2RS/KC$. Thus the economic order quantity Q is:

$$Q = \sqrt{\frac{2RS}{KC}}$$

The economic order quantity is usually developed using calculus; however, it is important to see that it is really selected according to the simple definition of the existence of inventories. Let's now briefly review the functions of inventories.

✕ What functions do inventories provide?

Regardless of their form (raw material, work in process, and finished goods), all inventories may be further described as performing one or more of transit, cycle, buffer, seasonal, and decoupling functions.

1. *Transit inventories.* These are primarily pipeline inventories, their existence arising because of the need to transport inventories from point A to point B in the production inventory system. Since this transit time is not instantaneous in most situations, significant quantities of transit inventories result.

2. *Cycle inventories.* These exist because of management's attempt to produce in lot sizes, either EOQs or other reasonable lot sizes. In order to facilitate such a plan, inventories accumulate at points in the system.

3. *Buffer.* Inventories in this classification arise mainly from decisions regarding risk. The higher the service level (the lower the risk we set of running out of stock) the greater are the quantities in buffer inventories required.

4. *Anticipation inventories.* Anticipation inventories exist because of expected changes in demand, supply, or price. A simple demand example would be a seasonal expectation for high requirements such as heating oil in the winter time. If supply shortages are expected or prices expected to rise, inventories may be acquired in anticipation of these developments.

5. *Decoupling.* Decoupling inventories provide the function of separating dependent production centers. The independent operation of these centers may be achieved over a limited period of time by the use of decoupling inventories.

A reasonable question at this time would be to ask why one would want to distinguish between five functions of inventories? At any one time, a transit, buffer, and decoupling inventory will all appear exactly the same, or one step further a single unit of inventory may in reality support all functions at once. One reason for dwelling on the functions of inventories as we have is to identify and highlight those inventories which are controllable and those which are essentially noncontrollable. The controllable/noncontrollable concept, of course, must pertain to a reasonable time period, for all inventories are controllable in the long run.

Before looking at management's decision variables which control these various inventories, let us first add the form dimension to these functions.

Inventory forms

Inventories can be classified by form as well as function. The three commonly recognized forms for production material are raw material, work in process, and finished goods. Scrap, or obsolete materials, although technically a form of inventory, will not be included in these basic forms here. (See Chapter 12 which deals with disposal.)

Supplies or MRO items are also a form of inventory and lend themselves to the same framework. In most manufacturing companies the size of the supplies inventory is relatively small compared to the other forms. The identification of inventory forms is relative in that the finished goods of one company often become the raw materials of the next company. This total system interdependence is well illustrated by Forrester's[3] interesting approach to industrial dynamics. However, within one organization they are easily distinguished.

Raw material inventories for manufacturers represent stocks of the basic material inputs into a company's production process. As material and labor is added to these inputs, they are combined and transformed into work-in-process inventories. When completed and stocked they become finished goods inventories.

In general, these inventory forms are distinguished by the amounts of materials and labor added by the organization. Finished goods inventories have more material and labor added than do work-in-process inventories. Again within any organization these forms are usually well defined.

For nonmanufacturing organizations other than retail institutions finished goods may not be a significant form and many of the inventories carried may properly be classified as supplies. Two main classes may be recognized here: prior to use and in service.

---

[3]J. W. Forrester, "Industrial Dynamics," *Harvard Business Review,* July–August 1955.

Inventory function and form framework

Pulling together the five functions and three forms, we have the 15 potential kinds of inventory making up the total inventory profile of a company. Figure 5–3 illustrates these, together with brief descriptions of the key management decision variables affecting the existence of these different kinds of inventories. All may not be present to the same degree in any one organization; however, those that are present in significant numbers exist because the cost of having them are less than the cost of not having them. It is useful to discuss some of the more common kinds of inventory at this point.

Transit inventories

In order to sustain operations, transit inventories are employed to stock the supply and distribution pipelines linking a company to its suppliers and customers respectively. On the procurement side some of the more common decisions affecting the size of this inventory deal with the supplier's location and the transport mode selected. A decision to use a supplier a long distance away and to use rail transportation may create far greater raw materials transit inventories than using a local supplier with daily truck deliveries. Trade-offs exist between transportation and inventory carrying costs as well. Obviously, a decision here may have further impact on the other functional inventories for the same material. If the likelihood of a rail strike is high, anticipation stocks may be forced up. And if the chances of variation in lead time are high, buffer stocks also may have to be enlarged. Total system design should recognize these trade-offs and assure their consideration in the decision making. Work-in-process transit inventories are determined by such factors as process design and plant layout as materials flow from operation to operation. Finished goods transit inventories are likewise related to marketing policies and channels of distribution. All are characterized as inventories in transit from one point to another.

For some organizations being located close to the source of raw materials is important. Others have to be close to markets. For others again location is less sensitive. Once an organization's site is established, however, operational decisions involving transit inventories must be made with the locational context as given. For example, a number of steel companies situated on the Great Lakes use water transport for raw materials and find that during the winter this mode is not available. They are, therefore, forced to build an anticipation or seasonal inventory. So long as the cost of building up this inventory and carrying it over the winter is lower than the cost of switching to alternate means of transport in the winter, this practice will continue.

Cycle inventories

Rather than purchase, produce, or even transport inventories one unit at a time, we may choose to work in lots. As a direct result, inventories tend to accumulate at various points in the system. These are called cycle inventories:

Figure 5–3
Inventory forms and functions

INVENTORY FORM

		Raw material 1	Work-in-process 2	Finished goods 3
	1 Transit (pipeline)	Logistics Decisions		
		Design of supply system, supplier location, transportation mode	Design of layout and materials handling system	Design of plant location and product distribution system
	2 Cycle (EOQ, lots)	Product/Process Design Decisions		
		Order size, order cost	Lot size, set-up	Distribution costs, lot sizes
INVENTORY FUNCTION	3 Buffer (uncertainty)	Management Risk Level Decisions & Uncertainty		
		Probability distribution of price, supply & stock-out & carrying costs	Probability distribution of machine and product capabilities	Probability distributions of demand and associated carrying and stock-outs costs
	4 Anticipation (price) (shortage)	Price/Availability/Decisions & Uncertainty, Seasonality Capacity		
		Know future supply & demand price levels	Capacity, production costs of hire, fire, transfer, overtime, idle time, etc.	Demand patterns (seasonal)
	5 Decoupling (interdependence)	Production Control Decisions		
		Dependence/ independence from supplier behavior	Dependence/ independence of successive production operations	Dependence/ independence from market behavior

inventories required to support our decision to function in lot sizes. Although lot sizes may be determined in many ways, one lot size of special interest is the so-called economic order quantity. There are a large number and variety of economic order quantity models to take account of variations in demand, supply, or production rate, lead time, and costs. The derivation of the simple model $Q = \sqrt{2RS/KC}$ has been provided in an interesting way at the beginning of this chapter. This model presumes instant replenishment, standard usage throughout the year, and costs which do not change. From the procurement side the cost of ordering in itself is not easily determined. The principle behind almost all mathematical inventory models involves relevant or marginal costs which are balanced against carrying costs. Most accounting systems do not readily supply the necessary information for such calculations and it is foolish to base extensive models and fancy systems on shaky cost foundations. The theoretical trade-off

Figure 5–4
Material carrying and order costs

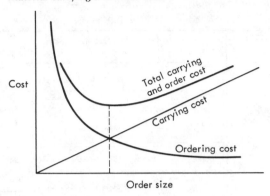

between ordering cost and carrying cost is readily seen from Figure 5–4. As the order quantity increases ordering cost decreases (because fewer orders are placed), and carrying cost increases (because the average inventory increases). Not all costs will behave as shown in Figure 5–4. It is proper to determine the costs relevant to the particular situation studied. Not all total cost curves are smooth parabolas with a nice flat bottom and little sensitivity to the lot size over a wide range of values.

Buffer inventories

The term buffer inventory or safety stock is undoubtedly familiar to many of us, each with our own concept of what it means. However, let us reserve this definition to represent inventories that exist at a point in a company as a result of uncertainties of the demand or supply of units at that point. Raw material buffer stocks give some protection against the uncertainties of supplier performance due to such factors as lead time, variation, shut-downs, strikes, late deliveries, and poor quality units that cannot be accepted. The determination of the level of buffer inventory carried may be of significant financial consequence to the organization. The average inventory carried is close to the sum of all of the buffer inventory but only half of the EOQ. If the level of buffer stock is at all large in relation to the EOQ very special attention may have to be paid to it. Since the normal reason for carrying buffer stock is to protect against uncertainties of demand or supply, management efforts to reduce these uncertainties may have substantial pay-off. For example, switching from one supplier to another with a more predictable lead time may make a lot of sense. The buffer inventory level should be determined by balancing carrying cost versus stock-out cost. Since our ability to measure stock-out costs is not particularly advanced, possibly because few managers are willing and able to think negatively and in terms of uncertainty, the mathematical models currently available generally outstrip by a long distance our ability to use them effectively.

Figure 5–5
Decision to inventory in anticipation of possible price increase

DECISION ALTERNATIVES   DECISION VARIABLES   OUTCOMES

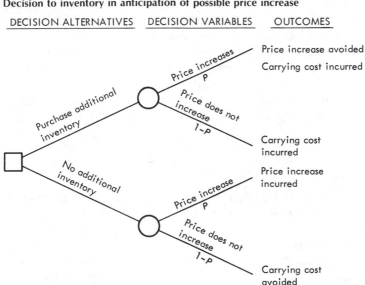

Buying in expectation of major market shortages falls into a different class from the normal type of buffer inventory discussed so far, which is oriented to a shorter time span and normal variation in lead time and availability. The dollar commitments may be so large as to require top management strategic moves. Chapter 10 on forward buying discusses this topic more fully.

A different class of buffer stock deals with price uncertainty. In the expectation, but not certainty, that prices may rise, a decision may be made to purchase in advance. In this case, the trade-off would be between carrying costs and price increases. The decision tree illustrating this situation is shown in Figure 5–5.

Finished goods buffer inventories provide protection against the possibility of lost sales due to unexpected upturns in customer demands or production failures. The location and quantities of buffer stocks are related to the risks and costs of being out of stock. These stocks provide a margin of safety and are often called safety stocks.

Anticipation inventories

Anticipation stocks are accumulated for a well-defined future need. The difference between buffer and anticipation inventory is that the latter is committed in the face of reasonable certainty and, therefore, has far less risk attached to it. Seasonal inventories are an excellent example; the summer work-in-process stocking of tomato paste for further processing during the winter is a typical case. Anticipation stocks of raw materials may include availability reasons like strikes, or definite shortages, or price when definite increases are announced. The managerial decision is considerably simplified, however, compared to the buffer situation, because the model becomes a simple deterministic one without probabilities attached. Unfortunately, in periods of shortages and rapidly rising prices, although the need to increase inventory in the form of buffer and anticipation stocks is clear, the ability of the organization to commit the necessary funds may be severely taxed. Public organizations working under control of regular budgets may find it difficult to obtain authorizations and funds, and many private organizations short of working capital may be frustrated in their attempts to find the money.

Spare parts inventory

A form of buffer and anticipation inventory related to capital equipment is that of spare parts. A simple example will illustrate the basic decision format.

In a certain factory one of the major pieces of equipment has two main shafts. If either shaft wears out, the machine has to be shut down and with it the whole plant. If new shafts are in stock, the machine can be repaired in four hours. Without sufficient stock it will take 48 hours to get emergency replacements and repairs. Each shaft costs $2,000. The additional cost of factory shutdown in excess of four hours (for 44 hours) is $2,500, and additional emergency costs for transportation, etc., are $500 per shaft. The factory normally operates for eight months a year. During the remaining four months maintenance and repairs and equipment replacements are performed. The decision facing the manager is,

Figure 5–6
Typical maintenance part inventory decision

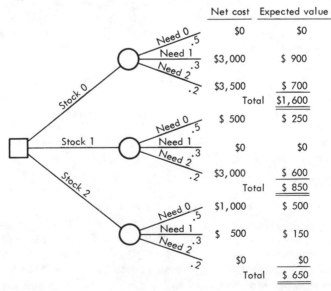

therefore, how many shafts should be stocked for the eight-month season? Because capital is tight, the manager figures inventory carrying cost at $500 per shaft per season and thinks the probability is .50 none will be needed; .30 one will be required; and .20 two will be needed. For simplicity's sake, we will assume at the most only one breakdown is likely to occur which may require one or two shafts. See Figure 5–6 for the decision tree covering this example. As it shows, putting expected values right at the tips and summing them for each alternative shows that stocking none is the worst choice and that the manager would be slightly better off with two shafts than one shaft in stock.

Decoupling inventory ✗

The existence of inventories at major linkage points makes it possible to carry on activities on either side of the point relatively independently of each other. These inventories tend to reduce the dependence of one activity on the other. The amounts and locations of raw material, work-in-process, and finished goods decoupling inventories depend upon the relative advantages of increased flexibility in operations over the costs of maintaining these inventories. The ability to plan the plant's operations independent of suppliers short run behavior is highly valued by most managers. Many contracts specify that the supplier shall maintain an inventory for just this reason. The size of such inventory and its appropriateness will vary from situation to situation. It is possible that a transit, cycle, buffer, or anticipation inventory may perform the double function of decoupling at the same time. It may be just as much in the supplier's interest as the purchaser's that decoupling inventory exists. It gives flexibility and independence to both parties and is an excellent area for negotiation. Work-in-process decoupling inventory may become substantial in situations where a large number of operations are planned for the same product. One reason for the line as opposed to the process layout in plants is to cut down on this type of inventory. The trade-off lies between carrying cost and operations costs and/or flexibility. One of the costs of flexibility is decoupling inventory. Since degree of flexibility is clearly a managerial decision and frequently a strategic one, decoupling inventories tend to play a larger role than may at first glance be apparent.

By examining the functions of inventories, it is now clear that inventories are the result of many interrelated decisions and policies within an organization. A management directive to reduce total inventories by 20 percent could, because of purchasing and marketing policies and a prior commitment on cycle and seasonal inventories, cause the virtual elimination of all decoupling and buffer inventories with potentially disastrous results.

Implications for the control of inventories

Because we are now dealing with up to 15 different kinds of inventories, the problem of control becomes a little more complicated. First, we should recognize that the behavior of inventories is the direct result of diverse policies and decisions within a company. Marketing, production, finance, and purchasing decisions directly influence the level of inventories throughout the organization.

For example, an inventory control manager within a staff production planning and control group may have little control over finished goods transit (marketing) and raw material cycle (purchasing) inventories. Thus, many firms have created material control executives to improve the coordination of marketing, purchasing, and production activities with respect to inventories.

Second, not all inventories are equally controllable for other reasons. Long-term marketing commitments in terms of distribution networks may render transit finished goods inventory levels quite inflexible, whereas the relatively shorter term production scheduling plans may provide a great deal of flexibility in the control of decoupling work-in-process inventories. Consider another case. Short-term production scheduling may provide a great deal of flexibility in work-in-process cycle inventories; relatively longer term supplier development and purchasing commitments may result in rigid raw material cycle and transit inventories. How often has the total value of inventories risen due to the unavoidable accumulation of raw materials as production schedules and product demand drop rapidly? To be effective, inventory control managers must recognize the controllability of each kind of inventory in the short and long run.

Third, why haven't EOQs worked? Very simply, EOQs are cycle inventories and may be only a small part of the total inventory picture. Managers who produce only in EOQs are ignoring the potential benefits of transit, anticipation, and decoupling inventories. Often the production in noneconomic order quantities may be more profitable.

Finally, let's consider the simple "rules of thumb"—for example, turn-over defined as the ratio of total sales to average inventory. Acceptable turnover values can be obtained from past performances or industry norms. Assume a company has $1 million annual sales and an average inventory level of $250,000 creating a turnover of four. If this is acceptable now, then as sales double inventories should rise to $500,000. However, let's take a closer look at the components of the inventory.

Cycle EOQ inventories vary as the square root of demand, so that as demand doubles EOQ rises by the square root of two which is less than doubling. In addition raw materials (purchasing in EOQ) need not be the same. The costs of carrying raw materials versus finished goods may be quite different. Thus, cycle inventories, if doubled, may not be optimal.

Further, transit inventories are more dependent upon the supply and distribution network than simply annual sales. A change in the distribution system to accommodate the doubled sales could result in more than a double finished goods transit inventory.

Anticipation finished goods stocks depend more upon the pattern of demand, rather than its total value. Decoupling stock requirements may remain unchanged and so on through the list.

The point that should be stressed here is this. Although a turnover of four was desirable for a sales level of $1 million the optimal turnover could legitimately drop to two for an annual sales of $2 million. All 15 kinds of inventories do not vary directly with sales volume, and therefore the rules of thumb can often be misleading.

During the 13th Annual International Conference of the American Production and Inventory Control Society, Professor Richard Shell[4] put it this way.

> For a long time top executives of certain companies have used the inventory ratio as a "standard measurement" to determine if inventory levels are "proper." The inventory ratio is obtained by simply dividing the total dollar value of inventory by the total dollar asset value of the company. Within a company, comparisons can be made between the inventory ratio for one year and the inventory ratio for another year. It is absurd to consider this relative comparison a true standard of measurement. Yet today many inventory control managers are in-part evaluated on this ratio. Countless other ratios have been devised in an attempt to quickly "evaluate" inventory levels within a particular company. These include such questionable values as the total number of parts produced divided by the total number of parts in inventory and the total physical area occupied by inventory divided by the total manufacturing area. Even the time tested number of inventory "turns" each year is not a fair measure of correct inventory level. This discussion might lead to the conclusion that we should not use ratios or rules of thumb to evaluate inventory levels. Generally, this is true. However, it is suggested that the inventory ratio can be useful in evaluating total inventory levels within a specific company if the ratio is properly developed. Proper development consists of determining individual product inventory levels, raw material through finished goods, and then summing their dollar value equivalent and dividing by total dollar assets. Stated another way, the inventory ratio is obtained after all individual requirements have been properly assessed as compared to the traditional method of obtaining the inventory ratio before assessing individual item requirements.

Most executives have rules and have learned from experience that desirable outcomes result as these rules ae followed. The danger is, of course, that executives never know if the rules they have are the best available. Any set of rules used for inventory control should be reevaluated regularly.

The control of inventories is complex because of the many functions and forms. Inventory levels are the result of many short- and long-term decisions and policies of all functional areas (i.e., production, marketing, purchasing) within the organization. The control of inventories represents a shared responsibility and must be viewed as such.

The price-discount problem ✕

A normal situation in purchasing occurs when a price discount is offered if purchases are made in larger quantities. Acceptance of a larger quantity provides a form of anticipation inventory. The problem may be solved in several ways. Marginally, the question is: should we increase the size of our inventory so that

---

[4]Richard L. Shell, "Principles of Inventory Control," *Proceedings, International Technical Conference, American Production and Inventory Control Society,* 1970.

we obtain the benefits of the lower price? Put this way, it can be analyzed as a return on investment decision. The simple EOQ model is not of much assistance here since it cannot account for the purchase price differential directly. It is possible to use the EOQ model to eliminate some alternatives, however, and to check the final solution. Total cost calculations are required to find the optimal point.

The following problem is illustrative of the calculation.

Sample price-discount problem

R = 900 units (annual demand)
S = $50 (order cost)
K = .25 (carrying cost) or 25 percent
C = $45 for 0–199 units per order
      $43 for 200–399 units per order
      $41.50 for 400–799 units per order
      $40.00 for 800 and over units per order

Sample calculations for the price-discount problem

	100	200	400	800
Total annual price paid	$40,500	$38,700	$37,350	$36,000
Carrying cost	562	1,075	2,075	4,000
Order cost	450	225	112	56
Total cost	41,512	40,000	39,537	40,056
Average inventory	2,250	4,300	8,300	16,000
EOQ	Units 89	92*	93*	94*

*Not feasible.

A simple marginal analysis shows that in moving from 100 per order to 200 the additional average investment is $4,300 − $2,250 = $2,050. The saving in price is $40,500 − $38,700 = $1,800, and the order cost saving is $450 − $225 = $225. For an additional investment of $2,050 the savings are $2,025 which is almost a 100 percent return and is well in excess of the 25 percent carrying cost. In going from 400 to 800 the additional investment is $7,700 for a total price and order savings of $1,406.25. This falls below the 25 percent carrying cost and would not be a desirable result. The total cost figures show that the optimal purchase quantity is at the 400 level. The largest single saving occurs at the first price break at the 200 level.

The EOQs with an asterisk are not feasible because the price range and the volume do not match. For example, the price for the second EOQ of 92 is $45. Yet for the 200–400 range the actual price is $43.00. The EOQ may be used, however, in the following way. In going from right to left on the table (from the lowest unit price to the highest price) proceed until the first valid EOQ is obtained. This is 89 for the 0 to 199 price range. Then the order quantity at each price discount about this EOQ is checked to see whether total costs at the higher order quantity are lower or higher than at the EOQ. Doing this for the example shown gives us a total cost at the valid EOQ level of 89 of:

Total annual price paid $40,500
Carrying cost   500
Order cost   500

Total cost $41,500

Since this total cost at the feasible EOQ of 89 units is above the total cost at the 200 order quantity level and the 400 and 800 order levels as well, the proper order quantity is 400, which gives the lowest total cost of all options.

The discussion so far has assumed that the quantity discount offered is based on orders of the full amount, forcing the purchaser to carry substantial inventories. It is preferable, of course, from the purchaser's standpoint to take delivery in smaller quantities but to still get the lower discount price. This could well be negotiated through annual contracts, cumulative discounts or blanket orders. This type of analysis can also identify what extra price differential the purchaser might be willing to pay to avoid carrying substantial stocks.

Inventory models

Most procurement inventory models fall into four basic classes.

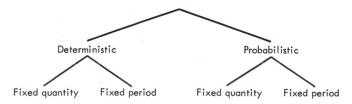

Deterministic models are different from probabilistic models in that they assume conditions of certainty regarding demand, price, and costs. For example, demand is 900 units, not 900 ± 200; prices and costs are similarly fixed at specified dollar amounts which do not change over time. These conditions seldom prevail in reality; nevertheless, deterministic models are useful in conceptualizing the problem and in a large number of low-cost situations where the additional accuracy of probabilistic models is not worth the extra effort. Fixed quantity models use a standard order quantity but vary the time between orders. The reorder point depends on usage. Fixed period models use a standard time between orders but vary the order quantity. All four models attempt to minimize cost (or maximize contribution) through trading off carrying costs, order costs, and stock-out costs.

X **Deterministic-fixed quantity models.** One of the simplest deterministic fixed quantity models is shown in Figure 5–7.

Figure 5–7
Simple fixed quantity model

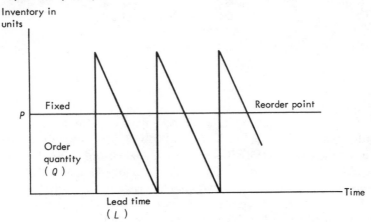

In this example demand (R), lead time (L), price (C), order or set-up (S), and carrying cost (K) are all constant. When the inventory drops to the reorder point (P) a fixed order quantity Q is ordered which arrives after a lead time (L). There are no stock-outs and no back orders.

The objective is to minimize total cost (C_t) which is:

$$C_t = RC + \frac{R}{Q}S + \frac{Q}{2}KC$$

This may be done using calculus by taking the derivative of total cost with respect to Q and equating this to zero.

$$\frac{dC_t}{dQ} = 0 + \frac{(-RS)}{Q^2} + \frac{KC}{2}$$

This is equal to zero when:

$$Q = \sqrt{\frac{2RS}{KC}} \text{ or EOQ} = \sqrt{\frac{2RS}{KC}}$$

This is the EOQ (Economic Order Quantity) or Qopt (Optimal Order Quantity). (See also the different derivation of EOQ shown under the heading "Why Do Inventories Exist?" in this chapter.) The cost curve for this model are shown in Figure 5–8.

An example of the calculations that may be performed using this model follows:

R = Annual demand = 900 units
C = Delivered purchase cost = \$45 unit
K = Carrying cost = 25 percent
S = Order cost = \$50 order

**Figure 5–8
Inventory costs**

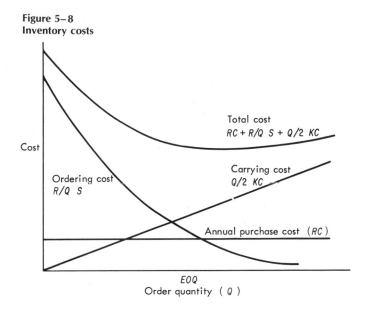

$$EOQ = \sqrt{\frac{2RS}{KC}} = \frac{2 \times 900 \times 50}{.25 \times 45}$$
$$= \sqrt{8,000} = 89$$

Algebraically, $P = L \times$ the daily demand. The daily demand is 4 units for 225 working days per year. The lead time (L) is 10 working days. The reorder point (P) is, therefore, $10 \times 4 = 40$ units. The average inventory carried in EOQ form is $89/2 = 44\frac{1}{2}$ units at an average investment of $44.5 \times \$45 = \$2002$ and annual carrying cost of $.25 \times \$2002 = \$500$. This needs to be added to the safety stock which is not specified in this example.

Further deterministic models exist to account for usage during replenishment and stock-outs. A price discount deterministic model is discussed elsewhere in this chapter.

Fixed period models. There are many situations where fixed period models are more desirable from an operations management point of view than fixed order quantity models. The scheduling of tasks for employees is facilitated when, for example, they know they can be assigned to check on certain classes of inventory items with a predetermined time span of a day, a week, two weeks, a month, and so on.

Fixed period systems tend to require a higher safety stock level than fixed order quantity systems, because they receive less monitoring. In a fixed order quantity system a new order is theoretically placed the moment the reorder level is reached. In fixed period systems the inventory level is recorded only at review time. The inventory on hand must, therefore, cover against stock-outs during the review period and also the lead time which follows the placing of an order.

In fixed period models the problem becomes one of determining what the optimal time period (Topt) should be. Theoretically, both T and Q are variables. The minimum cost point can be determined as follows. There are R/Q cycles per year and, therefore, T (the fraction of the year) $= Q/R$ and $Q = TR$. This value for Q may be substituted in the conventional total cost formula of:

$$C_t = RC + \frac{R}{Q}S + \frac{Q}{2}KC$$

giving:

$$C_t = RC + \frac{RS}{TR} + \frac{TR}{2}KC$$

When this is differentiated with respect to T and solved for Topt we obtain Topt $= \sqrt{2S/RKC}$. If we check this against our earlier example of $R = 900, C = \$45\,K = \$25\%$ and $S = \$50$, we obtain:

$$\text{Topt} = \sqrt{\frac{2 \times 50}{900 \times .25 \times .45}}$$
$$= \sqrt{\frac{100}{10,125}} = \sqrt{.01} = .10$$

for 225 working days. This is once every 22½ days and EOQ $= R$ Topt $= 900 \times .10 = 90$. The proper decision, then, would be to order 90 units every 22½ days. This is the same decision as reached in the earlier example.

✗ **Probabilistic models.** Probabilistic models take into account variations in the model variables. This increases their complexity but also their accuracy. To illustrate the principle involved, the fixed order quantity model with variation in demand (usage) will be discussed in some detail. A buffer stock needs to be maintained to give protection against stock-outs. This raises the question on the criterion to be used for safety-stock level and stock-out policy. Shall it be minimization of cost or optimization of service level?

Minimization of cost for buffer inventory would seek the point at which total cost of carrying the inventory and stock-out costs would be lowest. This, in turn, would require some reasonable knowledge of stock-out costs, something which, as discussed earlier in this chapter under buffer inventory, still leaves much to be desired. The principle is clear, however, and parallels the ordering cost versus carrying cost situation discussed under the fixed order quantity model. As buffer inventory decreases stock-out costs soar; as buffer inventory increases holding costs go up and stock-out costs drop.

Service level. The service level is another method of describing the performance management expects from a buffer inventory. How many stock-outs are acceptable? A prominent manufacturer of sewing machines, for example, set a policy that 94 percent of all orders coming in for spare parts for commercial machines should be filled from stock on hand. A 92 to 96 percent service policy is relatively common in most industries. Experiments have shown that increasing the service level above 95 percent tremendously increases holding costs. A

100 percent service level is not only very difficult to achieve but also extremely expensive. A further refinement in definition of service level should be made. It can be defined as the ratio of users (customers) who are fully satisfied to the ratio of total users asking for the item. Suppose there are 400 using department requests for a certain item during a year, and 372 were immediately satisfied. This would amount to a 93 percent service level.

A second way of defining service level would be the ratio of number of units supplied versus the number of units demanded. For example, if in the 400 requests the 372 which were met were all for one unit each, while the 28 which were not met were all for five units each, the service level would be:

$$\frac{372 \times 1}{28 \times 5 + 372 \times 1} = \frac{372}{512} = 73 \text{ percent}$$

As long as we are discussing inventory levels internal to the organization and excluding finished goods, the customers are internal departments, and service level can be used as one measure of materials management's effectiveness. It is useful to stress that service level and investment required are not independent of each other, and a high expectation of the first without the financial back up for the second can only lead to frustration. Procurement is, of course, very interested in service levels as they pertain to supplier performance.

The fixed order quantity model with variation in demand and buffer inventory. In this model uncertainty exists only with regard to demand. Costs, lead time, and order quantity are all constant. The buffer inventory is necessary to protect against stock-out during the lead time between the time an order is placed and received. Figure 5–9 illustrates the situation.

Let: P = reorder point
B = buffer inventory
L = lead time
u = random variable, usage during lead time
$\bar{u}$ = average usage during lead time
σ_u = standard deviation of usage during lead time
$\bar{r}$ = average daily demand
σ_r = standard deviation of daily demand
α_r = number of standard deviations needed for a specified confidence level

The service level will be defined as percentage of satisfied customers. As can be seen from the diagram, the variation in demand can lead to four different positions of buffer inventory at the time of replenishment. They are from left to right in Figure 5–9.

1. There is buffer inventory remaining, but some has been used.
2. There is no buffer inventory remaining and no stock-outs.
3. There is no buffer inventory remaining and a stock-out.
4. All buffer inventory remains.

Figure 5–9
Fixed order quantity model with buffer inventory
and variation in demand

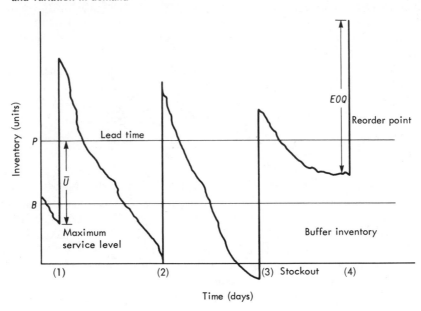

The reorder point P is equal to the average usage during lead time $\bar{u}$ plus the buffer inventory B. $P = \bar{u} + B$. The average usage during the lead time L is $\bar{u} = \bar{r}L$. Buffer inventory $B = \alpha\sigma_u$. Assume the demand is normally distributed and a 94 percent service level is desired. This corresponds to 1.555 standard deviations resulting in a reorder point $P = \bar{r}L + 1.555\,\sigma_u$. The standard deviation of usage during the lead time depends on the variance of the individual days. If we assume each day's demand is independent, the standard deviation of the sum of the days demand is equal to the square root of the sum of the variances.

Thus:

$$\sigma_u = \sqrt{\sum_{i=1}^{n}\sigma r_i^2}$$

The complexity of probabilistic models increases as more variables are allowed to change under conditions of uncertainty. If the variations are all continuous distributions, joint probability distributions may be used to solve the problem. For discrete variations tables may be built showing the range of outcomes. The interaction between variables may require a number of iterations until convergence is achieved. The EOQ $= \sqrt{2RS/KC}$ where R is the average annual demand.

Let us use the same example as for the fixed quantity uniform demand situation. The additional information is that daily usage is normally distributed with a mean of 4 and a standard deviation of 1.5 units. The lead time is 10 working days and there are assumed to be 225 working days evenly spaced during the year. Stock-out costs are assumed to be zero and back orders are filled as soon as the new order arrives.

Thus: $\bar{R} = 900$ $\bar{r} = 4$
    $C = \$45$ $\sigma_{\bar{r}} = 1.5$
    $K = .25$
    $S = \$50$
    $L = 10$ days

$$\text{The EOQ} = \sqrt{\frac{2\bar{R}S}{KC}} = \sqrt{\frac{2 \times 900 \times 50}{.25 \times 45}} = 89$$

$$\sigma u = \sqrt{\sum_{i=1}^{10} \sigma r_i^2} = \sqrt{10(1.5)^2} = \sqrt{22.5 = 4.75}$$

$$P = \bar{r}L + 1.555\sigma_u$$
$$= 4 \times 10 + 1.555 \times 4.75 = 47.4$$
$$B = 1.555\sigma_u = 1.555 \times 4.75 = 7.4$$

Therefore, the buffer inventory should be 7 or 8 units, and an order for 89 units should be placed whenever the total inventory drops to 48 units.

Use of integrated data processing systems

The computer and its associated hardware and software has aided greatly in good inventory management. All of the concepts mentioned previously in this chapter can be applied in developing programs for computer-based inventory recording and control systems. Economic order quantity formulas can be programmed into the computer so that when reorder points are reached purchase orders will be prepared automatically. Because of fantastic speeds of operation of the computer even the most complex inventories including tens of thousands of items can be maintained on a basis which permits a daily or weekly report showing items on hand, on order, withdrawals, additions, and any other information needed for control purposes. On-line terminals and visual displays may be effectively used in situations where continuous monitoring is desirable.

Most of the computer manufacturers make available software packages which provide sound inventory control programs.

Stores

Stores are often placed under direct purchasing responsibility. This is normal for hospitals, educational and public institutions, and 15 percent–45 percent of manufacturing firms place stores under purchasing.

Emphasis needs to be placed on the importance of good storeskeeping as distinct from inventory control. After all, the only material that can be used is that which is "on hand" in stores—not what the inventory control records say is available. It is always to be hoped that the stores and the inventory records will agree, as theoretically they always should, and it is for ensuring they do agree that physical stock inventory must be taken periodically. If the two records do not agree, then the inventory record must be adjusted. True as this is, decisions as to when and how much to order are based on the inventory record. And, regardless of how carefully, accurately, and adequately these records may be kept, their value is vitiated if the storeskeeping is badly handled. If stock records are inadequate or poorly kept; if material is withdrawn from stores without the proper notations being made; if items, though in stores, cannot be located or, if located, cannot be obtained; if stock clerks are dishonest, incapable, or just simply careless—if these conditions prevail, quite regardless of whose fault it may be—then the storeskeeping function is not carrying its share of the load.

Certain conditions are essential to good storeskeeping. These indicate the need for adequate and qualified personnel for centralizing responsibility for all stores in a chief storeskeeper and for adequate physical facilities.

The problem of the extent to which all stores should be kept in a central storesroom is often perplexing, particularly with reference to the matter of centralizing or decentralizing stores. The tendency toward decentralizing stores is quite widespread. Every effort is made, consistent with economical purchasing, materials handling, and storage, to keep materials as close to the machines or users as possible. This may be done by a series of shop storesrooms adjacent to the centers; sometimes no storesrooms may be maintained, but here also the material is kept near the point where it is to be used. Needless to say, control must be exercised even under these circumstances to show definitely what is on hand. In many cases, shop storesrooms are used only for storing material released on requisition for a definite factory order and not part of unassigned raw material. Obviously, there are limits beyond which decentralization must not be carried, however advisable it may be under other circumstances. Some materials may require special warehousing facilities because of the difficulties inherent in their handling, because of their perishable character, or because of some other characteristic that may necessitate special storage facilities. Regardless, however, of where stores are kept or the conditions under which they are kept, proper classification of stores is a prerequisite to good storekeeping. Standard nomenclature is also essential. With carefully classified stores, designated by standard items or symbols, a system of records can be established which will indicate at all times what material is on hand, what is expected, and where it is. Only in this manner can close cooperation between stores and production, on the one hand, and stores and purchasing, on the other, be maintained.

Stores should be carefully classified into major groups. Although the actual classification of stores used must of necessity vary tremendously from one industry to another and from one company to another in the same industry, such a classification might be made on the following basis: (1) raw materials, (2) material parts, (3) supplies, (4) in-process material, (5) tools, (6) miscellaneous stores, and (7) finished goods. Each of these groups would be divided into subgroups according to the nature of the stock, and, finally the subgroups might be broken down into types and sizes. Each of the groups might be assigned a series of numbers, such as 100–199, 200–299, and the subclasses be numbered 100–109, 110–119, and so forth. In this way, each item of stock would be identified by a number. Instead of assigning numbers, many persons prefer to use the letters of the alphabet. Under such a system, all stores are represented by capital letter "S." "SM" may stand for maintenance stores, "SP" for production material stores, and so forth. In the symbol, "SMA," "SM" would stand for maintenance stores and "A" for the supplies. Usually, figures are combined with the letters to designate sizes.

Practically, the method of classification used in stores should correspond as closely as possible with that followed by those in charge of inventory. The actual arrangement of the stock in the storesroom, however, need not and usually does not follow this same arrangement. The nature of the item, its accessibility, and the frequency with which it is called for will obviously affect the decision on where the stock itself is placed.

Stores may be priced in any one of several ways, the choice of method being a matter for top management to decide. (1) One method is to use the average unit price paid for the material. Thus if, of the stock on hand, 100 units were bought for $50 and subsequently 500 units were purchased for $225, the entire lot would be valued at $45.83 per 100 units. (2) A second method is to value the stock in accordance with a standard cost figure set by the cost accounting department. (3) Some companies use the well-known first-in, first-out method commonly referred to as "Fifo." (4) Others use "cost or market," whichever is lower. (5) A method which has grown in popularity in recent years is "Lifo," or last-in, first-out.

A discussion of the relative merits of these various methods would carry us too far afield of our present purpose. Furthermore, the particular manner in which stores are valued has but little bearing on the actual operation of the stores-room.

Materials requirements planning (MRP)

A relatively recent phenomenon has been the emergence of Materials Requirements Planning (MRP) or Requirements Planning as a way of planning for the production of dependent demand items. Since MRP requires substantial computer capacity, its original applications have been in those organizations able to afford it, normally those of medium or large size. MRP advocates claim substantial benefits to their system including: increased sales, reduced sales price, reduced inventory, better customer service, better response to market demands, ability to change the master schedule, reduced setup and tear-down costs, and reduced idle time.[5]

Aside from these potential benefits, MRP also impacts substantially on many

[5]Statements attributed to Oliver Wight of Oliver Wight Associates, Inc., and Joseph Orlicky of IBM.

areas of management, including the procurement function. For this reason, a close look will be taken at the system and its implications for purchasing.

Dependent demand items. Dependent demand items, the ones for which MRP is supposed to be tailor made, are those which form part of a higher level demand item. For example, wheels, the dependent demand items are part of the higher level independent demand item: bicycles. The demand for bicycles may be forecast using any of the forecasting techniques already described in this chapter. The demand for the parts of the bicycle really depend on the production scheduling decisions taken to plan the assembly of the finished bikes. Only if assembly production is scheduled to coincide perfectly with the demand for bikes would the demand for parts match the demand for the finished product. Frequently, however, decisions are made to produce certain finished products at intervals. These "production runs" will then often result in finished goods inventory which is supposed to supply market demand until the next production run is scheduled. Thus, the demand for parts used in production comes at intervals and is called "lumpy". Lumpy demand implies that extra parts will not be used at all for some time—creating costly and needless inventory (or that a shortage of parts will result in stock-outs, shortening the planned production run and/or creating extra costs for such things as overtime, rush orders, expediting, lost sales opportunities or capital tie-ups). Using statistical techniques for dependent demand items may, therefore, not be optimal. For example, we may plan to assemble ten-speed bicycles of a certain type only three times a year, 10,000 at a time over three 20 working day periods in February, June and October. We would show total yearly demand to be 30,000 bikes, requiring 60,000 wheels or 5,000 per month on the average. But there are nine months we don't want any, and three months for each of which we need 20,000 wheels. The philosophy behind MRP, then, is to call for the supply of wheels only for those three months in which they are actually required. That sounds simple enough and makes a lot of intuitive sense. What makes the problem messy is the magnitude of the tasks. Bikes have a lot more parts than just wheels. The same wheels may be used in different model bikes. Some wheels may have to be available as spare parts (in which case they might have to be treated as independent demand items). It may be more economical to produce wheels at a rate and in quantities different from the lumpy demand forecast. There may be price considerations or transportation or market conditions which may make different quantities more reasonable or desirable. In large, multiproduct companies the total number of dependent demand items may run into the tens of thousands. To try to keep track of each individual part which may well be included in a variety of sub-assemblies as well as a number of final assemblies is an impossible task without a computer. The normal place to start with the MRP computer program is with the master production schedule.

The master production schedule. The planning for MRP must begin with a production plan (or a use plan for non-manufacturing organizations) which is developed to make sure that the market demand for the finished products will be reasonably met. Thus, a simplified master production schedule for the assembly line in a bicycle factory could look like this:

Model	February	March	April	May	June	July
Children's	5,000	—	7,000	—	—	4,000
Regular	3,000	—	5,000	—	—	3,000
3–speed	5,000	—	—	10,000	—	—
5–speed	—	2,000	—	1,000	—	2,000
10–speed	—	10,000	—	—	10,000	—

This master production schedule will have to be checked to assure that sufficient capacity is available to meet it, allowing for setup changes and machine and labor availability. Once a feasible master production schedule has been developed, it is possible to start the next step of material explosion.

Materials explosion. In the bill of materials file the components of every bike are identified. These can now be exploded and aggregated to show the total requirements for every part required for each planning period. Thus, a weekly requirements plan could be developed showing exactly which parts would be required and how many. On a monthly basis, we can see from the master schedule that we need for February 10,000 wheels for children's bikes, 6,000 for regulars, and 10,000 for 3–speeds. If all of these wheels are different, this would result in three different requirements for February. If the speed bikes all used the same wheels, we would require 24,000 wheels for March. These requirements can now be fed into the inventory records file and the MRP program to check for availability and lead time.

The inventory position. The inventory records file keeps track of all items in inventory and on order. The MRP program works backwards from the master production schedule, using known lead times to schedule into production the dependent demand items for which the on hand inventory and on order quantities are insufficient to meet the scheduled requirements. Let us assume that no children's bike's wheels are on hand and on order beyond the 10,000 scheduled for February. Thus, we need 14,000 for April. Given a lead time of one month, these must then be ordered into production from suppliers in March, one month ahead of the final assembly schedule.

MRP reports. The output from the MRP program can be divided into two main classes. The first includes the basic reports necessary to engage in production and purchasing such as:

1. Planned orders to be released at a future time.
2. Order release notices to execute the planned orders.
3. Changes in due dates of open orders due to rescheduling.
4. Cancellations or suspensions of open orders due to cancellation or suspension of orders on the master production schedule.
5. Inventory status data.

It is also possible to get additional reports which might include:

1. Planning reports to be used, for example, in forecasting inventory and specifying requirements over some future time horizon.
2. Performance reports for purposes of pointing out inactive items, and de-

termining the agreement between actual and programmed item lead times and between actual and programmed quantity usages and costs.

3.   Exceptions reports, which point out serious discrepancies such as errors, out-of-range situations, late or overdue orders, excessive scrap, or nonexistent parts.[6]

Some general MRP implications. Since the area of production scheduling and inventory control has always been a complex and troublesome one, it is only logical that a concept like MRP should have a lot of appeal. It should be recognized, however, that the system is expensive and has certain prerequisites which a number of organizations may fail to meet. For example, the bill of materials file needs to be right up-to-date and of high quality as does the inventory records file. Information must be correct about lead times, plant, department and machine capacity, and setups. These are all stiff prerequisites and may not only require a considerable amount of planning, but also substantial changes in the ways some functions are performed. Some of these, as they apply to purchasing and stores are detailed further below. A great degree of organizational discipline is required to make MRP work. Marketing must be willing to live with its contraints and resist the temptation to "please a good customer and change the master production schedule at the last minute." Too much meddling with the immediate schedule means that the carefully laid out plan will not work and that excess inventories and shortages will be created that may become greater problems than the ones we are trying to correct.

Purchasing and stores implications. MRP has extensive impact on purchasing and stores operations and management compared to what might normally be expected under more traditional scheduling and inventory control means. The necessity for tight control in stores in all likelihood means centralization of the stores function and controlled access stores with wire fences. The total amount of work in process inventory should be substantially less and the total dollar tieup in inventory also less. Records about lead times, specifications, and quantities must be impeccable.

In purchasing, the trend is to contract buying from reliable sources with whom excellent relations exist. What may be purchased is, in many cases, a commitment for future capacity rather than for specific products. It is up to the buyer to specify the use of that capacity at a later time. Supplier education may have to be extensive, so that sellers realize how important quantity commitments and delivery promises really are to the purchaser. Expediting under MRP is serious, because items which need to be expedited are clearly identified, and it is unlikely that safety stock back-up exists.

The old purchasing trick of buying larger quantities at one time to secure lower unit price, but resulting in higher inventory, is less attractive with MRP. Pressure is on purchasing to secure progressive or annual volume discounts instead, allowing for specific releases in varying quantities during the year. More frequent ordering is a natural result of MRP. Thus, purchasing is forced to move

---

[6]Chase and Aquilano, *Production and Operations Management.* (Homewood, IL: Richard D. Irwin, 1977), pp. 431–32. © Richard D. Irwin, Inc., 1977.

into a longer range planning mode. Also MRP may force a reassessment of suppliers in which on time delivery assurance may obtain higher priority. Purchasing may wish to encourage suppliers to improve their own scheduling and inventory control procedures and to use MRP where appropriate.

CONCLUSION

Today's inventory systems are in the midst of great change. Early applications centered on the determination of order size and order points, sometimes using theoretical models, though more often than not using "seat of the pants" analysis. In any event, it was all done by hand, using a series of cards and files. Now, however, the field is changing to computerized record keeping and computer-aided decisions.

In taking over many of the inventory decision chores, computer procedures have progressed from simple data processing tabulations to large-scale information systems encompassing the entire firm. This evolution from simple hand methods to an integrated computerized system seems to develop along the following lines. First, data processing is introduced and is applied to record keeping, the primary output being printouts of inventory status. Then some elementary forecasting and inventory rules are incorporated into a simple computer program. Next is the inclusion of more sophisticated forecasting techniques, refinement of ordering rules, and programmed monitoring of the form and location of inventory items.

From here on the system begins to overflow into other functional areas. Inventory control becomes part of the production-inventory program, which specifies material requirements and schedules the order of work to be done. As the system's size expands further, central files are formed which give ready access to complete item description, engineering changes, costs, vendors involved, and production schedules, as well as complete stock data. Ultimately, the company might consider a system in which the production-distribution system is integrated with finance, marketing, and personnel along the lines of a modular simulation approach.

QUESTIONS FOR REVIEW AND DISCUSSION

1. What are the main files in an MRP system and why are they required?
2. Of what use is ABC analysis in purchasing? In inventory control?
3. What is the rationale behind a quantity discount?
4. Why should anyone carry inventory?
5. Why should a buyer be concerned with whether actual requirements are above or below forecasts given to suppliers?
6. What are the normal costs associated with the carrying of inventory?
7. What are the main advantages of fixed-period inventory models over fixed-quantity models?

CASE 5-1
✗SEATIDE CRAFTS INC. (A)

Donna Jackson had recently been hired as a buyer at Seatide Crafts, a reputable producer of high-quality gifts located on the Maine coast. Donna reported directly to the president, who until recently had looked after all purchases personally. She was a business school graduate and had worked in the purchasing office of an automotive parts manufacturer before moving to Seatide. In her previous job she had been well aware of economical order quantities and had done a special study which had resulted in alterations in the computer program and some substantially different buying patterns. Donna wondered about the possibility of using a microcomputer for purchasing, scheduling, and inventory control at Seatide. However, it was still too early for such a move since she had been on the job for only eight months and was still becoming better acquainted with the organization and its requirements.

During the last two weeks, Donna had conducted an informal study to get some feel for the marginal cost of a typical purchase order and she estimated it to be about $60. She also believed carrying costs to be about 2 percent per month since Seatide was still expanding rapidly and projects were available which would return at least that amount. Since the president had always bought hand to mouth, only as required, Donna found herself ordering the same items frequently and she wondered if this really was the most economical way to proceed.

A typical example were the cheese knives which were part of every cutting board sold. These polished stainless steel knives cost $3.00 each f.o.b. Seatide. Seatide produced cutting boards twice a month in order quantities ranging from 200–300 per manufacturing order. Donna suspected the current order quantity and frequency were not optimal and decided to see if she could determine what they should be.

CASE 5-2
SEATIDE CRAFTS INC. (B)

Donna Jackson, buyer at Seatide Crafts, was examining the purchase of cheese knives for the company's cutting board line. (See Seatide Crafts (A) for further details). In discussing this item with the supplier's sales representative, she found out that the supplier incurred significant setup costs for this specialty item, amounting to about $200 for every run. The sales representative also explained that they currently produced these knives once per month in average quantities of about 500 per run. Seatide was the only customer for this type of knife. Since the supplier was in a tight working capital position it was this company's policy not to carry any excess inventories. Donna tried to find out how much direct labor and material costs were per knife, but she could not get the sales representative to disclose this. Seatide's production superintendent guessed that direct labor and material cost per knife would amount to about $1.25, but he said he could be off by 25¢ either way. Knives are currently delivered twice per month to Seatide in average quantities of 250 knives per order. Donna estimated current delivery charges to be about $20 per order, but she did not know what the impact of larger or smaller order sizes would be on delivery charges.

Donna wondered if she could not use the above information to obtain a quantity discount from her supplier, recognizing that Seatide's own carrying costs were about 2 percent per month.

CASE 5–3
SEATIDE CRAFTS INC. (C)

Donna Jackson, buyer at Seatide Crafts had recently investigated the company's purchases of cheese knives. (See Seatide Crafts (A) and (B) for further background.) She had located an alternate source for knives which gave her the following quotation:

Order quantities	Price
500– 999	. . . .$3.00 ea. f.o.b. Seatide
1000–2999	. . . . 2.75 ea. f.o.b. Seatide
3000–5999	. . . . 2.50 ea. f.o.b. Seatide
6000–9999	. . . . 2.25 ea. f.o.b. Seatide

Donna was satisfied the quality of these knives was equivalent to those from the current supplier. She wondered about three specific aspects of this offer:

1. Were the discounts offered interesting enough to be seriously considered by Seatide?
2. Compared to her calculations in Seatide (B) were the prices attractive enough to switch from her current source?
3. Should she have two suppliers for knives, and if so, in what quantity should she buy from each?

CASE 5–4
CANADIAN GAMES

In early April, 1977, Paul Brock, materials manager for Canadian Games of Cambridge, Ontario, received a requisition to purchase the June production requirements for the "Trap" game. This would be the third time he had ordered Trap components in 1977 and he wondered if current company ordering policies and procedures really made sense. Paul had joined Canadian Games eight months previously and had spent a considerable amount of time familiarizing himself with the company. He believed the "Trap" requisition was typical and wondered whether improvements were possible.

Company background

Canadian Games was a family owned business incorporated in 1897. Originally toys were the only products produced but games and hobby kits were added to the line after 1920. Canadian Games was a leader in the industry, had a well-known brand name and a reputation for quality and new product innovation.

Current projected sales for 1977 were estimated at $22 million or 17 percent over 1976 sales. Approximately 75 percent of sales were manufactured and assembled in house and 25 percent were finished product resale items imported from the Far East. Raw material purchases were estimated to exceed $6.5 million for 1977.

The organization at Canadian Games consisted of a president, an executive committee, a middle management group, salaried support personnel, and approximately 150 hourly paid workers. (See Exhibit 1 for an organization chart.)

The manufacturing process for games usually involved equipment to make boxes and playing boards augmented by packing lines. Most of the printing requirements were met by an outside supplier under a long term agreement.

Since 1974, the efficiency in manufacturing had been improved through capital expenditures for modern machinery and the intensive use of industrial engineering in order to reduce the hourly paid work force.

In 1976, the company had changed to the "product manager" concept and added two managers. At the same time, a technical manager and a materials manager (Paul Brock) had also been hired. Part of Paul's mandate was to improve the efficiency of the materials department.

The company plant was at capacity and suffered from a shortage of space in spite of a new warehouse that had been recently built for finished goods inventory. The labor force was kept fairly stable throughout the year by building inventory during slack times.

Exhibit 1
Organization chart

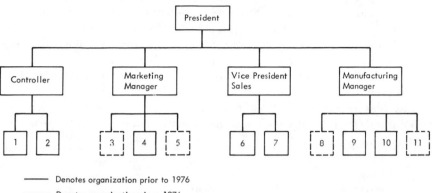

——— Denotes organization prior to 1976

– – – Denotes organization since 1976

Key:
1. Chief accountant
2. Credit manager
3.4.5. Product manager
6.7. Sales manager
8. Technical manager
9. Plant manager
10. Production control manager
11. Materials manager

New program development

Of prime importance to Canadian Games was the need to develop a series of new programs annually; each program referred to a new game, hobby kit, or toy, introduced for distribution. The organization had to react quickly to determine (1) market desires, (2) the elements of competition, (3) concept development, (4) defined program requirements, and (5) goods and services required to manufacture these items. Failure to comply with this rigid schedule could result in the loss of sales and market position, especially in view of the seasonal buying pattern of the consumer. (See Exhibit 2 for an overview of new program introductions since 1973.)

Sales forecasting and production planning

An annual sales forecast was developed by the sales and marketing departments reflecting anticipated sales for a calendar year. This forecast was initially issued in October, prior to the start of a new calendar period which would commence the following January and run to December. This sales forecast was reviewed four to six times annually, with upward or downward revisions by program reflecting current sales and anticipated trends. Some programs could be revised upward as much as 300 percent of the initial forecast, or be decreased as much as 70 percent. Many toys and games were directly tied to current TV programs and might have very short lives. Generally, sales peaked at Christmas. Regular yearly demand came from sales for birthdays and gifts as well as from special department store and chain promotions. For instance, a big discount store could decide to run a "special sale". There were penalty clauses for not keeping larger, regular customers supplied. The big retail sales month was December, and, if the goods were not produced by October 1, management figured the Christmas market would be missed.

The sales forecast was refined into a manufacturing plan by the production control department which scheduled manufacturing runs by program, balancing the needs of sales and plant loading capacity.

Exhibit 2
Program category totals by year and related data

	1973	1974	1975	1976
Number of programs carried over from prior year	860	956	905	967
New program introductions	182	156	310	391
New program introductions as a percent of carryover	21	16	34	40
Total program (new and carryover)	1,042	1,112	1,215	1,357
Average number of hourly personnel employed	242	187	165	154

The manufacturing plan was then issued to the materials department for inventory control and procurement purposes.

There were seven major considerations which guided Paul Brock's work. These were:

1. Company policy dictated that all components and materials required for production must be in house four weeks ahead of a scheduled run. This policy was developed to allow for flexibility in the scheduling and manufacturing process.

2. Company policy dictated that a safety stock of finished goods required at a given month end had to be 15 percent of the next month's sales forecast. This responsibility for setting the safety stock level rested with sales (i.e., the corporate philosophy was to be in an "in stock" position at all times on finished products).

3. Inventory carrying charges were calculated at 2 percent per month.

4. Normal lead time for printed components was four weeks after receipt of order on repeat programs; 8–12 weeks on new program introductions.

5. A computer printout was issued weekly indicating the following data *for finished or completed units only:*

a. Sales forecast this year.

b. Revised sales forecast this year.

c. Last year sales by month (actual).

d. This year sales by month (actual).

e. Manufacturing schedule by month this year.

f. Opening inventory as at January 1.

g. Free balance by month: finished goods inventory left over after fulfilling booked orders during a given month.

h. Commit quantity: the degree of confidence relative to the sales forecast indicated in units. For example, the sales forecast for a particular program might read 100,000 units; the commit quantity might read 70,000 units.

i. Program category: defined the program as a no.1, or no.2, or no.3 category. No. 1 referred to a program considered staple and sufficient materials had to be in stock at all times. No. 2 category was a program considered semi-staple; sufficient materials should be in stock at all times, but less significant than no. 1. No. 3 category referred to a sensitive product about which no automatic decisions should be made. An audit of current program categories indicated that 66 percent of the total product line of manufactured programs were classified in the no. 3 category.

6. Production runs could not be smaller than 10,000 units, as setup costs were significant.

7. Authority to purchase was limited to buying, or having on hand, that number of components and materials required to produce finished goods not exceeding the commit quantity indicated by program. From the materials department's point of view, the term used to denote this situation was the "net commit quantity". This number was derived by taking the indicated "commit quantity" (i.e.: 50,000 units) less the "opening inventory" of finished units as at January 1, (i.e.: 10,000 units). This figure equalled the "net commit quantity", or "authority to purchase". In effect, for the example cited above, authority was limited to purchase, or have on hand, that number of components or materials to produce 40,000 finished units only.

The authority to purchase, and the development of commit quantities, had been recently initiated. Usually, the majority of purchases were made to meet the requirements of each scheduled production run only. This practice was a direct response to the wide fluctuations experienced with sales forecasts to avoid excessive obsolete and surplus inventories.

Materials department

In the materials department, the inventory controller/buyers were responsible for the maintenance and control of the inventory system as well as all the raw material purchases of the company within established guidelines. (See Exhibit 3.)

Exhibit 3

MATERIALS DEPARTMENT ORGANIZATION

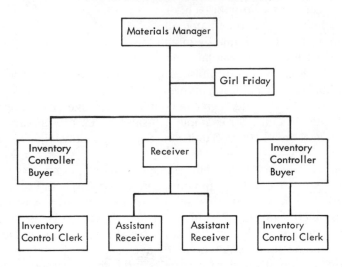

The receiver received and verified all incoming goods, and processed shipping memos on outgoing sub-assembly raw materials which were sub-contracted to outside vendors.

One secretary performed all secretarial duties for the department and assisted in all clerical functions, including the typing of purchase orders and miscellaneous correspondence, and was also responsible for procuring MRO items and fulfilling miscellaneous purchase order requests.

The inventory control clerks maintained the perpetual inventory control records by manually posting the receipts and withdrawals of materials and components on a daily basis.

Purchasing performance in the materials department was evaluated by two major criteria. First was the ability to have the necessary components and materials in house four weeks ahead of the scheduled production run. The second was based on the ability to purchase components and materials at a cost less than, or not exceeding, the standard costs developed. This evaluation was provided by a purchase variance report issued monthly by the accounting department. Purchase prices were compared to standard cost levels to show positive or negative variances.

Standard costs were developed annually, usually in late September, for use in the following calendar year commencing January 1. The basis for setting standard costs for components and materials was to take the most recent invoice price and add on the appropriate duty, exchange, freight and royalty factor. In addition, the accounting department (based on historical trends) factored in any anticipated increases or decreases.

Paul Brock realized that the materials department did not provide any input into developing standard costs. Furthermore, he had no opportunity to examine standard costs prior to issue. He also recognized that no consideration was given during the setting of standards to the size of purchase indicated on the base invoice price.

The "Trap" situation

Paul took another look at the "Trap" requisition order and decided to calculate the total cost for the August and June requirements under current company policy. He gathered the following information from the computer:

Program: "Trap"   *Sales forecast = 65,000 Units*
Commit Qty: 50,000 Units   *Category 1   Open Inv: 10,000*
Manufacturing schedule: 10,000 units February/77 (Complete)
                          10,000 units April/77 (Complete)
                          10,000 units June/77
                          10,000 units August/77
                          10,000 units October/77
Net authority to purchase: Confidence level 50,000 less opening inventory
                          of 10,000 units = 40,000 units (less individual
                          components and materials on hand or on order).

The on hand inventory of unique components as at April 1, 1977, was as follows: (a) lid wrap—10,000, (b) face label—6,000, (c) box wrap—11,000, (d) rules—8,000, (e) printed deck—7,000, (f) playing cards—20,000 sets, (g) trays c/w lid—9,000 sets, (h) triangles and stars—9,000 sets.

Then he made the following summary of the purchases that would have to be made:

a. Purchase 4,000 face labels for delivery May 1. Cost is $62.30/M + $384.00 set up cost + $35.00 to issue purchase order[1] and carrying costs of 2% = $681.56.
   (i) Purchase 10,000 face labels for delivery July 1. Cost is $62.30/M + $384.00 set up cost + $35.00 to issue purchase order and carrying costs at 2% = $1062.84.
   Total cost incurred: $1,744.40 or $124.60/M.
b. Purchase 2,000 rules for delivery May 1. Cost is 2,000 × $88.90/M + $148.00 set up and $35.00 to issue purchase order and carrying costs @ 2% = $368.02.
   (i) Purchase 10,000 rules for delivery July 1. Cost is 10,000 × $88.90/M + $148.00 set up + $35.00 to issue purchase order and carrying costs @ 2% = $1093.44.
   Total cost incurred: $1461.46 or $121.79/M.

---

[1]Purchase order cost of $35 was determined by dividing the total budget for the materials department by the total number of purchase orders.

c. Purchase 3,000 printed decks for delivery May 1. Cost is $96.50/M + $124.00 set up + $35.00 to issue purchase order and carrying charges @ 2% = $457.47.

   (i) Purchase 10,000 printed decks for delivery July 1. Cost is $96.50/M + $124.00 set up + $35.00 to issue purchase order and carrying charges @ 2% = $1,146.48.

   Total cost incurred: $1603.95 or $123.38/M

d. Purchase 1,000 sets of trays c/w lids for delivery May 1. Cost is $39.20/M + $100.00 set up + $35.00 to issue purchase order and carrying charges @ 2% = $177.68.

   (i) Purchase 10,000 sets of trays c/w lid for delivery July 1. Cost is $39.20/M + $100.00 set up + $35.00 to issue purchase order and carrying charges @ 2% = $537.54.

   Total cost incurred: $715.22 or $65.02/M.

e. Purchase 1,000 sets of triangles/stars for delivery May 1. Cost is $139.88/M + $100.00 set up cost + $35.00 to issue purchase order and cost of carrying inventory @ 2% = $280.38.

   (i) Purchase 10,000 sets of triangles and stars for delivery July 1. Cost is $139.88/M + $100.00 set up cost + $35.00 to issue purchase order and cost of carrying inventory @ 2% = $1,564.48.

   Total cost incurred: $1,844.86 or $167.71/M.

f. Purchase 9,000 box wraps for delivery July 1. Cost is $52.30/M + $74.00 set up + $35.00 to issue purchase order and carrying costs @ 2% = $591.29.

   Total cost incurred: $591.29 or $65.69/M.

g. Purchase 10,000 lid wraps for delivery July 1. Cost is $78.10/M + $434.00 set up cost + $35.00 to issue purchase order and carrying cost @ 2% = $1,275.00.

   Total cost incurred: $1,275.00 or $127.50/M.

Thus, the total costs incurred would come to $9,236.18.

Conclusion

Paul was concerned that this would be the third time this year he would be purchasing parts for "Trap" and wondered what he could do to improve the situation.

CASE 5-5
MYERS DIVISION (R)*

On August 15, 1974, the Myers Division of the Young Corporation began negotiating the annual contract with its employees' union representatives. In 1973 and 1974 Myers had refused to accept the union's demands, and the union bargaining committee had advised the workers to strike. In each instance, however, the workers had voted against the committee's recommendation and had accepted the company's contract terms. For the third consecutive year, neither the union nor company representatives seemed willing to accept the others' demands. In preparing for the negotiation of the 1974 contract, however, the union bargaining committee had received a vote of confidence from the employees previous to the negotiations which, for all practical purposes, gave the committee the authority to call a strike against Myers without another employee vote. Therefore, a strike commencing October 1 appeared to be a foregone conclusion. Myers' management notified all executives of the situation and added that in their opinion, "the strike would probably be a long, drawn-out affair . . . possibly lasting several months."

The Myers Division was one of the major producers of dictating machines, with 1973 sales approximating $19,800,000 and profits after taxes of $1,006,000. Approximately 66 percent of the company's sales volume came from the sale of dictating machines, 13 percent from government contracts, 12 percent from repair parts and supplies, and 9 percent from repair service.

To Mr. Arthur, the manager of purchases, a potential work stoppage presented several problems regarding outstanding purchase orders and future purchasing commitments. He believed that if the strike became a reality the entire inventory investment excluding finished goods would be largely under his control. The finished goods inventory would probably be depleted during a strike because all sales orders would have to be shipped from inventory since there would be no production. With the production lines shut down, there would be no problems concerning work-in-process inventory. Consequently, the raw materials inventory would not be reduced by production requirements but would be continually increased by the material flowing in from suppliers if the company continued its normal purchasing operations. He realized if a strike was called it would have to be determined for how long the company could finance an inventory accumulation and what action the purchasing department could take to limit its purchases during work stoppage. Limiting purchases presented two additional problems to Myers' manager of purchases: what effect will canceling outstanding pur-

chase orders and delaying future purchases have on the relationship between Myers and its suppliers? and, how will cancellations and delays affect
the availability to the company of critical materials after the strike ends? Mr.
Arthur also understood that the truck drivers might refuse to deliver and
unload incoming material at Myers' plant, which introduced the problem of
what effect action taken by the purchasing department would have on strike
activities. Since Mr. Arthur's decisions involved considerations of finance
and labor relations, he felt he should bring the problem of inventory control
during a strike to the attention of management. However, he realized that he
was probably better acquainted with the details of the problem than any
other executive and that management would expect a recommendation
from purchasing on what action would be most appropriate under the circumstances.

Mr. Arthur first attempted to analyze the outstanding purchase orders. For
his purposes, he separated the orders into three categories: basic raw materials such as steel, aluminum, magnesium, and so on; purchased parts such
as small castings, forgings, circuit boards, transistors, injection molded parts
and assembled controls of various types, and so on; and miscellaneous materials such as office supplies, maintenance supplies, and standard items that
were usually procured from the stocks of local sales branch offices, mill
supply houses, and so on. The breakdown was as follows:

Raw materials	$1,200,000
Purchased parts	400,000
Miscellaneous materials	75,000
Total	$1,675,000

Mr. Arthur also determined that Myers' normal monthly purchases totaled
$750,000. He separated these purchases into the same classifications and
found that each month the following materials were purchased from
suppliers:

Raw materials	$300,000
Purchased parts	375,000
Miscellaneous materials	75,000
Total	$750,000

By reviewing the previous six months' inventory levels, Mr. Arthur found
that Myers' inventory excluding finished goods and work-in-process had av-
eraged $1.5 million. However, he estimated that the inventory was approx-
imately $1 million on September 1, a month before the date the strike would
probably begin. The normal inventory and August 15 inventory were broken
down as follows:

	Normal inventory	Inventory on August 15
Raw materials	$ 700,000	$ 600,000
Purchased parts	520,000	320,000
Miscellaneous materials	80,000	80,000
Total	$1,300,000	$1,000,000
Work-in-process	$1,000,000	$1,000,000

After investigating the company's balance sheet (see Exhibit 1), Mr. Arthur believed that if normal buying operations continued during a work stoppage, Myers would be able to finance the normal inventory level for about two weeks but afterward would be forced to borrow money to cover the increasing investment in inventory.

Exhibit 1

Balance sheet
As of August 15, 1974

Assets

Current Assets:	
Cash	$ 1,163,313
Securities	4,200
Accounts receivable—net	3,015,961
Inventories (raw materials; work-in-progress; finished goods and branch sales offices' stocks)	4,190,381
Total current assets	$ 8,373,855
Investments	397,110
Sinking fund	75
Land, buildings, and equipment	1,455,467
Prepaid expenses	85,563
Patents	1
Total assets	$10,312,071

Liabilities

Current Liabilities:	
Notes payable	$ 350,000
Accounts payable	838,580
Sinking fund payments	140,000
Accrued liabilities	566,599
Accrued taxes	1,661,376
Advanced payments received	47,681
Total current liabilities	$ 3,604,236
Sinking fund note at 4% interest	980,000
Capital	5,727,835
Total liabilities and capital	$10,312,071

Myers' production process normally required about $750,000 of purchased materials a month. The requirements included approximately 40 percent raw materials, 50 percent purchased parts, and 10 percent miscellaneous materials. Since the sales department would probably deplete the inventories of finished goods during the strike, Mr. Arthur understood that management was scheduling an increased rate of production after the strike ended to rebuild sales inventories. The increased manufacturing schedules would, according to Mr. Arthur, probably require $1,125,000 of purchased materials per month until normal operations could be resumed.

It was expected that overtime would be used until finished goods inventories were built up to prestrike levels. Mr. Arthur also knew that substantial increases in future sales were expected. Forecasts for 1975 and 1976 called for annual increases of about 20 percent per year.

What made Mr. Arthur's planning task difficult was that a strike was not a foregone conclusion. There could be no strike at all, a short strike, or a long one. The purchasing department was expected to assure sufficient supply of raw materials and parts and supplies no matter what happened. Availability of equipment was one of the key sales factors of success in the dictating machine business.

The buyer of raw materials informed Mr. Arthur that he had been experiencing difficulty in procuring items in tight supply such as steel, copper, and magnesium. Purchase orders were being issued for these materials at least five months before the material was required for production schedules. The buyer had been informed by the suppliers that if the orders scheduled to be shipped within the next few months were canceled, it would be about four months after reinstatement before Myers' requirements could be fulfilled. Mr. Arthur believed that to be conservative, all basic raw material purchases should be regarded as in tight supply. If the outstanding orders for critical materials were canceled, the buyer informed Mr. Arthur, the cancellation charges woul only be about ½ to 1 percent of the value of the orders.

This cancellation charge was not to reimburse the producer for work invested in manufacturing Myers' orders, since these orders called for basic raw materials and the suppliers would have no difficulty with the tight market situation in selling the canceled material to other users. However, a trade practice had existed for many years in the basic raw material industry stipulating that any orders canceled within two months of delivery would be penalized with a nominal cancellation charge. Mr. Arthur also considered placing orders for raw materials in the normal pattern and then canceling the orders just before delivery if the strike was still continuing. However, the raw material suppliers were strongly opposed to such a policy, and Mr. Arthur decided not to buy in this manner because of the necessity of maintaining excellent relationships with the raw material suppliers if Myers was to be assured a supply of these materials once the strike ended.

Mr. Arthur also learned that the buyer of purchased parts was concerned about the effect of cancellations and delays on many of his suppliers. Most of these orders were placed with relatively small, local firms that had scheduled a large part of their facilities to fulfill Myers' requirements. The buyer felt that most of his suppliers were so dependent on Myers' business that they would be forced to locate other work to fill the void resulting from cancellations or delays in future purchases. The only other alternatives for these companies, in the buyer's opinion, would be to close a portion of their factories—a costly process—or go completely out of business. Because of market shortages of raw materials in 1972, 1973, and 1974 many of these smaller sources had committed substantial amounts of working capital to raw material inventories to be able to supply Myers' rapidly growing needs. In any case the buyer believed that the relationships established between Myers and many of these suppliers would be endangered or eliminated. The company would, therefore, be forced to develop several new sources of supply which might prove to be a costly and time-consuming procedure. The purchased parts buyer was not convinced that Mr. Arthur's suggestion that Myers could probably work with these suppliers in an attempt to reduce these orders by 20 percent and still save the suppliers from large-scale inactivity would be successful. From past experience Mr. Arthur estimated that the cancellation charges on the orders for purchased parts would approximate 10 percent of the total price.

The final classification of purchases presented few if any problems concerning cancellation in Mr. Arthur's opinion. He estimated that 20 percent of the miscellaneous materials would be required by the office force and maintenance personnel irrespective of a work stoppage. The buyer for miscellaneous materials believed that the remaining 80 percent could be cancelled without any complications. Since these orders called for items stocked by local suppliers, delivery could be obtained in two weeks or sooner if the strike ended abruptly and certain materials were required immediately.

Mr. Arthur next discussed the strike situation with the industrial relations manager and was told that there was a definite possibility that the union would not allow incoming material to be unloaded at Myers' plant. If a picket line were established around the receiving docks, the truck drivers' union would probably refuse to handle Myers' shipments. The only alternative available, if all orders were not canceled, was to receive and store all shipments at independent warehouses within the city. Mr. Arthur estimated that the additional costs accruing from this arrangement would average approximately $3,000 a week.

Before Mr. Arthur had determined what action the purchasing department should take if the union decided to strike, he received the following memorandum from the company's treasurer:

> All company executives should attempt to keep the expenses of the operations under their direction at a base minimum for the duration of a work stoppage. A strike is always costly to everyone involved, and it is extremely important that Myers refrain from absorbing any unnecessary costs which would prevent the company from pursuing the contract negotiations to a successful conclusion.

CASE 5–6
LAMSON CORPORATION

In this game you will have the chance to try your skill at inventory and operations planning using information similar in type to that available to Mr. Marino, the operations manager of Lamson Corporation, a large multi-plant manufacture of sewer pipes. Every two weeks in the summer sales period

Mr. Marino had to decide how many tiles of each type and size should be produced during the coming two weeks. In doing this, he took into account sales trends, the time of the year, the capacity of Lamson's tile making machinery, the stock of the various size tiles on hand, the cost of overtime production and the cost of missed deliveries. In this game you will be able to make similar decisions although the game will be a simplified version of the actual situation. The most important feature of this simplification is that you will be dealing with only two sizes of sewer tile—the 18" diameter size and the 36" diameter size. Mr. Marino, in contrast, had to decide on production levels for 13 different sizes of tile and which plants would produce what mix.

Sales patterns

Company sales, and industry sales in general, were very much influenced by general economic as well as seasonal factors. Since weather affected tile laying conditions and the number of construction starts, sewer tiles exhibited a yearly sales trend of the following general shape (Exhibit 1). Sales were low for six months from October 1 to April 1 and rose rapidly in the spring to a summer peak and then tapered off again. About one-third of all annual sales were made in the two middle months of the year while about three-fourths were made in the summer sales season. However, there was not necessarily a smooth rise and fall in sales in any particular year. The curve shown is only the average of the experience of many years. In any given year, biweekly sales might vary ± 25 percent from levels they would assume if a smooth sales curve existed. The maximum number of 18" tiles sold in any two week period between April and October of last year was 4,550. The similar figure for 36" tiles was 2,000. Major fluctuations in annual levels of sales and mix were caused by economic conditions.

In the game you are about to play, Period 1 refers to the first two weeks in April. Thus, company sales are just leaving the low part of the annual swing.

Exhibit 1

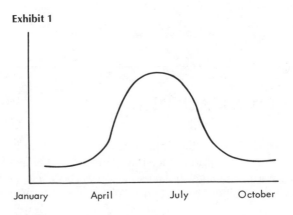

| January | April | July | October |

The game culminates in Period 12, the last two weeks in September. At this point sales are reentering the low winter period. Between Periods 1 and 12, sales follow the general shape of the curve shown in Exhibit 1.

All sales made by Lamson are booked for delivery within the period being considered. That is, there is no advance ordering. Mr. Marino has no idea what the sales for any coming period will be other than from judgement of the sales level of prior periods and from consideration of the general shape of the sales trend curve.

Production constraints

The most popular sizes of concrete tile sold by Lamson were the 18" diameter and the 36" diameter sizes. Mr. Marino had found that together these tiles accounted for a large part of tile sales; in fact, roughly one half of each period's production was devoted to one or other of these sizes. The other half of each period's production was used for the other sizes of tiles produced by Lamson. In order to simplify the game, it has been assumed that Mr. Marino will continue to schedule the production of the less popular eleven tile sizes and that he will use half the production time each period for these sizes. Each participating group will be asked to schedule the numbers of 18" and 36" tile to be produced during each period. Thus, each group will in fact schedule the production of a summer season's supply of 18" and 36" diameter tile.

There are nine possible volume combinations of 18" and 36" tile for the output of the tile-making machines. Four of these output values involved the normal capacity output of the plants. The other five values called for 50 percent overtime production (50 percent overtime represented maximum output possible at Lamson).

The nine production levels possible for 18" and 36" tile in each two week period are shown in Exhibit 2.

Please notice that tradeoffs are involved in choosing a production level for a period. If the number of 18" tiles to be produced is increased, the number of 36" tiles that can be produced will necessarily decrease unless overtime is used.

Exhibit 2
The nine possible production choices open to Mr. Marino each two week period

Normal capacity		50 percent overtime	
18" tiles	36" tiles	18" tiles	36" tiles
6,000	0	9,000	0
4,000	600	7,000	600
2,000	1,200	5,000	1,200
0	1,800	3,000	1,800
		1,000	2,400

Costs involved

Inventory costs. In deciding on production alternatives, Mr. Marino bore in mind several costs which he knew to be fairly accurate. For instance, storage costs of 18" tile for one period were an average of $2.00. This amount took into account interest on tied-up capital, insurance against breakage and direct handling expense. The inventory carrying costs on each 36" tile were higher and averaged $6.00 per tile per period. Mr. Marino had found that over the period of a season, inventory carrying charges could reasonably be calculated on the basis of inventory on hand at the end of each period.

Stock-out costs. Stock-out costs also had to be considered by Mr. Marino. A stock-out occurred whenever a sales in a particular period could not be filled because there were insufficient tiles of the required diameter on hand or in production during that period. For instance, if 100 tiles were on hand at the beginning of a period, 2,000 tiles were produced during the period, and sales during the period totalled 2,200, then a stock-out of 100 tiles would occur. When such a stock-out occurred there was a chance that a future customer of Lamson would be lost. Furthermore, Lamson lost the profit potential on the missed order. Mr. Marino had assessed the risks and costs involved and thought that a stock-out cost Lamson $20 for each 18" tile and $60 for each 36" tile. This figure took into account the fact that the larger the number of tiles that could not be delivered, the more apt the customer was to take future business elsewhere. Stock-outs could not be made up in subsequent periods. If a stock-out occurred, the sale was lost forever to the firm and the above costs were incurred.

Overtime costs. If overtime was used in any period, a fixed charge of $20,000 was incurred. This charge was used mainly to pay extra wages to the employees. The amount was fixed because the employees had been guaranteed a minimum amount each period overtime was used.

How to play the game

In the actual conduct of this game, teams will be used to make the production decisions normally made by Mr. Marino regarding the 18" and 36" diameter tile. Before each period, each team will be required to decide on the production level that will be used in the plant. This decision will be made by the team by whatever means it chooses. Thus, a prediction from a plot of past period sales might be used by some teams, a pure guess by others. In making the decision, teams will want to consider both the possibilities of future sales and the inventories of tiles now on hand.

After each team has decided on the production level it desires for the coming period, the instructor will announce what sales have been for this period. Given this information, teams will then be able to calculate inventory on hand, inventory, stock-out, and overtime costs. These add up to a total period cost which is added to a cumulative total of costs.

The object of the game is to keep the total costs incurred over 12 periods to a minimum. This means that teams will have to decide whether it would be cheaper in the long run to incur overtime costs, inventory carrying costs, or stock-out costs. It is impossible to avoid all three. At the end of the twelfth period the game will be stopped and final costs figured. Your team's results will be compared to those of other teams. During subsequent discussions the merits of various inventory and production policies can be evaluated. Teams will probably find it advantageous to split the work of making sales estimates, calculating costs and keeping records among the various members.

Result form used. To make the keeping of results easier for all teams, Exhibit 3 will be used. The exact steps in using this form are:

1. Decide on the production level to be used in the forthcoming period.
2. Enter number of tiles to be produced in Columns A (18") and J (36").
3. Fill in stock on hand at start of period in Columns B (18") and K (36"). These figures come from Columns E (18") and N (36") of the previous period.
4. Enter total stock available for sale in the period in Columns C and L.
   Entry in Column C (18" tiles) = Entry in Column A +
                              Entry in Column B.
   Entry in Column L (36" tiles) = Entry in Column J +
                              Entry in Column K.
5. Obtain actual sales in period from Instructor. Enter in Columns D (18") and M (36").
6. Compute inventory remaining at the end of the period. Enter in Columns E and N.
   Entry in Column E (18" tiles) = Entry in Column C −
                              Entry in Column D.
   Entry in Column N (36" tiles) = Entry in Column L −
                              Entry in Column M.
   Enter zero if an entry is calculated as negative. There can be no negative inventory on hand.
7. Compute inventory carrying costs and enter in Columns F and O.
   Entry in Column F (18" tiles) = $2.00 × No. in Column E.
   Entry in Column O (36" tiles) = $6.00 × No. in Column N.
8. Compute stock-outs incurred in period, enter in Columns G and P if zero or a positive number. Enter zero if an entry is calculated as negative; there can be no negative stock-outs.
   Entry in Column G (18" tiles) = Entry in Column D −
                              Entry in Column C.
   Entry in Column P (36" tiles) = Entry in Column M −
                              Entry in Column L.
9. Compute stock-out costs, enter in Columns H and Q.
10. Compute total period inventory cost, enter in Column R.
    Entry in Column R = Entry in Column F (18" tiles) + Entry in Column O (36" tiles).

11. Compute total period stock-out costs, enter in Column S.
    Entry in Column S = Entry in Column H (18" tiles) + Entry in Column Q (36" tiles).
12. If overtime was used, enter $20,000 in Column T. If no overtime used, enter zero.
13. Compute total period cost and enter in Column U. Entry in Column U = Entry in Column R (total period inventory cost) + Entry in Column S (total period stock-out cost) + Entry in Column T (overtime cost).
14. Compute cumulative total to date, enter in Column V. Entry in Column V = Entry in Column U for current period + Entry in Column V for last period.

Example. Each team member should carefully trace the proceedings as outlined in the following example to understand fully all of the steps involved in playing and recording the game.

Mr. Marino has already used the form to record the operating results of the two periods prior to the first period for which you will be required to decide the production level (Period 1). Lamson started Period 1 with 400 18" tiles (Column B) and 100 16" tiles on hand (Column K). Because he knew that a special, large order for 18" tiles would be placed in Period 1, (a most unusual size of order at this time of year), Mr. Marino decided to go to overtime and to produce 7,000 18" tiles (Column A) and 600 36" tiles (Column J). Thus 7,400 18" tiles (Column C) and 700 36" tiles (Column L) were available for sales during Period 1.

In actual fact, the special order was smaller than Mr. Marino had anticipated and total sales turned out to be 6,000 for the 18" tiles (Column D) and 800 for the 36" tiles (Column M). Because 18" inventory available for sale exceeded sales, Mr. Marino entered 1,400 in Column E to show there was inventory remaining at the end of the period, and then entered zero in Column G to show that there had been no stock-out of 18" tiles. Column F then shows the inventory cost incurred by having 1,400 18" tiles on hand at the end of the period ($2.00 × 140 = $280.00). Column H shows that no stock-out cost was incurred. Because demand for the 36" tiles (800) exceeded the total available for sale (700), a stock-out of 100 occurred and no tiles were left in inventory at the end of Period 1. To show this, zero was entered in Column N and 100 was entered in Column P. There was a zero inventory carrying cost entered in Column O while a stock-out cost of $6,000 was entered in Column Q ($60 × 100 = $6,000).

The total inventory carrying cost was entered in Column R ($2,800 + 0 = $2,800) and the total stock-out cost in Column S (0 + $6,000 = $6,000). A sum of $20,000 was entered in Column T because overtime was used. The total period cost was calculated to be $2,800 + $6,000 + $20,000 = $28,800. This amount was then entered in Colunn U and also Column V.

Lamson began Period O with 1,400 18" tiles (Column B) and zero 36" tiles on hand (Column K). These totals had been brought down from Col-

Exhibit 3

NUMBER	MONTH	(A) Number produced	(B) Stock on hand at start of period	(C) Total available for sale (C = A + B)	(D) Sales in period	(E) Inventory remaining at end of period (E = C−D) (Minimum = 0)	(F) Inventory carrying cost ($2 × E)	(G) Number of stock-outs (G = D−C if greater than 0)	(H) Stock-out cost (H = $20 × G)	(J) Number produced	(K) Stock on hand at start of period	(L) Total available for sale (L = J + K)	(M) Sales in period	(N) Inventory remaining at end of period (N = L−M) (Minimum = 0)	(O) Inventory carrying cost ($6 × N)	(P) Number of stock-outs (P = M−L if greater than 0)	(Q) Stock-out cost (Q = $60 × P)	(R) Total inventory cost (R = F + O)	(S) Total stock-out cost (S = H + Q)	(T) Overtime cost $20,000 (if used)	(U) Total period cost (U = R + S + T)	(V) Cumulative total to date
		18" Tiles								36" Tiles								TOTALS				
−1	March	7,000	400	7,400	6,000	1,400	$2,800	0	0	600	100	700	800	0	0	100	$6,000	$2,800	$6,000	$20,000	$28,800	(28,800)
0	March	2,000	1,400	3,400	1,400	2,000	$4,000	0	0	1,200	0	1,200	500	700	4,200	0	0	$8,200	0	0	$ 8,200	(37,000)
1	April																					
2	April																					
3	May																					
4	May																					
5	June																					
6	June																					
7	July																					
8	July																					
9	August																					
10	August																					
11	September																					
12	September																					
	Total																					

umns E and N respectively of Period 1. At the beginning of Period O, Mr. Marino elected to produce 2,000 18" tiles (Column A) and 1,200 36" tiles (Column J). No overtime was called for. Thus there were 3,400 18" tiles (Column C) and 1,200 36" tiles (Column L) available for sale in Period O.

In Period O, sales totaled 1,400 18" tiles (Column D) and 500 36" tiles (Column M). Thus the inventory remaining at the end of the period was 2,000 18" tiles (Column E) and 700 36" tiles (Column N). There were zero stock-outs (Columns G and P). Inventory carrying costs were computed to be $2.00 × 2,000 = $4,000 (Column F) and $6.00 × 70 = $4,200 (Column O). There were no stock-out costs (Column H and Q) because stock-outs equalled zero in this period.

The total inventory carrying cost for Period O was $8,200 ($4,000 + $4,200). This amount was entered in Column R, while zero was entered in Column S since there had been no stock-outs in the period. There was no overtime used, consequently a zero was entered in Column T. The Column U entry shows that the total period costs incurred were $8,200. The Column V entry was $28,800 + $8,200 = $37,000. Since your team did not incur these costs we will wipe them off the slate and have you start with a zero cost at the beginning of Period 1 in Column V.

A few operating rules during the game

1. The only production combinations your team may choose are those given in Exhibit 2.
2. If your team makes a calculation mistake, a penalty of $25,000 will be assessed and all figures will be corrected.
3. If your team is unable to reach a decision by the time called for by the instructor, it will automatically be decided that you produce 2,000 18" tiles and 1,200 36" tiles.
4. Normally, at the beginning of the game, each team will have approximately ten minutes to make a decision. This time will decrease as the game progresses.

Start of game. The game proper starts in Period 1. At the beginning of the game there are 2,000 18" tiles on hand (brought down from Column E of Period O) and 700 36" tiles on hand (brought down from Column N of Period O). It is now up to each team to pick the production level most appropriate for Period 1 and thus start the playing of the game.

SELECTING ADEQUATE SOURCES OF SUPPLY

6

Introduction

The selection of sources of supply is a key decision area in the acquisition process. The expressed purpose of industrial marketing is to influence this decision in favor of one source over another. Supplier selection is purchasing's most important responsibility. The purchasing department must be able to locate dependable and progressive sources of supply and to secure and maintain their active interest and cooperation. All other purchasing contributions to the organization are secondary to the competent selection of suppliers.

Even though in sequence of preparation it is logical to consider matters of quality and quantity first, these can seldom be settled without consideration of available sources. One of the signs of a good supplier is the ability to be of assistance to the purchaser in establishing what constitutes the proper quality and quantity for the intended use.

The supplier selection decision •

The decision to place a certain volume of business with a supplier is always based on some rationale. The art of good purchasing is to make the reasoning behind that decision as sound as possible. An interesting study by G. W. Dickson listed 23 factors which might be considered in evaluating potential vendors. (See Table 6–1.) That the type of product purchased influenced the ranking of importance of these factors was clear. (See Figure 6–1.)

The supplier selection decision may be modeled using a decision tree format as shown in Figure 6–2.

This is, obviously, a very simple, one-stage situation with only two suppliers seriously considered and two possible outcomes. It illustrates, however, the uncertain environment present in almost every supplier choice and the risk inherent in the decision. David Wilson[1] conducted his thesis research on the treatment of this risk factor. He tried to relate personality variables of the purchasing agents to their willingness to take risks and their need to seek additional information. His work and that of a number of others show that the perceived risk of placing

[1] D. T. Wilson, *An Exploratory Study of the Effects of Personality and Problem Elements upon Purchasing Agent Decision Styles,* Unpublished doctoral thesis, London, Ontario, Canada, The University of Western Ontario, 1970.

Table 6-1
Aggregate factor ratings

Factor	Mean rating	Evaluation
Quality	3.508	Extreme importance
Delivery	3.417	
Performance history	2.998	
Warranties and claims policies	2.849	
Production facilities and capacity	2.775	Considerable
Price	2.758	importance
Technical capability	2.545	
Financial position	2.514	
Procedural compliance	2.488	
Communication system	2.426	
Reputation and position in industry	2.412	
Desire for business	2.256	
Management and organization	2.216	
Operating controls	2.211	
Repair service	2.187	Average
Attitude	2.120	importance
Impression	2.054	
Packaging ability	2.009	
Labor relations record	2.003	
Geographical location	1.872	
Amount of past business	1.597	
Training aids	1.537	
Reciprocal arrangements	0.610	Slight importance

Figure 6-1
The most important factors by situation

Importance rank	Case A: paint	Case B: desks	Case C: computer	Case D: art work
1	Quality	Price	Quality	Delivery
2	Warranties	Quality	Technical capability	Production capacity
3	Delivery	Delivery	Delivery	Quality
4	Performance history	Warranties	Production capacity	Performance history
5	Price	Performance history	Performance history	Communication system

Source: G. W. Dickson, "An Analysis of Vendor Selection Systems and Decisions," *Journal of Purchasing* 2, no. 1 (February 1966): 10–11.

substantial business with an untried and unknown supplier is high. A distinction between routine repetitive purchases and less standard acquisitions needs to be made. The risk is seen to be higher with unknown suppliers as well as unknown materials, parts, or equipment and with increased dollar amounts. Purchasers attempt to share the risk with others by asking for advice, such as engineering judgment, and by seeking additional information which includes the placing of a trial order.

The more normal situation is shown in Figure 6–3 where a continuing need for the product or service exists. Whether the chosen source performs well or not,

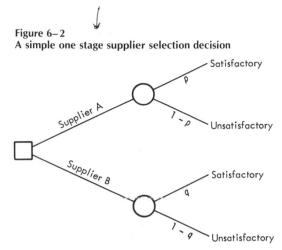

Figure 6–2
A simple one stage supplier selection decision

the future decision on which supplier to deal with next time around may well affect the present decision. For example, if we place the business with supplier C and C fails, then this may mean that only A could be considered a reasonable source at the next stage. If we don't like the idea of being tied to supplier A by necessity, without alternatives, we may not choose C as the supplier at the first stage.

Necessity for supplier goodwill

It has long been considered sound marketing policy to develop goodwill on the part of customers toward the seller. This goodwill has been cultivated through the development of trademarks and brands, through extensive advertising, through missionary efforts as well as through regular calls by sales personnel, and through the many other devices which have appealed to the imaginations of marketing managers. Sellers are jealous of this goodwill, considering it one of their major assets. It has real commercial value and is so recognized by courts of law. Goodwill between a company and its suppliers needs to be just as carefully cultivated and just as jealously guarded. When purchasing directors and the management behind such directors are as aggressive in their attempts to maintain proper and friendly relations with suppliers as sales managers are in their relations with customers, many a costly error will be avoided. Failure to maintain these relations is often more serious than is sometimes believed. Concerns have even been forced to engage in the manufacture of their own supplies because of an unwise attitude toward former sources of supply. Since corporate strategic plans are so often based on the assumption that supply sources will be cooperative, it makes sense to assure that such cooperation will be forthcoming.

No matter how carefully a purchasing, using, or production department may plan, it is inevitable that emergencies will arise and that actual needs will be different from anticipated requirements.

The shortages of many basic materials in recent years had the most serious

Figure 6–3
Simplified three stage decision tree for supplier selection

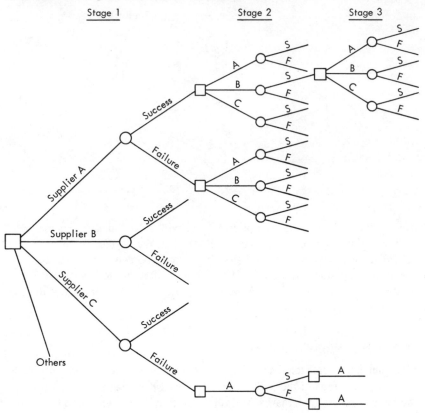

effects on companies which had ignored developing good vendor relations during past periods of a buyers' market.

The purchasing manual from a large corporation states:

> The Purchasing Department has more contacts with other companies than any other department except sales. An opinion of a company is formed by contacts with its employees. The buyer has it in his hands to enhance or detract from the Company's good name in his relations with vendors and their salesmen and has a major responsibility to form a good reputation for the Company and for the goodwill it commands." Another manual states: "Friendship can be cultivated even through the very manner in which a salesman is told that he has lost, or cannot have, an order. These may seem small things, but courtesy, square dealing, honesty, and straightforwardness beget friendship. They are appreciated by sellers, and the buyer benefits largely from them.

Qualifications of a good supplier

The selection of a supplier will be influenced by the purchaser's conception of what a good supplier is. What, then, is a good supplier?

A good or preferred supplier should be one which does the following for its customers. It provides the quality specified and delivers on time as promised; has an acceptable price; reacts to unforeseen needs such as suddenly accelerated or decelerated volumes of business, changes in specifications, service problems, and any other legitimate requests. The good supplier takes the initiative in suggesting better ways of serving customers and attempts to find new way of developing products and services which will allow customers to perform their operations more economically. The good supplier will warn ahead of time of material shortages, strikes, and anything else that may affect the purchaser's operations. It will provide technological and other expertise when requested by customers. It will remain competitive on a continuing basis. Suppliers like this are hard to find. In many industries there may only be one, two, or three that fit this bill. The art of a good purchasing department is to find and keep top suppliers over time. Many of the qualities listed in the above mentioned requirements create additional cost for the supplier in the short run. To make it worthwhile for the supplier to incur these costs, there must be assurance that special care will be rewarded with additional future business. The greatest reward a customer can give is assurance of future business in response to satisfactory performance. It is important to avoid a very high and rapid supplier turnover. Occasionally, preferred suppliers have been given the axe on the basis of incomplete information. The reactions of suppliers are understandable if they lose the next order after they have gone to great lengths to please a customer's special demands in terms of overtime, quick delivery, or unusual quality because someone else bids a few hundred dollars lower. Every supplier switch costs the customer something. Quality assurance needs to inspect the new premises, new contacts need to be established with supplier personnel, and new data inputs are required for the various computer systems. A supplier switch may well have substantial costs attached, depending on the commodity and supplier. If a supplier does not have the expectation of getting a contract renewal it may well choose not to make long-term raw material commitments so necessary to the continued running of the business. If purchasing is late in terms of contract renewal, even continuing with the same source may result in a period of stock-outs. Although uncertainty regarding future business is certainly one of purchasing's powerful tools to keep suppliers on their toes, it does have its drawbacks. Should some of the current predictions regarding shortages of basic raw materials hold up, some customers may well be in a very difficult position when suppliers establish priorities of customers on vital requirements.

Suppose that the above premise is granted. The real danger clearly lies in becoming puppets of suppliers. Suppliers know that customers depend on them, and they will charge excessively. This is where careful supplier management becomes important. In the first place it requires an understanding and identification of value. Value is the ultimate long-term cost to the user of the product or service acquired. It does not mean lowest purchase price, or lowest investment in inventory, or fastest delivery time, or lowest delivery cost, or longest life, or highest disposal value, or even the highest attainable quality; it is an optimal amount cutting across all of these. The purchase price frequently is one important part of this total. It is the duty of the purchasing department to make sure that the price quoted is reasonable in view of the total set of circumstances surrounding the purchase of the particular product.

Information is required on the actual performance of the supplier. Is quality acceptable and delivery on time? Is there initiative to make suggestions for changes and improvements? Do the quantities delivered conform with those requested? Without such information supplier management is impossible. Action needs to be taken immediately in response to feedback. Frequently, the marketing people of the supplier do not know what is going on with individual customers. Letting them know quickly that problems exist can solve many future headaches. This requires a good supplier performance record. Subsequently, at quotation time, purchasing can make a good case for one supplier versus another, and it is illogical to let price have an unusually large bearing. In all fairness in some markets the segments do exist where the lowest bidder can be given the business in the expectation of satisfactory performance. The problem is that even here the market segment may change, conditions may vary, and what is satisfactory one year may not be satisfactory at a future time.

Good sources of supply are one assurance of good quality production today, and their progressive thinking and planning is a further assurance of improved quality tomorrow. Good souces of supply, therefore, are an important company asset that no one individual, no emergency of the moment, no opportunity of the moment should be allowed to jeopardize. As a means of carrying out this policy, one company's bulletin states that it intends:

> . . . to give full management support and authority to our Director of Purchasing so that he may carry out to the fullest degree the purpose and spirit of our source relationship policy and to maintain a *Source Relationship Committee* consisting of Director of Purchasing, Director of Research, Treasurer, Vice President in charge of Marketing, Vice President in charge of Production, Vice President in charge of Paper Mill Operation, and the President. It will be the responsibility of this committee to periodically review our source relationships with the continuing aim to improve present relationships, review any deficiencies, and recommend corrective action. Occasional reports on our source relationships will be made to the Board of Directors.

In a similar effort to strengthen its source relationships, Pillsbury Company, of Minneapolis, engaged an outside consultant to interview the company's suppliers to learn what the vendors thought of the company's purchasing policies and procedures and what complaints the suppliers had either of the Pillsbury Company or of its buying habits. The interviews covered salespeople who had personal contact with the company's purchasing agents and also the top management of the supplier companies. It was hoped that the results would show a mass-attitude answer to the question of how Pillsbury stood with its suppliers and provide a guide to its future purchasing policies and to the building of good supplier relationships.

Sources of information about suppliers ♪

Having in mind the characteristics of a supplier, the next step is to ascertain the available sources. Knowledge of sources is a primary qualification for any effective buyer. Some buyers rely solely upon their experience and memory for their knowledge of sources. Perhaps in a very limited number of instances this practice may be satisfactory; when the requirements are exceedingly simple, obtainable from a limited number of suppliers, it may not be worthwhile to maintain elaborate records. These cases, however, are so few as to be almost negligible. The normal principal sources consist of catalogs (both printed and microfilm), trade journals, advertisements of various sorts, vendor and commodity directories, salespeoples' interviews, and the purchasing department's own records.

Catalogs. Catalogs of the commonly known sources of supply, covering the most important materials in which a company is interested, are properly considered essential in any well-managed purchasing office. The value of such catalogs depends largely on the form in which they are presented (a matter for the most part beyond the control of the purchasing officer), the readiness with which the material contained in them is available, and the use which is made of such information.

Jobbers' catalogs contain many items from a variety of manufacturing sources and offer, to a certain extent, a directory of available commodities within the jobbers' fields. Equipment and machinery catalogs provide information as to the specifications of, and the location of a source of supply for, replacement parts as well as new equipment.

Catalogs frequently provide price information. Many supplies and materials are sold from standard list prices, and quotations are made by quoting discounts only. Catalogs also are reference books called for by department heads and engineers.

The availability of the material in the catalogs is largely a matter of the manner in which they are indexed and filed, a not so simple task. Catalogs are issued in all sorts of sizes and in binders which make them difficult to handle.

In some cases all catalogs, regardless of size, thickness, or specification are filed together. In other cases catalogs are grouped and filed in comparable sizes, as nearly as may be. The identification of individual catalogs is commonly achieved by numbering them consecutively, frequently with the number pasted on the back of the catalog. A number of influential associations have endorsed a standard size of 7¾ × 10⅝, among them the National Association of Purchasing Management, American Society of Mechanical Engineers, Southern Supply and Machinery Dealers Association, and Automotive Jobbers Association. The general use of a standard size would simplify the filing problem.

Proper indexing of catalogs is essential. Some firms use loose-leaf ledgers with sheets especially printed for catalog filing; others use a form of card index. Indexing should be according to suppliers' names as well as products listed. It should be specific, definite, and easily understandable.

A proper catalog has the advantage of being a permanent record, always in the office of the buyer. Salespeople are not always available; advertisements are frequently forgotten; but the catalog is an ever-present reminder of the existence of the vendor issuing it.

Microfilm files. Several companies have issued catalogs of suppliers with all information recorded on microfilm. An example of this service is that provided by VSMF (Visual Search Microfilm File). Information about more than 3,100 suppliers and their products serving the aerospace and electronics industries has been recorded on over 100,000 frames of 16 mm. microfilm. A comprehensive indexing system, a reader for the films, and a printer which permits a full-size sheet reproduction of the information on the film are included in the service.

Trade journals. Trade journals also are a valuable source of information as to potential suppliers. The list of such publications is, of course, very long, and the individual items in it vary tremendously in value. Yet, in every field there are worthwhile trade magazines, and buyers read extensively those dealing with their own industry and with those industries to which they sell and from which they buy. These journals are utilized in two ways. The first use is a study of the text, which not only adds to buyer's general information but suggests new products and substitute materials.

The trade gossip provides information about suppliers and their personnel. The second use has to do with advertising. A consistent perusal of the advertisements in such publications is a worthwhile habit cultivated by all keen buyers.

Industrial advertising. As a general source of information to the purchasing officer, the exact value of industrial advertising is a matter of dispute. Advertising people generally, even professional teachers of the subject, are definite in their opinion that in spite of many weaknesses, industrial advertising has value; buyers generally read it and are, perhaps unconsciously, influenced by it.

Trade directories. Trade directories are another useful source of information. They vary widely in their accuracy and usefulness, and care must be exercised in their use.

Trade registers, or trade directories, are volumes which list leading manufacturers, their addresses, number of branches, affiliations, products, and, in some instances, their financial standing or their position in the trade. They also contain listings of the trade names of articles on the market with the names of the manufacturers, and classified lists of materials, supplies, equipment, and other items offered for sale, under each of which is given the name and location of available manufacturing sources of supply.

These registers, then, are so arranged that they may be consulted either by way of the commodity, the manufacturer, or the trade name.

Such standard directories as, for example, *Thomas' Register of American Manufacturers* and *MacRae's Blue Book* and the Kompass publications in Europe, not to mention the more specialized directories, serve a useful purpose, and no purchasing officer's library is adequate without a file of the more standard directories. The Yellow Pages of telephone directories provide lists of local suppliers.

Sales representation. Sales representation may constitute one of the most valuable sources of information available to the purchasing manager, with references to sources of supply, types of products, and trade information generally. Today an alert purchasing official makes it a point to see as many sales representatives as possible without neglecting other duties. It is essential to develop good supplier relations which begin with a friendly, courteous, sympathetic, and frank attitude toward the vendor salesperson. The buyer endeavors not to waste any time. After the visit, a record is made of the call together with new information obtained. Some purchasers make it a point to see personally every sales representative who calls at the office; others, because of lack of time and the pressure of other duties, are unable to follow such a rule, but they do make sure that someone interviews every visitor in order that no one may go away feeling rebuffed. The representative who receives brusque treatment is less likely to make extra effort to render special services, or to offer new ideas readily.

Most companies have policies and procedures guidelines concerning the relations between the purchasing office and vendors' representatives. For example:

> In negotiating with vendors and their sales representatives, there are certain points of personal character and ethical conduct that are requisites of a good purchasing agent or buyer. Courtesy, honesty, and fairness each has its place in this activity.

To the Sales Representative:

1. See them without delay. If, however, someone has violated routine rules, call the matter to his or her attention.
2. Let them tell their story and analyze it while listening.
3. Talk business.
4. Answer ethical questions.
5. Be truthful in all statements.
6. In all negotiations cover all elements of purchasing in order that the final understanding may be complete.

To the Vendor:

1. Do not ask any vendor to quote unless you conscientiously expect to consider the supplier at final determination.
2. Keep specifications fair and clear.
3. Keep competition open and fair.
4. Respect the confidence of vendors and sales representatives in all quotations and other confidential information.
5. Do not take improper advantage of sellers' errors.
6. Discourage revision of bids by insisting on best price on first bid. If, however, second bids are accepted, all bidders must have equal opportunity.
7. Cooperate with vendor in solving vendor's difficulties.
8. Negotiate prompt and fair adjustment in handling material below quality.
9. Be courteous in stating rejection of bids with explanations that are reasonable but do not betray confidential information.
10. Answer letters promptly.
11. Handle samples, tests, and reports concerning them with prompt, complete, and truthful information.

12. Submit shipping schedule to vendor and follow up efficiently.
13. Avoid all obligations to seller except strict business obligations.

Were we concerned primarily with industrial marketing instead of industrial buying, much would be said at this point concerning the mistaken attempt on the part of both sales representatives and sales managers to bypass the purchasing executive. Such attempts are unfortunate from everyone's point of view. Here, we are forced to omit an extended analysis of this problem. However, this much must be said. Although the purchasing executive is expected to be well acquainted with the company's operation, equipment, materials, and production and to be qualified to pass on the practicality of suggestions and proposals that may be made by sales representatives and technical people, the purchaser does not, as a rule, have the background that constitutes the basis for the technical person's special knowledge. Therefore, it is often necessary for the purchasing agent to refer such proposals to others better qualified to handle them. The best way to reach the right people in any company is through the purchasing agent. One sales manager said in effect:

> It is easy for a sales manager to ask the question, "What does the Technical Service Department do to help me get the business?" The average sales manager would answer the question quickly by giving this definition of technical service: It is the means of selling the customer's technical people without hurting the purchasing agent's feelings. . . . But this is a misconception of the true situation. Centralized purchasing is based on management policies that channel all procurement through the purchasing department. This is indispensable if a company is to reap the full benefit of controlled purchasing. In order that the purchasing agent may function in the best interests of the company and its departments, all transactions must be screened through the purchasing department from their inception. Suppliers find that adherence to this policy best serves their interests. Bypassing the purchasing agent is not a matter of hurting feelings. It is a matter of violating sound rules of procedure and company policies that experience has proved to be of greater value to all concerned—buyer and seller alike.

There are scores of sales representatives, sales engineers, technical experts, and others making "cold" calls who fail to recognize that the members of today's modern purchasing department are fully conversant with the company's production and material requirements and quite capable of determining whether a new product has potential use in the firm. Purchasing is part of a cooperative group within a company, made up of engineering, planning, production, procurement, and sales and is duty-bound to see to it that technical people or sales representatives with products of interest are given a full hearing and referred to the correct insiders when necessary.

Vendor files. Information from any source, if of value, should be recorded. One such record has already been mentioned, the index accompanying the catalog file. Another common record is the vendor file, commonly on small cards or simple computer file, classified by names of vendors. Such files contain information concerning the address of the vendor, past orders placed with the company, data concerning its general fitness and reliability and the company's willingness to meet the particular requirements of the purchaser, and other pertinent information of any sort that might be of value to the buyer. A third record of importance kept in many companies is a commodity file, in which material is classified on the basis of the product. The information on such cards relates to the sources from which the product has been purchased in the past, perhaps the price paid, the point of shipment, and a cross-reference to the vendor file. Miscellaneous information is also given, such as whether specifications are called for, whether a contract already exists covering the item, whether competitive bids are commonly asked for, and such other data as may be of importance. Accompanying such files as those dealing with sources are, of course, those relating to price and other records. Some of these have already been discussed in earlier chapters, and others will be discussed later. Proper use of DP equipment facilitates the compilation of the above records.

From any or all of these various sources of information, the purchasing officer is able to make up a list of available vendors from whom the items required can be acquired. The next step is to reduce this list to workable length, retaining only the most likely sources of supply. From the resulting list, usually a comparatively small one, the best source (or sources, if more than one are to be used) must be selected. Obviously, the extent to which the investigation and analysis of sources are carried will depend upon the cost and the importance of the item involved. A large number of items which the purchasing department is called upon to buy are so inexpensive and are consumed in such small quantities as to render any studied investigation clearly unwise.

In reducing the number of potential suppliers to a practical list or in passing upon the desirability of a new supplier (either for a new product or for one already being used), it is obvious that an adequate study must be made of each vendor's qualifications. The points to check have already been listed and will not be repeated. The investigation required may be drawn out and extensive. It may well require joint inquiry by the buyer, cooperating with representatives of the engineering and production departments.

Personal visits to suppliers' plants. In some instances, a representative of the procurement department may visit the potential supplier in order to form, through actual observation, an opinion as to the supplier's equipment, personnel, and similar matters. Few purchasing managers or buyers follow a practice of making such visits regularly, but the percentage of those who do no visiting whatsoever is equally small. It is good practice to "team visit" with technical and financial experts where a major corporation assessment needs to be made. There are, of course, a number of reasons for plant visits other than merely to check up on a potential supplier. Visits to suppliers already being utilized are sometimes equally worthwhile, perhaps to learn why delivery promises are not being kept, to settle an adjustment that has long been pending, or to discuss the terms of an important order or contract. Another important objective is to become personally acquainted with the personnel and habitat of a firm with which the purchasing officer is doing business.

In this connection it should be pointed out that some purchasing executives feel that visits to suppliers are particularly useful when there are no difficulties to discuss. By such friendly visits the purchasing officer frequently can talk with higher executives rather than confining oneself to someone who happens to be directly responsible for handling a specific complaint. This helps to cement good relations at all levels of management and may reveal much about a supplier's future plans that might not otherwise come to attention. Such a visitation policy does raise certain problems not found in the more routine types of visits, such as who should make the visits, how best to get worthwhile information, and the best use to put the data to, once obtained. Experience has indicated that in order to get the best results from such trips, it is desirable (1) to draw up in advance a general outline of the kinds of information to be sought; (2) to gather all reasonably available information, both general and specific, about the company in advance of the trip; and (3) to prepare a detailed report of the findings, once the visit is completed. When the visits are carefully planned, the direct expense incurred is small compared with the returns.

Motion-picture films or video-tapes of suppliers' plants. Profitable use can be made of well-selected motion-picture films as an aid in adding to a buyer's general fund of knowledge about major commodities and sources of supply. One of the reasons for plant visits is to learn more about commodities and manufacturing processes. Visits for such purposes are to be commended. Actual visits, however, have their limitations. They may be expensive or, if not, may be available to but a portion of the procurement staff of a particular company. They are also fatiguing physically. Much of the process may not be observable because it goes on hidden from the observer's sight. The visitor may not know what should be looked for, or what questions should be asked. Many of these difficulties are overcome with a good film. Cross-sections of machines and diagrammatic presentation of processes, coupled with actual "shots," can tell an informative story. Films by themselves can never tell the whole story—the plant itself must be visited in addition to viewing the film if the very maximum is to be gotten from the study. Of course, too, the film or tape tells little or nothing of the reliability of a vendor or of prices. It is limited by its very nature to a fairly brief presentation. It shows to the observer only what the sponsor wants. However, in spite of these disadvantages, properly used, well-chosen, properly presented films can add to a purchaser's fund of knowledge.

Samples. In addition to the usual inquiries concerning the potential supplier and to a plant visit, samples of the vendor's product can be tested. Some thought may well be devoted, therefore, to the problem of how to handle what may be called the "sample problem." Frequently a sales representative for a new product urges the buyer to accept a sample for test purposes. This raises questions as to what samples to accept, how to ensure a fair test of those accepted, who should bear the expense of testing, and whether or not the vendor should be given the results of the test.[2]

---

[2]For a discussion of the use of samples, see Chapter 4.

Supplier evaluation—existing and potential sources

The evaluation of suppliers is a continuing purchasing task. Current suppliers have to be monitored to see if expected performance materializes. New sources need to be screened to see if their potential warrants serious future consideration. Since most organizations tend to place a significant portion of repetitive business with the same suppliers, evaluation of current sources will be discussed first.

Vendor rating and evaluation

Some procurement executives have attempted to establish formal vendor rating procedures as an aid in selecting suppliers. Inasmuch as price can usually be determined objectively if a way can be found to measure quality, delivery, and service, the attempt at rating is usually confined to these three factors.

One method which has been found effective in rating quality is to make a monthly tabulation of the invoices from each supplier and the value of the supplier's materials which were rejected during the month. This latter figure is then divided by the value of the materials shipped, and the resulting percentage indicates the rate of rejection.

Comparison of rejection rates among competing suppliers or against an average of the rejection rates shows those suppliers who are providing the proper quality.

Delivery and service can be rated by having whoever does the expediting keep a continuing tabulation for each supplier covering the following points:

Top rating:	a. Meets delivery dates without expediting.
	b. Requested delivery dates are usually accepted.
Good:	c. Usually meets shipping dates without substantial follow-up.
	d. Often is able to accept requested delivery dates.
Fair:	e. Shipments sometimes late, substantial amount of follow-up required.
Unsatisfactory:	f. Shipments usually late, delivery promises seldom met, constant expediting required.

In addition to the above tabulation the buyer records an opinion of the technical help the supplier is able to furnish, the willingness to furnish such help, and the general attitude in meeting any situation which may arise.

Point ratings can be applied to any of these factors and are used by a number of computer based systems. G. W. Dickson in his study[3] found that over one third of the responding firms in his sample did not retain formal records on actual supplier performance. For those who did, the most common types of information retained were:

Delivery experience	45.8%
Defective material experience	44.6%
Repair service rendered	22.6%
Technical service rendered	20.8%
All service rendered	17.8%
None of the above	35.0%

[3] G. W. Dickson, "An Analysis of Vendor Selection Systems and Decisions," *Journal of Purchasing* 2, no. 1 (February 1966): 5–17.

Some companies have found it advisable to inform the chief executives of the suppliers periodically on how their companies stand on the rating scale. Improved performance on the part of the supplier often results from the knowledge that its rating is lower than some competitors.

Each vendor is rated either by formal or informal methods. Where formal methods can be established at reasonable costs, results probably warrant the expenditure.

Evaluation of potential sources

In evaluating potential sources, the four most common major factors are technical or engineering capability, manufacturing strengths, financial strengths, and management capability.[4] Potential sources need to be examined to determine their suitability as future sources of supply. A list of 23 common evaluation factors has already been discussed in this chapter. (See Table 6–1.) The quality capability survey was covered in Chapter 4. Price will be discussed separately in later chapters. The use of trial orders has been mentioned as a popular means of testing a supplier's capability, but, popular as this may be, it still begs the question as to whether the trial order should have been placed with a particular source at all. Even though a supplier may complete a trial order successfully, it may not be an acceptable source in the long run. Two prime reasons may be its doubtful financial and management capability.

Financial evaluation

The financial strengths and weaknesses of a supplier obviously affect its capability to respond to the needs of customers. There are often substantial opportunities for negotiation if the purchaser is fully familiar with the financial status of a supplier. For example, the offer of advance payment or cash discounts will have no appeal to a cash rich source but may be highly attractive to a firm short of working capital. A supplier with substantial inventories may be able to offer supply assurance and a degree of price protection at times of shortages which cannot be matched by others without the materials or the funds to acquire them.

A study at the Bell Helicopter Company showed that purchasing managers ranked financial evaluation third in importance, behind management and manufacturing, but ahead of technical and other considerations. Special factors considered included:

This study was done in conjunction with a supplier classification system.

> In reviewing procurement policies, practices, and procedures and the controls and requirements of the different governmental agencies, it was readily apparent that the most-stringent requirements were for suppliers which furnished materials to design criteria. This, then, comprises one classification of suppliers for which the

---

[4]M. G. Edwards and H. A. Hamilton, Jr. (eds.), "Guide to Purchasing," vol. 1 (New York: National Association of Purchasing Management, Inc., 1969).

	Importance ranking percentage
Net worth	8.5
Profitability	6.9
Bid rates	12.0
Working capital	10.7
Current ratio	9.0
Net quick assets ratio	6.5
Capitalization	5.8
Equity of business	5.8
Past financial record	9.5
Debt structure	7.7
Ability to finance contracts	17.7

most-stringent evaluation techniques and monitoring policies are required. These will be known as Class I suppliers.

The second most-important items procured are those purchased for production, and not necessarily to a design criterion. Generally speaking, these will be supplier-designed items requiring little or no modification. This group will be known as Class II suppliers.

The third and largest classification is for those suppliers which furnish non-production items, such as MRO materials, supplies, and services. This group will be known as Class III suppliers.

By segregating proposed suppliers into these three classifications, it becomes apparent that the Class I supplier requires the most-thorough evaluation and the greatest amount of control. The purpose of this study, then, was redefined as a concentrated effort to improve the techniques utilized in the evaluation, control, and monitoring of Class I suppliers.[5]

According to A. K. Stewart there is a similarity between credit rating and financial analysis of supplier.

Combining the implications of the recommendations already made suggests an area where additional research would be of value. The basis for a vendor rating should be an evaluation of this technical, financial, production, and managerial ability. The credit rating makes an evaluation of financial and managerial ability. If technical and production ability are mainly dependent on the ability of the managers, the evaluation of financial and managerial ability, made for credit rating, would provide a very accurate estimate of the company as a supplier. If actual performance data on suppliers could be gathered from purchasing agents and if the credit rating of the supplier could be obtained from a credit reporting service (such as Dun and Bradstreet), a correlation analysis could be made. Such an analysis would show the reliability of the credit rating as an indicator of vendor performance. If reliability could be established, it would save many man-hours now spent in vendor surveys.[6]

---

[5]H. L. Payne, "Development of a Supplier Evaluation Technique Utilizing Financial Information," *Journal of Purchasing* 6, no. 4 (November 1970): 23.

[6]A. K. Stewart, "Vendor Rating and Credit Rating: A Comparison and Analysis," *Journal of Purchasing* 4, no. 3 (August 1968): 69.

Management evaluation

There is general agreement among purchasing executives that a supplier's management capability is a vital factor in source evaluation and selection. According to M. G. Edwards there is also general agreement that supplier management is considered most significant in high-risk, large dollar volume, and long-term situations. Few formal management evaluation systems exist and considerable work still needs to be done in this area. Three normal sources of information are: personal visits, financial reports, and credit reports. An interesting formal program is one initiated by the Boeing Company named the "Supplier Performance Evaluation and Rating System (SPEAR)."[7]

A brief description of this plan by their director of material follows:

> On major subcontracts we appoint a Source Selection Board which establishes the criteria and subcriteria which will be used in the evaluation, and determines the weight factors for the major elements of consideration.
>
> The supplier is requested to submit as part of his proposal a management plan covering: plan of management, organization of management, corporation structure and relationship, plan of assignment of personnel, and management controls. In addition to the proposal, a source selection survey is conducted which, among other things, evaluates the effectiveness of the supplier's management. As a result of discussions with supplier's management, the Boeing team completes a summary in which they are required to:
>
> 1. Discuss the company organization and staffing structures for the potential contract.
> 2. Evaluate planning and program control for the project, including its integration with present work.
> 3. Generally evaluate management, particularly the personnel to be assigned to the project, with emphasis on approach to and knowledge of the project, past performance, and other aspects pertinent to accomplishment of the contract.
>
> The results of the survey and the team summaries are used during the evaluation process.
>
> Also, management is one of the factors evaluated and rated regularly during the life of purchase orders of $25,000 or more. Each six months, and at the time of order completion, the buyer rates the supplier's management performance as excellent, good, fair, poor, or not acceptable.

The total SPEAR program is quite elaborate, with considerable emphasis placed on management and its ratings. One of the first steps is for the source selection board to establish the criteria to be used in the evaluation. Although this will vary from one procurement to another, the major elements which likely are to be considered are engineering, management, finance, material, manufacturing, quality, and reliability. Each of these six major elements will have appropriate subelements, and under management the five subelements are:

---

[7]M. G. Edwards, Supplier Management Evaluation," *Journal of Purchasing* 3, no. 1 (February 1967): 28–41.

1. Plan of management.
2. Organization of management.
3. Corporate structure and relationship.
4. Plan of assignment of personnel.
5. Management controls.

A typical management evaluation summary is shown in Table 6–2.

Table 6–2
Typical management evaluation summary*

Company	Plan of management	Organization of management	Corporate structure and relationship	Plan of assignment of personnel	Management controls	Total
	20	30	10	10	30	100
A	19	27	9	9	28	92
B	20	30	10	9	28	97
C	18	28	7	10	20	83
D	17	24	10	10	18	79
E	18	23	10	8	19	78
F	19	22	10	7	18	76

*In this particular supplier evaluation example, of the six elements included in the total evaluation, management was assigned a weight of 100 out of a total of 500 points.

Although this has been a rather brief explanation of the Boeing SPEAR system, it seems clear that its main points are:

1. A systematic check list of factors to be considered regarding each procurement and each supplier.
2. Flexibility to provide weights for each factor in accordance with its importance as decided by the source selection board.

Performance information is fed into a data processing system and periodic reports are prepared.

Some questions which may be raised with respect to management evaluation follow. Is the purchaser's viewpoint of management the same as a stockholder's or creditor's? Should management attitudes be measured? What weight should management be accorded in relation to other factors? Should the purchaser try to overcome a supplier's management deficiencies? There are no easy answers to these questions, and their resolution will depend to a large extent on the quality of purchasing personnel assigned to this task.

Many examples exist illustrating the need for supplier management strength. Many of these are those normally related to the long-term survival of the company. Small suppliers are frequently dependent on the health, age, and abilities of the owner-manager. Every time this individual steps into an automobile the fate of the company rides along. The attitudes of this individual to certain customers may be very important in supply assurance.

Most long-term and significant supplier-purchaser relationships are highly dependent on the relationships and communication channels built by the respective managers in each organization. Unless each side is willing and able to listen and react to information supplied by the other side, problems are not likely to be resolved to mutual satisfaction.

Some problems in source selection. One might think that after a vendor had been found who could meet all the requirements, the search would be over. Such is not the case. Shall the buyer, in buying a given item, rely upon a single supplier, or utilize several? Shall the buyer buy directly from manufacturers or through distributors? Shall the buyer confine orders to local sources? Consider minority groups and environmental and political concerns? What shall be done about the problem of commercial bribery in any one of its various forms? To understand the difficulties involved in making a final selection of source, it is necessary to consider some of these problems. In doing so, we shall assume that adequate investigation has been made of the vendor's financial standing, general reputation for fairness, and capacity to meet the requirements as to quality, quantity, and delivery, and that prices are not unreasonable.

Concentration of purchases with one source

Shall the buyer rely upon a single supplier, or utilize several? The answer to this question must be the very unsatisfactory one, "It all depends."

Briefly, the arguments for placing all orders for a given item with one supplier are as follows:

a. The supplier may be the exclusive owner of certain essential patents or processes and, therefore, be the only possible source. Under such circumstances the purchaser has no choice, provided that no satisfactory substitute item is available.

b. A given supplier may be so outstanding in the quality of product or in the service provided as to preclude serious consideration of buying elsewhere.

c. The order may be so small as to make it just not worthwhile, if only because of added clerical expense, to divide it.

d. Concentrating purchases may make possible certain discounts or lower freight rates that could not be had otherwise.

e. The supplier is more cooperative, more interested, and more willing to please having all the buyer's business. This argument, of course, loses much of its weight if even the total order amounts to but little or, although fairly large, represents but a very small proportion of the seller's total sales.

f. A special case arises when the purchase of an item involves a die, tool, mold charge, or costly set-up. The expense of duplicating this equipment or set-up is likely to be substantial. Under such circumstances, probably most buyers confine their business to the possessor of the die, tool, or mold.

g. When all orders are placed with one supplier, deliveries may be more easily scheduled.

h. The use of the stockless buying or systems contracting concept provides many advantages which are not possible to obtain unless business is concentrated with one or at best a very few suppliers.

On the other hand, there are strong arguments for diversification—provided, of course, that the sacrifice is not too great:

a. It is common practice among the majority of buyers to use more than one source, especially on the important items.
b. Knowing that competitors are getting some of the business tends to keep the supplier more alert to the need of giving good prices and service.
c. Assurance of supply is increased. Should fire, strikes, breakdowns, or accidents occur to any one supplier, deliveries can still be obtained from the others.
d. Even should floods, railway strikes, or other widespread occurrences develop which may affect all suppliers to some extent, the chances of securing at least a part of the goods are increased.
e. Some companies diversify their purchases because they do not want to become the sole support of one company, with the responsibility that such a position entails.
f. Assigning orders to several suppliers gives a company a greater degree of flexibility, because it can call on the unused capacity of all the suppliers instead of only one.

Numerous examples exist showing the advantages of one approach over another. A typical example favoring sole sourcing was as follows.

A very high-quality custom printer found that none of the company's ink suppliers could satisfactorily meet the exacting requirements of the unusual jobs the firm was called on to perform. A special arrangement with one supplier which involved extensive research and development resulted in a satisfactory, but expensive, product. Since the printer was in a position to pass ink costs to its customers who were more interested in quality and delivery than price, the printer found working with this one source advantageous in several ways. To protect against shortages, strikes, and other interference, the supplier agreed to maintain a special inventory in both the supplier's and customer's plant. When market shortages developed, the supplier put all customers except this printer on quotas.

A typical example favoring multiple sourcing was the purchaser of recreational equipment. One supplier, a sole source for a large segment of equipment, was strongly favored by engineering and production and had provided excellent service over the years. However, prices had increased substantially despite large volume increases. Only when a second source was brought in by the purchasing agent, over strong initial engineering and production objections, did the first supplier become concerned over price performance. Both suppliers performed well and competed strongly with the result that savings over the following five years ran into millions of dollars.

Genuine concern exists among purchasing executives as to how much business should be placed with one supplier, particularly if the supplier is small. It is feared that sudden discontinuance of purchases may put the supplier's survival in jeopardy, and, yet, the purchaser does not wish to reduce flexibility by being tied to dependent sources. One simple rule of thumb is that no more than a certain percentage, say 20 or 30 percent, of the total supplier's business should be with one customer.

If a decision is made to divide an order among several vendors, there is then the question of the basis on which the division is to be made. The actual practice varies widely. One method is to divide the business equally. Another is to place the larger share with a favored supplier and give the rest to one or more alternates. In the chemical industry as in several others it is common practice to place business with various vendors on a percentage of total requirements basis. Total requirements may be estimated, not necessarily guaranteed, and there may not even be a minimum volume requirement. Each supplier knows what their own percentage of the business amounts to, but may not be aware who the competition is or how much business each competitor receives if the number of sources exceeds two. There is, and can be, no common practice or "best" method or procedure.

● Purchase through manufacturer or distributor

The question sometimes arises whether to purchase from a manufacturer directly or from some middleman. Occasionally, pressure is brought to bear, by various types of trade associations particularly, to induce the purchaser to patronize the wholesaler, jobber, or mill supply house. The real issue involved here is closely related to buying from local sources. The question is not primarily one of proximity to the user's plant but rather one of buying channels.

The purchaser for a candy manufacturing company had been buying transparent gelatin paper from a wholesale distributor. This distributor had up to that time been able to render the better service, with the price practically identical. It appeared likely, however, that there might be a shortage in the supply of this item and also that the manufacturer might undertake direct distribution. In the event of a shortage, the buyer felt that those who bought directly from the manufacturer would probably receive preference on their orders. His belief that this situation might develop was so pronounced that he abandoned the use of the wholesale distributor and purchased directly from the manufacturer.

Another example may be cited to illustrate an opposite decision. An insurance company decided to purchase loose-leaf binders from a wholesale distributor and, when urged by the manufacturer to purchase directly at a lower price, refused to do so. The basis for this action was that the manufacturer had neglected to notify the wholesale distributor of his intention to canvass the latter's customers directly, and the purchasing director thought this was unethical.

Another company made addressing machines. The buyer acquired glue directly from a manufacturer, even though the local wholesaler could make more prompt delivery and quoted the same price. The reason was that the wholesaler occasionally followed the very unwise policy of substituting glue inferior in quality to that demanded by the buyer's specifications. Since appearance did not indicate quality, this substitution was rather easy to effect. Although brands were usually marked on the barrels, occasionally they were indistinct; and if the supplier wished to deceive, he could alter the brand markings. The purchaser felt that refusal to give further orders for glue to the wholesaler would be a warning to guard against substitutions on other products which he continued to purchase.

The justification for independent middlemen is found in the services which they render. If wholesalers are carrying the products of various manufacturers and spreading marketing costs over a variety of items, they may be able to lay down the product at the buyer's plant at a lower cost, particularly when the unit of sale is small and customers are widely scattered or when the demand is irregular. Furthermore, they may carry a stock of goods greater than a manufacturer could afford to carry in its own branch warehouse and therefore be in a better position to make prompt deliveries and to fill emergency orders. Again, they may be able to buy in carload lots, with a saving in transportation charges, and a consequent lower cost to the buyer.

Local sentiment may be strongly in favor of a certain jobber. Public agencies are particularly susceptible to such influence. Generally, concerns that sell through jobbers tend, as a matter of policy, to buy whenever possible through jobbers.

On the other hand, some large organizations often seek ways of going around the supply house, particularly where the buyers' requirements of supply items are large, where the shipments are made directly from the original manufacturer instead of from the middleman's stock, and where no selling effort or service is rendered by the wholesaler. Some manufacturers operate their own supply houses to get the large discount. Others have attempted to persuade the original manufacturers to establish quantity discounts—a practice not unlike that in the steel trade.

Still others have sought to develop sources among small manufacturers not having a widespread distributive organization. Some attempts have been made to secure a special service from a chosen middleman, such as an agreement whereby the latter would add to his staff "two people exclusively for the purpose of locating and expediting nuisance items in other lines."

Geographical location of sources

Shall purchases be confined as largely as possible to local sources, or shall geographical location be largely disregarded? Seventy-five percent of buyers *prefer* to buy from local sources, and a substantial percentage of these indicate that they are willing to pay more or accept less satisfactory quality or service to do so. This is particularly true of the larger companies.

This policy rests on two bases. The first is that a local source can frequently offer more dependable service than one located at a distance. For example, deliveries may be more prompt both because the distance is shorter and because the dangers of interruption in transportation service are reduced. Knowledge of the buyer's peculiar requirements, as well as of the seller's special qualifications, may be based on an intimacy of knowledge not possessed by others. There may be greater flexibility in meeting the purchaser's requirements; and local suppliers may be just as well equipped as to facilities, know-how, and financial strength as any of those located at more distant points. Thus, there may well be sound economic reasons for preferring a local source to a more distant one.

A second basis for selecting local sources rests on equally sound, although somewhat less tangible, grounds. The organization owes much to the local community. The facility is located there, from it is drawn the bulk of the employees, and often a substantial part of its financial support, as well as a notable part of its sales, is local in character. The local community provides the company's personnel with their houses, schools, churches, and social life. To recognize these facts is good public relations, which have financial as well as social value. Therefore, if a local source of supply can be found that can render a buyer as good a value as can be located elsewhere, it should be supported.

This policy has two complicating elements. One is that the purchasing agent's primary responsibility is to buy well. Emotion should rarely supplant good business judgment, for to do so, in the long run, is to render the local community a poor service indeed. A second complication arises through the difficulty of defining "local." Technological changes have affected not only the size and distribution of the centers of population but also the commercial and business structure, resulting, among other things, in a widening of market areas and hence the sources from which supplies can be obtained. These boundaries are constantly expanding. Sellers can now profitably cover a much wider area than they once could. With radio and television, increased national advertising, and wider newspaper coverage, "local promotion" has taken on a new meaning. Improved packaging, improved roads, and speedier delivery by truck and plane have had a similar effect. Therefore, what once might properly have been called "local" has, for many areas and many items become state or federal. There is no easy rule by which a buyer can decide the economic boundaries of the local community.

Despite the validity of the arguments for giving preference to local sources, it would be folly to carry them too far. The wisdom of stimulating healthy competition, the assurance which comes from having a diversity of sources, actual inefficiency of local sources—these and many other reasons lead purchasing officers to seek a proper balance with reference to the geographical location of suppliers. No vendors should expect to get orders merely because they represent local firms. Mr. W. G. Morse, formerly purchasing agent for Harvard University, has said, "I am asked to buy because the dealer is a Harvard graduate; because at some time or other he made gifts to Harvard; because it is his policy to employ Harvard men; because he happened to pay rent to Harvard; and because Harvard is in Cambridge." No reliable vendor is likely to seek business on such grounds as these.

Reciprocity ✒●

Under what circumstances, if at all, shall reciprocity be practiced? A workable, though none too exact, definition of reciprocity is as follows: "Reciprocity is the practice of giving preference in buying to those vendors who are customers of the buying company as opposed to vendors who do not buy from the company." This broad statement, however, is scarcely the form in which the problem arises. Much fruitless criticism has been advanced on the part of those who apparently do not fully realize that so far as purchasing departments, at least, are concerned, reciprocity is not a debatable policy to the extent that it involves purchasing requirements under conditions which will result in higher prices or inferior service. Purchasing directors do debate the issue as to how far it can be practiced, *assuming that conditions of price, service and quality are substantially the same.*

The use of reciprocity as a basis for obtaining sales is a practice of long standing, the essential soundness of which has been argued pro and con at great length. It is probable that the policy originated simply from a desire to increase goodwill. Quality, service, and price being equal, it was natural for a company to distribute some of its orders for materials and supplies among its better customers as a friendly gesture of appreciation, realizing that at no added cost to itself it might strengthen good relations already existing. Many refuse to practice it, even to this extent, because they are not satisfied that in the long run it is essentially sound. Others do not feel the need of it, as, for instance, those who do a large amount of special order business, have an outstanding reputation for service, or sell a product widely recognized as superior. However, many companies have come to use it as a basis for soliciting and even for demanding orders. Thus, a definite issue on policy has developed. Should sales depend solely on the ability of the sales force to obtain orders without any assistance from the purchasing department, or should the purchasing power of the company be used as a means to increase the sales volume and presumably the net profits of the company even at some added cost or sacrifice at other points?

Reciprocity is not either a purchasing or a sales problem; it is a management problem—and management can build an excellent case for reciprocity. Thus, there are cases—real or fancied—in which a company is, to all intents and purposes, forced to practice reciprocity to survive.

The case against any general use of reciprocity rests on the belief that the practice is at variance with the sound principles of either buying or selling. The sale of a product must be based on the qualities of the product sold and of the service attending the transaction. There is only one permanent basis for a continuing customer-supplier relationship: the conviction on the part of the buyer that the product of a particular seller is the one best adapted to his need and is the best all-around value available. As long as the sales department concentrates its attention on this appeal, it will find and retain permanent customers.

Few purchasing officers would object to reciprocal buying on the basis that quality, service, and price must be equal. In practice, abuse is practically certain to creep in. For instance, buyers are urged to buy from X not because X is a customer but because X is Y's customer and Y is our customer, and Y wants to sell to X.

The normal expectation of a seller using reciprocity as an argument is that the purchaser is willing to grant price, quality, or delivery concessions. In North America reciprocity is on shaky legal grounds and the Supreme Court has upheld the Clayton Act under Section 7 that reciprocity may be restrictive to trade and create unfair competition.[8]

Attitude toward gratuities [4][9]

How shall the purchasing manager deal with the problem of excessive entertainment and gifts in any one of their varied and subtle forms? Here is a practice that seeks, through gifts, entertainment, and even open bribery, to influence the decision of persons responsible for making a choice between suppliers.

There can be no justification for accepting such gratuities. Fortunately, the purchasing manager today is not open to any general criticism on this basis. Sometimes buyers have been permitted to benefit from a speculative stock or commodity account (carried by the seller of supplies for the buyer) giving the buyer margin facilities which he or she would not otherwise have been entitled to receive; in some cases the buyer has even been allowed to trade and reap the benefit of all the profits, while all losses have fallen on the party sponsoring the account.

Such attempts to influence decisions unfairly are directed not only toward purchasing personnel. Work managers, foremen, and others in production or engineering who are directly responsible for or largely influence decisions regarding types of materials to be procured are also approached. In such cases, even though the purchasing officer is not directly influenced, the buyers' task is affected. So serious do some companies consider this whole problem that they forbid any employee of the company to receive any gift, no matter how trivial, from any supplier, actual or potential.

It is, of course, difficult always to distinguish between legitimate expenditures by suppliers in the interest of goodwill, and illegitimate expenditures made in an attempt to place the buyer under some obligation to the vendor. In these borderline cases, only ordinary common sense can provide the answer.

The National Association of Purchasing Management (NAPM) and the Purchasing Management Association of Canada (PMAC) in their codes of ethics strongly condemn gratuities. It is true, however, that every year a small number of cases are uncovered of individuals who do not abide by this code, thereby placing the whole profession under suspicion. Part of the blame must clearly lie with those who use illegal enticements to secure business. For example, a salesperson calls on a purchaser and invites him or her out to lunch so they may

---

[8]The case is *FTC* v. *Consolidated Foods* (1965) 380 U.S. 592.

discuss a transaction without losing time or as a matter of courtesy. Such action is presumed to be in the interests of goodwill, although the cost of the lunch must be added to the selling price. An attractive but inexpensive gift may be given by the vendor's company to adorn the desk of the procurement officer. The vendor's name appears on the gift, and therefore it is construed as advertising. The sales representative may send a box if cigars, bottle, or sporting event tickets after a deal has been completed, merely as an expression of personal appreciation, paying for them personally.

It is but a step from this type of effort to entertaining a prospective buyer at a dinner, followed perhaps by a theater party. The custom of giving simple gifts may develop into the granting of much larger ones. It is because of the difficulty of drawing the line between these different situations and because of an appreciation of the desire to keep the buyer wholly without any sense of obligation toward a possible vendor that some companies, as has been indicated, refuse to permit their employees to accept gifts of any sort. The purchasing manager not infrequently refuses to allow sales personnel to pay for luncheon or at least insists upon paying for as many luncheons as do prospective sellers. These situations are referred to because of the difficulty, and yet the necessity, of drawing some practical line between bribery, on the one hand, and the legitimate development of goodwill, on the other.

Aside from its economic aspects, the practice of commercial bribery is involved in many legal cases. Fundamentally, the rulings on commercial bribery rest on the doctrine of agency. Any breach of faith on the part of the agent, who has always been recognized by law as keeping a fiduciary position, is not permitted; therefore, the agent's acceptance of a bribe to do anything in conflict with the interests of its principal is not permitted by law.

The evils of commercial bribery are more far-reaching than would at first appear. Although originating with only one concern, bribery is rapidly likely to become a practice of the entire industry. A producer, no matter how superior the quality of its goods or how low its price, is likely to find it extremely difficult to sell in competition with concerns practicing bribery. The prices paid by the buyer who accepts bribes are almost certain to be higher—in some cases, two or three times as much as they would be under other circumstances. Defects in workmanship or quality are likely to be smoothed over by the buyer who accepts bribes hidden from his or her employer. Materials may be deliberately damaged or destroyed to make products of some manufacturers who do not offer bribes appear unsatisfactory. There is no occasion for going further into an analysis of this practice. It takes many forms, but regardless of the guise in which it appears, there is nothing to be said for it.

Even though bribery is outlawed in North America, it may flourish in other parts of the world, legally or not. The spectacular revelations about the bribed sales of U.S. aircraft to other countries during the mid 70s were a sad reminder of the pervasiveness of such practices in our world.

There is a noticeable trend away from Christmas bottles, fishing trips, sporting event tickets, and other enticements that used to be common. Hopefully, this trend will continue, and, perhaps, this will be a small side benefit of recent sellers' markets.

Joint purchasing with supplier *

Sometimes a purchasing department becomes involved with buying certain items for suppliers, believing it can purchase more efficiently than they. Since the suppliers would realize substantial savings, some of these might be passed along to the purchaser. Although the purchasing department will incur some additional expense, there would be a net gain to both parties in the transaction. The close relationship that would exist between the suppliers and purchasers, furthermore, would enable purchasers to know more about the production costs of those companies and to ascertain whether or not it was paying a fair price for the products. The purchaser would, moreover, be sure of the quality of the materials used and would increase buying power. With a reduction in the number of buyers in the market of the raw materials, there would be less false activity and thus greater price stability. This last reason is rather important. Not infrequently, when a large company requests bids from individual suppliers, they in turn enter the material markets to make inquiries about prices and quantities available. If six suppliers are bidding on an offer, their preliminary inquiries for material required to fill the prospective order will be multiplied six times.

Purchasing for company personnel * ●

Still another problem faced by most purchasing departments is that of the extent to which it is justified in using its facilities to obtain merchandise for employees of the company or for its executives at better terms than they could individually obtain through their own efforts. Many companies not only sell their own merchandise to their employees at a substantial discount and also allow them to buy at cost any of the merchandise bought by the company for its own use but go even further and make it possible for employees to obtain merchandise which the company itself neither makes nor uses.

There are many reasons why a company should pursue a policy of employee purchasing. Under certain circumstances, of course, it is imperative that a company make some provision for supplying its employees with at least the necessities of life, a condition particularly true in mining and lumbering towns. A policy of employee purchasing, it is also argued, provides the means for increasing real wages at little or no cost to the company. It may increase the loyalty of the employees to the organization and thus form a part of the general company policy with reference to old-age pensions, thrift plans, and so on. Many times, employees feel they are entitled to any considerations or advantages the company can obtain for them. Furthermore, whatever the procurement manager may think about the general practice, it is often somewhat difficult to refuse a request from a top executive to "see what can be done about a discount."

Many companies, on the other hand, have steadfastly refused to adopt such a policy. If used as a wage expedient, there is some additional expense connected with it. Employees prefer cash if increases in wages are called for. Such a wage policy may be inequitable, because only those in a position to take advantage of the discounts realize the wage increases. Even for those who do buy through the company, there is some question of just how much prices are really reduced compared with the prices of the chain store, the supermarket, the discount store, and other low-cost distributive outlets. Some ill will toward the company may be aroused, since the ordinary retailer is likely to feel that the manufacturer is entering into direct competition or at least is bringing pressure to grant discounts to the manufacturer's employees.

Unfortunately, few people realize how difficult it is for a purchasing department to handle numerous small requests of a personal nature. It is a time-consuming and unrewarding task, since a complete market search is almost impossible, and any quality, price, or service troubles arising from the purchase are always brought back to those involved.

Social, political, and environmental concerns

Recognition has come, rather belatedly, that certain noneconomic factors may have a significant bearing on procurement sourcing decisions. These fall into the social, political, and environmental areas.

Social. Most organizations recognize that the carrying on of its existence may affect the social concerns of society. It is possible to address some social problems through purchasing policy and actions. For example, it is possible to purchase from agencies employing addicts and the physically and mentally handicapped certain items or services which assist in the employment of these people. It is possible to purchase from suppliers located in low-income or certain geographical areas of high unemployment. The U.S. Federal Government has tried in a variety of ways to encourage purchasing from minority suppliers. [See also the Detroit Edison case at the end of this chapter.] Most larger organizations recognize the problems and opportunities present through the exercise of purchasing power in the social area. It is not easy for a hard-nosed purchasing manager, used to standard, low-risk, reputable sources, and extensive competition, to consider dealing with the high-risk sources often represented by this class. Most purchasing managers agree that the "deal" must make good business sense and that an arrangement based on charity will sooner or later collapse. Without purchasing initiative to seek out those suppliers who might have reasonable potential, it is unlikely that much can or will be accomplished. Too many of the potential sources are small, have few resources, and low marketing skills. Recognition of supplier weaknesses and the willingness to be of assistance are, therefore, necessary ingredients. Normally, sources like these will be local allowing for personal contact, watchfulness, and support through the development stage.

Political. The basic question in the political area is: should the acquisition area be seen as a means of furthering political objectives? Public agencies have long been under pressure of this sort. "Buy local" is a common requirement for city and state purchasing officials. "Buy American" is a normal corollary requirement. The recent attempt by the Canadian Government to direct the department of supply and services to spread purchases across the country, approximately in line with population distribution is another example. For military purposes the U.S. Federal Government has a long-standing tradition of support and development of a national supply base to afford protection in the case of conflict.

The question always arises as to how much of a premium should be paid to conform with political directives. Should a city purchasing agent buy buses from the local manufacturer at a 12 percent premium over those obtainable from another state or other country?

For private industry political questions are also present. Should the corporation support the political and economic aims of the governing body? In the construction industry there has often been a form of patronage. The contract is awarded on the basis of specified subcontractors who might otherwise not have received the business. Governments have little hesitation on large business deals to specify that a minimum percentage should have domestic content. In the aerospace industry, for example, foreign plane orders are often contingent on the ability to arrange for suitable subcontracting in the customer's home country. It is interesting that governments have no fear to tread where private industry is forbidden to walk. Multinationals often find themselves caught in countries with different political views. American companies for many years had not been allowed to trade with China and Cuba. American subsidiaries in other countries face strong national pressure to export to Cuba or the USSR the same products that the American parent is not allowed to sell from American soil. The same holds for purchasing from countries with whom trade is not encouraged by the government. American subsidiaries frequently find themselves caught between the desire of the local government to encourage local purchases and the U.S. Government which encourages exports from the parent or the parent's suppliers. The growing role of government in all business affairs is likely to increase difficulties of this kind in the future. Their resolution is far from easy and will require a great deal of tact, understanding, and freedom to make decisions in which the political consideration may be an overriding factor.

Environmental. Although environmental concerns are not new to our society, genuine purchasing concern as a potential area of influence is. The first problem is: should our organization purchase materials, products, or equipment which may directly or indirectly increase environmental concerns? Should the purchasing group raise the environmental question when others in the organization fail to do so?

The second problem is: Should we purchase from sources, domestic or international, that we know are not following sound environmental practices? These are not easy questions answered glibly out of context. It is possible to evade the issue by putting government in the control seat, saying, "as long as government allows it, it must be all right." A practical purchasing consideration is that government may shut down a polluting supplier with little notice, endangering supply assurance. The report of the Club of Rome reinforces the potential dangers of pollution to our world and the real question in the environmental, as in the political and social areas is: what stand should our organization take on this issue?

Before a purchaser can make a final vendor choice, a decision on all the important questions of policy just discussed must be reached: whether to patronize a single or several sources of supply; whether to buy directly from the manufacturer or through a distributor; whether to buy wholly from local sources; to what extent, if at all, to practice reciprocity; what weight to give social, political, and environmental concerns; and how to deal with the problem of commercial bribery. Having formulated a policy with reference to these matters the basis has been laid for settling the specific issues as they arise later on. Most purchasing managers are compelled sooner or later to take a position on these issues and, having done so, have gone a long way toward selecting their sources.

SUPPLIER DEVELOPMENT[9]

Supplier selection is an important procurement task. Supplier development implies a degree of executive involvement not normally encountered in supplier selection. For example, it frequently places a purchasing manager in a position where a prospective supplier must be persuaded to accept an order.

The need for supplier development

That purchasing executives need to find new sources of supply and to develop such sources when there are none available is a topic that has been discussed for many years. The classicial point of view about this need for supplier development has been well expressed by S. F. Heinritz and J. Farrell in *Purchasing*. They state:

> Products or parts that have not previously been made, intricacies of special design, unusual requirements in the specification or difficult conditions and use, and the utilization of unfamiliar materials for which there is little precedent in treatment and fabrication are some of the factors that may lead to a situation for which no established supply source stands ready to hand. Or from the standpoint of practical procurement, the only available sources may be too distant, prices may be exorbitant or out of line with budgeted costs for the product, production capacity may already be fully occupied so that no new customers may be accommodated, or the potential suppliers may simply be unwilling or uninterested in additional business.
>
> Under any of these circumstances, the buyer's responsibility is not to select, but to create a satisfactory source.[10]

This point of view may be summarized as stating that the development of new sources of supply may be forced on the purchaser by circumstances beyond direct

---

[9]M. R. Leenders, *Improving Purchasing Effectiveness through Supplier Development* (Boston, Harvard University, 1965).

[10]S. F. Heinritz and P. J. Farrell, *Purchasing*, 5th ed. (Englewood Cliffs, N.J.: Prentice-Hall, Inc., 1971), p. 236.

control. The purchaser does not initiate supplier development as an appropriate technique or tool; it is the only alternative other than making the part himself.

Our definition of supplier development takes a broader point of view. It defines the need for developing new suppliers as follows: the purchaser is aware that benefits will accrue to both the supplier and the purchaser, benefits of which the supplier may not be aware. These benefits may be limited to the particular order at hand, or they may include more far-reaching results, such as technical, financial, and management assistance; future business from the same purchaser as well as from others; training through learning about new manufacturing processes, skills, or quality levels; reduction of marketing effort; use of long-term forecasts permitting smoother manufacturing levels and a minimum of inventory; and so on.

It is true that this wider view includes all the factors for supplier development advanced by Heinritz and Farrell. In contrast with the view that this is the last resort of the purchasing executive, however, the broader definition allows for opportunities inherent in the method itself to give it greater scope.

It is the aggressiveness and initiative by the purchaser that makes the difference (see Figure 6–4). In the normal market context the purchaser responds to marketing efforts. In supplier development, the purchaser, not the marketer, has the initiative and may quote prices, terms, and conditions as part of the aggressive role. Numerous examples show that high pay-offs are possible from this purchasing initiative and that suppliers of all sizes may be approached in this fashion.

A further reason for supplier development not advanced by Heinritz and Farrell is that there are bound to be deficiencies in the normal industrial marketing-purchasing process in which the marketer traditionally takes the initiative. Numerous examples of such deficiencies exist. Even when a supplier and a purchaser have entered into a regular vendor-vendee relationship, often neither party is fully aware of all the opportunities for additional business which may exist between them. This might arise because of salesperson and buyer specialization, a lack of aggressiveness by the salesperson, or a lack of inquisitiveness by the purchaser.

FIGURE 6–4
Supplier development initiative with the purchaser
THE MARKETING CONTEXT

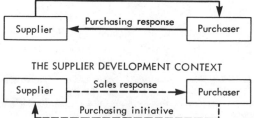

If gaps are evident even where an established vendor-vendee relationship exists, there must be even greater shortcomings where no such relationship has yet been established. For example, a company may be unable to cover its full market because of geography, limited advertising, or lack of coverage by its sales force, distributors, or agents. Most companies have lines of products which receive more management attention and sales push than other products also made by the same company. It is always difficult to keep entirely up to date. A time lag may exist between the time of product introduction and the time the purchaser finds out about it. By filling these gaps through his own intiative, the purchaser effectively strengthens this whole process.

One of the most important arguments in favor of supplier development not yet mentioned arises from future considerations. If the procurement role is envisaged as encompassing not only the need to fill current requirements but also the need to prepare for the future, supplier development can be valuable in assuring future sources of supply.

There are at least two outside forces which would suggest the increasing necessity for purchaser involvement in the creation of future sources of supply. One of these forces is technological. The increasing rate of development of new products, materials, and processes through research will tend to make the industrial marketing task even more complex and more open to shortcomings. In addition to this, the stepping up of international trade will tend to widen supplier horizons and may create a need for purchaser aggressiveness in the development of foreign sources of supply. One of the most demanding and important tasks of management of a subsidiary in an underdeveloped country is the problem of supplier development.[11]

The supplier development decision

The nature of supplier development is such by definition that the responsibility for the decision of whether to engage in this development rests with the appropriate executives of the vendee company. This decision should be made on the basis of conscious analysis. Actual field research indicated, however, that this decision is seldom consciously made by the buyer. Apparently most source development decisions are still the result of a negative rather than a positive approach. "It is the only alternative left open to us" seems to be the general attitude. Recent market shortages, however, have reawakened purchasing's interest in aggressive acquisition.

Ideally, the choice of whether or not to engage in supplier development should be based on a sound analysis of the alternatives available. Were this the case, it would seem that far more frequent use of supplier development could be made. The examples near the end of this study show the successful use of supplier development by several purchasing executives in other than "avenue of last re-

---

[11]C. W. Skinner, *Production Management of U.S. Manufacturing Subsidiaries in Turkey*. Published doctoral dissertation, Harvard Business School, 1961.

sort'' situations. The analysis of the alternatives should be made on a basis similar to an investment or a make-or-buy decision. The problem is to select the alternative giving the best return for the investment in time, money, and effort involved.

When viewed in this way the supplier development decision involves the evaluation of many opportunity costs. The effort expended in developing one new source might have been used to develop another source, to encourage manufacture in the purchaser's own plant, or to sharpen internal control within the purchasing department. The decision not to engage in supplier development, so often made without full appreciation of its possibilities, presumes that another alternative will be in the end bring better over-all results.

Foreign sources of supply ✿

Until comparatively recent times, industrial buyers have sought sources of supply outside of the United States only when the products needed were not readily available domestically. Since the close of World War II, many different events and forces have set in motion developments aimed at expanding world trade. In the efforts to build the economies of Western Europe and Japan after the war's massive destruction, international agreements included provisions for encouraging trade between the free nations. U.S. government leaders played a major role in working for the reduction of tariffs and other commercial restrictions among the countries of the free world.

Many American companies became multinational in capitalizing on their technical know-how in foreign markets. Licensing agreements, joint ventures, acquisitions, and mergers led many companies into worldwide operations.

Competitive pressures stimulated many executives of American companies to seek new and lower cost sources of supply in order to protect or increase profit margins. Many foreign manufacturers had modern plants built after the end of the war, and foreign labor rates were substantially lower.

While problems of communication, language, differences in cultural background, and the metric system of measurement create some difficulties, the benefits to be obtained frequently compensate for the difficulties.

Large companies with ownership interests in foreign companies have frequently found it desirable to establish a purchasing office in a foreign country. Other companies have worked through the purchasing departments of their foreign subsidiaries.

Small American companies have been able to obtain most of the benefits of buying from foreign sources of supply by using the services of importers, trading companies, or the agents representing foreign manufacturers.

There are a number of significant obstacles and constraints to international trade. The different languages, customs, red tape, long lead times, and transportation modes as well as the uncertainties of the international monetary market are real difficulties for the novice. P. Combs[12] advises a two-step approach. First,

---

[12] P. H. Combs, *Handbook of International Purchasing* (Boston: Cahners, 1971.)

use an importer to get started and to answer questions of quality, availability, corporate acceptance, etc. Then, subsequently, deal directly with foreign sources.

As of 1974, worldwide inflation, the devaluation of the U.S. dollar, greatly increased foreign labor rates, and rapid changes in foreign exchange rates have reduced some of the advantages of buying in worldwide markets.

Foreign trade zones

Foreign trade zones provide an interesting opportunity for channeling foreign trade.

How foreign-trade zones function

Geographically, a foreign-trade zone is located in a designated area(s) or its port of entry (see Figure 6–5). Each zone differs in character depending upon the functions performed in serving the pattern of trade peculiar to that trading area. The major functions which may be conducted within a zone are:

1. Transshipment. Goods may be stored, repackaged, assembled or otherwise manipulated while waiting shipment to another port, without the payment of duty or posting a bond.

2. Storage. Part or all of the goods may be stored at a zone indefinitely. This is especially important for goods being held for new import quotas or until demand and price increase.

3. Manipulation. Imported goods may be manipulated, or combined with domestic goods, and then either imported or reexported. Duty is paid only on imported merchandise.

4. Refunding of Duties, Taxes, and Drawbacks. When imported merchandise that has passed through customs is returned to the zone, the owner immediately may obtain a 99 percent drawback of duties paid.[13] Likewise, when products are transferred from bonded warehouses to foreign-trade zones, the bond is cancelled and all obligations in regard to duty payment and time limitations are terminated. Also, exporters of domestic goods subject to internal revenue taxes receive a tax refund as soon as such products move into a foreign-trade zone.

5. Exhibition and Display. Users of a zone may exhibit and display their wares to customers without bond or duty payments. They can quote firm prices (since they can determine definite duty and tax rates in advance) and provide immediate delivery. Duty and taxes are applicable only to those goods that enter customs territory.

6. Manufacturing. Manufacturing involving foreign goods can be carried on in the zone area. Foreign goods can be mixed with domestic goods and, when imported, duties are payable only on that part of the product consisting of foreign

---

[13] Under the drawback arrangement, exporters may apply for a refund of 99 percent of the duty paid on imported material used in the manufacture of exported products.

Figure 6–5
How foreign-trade zones work

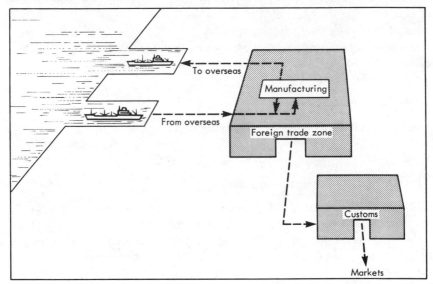

goods. This activity, made possible by the 1950 amendment to the original Celler Act, offers an excellent opportunity for use of foreign-trade zones.

If the purchasing executive has large overseas suppliers or is contemplating importing substantial amounts of dutiable products, savings can be realized on duties or drawbacks, and on the cost of shipping both imported materials to plants in the hinterland and manufactured products back to the same port for export.[14]

The functions actually performed in any zone, in the last analysis depend upon the inherent nature of the trading and commercial community and demands made by users of zone facilities.

Foreign-trade zones compared with bonded warehouses

The purpose of bonded warehousing is to exempt the importer from paying duty on foreign commerce that will be reexported. The bonded warehouse allows for delay of the payment of duties until the owner moves the merchandise into the host country. Goods can be stored for three years.[15] At the end of the period, if duty has not been paid, the government sells the goods at public auction.

---

[14]William A. Dymsza, *Small Business Opportunities in Foreign-Trade Zones and International Business,* Small Business Administration Management Research Summary (Washington: U.S. Government Printing Office, 1964), p. 2.

[15]Extensions may be granted upon application.

All merchandise exported from bonded warehouses must be shipped in the original package unless special permission has been received from the collector of customs. Any manufacturing must be conducted under strict supervision and the resulting items must be reexported.

Zones in the U.S.A. include Cleveland, New York, Kansas City, New Orleans, San Francisco, Seattle, and Toledo.

Sourcing in the multinational company

The multinational company is automatically involved in worldwide procurement through the location of its various subsidiaries. It is practically impossibile to supply every subsidiary need through the parent company. A relevant problem, then, becomes what should be purchased where and for whom. That many multinationals still fail to recognize the problems and opportunities of operating in worldwide markets is evident from a number of writers. R. G. Acknoff said:

> . . . it is not uncommon for firms to assume, even implicitly, that there will always be enough raw material and other required supplies at an acceptable price. Sometimes this leads to lack of anticipation of major changes in the "supply picture." . . .
>
> In short, a firm should have some understanding of the markets in which it operates as a consumer. Perception of impending changes in these markets and its suppliers' activities can indicate either the need for research and development, acquisition of sources of supply, redesign of old products, or design of new ones."[16]

D.H. Farmer adds:

> That an increasing number of constraints are affecting the scope of action of the multinational company in this area; if they are to be mitigated, careful planning of sourcing decisions will be required.
>
> An illustration of the constraints upon multinational companies relates to the increasing intervention of governments in the business patterns of their countries. Transfer of funds and "arms length" pricing are two of the areas where governmental attention has been directed. Now as more governments face up to economic and socio-political pressures, the scope of their search for greater inputs increases.
>
> This is particularly true in the developing countries and soft currency areas where there is competition to attract larger contributions from the multinational companies. In looking for this larger share, an obvious area of considerable significance is the supply market of the multinational company. On the average in a manufacturing company, over 50 percent of the gross money received by the concern is disposed of in purchasing raw materials and components. Clearly, by directing a flow of business of that extent into their own economy a government could make a worthwhile contribution to its gross national product and to the prosperity of its people.
>
> The traditional method of "encouraging" such action was to manipulate tariffs

---

[16]Russell L. Ackoff, *A Concept of Corporate Planning* (New York: Wiley-Interscience, 1970), pp. 48–49.

to make importing unattractive. While not abandoning this ploy, many governments now are taking a more positive line; they are soliciting reciprocal business. In effect they are saying to the multinationals, "If you wish to sell a large volume of goods in this country, then you must manufacture here and purchase components or materials from our national sources."

Where suitable sources do not exist, governments appear to be setting out to persuade the international companies to develop local sources. And where that is not feasible, they encourage the current source of supply of major items to set up a factory in the country.

In Eastern Block countries the previous preparedness to exchange things like fresh fruit for manufactured goods is now being superceded by requests to make purchases equal to the sales in the area concerned. One European coordinator of procurement for a multinational company told the writer that once sales equal to 1 million per annum were achieved the pressure for reciprocal business increased.

One author has suggested that "these new efforts (pressures from governments) tend to influence the initiative that the international manufacturer can take to plan and control the availability and the flows of his nonmonetary (as well as financial) resources."* Developments since then have heightened these pressures, particularly in certain countries. For example, supplies executives in seven multinational companies recently have reported to this author approaches from the Spanish government regarding their requirements of reciprocal business.[17]

Supply market differences

It is a common marketing concept that marketing approaches be planned to suit the various market segments, while maintaining an integrity with the overall marketing plan. International procurement needs to be approached in much the same way, in full recognition of the differences between various markets, particularly their opportunities and constraints. David Farmer prepared an interesting table listing the constraints under the headings of internal, economic, sociological, market size, political and legal. (See Figure 6–6.)

The opportunities stem from differences in price, availability, and the various cost components of any material or product, as well as different levels of constraint. Theoretically, a multinational company should be in a much better position than a national organization to purchase intelligently on the international market. It is surprising how few multinationals use local contacts as information about local opportunities.

The idea of bringing together those who head purchasing operations in subsidiaries is still relatively new. Even where such corporate conferences have been held, they've often tended to focus on communicating the parent's will rather than the subsidiary's input.

An interesting development arose at one such conference for a multinational company with at least one common raw material used extensively throughout the

    *Robert E. McGarrah, "Logistics for the International Manufacturer," *Harvard Business Review* 44 (March–April 1966): 154.

    [17]D. H. Farmer, "Source Decision-Making in the Multi-National Company Environment," *Journal of Purchasing* 8, no. 1 (February 1972): 6.

world. This material was supplied by another large multinational firm at substantially different prices in different world markets. It was agreed to purchase the total corporate requirements in the most favorable market. Clearly, these requirements were far too large for that market, so that extensive negotiations were started in both multinationals in an attempt to resolve their differences. Developments like this might well lead to different pricing behavior. David Farmer quotes four interviews with supplier executives showing that increased interest is being shown in the opportunities of international markets by multinationals and how they approach the coordination task.

Figure 6–6
Constraints affecting the multinational company supply market complex

Internal	Sociological	Political
Make or buy	Attitudes toward authority	National defense and military policies
Effectiveness of communications and interrelationships	Attitudes to status of delivery/quality specifications	National foreign policies
Creativity and general effectiveness of procurement staff	Attitudes to work and wealth	Union strengths
Forecasting and planning effectiveness	Attitudes toward inter-company cooperation (buyer-seller)	Political stability
Finance	Religious and ethical beliefs	Government intervention re:
Plant location decision	*Market Size*	Markets (sales and supply)
Nature of product line (e.g., volatile)	Sales market size and extent of competition	Imports (licenses and permits)
Manufacturing strategy	Supply market size and extent of competition	Location of industry
Attitude to risk taking	Skills available in supply market	Fund management
Economic	Technical	Reciprocal business demands
National economic frame-work and system	Management	Political/economic alliances
Economic stability	Support research	*Legal*
Organization of capital markets		National legal rules
Social overhead(s)		International legal rules
Political/economic alliances		

Source: D. H. Farmer, "Source Decision-Making in the Multi-National Company Environment," *Journal of Purchasing* 8, no. 1 (February 1972): 12.

Interview 1:

Until 1965 there was no attempt even to co-ordinate purchases where there was commonality. In one case we discovered, just in time, that we had been bidding against our French associate for a parcel of a certain material which was then in short supply. As a result of this and of a number of similar happenings there was an attempt to set up a European office in 1966. This was closed in 1967 because "its presence was not justified by events." Only in 1971 has the idea been revived and now on a far broader scale.

Interview 2:

Until this year (1971), all our companies throughout the world were independent of our U.S. parent, save for financial control. Now we are organized into three zonal areas: Europe, The Americas, and Asia. In each area there is a purchasing controller among whose functions it is to utilize our purchasing power in that region to the full, while maintaining local flexibility.

Interview 3:

In the late 50s our policy was to buy for our European factories from the U.S. This was changed in 1961 to allow local purchasing, but it was then carried on by each plant in isolation. In 1966 we realized that we were not using our corporate purchasing strength to the full and, on 1968, following a survey, this office [that of the European Procurement Controller] was set up.

Interview 4:

There was no coordination between our U.S. headquarters and the rest of the world on purchasing. As a matter of fact, there was some animosity and distrust about what we were doing in trying to bring some kind of cohesion to the European end. Only in 1970 did the first break appear in the ice and that was when our East European sales started to go well. Only last month (April 1971) we held our first corporate supplies meeting and we are now at the stage of putting forward draft procedures for collaboration. But we have a long way to go.[18]

Developing countries

In developing countries sourcing problems are particularly difficult. D. H. Farmer lists eleven areas:

1. Lack of local technological back up.
2. License and foreign exchange difficulties.
3. Poor service from indigenous supply sources (e.g., poor delivery schedule performance, quality failure, limited variety, etc.).
4. Political instability or risk, affecting investment (either with respect to the company itself or potential suppliers).
5. Tariffs and host government pressure to buy within the country.
6. Governmental pressures regarding their own purchasing from the company.
7. Necessity for carrying higher inventories.
8. Necessity for intensifying goods inwards inspection activity.
9. "Home" derived specifications not available from local supply markets.
10. Quality inconsistency with certain imported components.
11. Lack of trained local staff, affecting supply department performance. (Even though this could be said to apply to all company staff, it was said in more than one case to affect purchasing in particular.)[19]

Apparently, few companies recognize these difficulties at the project planning stage, and operations of subsidiaries may be severely hampered by this lack of adequate concern.

Satisfaction and stability in purchaser-supplier relationships

Certainly one of the major assessments a purchaser must make is whether the

---

[18]Ibid., pp. 34–35.
[19]Ibid.

current relationship with a supplier is a satisfactory one or not. This relationship is highly complex and different people inside the purchasing organization may have different perceptions of it. In the simplest form, with a new supplier just after a relatively small order has been placed but no deliveries have yet been made, it may consist only of an assessment of the agreement just reached and the buyer's quick impression of the sales representative. For a long-term supplier of major needs the assessment will be based on past and current performance, personal relationships with a number of personnel in both organizations, and even future expectations. Such assessments may well change as a result of competitive action in the marketplace. What may look like a good price deal today may not look so attractive when information comes to light that a fully competent competitor could have supplied the same materials or items for substantially less.

The following model (Figure 6–7) attempts to provide a simple framework for clarifying the current purchaser-supplier relationship in terms of satisfaction and stability. The assumptions behind it are:

1. That satisfaction with a current supplier relationship can be assessed, however crudely, at least in macro-terms, whether it is satisfactory or not.
2. That an unsatisfied party (seller or purchaser or both) will attempt to move to a more satisfactory situation.
3. That attempts to move may affect the stability of the relationship.

Figure 6–7
A simple purchaser-supplier satisfaction model

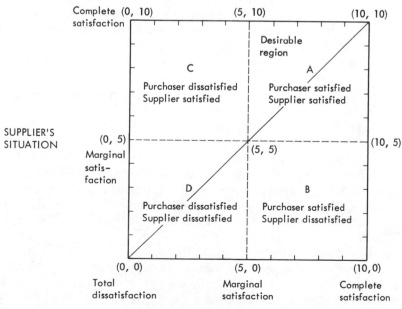

PURCHASER'S SITUATION

4. That attempts to move may fall in the win-lose, as well as the lose-lose, lose-win, and win-win categories.
5. That purchaser and seller may well have different perceptions of the same relationship.
6. That many tools and techniques and approaches exist which will assist either party in moving positions and improving stability.

   A.   The upper right hand quadrant.   (5,5–10,5–10,10–5,10) Region. Considerable satisfaction exists on both sides and stability is likely. Long-term relationships may be built on this kind of foundation. Considerable room for improvement is still possible within this quadrant in moving from a (5,5) situation toward a (10,10) objective.

   B.   The lower right hand quadrant.   (5,0–10,0–10,5–5,5) Region. In this region the buyer is at least marginally satisfied, but the seller is not. This is the mirror image of the *C* region, and the seller is likely to initiate action for change which may end up subsequently in any of the four regions. Stability is not likely over the long run.

   The above comments are, of course, general in nature. It is entirely possible for a powerful purchaser or a powerful supplier to maintain a *B* or *C* region position respectively for a long time with a weak counterpart.

   C.   The upper left hand quadrant.   (0,5–5,5–5,10–0,10) Region. The supplier is at least marginally satisfied, but the purchaser is not. The purchaser will attempt to improve the buying situation. If this is done at the expense of the seller, a see-saw may be created whereby the purchaser's efforts result in the supplier's moving down the satisfaction scale into the *D* region. The assumption is that the most dissatisfied party is the most likely instigator of change. It is also possible that such instigations may reduce satisfaction for both parties so that both end up in the *D* region. Hopefully, changes might result in both parties moving into the *A* region.

   D.   The lower left hand quadrant.   (0,0–5,0–5,5–0,5) Region. Both parties agree that significant dissatisfaction exists on both sides. This kind of situation is not likely to be stable for any length of time, since each side will be striving to improve at least its own satisfaction.

   The diagonal line.   The diagonal in the diagram may be seen as a "fairness or stability" line. As long as positions move along this line both purchaser and supplier are at least equally well off. Its end points of (0,0) and (10,10) represent two extremes. The (0,0) position is completely undesirable from either standpoint and is a "total war" picture which is extremely unstable. It represents an unlikely starting point for any long-term stable position since memories of this unhappy state of affairs are likely to prevent substantial improvements. The obvious solution is disassociation and the seeking of a new source by the purchaser.

   The (10,10) position represents a utopian view rarely found in reality. It requires a degree of mutual trust and sharing and respect that is very difficult to achieve in our society of "buyer beware" and where competition and the price mechanism are supposed to work freely. Perhaps, as more and more governmental controls are imposed on both purchasers and sellers, the (10,10) state may become more approachable. In some systems contracting situations a relationship close to the (10,10) state has been developed. Buyers are willing to share risks and information with the seller, and the seller is willing to open the books for buyer inspection. Problems are ironed out in an amicable and mutually acceptable manner and both parties benefit from the relationship.

The middle position of (5,5) should really be considered as a minimum acceptable goal for both sides, and few agreements should be reached by the purchaser without achieving at least this place. Adjustments in positions should, hopefully, travel along the diagonal and towards the (10,10) corner. Substantial departures from the diagonal raise the difficulty that the agreement may be seen as less beneficial to one party than the other, with the possibility of jealousy and the attempt by the less satisfied party to bring the other down to a more common denominator. The region of greatest stability will, therefore, lie close to the (5,5)–(10,10) portion of the diagonal line.

Perceptions

This model becomes more complex when the perceptions of both parties are considered, both with respect to their own position as well as the other side's. For example, the purchaser's perception may be that the relationship is in the A region. The supplier's perception may or may not match this view. Let us look at the congruent side first.

Congruent situations

Where both buyer's and supplier's perceptions agree, congruence exists and both parties would record their own and the other side's satisfaction on the same place on the chart. This does not necessarily mean that both parties are satisfied with the situation. Both at least have the same starting point, and mutual agreement on this is useful. For example, take a (8,6) situation, and both buyer and seller agree that the buyer is better satisfied with the current arrangement than the seller. Chances that both will be willing to work towards a corrective solution are reasonable (see Figure 6–8).

Noncongruent perceptions

Lack of congruence in perceptions of relative positions will present a problem in itself. Take, for example, the situation where the buyer's perceptions of the situation is (2,8), but the seller's perception is (9,1). (See Figure 6–8.) The buyer thinks the supplier has a pretty good deal but is quite dissatisfied with the purchaser's situation. The seller's opinion is the exact opposite. So both parties are dissatisfied, but their actions are likely to lead to even further dissatisfaction on the other side. This would normally be a highly unstable situation. It may be possible to settle differences of perception through discussion among the mana-

Figure 6–8
Purchaser—supplier satisfaction model showing
(1) congruent (2) noncongruent perceptions

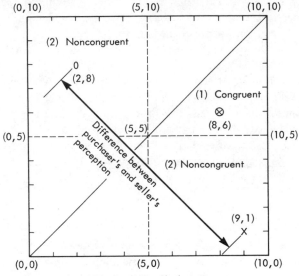

O = Buyer's perception of position of both parties.
X = Seller's perception of position of both parties.

gers involved. Such resolution will be necessary before any attempts can be undertaken to improve the position of either side.

Using the framework

The model is based on the assumption that both purchaser and seller are capable of expressing a view on the degree of satisfaction that exists with a relationship. Essential elements of this relationship would include perceptions on prices paid, service, delivery, and quality performance, and whether the demands and cooperation of the other party are reasonable in view of the circumstances. Personality factors are also a likely component. These measures are, of course, difficult to quantify, but ranking of relative positions compared to other suppliers (or customers) may well be possible. For example, Boeing's SPEAR system attempts to quantify the management component. Even though absolute quantification is difficult, this model may be useful in a number of ways.

From a purchasing point of view it is possible to assess the total package of current supplier relationships and to determine how many fall inside the desirable region and how many outside. A significant percentage of unsatisfactory or marginal situations will mean a substantial amount of work to restructure current arrangements. The purchasing perception of a relationship may be shared with a supplier to check on congruence and as a starting point for mutual diagnosis and plan for change. Even the process of attempting to assess contracts and suppliers against the model's framework may be useful in establishing the key variables which are relevant for the particular commodity under study. Finally, the severity of the situation is a good indicator of the need for action and the tools and techniques which might be applied. For example, a purchaser may wish to work harder at a (1,5) than a (5,5) situation of equal dollar value and corporate impact.

Tools and techniques for moving positions

There are a number of purchasing and marketing means which may be employed to shift positions on the satisfaction chart. The use of some of these will adversely affect the perceptions of the other party, and these might be called "crunch" tools or negative measures. Others are likely to be viewed in less severe terms and might be considered "stroking" methods or positive approaches. For example "crunch" tools for the purchaser include:

1. Complete severance of purchases without advanced notice.
2. Refusal to pay bills.
3. Refusal to accept shipments.
4. Use or threat of legal action.

For the supplier examples would include:

1. Refusal to send shipments as promised.
2. Unilateral substantial price increase without notice.
3. Insistence on unreasonable length of contract, take or pay commitments, escalation clauses, or other terms and conditions and use of take it or leave it propositions.

"Stroking" techniques by the purchaser would include:

1. Granting of substantial volumes of business or long-run commitments of 100 percent requirement contracts.
2. Sharing of internal information on forecasts, problems, and opportunities to invite a mutual search of alternatives.
3. Evidence of willingness and ability to work towards changed behavior in the purchasing organization to improve the seller's position.
4. Rapid positive response to requests from suppliers for discussions and adjustments in price, quality, delivery, and service.

On the marketing side examples could be:

1. Willingness and ability to make rapid price, delivery, and quality adjustments in response to purchasing requests without a major hassle.
2. Invitation to the purchaser to discuss mutual problems and opportunities.
3. The giving of notice substantially in advance of pending changes in price, lead times, and availability to allow the purchaser maximum time to plan ahead.

It is interesting that "stroking" techniques are more likely to be used in the A region, further strengthening the stability of the relationship, whereas the use of "crunch" tools may well accomplish short-term objectives but may impair future chances of a desirable stable relationship.

The perception of a relationship is based on both the results obtained as well as the process by which they have been achieved. For example, a price concession extremely grudgingly granted by a supplier and continually negatively referred to by supplier's personnel may create less satisfaction for the purchaser than one more amicably reached. "Crunch" methods pleasantly applied may be far more palatable than the same tool used in a hard-nosed way. For example, an unavoidable price increase can be explained in person by a supplier's sales manager well in advance more palatably than by circular letter after the increase has been put into effect. A purchasing manager can visit a supplier's plant to determine ways and means of solving a quality problem and explain that no deliveries can be accepted until the problem is solved, instead of sending back shipment after shipment as unacceptable. The results-process combination puts a heavy emphasis on managerial judgment and capability to accomplish change effectively.

QUESTIONS FOR REVIEW AND DISCUSSION

1. What is a good supplier?
2. Why would a buyer wish to multiple source for the same item? What would make this difficult?
3. Why should a buyer consider sourcing locally?
4. What is "supplier goodwill"?
5. What is the traditional reason for developing a supplier?
6. What rating factors are normally included in a vendor rating system?
7. Is a silver paperweight a gratuity? Tickets to a sports event? A keychain? A discount on tires for a personal automobile?
8. What are four typical sources of information about suppliers? Are there more?
9. If a supplier is dissatisfied with a customer, what actions might the supplier consider taking to improve the situation? What would the purchaser do in return?

CASE 6–1
DORSON INC.

Jim McBirnie was a buyer of accessories at Dorson Inc., a well established small manufacturer of consumer appliances. He was particularly concerned about one of the items he purchased, a specialized cotton filter wick for a line of humidifiers Dorson used to make. Mr. and Mrs. Carrothers had supplied these wicks for years, operating a small business out of their garage. However, they were approaching retirement age and their health was failing. Jim wondered, therefore, if he could count on them as a reliable source much longer.

Dorson Inc.

Dorson Inc. had been established by Mr. Dorson in 1911 as a small manufacturer of household fans. The company had added a variety of other products to its lines over the years and in 1936 had developed a humidifier of high quality and advanced design. Since then, humidifiers had grown to become a major share of total sales and the company continued to increase the number of different types available. It had been company policy to supply parts and accessories for all humidifiers made, and the sales staff believed this to be a continuing strong selling feature with customers and dealers.

The filter wick

The humidifier filter wick Jim was concerned about was used in a line of humidifiers Dorson had discontinued manufacturing seven years earlier. Wicks had to be replaced, according to Dorson instructions, once a year, but Jim believed many customers kept their wicks longer than this. No substitute or competitive product was available and Dorson still sold 70,000 wicks per year currently. In Jim's opinion, demand for wicks was likely to last at least another five years.

Mr. and Mrs. Carrothers

Mr. and Mrs. Carrothers had supplied wicks to Dorson for at least 20 years. The equipment used was antiquated in Jim's opinion, but he knew that no modern machinery was available on the market to replace it. Dorson was the only customer of Mr. and Mrs. Carrothers, who employed three women and one weaver in their small plant during the period from July to February. These workers were laid off for the rest of the year. The Carrothers were about 65 years old and Jim knew their health had been failing for some time. The current purchase price was $1.60 per wick and the retail selling price about $4.50.

In an effort to find an alternative source, Jim had talked with respresentatives from several textile firms to see if they could supply. After initial interest from the sales representatives, Jim received negative replies from all, stating that the equipment was not available, the production process too complex, and the amount of hand sewing required prohibitively expensive.

Thus, faced with the problem of an uncertain sole source, Jim wondered what further action, if any, he should take to resolve the wick situation.

CASE 6–2
SUFFOLK POWER CORPORATION (A)

Suffolk Power Corporation was building three additional generating stations to serve its rapidly expanding energy market. To link these stations with the total area grid, a new method of carrying the power lines using ornamental tubular poles instead of towers had been adopted. Suffolk had had no previous operating experience with poles and decided to subcontract the design engineering, fabrication, and erection of the new line.

For the first phase engineering design, Mr. Carter, the director of purchasing, faced the responsibility of deciding with which supplier the business was to be placed after his staff had developed the information needed. He was aware that Suffolk had only three years in which to complete the entire project, and yet he had to ensure high-quality work.

Company background

Suffolk Power Corporation had been established before the turn of the century and was now one of the largest power utilities in the eastern United States. It serviced a highly industrialized area from ten fossil-fueled plants. It was expanding into nuclear generation. With assets of over $3 billion and demand doubling every decade, it had already earmarked funds to increase its kilowatt capacity from 8.4 million to 13 million over a four-year period.

The company was well known for its advanced technology and its good public relations. Both purchasing and engineering departments were centralized and located in the head office in the area's largest city. The new construction program was a heavy strain on both the professional and financial resources of the company, placing increased emphasis on the use of qualified people and suppliers outside the corporation.

Transmission line background

Although Suffolk was stepping up its older lines to 230 KV, by management decision and in accordance with the technological trend, 345 KV was adopted for the new line. It was to link the new generating stations in Addison, Smithfield, and Mesa Valley with the area grid, some 140 miles all told. As the atomic plants came on stream, voltages twice as high were foreseen.

Until now, Suffolk had used structural steel towers exclusively for carrying its power lines. (See Exhibit 1.) These were strong but visually prominent and attracted adverse comments from a public daily growing more aesthetically sophisticated. A relatively new development in the transmission field was the introduction of the ornamental tubular power pole. (See Exhibit 2.) Approximately 200 miles of line using these poles had been installed with good success in various parts of the country. Most installations were relatively short sections in densely populated areas. A line using poles cost twice

Exhibit 1

as much as the conventional towers but was still substantially cheaper than underground installation. Conscious of the great strides made in power pole design and use, Suffolk management decided to specify poles for the new line.

Because of the volume of conversion and projected expansion work Mr. Carter and the project engineers knew that the tower manufacturers and erection companies with whom they had dealt in the past would not have the capacity to handle all the elements of the new pole concept. Furthermore, with no experience in 345KV or pole suspension, Suffolk had to rely on the know-how of others for the new line and needed the services and guidance of competent subcontractors.

Exhibit 2

The total job involved three major phases:

1. Engineering design called for layout as well as a functional pole specification and project guidance.
2. Pole manufacture involved a manufacturing proposal consisting of a specific design to meet the functional specifications as well as manufacturing volume and schedule deadline capabilities.
3. Pole installation involved excavation foundation setting, pole erection, and line stringing. Preliminary cost estimates for the total project were as follows:

> Phase 1—Engineering—$250,000–$300,000
> Phase 2—Pole manufacture—$15 million
> Phase 3—Installation—$13 million

Mr. Carter and the chief engineer were not satisfied that any individual supplier could handle the total contract well. They decided, therefore, to subcontract each phase to a reliable source of high expertise within that phase, so that optimum overall benefits would accrue to Suffolk. The first sourcing decision dealt with the engineering phase.

Design engineering selection

All through the spring and half of the summer Mr. Oliver Dunn, the buyer, worked with the transmission engineering section of the system engineering department of the company to establish parameters and locate a suitable design source. By late July he was able to make his recommendation to the director of purchases. (See Exhibit 3.)

It was normal practice at Suffolk to provide a very brief summary for the director of purchases on all major contracts. A large file containing detailed information was built up by the buyers and purchasing agents involved. Normally, some preliminary discussions were held as the project progressed, so that Mr. Carter was reasonably informed by the time the official recommendation was prepared. Should he wish to see more information he could request the file at any time.

All three of the engineering firms considered were large and engaged in a wide variety of engineering consulting services. Travers & Bolton and Crown Engineering had both done considerable work for Suffolk in the past and had performed satisfactorily. Pettigrew Associates had its head office in New York and maintained branches in ten American cities. Pettigrew employed over 3,800 people, had a good credit rating, and had annual sales in excess of $80 million per year. Suffolk had never used Pettigrew in any of its projects. All three engineering firms had some tubular pole experience with short-line sections in other parts of the country. Aside from the design requirements, the consulting engineering firm was also expected to evaluate the bids from pole manufacturing and erection subcontractors.

Exhibit 3
Quotation summary

Description:	Design 140 miles 345KV transmission line for Addison-Smithfield-Mesa Valley
Recommended vendor:	Pettigrew Associates, New York, N.Y.

Location: Their premises   Using department: General engineering
Buyer: O. Dunn.   Total Value: Established $290,000 salaries
                                              + burden

P.O. No: Date: Approval:

Additional information:

1. The transmission section of our general engineering department is unable to perform the design work of all the planned transmission work for the next three years, and it is necessary to contract some portions of this work. Travers & Bolton are already assigned the conversion of the 120KV to 230, and it is recommended that this 140-mile Addison-Smithfield-Mesa Valley 345KV be contracted to some competent engineering firm.
2. We had sessions with each of three below mentioned engineering firms to acquaint them with our needs and learn of their capabilities. The work they will perform is as follows: make route sections; make subsurface investigations; make electrical hardware and general project designs; and furnish miscellaneous specifications, drawings, and technical data required to procure the right of way, hardware, structural steel and for the awarding of contracts for construction. It is estimated this work will total 12,300 man-hours. There would also be approximately $24,000 worth of computer services and general out-of-pocket expenses in addition to the man-hours.
3. Bid comparison is:

Supplier	Estimated man-hours	Basic average cost per man-hour (w/o fringes)	Approximate fringes (assumed same for all)	Overhead and profit	Estimated $/hour
Travers & Bolton	14,350	$10.00	20%	67.5%	$20.00
Crown Engineering	—	10.00	20	80.0	21.60
Pettigrew Associates . . .	12,190	10.00	20	85.0	22.20

It is recommended that this contract be awarded to Pettigrew even though their cost per hour is higher than the others. Total cost will be influenced by the capability and productivity of the company chosen, and, therefore, Pettigrew may not cost us any more; it is the desire of Suffolk management to have Pettigrew perform such a job with Suffolk as our first experience with them. Both T&B and C.E. have done considerable work for Suffolk.

CASE 6–3
SUFFOLK POWER CORPORATION (B)

Suffolk Power Corporation was building three additional power generating stations to serve the rapidly expanding energy market. To link these stations to the existing area grid, a new method of carrying the power lines using ornamental tubular poles, instead of towers, had been adopted. The second phase of the project involved pole manufacture to a functional engineering design with parameters. Mr. Carter, director of purchasing, had to evaluate the proposal from his purchasing supervisor as to which supplier should be chosen. [For company and transmission line background see Suffolk Power Corporation (A).]

Bidding procedures—preselection

Mr. Carter had given the responsibility to recommend a pole manufacturer to Gordon Yarrow, supervisor of materials purchasing. Gordon had the consulting engineers' services and the experience of his own engineering department to assist him. The consulting engineering firm on the project had been selected in August, and by early spring of the following year it had furnished Suffolk with functional specifications for the poles, cross-arms, and hardware. Suffolk engineers recommended that quotations should first be obtained on the most pressing portion of the line linking Addison to Smithfield. This amounted to about half of the total project distance. The expectation was that the experience gained on this first section would guide the contracts on the remaining half. Mr. Yarrow had to ensure a start on the 345KV line by the fall. This left not much time in which to develop pole prototypes and to perform the engineering tests in advance of erection. The number of potential suppliers was severely limited by two major requirements. Each supplier had to have a design computer program and a large press-brake for heavy metal.

First progress report

In May, after extensive negotiations with eight potential suppliers, Gordon Yarrow was able to give his superior a brief run-down on his progress. He told Mr. Carter he had encountered quite a spread in prices and that there were disturbing gaps in engineering information in some cases, but he believed the time-table could be met.

MR. CARTER: Try anyone abroad? There's a lot of high voltage experience on the outside, but perhaps it's mainly tower transmission?

GORDON YARROW: I don't know about that so much, but I've one bid definitely in the ballpark from a Canadian outfit, and what looks like rather a wild one from Japan. I think we can whittle these quotes down to a few fairly quickly when we get together with the engineers as some of them are a bit off the mark on first inspection.

MR. CARTER: Good. I take it that you don't think it will be necessary to let the consulting engineer see all the quotes, but only those that look most likely?

GORDON YARROW: Exactly, I shall let you know the outcome of our preliminary selection after I see our project engineers, and then we'll get the consulting engineer's evaluation of the remainder.

Mr. Yarrow then went over all detailed information and prices in the following weeks with the system engineering department and reported rejection of four bidders for the following reasons (see Exhibit 1).

JORDAN POLE CO.: Q. Use a zinc metallic finish and do not galvanize. Prices not firm, based on all rates in effect at time of delivery. Design not satisfactory; two-section bolted pole. No Charpy impact value furnished. Would have to add to test costs.

H. B. SMITHERS, INC.: *R.* Price too high. No previous experience in transmission but only in street light poles. Some questionable manufacturing techniques that we feel can be corrected. Excellent prospect for future requirements.

MARTIN AND STEVENSON: *S.* Price too high. Best qualified on basis of experience but did not provide weights, drawings, or details or alternate prices on standard base plate.

KYUSHIMO, INC.: *T.* Price highest (100 percent over low). No previous experience in high voltage transmission poles but provided the most information on design, drawing specifications, etc. Japanese source.

He then sent engineering information only (no prices) on the four remaining bidders to Suffolk's engineering consultants for a complete analysis of the bids on the basis of the requested design, a comparison of designs furnished and exceptions to specifications.

Consultant's analysis

The engineering consultant's analysis were combined in six documents.

1. Covering letter
2. Design points considered
3. Pole data comparison
4. Comparison of designs
5. Comments on exceptions to specification by Henry Nelson Company
6. Recommendations (see Exhibit 2)

Project engineer's review and discussions on capabilities

At the end of May, Gordon Yarrow agreed with Mr. Northrup of transmission projects that the latter should meet with bidders *M, N* and *O* (Structures Canadian, Ltd.) to resolve the engineering and fabricating capabilities of each. This was not necessary for bidder *P* (Henry Nelson Company) as he was already working for Suffolk.

When the engineer had concluded his meetings, he called the supervisor of material buying to that effect. "Be right over," said Gordon Yarrow, "I'm very anxious to learn what transpired."

"Sit down, Gord," said Mr. Northrup, greeting the purchasing department representative cheerfully and at the same time sweeping aside a pile of blueprints to make more room on his desk.

YARROW: How did you make out?

NORTHRUP: Not too bad. At least let me say it's pretty clear in my mind what we should do. Let's take our Canadian friends first. They're prepared to order a 40', 2,000 ton press now with a July delivery promised and probable operation by August.

YARROW: But we're after 108 poles by October 1.

Exhibit 1

Quotation summary—poles and arms 345KV line Addison-Smithfield section

	M	N	O	P†	Q	R	S	T
				Bidders				
	Molson, Inc.	Norris Steel Co.	Structures Cdn., Ltd.	Henry Nelson Co.	Jordan Pole Co.	H. B. Smithers, Inc.	Martin & Stevenson	Kyushimo, Inc.
Bid (in $000)	$5,600	$6,040*	$6,160*	$6,974*	$5,940*	$7,930*	$9,580*	$9,940*
Extra for Nelson base	350	—	—	—	—	—	—	—
Escalation	63	Firm	Firm	125	307	Firm	118	Firm
Total	$6,013	$6,040	$6,160	$7,099	$6,247	$7,930	$9,698	$9,940
Revised total							$8,025	

Quantity: 390 type 3A, 61 type 3B, 24 type 3C, 7 type 3D, 8 type 3E. Total 490.
*On basis of Nelson base design.
†Recommended on basis of past service; engineering preference; delivery.

Buyer: G. Yarrow   Approval:

Exhibit 2
Recommendations for steel poles Addison-Smithfield Section

Our recommendations based on the information submitted for review are:

1. Award the contract for supplying the poles to Henry Nelson Company provided they will accept the terms and conditions of the specifications.
2. Award the contract to bidder O (Structures Canadian, Ltd.) if unable to obtain a satisfactory agreement with Nelson's.
3. Require that Structures Canadian provide arm details such that the 3A-type arms can be used on the 3B-type pole shaft.
4. Before awarding the contract to Structures Canadian, determine working hole arrangements, hot line maintenance requirements, and ladder details.
5. Require additional splice design overlap which will allow for a minus tolerance in field erection and still maintain the required splice overlap dimensions.
6. Resolve questions on design features such as designation of steels to be used in fabricating the poles, arm attachment plate details, electrical clearances, and data to be shown on drawings.
7. Perform time studies on steel pole assembly and erection activities to determine any increase or decrease in erection costs between Nelson and Structures Canadian poles which may be incurred by the erector.

If you should award the contract to bidder M and N, our comments would be essentially the same as for Structures Canadian. However, we may have some additional comments regarding their proposed arm connections.

NORTHRUP: Precisely. So they suggested subcontracting these along with the required test poles. This, of course wouldn't do because the whole purpose of the test is to prove out the fabrication as well as the design.

YARROW: Have they made poles like this before? I know they are competent enough in other structures.

NORTHRUP: No. And there would be a certain risk in placing an order this size with them. Still, they indicated a thorough understanding of the engineering and manufacturing details, and we have some confidence in their ability based on past structural experience.

YARROW: What did you think of bidder M?

NORTHRUP: They, too, had three representatives present, but their engineering was incomplete and left much unanswered. The designs covered only the 150' 3A and 3B poles and nothing on the remaining three types. Because of their press brake size, all sections greater than ½" thickness would have to be made in shorter sections.

YARROW: Meaning welding?

NORTHRUP: Right. And circumferential welds are so critical in the stability of the pole, it would be better if they were avoided.

YARROW: So this leaves us with bidder N. Things any brighter there?

NORTHRUP: Not really. While their fellows told me that they had a 30' 1,500-ton press in transit and could have it operating in five days after delivery, I don't like the underdesigning of the arm attachment and cross-arms. However, they agreed to review these. The lengths of the sections as shown on the designs can't be made in a single piece because of the length of the brake. This would require either more lap field splices or circumferential welds, neither of which is desir-

able, particularly the latter. I really would question giving an order of this magnitude to an inexperienced supplier.

YARROW: Well, you have serious reservations about all of them. I'm a little sorry. I
was hoping we could have uncovered a more positive new source of supply. I
take it, then, that you favor the present supplier, Henry Nelson?

NORTHRUP: Let me put it this way, and I'll confirm it in writing, based on engineering
and fabricating experience, our first recommendation is Nelson's. However, the
exceptions to our specifications would have to be resolved. Next would be the
Canadians, provided they fabricated all poles in their plant and delivery
schedules could be worked out. Our third choice is bidder N, but design details
must first be resolved. And we're still concerned about their lack of experience
in heavy steel fabrication.

YARROW: And bidder M?

NORTHRUP: Can't recommend them, based on the engineering data supplied. Considerable engineering work would be required in order to supply the missing
information.

YARROW: O.K., many thanks. We're reviewing all the bids because there are still a lot
of loose ends to be tied together. I'll be seeing a lot of you in the next month or
two.

Purchasing recommendation

On July 2, Gordon Yarrow made his recommendation to the director of
purchasing, Mr. Carter. He supplied the consultant's analyses and explained
what had transpired to his chief. "We wanted to encourage competition and
develop local suppliers as you instructed," he said. "Engineering and purchasing met several times with representatives of bidders M, N and O." He
related the engineer's side of it and said, "It is all here, confirmed by Tony
Northrup," and he laid the report on the desk. "Then I summarized the bids,
including the four we rejected earlier on, and here is how it looks (see
Exhibit 1)."

Mr. Carter studied the figures briefly and said, "Thanks, Gordon. I have a
meeting with the executives now, so I'll go over this later and get back to you
tomorrow. I'll give you a call, probably in the morning." The two went their
separate ways.

Next day the two resumed their discussion. "I see what you mean when
you talked of a large price spread," said the senior man, "I can't understand
how bidder S—that's Martin & Stevenson—were so far out of line. After all,
with their experience, they shouldn't have, in the first place, tried to get
away without drawings, weights, and alternatives. Were they not really interested?"

"It's hard to say" replied Gordon Yarrow. "But we went back at them and
got into all that detail. As a result they revised their design and prices from
$9,698,000 to an estimated $8,025,000 including steps and tests. We also
considered buying the Canadian design, but they ran into labor troubles and

withdrew their quote. Also gave serious consideration to buying Nelson's design and having companies such as *M* and *N* requote on the basis of using it."

"Why?"

"Because they have excellent shop facilities but they lack engineering ability and experience in this area. We inspected their plants. Bidder *M*, as you will recall, is making some of our low voltage poles—the 120 KVs—and is running into manufacturing difficulties. Bidder *N* had a hard job to come through with a test pole for this line. All in all, we felt it was the better part of wisdom to stay with someone more tried and true. Mind you, both these companies have potential and with more experience should be considered on future requirments."

"So that leaves Nelson?"

"Yes, Mr. Carter. The exceptions pointed out by our consultants have been resolved with them. In addition they will release to us for unrestricted use, the designs on all the 345KV poles."

CASE 6–4
SUFFOLK POWER CORPORATION (C)

Suffolk Power Corporation was building three additional generating stations to serve the rapidly expanding energy market. To link these stations with the total area grid a new method of carrying the power lines using ornamental tubular poles instead of towers had been adopted. Suffolk lacked experience with poles and decided to subcontract the design engineering, fabrication, and erection of the new line. [For company background and line project information and the selection of engineering consultants see Suffolk Power Corporation (A). For selection of pole manufacturers see Suffolk Power Corporation (B).]

Having selected its consultants for its first 345KV transmission line and placed its order for the fabrication of the poles and hardware, Suffolk Power was ready to locate a suitable contractor to do the foundation work, erect the poles, and string the lines.

Purchasing and engineering had been pursuing this concurrently with the search for a fabricator as Suffolk wanted to get started on the line by the fall. Mr. Gordon Yarrow, supervisor of materials purchasing, was responsible to the director of purchasing, Mr. John Carter, for the negotiations.

Construction selection

One company, T. D. Rapier, had done almost all Suffolk's transmission work for over the last five years, but, with the consultant's help, a good cross section of qualified line builders had been invited to bid. In addition several foundation companies were asked to quote on the subgrade work. This helped to test the market to determine whether foundation contractors could build foundations cheaper than line builders. Mr. Carter reserved the right to award separate contracts for above and below grade work.

Two meetings were held with the bidders, one for the line builders and another for the foundation contractors at which all aspects of the job were fully discussed. The unit prices were based on current wage rates and working conditions and were subject to adjustment by a percentage equal to .80 times the percentage change in the average wage rates.

By September the consulting engineers were able to provide purchasing with an evaluation of the bidding and computations enabling the attached summary to be compiled (see Exhibit 1).

Exhibit 1
Suffolk hydro 345 KV transmission line—Addition-Smithfield-Mesa Valley

Comparison of bids

Bidder	Line construction	Foundations installation	Total
Line contractors			
(D)	$7,850,640	$ 8,846,608	$16,697,248
(E)...............................	6,352,984	7,436,185	13,789,169
(F)...............................	6,898,440	6,296,413	13,194,853
(G) T. D. Rapier	6,247,560	6,332,312	12,579,872
(H) McTaggart Construction	7,238,950	4,612,134	11,851,084
(I)	6,032,012	No bid	
Consulting engineer's prior			
estimate........................	7,958,400	5,102,400	13,060,800
Foundation contractors			
(J)		12,295,929	
(K)		6,494,394	
(L)...............................		5,866,896	

Notes:
1. Two line contractors and one foundation contractor declined to bid.
2. The two lowest line constructors, Rapier and McTaggart, were evaluated, plus the possibility of a split award to (L) for foundations and (I) for above grade work. However, McTaggart is recommended for the following reasons:
   a. Lowest bid.
   b. High experienced. Built thousands of miles of line in mountain, desert, and swamp. Experience included 230, 345, 500 and 750KV construction.
   c. Presently working for several other power companies.
   d. Recommended by our design engineers and consultants.
   e. Have done considerable work in this state through a subsidiary although not for Suffolk.

CASE 6–5
THE DETROIT EDISON COMPANY

Introduction

In 1972 Mr. K. W. Hartwell, director of purchases at Detroit Edison was trying to encourage increased purchasing from minority sources. In 1966 the Booker T. Washington Association of Detroit had contacted The Detroit Edison Company to solicit discussions with their Purchasing department, as to the desirability of the white business community placing business with Detroit based black-owned businesses. There were a number of meetings and, with each, a growing understanding within Edison of the special attention the Edison buyers would have to exert if there was to be an Edison business relationship with black suppliers. Immediately following one of these meetings, there was the costly and unnerving Detroit race riot of July 1967.

Following this, the non-profit organization, Economic Development Corporation (EDC), was formed in Detroit, under the auspices of 15 of Detroit's largest companies, to aid the growth of minority business locally. EDC's basic belief had been that private business and financial communities were best equipped to help minorities. One of the aims of EDC, therefore, was the encouragement of corporations to buy the products and services of minority firms. To this end, a sub-division of EDC was formed in 1968, called the Industrial Purchasing Committee (IPC). Mr. Kenneth W. Hartwell, Director of Purchases at The Detroit Edison Company, along with 14 purchasing heads of the Detroit based industries made up IPC. One of the early tasks of the committee had been the publication of a minority supplier directory. Mr. Hartwell knew opinions among purchasing executives varied as to the best way of increasing the dollar volume placed with minority suppliers. He was convinced that the large corporations had to give leadership and perhaps take risks that the smaller organizations could not.

Company background

The Detroit Edison Company, an investor-owned utility, supplied electric power to 1.6 million customers in a 7,600 square mile area of Southeastern Michigan. It operated, or had under construction, a dozen power plants which generated nearly 11 million kilowatts. The company had 167,000 common shareholders owning 40 million shares. Its capitalization was about $2 billion. In 1972 alone, capital acquisitions amounted to about $400 million. It was undergoing the largest expansion in its history.

Over 15 percent of Detroit Edison's individual power consumers were members of minority groups. Purchasing management had set $350,000 as the 1973 target for purchases to be placed with minority suppliers.

Exhibit 1
Organization chart—Purchasing department

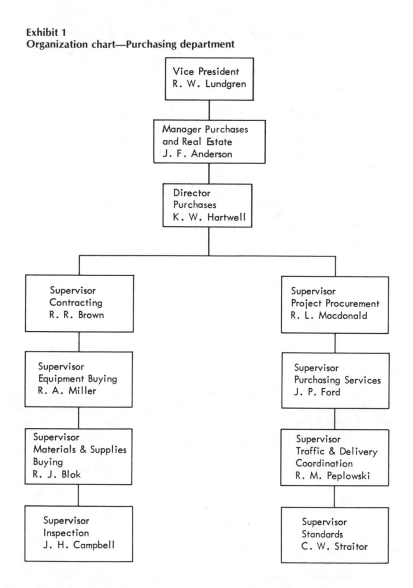

Purchasing department

Detroit Edison's purchasing is centralized in its head office in downtown Detroit. It was organized along commodity buying lines, but special project groups existed to cope with the extensive construction and capital expansion program.

Total purchases amounted to about $340 million in capital equipment per year and approximately $60 million in MRO type items. There were 80 people on the purchasing staff. Exhibit 1 gives the organization chart and

Exhibit 2 the purchasing policies as shown in a booklet for suppliers and employees.

Exhibit 2
Purchasing policies

The following policies govern our business relationships with the Company's suppliers. They are necessarily broad enough to allow for the reasonable exercise of judgment and discretion.

1. Develop and maintain the maximum competition compatible with the quality and service required by the Company and the degree of reliability we desire in our suppliers.
2. Develop and maintain dependable sources of supply—ask for quotations only from those suppliers from whom we are willing to buy.
3. Deal fairly—avoid favoritism and make each transaction both a good buy for the Company and a satisfactory sale for the supplier.
4. Do not bargain with suppliers—obtain each bidder's best price on the first quotation; don't ask for a second quotation to meet a competitive bid.
5. Pay no premium for reciprocal business—award orders to the lowest bidder, provided the elements of quality, service, delivery, and reliability are equal.
6. Keep prices confidential—do not divulge prices to competitors.
7. Receive supplier representatives promptly and courteously.
8. Establish good relationships with supplier representatives—this can be better accomplished when incidental social expenses are shared equally by buyer and seller.
9. Do not accept gratuities—it is not in accordance with Company policies and has no place in our purchasing transactions.

Minority business development

The United States government had, among other measures, encouraged the support of businesses operated or owned by minority groups for a number of years. The Small Business Administration and the Office of Minority Business Enterprise were the administration's main means of implementing its policy.

Mr. Hartwell, early in 1973, realized that his department had to undertake special steps if it were to satisfy his and Management's wishes to place a significant amount of business with minority suppliers.

Buying from minority sources

Mr. Hartwell had made a special effort as a member of the IPC, to become better acquainted with the question of buying from minority sources. His information included publications, as well as direct contact with purchasing managers outside and inside that organization. At a recent special meeting of the local National Association of Purchasing Management chapter a number of participants voiced the opinion that just because the government advised purchasing from minority sources this was hardly sufficient reason for a purchasing manager to risk the company's dollars where it did not make good business sense.

Mr. Hartwell heard from several colleagues in the automotive field that a very aggressive approach to minority source development had resulted in the placement of significant volumes of business. He also heard from many others that, despite genuine efforts, results had been largely disappointing. Mr. Hartwell talked informally with a number of purchasing managers and buyers inside his own organization and he found that his buyers were largely conditioned to being sold by suppliers. When he asked the mill supplies buyer why a certain black supplier was not considered, this typical buyer voiced the following contentions:

1. That no representatives of the minority supplier had called on him, and he therefore had no idea at all of their interest in Edison, which he believed was reason enough to assume that if a man doesn't think enough of his products to tell others about them, then the buyer is not willing to risk the Company's dollars on him.
2. He admitted that he did send inquiries to other outfits with whom he had never dealt before, but he had done so because they were listed in trade directories, or he had learned about them from others, and he was generally satisfied that they could meet the Company's needs. To gain the same information about minority suppliers seemed to be impossible, as he had no directories nor anyone with whom he could discuss this matter.
3. He reasoned that even if he did turn up a black supplier, he would have to be extra cautious except if he were a dealer for an established product.
4. He had not considered that he or the Company could go out of the way to encourage such suppliers, because he was well aware that the Company would not pay a premium in price, or lower the quality or service standards just to do business with minorities. The extent of his Company's willingness to find other ways to help minorities had not been evident, even though he knew the government had been encouraging the business community to deal more with minority groups.

Mr. Hartwell realized that purchasing from minorities was not exactly a high priority matter with his staff, but before taking further action he wanted to get the subject more into the open.

Mr. Peplowski, an experienced buyer, had recently taken part in an invaluable incident of doing business with minorities and this had excited him. The Company's normal distributor of some electrical fittings had announced a price increase of the products they distributed, which were manufactured by a certain company. When this increase was questioned by Mr. Peplowski, the answer was not too convincing as to the need to increase this price, so he had developed the names of other Detroit outlets for these same products. One of these companies was a minority business, and they offered the same items for the same forthcoming period 15 percent lower than the longtime supplier.

Mr. Hartwell asked Mr. Peplowski if he would head a special committee of four buyers, to investigate the ways to motivate the other buyers in this program. At the first meeting, he explained that the Company was anxious to deal properly with the problem of minority suppliers and not merely to give it lip service. He announced that Purchasing Management had adopted a goal of doing $350,000 of business with minorities in 1973. He also said he believed firmly in the desirability of this program and that the target could be met. Success would lead to a more stable community and this was not only in the best interest of Detroit Edison but of every Detroit resident as well. He frankly said that he did not know how to proceed, but thought open discussion would be useful. He asked what difficulties had been encountered in making a buying approach to minorities. Typical replies were:

"No one contacted the purchasing department." "They lacked financial stability." "There was no qualified minority supplier of major equipment." "Lack of persistence in selling, perhaps because they didn't know whom to contact and were too shy to inquire." "They don't know how to cost and bid a contract." "Often don't know enough about a product to sell professional purchasing agents."

Mr. Peplowski reported that approximately $50,000 had been expended during the previous year on minority businesses, mainly in painting, cleaning and appliance parts. This figure may have been greater, as there may have been much more business that had gone their way and not been recorded. He further stated that it may not be known if some suppliers are in the minority group.

Mr. Hartwell could see that one of the difficulties was in locating these people. He knew that EDC published a directory, and wondered if there might be others. When asking those present how many possessed such a directory, only one or two hands went up. Also, only a few hands went up when questioned as to how many kept records of minority purchases. He thanked the participants and asked for suggestions from all present to meet the target for 1973. He realized, however, he would have to take a strong position to get a significant change in the department. He knew he himself had to undertake the tasks of writing a policy for top level company approval and the outline of a positive action plan which would assure meeting his objectives.

CASE 6–6
SOUTHERN CHEMICAL PRODUCTS, INC. (R)*

Introduction

On May 15, 1979, Mr. William Todd, director of purchasing of Southern Chemical Products, Inc., of New Orleans, Louisiana, received a wire from Puritan Chemicals of Knoxville, Tennessee, in which he was informed that the price at which Puritan was selling muriatic acid to Southern Chemical's

Tulsa plant in Oklahoma was to be raised from $39.00 to $53.00 per net ton effective June 1, 1979. Although Mr. Todd had been aware of talk in trade circles about an expected sharp increase in demand for the chemical in the Tulsa region due to stepped-up buying by steel mills, he considered the price change "unjustified, arbitrary, and unacceptable." The director of purchasing observed:

> Puritan has been an important customer of Southern Chemical for some years. Frankly, we might have swallowed a price boost of, say, $4 or $6 per ton in view of our trade relationships with the firm. But pushing it to $53.00 per ton was outrageous. The magnitude of the price increase left us no choice but to reject the increase completely and with determination.

Southern Chemical's Tulsa plant was depending on Puritan as the sole source of supply for the acid under an annual contract covering the year 1979.

Company background

Southern Chemical Products was an industrial company producing and marketing commodity chemicals and chemical intermediates and specialities. Over 95 percent of the company's 700-odd products were sold primarily to industrial markets both in the United States and abroad. Sales were over $380 million in 1978, with net profits after taxes amounting to over $24 million. The company employed approximately 7,000 persons in over 30 geographically dispersed plants.

Commodity chemicals, sold principally to other large chemical producers, such as Puritan, accounted for approximately 40 percent of sales in 1978. Products included alcohols, benzenes, chloroform, camphor, esters, ketones, purines, phenols, acetic and oxalic acids, caustic soda and potash, amines, and ammonia. In addition to other chemical companies, Southern Chemical's customers for commodity chemicals included petroleum companies, food processors, pulp and paper manufacturers, textile companies, and steel mills.

Muriatic acid

Southern Chemical's Tulsa plant used muriatic acid, 20° Baume (31.45 percent HCl), for purification of NaCl brines fed to electrolytic cells. This application called for a low concentration of heavy metals, iron, and other impurities. Strict and consistent adherence to specifications was important for the prevention of improper cell operation and also for storage in rubber-lined equipment. The specifications set up by Southern Chemical chemists required that the liquid acid be essentially colorless (35 APHA max.), with iron content of 1 ppm. max., hydrochloric acid content of 31.45–32.56 percent, sulfate content of 50 ppm. max., arsenic content of 0.2 ppm. max., and lead content of 1 ppm. max.

The Tulsa plant preferred to purchase the material as a prime asset rather than as a by-product of ethyl silicate production.

Southern Chemical—Puritan trade relations

Southern Chemical Products and Puritan Chemicals had been buying from, and selling to, each other a variety of commodity chemicals for a number of years. Thus, for instance, in 1974, Puritan had bought from Southern commodity chemicals amounting to $3.3 million, while Southern had placed orders with Puritan totaling $1.7 million. Between 1974 and 1978, this balance had changed as Southern doubled its purchases from Puritan to reach a total of $3.6 million, whereas the latter firm's purchases from Southern had increased during the same period from $3.2 million to a total of $4.9 million by 1978. Of the two companies, Puritan was by far the larger one, with sales of $3.6 billion and net earnings after taxes of $318 million in 1974. Puritan employed approximately 74,000 persons in over 60 domestic and overseas plants.

Procurement of muriatic acid

The need to purchase muriatic acid for Southern Chemical's Tulsa plant had arisen in November, 1977, when the plant discontinued its own production of the material because of an unfavorable cost structure. By the end of 1977, the company's director of purchasing had negotiated a contract for 1978 with Puritan for the supply of "the buyer's requirements of muriatic acid estimated at 4,000 tons and not to exceed this quantity without the seller's consent" at $39.00 per net ton, delivered Tulsa plant. This contract was renewed on the same terms in December 1978, for the 1979 calendar year. The contract specified that shipments were to be made from Puritan's plants in Springfield, Missouri, or Dallas, Texas, by tank truck. The terms and conditions under which Puritan accepted the contract stated, among other things, that "price . . . may be revised as of the beginning of a new quarterly period commencing on the first of January, April, July, and October . . . by a written notice from the seller not less than 15 days prior to the date on which the new quarterly period is to commence. . . ." Puritan had further stipulated that:

> . . . the buyer's written objection to a price revision served upon the seller prior to its effective date shall permit the buyer to purchase elsewhere quantities due during the ensuing quarterly period if the buyer is able to purchase from a responsible U.S. manufacturer and to furnish the seller with satisfactory written evidence of a bona fide offer, and the seller shall have elected not to meet such offer in which event the seller shall be released from his obligations. . . .[1]

---

[1]These and other terms and conditions were printed on the back of Puritan's contract forms.

Because of high transportation costs for the acid over long distances, Mr. Todd had been severely restricted in the choice of sources of supply. With the exception of Lee Chemical Company, a jobber in Nashville, Tennessee, that had solicited the plant's muriatic acid business late in 1977 he had been unable to locate other suppliers with plants sufficiently near Tulsa to sell to Southern Chemical at prices competitive with those of Puritan. Mr. Todd said:

> The nearest supplier quoted us a price of $60 per ton delivered plant. The only way to get the acid at competitive prices over a longer distance might have been by barge. This we ruled out because we had no facilities for unloading. Of course, the price we were paying to Puritan was very advantageous, and, in this sense, the absence of other suppliers was not considered to represent a particular problem at the time the contract was negotiated. In fact, when Lee Chemical solicited the business. I told them that we were very satisfied with our supplier. Normally a buyer doesn't shop around for deals as long as he is convinced that the existing source of supply is excellent.

Unloading facilities available at the Tulsa plant required that the acid be shipped by tank trucks. The material supplied by Puritan was pumped by the truck driver from the truck into storage. Tank cars, by contrast, required additions to the existing railroad siding to reach the acid storage area, and the use of company yard crews. Plant engineers had estimated that the additional investment and labor required would add costs of up to $2 per ton of acid. The engineers had also noted that this cost figure presumed a full utilization of the facilities which could only be achieved by switching other incoming liquid chemicals from transport by tank truck to transport by tank car. The question of whether such switching would create other production problems had not been examined by the engineers. Tank car schedules were considered less flexible than truck schedules.

Developments subsequent to Puritan's announced price increase

Following the receipt of the wire sent by Puritan, Mr. Todd telephoned the general sales manager of Puritan's chemical division producing and marketing the acid and expressed his deep dissatisfaction with the price increase. The director of purchasing commented: "I told the man in no uncertain terms what I thought about the $53.00 price and that we refused to accept it. But I made little headway, and at the end of our conversation it was perfectly clear that we couldn't just talk Puritan into rescinding the increase."

On May 17, 1979, Mr. Todd, by letter, invited the Lee Chemical Company to submit a price quotation for muriatic acid and to indicate available tonnage, lead time, and means of delivery. On May 21, Lee Chemical submitted a bid of $44.30 delivered Tulsa by tank car. The quotation indicated that Lee could deliver up to 3,500 tons per year and that the first shipment could arrive at Southern Chemical's Tulsa plant within four days following the signing of a contract. In a cover letter accompanying the quotation, Lee's president stated that a contract would have to be signed on a must-take basis for no less than 3,000 tons. The offered acid was a by-product from a chlorination process. The specifications given by Lee were as follows:

Appearance .... Clear
Color—APHA 40–50
HCl^2 .... 31.5%
Free Cl .... Nil
Organics .... 5–7 ppm.
Fe .... 0.8 ppm.
Ni .... Nil
Arsenic .... Nil

In discussing Lee's quotation with the general production manager of Southern's industrial chemical division and the production manager of the Tulsa plant, Mr. Todd encountered considerable skepticism. He observed:

> Because Lee was a jobber and the real source of supply was unknown, the production people were extremely wary of quality problems. The minimum-requirement and must-take features met with no enthusiasm, and delivery by rail was considered inadequate. There was no argument that the price was good. But we were all quite aware of the fact that disregarding the unreasonable price boost, Puritan was a top-rate supplier. And no one likes to dump an excellent supplier for some unknown outfit that might not be able to meet delivery schedules or adhere to specifications.

At the request of Southern Chemical, Lee submitted to the Tulsa plant a quarter sample of the acid, which was analyzed and found to meet specifications. In a memorandum to Mr. Todd, the plant manager emphasized, however, the short of a trial run with a full tank truck the production department remained unconvinced about Lee's material quality and that delivery by tank car, as well as the minimum-requirement and must-take conditions, was unsatisfactory.

On May 22, Mr. Todd arranged for a meeting with Puritan representatives in which he reiterated in strong language his company's unwillingness to accept the announced price increase. He disclosed to the Puritan representatives that, as a result of Puritan's action, he had sought and received a highly attractive, competitive offer for the supply of acid. He, however, was careful to avoid searching questions by the Puritan representatives regarding any details of the offer and to avoid identifying the source of supply. Mr. Todd gained the impression that the Puritan representatives seemed particularly anxious to get information leading to an identification of the alternate source of supply. They pointed out that their company's action was strictly within the bounds of the terms and conditions of the contract and reminded Mr. Todd that the contract called for the supply by Puritan of the Tulsa plant's *entire* muriatic acid requirement. The representatives stated their belief that this condition prevented Southern from using a second supplier during the term of the contract. They emphasized through the meeting that any serious consideration of an alternate source of supply for the acid by Southern was likely to have detrimental effects on the company's trade relationships with Puritan. Mr. Todd commented:

> There was no direct suggestion that we might lose some of Puritan's business, of course. Reciprocal business today is not handled on the basis of cold turkey deals, at least not in our business. But when the other guy keeps wondering about how this or that could have an adverse impact on trade relations, you know perfectly well what he is talking about. I pointed out to them that we had made tremendous efforts since 1974 to increase our purchases from Puritan and would continue to do so. As far as the clause "buyer's requirements" was concerned, I took the position that this meant the Tulsa plant's requirements *from Puritan* rather than the plant's total requirements of the acid. I made it quite clear that we saw nothing in the contract that would compel us to stay with Puritan as the exclusive supplier for the Tulsa plant during 1979. Of course, I must admit that the term "buyer's requirements" was ambiguous and open to different interpretations. It was loose language that I should have caught at the signing of the contract. But, then, our relationships with the major chemical producers in the United States to whom we sell and from whom we buy are of a long-range nature, and the ties are frequently quite closely knit, so that the fine print on contract forms is not too important. At any rate, the meeting produced no results, and Puritan stuck with the new price.

On the following day (May 23), Mr. Todd contacted the president of Lee Chemical and informed him that, although the small sample of acid submitted by Lee had been found satisfactory, the production department of the Tulsa plant had expressed considerable concern over the need for a consistent adherence to specifications, particularly since there was no knowledge of the producer of the acid. In addition, he pointed out that any price in excess of $38 per ton was unsatisfactory, that delivery by tank car was viewed with disfavor by the Tulsa plant, and that the minimum-requirements and must-take conditions attached to the quotation represented a significant obstacle to a serious consideration of the offer. Shortly after this conversation, Mr. Todd received a letter from the jobber offering a new price of $42 per ton delivered by truck. The letter pointed out, however, that the minimum-requirements and must-take conditions could not be dropped in view of the favorable price. The letter furthermore suggested that Southern Chemical accept a full tank truck of acid for a trial run. After conferring with the Tulsa plant manager, Mr. Todd ordered from Lee such a tank truck for testing purposes, and it arrived at the plant on May 28.

On June 1, before the Tulsa plant had tested the new trial shipment of acid, Mr. Todd received a letter from Puritan informing him that the announced price increase had been canceled and that shipments of the acid would continue at $39.00 per ton. The letter reemphasized that under the existing contract Puritan was to supply all of the Tulsa plant's muriatic acid requirements. Mr. Todd communicated Puritan's price rescission to the Tulsa plant. In response, the plant manager suggested that Mr. Todd drop the jobber from further consideration in light of Puritan's action and also in view of Lee's insistence on delivery of at least 3,000 tons of acid on a must-take basis. The plant manager pointed out to Mr. Todd that the total quantity offered by Lee was not sufficient to fill the plant's needs, thus forcing Southern to rely on a second supplier even if a contract with Lee were to be signed.

On June 8, the director of purchasing sent a memorandum to the Tulsa plant manager inquiring about the results of the trial run with the carload of acid supplied by Lee. Mr. Todd concluded the memorandum with the following statement:

> In thinking about the present and also the future supply situation, with respect to muriatic acid for your plant, I cannot help but think that if it had not been for Lee's offer, Puritan would now charge $53.00 per ton and this price would probably be the basis for the imminent negotiations for 1980.

It was not until August 10 that Mr. Todd received a memorandum from the Tulsa plant manager stating that the results of the trial run had been satisfactory. The plant manager added that while he could not be absolutely certain, he had good reason to believe that the jobber was buying the acid from the National Chemical Corporation of St. Louis. This information was of interest to Mr. Todd, since he knew that Puritan was a large buyer of several commodity chemicals produced by National Chemical.

Before Mr. Todd came to a conclusion about how to proceed with the offer made by Lee, he received a phone call from Lee's president, who was anxious to learn about the results of the trial run. Upon being informed by Mr. Todd that the results had been satisfactory, the president of Lee expressed his desire to sign a contract, indicating that he would be prepared to take a partial requirement contract of less than 3,000 tons and to drop the must-take condition. He reiterated that he considered a price of $41.00 per ton delivered tank truck to be a very competitive price and that he was also prepared to sell at $39.00 per ton delivered tank car.

Early in September, while Mr. Todd was still undecided as to how to continue negotiations with Lee, Puritan representatives informed him that their company was extremely anxious to sign a contract for 1980 in view of tightening supply. The representatives offered a price of $39.00 per ton and told Mr. Todd that they would allow him three days to accept the offer on an "entire requirements basis." They also informed him that Puritan was prepared to increase the dollar volume of purchases from Southern in 1980 by approximately $400,000 through the placement of orders for several chemical commodities not previously purchased from Southern.

CASE 6–7
LOCAR CORPORATION (R)

Mr. John Palmer, manager of purchasing for Locar Corporation, became, in early 1979, increasingly concerned about the shortage of supply of PL75, a major pipe resin. Several PL75 suppliers had approached Mr. Palmer requesting long-term supply contracts. Mr. Palmer was attempting to assess the advisability of such commitments.

Company background

Locar, a long established company in Cincinnati, Ohio, sold industrial piping and plumbing supplies.The company's four plants were located in the eastern United States. A series of regional warehouses provided an extensive distribution system which serviced customers throughout the domestic U.S. market. Total company sales for 1978 exceeded $300 million; piping products totaled $102 million. PL75 pipes and fittings made up 80 percent of piping products sales by Locar. Locar had experienced rapid growth; total company sales had increased at 20 percent a year and were expected to continue at that rate for at least the next four years. The corporate five-year plan called for pipe and fitting sales to exceed $240 million by 1982.

PL75 piping

Locar used PL75 in manufacturing piping products; compounds and stabilizers were added to the PL75 polymer, which was then extruded into pipe and pipe fittings. The manufacturing cost of PL75 pipe amounted to 35 percent of its selling price.

PL75 polymer was a versatile nonburning resin used in significant quantities in nearly every major segment of the pipe market.

Pipes produced from PL75 had remarkable long-life characteristics. Chemically, these pipes had not yet been known to break down or deteriorate. Another reason for the enthusiastic adoption and use of PL75 piping, and plastic piping in general was the ease of both installing and fastening of the pipe joints with a cement. These characteristics made resin piping far superior to cast iron and copper piping which required soldering. However, PL75 pipe was difficult to stabilize during the extrusion process. The larger the diameter of the pipe or fitting, the more technically competent the extruder had to be. John Palmer believed much of the future market growth would be toward larger pipe sizes and pipe applications which required a high degree of extrusion ability.

The plastic pipe industry

In 1977 the plastic pipe industry consisted of about 60 companies which shared a business volume of approximately $1200 million at retail. Of the 60 companies, no more than 25 had any major market impact as plastic pipe manufacturers; as few as six companies had annual volumes exceeding $60 million. The top four companies accounted for approximately half of the plastic pipe market, and were the only ones supplying a complete range of pipe and pipe fittings. Pipe made from PL75 constituted 50 percent of the total plastic pipe market in 1977 with approximately one third of the industry processing PL75.

Due to a relatively high cost of shipping plastic pipe, many small pipe companies cropped up throughout the country, each serving a small local market, thereby keeping their shipping costs down. There were several other reasons why so many small companies were in the PL75 pipe market. Very little capital was required to become a pipe extruder. Although the more sophisticated equipment, recently introduced, raised the investment requirements, companies still could set up an extrusion line for $80,000 to $100,000. A prospective extruder did not have to be technically proficient. Resin suppliers gave advice about the type of equipment to buy and how it was to be used. Many resin suppliers had, in the past, boasted about the ease of setting up a plastic pipe shop.

As the market matured in 1977 and 1978, small extruders were being forced out of the market, amalgamated, or left to concentrate on a few small sizes of pipe and pipe fittings. In Mr. Palmer's opinion, the future competitive situation in the industry would be based on sales and merchandising strengths rather than on manufacturing capability.

Future demand for PL75

In the United States, PL75 had experienced an extraordinary growth along with other plastic pipe materials during the seventies. European building specifications had during the 60s, quickly adopted resin pipe to replace cast iron, lead, and copper. In the 1960s the problems holding back quick adoption in North America were the needs for greater product standardization and the lack of acceptance by local building codes for use of PL75 pipe. Since building standards were normally controlled by local as well as state or federal agencies, the job of gaining plastic piping acceptance was time-consuming. Mr. Palmer expected that after 1978 a steady industry growth would stabilize between 10 and 12 percent per year for PL75 pipe. Some experts in the market predicted a glut on the market of resins, including PL75, by 1981 but the manufacturers of PL75 polymer strongly denied this.

Supply of PL75 polymer

Suppliers of PL75 had built up loyalties with their customers over the years when the market was soft and prices were low. However, since the beginning of 1979, they had set quotas for all their present customers, thereby making PL75 still available to many small extruders. Mr. Palmer thought that in a few years these loyalties would be terminated. Other polymer suppliers, who were also extruders of PL75, had stopped selling PL75 polymer during the last year and were using all of their own production.

Suppliers located within a 1,000-mile radius of Locar's plants were considered by Mr. Palmer to be within the maximum shipping distance. Since PL75 was delivered in bulk by rail or truck, all current contracts were f.o.b. Locar plants. Suppliers further than 1,000 miles away would not submit an f.o.b. quote. Mr. Palmer estimated that within this shipping distance, 15 potential suppliers of PL75 polymer existed. If suppliers were to be switched or lost, freight charges could play a critical role in alternative supplier selections.

Locar purchases and suppliers of PL75

Locar started extruding resin pipe in 1965. Increasing quantities of PL75 had been purchased since then. Past purchases, future demand, forecasts, and price increases are outlined in Exhibits 1 and 2.

Exhibit 1
PL75 purchase forecasts by Locar
(volume—millions pounds)

1976	*			
1977		*		
1978			*	
1979				*
1980				35 million
1981				47 million
1982	20 million	35 million	45 million	60 million

*Year forecast was made.

Exhibit 2
PL75 actual purchases and prices per pound

	Volume (in million pounds)	Price per pound (paid by Locar)
1965	3	8
1976	12	20
1977	15	21
1978	20	22
1979	(28) projected to year end	24

Exhibit 3
1979 supply of PL75 to Locar

Company	1979 capacity (in million pounds)	Locar purchases (in million pounds)
Clark	85	8.4
Solvay*	60	8.4
Imperial*	20	5.6
Acro	40	2.8
Albis	60	2.8
		28.0

*Capacity available for sale. Other capacity exists which is used within the company.

In 1979, five companies supplied Locar with PL75. Clark and Solvay had supplied PL75 to Locar since 1965. These two companies also supplied other chemical stabilizers and compounds to Locar in addition to PL75, and were considered by Mr. Palmer to be "old, reliable suppliers." The other three companies had supplied PL75 only and were relatively new, having commenced business with Locar during the last three years. One of these three, Imperial, manufactured PL75 polymer and also extruded industrial food and beverage piping made of PL75. Exhibit 3 outlines the percentages and volumes expected to be supplied by these five companies for 1979.

Prices had always been the same from all suppliers. Mr. Palmer noted that with the general tightening of supply, the price had quickly increased to a higher level. Until 1979, it had been standard industry practice to buy on a hand-to-mouth basis at the current market price.

Long-term contract proposals

In February 1979, Mr. Palmer was stunned by the rapid alteration of the supply situation. Within the same week, three of the present suppliers (Clark, Solvay and Imperial) had approached Mr. Palmer with proposals to supply Locar with present and future requirements of PL75.

Clark, a large international producer of a wide range of chemical products, was generally perceived as a leader in the monomer and polymer field. Clark had asked for a five-year contract extending until 1984 with escalation clauses for labor, energy, and feedstock based on a current price of 24 cents a pound. Clark pointed out the danger of future capacity shortages by showing Mr. Palmer projected capacity and sales figures. Minimum contract volumes would be based on Clark's present percentage of Locar's total purchases (30 percent) projected over Locar's 60 million pounds forecast. The commitment would be on a firm volume guaranteed contract with an escalated price. Locar would be contractually obligated to pay for that volume at the agreed price. A cancellation penalty was available which would amount to 60 percent of the selling price at the time of cancellation. Clark's sales representative stated that without this long-term contract, no supply guarantees could be given after August 1979.

Solvay, another large international concern, manufactured PL75 polymer as a raw material for some of its own end products as well as selling the polymer on the open market. Solvay's proposal was similar to Clark's except that it asked for a three-year contract instead of a five-year contract.

Imperial, like Solvay, was a large international corporation selling a wide range of end products using PL75 polymer. Imperial asked for a purchase agreement which could be dropped at any time by either party. Mr. Long wondered if imperial's reluctance to offer a long-term contract indicated that Imperial was planning to use all production of PL75 polymer itself within a few years.

Acro and Albis, both small PL75 polymer producers, had not asked for any special considerations and had not initiated discussions of future purchases with Mr. Palmer.

It was clear to Mr. Palmer that the suppliers were trying to protect future capacity increases by signing customers to long-term contracts. Purchasing practice at Locar had never included the use of long-term contracts. Most contracts for materials were on a yearly or monthly basis. During the last few years, contracts for PL75 were short-term, three or six month blanket contracts. Availability was such that a telephone call would be all that was required to obtain supply. This situation had changed over the last month with the introduction of quotas by suppliers. Generally, expansion of PL75 production was expected to continue strongly. Mr. Palmer believed that demand would continue to climb as the full potential of PL75 was recognized.

To explore other alternatives during this unusual situation, Mr. Palmer inquired about PL75 polymer production. He learned that to bring a PL75 monomer plant on-stream and producing would take approximately 18 months. Investment would be close to $14 million for a monomer plant with a capacity of 150 million pounds per year. For a polymer plant of 50 million pounds per year capacity, $8 million would be required and $12 million for a 100 million pound capacity plant.

He had also looked into the possibility of contracting PL75 feedstock, which Locar could then provide to its existing five polymer suppliers. Present monomer plants were, however, heavily invested in by the petrochemical companies, making any control over the feedstock difficult. These companies also controlled ethane, itself a by-product accounting for only 1 percent of their sales but a major component of the monomer. Unsure about Locar's present suppliers' reactions, Mr. Palmer hesitated to act in this area. He was uncertain about the dangers of becoming too deeply involved in the problems of polymer and monomer producers.

In a recent article, Mr. Palmer had read that a laboratory had successfully developed a better manufacturing method for PL75 monomer. Should this method be proven commercially, it might be expected to reduce the manufacturing cost of PL75 by about two cents per pound by 1982.

On March 5, 1979, Clark's sales representative telephoned Mr. Palmer to ask if he could bring his sales manager to a meeting on March 9 to discuss future business. Mr. Palmer knew that the long-term proposals would have to be decided upon before then. He was not sure if it was in his company's best interest to make the kind of commitment the suppliers were currently requesting. Nevertheless, he was most anxious to assure adequate supply for the future.

PRICE DETERMINATION

 Determination of the price to be paid is one of the major decisions to be made in purchasing. Indeed, the ability to get a "good price" is sometimes held to be the prime test of a good buyer. If by "good price" is meant greatest value, broadly defined, this is true.

While price is only one aspect of the overall purchasing job, it is extremely important. Basically, the purchasing department exists to satisfy the firm's purchase requirements at a lower overall cost than could be accomplished through decentralized purchasing. The purchasing department must be alert to different pricing methods, know when each is appropriate, and use skill in arriving at the price to be paid. There is no reason to apologize for emphasizing price or for giving it a place of importance among the factors to be considered. The purchaser rightly is expected to get the best value possible for the organization whose funds are spent. Any price quoted should be analyzed, irrespective of who the supplier is or what the item may be. The price paid by the purchaser is as much a factor in the final decision on what is the "best buy" as are the technical properties of the product.

Relation of cost to price ✍

Every purchasing manager believes the vendor should be paid a fair price. But what does "fair price" mean? A fair price is the lowest price that ensures a continuous supply of the proper quality where and when needed. A fair price makes it possible for the user to be reasonably assured of a material cost such that an end product or service can be sold in a competitive market at a profit or can be provided by a not-for profit organization at a satisfactory cost benefit ratio over the long run.

A "continuous supply" is possible in the long run only from a vendor who is making a reasonable profit. The vendor's total costs, including a reasonable profit, must be covered by total sales in the long run. Any one item in the line, however, may never contribute "its full share" over any given period, but even for such an item the price paid should at least cover the direct costs incurred.

A fair price to one seller for any one item may be higher than a fair price to another or for an equally-satisfactory substitute item. Both may be "fair prices" as far as the buyer is concerned, and the buyer may pay both prices at the same time.

Merely because a price is set by a monopolist or is established through collusion among the sellers does not, in and of itself, make that price unfair or excessive. Likewise, the prevailing price need not necessarily be a fair price, as, for example, when such price is a "black" or "gray" market price or when it is depressed or raised through monopolistic or coercive action.

The purchasing manager is called upon continuously to exercise judgment as to what the "fair price" should be under a variety of circumstances. To determine this "fair price," he or she must have experience (data) and common sense. In addition to these qualifications, some people seemingly possess an intuitive ability to judge prices—and the suppliers offering them—to an unusual degree; others appear to possess far less of this particular capacity. In part, of course, accuracy in weighing the various factors which culminate in a "fair and just price" is a matter of capitalizing on past experience.

Meaning of "cost" ⊙

Assuming this concept of a fair price is sound, what are the relationships between cost and price? Clearly, to stay in business over the long run a supplier must cover total costs, including overhead, and receive a profit. Unless costs, including profit, are covered, eventually the vendor will be forced out of business. This reduces the number of sources available to the buyer and may cause scarcity, higher prices, less satisfactory service, and lower quality.

But what is to be included in the term "cost"? At times it is used to cover only direct labor and material costs, and in times of depressed business conditions, many a seller is willing merely to recover this amount rather than not make a sale at all. Or cost may mean direct labor and material costs with some contribution toward overhead. If the cost for a particular item includes overhead, is the latter charged at the actual rate (provided it can be determined) or is it charged at an average rate? The average rate may be far from the actual.

Most knowledgeable business people realize that determination of the cost of a particular article is not a precise process. However, it is common practice to refer to the cost of an article very precisely. In manufacturing industries there are two basic classifications of costs—direct and indirect.

Direct costs usually are defined as those which can be specifically and accurately assigned to a given unit of production; i.e., materials, such as ten pounds of steel; or labor, such as 30 minutes of a person's time on a machine or assembly line. However, under accepted accounting practices the actual price of the specific material used may not be the cost that is used in figuring direct material costs. Because the price paid for material may fluctuate up or down over a period of time, it is common practice to use a so-called standard cost. Some companies use as a standard cost for materials the last price paid in the immediately prior fiscal period. Other companies use an average price for a specific period.

Indirect costs are those incurred in the operation of a production plant or process but which normally cannot be related directly to any given unit of production. Some examples of indirect costs are rent, property taxes, machine depreciation, expenses of general supervisors, power, heat, and light.

Classification of costs into variable, semivariable, and fixed categories is a common accounting practice and a necessity for any meaningful analysis of price/cost relationships. Most direct costs are variable, because they vary with the units produced. For example, a product which requires 10 pounds of steel for one unit will require 100 pounds for 10 units. Semivariable costs may vary with the number of units produced but are partly variable and partly fixed. For example, more heat, light, and power will be used when a plant is operating at 90 percent of capacity than when operating at a 50 percent rate, but the difference is not directly proportional to the number of units produced. In fact, there would be some costs (fixed) for heat, light, and power if production were stopped completely for a period of time.

Fixed costs generally remain the same regardless of the number of units produced. For example, real estate taxes will be the same for a given period of time regardless of whether one unit or 100,000 units are produced. There are several accounting methods of allocating fixed costs. A common method is to apply a percentage of direct costs in order to allocate the cost of factory overhead. Full allocation of fixed expenses will depend on an accurate forecast of production and the percentage used. Obviously as full production capacity is reached, the percentage rate will decline.

From the foregoing, we can define cost as so many dollars and cents per unit based on an average cost for raw material over a period of time, direct labor costs, and an estimated volume of production over a period of time on which the distribution of overhead is based.

If this definition of cost is acceptable, then a logical question is, whose cost? Some manufacturers are more efficient than others. Usually all sell the same item at about the same price. But should this price be high enough to cover only the most-efficient supplier's costs, or should it cover the costs of all vendors?

Furthermore, cost does not necessarily determine market price. When a seller insists that the price must be a given amount because of costs, this position is not really justified. In the final analysis, goods are worth and will sell for what the market will pay.

Moreover, no seller is entitled to a price that yields a profit merely because the vendor is in business or assumes risk. If such were the case, every business automatically would be entitled to a profit regardless of costs, quality, or service. Unless a seller can supply a market with goods that are needed and desired by users and can supply them with reasonable efficiency, that seller is not entitled to get a price that even covers cost.

Adjusting purchases to meet changing prices

Frequently, an organization is unable in the short term to raise the selling price of its own products, and yet the prices of the components and raw materials fluctuate. Animal feeds, candy, and flour are examples. If the mix of ingredients can be changed without adversely affecting the quality, taste, nutrition, or performance of the final product, there may be an opportunity to buy low-cost items to substitute for at least some of the high-cost ingredients. Linear programs have been developed for a number of animal feeds, for example, in an effort to maintain nutrition with a large number of formulations. The rapidly-fluctuating prices of ingredients force the manufacturer to plan production according to market availability and prices. If all ingredients rise substantially in price at the same time, as is common at a time of shortages, such substitutions will not solve the problem, and the manufacturer will be forced to raise prices or absorb the extra costs.

HOW VENDORS ESTABLISH PRICE

Depending on the commodity and industry, the market may vary from almost pure competition to oligopoly and monopoly.[1] Pricing will vary accordingly. Most firms are not anxious to disclose just how prices are set for competitive reasons, but the two traditional approaches are the cost and the market approach.

The cost approach

The cost approach to pricing says that the price should be a certain amount over direct costs, allowing for sufficient contribution to cover indirect costs and overhead and leaving a certain margin for profit. For the purchaser, the cost approach offers a number of opportunities to seek low-cost suppliers, to suggest lower cost manufacturing alternatives, and to question the size of the margin over direct costs. Negotiation, used with cost analysis techniques, is a particularly useful tool.

The market approach

The market approach implies that prices are set in the marketplace and may not be directly related to cost. If demand is high relative to supply, prices are expected to rise; when demand is low relative to supply, prices should decline. This, too, is an oversimplification. Some economists hold that large multinational, multiproduct firms have such a grip on the marketplace that pure competition does not exist and that prices will not drop even though supply exceeds demand. In the market approach, the purchaser must either live with prevailing market prices or find ways around them. If nothing can be done to attack the price structure directly, it may still be possible to select those suppliers who are willing to offer nonprice incentives, such as holding inventory, technical service, good quality, excellent delivery, transportation concessions, and early warning of impending price and new product changes. Negotiation, therefore, may center on items other than price.

There are a number of ways around market pricing. One is for the purchaser to seek the same product in a different market where the price is lower. This often

---

[1] Fearon, Harold, *Purchasing Economics* (New York: American Management Association, 1968).

means purchasing from foreign sources. As the tendency to world trade increases and multinational firms grow, substantial differences between markets may well disappear, except for freight and tariff differentials.

Many economists hold that substitution of like but not identical materials or products is one of the most powerful forces preventing a completely monopolistic or oligopolistic grip on a market. For example, aluminum and copper may be interchanged in a number of applications. The aluminum and copper markets, therefore, are not independent of one another. The purchaser's ability to recognize these tradeoffs and to effect design and use changes to take advantage of substitution is one determinant of flexibility. Make or buy is another question. If access to the raw materials, technological process, and labor skills is not severely restricted, one alternative may be for an organization to make its own requirements to avoid excess market prices.

Sometimes purchasers use long-term contracts as an inducement for the supplier to ignore market conditions. This approach may be successful in certain instances, but it is normal for suppliers to find ways and means around such commitments once it becomes obvious that the prevailing market price is substantially above that paid by their long-term customers.

Government influence on pricing

During recent years, the role of government in establishing price has changed dramatically. Where belief in private enterprise and the market mechanism has been particularly strong, the increasing degree of government intervention has been viewed with considerable alarm by many industrialists. The role of government has been twofold. Not only has the government taken an active role in determining prices by establishing ceiling prices, production quotas, and instituting various forms of price/wage controls as part of an anti-inflationary battle, but also in the ways that buyer and seller are allowed to behave in agreeing on prices. The price control role is likely to vary with economic, political, and international conditions. The energy crisis and the dramatic increase in fuel prices has created a very serious challenge for both government and business. Since other governments are active in price control and have in a number of situations created dual pricing for domestic use and exports, it is difficult to see how North American governments will be able to ignore their position. Prices may be determined by review or control boards or by strong moral suasion. They are likely to be augmented by governmental controls like quotas, tariffs, and export permits.

The purchaser's role in affecting the price of items under direct government control may vary. Any purchaser may try to influence government directly. Substitution is still a possibility. The temptation of a gray or black market may well present itself, particularly if the governmental official price is so low that producers are loath to supply all the quantities the market needs. Copper scrap in the 1970s is a good example of what happens. With the price of virgin copper under control at 60 cents a pound and a world price of at least 90 cents a pound, copper scrap, which was not price controlled, rose to as high as $1.30 a pound domestically. The purchaser is in a very difficult position when supplies are not sufficient to meet internal demand and the pressure to acquire material at almost any price is extremely strong.

Legislation affecting price determination ✔

The government also has taken an active interest in how a buyer and seller agree on a price. The government's position largely has been a protective role to prevent the stronger party from imposing too onerous conditions on the weaker one or preventing collusion so that competition will be maintained.

The two most important Federal laws affecting competition and pricing practices are the Sherman and Robinson-Patman Acts. The Sherman Antitrust Act of 1890 states that any combination, conspiracy, or collusion with the intent of restricting trade in interstate commerce is illegal. This means that it is illegal for vendors to get together to set prices (price fixing) or determine the terms and conditions under which they will sell. It also means that buyers cannot get together to set the prices they will pay. The Robinson-Patman Act (Federal Price Discrimination Act of 1936) says that a vendor must sell the same item, in the same quantity, to all customers at the same price. It is known as the "one-price law." Some exceptions are permitted, such as a lower price (1) for a larger purchase quantity, providing the seller can cost-justify the lower price through cost accounting data, (2) to move "distress" or obsolete merchandise, or (3) to meet the lower price of local competition in a particular geographic area. The Act also goes on to state that it shall be illegal for a buyer knowingly to induce or accept a discriminatory price. However, the courts have been realistic in their interpretation of the law, holding that it is the job of the buyer to get the best possible price for his or her company, and that as long as he or she does not intentionally mislead the seller into giving a more favorable price than is available to other buyers of the same item, the law is not being violated.

If the buyer feels a seller is violating either the Sherman Act or the Robinson-Patman Act, a charge detailing the violation can be made to the Federal Trade Commission, which was set up to investigate alleged improprieties. From a buyer's standpoint, bringing a seller's actions to the government's attention has few advantages. Since most of the time government's reaction is relatively slow, the need for the item may be gone and conditions may be substantially changed by the time the complaint is decided. Most sellers would view the lodging of a complaint as a particularly unfriendly act, making it difficult for the organization to maintain a reasonable future relationship with the particular vendor. For this reason, complaints are not common, and most are lodged by governmental buying agencies rather than corporations.

TYPES OF PURCHASES AND METHODS OF PRICE DETERMINATION

Analysis of suppliers' costs is by no means the only basis for price determination. What other means can be used? Much depends on the type of product being bought. There are four general classes:

1. *Raw materials*. This group is made up of the so-called sensitive commodities, such as copper, wheat, crude petroleum, and jute.

2. *Special items*. This group includes items and materials which are special to the organization's product line and, therefore, are custom ordered, as well as purchases of equipment and items of a nonrepetitive nature.

3. *Standard production items*. This group includes such items as bolts and nuts, many forms of commercial steel, valves, and tubing, whose prices are fairly stable and are quoted on a basis of "list price with some discount."

4. *Items of small value*. This group includes items of such small comparative value that the expenditure of any particular effort to check price prior to purchase is not justified.

Sensitive commodities. For the sensitive commodities, the price at any particular moment probably is less important than the trend of the price movement. The price can be determined readily in most instances because many of these commodities are bought and sold on well-organized markets. Prices are reported regularly in many of the trade and business journals, such as *Iron Age* and *The Wall Street Journal*. To the extent that such quoted prices are a fair reflection of market conditions, the current cash price is known and is substantially uniform for a given grade. Yet it is common knowledge among buyers that such published market quotations usually are on the high side, and the astute buyer probably can get a lower price. With commodities of this sort a company's requirements usually are sufficiently adjustable, so that an immediate order is seldom a necessity and purchase can be postponed if the trend of prices is downward.

The trend of price is a matter of importance in the purchase of any type of commodity, but it is particularly important with this group. Insofar as "careful and studious timing" is essential to getting the right price, both the types of information required as a basis for such timing and the sources from which the information can be obtained differ from those necessary in dealing with other groups of items. Commodity study research, discussed in Chapter 15, is particularly useful in buying these items.

Special items. Special items include a large variety of purchased parts or special materials peculiar to the organization's end product or service. Make or buy is always a significant consideration on these items because of their proprietary nature. Prices normally are obtained by quotation because no published price lists are available. Subcontracts are common, and the availability of compatible or special equipment, skilled labor, and capacity may be significant factors in determining price. Since large differences may exist between suppliers in terms of these factors and their desire for business, prices may vary substantially between bidders. Each product in this group is unique and may need special attention. A diligent search for suppliers willing and able to handle such special requirements, including an advantageous price, may pay off handsomely.

Equipment and nonrepetitive purchases also normally are handled with extensive use of quotations.

Standard production items. The third group of items includes those standard production items whose prices are comparatively stable and are likely to be quoted on a basis of list less certain discounts. This group includes a wide range of items commonly obtainable from a substantial list of sources. The inventory problems related to this class of requirements are largely routine. Changes in price do occur, but they are far less frequent than with raw materials and are likely to be moderate. Prices usually are obtained from catalogs or similar publications of vendors, supplemented by periodic discount sheets.

It should not be concluded from this that such purchases are unimportant or that the prices quoted should not be examined with care. Quite the contrary is true. The items are important in themselves; the annual dollar volume of purchases is often impressive; and real attention needs to be paid to the unit price. When a requisition is received by the purchasing department, the first step commonly would be to refer to past purchase records as the first source of information. If the material in question has been regularly purchased or orders have been placed for it recently, an up-to-date price record and catalog file will give all the information pertaining to the transaction, such as the various firms able to supply the commodity, the firms from which purchases have been made, and the prices paid. This information will be sufficiently recent and reliable to enable the buyer to place the order without extended investigation. However, if the buyer does not feel justified in proceeding upon the basis of this information, a list of available suppliers from vendor files, catalogs, and other sources can be assembled and quotation requests can be sent to selected sources.

One of the best sources for current prices and discounts is sales representatives. Few manufacturers rely wholly upon catalogs for sales but follow up such material by visits from their salespersons. Much useful data can be obtained from such visits. The buyer learns of price revisions, which should be noted in the appropriate catalog, ascertains the probable date of publication of new editions, and is assured that the corporation is on the proper mailing lists. In some lines confidential discounts, usually based on quantity, are uncovered. Advance notice of intended price changes sometimes is given. It is the buyer's duty to be alert to the possibilities of such information in order that full advantage may be taken of them.

A sales representative may quote the buyer a price while in the buyer's office, and the buyer may accept by issuing a PO. There likely will be no problem, although legally the salesperson probably doesn't have agency authority, and the offer made by the salesperson does not legally commit the selling company *until* it has been accepted by an officer of the selling company. If the buyer wishes to accept such an offer, and to know that the offer is legally binding, he or she should ask the salesperson to furnish a letter, signed by an officer of the selling company, stating that the salesperson possesses the authority of a sales agent.

Items of small value. The fourth group of commodities for the purpose of price determination includes items of such small value, comparatively speaking, that they do not justify any particular effort to analyze the price in detail. Every purchasing department must buy numerous items of this sort from time to time; yet these items do not in themselves justify a catalog file, even when such catalogs are available, nor do they represent enough money to warrant sending out for individual quotations. Actually, the pricing problem on such items is handled in a variety of ways; the following constitutes an excellent summary of these procedures:

It is common practice to send out unpriced orders for such items. Another common practice is to indicate on the order the last price paid, this price being taken from the record of purchases or past purchases if the last purchase was not too far back. Other purchasing agents make a practice of grouping these small items under some contract arrangement or on a cost-plus basis with suppliers who undertake to have the materials on hand when needed, and who are willing to submit to periodical checking as to the fairness of the prices they charge.

In most cases, sources of supply for these items are local and current prices often are obtained by telephone and then placed on the face of the purchase order so they become a part of the agreement of purchase. The most common practice of all, however, is perhaps to depend upon the integrity of the suppliers and to omit any detailed checking of the proper price on items of small value. Many purchasing agents believe that their best assurance is the confidence they have in carefully selected sources of supply and they feel secure in relying upon the vendors to give them the best available price without requiring them to name the price in advance, and without checking it when the invoice is received.

Another and final method for controlling prices for these small dollar items consists of the practice of "spot-checking." This means the selection of an occasional item which then is carefully investigated to develop the exact basis upon which the supplier is pricing. Discovery of unfair or improper prices by such spot checks is considered a reason for discontinuing the source of supply who is discovered to be taking advantage of the nature of the transaction in pricing.

Perhaps a more effective way to buy items of small value, such as those included in the MRO group is to use the systems contracting techniques described earlier.

Somewhat similar to the small value purchase problem is the emergency requirement. Here, as for example with equipment breakdown, time may be of much greater value than money and the buyer may wish to get the vendor started immediately, even though price has not been determined. Here the buyer may decide merely to say "start" or "ship" and issue an unpriced purchase order. If the price charged on the invoice is out of line, it can be challenged before payment.

The use of quotations and competitive bidding •

Quotations normally are secured when the size of the proposed commitment exceeds some minimum dollar amount: e.g., $1,000. Governmental purchases commonly must be on a bid basis; here the law requires that the award shall be made to the lowest responsible bidder. In industrial practice, proposals may be solicited with a view to selecting those firms with whom negotiations as to the final price will be carried on.

The extent to which competitive bidding is relied upon to secure an acceptable price varies widely. On the one hand, it is a common practice for buyers of routine supplies, purchased from the same sources time after time, to issue un-priced orders. The same thing occasionally happens in a very strong seller's market for some critical item when prices are rising so rapidly that the vendor refuses to quote a fixed price. Wherever possible, however, price should be indicated on the purchase order. In fact, from a legal point of view, a purchase order *must* either contain a price or a method of its determination for the contract to be binding.

When it is decided to ask for competitive bids, certain essential steps are called for. These are a careful initial selection of dependable, potential sources; an accurate wording of the request to bid; submission of bid requests to a suffi-cient number of suppliers to assure a truly competitive price; proper treatment of such quotations, once received; and a careful analysis of them prior to making the award.

The first step is to select possible vendors from whom quotations are to be solicited; this amounts, in fact, to a preliminary sorting of the sources of supply. It is assumed that the bidders must (1) be qualified to make the item in question in accordance with the buyer's specifications and to deliver it within the desired date, (2) be sufficiently reliable in other respects to warrant serious consideration as suppliers, (3) be numerous enough to ensure a truly competitive price, but (4) not be more numerous than necessary. The first two of these qualifications have been considered in our discussion of sources. The *number* of suppliers to whom inquiries are sent is largely a matter of the buyer's judgment. Ordinarily, at least two vendors are invited to bid. More often, three or four are invited to submit bids. A multiplicity of bidders does not ensure a truly competitive price, although under ordinary circumstances it is an important factor, provided that the bidders are comparable in every major respect and provided that each is suffi-ciently reliable so that the buyer would be willing to purchase from that vendor.

The buyer normally will exclude from the bid list those firms with whom it is unlikely that an order would be placed, even though their prices were low. Occa-sionally, a vendor may insist on being given an opportunity to quote, and it may be good diplomacy on the part of the buyer to grant this request. So, too, it is wise to test out new and untried suppliers for the purpose of locating new sources. Sometimes bids are solicited solely for the purpose of checking the prices of regular suppliers or for inventory-pricing purposes. It should be re-membered, however, that a company is put to some expense—at times, a very considerable one—when it submits a bid. It should not be asked to bear this cost without good reason. Moreover, the receipt of a request to bid is an encourage-ment to the vendor and carries with it the implication that an order is possible. Therefore, purchasers should not solicit quotations unless placement of a pur-chase order is a possibility.

Having decided on the companies that are to be invited to bid, a general inquiry is addressed to them, in which all the necessary information is set forth. A complete description of the item or items, the date on which these items are wanted, and the date by which the bid is to be returned are included. In many instances, a telephone inquiry is substituted for a formal request to bid.

Subsequent to the mailing of an inquiry but prior to the announcement of the purchase award, bidders naturally are anxious to know how their quotations compare with those of their competitors. Since sealed bids, used in governmental purchasing, are not commonly used in private industry, the purchaser is in a position to know how the bids, as they are received, compare with one another. However, if the bids are examined upon receipt, it is important that this information be treated in strictest confidence. Indeed, some buyers deliberately keep themselves in ignorance of the quotations until such time as they are ready to analyze the bids; thus they are in a position truthfully to tell any inquiring bidder that they do not know how the bid prices compare. Even after the award is made, it probably is the better policy not to reveal to unsuccessful bidders the amount by which they failed to meet the successful bid.

Firm bidding ✦✦

The reason for the confidential treatment of bid price information is its connection with a problem practically all buyers have to face, namely, that of "firm bidding." Most firms have a policy of notifying suppliers that original bids must be final and that revisions will not be permitted under any circumstances. Exceptions are made only in case of obvious error.

Particularly in times of falling prices, suppliers, extremely anxious to get business, try by various devices to assure that their bids will be the lowest. Not infrequently they have been encouraged in this procedure by those purchasers who have acceded to requests that revisions be made. Unfortunately, it is also true that there are buyers who deliberately play one bidder against another and who even seek to secure lower prices by relating imaginary bids to prospective suppliers. The responsibility for deviations from a policy of firm bidding must be laid at the door of the purchaser as well as of the supplier.

A policy of firm bidding is sound and should be deviated from only under the most unusual circumstances. To those who contend that it is impossible to adopt such a policy, the answer is that it actually is the practice followed in many concerns. The advantages of firm bidding as a general policy, however, need no particular explanation. If rigidly adhered to, it is the fairest possible means of treating all suppliers alike. It tends to stress the quality and service elements in the transaction instead of the price factor. Assuming that bids are solicited only from honest and dependable suppliers and that the buyer is not obligated to place the order with the lowest bidder, it removes from suppliers the temptation to try to use inferior materials or workmanship once their bid has been accepted. It saves the purchaser time by removing the necessity of constant bargaining with suppliers over price.

Occasionally the buyer may, after reviewing the bids submitted, notify the bidders that all bids are being rejected, and that another bid request is being issued or that the item will be bought through a means other than competitive bidding. This may be done if it is obvious that the bidders did not fully understand the specifications; if collusion on the part of the bidders is suspected; or if it is felt that all prices quoted are unrealistically high.

Determination of most advantageous bid

After the bids have been submitted and compared, which should be selected? The lowest bid customarily is accepted.[2] The objective of securing bids from various sources is to obtain the lowest price, and the purpose of supplying detailed specifications and statements of requirements is to assure that the buyer receives the same items or services irrespective of whom the supplier may be. Governmental contracts must be awarded to the lowest bidder unless very special reasons can be shown for not doing so.

However, there are several cases in which the lowest bidder may not receive the order. Information received by the buyer subsequent to the request for bids may indicate that the firm submitting the lowest bid is not reliable. Even the lowest bid may be higher than the buyer believes justifiable. Or there may be reason to believe that collusion existed among the bidders.

There are other reasons why the lowest bid is not always accepted: plant management, engineering, or using departments may express a preference for a certain manufacturer's product. Possibly a slight difference in price may not be considered enough to compensate for the confidence insured by a particular supplier's product. A small difference in price may not seem to justify changing from a source of supply that has been satisfactory over a long period; yet the bid process may have been considered essential in assuring that the company was receiving the proper price treatment.

Selecting the supplier, once the quotations are received, is not a simple matter of listing the bidders and picking out the one whose price is apparently low, because the obvious price comparisons may be misleading. Of two apparently identical bids, one actually may be higher than the other. One supplier's installation costs may be lower than another's. If prices quoted are f.o.b. origin, the transportation charges may be markedly different. One supplier's price may be much lower because it is trying to break into a new market or is trying to force its only real competitor out of business. One vendor's product may require tooling which must be amortized. One supplier may quote a fixed price; another may insist on an escalator clause that may push the price above a competitor's firm bid. These and other similar factors are likely to render a snap judgment on comparative price a mistake.

Collusive bidding. A buyer also may reject all bids if it is suspected that the suppliers are acting in collusion with one another. In such cases the proper policy to pursue is often difficult to determine but there are various possibilities. Legal action is possible but seldom is feasible because of the expense, delay, and uncertainty of the outcome. Often, unfortunately, the only apparent solution is simply to accept the situation with the feeling that there is nothing the buyer can do about it anyway. Another possibility is to seek new sources of supply either inside or outside the area within which the buyer customarily has purchased materials or services. Resort to substitute materials, temporarily or even permanently, may be an effective means of meeting the situation. Another possibility is to reject all the

---

[2] This statement is made on the assumption that the lowest bid comes from a reliable supplier; presumably, of course, only reliable firms have been invited to bid.

bids and then to attempt, by a process of negotiation or bargaining with one or another of the suppliers, to reduce the price. If circumstances make the last alternative the most feasible, a question of ethics is involved. Some purchasing officers feel that when collusion among the vendors exists it is ethical for them to attempt to force down suppliers' prices by means which would not ordinarily be adopted.

The problem of identical prices

It is not unusual for the buyer to receive identical bids from various sources. Since such bids may indicate intensive competition, on the one hand, and discrimination or collusion, on the other, the purchaser must take care in handling such situations. Wolf lists eight factors which tend to make identical or parallel prices suspect.[3]

1. Identical pricing marks a novel break in the historical pattern of price behavior.
2. There is evidence of communication between sellers or buyers regarding prices.
3. Sellers refuse to sell at a higher price even if a buyer makes the offer.
4. Meetings are held which result in "artificial" standardization of the product.
5. Identical prices are submitted in bids to buyers on complex, detailed, or novel specifications.
6. Identical prices result from adherence to an "artificial" delivered pricing system.
7. Parallel pricing is associated with an "open price plan" or "price reporting plan" carried on by the industry's trade association.
8. Deviations from uniform prices are not ignored or endured in the same way as changes in the weather but become the matter of industry-wide concern—the subject of exhortations, meetings, and even organized sanctions.

According to Wolf, the purchaser can take four different types of action to discourage identical pricing. The first is the encouragement of small sellers who form the nonconformist group in an industry and are anxious to grow. The second is to allow bidders to bid on parts of large contracts if they feel the total contract may be too large. The third is the encouragement of firm bidding without revision. And the fourth is to choose criteria in making the award, so as to discourage future identical bids. "Drawing names from a hat, sharing the business among all the identical bidders, or dividing the business according to the historic market shares of the bidders are not conducive to breaking a pattern of identical bidding because such procedures are exactly what the firms hope will be done if bids are identical."[4]

---

[3]R. H. Wolf, "Purchasing in a World of Identical Prices," *Journal of Purchasing* 2, no. 1 (February 1966): 82.
[4]Ibid., p. 86.

Various alternatives for awarding the bid are available. It may be given to:

1. The smallest supplier.
2. The one with the largest domestic content.
3. The most distant firm, forcing it to absorb the largest freight portion.
4. The firm with the smallest market share.
5. The firm most likely to grant nonprice concessions.

Executive Order No. 10936, April 24, 1961, directed the reporting and analysis of identical bids received by federal and local levels of government. The Department of Justice must be informed by all agencies purchasing for the federal government of identical bids on contracts exceeding $10,000. State and local purchasing agents also were asked to report identical bids. Although most industrial purchasing managers are reluctant to use the courts to address identical bids, governmental employees are required to report them and their action has had significant results.

Negotiation as a method of price determination

Competitive bidding is the most efficient means of obtaining a fair price for items bought, for the forces of competition are used to bring the price down to a level at which the efficient vendor will only be able to cover production and distribution costs, plus make a minimum profit. If a vendor wants the order, that vendor will "sharpen his pencil" and give the buyer an attractive quote. This places a good deal of pressure on the vendor, and competitive bidding should be used whenever possible.

However, for the bid process to work efficiently, several conditions are necessary: (1) There must be at least two, and preferably several, qualified vendors; (2) The vendors must want the business; competitive bidding works best in a buyer's market; (3) The specifications must be clear, so that each bidder knows precisely what is being bid on, and so the buyer easily can compare the quotes received from various bidders; and (4) There must be honest bidding and the absence of any collusion between the bidders. When any of these conditions is absent; i.e., a sole source situation, a seller's market, specifications not complete or subject to varying interpretations, or suspected vendor collusion, then negotiation is the preferred method of price determination.

Negotiation is the most sophisticated and most expensive means of price determination. It is used on large dollar purchases where competitive bidding is not appropriate. Negotiation requires that the buyer sit down across a table with a vendor, and through discussion they arrive at a common understanding on the essentials of a purchase/sale contract, such as delivery, specifications, warranty, prices, and terms. Because of the interrelation of these factors and many others, it is a difficult art and requires the exercise of judgment and tact. Negotiation is an attempt to find an agreement which allows both parties to realize their objectives. It is used most often when the buyer is in a sole-source situation; in that case, both parties know that a purchase contract will be issued and their task is to define a set of terms and conditions acceptable to both. Because of the expense and time involved, true negotiation normally will not be used unless the dollar amount is quite large, $50,000 or more is the general minimum set by some organizations.

Reasonable negotiation is expected by buyer and seller alike. It is within reasonable bounds of negotiation to insist that a supplier:

1. Operate in an efficient manner.
2. Keep prices in line with costs.
3. Not take advantage of a privileged position.
4. Make proper and reasonable adjustment of claims.
5. Be prepared to consider the special needs of the buyer's organization.

While negotiation normally is thought of as a means of establishing price to be paid, and this is the main focus, many other areas or conditions can be negotiated. In fact, *any* aspect of the purchase/sale agreement is subject to negotiation. A few of these areas are:

1. Quality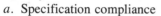
   a. Specification compliance
   b. Performance compliance
   c. Test criteria
   d. Rejection procedures
   e. Liability
   f. Reliability
   g. Design changes
2. Support
   a. Technical assistance
   b. Product research and development
   c. Warranty
   d. Spare parts
   e. Training
   f. Tooling
   g. Packaging
3. Supply
   a. Lead times
   b. Delivery schedule
   c. Consignment stocks
   d. Expansion options
   e. Vendor inventories
   f. Cancellation options
4. Transportation
   a. Terms f.o.b.
   b. Carrier
   c. Commodity classification
   d. Freight allowance/equalization
   e. Multiple delivery points

5. Price
   a. Purchase order price
   b. Discounts (cash, quantity, and trade)
   c. Escalation provisions
   d. Exchange terms (monetary rate fluctuation)
   e. Import duties
   f. Payment of taxes

Price haggling. Negotiating a fair price should not be confused with "price haggling," for which there is little justification. Purchasing managers generally frown upon haggling, and properly so, for in the long run the cost to the buyer far outweighs any temporary advantage. For a purchaser to tell a sales representative that he or she has received a quotation that was not, in fact, received or that is not comparable; to fake telephone calls in the sales representative's presence; to leave real or fictitious bids of competitors in open sight for a sales representative to see; to mislead as to the quantity needed—these and similar practices are illustrations of that "sharp practice" so properly condemned by the Code of Ethics of the National Association of Purchasing Management.

Revision of price upward. Negotiation need not result in a lower price. Occasionally, there may be revision upward of the price paid, compared to the vendor's initial proposal. If in the negotiation it becomes clear that the vendor has either misinterpreted the specifications or underestimated the resources needed to perform the work, the buyer will bring this to the vendor's attention so the proposal may be adjusted accordingly. A good contract is one that both parties can live with, and the vendor should not lose money, providing the operation is efficient. When a purchaser cooperates in granting increases not required by the original vendor proposal, the buyer is in a position to request decreases in prices if unforeseen events occur which result in the vendor's being able to produce the material or product at a substantial saving.

Cost/price analysis

The party in the strongest position in a negotiation session is the one which has the best data. Recognizing the importance of cost, it is common practice for the purchasing manager to make the best estimate possible of supplier's costs as one means of judging the reasonableness of the price proposed. When the supplier is given a request for proposal (RFP), which is an invitation to make an offer which both parties agree will be subject to further negotiation, it is normal for the buyer to also request that the proposal be accompanied by a cost breakdown. If the vendor has nothing to hide and is confident in the work of its estimating departments it should be willing to supply the requested cost breakdown. But, if a cost breakdown cannot be obtained, then the buyer must do a cost buildup, which is far more time consuming and difficult to do.

Many larger firms have within the purchasing department cost analysts to assist the buyer in analyzing vendor costs in preparation for negotiation. (See also Chapter 15 on purchasing research.) These cost estimates must be based on such data as are available. The prices of raw material entering into the product are commonly accessible and the amounts required are also fairly well known. For component parts, catalog prices often offer a clue. Transportation costs are easily determined. The buyer's own engineers should provide data on processing costs. Burden and general overhead rates can be approximated.

Overhead costs generally consist of indirect costs incurred in the manufacturing, research, or engineering facilities of the company. Equipment depreciation typically is the largest single element in manufacturing burden. It is important to know how these burden costs are distributed to a given product. If overhead is allocated as a fixed percentage of direct labor costs and there is an increase in labor costs, overhead costs can be unduly inflated unless the allocation percentage is changed.

The growing tendency for industry to become more capital intensive has increased the relative percentage of overhead versus direct labor and materials. Since some items in the overhead such as local real estate taxes are attributable to the location of the supplier and others are properly seen as depreciation or investment at varying technological and economic risk levels, the analysis and allocation of these costs to individual products is particularly difficult.

Both tooling costs and engineering costs often are included as a part of general manufacturing burden, but it probably is wisest to pull them out for analysis as separate items, since each may account for a relatively large amount of cost. The buyer wants to know what it should cost a reasonably efficient vendor to build the tooling, ownership of completed tooling, life expectancy (number of units), and whether the tooling can be used with other equipment than that owned by the vendor. Only with such information can the buyer guard against being charged twice for the same tooling. In the case of engineering labor, it usually is quite expensive on an hourly basis and the buyer does not want to pay the vendor for engineering work which really isn't necessary.

General and administrative expense includes items such as selling, promotion, advertising, executive salaries, and legal expense. Frequently there is no justification for the supplier to charge an advertising allocation in the price of a product manufactured to the buyer's specifications.

Material costs can be estimated from a bill of material, a drawing, or a sample of the product. The buyer can arrive at material costs by multiplying material quantities per unit by raw material prices. Sometimes a material usage curve will be helpful. The purpose of the curve is to chart what improvement should occur from buying economies and lower scrap rates as experience is gained in the manufacturing process. Use of price indices and maintenance of price trend records is standard practice.

Direct labor estimates are not made as easily as material estimates. Even though labor costs are normally labeled direct for machine operators and assembly line workers, in reality they tend to be more fixed than most managers care to admit. Most organizations prefer not to lay off personnel and there are strong pressures to keep the so-called "direct labor" force reasonably stable and employed. This means that inventories and overtime often are used to smooth fluctuations in demand and also that labor cost becomes at least semivariable and subject to allocation.

Product mix, run sizes, and labor turnover may affect labor costs substantially. The greater the mix, the shorter the lot size produced, and the higher the turnover, the greater direct labor costs will be. These three factors alone may create substantial cost differences between suppliers of an identical end product. Geographical considerations also play a large part since differences in labor rates do exist between plant locations. Such differences may change dramatically over time, as the rapid increases in direct labor rates in Japan, Puerto Rico, and Germany have demonstrated. The astute cost analyst will estimate the supplier's real labor costs, taking the above considerations into account.

The learning curve •

The learning curve provides an analytical framework for quantifying the commonly recognized principle that one becomes more proficient with experience. Its origins lie in the aircraft industry in World War II when it was empirically determined that labor time per plane declined dramatically as volume increased. Subsequent studies showed that the same phenomenon occurred in a variety of industries and situations. Although conceptually most closely identified with direct labor, most experts believe the learning curve is actually brought about by a combination of a large number of factors which include:

1. The learning rate of labor.
2. The motivation of labor and management to increase output.
3. The development of improved methods, procedures, and support systems.
4. The substitution of better materials, tools, and equipment or more effective use of materials, tools, and equipment.
5. The flexibility of the job and the people associated with it.
6. The ratio of labor versus machine time in the task.
7. The amount of preplanning done in advance of the task.
8. The turnover of labor in the unit.

We know the learning curve happens; its presence has been empirically determined a sufficient number of times that its existence is no longer in doubt. The reasons for it sound plausible enough; yet it is still not possible to determine in advance just what the learning rate should be for a brand new product or a novel task.

The learning curve has tremendous implications for cost determination, management by objectives, and negotiation. For example, take a 90 percent learning curve. Suppose we wish to purchase 800 units of a highly labor-intensive, expensive product which will be produced by a group of workers over a two-year period. The first 100 units have been produced at an average labor time of 1,000 hours. With a 90 percent learning curve the average labor time for the first 200 units would drop to 900 hours. Table 7–1 shows the figures.

Table 7–1
Learning curve example

	Units produced	Cumulative labor hours	Average labor hours per unit
100		100,000	1,000
200		180,000	900
400		324,000	810
800		583,200	729

These figures may be plotted on rectangular coordinates as shown in Figure 7–1. Using logarithmic coordinates this curve is a straight line, as shown in Figure 7–2.

It is important to recognize that the choice of learning curve, be it 95, 90, 85 or 80 percent of any other figure, is not an exact science. Normally the buyer, lacking past experience with a particular purchased item, will start with an 80 percent curve and then adjust it up or down to fit the particular situation. The new product situation can be compared to other situations where the same or similar circumstances were present. It can be readily established afterwards what really happened and what the actual curve was. It also is possible to wait for some preliminary production data, which can then be used to plot the curve since, theoretically, only two points are required to fix the curve's location (using log-log paper). Thus, for new products and relatively short runs, actual production information may be requested on the first significant run and renegotiation requested on the basis of actual data if uncertainty exists as to which learning curve is appropriate.

The learning curve or improvement function implies that improvement never stops, no matter how large the volume becomes. The potential of the learning curve in materials management has not yet been fully explored. It is a powerful concept and of great use to the buyer. Progressive discounts, shortened lead times, and better value should be planned and obtained through its use.

Some purchasing managers believe they are not justified in going very far into suppliers' costs. They take this position for several reasons: (1) In many cases suppliers do not know their costs, and it would be useless to inquire into them. (2) The interpretation of cost calls for an exercise of judgment and differences of opinion would arise even if all the figures were available. (3) Some suppliers will not divulge this information. (4) The seller's costs do not determine market prices. (5) The buyer is not interested in the supplier's costs anyway; the primary concern is getting the best price consistent with quality, service, and quantity. If a seller offers a price which does not cover costs, either in ignorance or with full recognition of what he or she is doing, the matter is the seller's problem and not the buyer's.

To a considerable extent, much of this reasoning is true. However, there are some limitations. In the first place, unless a buyer has some idea of a supplier's costs, at least in a general way, it is difficult to judge the reasonableness of the supplier's prices. Furthermore, the position that the buyer is neither concerned

Figure 7–1
Ninety percent learning curve plotted on standard graph paper

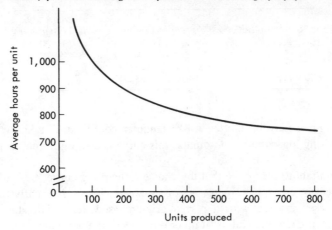

Figure 7–2
Ninety percent learning curve plotted on log–log paper

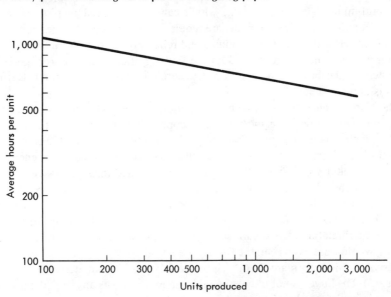

with nor responsible for vendors who offer merchandise below cost must recognize two things: first, that the buyer cannot complain if ruinous, vicious price cutting eliminates or handicaps efficient suppliers, and, second, that the buyer cannot maintain an attitude of indifference when the sellers offer merchandise below cost and then become intensely concerned when prices rise materially above cost as vendors fight for financial survival.

Negotiation strategy and practice ⦿

As the status of the purchasing function in well-managed companies has increased in importance, a more professional attitude has developed in the people responsible for the operation of the function. As the professional competence of the personnel has increased, greater use has been made of the more sophisticated tools available to the business decision-making executive. Negotiation is a prime example of this developing professionalism.

The discussion of some of the elements and considerations which affect the price of an item make it obvious that negotiation can be a valuable technique to use in reaching an agreement with a supplier on the many variables affecting a specific price. This is not to say that all buying-selling transactions require the use of negotiations. Nor is the intention to indicate that negotiation is used only in determining price. Reaching a clear understanding of time schedules for deliveries, factors affecting quality, and methods of packaging may require negotiations of equal or greater importance than those applying to price.

A list of some of the various kinds of purchasing situations in which the use of negotiations should prove of value follows:

1. Any written contract covering price, specifications, terms of delivery, and quality standards.

2. The purchase of items made to the buyer's specifications. Special importance should be attached to "first buys," since thorough exploration of the needs of the buyer and the supplier often will result in a better product at a lower price.

3. When changes are made in drawings or specifications after a purchase order has been issued.

4. When quotations have been solicited from responsible bidders and no acceptable bids have been received.

5. When problems of tooling or packaging occur.

6. When changing economic or market conditions require changes in quantities or prices.

7. When problems of termination of a contract involve disposal of facilities, materials, or tooling.

8. When there are problems of accepting any of the various elements entering into cost type contracts.

9. Problems arising under the various types of contracts used in defense and governmental contracting.

Success in negotiation largely is a function of the quality and amount of planning which has been done. Figure 7–3 presents a model of the negotiation process. The basic steps in developing a strategy for negotiation are:

1. Develop the specific objectives (outcomes) desired from the negotiation.

2. Analyze the vendor's bargaining position. What is the vendor's capacity, backlog, and profitability? How confident is the vendor of getting the contract? Is there any time urgency?

3. Gather pertinent data. Here is where cost analysis comes into play.

Figure 7–3
Model of the negotiation process

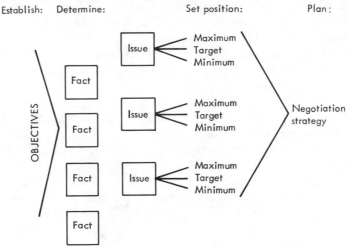

4.   Attempt to recognize the vendor's needs. In a successful negotiation, both parties must "win."

5.   Determine the "facts" of the situation. A fact is defined as an item of information about which agreement is expected. For example, if the vendor's cost breakdown states that the direct labor rate is $6.10 per hour, and you agree, that is a fact.

6.   Determine the "issues." An issue is something over which disagreement is expected. The purpose of negotiation is to resolve issues so that a mutually satisfactory contract can be signed. For example, if the vendor claims the manufacturing burden rate is 300 percent of direct labor costs, but your analysis indicates a 240 percent burden rate is realistic, this becomes an issue to be settled through negotiation.

7.   Set the buyer's position on each issue. What data will be used to support the buyer's position?

8.   Plan the negotiation strategy. Which issues should be discussed first? Where is the buyer willing to compromise? Who will make up the negotiation team (it frequently is composed of someone from both engineering and quality control, headed by the buyer)?

9.   Brief all persons on your team who are going to participate in the negotiations.

10.   Conduct a dress rehearsal for your people who are going to participate in the negotiations.

11.   Conduct the actual negotiations with an impersonal calmness.

Successful negotiators usually are extroverts who can express themselves well, have quick minds, and can analyze the position of the other party to a negotiation. A pleasant personality and a sense of humor go a long way in keeping negotiation sessions functioning.

Research into negotiation has not been extensive thus far, for obvious reasons. Most sellers and buyers are not anxious to have observers present during negotiations. But since considerable parallels exist between negotiation in purchasing and in labor relations, a large body of knowledge is, in fact, available. Some interesting observations by C. Karrass[5] dispel some of the old myths held about the negotiation process. He holds that deadlock or the threat of it can be very effective in forcing a party afraid of deadlock into agreement. He also believes in status as a powerful tool. It is no contest between a president and a clerk. This is another powerful argument for top management status for purchasing. Certainly marketing personnel have never shied away from using the vice president of marketing, the president, or even the chairman of the board as negotiators on key business deals. Lastly, the negotiator must have confidence in his or her negotiation skills. A skilled negotiator can spot lack of confidence and turn it to advantage. Although experience is a tremendous asset, and negotiation skills are learnable, a confident, inexperienced negotiator may well do better than an unconfident, experienced one.

Ground rules for successful negotiation

While negotiation still is more of an art than a science (although cost analysis techniques will provide the buyer a sound technical basis for setting the buying organization's position on key issues and planning and executing a strategy), the experience of many organizations and purchasing managers has resulted in some general negotiation ground rules. If the buyer is not following each of these ground rules, it is likely that, from a buying point of view, negotiation outcomes probably could be improved. These ground rules are broken down into three time phases—before, during, and after the negotiation session:

I. *Before the Session:*
   Preparation
   1. Establish possible sources.
   2. Analyze the vendor's position.
   3. Make a facilities survey.
   4. Make a financial analysis of the vendor.
   5. Analyze the vendor's proposal.
   6. Organize the negotiation team.
   7. Get a clear understanding of the work statement.
   8. Determine negotiation objectives.
   9. Prepare alternative action courses.
   10. Know your own authority.
   11. Provide adequate conference facilities.
   12. Set up the meeting room in advance.

---

[5]Karrass, Chester, *The Negotiating Game* (New York: World Publishing Co., 1970).

Basic Ideas
1. Be prepared to compromise.
2. You will have to "sell" your position.
3. Keep a poker face.
4. Don't ever underestimate your opponent.
5. Never let your guard down.
6. Take your time and do the job right.
7. Alcohol and negotiation don't mix.
8. Be reasonable; don't push too far.
9. Regardless of your offer, your opponent will want more.
10. Nervousness on your part will be interpreted as a sign of weakness.

II. *During the Session:*
Size Up Your Opposition
1. Watch for roving eyeballs—and your opponent can read upside down.
2. Spot their leader—who really can make concessions?
3. If they're hesitant to discuss an issue, it indicates a weakness.
4. If your opponent has no data on a key issue, it shows vulnerability.
5. Be intense; concentrate; look your opponent right in the eye and listen to what he or she has to say.

Strategy
1. Take command—sit at the head of the table.
2. Know names and pronunciation of vendor personnel.
3. Establish extent of vendor representatives' authority.
4. Assess supplier's minimum position.
5. Talk positive.
6. Phrase your questions to encourage a positive answer.
7. Compromise on minor points when advantageous.
8. If you compromise early in the session, you set the stage for the vendor to reciprocate.
9. Start with the easy issues first.
10. Avoid taking an "either-or" position. The vendor may get up and leave.
11. Never give anything away.
12. Don't go beyond your mental and physical endurance.

Tactics
1. Don't reveal maximum position.
2. Don't argue without reason.
3. Don't lose your cool.
4. Don't commit beyond your authority.
5. Remember, your opponent has to "win" too.
6. Don't interrupt; it is disrespectful and may "turn the other party off."
7. The best reply to a totally unacceptable offer is complete silence.
8. Don't go off on tangents—keep the discussion on track—time is valuable.

Resolving Negotiation Deadlocks
1. Go on to another point.
2. "I see your position—now try to understand mine."
3. "You suggest a solution."
4. "We've come too far to get bogged down now."
III. *After the Session:*
1. Make sure all items are covered in the final agreement.
2. Know how and when to terminate a session.
3. Keep complete notes on all points of agreement—both parties should initial or sign.
4. Analyze what happened and why.

Guarantee against price decline; providing for escalation ●

A guarantee against price decline frequently is provided in contracts for goods bought on a recurring basis and for process raw materials. The contract usually specifies a price in effect at the time the contract is negotiated and then provides for a reduction during a subsequent period if there is a downward price movement in the marketplace. The contract normally will specify that price movement will be determined by the list price reported in a specific business or trade journal. The buyer is more likely to be influenced by such guarantees when they are offered in an effort to overcome reluctance to buy, induced by a fear that prices are likely to drop still further.

Escalator clauses. The actual wording of many escalator clauses provides for either increase or decrease in price if costs change. Clauses providing for escalation came into common use during World War II when suppliers believed that their future costs were so uncertain as to make a firm quotation either impossible or, if covering all probable risks, so high as to make it unattractive, and perhaps unfair, to the buyer.

In designing any particular escalator contract, several general and many specific problems—such as the proportion of the total price subject to adjustment; the particular measures of prices and wage rates to be used in making the adjustment; the methods to be followed in applying these averages to the base price; the limitations, if any, on the amount of adjustment; and the methods for making payment—will be encountered. In times of price stability, escalation usually is reserved for long-term contracts, on the principle that certain costs may rise and that the seller has no appreciable control over this rise. In times of inflation, shortages, and sellers' markets, escalation becomes common on even short-term contracts as sellers attempt to assure themselves the opportunity to raise prices and preserve contribution margins. Finding a meaningful index to which escalation may be tied is a real problem in many instances. Since most escalation is automatic once the index, the portion of the contract subject to escalation, the frequency of revision, and the length of contract have been agreed to, the need for care in deciding on these factors is obvious.

The following is an illustrative escalator clause:

> *Labor.*   Adjustment with respect to labor costs shall be made on the basis of monthly average hourly earnings for the (Durable Goods Industry, subclass Machinery), as furnished by the Department of Labor (hereafter called the Labor Index). Adjustments shall be calculated with respect to each calendar quarter up to the completion date specified in contract. The percentage increase or decrease in the quarterly index (obtained by averaging the Labor Index for each month of the calendar quarter) shall be obtained by comparison with the Labor Index for the basic month. The basic month shall be _____, 198___. the labor adjustment for each calendar quarter as thus determined shall be obtained by applying such percentage of increase or decrease to the total amount expended by the contractor for direct labor during such quarter.
>
> *Materials.*   Adjustment with respect to materials shall be made on the basis of the materials index for Group VI (Metals and Metal Products), as furnished by the Department of Labor (hereafter called the Materials Index). Adjustments shall be determined with respect to each calendar quarter up to the completion date specified in contract. The percentage of increase or decrease in the quarterly index (obtained by averaging the Materials Index for each month of the calendar quarter) shall be obtained by comparison with the Materials Index for the basic month. The basic month shall be _____, 198___. The material adjustment for each calendar quarter shall be obtained by applying to the contract material cost the percentage of increase or decrease shown by the Materials Index for that quarter.

A buyer who uses escalator clauses must remember that one legal essential to any enforceable purchase contract is that it contain either a definite price or the means of arriving at one. No contract for future delivery can be enforced if the price of the item is conditioned entirely upon the will of one of the parties. The clauses cited above would appear to be adquate. So too are those clauses authorizing the seller to change price as costs of production change, provided that these costs can be reasonably determined from the vendor's accounting records. On the other hand, the following clause has been held unenforceable: "The prices and terms shall be as shown in the company's current price sheet and as established from time to time by the company. . . . Prices and discounts are subject to change without notice."

Discounts •

Discounts fall into two classes. The first class consists of inside prices and various other forms of price concessions that are not always defensible either legally or commercially. The second class consists of ordinary cash, trade, and quantity discounts which are thoroughly legitimate and fair.

The line of distinction between these two classes is difficult to draw for it is not always easy to define what is legitimate and what is not. Clearly there are certain types of apparent price concessions, such as "inside prices," which no responsible purchasing agent should even request and which under most circumstances should be refused if offered. A vendor who offers an "inside price" to one buyer will offer a similar or lower price to another. A seller who is not open and honest in pricing policy is not one with whom a purchaser can afford to do business.

The second class of discounts warrants more attention.

Cash discounts. Cash discounts are granted by virtually every seller of industrial goods, although the actual discount terms are a matter of individual trade custom and vary considerably from one industry to another. The purpose of a cash discount is to secure the prompt payment of an account.

Most sellers expect buyers to take the cash discount. The net price is commonly fixed at a point which will yield a fair profit to the vendor and is the price the vendor expects most customers to pay. Those who do not pay within the time limit are penalized and are expected to pay the gross price. However, variations in cash discount amounts frequently are made without due regard for the real purpose for which such discounts should be granted and are used, instead, merely as another means of varying prices. If a buyer secures a cash discount not commonly granted in the past, he or she may be sure that the net result is merely a reduction in the price, regardless of the name used. On the other hand, a reduction in the size of the cash discount is, in effect, an increase in the price.

Cash discounts, therefore, sometimes raise rather difficult questions of price policy, but if they are granted on the same terms to all buyers and if postdating and other similar practices are not granted some buyers and denied others, then the purchasing office's major interest in cash discounts is confined largely to being sure they are called to the attention of the proper financial managers. The purchaser ordinarily cannot be held responsible for a failure to take cash discounts, since this depends upon the financial resources of the company and is, therefore, a matter of financial rather than purchasing policy. The purchaser should, however, be very careful to secure such cash discounts as customarily are granted. It is a part of the buyer's responsibility to see that inspection is promptly made, that goods are accepted without unnecessary loss of time, and that all documents are handled expeditiously so all discounts quoted may be taken. A discount of two percent if payment is made within 10 days, with the gross amount due in 30 days, is the equivalent of earning an annual interest rate of approximately 36 percent.

Cash discounts generally have become less popular in the last decade. This may have been caused partly by buyers who paid the discounted price but not within the discount period. Also, the practice of sending invoices ahead of the actual goods has not helped this situation. Lastly, many sellers have found that removing cash discounts is an easy and little-noticed way of raising prices.

Trade discounts. Trade discounts are granted by a manufacturer to a buyer because the purchasing firm is a particular type of distributor or user. In general, they aim to protect the distributor by making it more profitable for a purchaser to buy from the distributor than directly from the manufacturer. When manufacturers have found that various types of distributors can sell their merchandise in a given territory more cheaply than they can, they usually rely on the distributors' services. To ensure that goods will move through the channels selected, the distributor is granted a trade discount approximating the cost of doing business.

However, trade discounts are not always used properly. Protection is sometimes granted distributors not entitled to it, since the services which they render manufacturers, and presumably customers, are not commensurate with the discount they obtain. Generally speaking, buyers dealing in small quantities who secure a great variety of items from a single source or who depend on frequent and very prompt deliveries are more likely to obtain their supplies from wholesalers and other distributors receiving trade discounts. With the larger accounts, manufacturers are more likely to sell directly, even though they may reserve the smaller accounts in the same territory for the wholesalers. Some manufacturers refuse to sell to accounts purchasing below a stipulated minimum.

Multiple discounts. In some industries and trades, prices are quoted on a multiple discount basis. For example, 10, 10 and 10 means that, for an item listed at \$100, the actual price to be paid by the purchaser is $(\$100 - 10\%) - 10\%(100 - 10\%) - 10\%[(100 - 10\%) - 10\%(100 - 10\%)] = \$90 - \$9 - \$8.10 = \$72.90$. 10, 10 and 10 is, therefore, equivalent to a discount of .271. Tables are available listing the most common multiple discount combinations and their equivalent discount.

Quantity discounts. Quantity discounts may be granted for buying in particular quantities and vary roughly in proportion to the amount purchased. From the seller's standpoint, the justification for granting such discounts is usually that quantity purchasing results in savings to the seller, enabling a lower price to the buyer who has made such savings possible. These savings may be of two classes: first, savings in marketing expense and, second, savings in production expense.[6]

In the late 1940s, the Federal Trade Commission in administering the Robinson-Patman Act from time to time proceeded against buyers who were alleged to have knowingly received lower prices from sellers than their competitors. It is obvious that in most cases it would be extremely difficult for the buyer to prove the seller had cost savings which could justify the lower price.

In one case the Federal Trade Commission found the Automatic Canteen Company of America, a large buyer of candy and other confectionery products for resale through automatic vending machines, guilty of receiving prices as much as 33 percent lower than prices quoted other purchasers. The Commission did not attempt to show that the price differential exceeded any cost saving that sellers may have enjoyed in their sales to Canteen, or that Canteen knew, or should have known, that they did.

In 1953, the U.S. Supreme Court ruled in the case of the Automatic Canteen Company of America that:

---

[6]The U.S. Supreme Court in May, 1948, ruled in the case of the Morton Salt Company (68 S. Ct.) that no wholesaler, retailer, or manufacturer whose product is sold to the public through these channels may grant quantity discounts unless they can be justified by (a) lower costs "due to quantity manufacture, delivery, or sale" or (b) "the seller's good-faith effort to meet a competitor's equally low price." Furthermore, it ruled that the Federal Trade Commission need not prove that discounts are discriminatory. The burden of proof is on the seller to prove the law is not being violated.

1. The mere inducement of receipt of a lower price is not unlawful.
2. It is lawful for a buyer to accept anything which it is lawful for a seller to give.
3. It is only the prohibited discrimination a buyer may not induce or receive.
4. It is not unlawful for a buyer to receive a prohibited discrimination unless he knows or, as a reasonably prudent buyer, should know that the differential is prohibited.

The court concluded that to prove cost justification according to the Federal Trade Commission's accounting standards would place a heavy burden on a buyer—it would require a study of the seller's business and "would almost inevitably," to quote the court, "require a degree of cooperation between buyer and seller, as against other buyers, that may offend other antitrust policies, and it might also expose the seller's cost secrets to the prejudice of arm's-length bargaining in the future." The court added: "Finally, not one, but as here, approximately 80 different sellers' costs may be in issue." The court dismissed the case against Automatic Canteen.

The savings in marketing expense arise because it may be no more costly to sell a large order than a small one; that the billing expense is the same; and that the increased cost of packing, crating, and shipping is not proportional. When these circumstances exist, a direct quantity discount not exceeding the difference in cost of handling the small and the large order is justified.

There are substantial savings in production costs as a result of securing a large order instead of a small one. For instance, placing orders in advance of the time when actual production begins is an aid in production planning.

From the buyer's viewpoint, the question of quantity discounts is intimately connected with that of inventory policy. While it is true that the larger the size of a given order, the lower the unit price likely will be, the carrying charges on the buyer's larger inventory are more costly. Hence, the savings on the size of order must be compared against the increased inventory costs.

The quantity discount question is of interest to many buyers for a second reason: all quantity discounts, and especially those of the cumulative type, tend to restrict the number of suppliers, thereby affecting the choice of source.

Since there is real justification for quantity discounts when properly used, the buyer should obtain such discounts whenever possible. Ordinarily they come through the pressure of competition among sellers. Furthermore, an argument may be advanced that such discounts are a matter of right. The buyer is purchasing goods or merchandise, not crating, or packing materials, or transportation. The seller presumably should expect to earn a profit not from those wholly auxiliary services but rather from manufacturing and selling the merchandise processed. These auxiliary services are necessary; they must be performed; they must be paid for; and it is natural to expect the buyer to pay for them. But the buyer should not be expected to pay more than the actual cost of these auxiliary services.

When an attempt is made to justify quantity discounts on the basis that they contribute to reduced production costs through providing a volume of business large enough to reduce the overhead expenses, somewhat-more-cautious reasoning is necessary. It is true that in some lines of business the larger the output, the lower the overhead cost per unit of product. It also may be true that without the volume from the large customers, the average cost of production would be higher. However, the small buyers may place a greater total proportion of the seller's business than do the large. So far as production costs are concerned therefore, the small buyers contribute even more toward that volume so essential to the per unit production cost than does the larger buyer.

Another contention is that large customers ordering early in the season, or even prior to the time actual production of a season's supply begins, should be granted higher discounts because their orders keep the mill in production. Such a buyer probably may be entitled to a lower price than one who waits until later in the season to order. However, such a discount, since it is justified by the early placement of an order and therefore should be granted to every buyer placing an early order regardless of its size, is not properly a quantity discount but is a time discount.

Cumulative discounts. Another type of quantity discount is cumulative and varies in proportion to the quantity purchased; however, instead of being computed on the size of the order placed at any one time, it is based on the quantity purchased over a period of time. Such discounts are commonly granted as an incentive to a company for continued patronage. It is hoped they will induce a purchaser to concentrate purchases largely with a single source rather than distributing them over many sources, thus benefiting the company offering the discount. Generally speaking, the purchaser should not scatter orders over too large a number of sources, for distributing one's orders over many sources is uneconomical and costly. No supplier, under such circumstances, is likely to give the same careful attention to the buyer's requirements as he would if he felt he were getting the larger portion of the purchaser's business.

The use of cumulative discounts must meet the same cost justification rules under the Robinson-Patman Act as other quantity discounts. However, as long as the buyer is not knowingly accepting or inducing discriminatory quantity discounts, then the responsibility for justification rests solely with the seller.

This discussion of discounts has oversimplified the problem. The discount structure in many individual companies and also in whole industries is extremely complicated—far more so than is justified. From the standpoint of the buyer, the whole purpose of the price discount is defeated when it becomes so intricate that it is impossible to compare the various quotations offered. The fault rests with the sellers. In some cases, it is the result of plain bad judgment. In other instances, there can be little doubt that the confusion is deliberate.

Reference has been made to the legitimate and illegitimate use of discounts. There is a reason for cash discounts. Trade discounts, as far as they are necessary to the well-being of a desirable source of supply, have their proper place. Quantity discounts may be earned and justified. However, discounts also may be used illegitimately. They may be used to grant price concessions, to pursue a policy of price cutting under a guise of legitimate business practice, or to play certain types of buyers against others. Indeed, under the Robinson-Patman Act, the buyer as well as the seller may be found guilty of the discriminatory use of quantity discounts.

Contract cancellation *

In practice, cancellations usually occur during a period of falling prices. At such times, if the price has declined since the placing of the order, some buyers may try to take advantage of all sorts of loopholes in the purchase order or sales agreement to reject merchandise. To avoid completion of the transaction, they take advantage of technicalities which under other circumstances would be of no concern to them whatever. One can have sympathy for the buyer with a contract at a price higher than the market. There is little justification, however, for the purchaser who follows a cancellation policy under this situation. A contract should be considered a binding obligation. The practice referred to is an instance of "sharp practice," which hopefully is becoming less and less prevalent as the years go by. There may be occasions when a buyer justifiably seeks to cancel the contract, but to do so merely because the market price has fallen is not one of them.

In some instances, the buyer knows when the purchase order is placed that the customer for whose job the materials are being bought may unexpectedly cancel the order, thus forcing cancellation of purchase orders for materials planned for the job. This is a common risk when purchasing materials for use on a government contract, for appropriation changes often force the government to cancel its order, and results then in cancellation of a great many purchase orders by firms who were to have been suppliers to the government under the now-cancelled government contract. Or, severe changes in the business cycle may trigger purchase order cancellations. If cancellation is a possibility, the basis and terms of cancellation should be agreed upon in advance and made part of the terms and conditions of the purchase order. Problems such as how to value, and what is an appropriate payment for, partially-completed work on a now-cancelled purchase order are best settled before the situation arises.

QUESTIONS FOR REVIEW AND DISCUSSION

1. What are the significance of the Sherman Antitrust and the Robinson-Patman Acts to the industrial buyer?
2. What advantages does the competitive bid process have as a method of price determination?
3. What are cash discounts, quantity discounts, trade discounts, and cumulative discounts? Should the buyer attempt to use these discounts? How?
4. When, and how, is negotiation used, and what can be negotiated?
5. What is a "learning curve" and how can it be used?

6. How is vendor cost related to vendor price?

7. What are the various ways by which prices are determined?

8. What methods can the buyer use to establish price for (1) sensitive commodities, (2) special items, (3) standard production items, and (4) items of small value?

9. Distinguish between direct and indirect costs. How can the buyer analyze these costs?

10. What can the buyer do if he or she suspects collusion on the part of vendors?

CASE 7–1
STEVENS CONSTRUCTION INC.

Eric Busch, purchasing agent for Stevens Construction Inc., faced a supplier selection decision on the bending of reinforcing rod for a major construction project. Should he select a local supplier or one more distant at a lower price?

Stevens Construction

Stevens Construction, located in the western part of the country was one of the largest construction companies in the region. The company was not involved in residential units, but built high-rise office towers, plants, government buildings, and roads. It had a reputation for high quality, on time work and the company had grown rapidly in the past 20 years, keeping pace with the general expansion of the region.

Reinforcing steel

Reinforcing steel, used in almost all of the projects in which Stevens was involved, was purchased by Eric Busch from several steel mills. During the past 18 months all of the bending required in preparation for the job site had been done by Adams & Adams, a small local steel fabricator. In the last year, total bending requirements had amounted to 4,000 tons. Adams & Adams had charged identical prices per ton for small and large jobs during this period. When a new construction job was undertaken and the steel requirements known, Eric Busch would request a quotation from Adams & Adams over the telephone, and invariably, the price per ton quoted was the same as for a previous job. Adams & Adams was also a supplier of reinforcing steel itself. Therefore, Eric Busch had worked out an arrangement of mutual help during periods of shortages or problems caused by the steel mills in not supplying certain sizes on time. Adams & Adams would use Stevens steel and Stevens would use Adams & Adams steel to satisfy all projects. This arrangement had worked very well with the result that no reinforcing rod shortages had occurred in any construction projects during the last 18 months. Adams & Adams also owned a major share in a detailing firm which did approximately 70 percent of the reinforcing detailing work required by Stevens. In the opinion of Eric Busch, Adams & Adams had done an excellent job on delivery and quality during the time it had been sole supplier of bending requirements for Stevens.

Recently, Stevens had successfully quoted on a large, two year, contract which would require about 3,000 tons of reinforcing steel. Because of the size of the job, Eric Busch decided to look for another quote for the bending of the steel once it became clear that Stevens would receive the contract. The contract price had included a bending estimate using the current prices of Adams & Adams. The closest reasonable other supplier Eric Busch could find was Blackstone Steel, a major fabricator in a city of 200 miles away. Blackstone quoted a price $7 per ton f.o.b. the Stevens plant lower than the one submitted by Adams & Adams. This quote was made on the condition that all transport would be in full loads, with no emergency short shipment transport charges. Eric Busch had checked Blackstone out very carefully and knew them to be a reputable firm, capable of doing good quality work. He now wondered if he should place the contract with them or whether he should stay with Adams & Adams.

CASE 7–2
SOUTHERN POWER CORPORATION (A)

Mr. Hanley, director of purchasing for Southern Power Corporation, faced an interesting problem on the insulation contract for a new nuclear reactor. Specifications were somewhat vague and subject to further changes. Firm bids requested from four contractors showed a wide variation in price. Mr. Hanley was, therefore, considering the use of a special contract allowing for price variation and incentive.

Company background

Southern Power Corporation was one of the larger electrical utilities in the southern United States. It employed over 8,000 people and had annual operating revenues in excess of $750 million per year. Annual plant and equipment expenditures exceeded $400 million. Purchases of noncapital items and fuel were over $180 million per year.

The insulation job

The insulation job for the new nuclear plant presented a difficult purchasing problem. The job involved coating of beams, ceilings, and piping and was subject to rigid inspection procedures. Access to some areas might be difficult, and the amount of material which might be required could not be easily determined. Not all construction details were clear yet, and Mr. Hanley had expressed some misgivings in going out for fixed bids when the contract came up. Al Williams, manager of contracts suggested that, if suppliers objected strongly to a fixed bid, something else might be worked out. Al preferred a fixed bid from a budgeting and ease of management point of view.

Special efforts were taken to assure that only reliable sources would quote. Four suppliers were approached, and, although none objected to using a fixed bid, the results showed a large price variation. Bob Cunningham, Inc., was high bidder at $225,000. Next came Hughes Corporation at ¡204,000 and Rennie Construction at $165,000. Stillcamp Construction was ow bidder at $103,000.

Al Williams discussed the bids with Mr. Hanley.

"I'm really unsure about using fixed bids on this new insulation job," said Mr. Hanley. "The scope and definition of this installation is still quite vague, leaving me very uneasy about these bids we received." Al Williams thought Stillcamp Construction might "get clobbered" once they got into the actual job and were subjected to Southern's high expectations. He raised this possibility with the sales manager of Stillcamp who replied that Stillcamp had included a safety margin in its bid. According to all of Stillcamp's calculations they felt they could meet a target price about 10 percent below the bid price. The sales manager confided that he thought his bid was on the high side rather than low. When Mr. Williams reported this rather startling finding to Mr. Hanley, Mr. Hanley wondered: "Perhaps we should be working on a form of incentive contract instead. You see, they're sure they're on the high side and that they can do better. We're sure they're on the low side and may get hurt. From everything we know, they're a good supplier, but they wouldn't be able to stand a bid loss if they turn out to be wrong. If they're willing to share some of the gains with us if they do better than the fixed bid, perhaps we can assist them a bit if they go over." Does this mean we'll have to go out for new bids all over again?" asked Mr. Williams. "Why don't we think about that while we work out a scheme?" replied Mr. Hanley.

The new proposal

Al Williams was intrigued by Mr. Hanley's remarks. As manager of contracts he had become aware of a number of situations where fixed bids did not seem to make sense from either the buyer's or the seller's point of view. He also realized that the frequency of contracts involving specification uncertainty was increasing. He wondered, therefore, if the insulation contract might not be an excellent vehicle for testing a different approach. Compared to most contracts in his office, the dollar volume was relatively low. All four suppliers were technically sound. The element of risk was, therefore, not particularly great. If, however, a new approach could be found it might be applied to a number of larger dollar contracts in the future.

Al Williams and one of the purchasing agents worked on the problem for several weeks and developed a scheme for Mr. Hanley's approval. It was a substantial departure from the traditional fixed bid approach, and the two originators were proud of their ideas.

The proposal called for a base price around which the contract provisions resolved. Suppliers would calculate the base price using detailed estimates of labor, material overhead, a contracting fee, and profit. Actual costs incurred, carefully audited, would form the basis for final price paid. If total

Exhibit 1

Memorandum for File

Subject: Martin Lee Insulation Contract

A variety of factors make it desirable for Southern to ask the bidders on the insulation work at our Martin Lee Power Plant to consider bidding an alternate to the lump sum price mentioned in their previous bids. This alternate bid is on the basis of sharing in savings up to base, contractors loss of profit mark-up for all costs between base and adjustment price, contractors loss of profit and overhead for costs over the adjustment price. Southern would like to evaluate the potential of such a contract using both the lump sum and time and material method of performing this work. Therefore, the alternate bid is to be on the following basis:

1. The bidders stipulate a base price from which the basic contract will center. (This could be your lump sum bid of the previous quotation) $103,000

The actual work to be performed on a time and material basis with the following items being established before the contract starts:

a. Labor—including all expenses based on labor (including all hourly supervision)		$ 48,500
b. Materials, cost to Contractor		36,500
c. Overhead—including all home, office and field cost not a part of labor 1 a. above		
(1) Overhead—labor (including all other supervision)	10%	4,850
(2) Overhead on material	10%	3,650
d. Profit (about 10%)		9,500
e. Total or base price		$103,000

2. If the contractor experiences cost of any of the items lised above that results in a total bill less than the base price, the savings would be shared between Southern and the contractor on the basis of 60 percent of the savings to Southern and 40 percent to the contractor.

3. If the cost of work reaches and starts to exceed the *base price,* Southern is to pay only the additional direct labor and taxes, insurance and benefits, cost of material and overhead as defined in 1 *a, b* and *c* above. The contractor offers as a limit to this arrangement the following adjustment price:

$115,000

4. If the cost of the work exceeds adjustment price Southern is to pay all direct labor and those items of taxes, insurance, and benefits directly based on labor payroll plus cost of items included in 1 *a* and *b* above but the contractor is to receive no compensation for overhead or profit, items *c* and *d* in 1. above.

5. All extra work to the contract which is not a part of the current bid in current drawings or specifications will be bid on by the contractor as a *lump sum* or *base price.* These individual amounts will be added to the *base* and *adjustment prices* as they occur and the accounting will remain on a time and material basis.

actual costs were less than the base price, Southern and the contractor would share in the savings. Sixty percent of the savings would go to Southern, 40 percent to the contractor.

The contractor would also bid an adjustment price above the base price. If actual costs incurred exceeded the base price but were below the adjustment price, Southern would pay all direct costs and overhead but no additional fee and profit. Should actual costs exceed the adjustment price, Southern would pay additional direct materials and labor only, but not overhead, fee, or profit.

The two designers of this scheme had used the Stillcamp bid as an example of how the system might work (see Exhibits 1 and 2).

Exhibit 2
Sample calculations to show impact of incentive formula

Situation A—Contractor Performs Below Base Price		
Actual costs incurred: Labor		$ 40,000
Material		32,000
Total		$ 72,000
Overhead allowed (10%)		7,200
Profit allowed		7,200
Total job cost		$ 86,400
Original base price:	$103,000	
Actual job:	86,400	
Difference	$ 16,600	
Therefore, incentive earnings to contractor @ 40%		$ 6,640
Therefore, savings to Southern @ 60%		9,960
Therefore, final job cost to Southern $103,000 − $93,040 =		93,040
Therefore, total contractor profit = $7,200 + $6,640 =		13,840
Situation B—Contractor Performs Above Adjustment Price		
Actual costs incurred: Labor		$ 66,000
Material		47,000
Total		$113,000
Overhead incurred		11,300
Profit at 10%		11,300
Total job theoretical price		$135,600

Southern's final job cost would be:

To adjustment price:	$115,100		
Labor and material	96,000	Actual labor and material	$113,000
Overhead allowed	9,600	Less labor and material	
Profit allowed	9,500	covered under adjustment	
		price	96,000
Total	$115,100	Additional labor and	
		material allowed	$ 17,000
Therefore, final job cost to Southern			$115,100
			17,000
			$132,100
Therefore, final profit to contractor			$ 9,500

Since it had been normal Southern practice in the past to reject all bidders on a contract if a major change in specifications or bidding procedure was planned, Al Williams thought he should go out for new bids from all four suppliers. He asked Mr. Hanley to review the plan and to give it approval as soon as possible so that he could get going on the insulation contract.

CASE 7-3
CARLYN CORPORATION

Mr. Bill Thomas, purchasing manager for Carlyn Corporation, became increasingly concerned about the purchase of MS-7, a special ingredient used in Stimgro, one of his company's new products. It appeared that a major cost increase might threaten the product's profitability, and Bill Thomas was anxious to explore any alternatives which promised at least some cost relief.

Carlyn Corporation was the U.S. subsidiary of Carlyn International, a U.K. based producer of veterinary products and feed additives. Total U.S. sales were expected to be about $5 million with profits before taxes of about $200,000. The Carlyn plant located in Chicago employed about 70 hourly rated people. The premises were leased, and primary activities involved the mixing of ingredients and the bottling and packing of finished products. About half of the $3 million worth of ingredients were imported from the U.K. parent, the remainder and all packaging were purchased in the U.S. The executive team consisted of Mr. Peters, president and treasurer; Mr. Grove, sales manager; Mr. Thomas, accountant and purchasing manager; and Mr. Harper, plant manager. Carlyn Corporation occupied a special niche in the U.S. market, concentrating on poultry medicines and feed additives. Three years earlier Carlyn had introduced Stimgro, a feed additive for turkeys, which had shown unusual promise in promoting rapid, healthy development in birds less than one month old. Sales prospects appeared extra promising, and, had it not been for the introduction several months later of a competitive product from Blondin, Carlyn might have captured the total U.S. market. Carlyn and Blondin had about equal shares in the Stimgro market with annual sales of about $350,000 each.

Carlyn imported the two primary ingredients for Stimgro from its U.K. parent and mixed and packaged them in the Chicago plant. The manufacturing cost for Stimgro is shown in Exhibit 1.
Carlyn's selling price of Stimgro was $90.00 per kilogram.

Mr. Thomas had tried to find a North American source for MS-7 over the past few years but had found that all potential sources, pharmaceutical, and specialty chemical firms had declined serious interest. They claimed the

Exhibit 1
Stimgro manufacturing cost/KG

MS-7 (500 grams)	$25.00
Other ingredients (500 grams)	12.00
Packaging	1.00
Labor	2.00
Overhead	5.00
Total	$45.00

volume was far too low, and the price would have to be at least $200.00 per kilogram before they could be persuaded to manufacture MS-7.

Blondin

Blondin Corporation was a U.S. owned manufacturer of products similar to those marketed by Carlyn. Blondin's range of products was greater than Carlyn's, and its annual sales volume was about $12 million. Blondin had originally obtained its MS-7 from a U.K. competitor of Carlyn International, but in the spring of the current year it had placed orders for equipment to manufacture its own MS-7. This action had surprised Mr. Thomas because, like Carlyn, Blondin had been relatively poorly prepared to take this step. For example, the North American market demand for MS-7 was limited to its use by Carlyn and Blondin. Although future growth might show a healthy increase, total current market demand certainly did not warrant the $250,000 investment Blondin had to make.

Moreover, MS-7 was tricky to produce requiring very careful temperature, pressure, and timing control. The main equipment item was a large glass-lined autoclave ingeniously instrumented and constructed to deal with the unusual demands of MS-7 production. The autoclave was normally a fairly general purpose type of equipment in the chemical industry. However, the special conditions required for the manufacture of MS-7 made this reactor a special purpose tool, certainly overdesigned and overengineered for the other uses to which Blondin might apply it. MS-7 manufacture was a batch production process, and the expected capacity of the equipment was about 40,000 kilograms per year based on two shift operation.

In Mr. Thomas' eyes, Blondin's action affected his own purchases of MS-7, which up to this point had been at an advantageous transfer price from the U.K. parent. Although the exact impact was still not entirely clear, Mr. Thomas expected at least a 40 percent increase in his laid down cost. He had no doubt that Blondin would aggressively seek customs protection from undervalued MS-7 imports and that at least a 20 percent duty would be applied on the American selling price.

Mr. Thomas, therefore, requested information from the parent company concerning manufacturing costs of MS-7. He added several other data from his own knowledge and prepared the following summary:

Summary of MS-7 cost and price data

Minimum equipment outlay	installed $250,000
Delivery on equipment...............................	9–12 months
U.K. normal market price	$56.00/kg.
Our laid down current cost from Carlyn U.K.	$50.00/kg.
Carlyn (U.K.) out of pocket cost (material, labor and variable overhead)	$40.00/kg.
Estimated minimum laid down cost in Chicago after Blondin starts production	$70.00/kg.

Mr. Thomas went to see Mr. Grove, Carlyn's sales manager, to discuss possible sales requirements for the future. Mr. Grove said:

> It's really anybody's guess. First, it depends on the popularity of turkeys. We are banking on continued growth there. Second, as soon as the feed companies can develop a suitable substitute for our product, they will go for it. We appear to be very expensive on a weight basis, although research and actual results show we represent excellent value. It takes such tiny quantities of Stimgro to improve the overall quality of a mix that it is difficult to believe it could have any impact. More competition can enter this market any day. We are just not large enough in the U.S. market to have any strong promotional impact. Each of our product lines is specialized, of relatively small volume, in an area where the big firms choose not to operate. Should a larger firm enter this market, they could flatten us. Blondin's entry after Stimgro took us by surprise, and those bastards stole half of our market already. Now you tell me how to turn this into a reasonable forecast.

Mr. Thomas replied:

> I'm glad that's your problem and not mine, Frank. Any time you feel you're ready to put some figures down, please let me know, because it may become very important for us in the near future.

In looking over past figures, Mr. Thomas estimated that the second half of this year's requirements would total about 1,000 kilograms of MS-7. Mr. Thomas decided that he had better think out the effect that Blondin's decision to make MS-7 might have on his future purchasing strategy.

CASE 7–4
MIDWEST UTILITIES

Mr. Lloyd Harbison, director of purchases for Midwest Utilities, was concerned about a major nuclear reactor contract. This $37 million contract extended over six years. Four suppliers had submitted bids including, as was normal practice, escalation clauses for labor and materials. Each contractor had used different indices tied to materials and labor, making direct comparison of the quotes difficult. A regression analysis of the past trend of these indices showed past annual increases ranging from 2.7 to 3.5 percent. Because of the magnitude of the contract and the major impact of the escalation clauses, Mr. Harbison had requested advice from Professor Roy Jones, a well-known economist. Professor Jones was surprised to see that escalation was even considered. He argued that improved productivity should offset future increases in labor and materials. Mr. Harbison knew he would have great difficulty persuading the four bidders to accept this productivity argument, but he was anxious to keep escalation, if any to a minimum.[1]

Company background

Midwest Utilities was a privately owned large supplier of electrical power serving a highly industrialized area of about 6,000 square miles in the midwestern United States. Total assets exceeded $4 billion and kilowatt capacity totaled about 10 million kilowatts. In response to the rapidly increasing demand for power, Midwest had moved into nuclear power in the 1960s and was planning at least five nuclear additions between 1970 and 1984.

Nuclear installations

The nuclear power unit under consideration in 1972 was to be installed in the Alta plant, for which an earlier similar power unit had already been contracted in 1970 and which was expected to be completed by 1975. The extended contract time on nuclear power units necessitated the use of progress payments, and for the utility the impact of the carrying cost of money was considerable.

The Alta 1 unit cost about $36 million and was expected to provide a capacity of approximately 1.1 million kilowatts. J&E Engineering had been awarded the Alta 1 job which included escalation clauses for labor and material.

In view of the volume of nuclear work ahead, Midwest was anxious to seek as many qualified suppliers as possible and at the same time assure a favorable price on each unit. For Alta 2, four possible suppliers were approached on June 15, 1972, by Joe Walton, equipment buyer, who sent out an inquiry along with extensive specifications and drawings (see Exhibit 1). Suppliers were requested to reply by August 15, 1972, on the understanding that the contract would be awarded during October or November 1972.

A nuclear reactor system could be considered as 60 percent mechanical equipment, including heat exchangers and piping and 40 percent electrical equipment and wiring.

Alta 2 bids

The four suppliers submitted acceptable proposals by August 15, 1972. The contract price for each was almost identical at $37 million. Differences

---

[1] It is important that the reader of this case recognizes that the high inflation rates encountered since 1973 were unknown at the time of this case.

Exhibit 1

June 15, 1972

Copies sent to: J & E Engineering
                 Malton Electric
                 Durnford Corporation
                 Ermi, Inc.

Subject: Inquiry No. B-2624
             Nuclear Stream Supply System and Nuclear Fuel Supply for Unit No. 2 for Alta
             Atomic Power Plant and a Two-Unit Unspecified Site

Gentlemen:

Please submit a complete and detailed quotation, in quadruplicate, by no later than August 15, 1972, to furnish each of the following:

One (1) 3300 Mwt—Nuclear Stream Supply System (NSSS) and associated Nuclear Fuel Supply for Unit No. 2 Alta Power Plant.

Two (2) 3300 Mwt—NSSS and associated Nuclear Fuel Supplies for a new Unspecified Site.

Options for two (2) additional identical NSSS and associated Nuclear Fuel Supplies for the Unspecified Site.

The above units are to have a guaranteed nominal nameplate rating of 1,100,000 electrical kilowatts, but the bidders may submit quotations on larger units as an alternative.

The Scope of Supply for these units shall be in strict accordance with the enclosed:

1. Midwest Specification 4194—1, dated 5/4/72, "NSSS and Nuclear Fuel, Alta Unit Two and Unnamed Two-Unit Nuclear Power Plant."
2. Midwest Specification 4194—3, dated 5/1/72, "Controls and Instrumentation for the NSSS, Nuclear Power Plant."
3. Midwest Specification 4148—A, dated 3/8/66, Addenda A, B, and C, "Horizontal and Vertical A.C. Electric Motors."

Inquiry No. B-2624

4. Midwest Specification 4178, dated 2/5/69, Addendum A, "460 Volt A.C. Motors."
5. Midwest Drawings:

6M-2263	3M-2287
5M-2278	3M-2288
5M-2279	6M-2290 sheet 2
3M-2285	3M-2300
3M-2286	

The scheduled date for Contract Award is approximately October–November 1972.

The commercial operating dates for the units have been established as follows:

Alta Unit 2—October 1, 1979
Unspecified Site Unit 1—October 1, 1980
Unspecified Site Unit 2—April 1, 1982
Optional Units:
Unspecified Site Unit 3—October 1, 1983
Unspecified Site Unit 4—April 1, 1985

The following requirements should be considered when preparing your proposal:

1. Proposals are requested for "equipment only" including technical direction on erection.
2. Itemize the "equipment only" prices, and state in detail the basis for escalation (if any). Include protection for a downward trend in the market. Also furnish total estimated escalation for each of the five (5) units specified above and the basis and accuracy for your estimate.
3. Submit quotations covering the initial fuel loading and fuel for a second core or for sufficient fuel to operate for six years on a requirement basis. Except for the initial fuel loading, the quote shall be on a batch by batch basis. Refer to Division 3—Nuclear Fuel Supply, Page 17, of Midwest Specification 4194—1 for additional information on fuel supply requirements.
4. Please note that we are preparing a "NSSS Commercial Specification" for transmittal to you in the very near future. This document will incorporate the commercial aspects for the purchase of this equipment, and all exceptions to this specification will be resolved and/or negotiated prior to contract award.
5. Do not include any cost for state sales and/or use tax. The state sales tax status will be determined at the time the contract is awarded. Your quotation *must* include, however, all other taxes and fees.

Exhibit 1 *(continued)*

6. Furnish schedules and dates of key points for required Midwest decisions on design, fabrication, and/or erection.
7. Rail facilities are available at both Alta and the Unspecified Site. Barge receiving facilities will be available at Alta 2 and for the Unspecified Site. It is required that all equipment be shipped f.o.b. plant site.
8. During the preaward period, Midwest may perform an in-depth audit of the bidders Quality Assurance Program to assess compliance with the requirements of Appendix B of 10 CFR 50.

If you have any questions concerning this inquiry, please feel free to contact me on 851-1099, extension 4839.

Sincerely,

Joe R. Walton
Buyer
Equipment Buying

JRW:bc
Enclosures (6) Six ccs all applicable specifications and drawings.

---

existed primarily in the escalation bases and percentages chosen. Two of the bidders were mechanical contractors who would subcontract the electrical equipment. J&E Engineering (company no. 1—see Exhibit 2) estimated labor at 55 percent of contract cost and used the primary metals index for escalation base. J&E estimated material at 35 percent and used two indicators, the iron and steel index and the nickel index, for escalation here. Ermi, Inc., (company no. 4) was the only bidder to estimate labor at 45 percent and material at 45 percent. Total employment was used as the index for labor escalation and the composite price of finished steel for the material. The two other bidders Malton Electric (company no. 2) and Durnford Corporation (company no. 3) were electrical equipment manufacturers. Both had chosen labor escalation clauses tied to the electrical equipment and supplies index. Both had estimated labor at 55 percent of the total contract and material at 35 percent. Malton had specified steel mill products for the material index and Durnford the metal and metal products index.

The confusion of indexes used made direct bid comparison difficult. Mr. Harbison, therefore, requested that two steps be undertaken. First, he requested the purchasing research group to analyze the individual indexes proposed by the four bidders, to establish a trend line, if possible, and to calculate the impact on each of the four bids over the length of the contract. Second, he wanted expert outside advice on the use of escalation. Although Midwest had allowed escalation on its Alta 1 nuclear contract (see Exhibit 3), he was particularly concerned about its possible impact and its future use on additional nuclear units.

Computations of escalation concepts

Bill Morris in purchasing research spent several weeks gathering data from various sources on the indices proposed by the four bidders. Most of the information was available from the Bureau of Labor Statistics in

Exhibit 2
Summary of contract bids on Alta 2 showing the variations in escalation

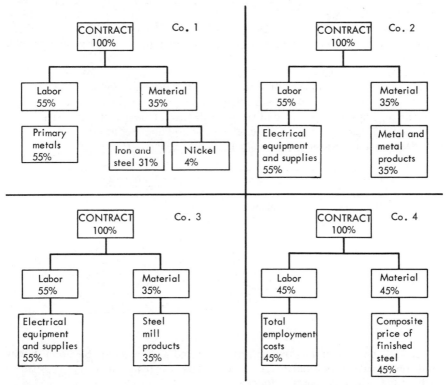

Washington, D.C. (See Exhibits 4, 5, 6 and 7.) Using the computer and regression formulae he obtained an estimate of average annual change per index (see Exhibit 8). Using the figures obtained in Exhibit 8 he calculated the impact of escalation and the cost of money to Midwest (see Exhibit 9). His calculations showed that escalation alone could account for a difference of $1 million between the lowest and highest figures. Variations in the cost of money, although affected by escalation, were primarily caused by the request for larger earlier payments by companies 1 and 4. (See Exhibit 3 for selected clauses from the 1970 Alta 1 contract with J&E Engineering, showing progress payment rates and the use of escalation.)

The outside consultant's view on escalation

Mr. Harbison was anxious to improve his understanding on the use of escalation in view of the large number of capital projects planned by Midwest. In the past he had not questioned the validity of escalation as it was a fairly standard concept, and he had accepted its use as a necessary evil of doing future business. He instructed Bill Morris to find an outside expert so

Exhibit 3
Selected clauses from the Alta 1 contract with J&E Engineering

A.   Price

The purchaser shall pay to the Seller $35,983,211.00 (contract price) for the materials and equipment furnished and services performed by the Seller pursuant to this contract.

B.   Terms of Payment

Progressive terms of payment shall apply to the system as follows:

1.   Purchaser shall make consecutive monthly deposits on account of the contract price, adjusted as provided in Section C below, at the percentages listed below in Column 3. Such deposits shall be refundable to Purchaser as provided in Article XII. The monthly deposits shall commence on October 1, 1969.

		Percent of price	
(1)	(2)	(3)	(4)
Monthly deposit no.	Number of deposits	Monthly	Cumulative
1–6	6	1	6
7–18	12	2	30
19–24	6	3	48
25–30	6	4	72
31–36	6	3	90
	36		

2.   The balance of the contract price, adjusted as provided in Section C below and consisting of the customary retention of 10 percent of the contract price, shall be paid in two equal payments as follows:

5%—30 days after date of shipment as defined in Section D below.

5%—30 days after successful completion of the 100-hour output performance test or on October 1, 1975 (as extended by delays established to the fault of Seller), whichever occurs first.

3.   In the event of any change in the contract price the new price shall be considered as having been in effect since April, 1969, for the purpose of payment.

4.   If the Seller's performance of the work is significantly delayed, the Purchaser and the Seller will mutually agree on an adjustment of the deposit schedule which will equitably reflect the effect of such delay provided that to the extent that such delay is nonexcusable as provided in Article XII.B, then pice adjustment as defined in Article V.C. below shall not apply to that portion of the agreed adjustment of the deposit schedule which is a result of the delay so caused.

C.   Price Adjustment

The contract price specified in Section A above is subject to adjustment upward or downward for changes in labor and material cost indices at the times when deposits are due and as of date of shipment for payments due after the date of shipment. Such adjustments shall be determined as set forth in this Section C.

1. Definitions. For the purpose of this provision, the following definitions apply:

a. The "Labor Index" shall be the Average Hourly Earnings in the Electrical

Exhibit 3 *(continued)*

Equipment and Supplies Industry (SIC 36) as finally determined and reported for the month in question by the Bureau of Labor Statistics of the U.S. Department of Labor in the publication "Employment and Earnings."

b. The "Materials Index" shall be the Steel Mill Products Index (Code 1013) as finally determined and reported for the month in question by the Bureau of Labor Statistics of the U.S. Department of Labor in the publication "Wholesale Prices and Price Indices."

c. The "Base Labor Index" shall be determined by averaging the Labor Indices for the months of March, April, and May, 1969.

d. The "Base Materials Index" shall be determined by averaging Materials Indices for the months of March, April, and May, 1969.

2. Adjustment for Labor Costs

a. For the purpose of price adjustment, 55 percent of the contract price and of each deposit and payment to be made on account thereof shall be deemed to represent the labor content.

b. The labor content of each deposit shall be adjusted for any increase or decrease in labor costs. The adjustment for labor shall be equal to the percent by which the Labor Index for the month in which such deposit is due is greater or less than the Base Labor Index.

c. The labor content of each part of the contract price due after the date of shipment shall be adjusted for any increase or decrease in labor costs. The adjustment for labor shall be equal to the percent by which the Labor Index for the date of shipment is greater or less than the Base Labor Index.

3. Adjustment for Material Costs

a. For the purpose of price adjustment, 35 percent of the contract price and of each deposit and payment to be made on account thereof shall be deemed to represent the material content.

b. The material content of each deposit shall be adjusted for any increase or decrease in material costs. The adjustment for material shall be equal to the percent by which the Materials Index for the month in which deposit is due is greater or less than the Base Materials Index.

c. The material content of each part of the contract price due after the date of shipment shall be adjusted for any increase or decrease in material costs. The adjustment for material shall be equal to the percent by which the Materials Index for the date of shipment is greater or less than the Base Materials Index.

4. General

a. In the event of any change in the contract price the new price shall be considered as having been in effect since April, 1969, for purpose of price adjustment.

b. For billing purposes, each periodic deposit and each payment shall include a tentative adjustment calculated in the manner prescribed above but based upon the Seller's estimate for the Labor Index and the Materials Index at the time such deposit or payment is due. Any further adjustment which may be required shall be made at the time the Indices are first published in final form. Billing rendered on the basis of indices published in such final form shall not be revised for a subsequent Index revision which may occur. Should the Indices specified in Paragraphs 1 a and 1 b above be discontinued, or should the basis of their calculation be modified, proper Indices shall be substituted by mutual agreement of the parties.

Exhibit 3 (concluded)

    c. The Base Labor Index shall be determined to the nearest second decimal place. The Base Materials Index shall be determined to the nearest first decimal place. In either case, if the next succeeding digit is five or more, the preceding digit shall be raised to the next higher figure.

    d. Both labor and material adjustments shall be calculated to the nearest one tenth of 1 percent.

D.   Shipment Date Defined

For the purpose of Sections B and C above, the phrase "date of shipment" shall mean the date the bill of lading is signed by the carrier covering the last to be shipped of the following items: reactor vessel, recirculation pumps (complete set) and control rod drive mechanisms (complete set).

Exhibit 4
Capital goods review
Indices of equipment prices and hourly labor costs (section A); ratio of the equipment index to the labor index and the long-term trend of the ratio (section B)* (indexes 1929–100)

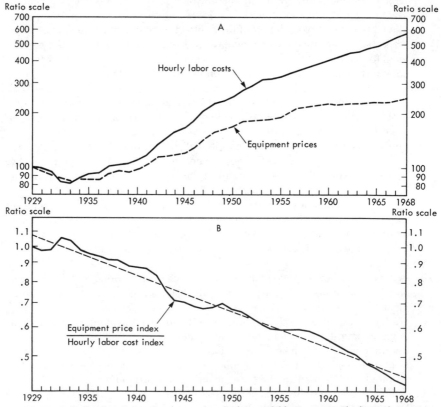

*A mimeographed description of sources and methods is available on request. The figures for 1968 are, of course, estimates.

Exhibit 5
Wholesale price index trends

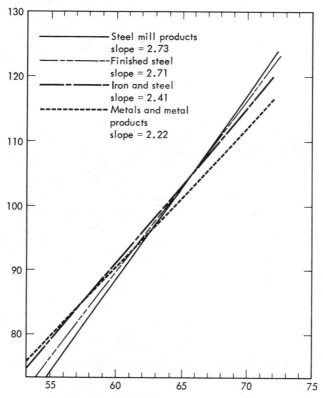

that the Midwest purchasing staff might benefit from his opinion. Bill Morris checked a number of sources and found out that Professor Roy Jones, employed at an internationally recognized local university, was considered one of the best economic experts on this subject. When Professor Jones visited Midwest he was surprised to see that escalation was even considered for the nuclear reactor at Alta 2. He claimed his calculations showed significant productivity increases in most industries through technological and management advances, removing the necessity for escalation altogether. He argued that the electrical industry as a whole had done extremely well in keeping consumer prices down on all appliances and saw no reason why the same principle could not be applied to large electrical equipment. In view of the popularity of nuclear reactors volume savings alone should warrant price decreases rather than escalation. The idea that escalation allowed for protection against increases in cost beyond management's control was not correct, according to Roy Jones. He said most labor and material costs were controllable through sound management and design. How Midwest could persuade

Exhibit 6
Average hourly earnings

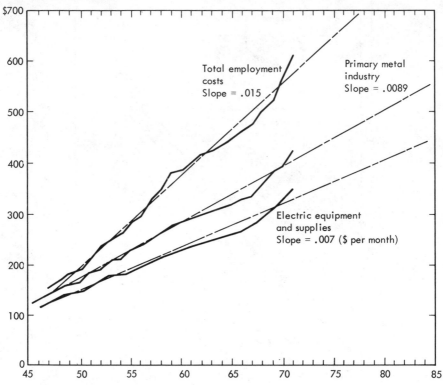

its suppliers to drop escalation charges was a problem Professor Jones could not answer.

Conclusion

Mr. Harbison was pleased with the work of Bill Morris and the advice of Professor Jones. He realized that the dollar impact of escalation was substantial and had largely been ignored in the past. In view of the short time left before the contract was to be awarded, he knew he would have to move quickly. His impression was that all four bidders believed escalation was legitimate and necessary, contrary to Professor Jones' opinion. He, therefore, wondered what he should do.

Exhibit 7   Wholesale price indexes

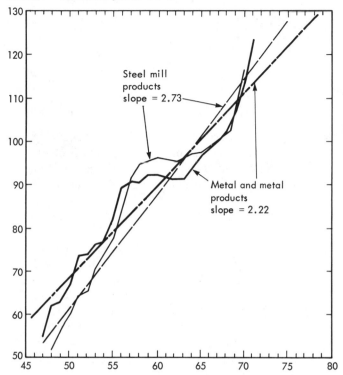

Exhibit 8 Computations of escalation concepts

Percent change per year in labor		Percent change per year in material		Total percent change per year
Concept no. 1	.......2.12	Iron and steel	.79	3.07
		Nickel	.16	
			.95	
Concept no. 2	.......1.96		.83	2.79
Concept no. 3	.......1.96		1.04	3.00
Concept no. 4	.......2.15		1.31	3.46

Computations based on the 10-year period, 1960–1970.

Exhibit 9 Escalation and cost of money analysis (average bid—$37,000,000)

	Company no. 1	Company no. 2	Company no. 3	Company no. 4	Maximum difference
Escalation	$ 3,054,017	3,588,165	3,296,244	4,099,476	1,045,459 (34%)
Cost of money (including interest on escalation) ..	$10,113,639	8,598,680	8,421,131	9,795,280	1,691,508 (20%)

FORWARD BUYING AND SPECULATION

 From the discussion up to this point, it should be clear that the determination of the proper price to pay is often far from being a simple task. It is even more difficult when the problem becomes one not merely of buying for immediate and known requirements but of buying for some period well in advance of these needs. Yet this is a situation with which every organization is faced. Under what circumstances and to what extent is forward buying justifiable?

A real distinction exists between ordinary forward buying, speculative buying, and a policy which is little short of gambling. While the border line between these three concepts at times is difficult to draw, they are by no means the same thing. Furthermore, the basic thinking of top management with reference to forward buying will be reflected in its procurement policy. If the management feels that its primary source of profit is to be derived from speculative purchases of raw material, it is likely to gear not only its procurement activities to that end but its sales, merchandising, and financial policies as well.

FORWARD BUYING VERSUS SPECULATION *

All forward buying involves some risk and is to some degree unavoidable. In ordinary forward buying, purchases are largely confined to actually known requirements or to carefully estimated requirements for a limited period of time in advance. The essential controlling factor is need. Anticipated trends are not disregarded but play a minor part in determining the amounts to buy. Thus, the inventory of an item may be controlled by a maximum-minimum method based on usage experience. Yet even here, when the reorder point is reached, the amount to be bought may be increased or decreased in accordance both with probable use and with the price trend, rather than automatically reordering a given amount. Temporarily, no order may be placed at all. On the other hand, a quantity somewhat larger than usual may be ordered. But the essential controlling factor is known need.

This may be true even where purchases have to be made many months in advance, as in the case of seasonal products, such as wheat, or those that must be obtained abroad, such as jute or carpet wools. Obviously, the price risk increases as the lead time grows longer, but the basic reason for these forward commitments is assurance of supply to meet requirements, and only secondarily price.

Speculation seeks to take advantage of price movements with need for supply

340

as a secondary concern. At times of rising prices commitments for quantities beyond anticipated needs would be called speculation. At times of falling prices speculation would consist of withholding purchases or reducing quantities purchased below the safety limits, and risking stock-outs as well as rush orders at high prices if the anticipated price decline did not materialize.

At best, any speculation, in the accepted meaning of the term, is a risky business, but speculation with other people's money has been cataloged as a crime. The position of a purchasing agent is a fiduciary one. The office should contain no throne for the Goddess of Chance. Its incumbent is a trustee for the wise employment of the funds belonging to the stockholders of the company. It is not within the purchasing agents province to expend any portion of those funds with the main object of future and uncertain gains, but only to provide for the immediate needs of the property, to the best advantage possible at the time, and to keep the investment in unused materials, the value of which is subject to fluctuations, at the lowest point consistent with safety of operation and economical maintenance.

Speculation versus gambling

Just where the line of distinction between speculation and gambling is to be drawn is a matter of individual judgment. There are certain practices, however, which can only be classified as gambling. If a person undertakes a venture in which there is an unknown chance to win, it is clear that that venture is not speculation. If a purchaser tries to guess what the market trend is likely to be for some commodity with which he or she has had no experience and practically no knowledge, he or she is a gambler. Others in the same category are those who, regardless of their experience with a particular commodity, lack adequate data upon which to forecast probable price movements. People who endeavor to anticipate price changes largely because of the thrill which they get out of such a practice are also to be placed in this same class.

The distinction between ordinary forward buying, speculative purchasing, and gambling should be reasonably clear. It is important to note that the three policies are quite different. The first policy is, in most cases, unavoidable. The second is debatable. If a company deliberately undertakes a policy of speculative buying, it is adopting a policy which it may feel is profitable, but which cannot be harmonized with the purpose for which most manufacturing concerns are organized. The third is never to be condoned.

Organizing for forward buying

The organization for determination and execution of policy with regard to long-term commitments on commodities whose prices fluctuate widely varies considerably from company to company, depending upon its size, the extent to which it desires to speculate, and the percentage of total manufacturing cost represented by those volatile commodities. In some instances, the president exercises complete control, based almost wholly on personal judgment. In other cases, although the president assumes direct responsibility, an informal committee provides assistance. There are companies in which the financial officer controls the raw materials inventory.

Some companies have a person other than the purchasing agent, whose sole responsibility is over "speculative" materials and who reports directly to top management. In a large number of firms the purchasing manager controls the inventory of such commodities. In a few companies almost complete reliance for policy execution is placed in the hands of an outside agency that specializes in speculative commodities.

The soundest practice for most companies would appear to be to place responsibility for policy in the hands of a committee consisting of the president or general manager, an economist, and the purchasing manager. Actual execution of the broad policy as laid down should rest with the procurement department.

Control of forward buying

Safeguards should be set up to ensure that the administration of a speculation will be kept within proper bounds. The following checks set up by one leather company are given merely as an illustration: (1) Speculative buying must be confined to those hides which are used in the production either of several different leathers or of the leathers for which there is a stable demand. (2) Daily conferences are held among the president, treasurer, sales manager, and hide buyer. (3) Orders for future delivery of leather are varied in some measure in accordance with the company's need for protection on hide holdings. Since the leather buyer is willing to place orders for future delivery of leather when prices are satisfactory, this company follows the practice of using unfilled orders as a partial hedge of its hide holdings. In general, the policy is to have approximately 50 percent of the total hides which a company owns covered by sales contracts for future production of leather. (4) A further check is provided by an operating budget which controls the physical volume of hides rather than the financial expenditures and which is brought up for reconsideration whenever it is felt necessary. (5) There is a final check which consists of the use of adequate and reliable information, statistical and otherwise, as a basis for judging price and market trends.

This particular company does not follow the practice of hedging on an organized commodity exchange as a means of avoiding undue risk, though many companies, including some leather companies, do. Nor does this company use any of the special accounting procedures, such as last-in, first-out, or reproduction-cost-of-sales, in connection with its forward purchases.

These various control devices, regarded as a unit rather than as unrelated checks, should prove effective. They are obviously not foolproof, nor do they ensure absolutely against the dangers inherent in buying well in advance. However, elasticity in the administration of any policy is essential, and, for this one company at least, the procedure outlined combines reasonable protection with such elasticity.

All such checks are designed in order that the combined judgment of those responsible for management may be exercised for the prevention of loss. A firm which operates to any substantial extent in the speculative markets without adequate financial backing is, in effect, gambling. A company always anticipates a profit from such operations or it would not engage in them. Yet losses do occur because mistakes are made, and luck does not favor the speculator consistently. No company should permit its resources to be so far committed to the uncertainties inherent in all speculative buying as to endanger its existence if heavy losses are incurred. Since losses are inevitable, ample reserves and reasonable caution are essential.

In manufacturing operations requiring large quantities of certain raw materials whose prices fluctuate widely, the risks involved in buying ahead may under some circumstances be substantially minimized through the use of the commodity exchanges. We must therefore devote some attention to these organizations, even though there is no need here to enter into a discussion of their technical operations and even though such organized exchanges exist for only a limited number of commodities.

THE COMMODITY EXCHANGES

The prime function of an organized commodity exchange is to furnish an established marketplace where the forces of supply and demand may operate freely as buyers and sellers carry on their trading. An exchange which has facilities for both cash and futures trading can also be used for hedging operations. The rules governing the operation of an exchange are concerned primarily with procedures for the orderly handling of the transactions negotiated on the exchange, providing, among other things, terms and time of payment, time of delivery, grades of products traded, and methods of settling disputes.

In general, the purposes of a commodity exchange will be served best if the following conditions are present:

1. The products traded are capable of reasonably accurate grading.
2. There is a large enough number of sellers and buyers and a large enough volume of business so that no one buyer or seller can permanently influence the market.

In order for a commodity exchange to be useful for hedging operations, the following conditions should also be present:

1. Trading in "futures"—the buying or selling of the commodity for delivery at a specified future date.
2. A fairly close correlation between "basis" and other grades.
3. A reasonable but not necessarily consistent correlation between "spot" and "future" prices.

All of these conditions usually are present on the major grain and cotton exchanges, and in varying degrees on the minor exchanges, such as those on which hides, silk, metals, rubber, coffee, and sugar are dealt in.

All these exchanges perform a real function. In most cases, the prices quoted on them and the record of transactions completed furnish some clue, at least, to the current market price and to the extent of the trading in those commodities. They offer an opportunity, some to a greater extent than others, of protecting the buyer against basic price risks through hedging.

Limitations of the exchanges

There are limitations upon the value of these exchanges as a source of physical supply for the buyer. In spite of a reasonable attempt to define the market grades, the grading is often not sufficiently accurate for manufacturing purposes. The cotton requirements of a textile manufacturer are likely to be so exacting that even the comparatively narrow limits of any specific exchange grade are too broad to serve his purpose. Moreover, the rules of the exchange are such that the actual deliveries of cotton made do not have to be of a specific grade but may be of any grade above or below basis cotton, provided, of course, that the essential financial adjustment is made. For the purpose of the cotton merchant or the cotton broker, these variables are of no practical importance. For them, the exchange serves a very useful purpose, but it is because their requirements are different from those of the cotton textile manufacturer.

This also holds true for wheat. Millers who sell patented, blended flours must have definite types of wheat. These types can be most satisfactorily procured only by purchase through sample.

There are other reasons why these exchanges are not satisfactory for the buyer endeavoring to meet actual physical commodity requirements. On some of the exchanges, no spot market exists. On others there is a certain lack of confidence in the validity of the prices quoted. Crude rubber, for example, is purchased primarily by tire manufacturers, a small group of very large buyers. On the hide exchange, on the other hand, the majority of hides sold are byproducts of the packing industry, offered by a limited number of sellers. An increase or a decrease in the price of hides, however, does not have the same effect upon supply that such changes might have upon some other commodities.

It is not asserted that these sellers use their position to manipulate the market artificially any more than it is asserted that the buyers of rubber manipulate the market to their advantage. In these two cases, however, there is likely to be a serious question in the minds of those who might otherwise wish to use the exchange as to the accuracy with which the prices quoted really reflect supply and demand conditions.

The large producers of nonferrous metals in this country do not use the metal exchange as largely as they might. The producers are said to be opposed to the use of the New York metal market because they wish to retain full control of their product and to sell to consumers only. They are especially anxious to keep it out of the hands of speculators because their past experience has indicated that buyers have refused to recognize the contracts when prices were falling and because the producers sometimes have found themselves in the position of competing "with their own products." They therefore feel that through constant contact with users better service to both parties in matters of brand, price, and delivery is obtained than if they were to deal through those who are interested primarily in the exchange. It is said, for example:

> Larger producers are interested primarily in having a stable copper market, something to which dealers and speculators are not committed, as speculators depend for a profit upon a rise or a decline in prices, and hence are anxious to have a fluctuating market. . . . The whole machinery of the metal business in this country is not built on lines which would work well with a large speculative exchange.

Hedging •

Perhaps the greatest advantage of the commodity exchanges to a manufacturer is that they provide an opportunity to offset transactions and thus to protect to some extent against price risks. This is commonly done by "hedging," which, broadly speaking, refers to transactions on the exchanges whereby a future sale or purchase of commodities is made to offset a corresponding purchase or sale on a spot basis. Hardy and Lyon say:

> The essence of a hedging contract is a coincident purchase and sale in two markets which are expected to behave in such a way that any loss realized in one will be offset by an equivalent gain in the other . . . The commonest type of hedging transaction is the purchase and sale of the same amount of the same commodity in the spot and future markets.[1]

Clearly, hedging can occur only when trading in futures is possible. A simple example of hedging to illustrate the above statement follows:

In the cash market	*In the futures market*
On September 1	
Processor buys	Processor sells
5,000 bushels of wheat shipped from country elevator at $4 per bushel (delivered Chicago)	5,000 bushels of December wheat futures at $4.10 per bushel
On October 20	
Processor sells	Processor buys
flour based on wheat equivalent of 5,000 bushels priced at $3.85 per bushel (delivered at Chicago)	5,000 bushels of December wheat futures at $3.95 per bushel
Loss of 15¢ per bushel	Gain of 15¢ per bushel

In the foregoing example it is assumed that the cash or spot price and the futures price maintained a direct correlation, but this is not always the case. Thus, there may be some gain or loss from a hedging operation when the spread between the spot price and the futures price does not remain constant. Hedging can be looked upon as a form of insurance, and like insurance it is seldom possible to obtain 100 percent protection against all loss, except at prohibitive cost. As the time between the spot and future declines, the premium or discount on the future

---

[1] Charles O. Hardy and Leverett S. Lyon, "The Theory of Hedging," *Journal of Political Economy,* vol. 21, no. 2, pp. 276–87.

declines toward zero (which it reaches when spot = future). On seasonal commodities, this decline in price differential usually begins six to eight months in advance. Under certain circumstances this phenomenon can make "risk-free" speculation possible. For example, when the speculator has access to a large amount of money, at least three times the value of the contract, and when a six- to eight-month future premium exceeds the sum of contract carrying cost and inventory and commission cost, the "speculator" can buy spot and short the future with a precalculated profit. Volume on the exchange should be heavy for this kind of operation.

While there are other variations to the techniques used in hedging, the one simple example is sufficient for our present discussion of forward and speculative buying.

The value to the manufacturer of hedging is open to debate. The issues involve the question of the net advantage to the buyer. Successful hedging on an exchange is a procedure requiring a great deal of skill and experience and capital resources. This suggests certain limitations imposed upon small manufacturers. It also explains why companies using large amounts of a certain commodity will often own seats on the exchange which deals in that commodity. A representative of the firm may then be constantly on the watch for advantageous opportunities for placing, withdrawing, or switching hedges between months and can translate this judgment into action immediately. To be successful, the actual procedure of hedging calls for the close observation of accumulating stocks of the commodity, the consequent widening or narrowing of the spreads between prices quoted on futures contracts, and the resulting opportunities for advance opening and closing of trades. These factors are momentarily shifting on the exchanges. The skill of the hedger is reflected in the ability to recognize and grasp these momentary opportunities.

Even assuming that the buyer is in a position to exercise this judgment and that the company is able to afford the administrative expenses and margin requirements there are other factors to consider. A close student of the commodity exchanges has summarized his conclusions relative to hedging as follows:

> Clearly it will not offset and should not offset expected basis gains or losses . . .
> cash prices normally rise relative to future prices as the crop year advances. They
> usually rise also with any improvement in the quality or position of supplies and it
> is through these sources that merchants derive the major part of their trade profit. It
> follows that if the cash commodity deteriorates in quality or position or is carried
> from an old crop year to a new in years when the on-coming crop is large, the hedge
> will not offset the loss sustained. Hedging is designed to protect only against un-
> foreseen major movements in price. . . . caused by factors having a common influ-
> ence on both cash and future prices.

It thus appears that hedging may not always be helpful or advantageous to the purchaser for a manufacturing plant. One obstacle to a wider use of the exchanges is the lack of understanding by manufacturers as to when and how to use them. Until this knowledge is gained, perhaps it is just as well that these industrial buyers proceed slowly. Another limitation is the vacuum effect when one of the relatively few large commodity brokers goes bankrupt, pulling some clients along.

Moreover, most brokers have not shown extensive interest in the industrial market. Most brokers probably will admit that they can barely afford to service a straight hedger, because they may have to send out six monthly position statements and four or more margin calls for a single round turn commission while their faithful "traders" will often maintain a substantial cash account and net them several round turn commissions per month with a minimum of bookkeeping.

According to G. J. Zenz[2] many managers still view futures trading with suspicion and tend to blame past mistakes on the system rather than managerial errors of judgment. The large increases in commodity prices in recent years may well have sensitized a number of managers to the opportunities of future trading, where before there seemed little need to be involved.

Business cycles and price forecasting

Underlying the entire discussion of forward and speculative buying is the problem of the business cycle and of price forecasting. In addition to secular and cyclical changes there are, of course, the ordinary seasonal movements, very pronounced in some fields of business, while practically nonexistent in others. These are looked upon more or less as the normal courses of events, and their influence is well recognized.

Some understanding of the nature of the business cycle should be part of the background of every purchaser. But, after all, it is only background, and the immediate task is much more specific. Theorists may argue about the causes of these fluctuations, and satisticians may evolve formulas and indices which will aid in foretelling price trends. The buyer cannot stop here, however, and must place definite orders at named prices.

Sources of information regarding price trends

Upon what is the buyer's judgment as to price trends based? Roughly speaking, there are three general sources of information. Any extended discussion of these sources is out of the question in this volume. The important thing to observe here is that all—even the highly organized and specialized forecasting agencies—are subject to marked limitations with respect to their value and dependability.

One source of information consists of the services of specialized forecasting agencies, such as the Babson Statistical Organization, Standard Statistics Company, Moody's Investors Service, and the Brookmire Economic Service.

The second includes a wide variety of governmental and other published data which are generally available. These include: the *Federal Reserve System Bulle-*

---

[2]G. J. Zenz, "Use of Hedging in Purchasing," *Journal of Purchasing* 8, no. 2 (1972): 47–53.

tin, the *Survey of Current Business,* the *Journal of Commerce, Business Week, Barron's,* and the *Wall Street Journal.* Trade magazines are also helpful in particular industries. They are typified by such publications as *Iron Age,* the *Oil, Paint, and Drug Reporter,* and *Engineering News-Record.*

The third comprises the highly unscientific—but nevertheless valuable, if properly weighted—information derived from salesmen and others with whom the buyer comes in daily contact.

One of the most valuable publications in this connection, although available only to members, is the *Bulletin* of the National Association of Purchasing Management. The Business Survey Committee of the association provides a useful service in compiling a composite opinion of purchasing agents throughout the country on commodity prices, inventories, employment, and commodity price changes.

Thus, from a variety of sources the purchaser gathers information concerning business conditions and price trends, sifts and weighs it, and finally acts. If asked to tell why a particular decision was reached the buyer might well have difficulty in explaining. Often the buyer acts upon what appears to be only a "hunch," although there is a substantial basis for that action. In the last analysis, it is judgment. The astonishing thing is not that the purchaser makes mistakes but that he or she is right so much of the time.

QUESTIONS FOR REVIEW AND DISCUSSION

1. Why might a buyer wish to hedge?
2. What is the difference between forward buying, speculation, and gambling?
3. Where might a buyer turn for information about commodities?
4. Does hedging remove all risk?
5. What is a commodity exchange?

CASE 8–1
EXERCISE IN PRICE FORECASTING*

Select one of the commodities listed below and report on it, giving:

1. Name of commodity selected.
2. Specific grade of commodity on which price is quoted.
3. Price of the commodity as of the present time. (Where the quotation applies only to a particular city, that point should be named; thus, gum

---

*© by the President and Fellows of Harvard College; all rights reserved.

turpentine at Savannah, or prime western zinc at St. Louis, or No. 2 hard, winter wheat at Chicago.)

4. Specific source of this quotation. (If the quotation is obtained from a printed source, give the name of the publication, date, and page. In a few cases, where a quotation is not available from a published source, give the name or names of the individuals from whom the quotation was obtained and their connections.)

5. Anticipated price (on comparable basis with that used in paragraph 3 above) as of six months from the present date.

Analysis of the reasons for anticipating the forecasted price will be accepted but not required.

Coconut oil, crude	Print cloth
Cotton linters	Rubber smoked sheets
Flaxseed	Sugar, raw
Hides (cattle)	Tin, pig
Paper, newsprint	Wool, carpet
Paper, waste	Wool tops
(No. 1 mixed)	

CASE 8–2
COMMODITY PURCHASING GAME

In this game you will have the chance to try your skill as a commodity purchaser. You will be using information similar in type to that available to Mrs. Martin, the purchasing manager of a well-known chocolate bar corporation.

Because raw material accounts for 50 percent of the cost of producing a chocolate bar, the purchasers in the chocolate bar business have a great deal of responsibility on their shoulders.

Among other functions, Mrs. Martin, at the beginning of each month has to decide how many pounds of cocoa should be purchased during the coming weeks of that month. When doing this, she takes into account the expected need of the production department, the time of the year, the inventory on hand, the cost of short supply, the cost of carrying inventory and, finally, the commodity market trends, more specifically, cocoa.

You will be able in this game to make similar decisions, although the game will be a simplified version of the actual situation. The most important features of this simplification are first, it will not be possible for you to buy cocoa after the first day of the month (you are allowed to purchase cocoa only once a month—on the first day); and, secondly, it will not be possible for you to buy cocoa on the futures market.

Cocoa need

Company sales, and industry sales in general, are very much influenced by seasonal factors. Because the chocolate has a tendency to melt in the warm months of the year, sales usually slow down during the summer months and rebuild very quickly in the fall when the manufacturers start their promotion again. For the last six years, July has been the slowest month for sales and September the biggest.

Because chocolate bars have a limited shelf life, and because it is company policy to supply freshly made chocolate bars to the retailers, it is company practice not to stockpile finished goods. Actually chocolate bars sold in one month have to be produced in that same month.

In the last five years, the company's cocoa need has grown almost constantly. Cocoa requirements have increased 200 percent in this five-year period. Last year's cocoa purchases were 4.76 million pounds. An average of the cocoa requirements for the last three years, broken down per month, is shown in Exhibit 1. The curve shown is only the average of the experience of many years. In any given year, the monthly percentage of total need might vary ± three percentage points from what is given by the curve. For example, January's figure of 10 percent is really the mid-point of a low of a possible low of 7 percent and a possible high of 13 percent.

From past experience, Mrs. Martin knows that the production department uses approximately 60 percent of the total yearly cocoa purchases in the last six months of the year. And, moreover, 55 percent of this last six months' need is used in September and October.

Production scheduling is done on a weekly basis. Mrs. Martin has no precise idea of what the actual total monthly production need for cocoa will be on the first day of that month, other than from her judgment of need level of prior periods and from consideration of the general shape of the need curve shown in Exhibit 1.

Raw material

Cocoa, the basic raw material in chocolate, has an especially volatile price, and there is no way to hedge completely against the wide price swings. Chocolate comes from cocoa beans, a crop subject to wide production fluctuations with a stable and generally rising demand. Furthermore, it takes 7 years for new cocoa trees to come into production (15 years to reach full production), and drought and disease can sharply reduce supply in a matter of months or even weeks.

Using the company's expected sales and expenses for the year, Mrs. Martin estimates that when she pays 24 cents a pound for cocoa, the contribution per pound purchased to profit is 6.5 cents, and any increase in the price paid for cocoa has a direct reverse effect on the amount of contribution and vice versa. (If she pays 25 cents per pound, then the contribution would be one cent less or 5.5 cents, and so on.)

Exhibit 1
Cocoa need per month by the production department

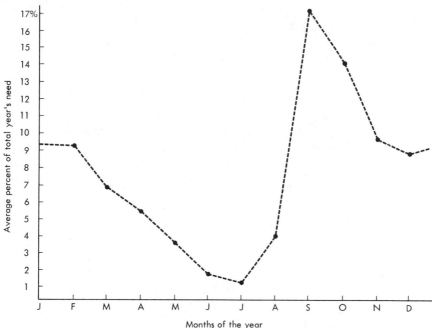

Months of the year

In order to be as efficient as possible in her predictions of future cocoa prices, Mrs. Martin keeps informed by means of trade journals; she follows the futures market closely and studies the past performance of cocoa prices.

As of October 1, Mrs. Martin has assembled the information given in Exhibits 2, 3 and 4. Company policy does not allow her to carry an inventory of more than 1,200,000 pounds of raw cocoa in her monthly ending inventory. The company is short of funds, and the president is not anxious to exceed borrowing limits set by the bank.

Costs involved

In deciding on purchasing alternatives, Mrs. Martin bears in mind several costs which she knows to be fairly accurate. These costs are inventory costs and stock-out costs.

(A) Inventory costs. Storage cost for one pound of raw material is 0.2 cents per month. This amount takes into account interest on tied-up capital, insurance against breakage of finished product or deterioration of raw material, and direct handling expense. Mrs. Martin knows that over the period of a season, inventory carrying charges can reasonably be calculated on the basis of inventory on hand at the end of each month.

Exhibit 2
Size of upcoming crops hold key to cocoa prices
(October 1)

Prices of cocoa beans have risen 8 percent since September 22. The increase follows a roller-coaster ride which took the market from a long-time low in July of last year to a 39-month peak in mid-July of this year, then down again by some 21 percent.

Harvesting of the main crop in Ghana, the world's largest cocoa producer, reportedly has been delayed by adverse weather. In addition, recent rains may have reduced yields in several African-producing areas. Black pod disease reportedly has hit the Brazilian crop, and Russia has told Ghana it wants early deliveries of the 100,000 long tons of cocoa pledged for this season and of cocoa on which Accra defaulted last season. Ghana, in turn, has requested an extension of one month or more for deliveries on sales contracts with the United States and Europe that were originally scheduled for the current quarter.

Future boost

Renewed buying interest by large manufacturers, coupled with trade and speculative purchases, helped boost cocoa futures. However, the extent to which supplies tighten in the next month or two will depend greatly upon the size of invisible stocks and of future government purchases from African growers, who have been given an incentive through purchase price increases by the Cocoa Marketing Boards.

The current New York spot prices of Accra (Ghanaian) cocoa beans, at 24 cents per pound compares with quotes of 22.25 cents on September 22, 16.75 cents a year ago, and a peak 28.25 cents on July 14 of the current year. During the ten-week price slump, the open interest in New York cocoa futures shrank from a record 38,054 contracts (30,000 pounds each) on August 10 to fewer than 28,700 contracts; it now aggregates 29,500 contracts.

On the New York Cocoa Exchange, the December future currently is selling at around 22.52 cents, up from 20.22 cents on December 22. The March option is quoted at around 23.11 cents, against 20.92 cents on September 22. The May future is selling at 23.54 cents. The distant December option is at 24.72 cents.

British bean experts

According to London's Gill and Duffus, Ltd., unfavorable weather held this year's would cocoa bean crop to 1,214,000 long tons, 20 percent below a year earlier. In the face of this dip, relatively attractive prices and rising incomes are expected to push the current year's world cocoa bean grindings (not to be confused with actual consumption) to a record 1,414,000 long tons, 83,000 (6.2 percent) above that of last year.

Allowing 1 percent for loss in weight, output seems to be lagging anticipated grindings by a record 212,000 long tons. This being the case, the October 1 would carry-over of cocoa beans, which is estimated at around 366,000 long tons, is barely a three-month supply. Nine years ago, a similar drop to a three-month supply saw prices averaging 34 cents, far above the current market.

On the eve of the coming season, the trade lacks accurate information on the size of the major new African crops. During recent months, African governments have sold ahead a large portion of the prospective new main crop at prices well above those of a year ago. Ghana's advance sales are placed above 275,000 long tons,

Exhibit 2 *(continued)*

some 100,000 more than last year, at prices ranging between 23 cents and 26 cents a pound.

Prior to the recent reports of adverse weather, the trade generally estimated the coming season's world cocoa output at around 1,300,000 long tons, some 60,000 to 86,000 tons above last season. This includes this year's prospective main and mid crops in Ghana of between 435,000 and 475,000 long tons versus 410,000 tons last year, and a record 572,000 long tons two years ago. Guess estimates for Nigeria range between 200,000 and 210,000 tons, against 182,000 last season, and a record 294,000 tons two years ago but may fail to account fully for losses due to the country's tribal unrest. Output from the Ivory Coast is tentatively forecast at between 120,000 and 150,000 tons, up from 112,000 tons last season, and close to its record of 145,000 tons.

Bad weather and pod rot, a fungus that causes seed to rot, have caused the experts to drop their estimates on the Brazilian crop to 130,000 or 135,000 long tons, down from 158,000 tons of last season. Recent reports indicate that the crops in other Latin American countries also will lag last season's levels, which may drop next season's yields for our southern neighbors some 60,000 to 75,000 tons below the 283,000 tons of last year. Adding everything together, the coming season's cocoa bean harvest is likely to range between 1,250,000 and 1,350,000 long tons, which would be a good deal smaller than the current year's anticipated world cocoa bean grindings.

How closely output matches next year's consumption is the key to the cocoa market. Bulls on cocoa believe that prices have not been high enough long enough to discourage the steady rise in usage. They attribute the July to September slump mainly to forecasts of increased crops, tight money, and the large open interest which invited volatile prices.

Exhibit 3
Cocoa spot price and cocoa futures market (October 1)

Spot Price: 24.0 cents per pound

	Futures market
December	22.52
March	23.11
May	23.54
July	23.92
September	24.31
December (next year)	24.72

(B) Stock-out costs. Mrs. Martin also considers stock-out costs. A stock-out cost occurs whenever the production demand for raw cocoa in a particular month is greater than the available raw cocoa in inventory. For example, if 50,000 pounds of raw cocoa are on hand at the beginning of the month, 50,000 pounds are purchased, and the need during the month totals 110,000 pounds, then a stock-out of 10,000 pounds occurs. The company then has to place rush orders for raw cocoa and, consequently, is forced to pay a three-cent per pound premium.

Exhibit 4
Past performance of cocoa on the commodity market

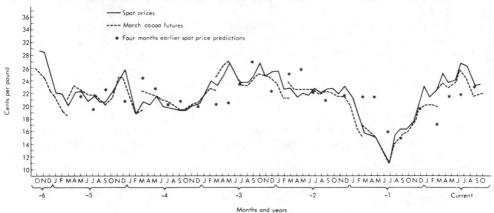

Mrs. Martin's commission

The president of the company was convinced that incentives for executives were important. Therefore, part of Mrs. Martin's salary was based on her performance as a cocoa purchaser. She received a 5 percent commission on the monthly net contribution to profits.

Net Monthly Contribution = Monthly contribution less
monthly stock-out costs
(or monthly inventory carrying costs)

Closing inventory target

At the end of the game, each group is expected to have a closing inventory of 200,000 pounds of raw cocoa. Every group who fails to reach this 200,000 pound target will be penalized in the following way.

a. For every pound in excess of the aforementioned target:

As in every other month, the company will have to pay an inventory carrying cost, and, moreover, there will be an extra charge of 2.8 cents per pound over the 200,000 pound target.

b. For every pound short in relation to the aforementioned target:

The company will have to pay 3.0 cents per pound and will have to buy sufficient cocoa at the September 1 spot price to bring the inventory level to 200,000 pounds.

How to play the game

In the actual conduct of this game, teams will be used to make the purchasing decisions normally made by Mrs. Martin. On the first day of each month, each team will be required to decide on the quantity of cocoa to be purchased. This decision will be made by the team by whatever means it chooses. Thus, a prediction from a plot of past months' performance might be used by some teams, a pure guess by others. In making the decision, teams will want to consider both the possibilities of future needs and the inventories now on hand as well as their forecast of cocoa spot prices behavior.

After each team has made its purchasing decision for the coming month, the instructor will announce what the month's need has been. Given this information, teams will then be able to calculate, using Exhibit 5, all of the necessary costs and, finally, the "net commission of the purchaser."

The object of the game is to increase as much as possible the purchaser's cumulative commission over 12 months. This means that teams will have to decide whether it would be cheaper in the long run to incur some inventory or stock-out costs, depending on their predictions of the cocoa behavior on the commodity market. At the end of each month, every team's results will be shown on the screen in front of the class and, at the end of the 12th month, the class will discuss each team's method of predicting sales and cocoa prices. Teams will probably find it advantageous to split the work of making sales estimates, calculating costs and profit, and estimating the next period cocoa spot price.

Exhibit 5
Result form

	Stock on hand at start of month in lbs. = ending inventory of previous month	Purchases in lbs.	Total available for production in lbs. (3 = 1 + 2)	Production requirements in lbs.	Ending inventory in lbs. (5 = 3-4) Cannot be less than 0 or greater than 1,200,000 lbs. Penalty for any excess of $1,000 in commission	Stock-out in lbs. (6 = 4 - 3 if greater than 0)	Stock-out costs (7 = 6 x $.03)	Inventory carrying costs (8 = 5 x $.002)	Contribution per lbs. purchased ($.065 - ($SPOT - $.24))	Total monthly contribution (10 = 2 x 9)	Total monthly costs (11 = 7 + 8)	Net monthly contribution (12 = 10 - 11)	Monthly commission on contribution (13 = 5% x 12)	Cumulative commission (14 = 13 + 14 previous month)
	1	2	3	4	5	6	7	8	9	10	11	12	13	14
August	50M	350M	400M	450M	0	50M	$1,500	0 .	3.5c	$12,250	$1,500	$10,750	$537	($537)
September	0	1,100M	1,100M	900M	200M	0	0	$400	6.4c	$70,400	$400	$70,000	$3,500	($4,037)
October	200M													
November														
December														
January														
February														
March														
April														
May														
June														
July														
August														
September														

Exhibit 5 *(continued)*

	15.	Stock at end of September (15 = 5 of September)
	16.	Purchases in quantity
	17.	September contribution per pounds purchased ($.065 – ($SPOT – $.24)
If (15) is less than 200,000 lbs.	18.	Final added contribution (18 = 16 × 17)
	19.	Extra cost (19 = line 16 × $.03)
	20.	Net September contribution (20 = 18 – 19)
	21.	September commission (21 = (.05 × 20) – 13 of September)
	22.	Total cumulative commission (22 = 21 + 14 of August)
If (15) is greater than 200,000 lbs.	23.	Extra cost (23 =(15 – 200,000) × $.028)
	24.	Net September contribution (24 = 12 of September – 23)
	25.	September commission (25 = .05 × 24)
	26.	Total cumulative commission (26 = 25 + 14 of August)

Summary of important points to remember when playing the game

1. Purchases can be made only on the first day of the month.
2. You cannot buy cocoa on the "futures market."
3. It is a company practice to purchase at least all the production requirements of the current month on the first day of that month.
4. It is not possible to carry an inventory of more than 1,200,000 pounds of raw cocoa.
5. At a purchased price of 24 cents per pound, the cocoa will bring a contribution to profit of 6.5 cents. This contribution is directly related to the purchased price. (A one-cent increase in the cost results in a one-cent decrease in the contribution, and vice versa.)
6. There is an inventory carrying cost and a stock-out cost which are directly deducted from the contribution amount to give the net contribution.
7. There is a closing inventory target of 200,000 pounds.

Result form used

To make the keeping of results easier for each team, a form has been distributed (see Exhibit 5). The exact steps in using this form are shown on the form itself.

Concluding result form

Because there is a closing inventory target of 200,000 pounds, you will be required to fill the concluding result form (see Exhibit 5) at the end of September. The steps in filling this form are as shown on the form itself.

Example

Each team member should carefully trace the proceedings as outlined in the following example so that he fully understands all of the steps involved in playing and recording the game.

Mrs. Martin has already used the "Result Form" to record the operating results of the two months prior to October. On August 1, Mrs. Martin had to decide how many pounds of cocoa should be purchased. Knowing the spot price on August 1 was 27 cents a pound, she thought, after consulting the trade journals and studying the "futures market," that the prices would go down; therefore, she decided to purchase cocoa to supply the need of the current month only. She then consulted the production need curve and came to the conclusion that the need of that month would be approximately 300,000 pounds. Knowing that she had 50,000 pounds of cocoa in inventory, and wanting to keep a safe margin, she purchased 350,000 pounds of cocoa at the price of 27 cents per pound. She then entered the following figures on the "Result Form."

Column (1) = 50,000 pounds (from column (5) previous month)
Column (2) = 350,000 pounds
Column (3) = 400,000 pounds
Column (9) = $.035 = $.065 − ($.27 − $.24)
Column (10) = $12,250

At the end of the month of August Mrs. Martin received from the production department the exact figure of the month's requirements, 450,000 pounds. Since there were only 400,000 pounds of cocoa in inventory, the company had had to make a last minute order to another user of cocoa at a premium of $.03/lb. With this information, Mrs. Martin could now calculate her net commission according to the company's norms. She entered the following figures on the "Result Form."

Column (4) = 450,000 pounds
Column (5) =   0   pounds
Column (6) =   50,000 pounds
Column (7) = $ 1,500

Column (8) = $ 0
Column (11) = $ 1,500
Column (12) = $ 10,750
Column (13) = $ 537
Column (14) = $ 537

On September 1, she received the latest information on the cocoa market (spot price, futures market, and trade news), and she went through the same process to purchase the raw cocoa for the month of September.

Start of the game

The game proper starts on October 1. At the beginning of the game there are 200,000 pounds of cocoa on hand. It is now up to each team at this time to decide on the coming year's purchases and, thus, start playing the game. We will assume that the cumulative commission of $4,037 to the end of September has been paid to Mrs. Martin and that each team will start again from zero. Please use Exhibit 6 as the sample for your group's reporting form which should be handed in to the instructor each period.

Exhibit 6
Report form

```
             DECISION REPORT

   Month i ........... Group # ........

   Purchases ........ Pounds of cocoa

             RESULT REPORT

  Last month's        Cumulative
  results             Commission
  net commission      to date
  $............       $............
```

References

From M. Jiler, ed. *Guide to Commodity Price Forecasting.* New York: Commodity Research Bureau, Inc., 1967. With permission from the Commodity Research Bureau, Inc.

Jiler, Milton W. "Understanding the Commodity Futures Markets"; pp. 5–22.

Shishko, I. "How to Forecast Cocoa Price," pp. 98–108.

PROCUREMENT OF EQUIPMENT

9

We have been concerned thus far primarily with the procurement of materials, component parts, and supplies. We turn now to the purchase of equipment, a decision which in most organizations is closely controlled at the top executive level. Many interrelated problems should be considered if a sound equipment policy is to be formulated:

1. Will the new equipment make the best use of available capital funds?
2. Will a desired return on invested capital be received if the new equipment is purchased?
3. Is the equipment flexible in that it has alternate uses?
4. Are technical advances being made which make it likely that better equipment will be available soon?
5. Will the necessary volume be maintained to realize fully the operating cost advantages of the new equipment?
6. What is the effect of taxes?
7. Will the company's competitive position be affected if the new equipment is not purchased?

These questions may be difficult to answer and may raise doubts about the feasibility of having a stated equipment policy rather than considering each new equipment purchase separately.

DEFINITION OF EQUIPMENT

Throughout this discussion, the term "equipment" will be applied broadly to those items the cost of which is more properly chargeable to a capital account than to expense. They are essential "durable" or "capital" goods. We shall exclude, however, building and similar construction, which, although both "durable" and "capital," falls into a class by itself. Although the questions relating to any particular piece of equipment will be common to all types of capital goods, the degree to which any broad conclusion will apply must vary with each individual case.

A useful classification of equipment is the division into multipurpose and single purpose. Multipurpose equipment may have a variety of uses, may be used in several or many industries, tends to have longer technological life, and may have considerable salvage value. Fork lift trucks, certain classes of computers, and standard lathes are typical examples.

Single purpose equipment is designed to do one or several operations well, normally, substantially better than a multipurpose piece of equipment could. On the other hand, its specificity limits its potential use, and its usefulness is closely tied to the need for the operations it performs. Such special equipment is normally limited to one industry and may even be limited to one customer. The purchaser's specifications are important, requiring extensive consultation between the technical personnel of both buyer and supplier. The salvage value of special equipment may be low, and chances are that the need for the tasks disappears before the equipment is physically worn out.

Minor or accessory equipment is normally used in an auxiliary capacity and tends to be of much lower dollar value. Its cost may not even be capitalized, and much of it tends to be standardized. Small pumps and motors are typical examples.

Special problems of equipment buying

Equipment procurement raises special problems, as follows:

1. The buying of equipment usually requires that substantial amounts of money be expended for a single purchase. Sometimes the sum is so large as to call for a special form of financing, such as a bond issue, leasing, or payment on the installment plan.

2. Because of their comparatively long life, equipment items are likely to be bought less frequently than other types of industrial purchases.

3. The final cost of equipment is more difficult to determine with exactness than, for example, the final cost of raw materials. The initial cost of equipment is but part of the total cost, which involves a whole series of estimates, such as the effects of idle time, of obsolescence, of maintenance and repair, of displaced labor, and even of direct operation factors. Some of these items may never be known exactly, even after experience with the particular piece of equipment in question. Moreover, many of the costs, such as insurance, interest, and obsolescence, continue even when the equipment is not in actual use. The income to be derived is also problematical, and, thus, even when it is possible to compute approximate costs, it is often difficult to determine how soon they will be met. These comments are particularly applicable to so-called nonproductive equipment, such as cranes and hoists.

4. Equipment purchases are often less affected by current price trends than, for instance, raw materials. The demand for industrial equipment more than the demand for any other type of industrial goods is a derived demand. Pricewise, the best time at which to buy is, therefore, particularly hard to determine. "Only when the need and the justification of the equipment has been established is there a possibility that its actual purchase may be delayed or hastened by price considerations." Since equipment is not commonly bought until needed, it is seldom bought during periods of business recession, although prices for equipment normally are low at such times and many good arguments can be advanced for buying then. Aside from absence of immediate need, manufacturers in periods of

slack business tend to watch their assets carefully. Also, labor may be cheaper during recessions, and there is less incentive to substitute machinery for labor. The reverse conditions prevail in times of prosperity.

5.   The purchase of equipment frequently involves problems concerning the wisest method of disposition of the displaced item, a consideration which almost never arises in connection with materials or supplies.

6.   A decision to purchase equipment, is therefore likely to require a careful consideration of many factors involving broad management policy. The decision once made may well commit the company to a series of other decisions of a permanent nature, such as the type of product to be manufactured, the method of its production, and the cost of operation. Put in other words, it is much easier "to get in and out" of a situation involving the purchase of raw materials than one involving the purchase of major equipment. Furthermore, the company's labor and financial policies may be affected. In short, equipment questions are likely to be procurement decisions of prime importance to management.

We turn now to a brief consideration of some of the specific problems involved in equipment procurement decisions. There are many of them, inevitably, but for purposes of our present discussion, we shall consider only the following:

1. The general principles which should control the selection of equipment.
2. The cost factors immediately applicable.
3. The problem of engineering service.
4. The timing of the purchase.
5. The selection of the source.
6. Some legal questions.
7. The financing of the purchase.
8. The disposition of obsolete or replaced equipment.
9. The purchase of used equipment.
10. Leasing.

General principles which should control the selection of equipment

The selection of major equipment is clearly based upon due consideration of a wide range of factors, so coordinated that the net result is efficient manufacture of the desired product at the lowest net cost per unit. To achieve this, it is necessary to analyze not only the price of the particular equipment in question but also such elements as plant layout, kind of power used, types of machines used for other operations, and the like. In short, the proposed installation must be looked upon as an integral part of an established process; and its coordination with the existing facilities must be obtained, even though extensive changes may be required to effect economical production.

Equipment purchases involve in part engineering and production considerations and in part factors largely outside the scope of these functions. From the former standpoint, there are six commonly recognized reasons for purchase: economy in operation, increased productivity, better quality, dependability in use, savings in time or labor costs, and durability. To these safety, pollution, and emergency protection should be added.

Beyond these engineering questions are those which only the marketing purchasing or financial departments, or general management itself can answer. Are style changes or other modifications in the present product essential or even desirable? Is the market static, contracting, or expanding? Does the company have the funds with which to buy the machine which theoretically is most desirable, or is it necessary, for financial reasons, to be satisfied with something that is perhaps less efficient but of a lower initial cost? What should be done in a case in which the particular equipment most desirable from an engineering standpoint is obtainable only from a manufacturer who is not thoroughly trustworthy or perhaps is on the verge of bankruptcy? Such questions are quite as important in the final decision as are the more purely engineering ones, and they are not questions which the engineer is qualified to answer. This merely emphasizes once more the many-sided nature of the problem and the many types of judgment required in reaching a sound solution of it.

For this reason it is sound practice to form a team including representatives from engineering, using departments, finance, marketing, and purchasing to work jointly on major equipment purchases. Unfortunately, in some organizations purchasing gets excluded from these decisions on the grounds that they have no contribution to make. The fallacious assumption behind this is that the decision is basically an engineering one.

In some organizations the volume of equipment purchases is so great that a special person or team of employees in purchasing is assigned the equipment purchasing task exclusively. The title of equipment buyer is a common one in such instances as is manager of equipment purchases.

Importance of cost factors

Once the need for new equipment has been determined, one of the first questions to be considered is that of cost. To arrive at the right answer to cost is likely to be difficult, calling for a careful balancing of several factors. For example, among the facts called for are the following: Is the equipment intended for replacement only or to provide additional capacity? What is the installed cost of the equipment? What will start-up costs be? Will its installation create problems of plant layout? What will be the maintenance and repair costs? Are accessories required, and, if so, what will their cost be? What will be the operating cost, including power and labor? What is the number of machine-hours the equipment will be used? Can the user make the machine in his own plant, or must it be bought outside? At what rate is the machine to be depreciated? What financing costs are involved? If, as is usually the case, the equipment is for production, what is the present cost of producing the product compared with obtaining the item from an outside supplier and of producing the unit with the new equipment?

Since the middle 1950s, there has been a substantial growth in the use of quantitative methods in the analysis of capital investment and capital equipment purchases. Research in mathematics and the increasing availability of computers have provided tools for a depth of economic analysis not feasible in the past. The increased sophistication of business managers in using such concepts as "discounted cash flow," "return on investment," and "present value" in making capital equipment and investment decisions has probably resulted in greater understanding and improved decisions.[1]

Life cycle costing ¢

The Department of Defense has strongly encouraged the use of Life Cycle Costing (LCC) as a decision approach to capital investments. The philosophy behind LCC is relatively simple. The total cost of a piece of equipment goes well beyond the purchase price or even its installed cost. What is really of interest is the total cost of performing the intended function over the life time of the task or the piece of equipment. Thus, an initial low purchase price may mask a higher operating cost, perhaps occasioned by higher maintenance and downtime costs, more skilled labor, greater material waste, more energy use, or higher waste processing changes. Since the low bid would favor a low initial machine cost an unfair advantage may accrue to the supplier with possibly the highest life cycle cost equipment.

The Logistics Management Institute defines LCC as "the total cost of a system during its operational life."[2] It is the inclusion of every conceivable cost pertaining to the decision that makes the concept easier to grasp theoretically than practice in real life. Since many of the costs are future ones possibly even 10 to 15 years hence of a highly uncertain nature, criticisms of the exactness of LCC are well founded. Fortunately, computer programs are available varying from simple accounting programs, which compute costs from projected life cycles, to Monte Carlo simulation of the equipment from conception to disposal. The computer allows for testing of sensitivity, and inputs can be readily changed when necessary. The normal emphasis, particularly in governmental acquisition, on the low bid finds, therefore, a serious and preferable alternative in LCC. The experience with LCC has shown in a surprising number of instances that the initial purchase price of equipment may be a relatively low percentage of LCC. For example, computers, if purchased, seldom run over 50 percent, and most industrial equipment falls into the 20-percent–60-percent range.

There are eight steps in LCC formulation. In practice, one may combine some of the following eight steps:[3]

1. Establish the operating profile.
2. Establish the utilization factors.
3. Identify all cost elements.

---

[1] For an explanation of these concepts, see George Willard Terborgh, *Business Investment Management* (Washington, D.C.: Machinery and Allied Products Institute, 1967).

[2] *Logistics Management,* Institute Report, 4C-5, April 1965.

[3] R. J. Kaufman, "Life Cycle Costing: Decision Making Tool for Capital Equipment Acquisitions," *Journal of Purchasing* 5, no. 3, (August 1969).

4. Determine the critical cost parameters.
5. Calculate all costs at current prices.
6. Escalate current labor and material costs.
7. Discount all costs to base period.
8. Sum up all discounted and undiscounted costs.

An interesting example provided by Kaufman includes two automatic palletizers X and Y for which the critical costs are shown in Table 9-1.[4]

The result of this study was that palletizer X with a substantially higher initial
purchase cost of $200,000 (versus Y at $170,000) showed a lower LCC of
$289,000 versus $306,000 for Y. Since this company intended to purchase six
machines the magnitude of the savings, beyond the normal return on investment
of the equipment, amounted to about $100,000.

Table 9–1
Critical cost parameters

	Palletizer X			Palletizer Y		
Cost parameter	Value	CL %	Srce	Value	CL %	Srce
Acquisition cost	$200,000	100	mfgr	$170,000	100	mfgr
Equipment life	12 years	100	mfgr	12 years	100	mfgr
Initial engineering	$3,000	100	mfgr	$2,000	100	mfgr
Installtion cost	$3,000	100	mfgr	$4,000	100	mfgr
Manning	⅓ man	100	mfgr	½ man	100	mfgr
MTBF	500 hrs	80	ee	100 hrs	90	ee
MTTR	.5 hrs	80	ee	2.0 hrs	90	ee
PM cycle	16 hrs	100	mfgr	16 hrs	100	mfgr
PM downtime	.5 hrs	100	ee	.84 hrs	70	ee
Time between overhauls	2 years	100	mfgr	2 years	100	mfgr
Cost to overhaul	$1,000	80	ee	$3,000	100	ee
Parts cost per year	1% NOHY	60	ee	2% NOHY	70	ee
(Percent of acquisition cost)	2% OHY	60	ee	2.5% OHY	80	ee
Input power	3.0 kw	90	mfgr	5.0 kw	100	mfgr

CL	= Confidence level	MTTR	= Mean time to repair
Srce	= Source of information	PM	= Preventive maintenance
mfgr	= Manufacturer	NOHY	= Nonoverhaul year
MTBF	= Mean time between failure	OHY	= Overhaul year
ee	= Engineering estimate	kw	= Kilowatt

Problem of engineering service

Most sellers of major equipment maintain an intimate and continuing interest
in their equipment after it is sold and installed. Two major questions are involved
in providing engineering service: why the service is given and accepted, and
what the cost of such service is.

Technical sales service is provided by a vendor to a potential or actual pur-

---
[4]Ibid., p. 25.

chaser of equipment, to determine the designs and specifications of the equipment believed best suited to the particular requirements of the buyer and also to ensure that, once bought, the equipment functions properly. It is nearly always related to the "individualized buying problem of particular users." Some sellers feel that the equipment they sell is so complicated or requires such fine adjustment that none but their own experts can either install the machines or service them after installation. The vendor may feel further that the buyer's operatives need to be specially trained, perhaps for weeks or months, before they can be trusted to handle the equipment themselves. Occasionally, equipment is sold which carries with it a production guarantee, an additional reason for supervising both the installation and the operation of the equipment. Even after this initial period, the seller may provide for regular inspection to ensure the proper operation of the machine.

In many instances, services of these various types are thoroughly warranted; and it is to the best interests of buyer and seller alike that they be offered by the vendor and utilized by the purchaser. Smaller companies may well be most in need of such assistance because they are unable to employ their own consulting engineers. Furthermore, regardless of the size of the company making the purchase, the greater the amount either of presale or postsale service rendered by the seller, the greater the responsibility of the latter for proper and satisfactory performance.

There is, however, another side to this question of sales service. For one thing, the prospective buyer may ask for and receive a great deal of presale service and advice without real intention of buying or knowing full well that the firm providing the service will under no circumstances receive an order. Not only is such a procedure unethical, but the buyer who pursues it will sooner or later find the organization's reputation for fair dealing has seriously suffered.

Yet abuses are by no means confined to buyers. It is well known that salespeople often solicit requests for expert consulting service from buyers without any real inquiry as to whether or not a sale is likely to materialize. Furthermore, the theory that such services are mutually advantageous is not always substantiated by the facts. The seller's claims as to the necessity of vendor-supervised installation and instruction are not always warranted.

The problem of engineering service is really twofold, both phases, however, involving cost. The first phase relates to the method followed by the seller in charging for presale service. Such service is clearly a matter of sales promotion, and, when no subsequent sale results or when the profit on the sale is insufficient to cover fully the cost of the service, some other means of recovery must be found. If the total costs of all such service are borne only by the firms which actually do buy, the price paid will appear unduly high; yet this method may prove the only feasible way of handling the charge. The problem is complicated further when a firm produces two lines of product, one requiring service and the other not. If presale service cost is charged into general sales promotion overhead, clearly the one product is likely to be overpriced and the other underpriced; this situation places the seller in an awkward competitive position. One suggestion for meeting this problem is that a specific charge, either a flat fee or one computed on the basis of actual cost, be made for presale engineering service, the recipient of the service paying this charge whether or not a purchase is made subsequently.

The second phase of the problem relates to postsale engineering service. The prime abuse of postsale services arises from those firms which insist upon furnishing it and upon charging for it, whether or not the buyer feels a need for it. Such charges naturally become a part of the price paid for the equipment, whether they are included in a single quotation or are billed to the purchaser separately. When the service is really needed, no objection to such charges can be raised by the buyer, provided, of course, that they are fair. The purchaser must see to it, however, that the service actually is necessary and that the charges are legitimate and reasonable. Such considerations are matters of price negotiation and should be settled before the purchase contract is signed.

Timing of the purchase

The determination of the proper time at which to make a purchase of equipment is significant. Productive equipment is usually bought on a basis of known requirements only when, after an analysis of all cost and other factors, it appears probable that the purchase will "pay for itself" within a definite period of time. The exact length of this period naturally varies widely, both with company policy and with the item in question. It may range from six months to several years or more. Obviously, in spite of all the formulas, this evidence is often somewhat difficult to produce, since it calls for judgment as to future sales and prices as well as cost figures.

For one thing, the need for expansion is normally felt during prosperous periods. Demand may be artificial at such times. Lead times for major equipment may be as high as five to ten years and predictions that far ahead are always difficult. Since most purchasers try to acquire equipment in prosperous times, lead times tend to be at their worst when the demand is the greatest, creating a cyclical effect for suppliers.

Selection of the source

Selection of the proper source requires careful consideration in any purchase of major equipment. In the purchase of raw materials and supplies, quick delivery and the availability of a continuous supply are important reasons for choosing a particular supplier. These characteristics are often not so important in equipment purchases. The reliability of the seller and a reasonable price are, of course, important, regardless of what is being bought. But, as contrasted with raw materials, what may be called "cooperation" in selecting the right type of equipment, proper installation, common interests in efficient operation—in short, a long-continuing interest in the product after it is sold—becomes very important. So, too, does the availability of repair parts and of repair services throughout the entire life of the machine. Satisfactory past relationships with the equipment supplier weigh heavily in the placing of future orders.

During the 1960s and early 1970s there was a substantial increase in foreign-made capital equipment sold in North America. Whether this was caused primarily by availability, price, technology, or other reasons is not entirely clear. The difficulties of obtaining service from nondomestic manufacturers may be considerable even for such simple reasons as poor translations of service manuals.

The interest of operations, engineering, or technical personnel in capital equipment is such that they usually have a strong supplier preference. For large companies, manufacturing equipment in their own shops has always been an alternative. Some even have subsidiaries specializing in equipment design and manufacture. Where secret processes give a manufacturer a competitive edge, such inhouse manufacture is almost essential.

Some legal questions

Attention should also be directed to the legal questions that arise in connection with equipment buying. The danger of liability for patent infringement constitutes one problem. The extent of liability for accidents to employees is another. Again, the equipment sales contracts and purchase agreements are often long and involved, offering many opportunities for legal controversies. Various forms of insurance coverage are used and are often subject to varying interpretations. Any purchased machine must comply fully with the safety regulations of the state in which it is to be operated, and these safety regulations vary greatly in the different states. Federal Government OSHA (Occupational Safety and Health Act) requirements have to be followed. The question of consequential damages is a particularly touchy one. Should the seller of a key piece of equipment be responsible for the loss of sales and contribution when the machine fails because of a design or fabrication error? Such losses may be huge for the buyer. In one company gross revenue of $1 million per day was lost for six months because of the failure of a new piece of equipment costing $800,000! These and many other situations exist which call for careful scrutiny and interpretation by qualified legal counsel. The importance of this phase of equipment buying should not be overlooked.

Financing the purchase

Before any commitment to buy a major item is authorized, careful thought must be given not only to the desirability of the purchase but also to the means by which payment is to be provided.

When the financial budget is set up, it is customary to make provision for two types of capital expenditure. The first type covers probable expenditures which, although properly chargeable to some capital account, are still too small to be brought directly to the attention of the finance committee or controller. Customarily, some limit is fixed, as, for example, $500 or $1,000.

The second type includes expenditures for larger amounts. The inclusion in the budget, however, constitutes neither an authorization to spend that amount of money nor an approval of any specific equipment acquisition. This authorization must be obtained subsequently from the executives concerned, and their specific approval is given only after they have examined carefully a preliminary analysis of the project. A formal appropriation request is called for, giving a detailed description of what is to be bought, estimates of the costs involved, the savings likely to result, the causes which have created the need, the effect of the purchase upon the organization as a whole, and whatever other information those initiating the request feel is pertinent. In the light of these facts, together with the data regarding other financial requirements of the company and its financial position, a decision is made as to wisdom of authorizing the particular expenditure under consideration.

In years past, no major capital expenditure was possible unless the company either had the necessary funds on hand or could secure them through what may be termed the "orthodox channels." More recently, however, sellers of equipment have made possible purchase on a deferred payment plan, and today there are very few types of standardized machinery that cannot be secured on this basis. The wisdom of buying equipment on such a plan is, of course, a matter which each individual organization must decide for itself and then only with reference to the particular purchase in question.

An interesting variation of the deferred payment plan has developed in recent years, particularly in some industries, based on the theory that the payments to the seller are dependent upon and proportional to the anticipated savings.

Leasing, a popular method of financing equipment, is described at the end of this chapter.

Disposition of obsolete or replaced equipment •

What to do with old or replaced equipment is an interesting question. One procedure is to trade in the old machine on the new, the vendor making an allowance and assuming the burden of disposal. A second procedure is to sell the old equipment to a used equipment dealer. A third is to find a direct buyer. A fourth is to sell the old machine as scrap. A fifth is to destroy the machine to assure no one else will have access to it. Some of these procedures will be discussed indirectly on the following pages. (See Chapter 11 for disposal of waste and surplus materials.)

Procurement of major equipment—used and leased

In our discussion of equipment purchases thus far, it has been assumed that the buyer was acquiring new equipment. An alternative is the purchase of used equipment which raises special issues. In general, the same rules of evaluation apply as in the case of new equipment. One important difference, however, may be that, ordinarily, manufacturers' services and guarantees do not apply to such purchases. The value of these intangibles is difficult to determine. Many buyers would say that they are more important with used equipment than with new and that their value may be greater than any differential in price.

Barring other considerations, the decision of whether to trade in or not is largely dependent on which will result in the lowest net cost to the purchaser. Since trade-ins are a form of price concession, they may not accurately reflect current market values of the old equipment. In some industries, old equipment may be in perfect operating condition and its disposal may well create unwanted competition. At other times, it may represent a health or environmental hazard, or contain special secret features. Destruction may be a reasonable solution in all these instances.

In large companies, equipment displaced in one plant may be of use in another within the same organization. It is normal practice for purchasing departments to circulate lists of items available within the organization before searching for other disposal alternatives. Transfer pricing is usually based on book value and the transportation charges are assumed by the receiving plant.

Reasons for buying used equipment

Some of the reasons for the purchase of used equipment follow:

1. When price is important either because the differential between new and used is vital or the buyer's funds are low.
2. For use in a pilot or experimental plant.
3. For use with a special or temporary order over which the entire cost will be amortized.
4. Where the machine will be idle a substantial amount of time.
5. For use of apprentices.
6. For maintenance departments (not production).
7. For better delivery when time is essential.
8. When a used machine can be easily modernized for relatively little or is already the latest model.
9. When labor costs are unduly high.

Why used equipment comes on the market

Used equipment comes onto the market for a variety of reasons. One obvious result of the modernization of a plant is the disposition of the displaced equipment. In addition to this somewhat general reason, there are other explanations as to the appearance of used equipment on the market. Some of these may be listed as follows:

1. Loss of contracts.
2. Change in process or in line of manufacturing.
3. Obsolescence in a specific use.
4. Insufficient productivity to meet the needs of the original owner.
5. Trade-in on a new machine.
6. Inadequacy to meet new requirements.
7. Discontinuance of entire manufacturing operations because of bankruptcy, insolvency, death of owner, etc.

Sales contract terms

Having used equipment either to sell or to buy, a manufacturer has at least two problems. The first relates to the terms of contract. Here there are three choices: (1) The equipment may be disposed of "as is," and perhaps "where is." A sale "as is" means that the contract carries essentially "no warranty, guarantee, or representation of any kind, expressed or implied, as to the condition of the item offered for sale." "Where is," of course, is self-explanatory. (2) The equipment may be sold with certain specific guarantees, preferably expressed in writing. This practice is found more generally among used equipment dealers, though they sometimes may offer equipment "as is." (3) Finally, the equipment may be sold "guaranteed and rebuilt." The desirable interpretation placed on this is that the equipment has been rebuilt or is in condition equivalent to that of a rebuilt machine and is invoiced as such; that it has been tested; and that it carries a binding guarantee of satisfactory performance for not less than 30 days from the date of shipment.

Organization of used equipment market ♦

There are various channels through which used equipment is bought and sold. Briefly, they are:

1. Trade-in as partial payment on new equipment.
2. Direct sale to a user.
3. Sale through a broker or liquidating agent.
4. Sale at auction.
5. Sale to a dealer in used equipment.

⊕ **Trade-in as partial payment on new equipment.** Generally manufacturers of equipment are unwilling to accept used equipment as part payment on new. Under certain circumstances, however, in the interest of customer goodwill, they may be willing to assist a prospective buyer of new equipment to locate a buyer for the used. This is most likely to be the case (1) when the item to be sold is noncompetitive with anything manufactured by the seller or (2) when the buyer is a regular customer of the particular equipment manufacturer. When the seller is unable to make delivery of a new item in time to meet the buyer's requirements, he may even go so far as not only to suggest a market for the equipment to be replaced but to indicate where it may be possible to locate a piece of used equipment of the type sought.

Except in the obvious case of direct sale to user, the utilization of one of these channels does not necessarily preclude the use of another. Thus, a used machine may be sold by the owner to a dealer, who in turn sells to another user. Or a liquidating agent may sell either to a dealer or to a user and may do so either directly or through an auction. Although direct purchase from the seller is an important method of acquisition, in the brief description which follows, major attention will be devoted to the dealer, probably the most important single agency in the market.

Direct sale to user. Direct sale through the company's own organization is often a profitable method of disposal. Through advertising in trade journals or some other media, the attention of potential buyers may be attracted to the offer, and negotiation initiated either by mail or by direct visitation. Used equipment is frequently disposed of in this manner. Since this procedure eliminates the use of an intermediary, it suggests a saving of the latter's profit. Finding a buyer, moreover, often does not appear to be a serious problem, particularly since the potential buyers are likely to be somewhat limited in number and the seller ordinarily has a sales organization already set up. However, experience has shown that in many cases the "saving of the middleman's profit" is illusory and that direct sale actually is time-consuming, troublesome, and ineffective so far as securing as high a return as can be secured through other methods is concerned. This is particularly true when, for instance, an entire plant is being closed down and the equipment sold.

Sale through broker. Brokers, in theory at least, do not take title to the equipment in which they are interested but seek only to bring buyers and sellers together. In fact, however, they may act in the capacity both of brokers and of dealers, though obviously not for the same equipment. Used equipment brokers are more important in some industries than in others. Comparatively few of them, for instance, specialize in general machine tools, largely because of the multiplicity of regular dealers. Brokers frequently employ personal selling and advertising to liquidate equipment and commonly realize a commission of 10 to 15 percent on the gross sale.

Sale at auction. Auction firms vary in type and character. Some are highly reputable. Others are not always so regarded. One type of auction firm is the trader who buys stock and auctions it off. This type of firm frequently has representatives both at its own sales and at other auctions to encourage bidding and to acquire good machines that, for one reason or another, do not bring high prices on the day of the initial auction. While the auction commission is less than that for a broker, the price realized on the merchandise frequently is lower, inasmuch as it is impossible to bring together in a local region as many interested buyers as can be reached through direct-mail advertising. Occasionally, it is possible to realize higher prices because the auction gives play to the emotional factors involved when bidders openly compete against one another.

From the standpoint of the buyer, both equipment and material can often be obtained economically through an auction sale. However, to buy well calls for a rare degree of ability on the part of the bidder, since it requires an intimate knowledge of one's requirements, judgment as to the economic worth of the items, and skill in the difficult art of bidding.

Sale to dealers. There are many types of dealers who buy and sell used machinery tools and other used equipment. Certain dealers act as brokers in handling some sales, while at other times they purchase outright. Another class of dealers stock new as well as used machines, but many—perhaps most—dealers specialize only in used equipment. In addition, many dealers rebuild equipment. The largest dealers of this type maintain plants which manufacture parts for used machinery, and they also employ an engineering staff to design improvements for the rebuilt machines. They then offer the machines "rebuilt," including guarantees which often are more comprehensive than those given by new machinery manufacturers. A different type is the merchant who buys machinery by placing a deposit against it and then sells it before moving it from the premises where it was purchased, thus eliminating the necessity of warehousing. Plants about to be closed down or liquidated following bankruptcy are sometimes bought by another type of large buyer, a speculator who attempts to keep a liquidated plant in operation for a time. Often these plants are operated only long enough to process the material on hand.

While many purchasing officers say they are opposed to purchasing used equipment, virtually all do buy it in larger or smaller quantities. The policy varies widely from company to company. Some apparently buy it only under unusual circumstances, while others buy used equipment in preference to new whenever a satisfactory purchase can be made.

Leasing equipment

Since the end of World War II, there has been a substantial increase in the number and diversity of manufacturers of capital equipment who lease as well as sell their equipment. Those who advocate leasing point out that leasing involves payments for the use of the assets rather than for the privilege of owning the asset.

Short-term rentals are a special form of lease with which everyone is familiar. Short-term rentals make a lot of sense when limited use of the equipment is foreseen and the capital and/or maintenance cost of the equipment is significant. Often an operator can be obtained along with the piece of equipment rented. The construction industry is a good example where extensive use is made of short-term rentals.

Most lease contracts can be drawn to include an "option to buy" after some stated period. It is important for anyone considering the lease of capital equipment to be sure that the Internal Revenue regulations are understood. On October 15, 1955, the Internal Revenue Service announced its position on ascertaining the tax status of leases as follows:

> In the absence of compelling factors of contrary implication the parties will be considered as having intended a purchase and sale rather than a rental, if one or more of the following conditions are covered in the agreement:
>
> 1. Portions of periodic payments are specifically applicable to any equity to be acquired by the lessees.
> 2. The lessees will acquire title upon payment of a stated amount of rentals.
> 3. The total amount which the lessee is required to pay for a relatively short period

constitutes an inordinately large proportion of the total sum required to be paid to secure transfer of title.

4. The agreed rental payments exceed the current fair-rented values.
5. The property may be acquired under a purchase option which is nominal in relation to the value of the property at the time when the option may be exercised, as determined at the time of entering into the original agreement, or which is a relatively small amount when compred with the total payments which are required to be made.
6. Some portion of periodic payments is specifically designated as interest or is otherwise recognizable as the equivalent of interest.

Unless the lease rental payments are allowed to be treated as an expense item for income tax purposes, some of the possible advantages of the equipment lease plan may not be realized.

In the past, some large manufacturers of machines and equipment employing advanced technology have preferred to follow a policy of leasing rather than selling their equipment. Government antitrust actions have aimed at giving the user the right to determine whether he wished to lease or purchase. The leasing may be done by the manufacturers of the equipment, by distributors, or by companies organized for the specific purpose of leasing equipment.[5] At times, as in the construction industry, an owner of equipment who has no immediate use for it may lease or rent it to other concerns that may have temporary immediate need for it.

An interesting phenomenon with leasing occurs in large organizations, including public agencies. Since lease costs are normally charged to operating instead of capital budgets, department heads may try to acquire equipment through the back door of leasing when the capital budget does not permit purchase. This can easily lead to abuse and some very high rental costs. In one government agency, the rental of recording equipment over a six-month period equalled the purchase cost. Buyers need to be aware of this practice and on the lookout for costly subterfuges involving leasing.

Advantages and disadvantages of leasing ●

The advantages of leasing may be listed as follows:

1. Lease rentals are expenses for income tax purposes.
2. Small initial outlay (may actually cost less).
3. Availability of expert service.
4. Risk of obsolescence reduced.
5. Adaptability to special jobs and seasonal business.
6. Test period provided before purchase.
7. Burden of investment shifted to supplier.

There are certain equally clear disadvantages, however:

---

[5]See Henry G. Hamel, *Leasing in Industry* (New York: National Industrial Conference Board, 1968), for a full discussion of professional lessors.

1. Final cost likely to be high.
2. Surveillance by lessor entailed.
3. Less freedom of control and use.

Many leases need to be watched with care since they are one-sided in their terms, placing virtually all the risks on the lessee. For instance, what are the arrangements for replacing equipment when it is obsolete or no longer service-able? Is the lessee free to buy supplies anywhere, such as paper for copying machines? Are the actual charges what they appear to be? Are there onerous limitations on either the maximum or the minimum output or other such opera-tional factors as the number of hours per day or number of shifts the equipment may be used or on using attachments? What limitations, if any, are there to the uses to which the equipment may be put?

Take for example, the question as to the freedom of a lessor to buy supplies from someone other than the owner of the leased equipment:

> In some cases manufacturers of both supplies and basic equipment have used their equipment installations as a method of promoting the sale of supplies by leas-ing the equipment at very low annual rates in order to secure the lessee's orders for supplies. From the user's standpoint this may have an important impact on purchas-ing. Selection of supplies may be based more upon the evaluation of the basic equipment installation than on the price and quality of supplies from competing sources. . . .
>
> Users must recognize that their choice of equipment introduces certain pressures for purchasing supplies and auxiliary equipment from the equipment manufacturer. A lease may serve to accentuate such pressures. . . . The effective performance of the machine, as well as its cost of maintenance and repair, *may be materially* af-fected by the type of supplies used. Obviously, the vendor's reputation is threatened if the equipment does not live up to performance claims. Consequently it may be argued that if the vendor's own supplies are used, the equipment will oper-ate at maximum efficiency. . . . But under the lease, the argument will be more forceful, since the lessor can show a direct interest in the particular equipment installation.
>
> A lessor has an interest in and responsibility for the servicing of leased equip-ment. Since ownership remains with the lessor under the lease, the lessor must take precautions against equipment damage resulting from improper use by the lessee. If an improper supply item is used, it may increase the amount and cost of servicing required. If the rental is based upon units of output, the use of inferior supply items can reduce the lessor's revenue from the lease. In either case, the lessor can argue a direct interest in the type of supplies purchased by the user. . . .
>
> Even if it is assumed that there is no contractual agreement concerning the purchase of supplies, the user should anticipate an inclination to assume that supplies provided by the company who makes the equipment will be superior for use with that particular type of equipment. . .[6]

---

[6]See Wilford J. Eiteman and Charles N. Davisson, *The Lease as a Financing and Selling De-vice*. Report No. 20 (Lansing, Mich.: Bureau of Business Research, School of Business Administra-tion, University of Michigan, 1951), pp. 80 and 100–101.

Types of leases ●

There are two main types of leases, the financial and the operational. The financial lease is primarily financial in nature and may be of the full payout or partial payout variety. In the full payout form the lessee pays the full purchase price of the equipment plus interest and, if applicable, maintenance, service, record keeping, and insurance charges on a regular payment plan. In the partial payout plan there is a residual value to the equipment at the end of the lease term and the lessee pays for the difference between original cost and residual value plus interest and charges.

The financial lease cost is made up of the lessor's fee, the interest rate and the depreciation rate of the equipment. The lessor's fee depends on the services offered and may be as low as .25 percent of the gross for straight financing without other services. The interest will depend both on the cost of money to the lessor and the credit rating of the lessee. The depreciation normally varies with the type of equipment and its use. For example, trucks are usually depreciated over a five-year period.

The operational lease is in its basic form noncancellable, has a fixed term which is substantially less than the life of the equipment and a fixed financial commitment which is substantially less than the purchase price of the equipment. Service is the key factor in the operational lease with the lessor assuming full responsibility for maintenance, obsolescence, insurance, taxes, purchase, and re-sale of the equipment, etc. The charges for these services must be evaluated by the lessee against other alternatives which may be open.

Categories of leasing companies ●

According to J. P. Matthews[7] careful analysis of how the lessor will profit from the leasing arrangement is vital in obtaining a satisfactory price. Since most leasing companies have standard procedures for calculating leases but are seldom willing to disclose these or the vital figures behind them, it behooves the buyer to search carefully before signing. Since lessors are more likely to disclose competitors' procedures and figures than their own, the search need not be seen as an impossible task. Matthews identifies four major different structures of leasing relationships, each with its special implications. (See Figure 9–1)

1. The full service lessor. Full service lessors are most common in the automotive, office equipment, and industrial equipment fields. The lessor performs all services, purchases the equipment to the buyer's specifications, and has its own source of financing. This type of lessor generally obtains discounts or rebates from the equipment manufacturers which are not disclosed to the lessee. Profits are also obtained on the maintenance and service charges which are included in the lease rate. Care should be taken on long-term leases which contain

---

[7]J. P. Matthews, "Equipment Leasing: Before the Cash-Flow Analysis, What Else?" *Journal of Purchasing* 10, no. 1, (February 1974): 5–11.

Figure 9–1
Four leasing structural relationships

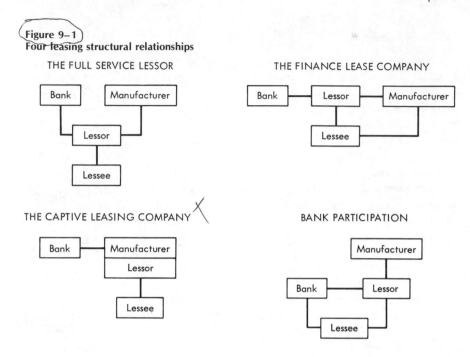

an escalation provision to allow such escalation only on that portion of the lease on which costs might rise.

2. The finance lease company. This type of lessor does not purchase or maintain the equipment, so that the lessee deals directly with the equipment manufacturer. The lessor frequently has access to funds at close to prime rate and is able to make its profit by lending above this. Occasionally, if a relatively short lease is involved, the lessor may wish to profit from the resale value of the equipment and may offer unusually low lending rates. A profitable lessor may benefit from the investment tax credits and depreciation which to a less profitable lessee may be meaningless. When a lessee has already reached the limits on its investment tax credits because of large capital expenditures but the lessor is not yet at the limit, leasing may similarly benefit both.

3. Captive leasing. The prime purpose of captive leasing is to encourage the sale and use of the parent's equipment. The reasons why the original manufacturer of equipment may choose to lease rather than to sell are several.

1. To secure either wider distribution or a higher margin.
2. To reduce the credit risk.
3. To sell a full line or to increase the volume of sales of supplies.
4. To control the secondhand market.
5. To stabilize the company's growth through securing distribution in times of recession when sales, especially of new as contrasted with used equipment, are difficult to make.
6. To control servicing.
7. To protect a patent position.

Obviously, a transfer price for the equipment holds between the parent and the lessor. Sometimes a lessor will quote a 2-percent sales tax figure on the rental value when in reality the lessor may only be charged with a use tax which applies to only 50 percent of the rental value. A lessee might expect to gain at least a 1-percent benefit from negotiation here.

4. Bank participation. There are advantages to bank participation in cases where the lessee has a good credit rating. The bank may be willing to finance part of the lease at rates slightly over prime, because it is a low-risk and low-nuisance lease. The lessor looks after the purchasing, servicing, and disposal of the equipment, relieving the bank of tasks it normally has little expertise in.

Conclusion

Quite aside from any weighing of the specific advantages and disadvantages and beyond the actual terms of the lease, any prospective lessee of equipment needs to exercise the utmost care in passing judgment on the lessor. Is the lessor:

1. Reasonable and fair in dealings with customers?
2. Devoting as much attention and money to research as alleged?
3. Strong financially?
4. Fully protected by patents?
5. If a sole source, prone to be arbitrary in the periodic adjustment of rental and other fees?

What effect would a fire in the lessor's plant have on the repair and servicing requirements of the user?

There is neither formula nor theory which can provide the right answer to all these questions. The solution to each particular problem can be found only in the sound judgment of the procurement personnel within the buyer's organization.

QUESTIONS FOR REVIEW AND DISCUSSION

1. In what ways is the purchasing of equipment different from the purchase of supplies?
2. What is Life Cycle Costing? What are the implications of using Life Cycle Costing in public purchasing?
3. Why might a buyer consider purchasing used equipment instead of new?
4. Give at least five reasons why leasing might be considered instead of purchasing equipment.
5. What is a full service lessor?
6. Why might an organization wish to destroy a piece of equipment rather than sell it as surplus?

CASE 9–1
KRAMER CORPORATION

Nick Walton was equipment buyer for the Kramer Corporation, a large manufacturer of construction and mining equipment. Part of Nick's responsibility was the rental of shop equipment as well as the purchase of new machinery. He was surprised to receive a requisition from Ray Scoles, assembly shop foreman, for a $9,000 steam generator.

Nick knew that a steam generator was only required for an occasional cleaning job. In the past it had been standard practice to rent one from A-1 Rentals, a reliable local firm. When Nick asked Ray why it was necessary to buy the generator, Ray answered: "That is none of your business, since the shop superintendent has approved the requisition." When Nick asked the superintendent for an explanation he replied "I don't care whether the equipment is bought or rented so long as Ray is happy with the arrangement."

On checking his files Nick found out that over the past four years A–1 Rentals had always supplied a good quality generator on time whenever requested. Current rental rates for the equipment were $75 per day or $300 per week, delivered and picked up by A–1 Rentals. Annual usage during the last four years had been as follows:

	Number of times rented	Number of days used	Total rental charges
4 years ago.... 5	5	19	$ 975
3 years ago.... 3	3	11	650
2 years ago.... 4	4	13	825
1 year ago.... 4	4	17	1050

The purchase requisition asked for immediate delivery, since a cleaning job was scheduled for the following week.

CASE 9–2
LINK SAND AND GRAVEL COMPANY

Mr. F. Wheeler, purchasing manager at Link Sand and Gravel was considering a proposal submitted to him by a local construction equipment leaser. Link was in the market to buy a wheel tractor scraper for its new quarry operation. Two decisions had to be made; one, which scraper model would suit the job best; and, two, should the scraper be purchased or leased.

Company background

Link operated a number of sand and gravel quarries throughout Ohio. Scrapers were used to remove the overburden and deliver the mixed sand and gravel to a sorting and screening plant. In the Wellfeld sand and gravel pit operation, an average scraper load carried 80 percent sand and 20 percent gravel. Sand after being sorted into different grades was sold for $10.00 to $17.00 a ton. The Wellfeld pit, typical of most Link sand and gravel quarries, used two scrapers, three loaders, and six large trucks.

Link had annual sales of $143 million. Last year the company had purchased 76 pieces of equipment valued at approximately $4 million.

The expected life of this equipment was between three and five years.

The Wellfeld operation

A year ago Link had purchased an elevator scraper to replace a grader and loader. The $150,000 elevator scraper had proved to be a poor purchase. Substantial downtime and increased maintenance had skyrocketed operating costs. The resulting production tonnages were 60 percent of the estimated 1 million ton target for the first operating year. The pit superintendent and general manager suggested that the scraper be traded in and replaced with a simple scraper tractor capable of producing one million tons a year. It had to be able to operate in dirt, sand, and gravel and be free of maintenance problems. Mr. Wheeler estimated that any piece of capital construction equipment would use 96 percent of its purchase price in parts and maintenance costs over its expected life. The Wellfeld pit was very rugged, limiting equipment life to a maximum of five years.

Search for the right scraper

Mr. Wheeler requested information and costs of scrapers from various manufacturers. The Wellfeld pit superintendent went to a number of other quarry operations to see what equipment was most popular and what type of equipment problems they were having. Caterpillar was known in the trade as the Cadillac of construction equipment, and the test results shown by Caterpillar in their testing fields warranted a Wellfeld on-site demonstration. Caterpillar had three scrapers which would be considered for the job. (See Exhibit 1.) Caterpillar model 633 had a purchase price of $143,000; model 637 cost $120,000, and model 627 cost $84,000. All purchase prices included options but no taxes. The pit superintendent was pleased with all three scrapers.

The Wellfeld quarry was 40 miles from the nearest company maintenance depot. On site maintenance was very expensive, therefore making unscheduled downtime an important consideration. An hour of downtime was

Exhibit 1

⊞ CATERPILLAR

MORE PLUS VALUES OF CAT TANDEM POWERED PUSH-PULL SCRAPERS

VARIOUS SCRAPER TYPES

TRACTOR FEATURES...

Semi-automatic 8-speed tractor transmission (standard on 637 and 657B, optional on 627). Highly efficient in the cut, haul and fill. Operator has option of automatic or manual power shifts in six haul road speeds, manually selects from two torque converter speed ranges to meet high rimpull needs.

Transmission hold pedal (semi-automatic transmission) locks machine in the gear in use—allows operator to maintain high engine RPM. For added hydraulic power and to prevent unwanted upshifts on favorable grades.

SCRAPER FEATURES...

Low wide scraper bowl picks up big loads fast. Wide cutting edge gathers volume loads from shallow cuts, incoming earth meets low resistance because the bowl is shallow.

Outboard-mounted scraper bowl cylinders (637, 657B) reduce stress on draft frame. Trunnion mounting allows fore, aft and sideways movement which eliminates bending forces that shorten cylinder, seal and rod life.

Power down apron slices through and holds hard materials. Double-acting hydraulic cylinder exerts powerful force. Apron lip protected from lodged rocks by hydraulic relief valve.

TRACTOR AND SCRAPER FEATURES...

Four cycle engines for tractor and scraper have high torque rise and excellent lugging characteristics, can burn non-premium, high energy fuels.

Exhaust muffler combines with silencing effect of turbocharger to keep engine noise to a minimum.

Fuel filler opening accepts adapter for high speed pressurized fueling attachments.

Automatic dust ejector uses engine exhaust gases to remove 95% of foreign matter from air entering the precleaner. Air cleaner requires less servicing time and effort.

Tractor differential lock reduces tire spin and improves traction on wet or slippery surfaces. Engaged by foot pedal.

Constant speed steering through working engine RPM range combines with stabilizing action of follow-up mechanism to give automotive "feel" to steering.

Louvered radiator guard (637, 657B) directs radiator heat to right side of tractor and away from operator compartment.

Cushion Hitch (optional on 657B, 637) absorbs road shocks, allows faster usable road speeds. Cuts haul road "washboarding," reduces wear and tear on machine parts. Combines with torsionflex seat for smooth ride.

Positive bulldozer ejection dumps wet or sticky material. Powered by fast double-acting hydraulics. Detent allows operator to take hand from control lever during ejector return. Lever automatically snaps to "hold" when ejector reaches rear position.

Positive down-pressure on bowl provides penetrating force on cutting edge. This reduces load time in hard materials and prevents the bowl from riding over and on blocky material which can accelerate bowl wear.

Multiple speed scraper transmission combines multi-speed gear box with torque converter. Accurately balances scraper engine to speed and load requirements.

Automatic positive locking type differential on scraper reduces wasteful tire spinning and rutting. Aids traction.

Horn and light alert operator to malfunction of rear engine cooling and lubrication systems or transmission synchronization problems.

XT-3 hydraulic hose made by Caterpillar will outlast any other make hose in high pressure, high temperature, high flexing applications. Significantly reduces hydraulic system downtime.

Multiple system hydraulic tank supplies all needs: steering scraper operation, Cushion Hitch and Push-Pull. One sight gauge checks all, simplifies servicing.

Variable rate tractor and scraper retarders (637, 657B, optional on 627) Tandem powered units provide virtually double retarding capacity over comparable single drive units—increasing downhill performance.

Separate brake circuits for tractor and scraper assure reserve braking is always available at one axle.

Automatic emergency braking automatically engages if brake pressure drops below safe operating level.

PUSH-PULL SCRAPERS
3 sizes...dual struck loading capacities from 28 to 64 cu. yd. (22-49 m³)

High returns from modest added investment. Team-load two tandem powered scrapers then separate on-the-go for haul. Can also be loaded separately by usual pusher.

TANDEM POWERED SCRAPERS
4 sizes...struck capacities from 14 to 40 cu. yd. (11-31 m³)

The added power and traction pay important productive dividends on a surprisingly wide range of jobs.

STANDARD SCRAPERS
6 sizes...struck capacities from 14 to 40 cu. yd. (11-31 m³)

Powerful engines, advanced transmissions and low, wide bowls make these machines the most productive units of their type on the market.

ELEVATING SCRAPERS
3 sizes...struck capacities from 11 to 32 cu. yd. (8.4-25 m³)

These units self load—eliminate a pusher and unproductive wait time. Another point worth considering: these are the most *durable* elevating scrapers you can buy.

estimated to cost the company $23. The company accountant had recently pointed out to Mr. Wheeler that investment in capital equipment must be recouped in three years in order to take the maximum tax credits. He also estimated that the company's cost of capital was 8.5 percent. Internal sources of funds were becoming increasingly scarce.

The lease alternative

Mr. Wheeler contacted Contract Leasing Company who had done business with Link previously on a satisfactory basis. Arrangements were made to bring a 637 model scraper to the Link Sand Pits at Wellfeld and substantiate manufacturer's previous operating figures. The results were favorable, and Contract Leasing outlined a proposal to lease and maintain any one of the three models for the Wellfeld quarry. (See Exhibit 2.) Mr. Wheeler

Exhibit 2

To: Link Sand & Gravel Co., Ltd.,   From: Contract Leasing, Ltd.,
    R.R. 1,   192 Eglington Avenue,
    Wellfeld, Ohio.   Wellfeld, Ohio.

We propose to rent to you the following equipment subject to the terms described below:

1—Caterpillar 633 Wheel Tractor-Scraper, Cushion-Hitch, series C, 32 cubic yard elevating scraper, semiautomatic, power shift transmission, direct electric starting, muffler, emergency brake system, ROPS fully enclosed cab, heater, windshield wiper, defroster fan, scraper floodlight, driving lights, 33.25-35 32 PR, Michelin tires. Elevator extended one foot to include 14 flights and scraper modified with sideboards and miscellaneous wear shields to adapt it for operation in gravel.

Base rental rate $5,170.00 per month plus any applicable taxes, from date of delivery until equipment is returned to Lessor, or satisfactory notification of rental termination is received. This rate is based upon 3,000 hours use in one year as measured by Sangamo Tachograph. If machine is rented in excess of 3,000 hours per year, all excess hours shall be on the basis of $20.00 per hour. Credit *will be issued* for use under 3,000 hours per year at $10.00 per hour; maximum 400 hours credit.

Minimum rental charge $62,040.00 based upon a guaranteed 12-month rental at the base rental rate renewable for a second year at the same rate.

1—Caterpillar 627 Wheel Tractor-Scraper, Cushion-Hitch, push-pull, series C, 20 cubic yard heap capacity, semiautomatic power shift transmission, direct electric starting, muffler, emerency brake system, ROPS fully enclosed cab, heater, windshield wiper, defroster fan, scraper floodlight, driving lights, 29.5-29 28 PR, Michelin tires.

Base rental rate $3,000.00 per month plus any applicable taxes, from date of delivery until equipment is returned to Lessor, or satisfactory notification of rental termination is received. This rate is based upon 3,000 hours use in one year as

Exhibit 2 *(continued)*

measured by a Sangamo Tachograph. If machine is rented in excess of 3,000 hours per year, all excess hours shall be on the basis of $12.00 per hour. Credit *will be issued* for use under 3,000 hours per year at $6.00 per hour; maximum 400 hours credit.

Minimum rental charge $36,096.00 based upon a guaranteed 12-month rental at the base rental renewable for a second year at the same rate.

1—Caterpillar 637 Wheel Tractor-Scraper, Cushion-Hitch, push-pull, series C, 30 cubic yard heap capacity, elevating scraper, semiautomatic power shift transmission, direct electric starting, muffler, emergency brake system, ROPS fully enclosed cab, heater, windshield wiper, defroster fan, scraper floodlight, driving lights, 33.25-35 32 PR, Michelin tires.

Base rental rate $4,512.00 per month plus any applicable taxes from date of delivery until equipment is returned to Lessor, or satisfactory notification of rental termination is received. This rate is based upon 3,000 hours use in one year as measured by a Sangamo Tachograph. If machine is rented in excess of 3,000 hours per year, all excess hours shall be on the basis of $18.00 per hour. Credit *will be issued* for use under 3,000 hours per year at $9.00 per hour; maximum 400 hours credit.

Minimum rental charge $54,144.00 based upon a guaranteed 12-month rental at the base rental rate renewable for a second year at the same rate.

Terms:

100 percent of the base monthly rental rate is payable monthly in advance. Monthly billings are to be recognized as an *estimate* of the actual use charges. Every 90 days, commencing 120 days after delivery to the Lessee, a supplemental invoice (or credit memo) will be issued adjusting the estimate for cumulative *Total Actual Use*. These supplemental adjusting invoices will be due for payment within ten days of receipt. Should a "credit balance" develop in excess of one "monthly estimate," Lessor will remit a check in the amount of such excess, insofar as these refunds do not infringe on the minimum annual guarantee or actual use charges.

Lessor will deliver and pick up machine at Link Sand and Gravel, Ltd. Lessee is to assume full responsibility for the equipment during the rental period and will return machine in as good condition as received, less wear incident to normal use in the hands of a competent operator and while operated in the manner the equipment was designed for. Lessor will be responsible periodically to inspect the machine and advise Lessee immediately if this requirement is not being met. Lessor is to deliver equipment in good working order. Lessor is to furnish all filters, parts, and labor necessary for maintenance and repairs necessitated either by normal wear and tear or by internal equipment failures, except that Lessee will assume full responsibility for all fuel and lubricants and for the proper lubrication of the equipment while renting machine. The scraper linkage rollers and pins will be pressure lubricated twice per shift.

Lessee will be responsible for all breakdowns and repairs occasioned by operator negligence or external job factors, except for those resulting from some poor design, weakness, or failure in the machine itself. No repairs are to be made by the Lessee without the specific permission of the Lessor. Lessor assumes no liability for loss or damage on account of accidents, delays due to defective material, engine or transmission troubles, delays in the delivery or removal of equipment or resulting from interruption of business or other consequential loss. Lessee agrees to indemnify Les-

Exhibit 2 *(concluded)*

sor against all loss, damage, expense, and penalty arising from any action on account of personal injury or damage to property occasioned by the operation, handling or transportation of this equipment during the rental period, unless due to some weakness of failure on the machine itself. Lessor reserves the right, if Lessee is in default under the terms of this agreement, or if in the Lessor's opinion the equipment is being damaged in excess of ordinary wear and tear, to take possession of the machine upon 24 hours notice.

Lessor agrees to perform all possible repairs during Lessee's nonworking hours and in case of long delays resulting from serious breakdowns. Lessor will endeavor to furnish a replacement machine on a "no extra cost" basis.
Location:

This rental rate is predicted on use of this machine in the Link Sand pit at R.R. 1 Wellfeld, Ohio.
Safety:

Unit will be equipped to meet applicable OSHA safety standards.
Production and Cost:

Based upon a field time study of one of our present 637's in your Link Sand pit we have arrived at hourly production over an approximate 1,800-foot one-way haul distance. These production figures, plus an annual production capability based upon 3760 hours per year, are listed below. To present reasonable costs we projected an average rental cost based upon 3,000 hours of use in a year at the base rental rate plus 760 hours at the "extra" rate. The average annual hourly cost is listed in the table below.

	Cat 627	Cat 637	Cat 633
Hourly production (tons)	255	370	385
Annual production (3,760 hours)	958,545	1,390,830	1,447,215
Average hourly rental cost	$12.03	$18.04	$20.54
Operator (category II)	7.50	7.50	7.50
Fuel	3.62	4.40	3.17
Total operated cost	$23.15	$29.94	$31.21
Cost per ton (in cents)	9.08	8.08	8.12
Total rental costs	$45,232	$67,830	$77,230

thought that the reputation of a leaser was the critical dimension in leasing. There were never enough guarantees and warranties in equipment leasing. Manufacturing warranties, tire warranties, and other parts problems were difficult to handle when purchasing equipment, but were compounded when a leaser was involved.

CASE 9–3
DEANS BREWERY (A)

In February, 1978, Mr. Simpson, chief engineer at Deans Brewery, Trinidad, was completing the design of a new bottling line. The last remaining major issue dealt with the materials handling situation at the end of the line. Currently, the company was using manual labor to put the full cases of beer on pallets. Mr. Simpson was considering the possibility of using automatic equipment.

Company background

Deans Brewery was located in the southern Caribbean island of Trinidad. Founded by John Deans in 1924, the company had established a high reputation. Deans beer had also become a favorite with tourists, and as a result a modest export business to the United States had started in 1959. In February 1978, sales reached the highest level in the company's history.

Four sales peaks occurred during the year: Carnival,[1] Christmas, Easter, and Independence.[2] Carnival was the highest sales period, but each peak caused the company to operate on tight schedules during which Deans hired more labor and scheduled extra shifts.

Brewing process

Beer brewing started with extraction of sugar from malt by an enzymic process. This sugar was boiled with hops, producing a sterilized and concentrated solution. The resins extracted from the hops during boiling acted as a preservative and gave the beer its bitter flavor. The hops were then removed, and the solution was cooled to a temperature of 50°F for bottom fermentation lasting seven days, during which yeast converted the sugar to alcohol and CO_2. After fermentation the beer was cooled to 30°F and stored for ten days (during which the yeast dropped out) and then roughly filtered through diatomaceous earth. After 24 hours storage it was put through a polish filtration process and was artificially carbonated ready for bottling. After bottling and case packing, the beer was stored in the finished goods warehouse ready for delivery to retail outlets.

Current operating in bottling and warehousing

The bottling department and warehouse were part of the same building separated by a wire fence (see Exhibit 1). The current bottling line had a

[1]Carnival took place two days before Ash Wednesday, which normally occurs during February and occasionally in early March.
[2]Trinidad gained its independence from Britain on August 31, 1962.

Exhibit 1
Warehouse layout showing proposed automatic palletizing system

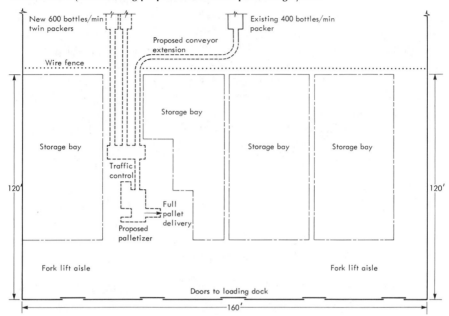

capacity of 400 bottles per minute and usually operated two eight-hour shifts, five days a week at 85-percent efficiency. For the past three months it had run at three shifts per day. This had meant that maintenance, previously done at night, had begun to interfere with production time. The third shift was difficult to staff and supervise, but the expanded bottling capacity would eliminate this need. At 1,000 bottles per minute demand could be met by a one-shift operation with occasional overtime.

The last operation on the current bottling line was the manual stacking of full cases (24 bottles per case) on wooden pallets. Each case weighed 45 pounds, and each pallet held 40 case (5 layers high of 8 cases per layer). Two men were employed at this task; normally it took 7½ seconds to load each case. Each man loaded his own pallet and earned $80.00 a week.

Currently two fork lifts carried the full pallets to the warehouse where they were stacked three high. The company owned 12 fork lifts and usually had at least two in the repair shop at any one time. The warehouse (ceiling height 15½ ft.) had four storage bays in total, and usually two were being unloaded while the other two were being loaded. Space was reasonably plentiful except before peak sales periods when extra pallets were stacked in the aisles for inventory build-up.

New bottling line

The bottling line which Mr. Simpson had designed called for major changes in the bottling shop. Line capacity was to be increased by 600 bottles per minute with the addition of twin packers which would unload onto two exit conveyors. Aside from this, a new empty bottle conveyor feed-in system was planned and would occupy all existing space between the bottling shop and the warehouse. As a result it would be necessary to move the unloading and palletizing operation into the warehouse. (See Exhibit 1.) The required conveyor system from the three lines in bottling to the warehouse for hand loading of pallets would cost $36,000 including installation. One advantage of the move to the warehouse was the shortening of the fork lift route. Mr. Simpson calculated that turnaround time from the new location would range from 35 seconds to 3 minutes and would probably average 1 minute.

Automatic palletizer

Mr. Simpson was considering the possibility of substituting an automatic palletizer for the hand loading operation in the new location (see Exhibit 2). The machine's operation was similar in concept to the manual loading procedure. It would take eight cases at a time and feed them onto the pallet in a predetermined pattern. The pallet was then lowered for the next layer. The full pallet was put onto the discharge conveyor which could hold up to three full pallets. The machine required one operator whose primary function was to make sure the machine shut off in case of trouble and to clear jams if they occurred at the feed-in point. He would probably be paid $100.00 per week. The palletizer would require a different feed-in system from manual loading because of the counting operation and machine height.

Mr. Simpson was considering two different makes of equipment, Perrin and Clark. He had received literature on both and had talked with sales representatives and also with executives in North American breweries. He was not sure how to choose between the two makes. Mr. Simpson wanted a palletizer which could handle 45 cases per minute, operate on a 50-cycle electrical supply, load at least 40 cases per pallet and have a stacking pattern identical to the present system. Both Perrin and Clark sales representatives said they could produce satisfactory equipment.

Perrin Conveyors, Ltd., was a Canadian subsidiary of an American firm. It handled all Canadian and Commonwealth sales and operated relatively autonomously from its parent. For over 50 years Perrin had enjoyed a high reputation for its conveyor systems which were light, easy to install, durable, and efficient. An additional feature was the ready convertibility of all conveyors to any of three basis types—live roller, gravity, or belt. Perrin had designed and manufactured many of the conveyor systems for Canadian grain handling and mineral processing installations. Perrin manufactured a variety of materials handling equipment including palletizers, although it had never built one which met all of Mr. Simpson's specifications. Maximum capacity was determined by the number of cases the machine could handle in a given amount of time, and Perrin had never manufactured

Exhibit 2
Automatic palletizer and pallet stacking pattern

Palletizer operating in different company

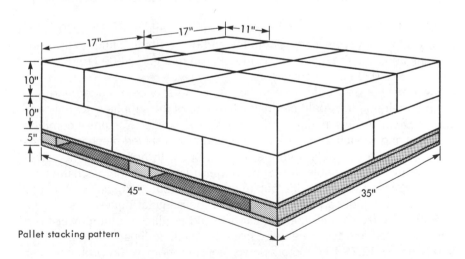

Pallet stacking pattern

a unit faster than 40 cases per minute. In answer to Mr. Simpson's request, Perrin had said they would design a machine especially for him, which could handle 45 cases per minute and stack 5, 6, or 7 layers high with 8 cases per layer. The machine would be strictly mechanical, consisting of gears, belts, etc., and would not require a foundation of any sort. It would require an air line at a pressure of 120 psi. which exceeded the 90 psi. in the current general shop lines, and, therefore, a separate small compressor would have to be added at a cost of about $800. Perrin would supply a skilled technician for ten days to help with installation after delivery. The equipment would carry a standard guarantee of one year. Deans Brewery had purchased Perrin conveyors in the past and had been fully satisfied. Perrin's quotation for the palletizer was $108,000,[3] including the air compressor.

Clark Loading Systems was an American company of high reputation in the palletizer field. It could supply a standard model which met all of Mr. Simpson's specifications and could stack five, six or seven layers high. The Clark palletizer would be hydraulic, with few mechanical parts, requiring a 12-foot hole in the floor for the piston in the pallet lift. The general shop air line pressure would be sufficient for the machine. Service and guarantee terms would be the same as Perrin's Clark also manufactured conveyors which tended to be heavier, bulkier, and more difficult to install than Perrin's but which also enjoyed an excellent reputation for quality and durability. Clark quoted a price of $136,000 for the palletizer.

If Mr. Simpson decided to use an automatic loader, he would have to combine the three exit lines into one line for delivery into the loader. He had asked both Perrin and Clark to quote on a traffic control system to join the lines. This system would have to jockey the cases into the single line and automatically count eight cases for delivery to the loader for each layer on the pallet.

Clark indicated that a traffic control unit would cost $24,000, plus $20,000 for conveyors leading from the end of the bottling lines to the control unit and from the unit to the loader. Perrin quoted $24,000 for the control and $16,000 for the conveyors.

Two mechanics would have to be trained to service a loader, and Mr. Simpson felt training could be done when one of the suppliers' technicians was at Deans for installation and start-up. A palletizer was not a complex machine and servicing should not be difficult for a skilled mechanic. Spare parts would be available from the makers, but with normal maintenance, costs would be negligible. Mr. Simpson felt that two of the mechanics already employed to service the bottling shop at about $120 per week could be trained to handle a palletizer as part of their regular duties.

Both palletizers under consideration would require electric power from lines extended into the warehouse from the bottling department. Each palletizer had a 12.75 h.p. motor; power consumption would probably cost $1,000 per year.

Installation costs would be substantial for either palletizer-conveyor system. Mr. Simpson estimated that a total Perrin System with traffic control could be installed by a local engineering contractor for $30,000. A complete Clark system would require $36,000.

Mr. Simpson wondered if he should change to a seven-layer pallet if an

---

[3]All prices quoted represent landed cost to Deans, including freight and duty but not including installation.

automatic palletizer were purchased, but he was not sure how he could quantify the advantages and disadvantages of such a move. In any case he wanted to find the best system possible for handling finished goods. Mr. Simpson was concerned about his lack of familiarity with this kind of equipment, but he realized he could not turn easily for help elsewhere. It had been standard practice at Deans Brewery to justify certain investments on the basis of meeting future demand. These investments would also have to show a reasonable return in the long run.

CASE 9–4
THE NEXT STEPS

Mr. Thomas thought he had three main alternatives of action in purchasing MS–7 once Blondin's equipment went into operation.

1. He could continue to buy from the parent company.
2. Carlyn could start manufacturing MS–7 itself.
3. He could purchase MS–7 from Blondin.

The fourth alternative of buying MS–7 elsewhere in North America appeared unrealistic because of MS–7's special properties.

The main disadvantage of the first alternative was that Carlyn would have to pay U.K. market price plus duty, plus exchange and transportation instead of the former preferred price. Mr. Thomas thought this might increase his laid down cost to at least $70.00/kg. The main advantage of this action would be the staying with a reliable high-quality preferred supplier and the U.K. parent company would continue to reap the benefits of the American business.

The second alternative was not too attractive in view of the uncertainty of demand, the relatively high cost of the equipment, the manufacturing skills required, and the lack of space in the Carlyn operation. This alternative would, however, mean that Carlyn should be able to operate on approximately the same cost structure as Blondin.

The third alternative also had its drawbacks. Mr. Thomas knew that he would have difficulty persuading his fellow company officers to buy from Blondin, a direct competitor on at least four of Carlyn's products. He knew that Blondin would be in the driver's seat regarding the setting of price, and he might end up losing out on three counts. First, by helping Blondin get some volume going on the reactor, he would enable them to achieve production savings and efficiencies. Second, by paying a price over Blondin's cost, he was putting Stimgro at a cost disadvantage to Blondin's competitive product. Third, he would be heavily dependent on the goodwill of Blondin, who would be a sole source on a vital item. One advantage to buying from

Blondin was the elimination of the investment risk. Another was the shortening of supply line. Perhaps the strongest point in favor was that it seemed to make economic sense. Why should both Blondin and Carlyn end up with expensive pieces of equipment running at an uneconomic level when they could pool their resources and requirements?

Mr. Thomas decided he would prefer to go after alternative three. He knew he could always buy from the parent company so that supply was at least assured. He also knew his fellow managers at Carlyn would never go for a deal with Blondin in which Carlyn paid a premium price. He, therefore, went back to his original cost and price figures to see if he could set some targets to use in discussion with the other Carlyn managers. He concluded that Blondin's out of pocket cost would probably be about $40/kg. He guessed Blondin would be anxious to charge the U.K. market price laid down in the United States which would be around $70/kg. He knew as long as he got a better price than $70/kg, he would be better off than with alternatives 1 and 2. He summarized his position as follows:

Summary of Our MS–7 Position
Maximum price: $70–75/kg.
Would possibly settle for as high as $65/kg.
Would strongly prefer: $50/kg (present cost).
Should offer: $44/kg (10 percent better than their out-of-pocket cost).
N.B.: The only way in which this can be sold is on the basis of a mutual sharing of the benefit.

Mr. Thomas thought he was now ready to discuss the proposition with the other Carlyn executives. An informal atmosphere existed among Carlyn's top team, and all major moves in any area were normally fully argued out before action was taken. Deliberations could be initiated by any individual with any other at any time. The group normally lunched together at least once a week, at which time shop talk was also normal.

It was common knowledge among all members of Carlyn's executive team that there was no love lost between Frank Grove and Blondin. Mr. Thomas knew that Frank in his capacity as sales manager saw Blondin daily as an adversary and had taken an extremely strong dislike to their aggressive marketing tactics. Mr. Thomas knew that Frank would strongly oppose any proposition which would involve buying anything from Blondin. He also knew that approaching the president or the production manager first would produce the automatic question: "Have you talked to Frank about this yet?" For this reason he thought he might as well talk to Frank first on the basis that if Frank would veto any approach to Blondin, there would not be much point in pressing this alternative further. He, therefore, went to Frank's office to see what he might be able to accomplish. Their conversation went like this:

MR. THOMAS: Frank, remember I asked you about Stimgro a while ago?

MR. GROVE: Sure, Bill, what's on your mind now?

MR. THOMAS: Well, did you know that Blondin had ordered their own equipment to start making MS–7 in the U.S.?

MR. GROVE: No, but so what? We're getting a good deal from the U.K., so why should we care what Blondin is up to?

MR. THOMAS: As soon as they get into operation, they will be able to force us to pay U.S. market dutiable and dumpable instead of our present prices.

MR. GROVE: How much are we talking about?

MR. THOMAS: At least $70/kg as opposed to our present $50.

MR. GROVE: That's too darn much. How much do you figure Blondin's cost will be to them?

MR. THOMAS: This depends on how you figure it. Their straight out-of-pocket cost should be around $40/kg. At their present volume their return on investment after tax is practically negligible.

MR. GROVE: I'm glad to hear that, but what are you leading up to?

MR. THOMAS: If Blondin can't really make any money making their own MS–7, neither can we, right?

MR. GROVE: I guess so.

MR. THOMAS: O.K., then we are automatically forced to pay at least $70 and you've already said that's too much.

MR. GROVE: I suppose the parent wouldn't mind that at all, but it would certainly give us a rough time on our Stimgro costs and profits.

MR. THOMAS: That's the way I figure it, too. That's why I would like a chance to play a long shot to see if we can't keep our cost down.

MR. GROVE: What are you talking about?

MR. THOMAS: I think we should go to Blondin and offer to buy our MS–7 from them. It . . .

MR. GROVE: (interrupting) Holy cow, have you gone crazy? Do you know what you are saying? For ten years I have been fighting those guys, and we are in with Stimgro and guess who else tried to horn in on a good deal. That's like the U.S. buying its atom bombs from Russia. Man, you sure come up with some real wild ones every once in awhile. Why don't you just forget about the whole thing, and, if and when Blondin gets their equipment going, we'll just have to pay the parent a bit more. After all, it's not as if we are shoving the dough down the drain.

MR. THOMAS: Now, just a minute. If I could get the stuff at a good price elsewhere in the U.S. would you care?

MR. GROVE: Well, now, that's something different altogether. If you can get a good price elsewhere in the U.S. I'm all for it.

MR. THOMAS: Fine, unfortunately, there is no chance of that. You know as well as I do that Blondin and we are the only users. But, if I could get a good price from Blondin, why shouldn't we take it?

MR. GROVE: *If* the old lady hadn't picked up the dime between the railway tracks, she would still be alive today.

Mr. Thomas: Sure, I am not guaranteeing a thing. I don't know if I can get a good price from Blondin. As a matter of fact, I have a feeling they might not be too anxious to sell to us, period.

Mr. Grove: And why not?

Mr. Thomas: Because we are their competition, too. If they feel they've got an advantage over us by making their own MS–7, why should they let us in on a good deal?

Mr. Grove: Because with us they might have a better total deal than without us.

Mr. Thomas: Exactly, that's why I want a chance to try them out. I want to sell them on the basis that we both share in the benefit from pooling our requirements. I have a feeling they may be worried about their efficiency at the low volume they are turning out, and we could double their volume.

Mr. Grove: Suppose, just suppose, and I am not committing myself to a thing here now, that Blondin let us talk to them, what makes you so sure they will give us a good deal?

Mr. Thomas: As I have said before, Frank, I can't guarantee a thing. They may just be too obstinate to give us even a chance of proposing anything. On the other hand, if we don't try it, we'll never know.

Mr. Grove: You really are a persistent joker. Just give it a chance, Bill, and tomorrow Blondin's trucks are delivering the stuff, and the next day we have a merger on our hands.

Mr. Thomas: No, sir, I want to approach this on a straight business basis. It so happens they are the only U.S. supplier of a product we need. Why we need that product should have nothing to do with them.

Mr. Grove: How much do you think we could get it for?

Mr. Thomas: I really don't know. Theoretically, we are better off as long as their price is lower than $70 or $75/kg. I would like to settle for less than $65.00. As a starter I think we should offer $44.00.

Mr. Grove: That starter is going to give us a really warm reception at Blondin.

Mr. Thomas: What do you mean?

Mr. Grove: Well, with that kind of an offer they are really going to wonder who is doing whom a favor.

Mr. Thomas: You are probably right. However, it's always easier to come up than to get down. Do you really think Blondin might give us a rough time?

Mr. Grove: I am positive. Unless you offer them $100/kg. and a gold-plated key to plant.

Mr. Thomas: Have you got any idea on how we might pitch this thing to them?

Mr. Grove: The only way would be to hit their top man. If he doesn't buy it, no one else in their organization will.

Mr. Thomas: That sounds like a good idea. Whom do you think should talk to him?

Mr. Grove: Bill, I know you can talk an old lady on a bus into giving her seat up for your briefcase, but I figure it's got to be our top man versus theirs.

Mr. Thomas: I fully agree. Let's go talk to the old man.

Mr. Grove: Now, just a minute . . . I was just hypothesizing . . .

Mr. Thomas: Sure you were, but we have gone too far now to drop this thing.

MR. GROVE: The old man will never go for it.

MR. THOMAS: Let's go and see.

MR. GROVE: Remember, this is your idea, not mine. How do you feel knowing the knife is coming and no anesthetic?

MR. THOMAS: It scares me to pieces, but I know you always enjoy a good side show.

The "old man," Mr. John Peters, a president of Cato of Canada, was to Mr. Grove's surprise fairly quickly won over to the general idea. He did want to enlist the ideas of Bob Harper, the production manager, and he instructed Grove, Harper, and Thomas to think ahead and to predict possible future demands so that he could have some idea of the length of period that a deal might be settled on. He said:

> If I were in Blondin's shoes, I would insist on a fairly long contract if the price seems favorable. I would insist on a reasonable guarantee of sufficient volume to make the deal at least half attractive. Then we might be talking a contract lasting as long as five or six years. Before I commit Carlyn to that kind of deal I want some indication of what our volume would be over that period. We don't want to find ourselves in the boat that we are committed to buy if we should be making it ourselves, for example.

Subsequently, Mr. Harper determined that the minimum production volume he would like of MS–7 to warrant plant expansion, labor training, etc., would be 20,000 kg. of MS–7 a year. Mr. Grove forecasted the following demands for the next six years.

Year 1 .... 4,000 Kg.
Year 2 .... 6,000 Kg.
Year 3 .... 9,000 Kg.
Year 4 .... 13,000 Kg.
Year 5 .... 18,000 Kg.
Year 6 .... 23,000 Kg.

On the basis of their forecast, Mr. Harper, Mr. Grove, and Mr. Thomas thought that the maximum contract length should be five years. Mr. Peters agreed. Mr. Peters warned the other three that he saw his main role as that of an ice breaker. He said:

> All I want to do is feel them out and possibly agree on a price. Bill Thomas and you guys can take over after that and clean up all the details.

MAKE OR BUY

 The "make or buy" question is an interesting one because of its many dimensions. Almost every organization is faced with it continually. For manufacturing companies the make alternative may be a natural extension of activities already present or an opportunity for diversification. For nonmanufacturing concerns it is normally a question of services rather than products. Should a hospital have its own laundry, operate its own dietary, security, and maintenance services, or should it purchase these outside? Becoming one's own supplier is an alternative that has not received much attention in this text so far, and yet it is a vital point in every organization's procurement strategy.

Make or buy–the strategy •

What should be the attitude of a company toward this issue of "make or buy?" Most companies do not have a consciously expressed policy with reference to this issue but prefer to decide each issue as it arises.

The strategic dimensions of the make or buy question are far reaching. "What kind of an organization or company do we want to be?" is a fair starting question. If the opportunities in the environment can be matched against the strengths and weaknesses of the firm, a preliminary stance on make or buy is likely to result. An organization seeing an environmental need for certain products may be anxious to make if it has considerable manufacturing skills. If the opportunity is primarily of a marketing nature and the firm is weak on the manufacturing side, it might not be wise to take a strong "make" stance. If it were possible to discuss the question in the aggregate for the individual firm, the problem should be formulated in terms of: "What should our organization's objective be in terms of how much value added as a percentage of final product or service cost and in what form?" Such a goal might never be reached or agreed on because of factors beyond the control of the decision makers. For example, vertical integration may be forced on a concern to protect its sources of key raw materials, even though the executive might have preferred purchasing these requirements on the open market. Political, social, and environmental concerns may also affect the desired stance. Despite the difficulties of formulating a strategic stance, an attempt to develop one may well have significant benefits. Few organizations recognize the quality of their materials management function as one variable to be considered. A strong purchasing group, capable of assuring supply at reasonable prices would favor a "buy" tendency when other factors are not of overriding impor-

394

tance. For example, one corporation found its purchasing ability in foreign markets such a competitive asset that it deliberately divested itself of certain manufacturing facilities common to every competitor in the industry.

In some ways it is rather futile to discuss this issue as a matter of general policy, only because the problems always resolve themselves into specific situations; each case must be settled on its own merits. The best that can be done, therefore, is to outline the advantages or objectives of procurement by manufacture; attempt to note the dangers; and, finally, try to reach some useful generalizations.[1]

Reasons for manufacture instead of purchase *

There are many reasons that may lead a manufacturer to produce rather than purchase required items. These include:

1. Occasionally, such small quantities of a special item may be required to make production of it by a vendor prohibitive because of the cost.

2. Manufacture may be undertaken to secure the desired quality. The quality requirements may be so exacting or so unusual as to require special processing methods that vendors cannot be expected to provide. Also, in a strong seller's market, vendors tend to grow careless and, although quite capable of meeting the specifications, simply do not do so. On the other hand, vendors may be selling only a quality far above that which would fully satisfy the need in question and may, at the same time, have so satisfactory a volume at the higher level as to have no interest in a lower grade. If any one of these various situations exists, the user may feel forced to start manufacturing the item. This decision may be quite sound. Before undertaking the experiment, however, the user should carefully reexamine specifications, check on inspection procedure and methods, and make every reasonable effort to secure the active cooperation of a vendor. If the manufacturer still decides to "make rather than buy," it is assuming responsibility for producing and maintaining a quality not obtainable from anyone else.

3. Manufacture may be undertaken as a means of greater assurance of supply. Under some circumstances, a closer coordination of the supply with the demand is possible when the item is manufactured by the user. A certain degree of self-sufficiency appears attractive, since it theoretically involves a freedom from transportation difficulties and costs and from interruption of delivery by vendors confronted with labor difficulties or "acts of God." Of course, this argument is not valid when the items in question are obtainable from a variety of sources, including local ones. Also, when but one qualified supplier exists—even though located geographically nearby—there is a substantial risk of delayed deliveries.

4. In some industries, manufacturers find it essential to make their own equipment because no suitable suppliers exist or because they wish to preserve technological secrets. One large chemical firm owns its own equipment making

---

[1] One of the most thoroughgoing and useful treatments of the topic is that of James W. Culliton, *Make or Buy*. 4th reprint (Boston: Harvard Business School, Division of Research, Business Research Study, No. 27, 1956).

plant where about 60 percent of all corporate requirements are manufactured. Experimentation in recent years showed it was possible to subcontract certain parts of equipment to various vendors leaving final assembly and manufacture of particularly "sensitive" components to the corporation's own shop.

5.   It may be cheaper to manufacture than to buy. There are conditions under which a company may temporarily or even permanently produce certain items more cheaply than they can be bought, due consideration being given to transportation and other costs. Thus, a company may, quite by accident, discover a new process by which it can produce some item at a substantially lower cost than its regular suppliers. So, too, a company may be able to acquire, at an exceptionally low price, certain equipment with which it can manufacture some part at a cost below that of its past suppliers. Also, the volume of certain items used may be so large that it is possible to manufacture them at a production cost as low as that of any accessible supplier and thus to save an amount equivalent to the latter's marketing expense and profit. The lower cost in any one of these cases may be real, computed in accordance with the best accounting practice, and not merely a juggled cost computed to justify a decision actually made on quite different grounds.

6.   Particularly in depression or recession the manufacturer with idle equipment may undertake production, rather than buy, to use surplus production facilities. Even in more normal times, when items of satisfactory quality can be obtained from reliable suppliers, manufacture by the company itself may be undertaken as a means of increasing the total volume of production over which the overhead burden can be distributed.

The make or buy decision can be an integral part of the overall production plan of a company. Any organization wishing to smoothe production or employment can use make or buy as one alternative. If a significant portion of total requirements is purchased, it may be possible to ensure steady running of the corporation's own facilities, leaving the suppliers to bear the burden of fluctuations in demand. If making is normally preferred and buying is only resorted to when all other alternatives to capacity expansion have been exhausted, it theoretically appears attractive. In reality, such subcontracting would occur normally at very busy times, making it difficult to find suitable and willing vendors. A number of interesting models have been developed using make or buy in the production smoothing context. Few still recognize the difficulties of jumping in and out of the marketplace on short notice.[2]

7.   Occasionally, although the cost of manufacturing an item may not be any lower for a user than those of vendors from whom it could buy, yet those vendors, through collusion, legislative protection, or unwise pricing policy, may be asking an exorbitant price. A company that is manufacturing even a small part of its requirements is in a strategic position to bargain with such suppliers. Its em-

---

[2]B. Shore, "Quantitative Analysis and the Make-or-Buy Decision," *Journal of Purchasing* 6, no. 1 (February 1970): 5–11.

ployees have had experience in making the article, and the company has a record of cost data that can be used effectively with vendors. The latter know that although the buyer may be reluctant to go further in making this particular item, the buyer can and will do so if necessary.

8.   Still another reason for manufacturing an item formerly purchased is to protect the personnel of the company and to maintain the oranization. This same contention is used as an argument against abandoning manufacture, once undertaken, in favor of buying outside. In organizations where ''hold the line'' policies are in effect with regards to hiring and which simultaneously are seeking to reduce the number of employees by better systems and technological change, normal attrition may not be fast enough to reduce the number of employees. Shifting employees to products or services formerly purchased may be one way to avoid direct firing or layoff costs.

9.   Competitive, political, social, or environmental reasons may force a company to make even when it might have preferred to buy. When a competitor acquires ownership of a key source of raw material, it may force similar action. Many countries insist that a certain amount of processing of raw materials be done within national boundaries. A company located in a high unemployment area may decide to make certain items to help alleviate this situation. A company may have to process further certain by-products to make them environmentally acceptable. In each of these instances, cost may not be of overriding concern.

10.   Finally, there is a purely emotional reason. The management of some organizations appears to take pride in size.

Dangers involved in decision to manufacture[*]

Thus, there is an imposing list of reasons for undertaking, under the proper circumstances, to manufacture certain items rather than to purchase them. Many times the reasoning in favor of such a policy is cogent and the conclusions are sound. It is also true, however, that not infrequently a company will succumb to the temptation to make its own items under conditions which do not warrant doing so and without full appreciation of the dangers involved in the decision.

1.   One of their dangers is lack of administrative or technical experience in the production of the items in question, which are often substantially unlike those which the company is manufacturing for sale. They have been bought from suppliers in the production of that line. What is now proposed assumes that the purchaser can produce this item as a sideline and can do a better job than the original manufacturer. The company undertaking manufacture lacks the experience of the supplier and the project may require new types of skilled labor, new supervisors, and new equipment. Moreover, every time another unrelated production unit is added to the original organization, there is bound to be some loss of cohesion and unity resulting in new technical operating and executive problems. In short, the company may well be launching upon a type of business not

originally contemplated, without experience and frequently without adequate or qualified personnel.[3]

2.   There may be a loss of goodwill that could have an adverse effect upon the sales volume of the company in a number of ways. If reciprocity plays a part in the selling program, the effect of ceasing to buy an item is obvious. The sales people from the former supplies cease to call. To sever business relations with former suppliers may arouse their actual resentment. This may prove particularly serious if the displaced supplier is one through whom the manufacturer's finished product was sold as well as one from whom the manufacturer had bought. The erstwhile buyer will find competitors prompt to take advantage of the ill will created. Finally, too, such action is likely to raise the question in the minds of those companies from which other items are still bought as to how long it will be before they, in turn, are dropped.

3.   Frequently, certain suppliers have built such a reputation for themselves that they have been able to build a real preference for their component as part of the finished product. Normally, these are branded items which can be used to make the total piece of equipment more acceptable to the final user. For example, most diesel engine manufacturers buy Bosch or Simms injection pumps, not because they are cheap, or difficult to manufacture, but because the ultimate consumers want them. The manufacturers of road grading equipment and other construction or mining equipment frequently let the customer specify the power plant brand and see this option as advantageous in selling their equipment.

4.   Companies wishing to maintain a leading position in their industry must be constantly engaged in some form of research so their product may be continually improved and production costs reduced. A concern that specializes in manufacturing a major line can do this. A company in which that product is merely a sideline can rarely afford to devote the same attention to it; consequently, no matter how great an advantage existed originally, it is likely to be only a matter of time before the company in which such an item is a sideline finds itself outclassed both as to product and as to cost. Often, the new department comes, perhaps unconsciously, to look upon itself as being in a favored position; in other words, it enjoys a "protected status." This attitude having once been established, every conceivable argument is advanced for retaining the department. The new department is seldom under the same competitive pressure either to keep costs down or to keep the product up to date, as is the independent supplier.

5.   Closer coordination of inventory with requirements is one of the arguments advanced for manufacturing rather than buying. Actually, this result is not as easy to obtain as might at first appear. To get the lowest costs, the production

---

[3]The problem is simplified somewhat since a marketing problem is not involved; at least, none is intended. Actually, a marketing problem may develop. If the company's requirements for the particular item in question subsequently become less than originally contemplated after auxiliary facilities have been built up to meet the larger demand expected, it naturally follows that the company has the option of producing a volume beyond its own requirements and disposing of the surplus in the general market or of finding itself with equipment which is excessive as far as its own needs are concerned. Under these circumstances the company may actually be confronted by a marketing problem as well as by a technical and an administrative one.

department must manufacture in the quantities set by the most economical run. It is possible that this quantity may be well above reasonable requirements. The alternatives are either higher costs or excessive inventory.

6.   A lack of flexibility in selecting possible sources and substitute items is likely to result. As a purchaser the company is able to buy from anyone, to obtain the best existing price, to shift from one source to another whenever conditions warrant, or, indeed, with the greatest freedom to cease using the product at all. Such is not the case once a concern has committed itself to a police of procurement by manufacture.

Some problems in costing

Whether or not a particular company can manufacture at a cost lower than that at which a given item can be bought is a question often very difficult to answer. The question is not whether this cost is lower than that of a high-cost supplier but rather whether it is lower than that of the firm (or group of firms) that set the actual market price. Indeed, it is frequently possible to obtain from a low-cost producer (as distinguished from the marginal one) a price that is lower even than the market price and at a profit to both buyer and seller, especially if such a producer is seeking additional volume or for some other reason finds the purchaser's business particularly attractive.

Further, it is always a moot question as to what *cost* really is. The answer depends upon what cost data are available, the purpose for which they are collected, and the form in which they are to be kept. Standard costs, for example, may be most helpful for control purposes and of no value whatsoever in attempting to answer the question: "At what cost can one manufacture a particular brass stamping or a metal container of given material and specification?" If new equipment is bought for the purpose, how is depreciation to be handled? Shall the usual burden of overhead factors be considered in arriving at a comparative cost figure? Since many costs vary with volume of output, what volume figure is to be used? Shall it be present or future volume? For total requirements or only for part? And if for only part, then how much? What allowance shall be made for the additional expense incurred by the purchasing department, if manufacture is undertaken, for such operations as assembling the new raw materials and performing the extra inspection required? Also, what allowance shall be made for the necessary training of the production personnel and the effect of the new product on the major production lines? Clearly, there are many debatable questions that must be settled before any progress at all can be made in actually arriving at a definite figure.

Normally, direct variable costs include labor and materials. Variable overhead costs may include: indirect labor and fringe benefits, taxes, overtime premiums, additional supervisory costs, additional power and security costs, equipment depreciation, and others. Fixed costs may include several of the above plus general taxes, building repair and depreciation, administrative costs, insurance, and others. The difficulty in deciding whether making or buying is justified on a cost basis lies in the identification and quantification of those costs relevant to the decision. Normally, in the short term, variable costs are of most concern. In the longer term fixed costs may become important. It is also useful to recognize that a difference exists between the individual decision and the cumulative effect of many make or buy decisions over a period of time. Since future costs are almost always uncertain, probabilistic estimates need to be made in any longer term make or buy decision. An interesting probabilistic model developed by D. A. Raunick and A. G. Fisher attempted to quantify such factors as the loss of trade secrets, employee morale, and communications and control if subcontracting were used instead of making. This allowed the calculation of a rate of return on investment with a probabilistic range permitting managers to make the decision with quantitative recognition of the risk involved.[4]

Experience has made is amply clear that once management has definitely committed itself to a policy of procurement by manufacture, it is not difficult for costs to be figured to justify both the original decision and a continuance of the practice.

Thus, it becomes increasingly evident that the make or buy decision is often a difficult one and that the decision to manufacture, once made, is likely to place the company in a position from which it is difficult to withdraw.

If an examination is made of the reasons why the problem is brought up in the first instance, it will often be discovered that it arises out of a temporary condition. The plant may be operating below capacity because of temporary business conditions. Vendor's current prices may appear out of line. The immediate needs of quality, volume, or service cannot be filled satisfactorily by suppliers at the moment. Or in a reverse situation, a war or some other unusual condition may force a company to concentrate on processes in which it is peculiarly qualified to a degree far beyond what is either necessary or desirable under ordinary circumstances, with the result that it has to "farm out" or subcontract many items it commonly both could and would produce in its own plant. Or it may, in such extraordinary situations, have requirements for such subcontractable items far beyond what is able to produce with its available equipment and manpower and, in consequence, be forced to "buy" where it normally would have "made." Such conditions may appear, and doubtlessly are, serious for the moment; but in many cases it is only a comparatively short time before the situation has been corrected.

There may be good reason for a company to undertake manufacture if the item is required in large volume, is substantially of the same nature as the regular product, is adapted to the existing productive facilities, is capable of production by the company at a cost low enough to allow a saving over the price charged for the item by a supplier, and is not protected by patents so sizable royalties have to be paid.

From this analysis of the problems involved in arriving at "make or buy"

---

[4]D. A. Raunick and A. G. Fisher, "A Probabilistic Make-Buy Model," *Journal of Purchasing* 8, no. 1 (February 1972): 63–80.

decisions, certain generalizations appear justifiable, although, as in all generalizations, exceptions must be made. Clearly it can be said that only in rare instances will any one argument be so conclusive as to dictate an obvious decision. Consequently, in most cases the solution will be a compromise based on judgment as to the course of action most conducive to the company's best interest. In a real sense, therefore, the correct answer to the question: "What is preferable, make or buy?" is that "it all depends upon circumstances." Nevertheless, balancing all the arguments, the burden of proof in most situations rests on those urging "make" rather than "buy." Dr. Culliton states the case well:

> Most of the arguments *for* making appear to be weaker than those *for* buying. They appeared weaker because in many instances they seemed to smack of rationalization. The argument, for example, that the impossibility of buying necessitates making was rarely used as a current argument but only in explanation of previous decisions to make. And quite frequently the conditions which were claimed to have rendered buying impossible changed with embarrassing rapidity. The number of instances in which a company *had* to make was small.
>
> This implies that in many instances where corporations began making, not because they had to but because they wanted to, the decision was wrong and that those corporations would be better off if they bought certain things now being made. This conclusion is based on several grounds.
>
> Make or buy problems are considered as unusual by many business executives, even though every purchase and every manufacturing schedule implies a decision to buy or to make. In other words, any executive machinery for discovering make or buy decisions is practically nonexistent. Consequently, the only make or buy problems ordinarily to receive any attention are those that come to management's attention by way of an accident, an emergency, or as the result of the addition of an entirely new final product to the company's line.
>
> Closely allied to the failure to recognize make or buy problems was the failure to review decisions once they were made. Companies were especially lax in reviewing those decisions which had led to the adoption of a make program.
>
> There is a general lack of attention to other possible solutions to the problem. A company, for example, claimed that it was unable to buy the quality needed. Yet, its procurement efforts were devoted almost entirely to negotiations with one supplier, despite the fact that there were several well-equipped prospective suppliers that, in appearance at least, were ony too anxious to work on the kind of technical problems faced by the company. Failure to secure from one supplier what was wanted offered an excuse for following a course of action already desired by the company. The real reasons were based principally upon the management's pride and desire to boast of the large number and variety of products which the company made.
>
> Finally, relatively few companies seem to give any attention to the change in their organization which will be caused by the addition of something new. A company's production men often favor a new program in the belief that they would be able to meet all the problems without loss of efficiency in their regular jobs.
>
> This last fact is a dramatic comment upon the narrow point of view many people take with respect to limitations in their own ability. The same fact is frequently overlooked by executives themselves when they keep adding new functions to their

portion of the business, with little thought to the possibility that their efforts might be less effective. . . .[5]

QUESTIONS FOR REVIEW AND DISCUSSION

1. Generally, can a better case be made for manufacturing or for buying? Why?
2. Give at least four reasons why purchasing might be considered instead of manufacturing.
3. Why is it not easy to purchase outside an item currently manufactured "in house"?
4. Why is it difficult to get an exact cost for an item manufactured "in house"?
5. Give at least four reasons why manufacturing might be considered instead of purchasing.

CASE 10–1
ERICSON-MORGAN INDUSTRIES, INC.

Recent problems with piston pin suppliers had created a tight supply situation resulting in unreliable deliveries. In view of this Mr. H. Irwin, manager of purchasing for Ericson-Morgan, had to decide whether or not he should propose to top management that the company further investigate the possibility to manufacture piston pins instead of purchasing them.

Company background

Ericson-Morgan, an international company, sold automotive parts to the domestic O.E.M. (original equipment market) and to the international as well as domestic replacement market, sometimes known as the "aftermarket." Current annual sales of $65 million were split 25–75 respectively, between these two markets. Over the years, the company had expanded with the rapidly advancing automobile market and was now a major auto parts supplier. The company had four manufacturing plants in the United States, one in Canada, and one in Europe. Approximately 50 percent of the products sold by Ericson-Morgan were directly manufactured by company plants. The remaining 50 percent were purchased and resold as part of the company's product line. Piston pins represented 15 percent or $9.75 million of the company's auto parts business. Piston pin sales were split, $8,800,000 to the aftermarket and $950,000 to the O.E.M. market. Piston pin sales, like other company products, had been experiencing a 15 percent annual growth rate over the last four years.

---

[5]Culliton, James W., *Make or Buy*. 4th reprint (Boston: Harvard Business School, Division of Research, Business Research Study, No. 27, 1956), pp. 98–99.

Piston pins

Piston pins were used in gas combustion piston engines for automobiles and trucks. A piston pin resembled a steel cylinder, approximately ⅓″ long with a ⅝″ diameter that could either be formed as an extruded blank or produced on a screw machine. Extrusion was substantially lower in cost of the two methods due primarily to the one step "blanking" nature of the process. The cylinder blank was then further machined and heat treated to very close hardness tolerances.

Ericson-Morgan had purchased $3.1 million worth of piston pins during the last year. The average purchase price was 32¢ per pin. Size and volume purchased changed the price from 18¢ to 54¢ per pin. Ericson-Morgan sold 50 different sizes of pins. Twelve pin sizes topped the 100,000 mark. Twenty-five pin sizes called for more than 50,000 pins. Order volumes ranged from 2,000 to 700,000 pins of one size.

In the United States, there were five suppliers of piston pins, four of which were small and did specialty work on high-cost, low-volume orders. The fifth supplier, Craig Manufacturing, was large and supplied a substantial share of the O.E.M. market. Craig supplied 85 percent of Ericson-Morgan's piston pin business; two smaller suppliers had 10 percent and 5 percent respectively. Last year's prices had remained constant, but this year a price increase of at least 5 percent or 6 percent was expected by Mr. Irwin.

Future demand for piston pins

Mr. Irwin felt that piston pin purchases would increase substantially over the next few years. In Europe, especially, the aftermarket was increasing rapidly as a result of the growing number of supermarket type stores for automobile replacement parts. Previously, European automobile manufacturers had monopolized the auto part replacement business by controlling the distribution system. In addition, domestic U.S. auto sales had hit unexpected new highs in the previous two years, resulting in a significant increase in demand for auto parts in both the O.E.M. and the aftermarket. At some point in time, major changes to the piston engine would be made because of antipollution legislation. Mr. Irwin felt that this or other advances into the piston market like the rotary engine were "too far down the road" to worry about. He did not expect a large proportion of the O.E.M. business to be affected for another five years. The aftermarket would then lag a significant number of years past that date. Piston pin customers, such as engine rebuilders or specialty garages, were expected to be in business for a long time to come.

Ericson-Morgan had, until now, considered the feasibility of making or buying pins based only on the amount of return that would be generated from the invested capital for such a project. Reliability of supply had in the past never been an issue.

Delivery problems

Craig, a division of a large corporation, had been experiencing new equipment problems and had found it difficult to meet the general increase in demand for piston pins. This had resulted in a one- to two-month backlog of orders. Craig was attempting to train workers to operate the special production equipment for the last 18 months but was not entirely successful. Competition was unable to take up the slack since Craig's prices and quality were highly superior. Craig had a reject rate that was less than 1 percent. Last year Craig's total sales had amounted to $100 million. The company also competed with Ericson-Morgan in the aftermarket for piston pin sales as well as other automotive parts.

Located 300 miles from Ericson-Morgan's main plant and head office, Craig Manufacturing was accessible to Ericson-Morgan's engineering and purchasing people. Close contact was maintained and Craig's progress was continuously monitored. Recent correspondence and field visits to Craig indicated that the company would resolve its backlog orders and the resulting unreliable deliveries within the next year. Similar assurances had been given by Craig's managers a number of times over the last two years. Craig management felt that once these production problems were solved, future capacity and deliveries would no longer present difficulties.

The old make or buy proposal

Six years earlier, the purchasing department had recommended to the vice president of operations that he further investigate the making of piston pins at Ericson-Morgan. At that time the study which cost hundreds of man-hours in engineering and production studies revealed that pins made entirely by screw machines would cost 30 percent more than purchased prices. On a few large-volume standard pins the prices would, however, be competitive. Capital investment would have been a substantial $4 million for plant and equipment. If extrusion equipment were purchased to make blanks, the net additional investment would amount to another $2 million. Other more favorable investments for company funds at that time resulted in the shelving of this proposal.

The new make or buy situation

In a recent meeting of the management committee reviewing new company undertakings, Mr. Irwin as member of the committee had raised the question of making piston pins. The vice president of operations said that presently Ericson-Morgan controlled 40 percent of the aftermarket in piston pins and expected at least to hold onto that share. Any market share loss would critically hurt company sales growth targets. He subsequently stated

that delivery of piston pins and not profit should be the primary consideration for the make or buy consideration.

This year a new plant was built by Ericson-Morgan, making extra production space available. Screw machine equipment was also available in the
surplus equipment stock. Mr. Irwin thought the necessary engineering and
production capabilities were available in the organization. In discussion
with engineering and production personnel, Mr. Irwin learned that, in
house, 90 percent of the piston pin requirements could be met. The other 10
percent would have to be purchased from an outside supplier because of
their low volume and extreme size dimensions.

Engineering estimated that an additional capital investment of $200,000
would be required to start the production of piston pins. The lead time to set
up production was estimated at six months.

The chief engineer said that a continuing problem was deciding upon
standard blanking sizes. Once a standard cylinder wall thickness was established, five or six different piston pins could be finish machined from one
blank. The number and size of blank determined, therefore, major production costs and, hopefully, savings.

A pin costing 32¢ previously purchased on an average run of 50,000
would have a primary material and blanking cost of 16¢ per pin. Finish
machining would cost 5¢ and heat treating another 2¢ per pin. The cost,
however, depended upon the size of run for any particular pin. Production
runs under 50,000 pins could boost the cost by at least 40 percent. Engineering's primary cost projections could be met with the in-house use of screw
machines. Extrusion equipment would reduce the primary material and
blanking cost from 16¢ to 11¢ per pin for a 50,000 production lot. This
difference would continue to increase as the production lot increased. Extrusion equipment was very expensive; however, one option was to have the
blanks extruded by an outside supplier. Mr. Irwin thought that Pearson, Inc.,
a well-known local extrusion company, would have the capabilities and
capacity required.

Pearson, Inc. had sales of $20 million and were expanding at a 20 percent
sales and profit growth rate. A majority of its business was with the big three
automobile manufacturers. Pearson, Inc., had followed a policy in recent
years of not committing itself to low volumes for any type of business. Any
quantity over 50,000 would offer no "difficulty" in cost or delivery. Mr.
Irwin estimated Pearson's prices for blanks would be close to Ericson-
Morgan's variable manufacturing costs, using screw machines for volumes
over 50,000.

Conclusion

Mr. Irwin was expected to report his findings and recommendations at the
next management committee meeting. A number of factors at this time were

very disconcerting to Mr. Irwin. First, with the long lead time required for the manufacture of piston pins, when should preparation for production be made in order to avoid a sudden shortage of supply? Secondly, Craig had stated that it hoped to be back on schedule within the next year but could still not promise anything definite in the way of delivery time. The one- to two-month delivery delays had caused low inventory stocks of specific pin sizes and slow delivery for Ericson-Morgan customers. Delivery, quality, and availability of piston pins were primary considerations in the O.E.M. and aftermarket. Thirdly, Mr. Irwin realized that if Ericson-Morgan should stop buying from Craig, this might help solve much of the current crisis and allow Craig to offer better service to Ericson-Morgan's competitors or its own customers. Finally, he was not sure if Ericson-Morgan could meet the high quality standards or efficiency set by Craig Manufacturing.

CASE 10–2
CHELMSFORD TOY COMPANY

Mr. Tom Denton, materials manager at Chelmsford Toy Company, was investigating alternate means of supply for a new plastic blister enclosure. Several years earlier Chelmsford had introduced a successful new line of toys called Micro Monsters in a tent package. For a variety of reasons a plastic blister was considered an improvement on this earlier tent package. Mr. Denton was seriously considering a local workshop for the retarded as a supplier for the new plastic blister. He was uncertain about the problems associated with catapulting such a workshop into this type of business and how his future alternatives of supply might be affected.

Company background

Chelmsford Toy was a large well-known manufacturer of quality toys sold under the Chelmsford label. It produced a full range of toys, although it was best recognized for its line of dolls. Chelmsford was known in the industry as an aggressive merchandiser, and it had secured wide distribution in a large number and variety of retail establishments from coast to coast.

Packaging history and development

The highly successful Micro Monster line used a package composed of a card with tapering cutouts. Two monsters were enclosed in each pack. By folding the thin cardboard over the two toys and stapling it at the top, a "tent" was formed, approximately 3¾" by 4¼" with a ½" wide floor. This could be displayed free standing or on a wire bar rack for which it was prepunched. The package was attractive, simple, cheap, and different from its competitors'. The fit was snug enough around the Micro Monsters to require some effort in removal. The packaging operation was largely a manual one utilizing automatic staplers. There were three different sizes of packages to accommodate the range of shapes of Micro Monsters. Total volume had grown to six million toys a year using three million packages. Each "tent" cost about 3.6¢.

The marketing manager had recently talked with Tom Denton indicating that an improved package was necessary for Micro Monsters. Retailers complained that youngsters were prying the monsters out of the packages hanging on the display racks. The small size of the monsters made them easy to hide. The tent also did not permit full disply of the monsters inside.

Mr. Denton proposed a blister type of enclosure and discussed various possibilities with several suppliers. He wanted a unique package that would not require high-cost skilled labor and which would be manuactured to meet sudden variations in demand. One of his suppliers, Green Plastipackers, Inc., had suggested an interesting option and supplied several prototypes made on a hand tooled mold. It was clear plastic enclosure made from transparent 7.5 mil P.V.C. sheeting formed on a vacuum mold. A graphics card printed on both sides and the twin monsters could be placed in position by hand. The plastic enclosure was then folded together and heat sealed. This gave a completely enclosed, pilfer-proof display that could be either free standing or hung on a wire counter rack (see Exhibit 1). One tremendous advantage of the blister pack was that only one size could handle the full range of Micro Monsters. The printed card inserts could still vary to contain different merchandising information.

Green's proposal

Green was well known in the packaging trade for selling domestically manufactured and imported plastics and other wrappers. To promote packaging material sales Green had started selling and leasing equipment produced by others for forming, wrapping, slitting, and sealing. Green also supplied packaging advice and packaging expertise. During the last decade Green had begun manufacturing machines of its own design. Chelmsford had purchased from and consulted with Green's in the past and found it to be a thoroughly knowledgeable and reliable supplier.

Green recommended one thermoforming machine, one die cutter, and at least three heat sealers as the minimum necessary equipment. This semiautomatic machinery was a well-known American line widely used for medium production demands, and it was carried in stock by Green. The equipment was demonstrated to Tom Denton. It did not require a highly skilled operator as automatic timers governed the cycles of the forming machine. The flat mold bed could accept any mold up to 24" by 36" and 2" to 3" in depth. The thermoforming machine occupied a floor space of 4' by

Exhibit 1
Proposed micro-monster package

8' and was little more than desk height. It contained its own vacuum pump and provision for water supply for cooling molds, but the small compressor stood separately. The die cutter, approximately the size of the mold bed, was adjacent to the thermoformer head. Heat sealers could be placed at sorting tables as required.

The operating procedures was as follows. An operator manually drew the film over top of the mold from a 100-foot roll of P.V.C. mounted on the left hand side of the machine. The glass-topped cover was manually lowered over the film, locking it in place and shearing it off the roll. Heat was applied automatically, then the vacuum, which sucked and stretched the soft film skin-tight over the mold. An air blast was applied automatically, both to release the film from the mold and to cool it. Next, the cover released automatically. The operator moved the molded sheet manually to the adjoining die press cutter which sectioned it automatically. Cut sections of two joined halves were manually removed by another operator to the sorting tables where workers inserted the monsters in their blister cavities and the graphics card in the surrounding space. They then folded over the section in the middle and applied it to a three-point heat sealer. Others packed the twin toys into cartons.

Green's sales manager estimated that after two weeks under their supervision (supplied free) an experienced operator could reach the maximum of nine sheets per minute made from a 24-impression mold. Each sheet would yield 12 packets. Chelmsford would be responsible for the design and purchase of the mold from others. The cost of a 24-impression mold was estimated at $2,000. Green Plastipackers quoted $15,000 for all of the equipment and were prepared to offer a conditional sales contract over a three-year period or less on annual payments of one third of the principal plus a 7½ percent carrying charge per annum.

When he asked about service and maintenance, Tom Denton was told that this was included, providing that the film was bought from Green. Current P.V.C. material costs were estimated at $15.00 per 1,000 blisters. The sales manager explained that his company had found it best for long-term satisfaction to operate on this basis, but he emphasized that he had to meet prevailing competition in plastics. If the P.V.C. was not bought from Green, maintenance and service could be purchased on an hourly rate basis of $25.00 per hour.

Green also had a more automated line available involving automatic feed of the sheet P.V.C., transfer to the die cutter and conveyor to filling, folding, and sealing. It had a capacity of 25 sheets per minute with a 64-unit mold processing 750 blisters per minute. Cost of this equipment was about $90,000. The mold would cost about $5,000.

The first alternative—make own

Tom Denton discussed the new blister package proposal with Lyle Stanley, Chelmsford's plant manager. Lyle was concerned about the changeover as he currently employed about the equivalent of ten women full time on the tent packaging line. Acutally, the line was not operating on a daily basis. Normally, about 30 or 40 employees would work for about a week and produce a month's output. Then the workers would switch to other packaging jobs. He favored purchasing the highly automated line proposed by Green but doubted he could get approval for that large an expenditure on a still unproven design. He also hoped the same line could be used for other products. He estimated he would need at least one machine operator and use a crew of 36 packers for the less automated line when it was running. With a card insert price of $4.00 per thousand, P.V.C. raw material cost of $15.00 per thousand and direct labor of $20.00 per thousand, he figured his direct variable cost at $39.00 per thousand. Normally, factory overhead was assessed at 230 percent of direct labor and was composed of 34 percent—fringe benefits; 20 percent—supervision; 120 percent—materials handling, maintenance, supplies, power and heat; and 55 percent—fixed charges such as depreciation, insurance and taxes.

Commercial packagers

Mr. Denton obtained quotations from several commercial firms specializing in custom packaging. For the blister package, card insert, filling, closing, and packing in Chelmsford supplied cartons, the lowest quote was from

Jarnes, Inc. Jarnes was a medium-sized local firm of good reputation, and Mr. Denton was satisfied he would receive a quality job. Jarnes quote $75.00 per thousand blisters on a guaranteed volume of at least 2 million blisters per year. Jarnes would purchase the card inserts with Chelmsford specified graphics. Chelmsford would own and supply the mold.

The Association for the Retarded

Mr. Denton was considering a third alternative, the Association for the Retarded. The Association operated several workshops within a 20-mile radius of the Chelmsford plant. The largest of these, employing about 50 people, was located only several blocks from Chelmsford's main warehouse. Mr. Denton had used this workshop for a variety of small packaging jobs in the past, often on an overflow basis, and had always been pleased with the quality and prices of the jobs done. In discussion with Chelmsford's president Tom Denton found that he was not averse to placing business with charitable institutions, although no company policy existed on this matter.

The Association had a progressive board of directors dedicated to make its charges active and happy members of the community. It was confident that its drive to expand its industrial section would go a long way to meeting the foregoing criteria. (See Exhibit 2.)

Exhibit 2
The Association for the Retarded treasurer's report

It is of interest to note the percentage breakdown and change in our sources of over the three-year period—the latter being based upon budget estimates.

	Two years ago (actual)	Last year (actual)	This year (budgeted)
Operating costs	$1,020,000	$1,391,240	$1,795,000
Recoveries:			
Government grants and subsidies	36%	37%	44%
United Way	30	25	19
Parents fees	17	17	21
Donations, local campaigns and membership fees	6	5	4
Sale of goods including Christmas cards	10	12	9
Use of capital funds	1	4	3

Operations:

The accompanying table shows a dramatic change in our total actual spending and our budgeted spending. Furthermore, there are significant changes in the sources of our operating funds. It must also be pointed out that a high proportion of recovery from Parents and Users is actually government allowance money, which in turn emphasizes that the Association is highly dependent upon government financing.

It is impossible for the United Way monies to keep up with our present rate of expansion, and in our opinion every effort must be made to increase future recov-

Exhibit 2 (*continued*)

eries from our industrial sales program. To do this, we will need additions to our managerial resources which, although very competent, are becoming strained. We believe this can be accomplished by mobilizing volunteer sales and production-oriented people.

Capital funds

You will note that our description of these has been changed to show, as clearly as possible, the amount of funds available for general use, as compared to specifically designated funds.

General capital available, at December 31 last year, to cover new projects and potential deficits was approximately $250,000.

Future expansion of services:

There is increasing pressure to spend money on:

a. Additional residences
b. More workshop space to accommodate:
   1. More workers.
   2. Better production equipment.
   3. More storage space for materials and finished product.

Thus, capital spending priorities must be carefully established.

The bricks and mortar of these facilities are not the only priorities to be considered. In the end it is people that make things happen, and we must carefully plan our expansion based on the capability of our staff to cope with the additional demands. If this is neglected, then the quality of our programs and services to the people we serve will suffer due to the overstretching of our human resources.

Mr. Denton visited Mr. Watts, the administrative director, to explore the new packaging proposal.

WATTS: First of all, let me tell you that we are determined to become as self-sufficient as possible. We have to absorb about 70 workers annually, aged about 20–23 years. Our cost deficit has been running to $500 per worker per annum, which the United Way met, but it is now becoming too much for them. So our only answer is to generate more business to close the gap. We have been digging into capital to improve our workshop facilities, and we are hungry for almost any kind of work.

DENTON: How do you cost your jobs?

WATTS: That's an interesting question. It was difficult to find a basis for measurement. Conventional time and motion studies and profit and loss factors were no good. We settled on a job-day return basis which gave us an earnings target for costing contracts. We ran a pilot project at one of our larger workshops, the one near your warehouse. We kept the shop going at full pressure under normal factory conditions for the study.

DENTON: How did your labor force react to that?

WATTS: Very well. Absenteeism dropped because each worker was anxious to see how well he did against the target, and a sense of competition was established.

We also evolved a set of ideal factory conditions for us. One hundred workers and 20,000 square feet of space is just about right. Below this, efficiency drops. Mind you, these fellows have to be organized more than normal people. Fifty percent normality is high. We need lots of jig work, for instance, but their ability to use equipment under close supervision is good. We've had to employ normal trained artisans rather than social service people as supervisors, because they must watch the work and the inmates. Another thing, everything has to be inspected, and is. No statistical checks for us. That's why we turn out better quality than an automated factory. Furthermore, we are flexible. If you need a rush job done, we can transfer people from any of our other workshops on short notice. Shortage of labor is one problem we don't have.

My philosophy is that we're not looking for handouts. I'm willing to sign a contract with normal safeguards for you for anything within our capabilities. Just tell me what you're after, and we'll quote.

Mr. Denton then explained to Mr. Watts the nature of the new blister package. He requested Mr. Watts to supply a full quote based on using Green's equipment and materials with Chelmsford supplied molds and cardboard inserts. He suggested Mr. Watts contact Green directly to see if his labor force might be capable of operating the equipment and whether Green might be able to offer training assistance.

Two weeks later, Mr. Watts quoted the following prices based on an annual order quantity of 3 million blisters.

Empty blisters ready for filling . . . . $20.00/thousand.
Fully packed blisters using Chelmsford supplied molds,
    inserts and packing carton . . . . $35.00/thousand.

Green would guarantee the packaging materials costs for the duration of this contract.

Tom Denton discussed the workshop quote with Lyle Stanley who expressed doubt about the contract. Lyle also wondered if he would have to supply quality control personnel to assure workshop performance.

Lastly, Lyle Stanley was worried he might lose shop flexibility if Micro Monster packing were done outside the plant.

Conclusion

Mr. Denton was pleased with the Association's quote as it would mean that a superior package could be obtained at almost the same price as the current "tent." Moreover, the quote was about 40 percent below the lowest commercial suppliers. He was not happy about the plant manager's reaction to the proposal. He also wondered if he might not be encouraging the Association to enter an area of risk taking not traditionally encountered. The new process was highly material and machine dependent, and the Association's real strengths lay in simple, labor intensive tasks. Moreover, marketing had just issued its forecast of Micro Monster sales for the coming year, and it called for 4 million packages. Finally, Tom Denton was not convinced that

Chelmsford's long-term manufacturing strengths should lie in the packing area.

CASE 10–3
THE ACCORD

Mr. John Peters, president of Carlyn Corporation, visited Mr. Doug Warden, executive vice president of Blondin as planned. They knew each other reasonably well, and Mr. Peters quickly got down to business.

MR. PETERS: Doug, I have come to you to discuss a proposition which I think makes a lot of sense for both of our companies. Are you interested?

MR. WARDEN: John, all I have to lose is some time. Your start intrigues me. What have you got up your sleeve?

MR. PETERS: It has to do with MS–7. We know you are preparing to make your own, and we would like to help you make it a success.

MR. WARDEN: What do you know about MS–7 that we don't know?

MR. PETERS: Perhaps not much. Maybe it's more a matter of what we both know. And that is that your present volume is way below a reasonable efficiency level for the investment you are shelling out.

MR. WARDEN: Suppose that's true, we would still be prepared to meet our growing sales requirements in the future.

MR. PETERS: Sure, but that's going to take time. Now you know that our parent has been supplying us with MS–7. We have all of their cost figures and experience behind us, and we know pretty well what your situation looks like from a financial and production point of view. That's why we were a little surprised to see you get into it. However, now that you are in the game it's probably wise to make the best of it. I want to be frank with you. We have no real interest in starting our own MS–7 manufacture because it is tricky, and our volume just doesn't warrant it. On the other hand, if we have to, we will. And then two of us are fiddling around with expensive equipment inadequately loaded. What I want to propose to you is that, since you have taken the step to start manufacture, you supply both of us with MS–7 instead of just yourself. I am willing to make a long-term commitment to you, four or five years, if necessary, but I want a good price in return.

MR. WARDEN: John, there is a heck of a lot of sense to what you are saying. I have been worried a little about our return on this investment. If your volume comes in with ours, we could certainly expect better operating efficiency. What are you willing to offer?

MR. PETERS: We are prepared to offer $44/kg.

MR. WARDEN: You must be kidding. You know that the current U.K. laid down price in the U.S. is close to $60/kg.

MR. PETERS: That may be, but that's certainly not what we have been paying. Look, if it really interests you, I'll tell you what we figure your variable cost is, and that's around $40. Now everything you make on top of that is contribution to your fixed expenses. That's why we are willing to give you a 10-percent contribution. We think we should approach this from a sharing of the benefits point of view rather than a market price proposition. What's market price anyway, with only two customers?

Mr. Warden: (After requesting a file from his secretary and scribbling on paper) Excuse me, John, I had to check a few things myself. Let's not kid ourselves, if I let you have the stuff at $44 my sales and production managers would kill me. At that price the sharing of the benefit you talk about is too one-sided. Now I know we can start horse trading and end up frustrated and feeling foolish. I'll be honest with you. I like the premise of your proposition. I like the idea. I don't like the price you quoted. Now, I am going to beat around the bush. I'll quote you what I think is a very good deal. You either take it or leave it. If you take it, we can settle a few details later. If you leave it, you'll never be able to buy MS–7 from us.

Mr. Peters: You are not giving me much choice but go on.

Mr. Warden: First, the length of time. You want five years, we'll give you five years. Now the price. I'm probably crazy, but I'll let you have it for $50/kg, f.o.b. our plant in St. Paul, Minnesota. Agreed?

Mr. Peters: Doug, you drive a hard bargain. If you feel that you need $50 to feel satisfied about our sharing agreement, $50 it is, and good luck to both of us.

Mr. Warden: Fine.

Mr. Peters: What I would like to suggest to you is that our Mr. Bill Thomas in purchasing get together with whoever you want to assign this to on your end to agree on further details. Is this acceptable to you?

Mr. Warden: This is agreeable. Since our equipment will not be coming in until late October, I would appreciate holding off on any follow-up until the beginning of October because we have our annual plant shut-down still coming up, and we are trying to introduce another new product which will take a lot of our staff's time until early October. Is this okay with you?

Mr. Peters: It's a little long, and I would like to get this thing tied up as soon as possible, but I guess we can wait until October in view of your special circumstances. I'd like to wish you good luck with your new product provided it's not going to compete with one of ours.

Mr. Warden: Thanks. No, this new one isn't another rival. Thank you for coming, John. I am sorry I don't have more time to spend with you now.

Mr. Peters: I want to thank you too. I'm glad we got a deal. Goodbye, Doug.

Mr. Warden: Goodbye, John.

DISPOSAL OF SCRAP, SURPLUS, OR OBSOLETE MATERIAL

Managers are concerned about the effective and efficient handling of the disposal of surplus, obsolete, and waste and scrap materials generated within the firm. In recent years, disposal problems have become more complex, as well as more important, as companies have become larger, more diversified in product lines, and more decentralized in management. More recently, a new dimension has been added to the overall disposal problem: the need to develop and use new methods to avoid the generation of solid waste products and better means of disposing of other wastes which are discharged into the air and waterways, causing pollution.

While this chapter will analyze and discuss the purchasing department's role in disposition of surplus and waste, the alert purchasing executive must also keep abreast of new technology concerned with avoiding and eliminating causes of pollution.

The salvage of all types of materials in U.S. industry is big business. It is estimated that sales of scrap and waste materials of all types are in excess of $10 billion per year.[1] Not only does the sale of scrap, surplus, and waste result in additional income for the seller, it also prevents pollution and serves to conserve raw material resources and energy. For example, every ton of iron and steel scrap recycled saves one-and-one-half tons of iron ore, one ton of coke and one-half ton of limestone.

Savings potential

It is surprising that more attention has not been given by more companies to the whole problem of disposal. The reasons are probably several. One of the most important is that scrap is suggestive of something which has no value and which the junkman can take away—in other words, something which a company is willing to sell if it can get anything for it, but which, if not, it is willing even to pay somebody to haul away. Another reason is that many concerns are not large enough to maintain disposal departments, since the amounts of scrap and surplus

---

[1] The Institute of Scrap Iron and Steel, Inc., 1729 H Street, N.W., Washington, D.C. 20006 is a national association of firms who are predominantly processors and brokers of scrap. The Institute publishes several reports on the scrap industry and provides much data.

415

they have do not appear great enough to warrant particular attention. Yet these items may be a source of potential profit.

An illustration may help. A man purchased old burlap and other items from the salvage department of a large organization. He then called on the sales department of the same company and disposed of the material at a substantial profit. He made $20,000 in these transactions merely because the salvage and the sales departments of the same company were not cooperating.

At times of raw material shortages, scrap is likely to command very high prices. England found in 1973 and 1974 that its domestically controlled price of waste rags of about $60 per ton was well below that of the European market, resulting in an exodus of this material for which a special domestic collection program had been set up to encourage local manufacture of toilet tissue. The result was a shortage of raw materials for the English mills, and a tissue shortage forcing imports of an item that could well have been manufactured locally.

The disposition of all kinds of scrap and surplus materials should always be handled to reduce the net loss to the lowest possible figure or, if possible, achieve the highest potential gain. The first thought, therefore, should be to balance against each other the net returns obtained from each one of several methods of disposition. Thus, excess material can frequently be transferred from one plant of a company to another of the same company. Such a procedure involves little outlay except for packing, handling, and shipping. At other times, by reprocessing or reconditioning, the material can be salvaged for use within the plant. Such cases clearly involve a somewhat larger outlay, and there may be some question as to whether, once the material has been so treated, its value, either for the purpose originally intended or for some substitute use, is great enough to warrant the expense. Since the decision whether to undertake the reclamation of any particular lot of material is essentially one of production costs and of the resultant quality, it should be—and commonly is—made by the production or engineering departments instead of by the scrap department. The most the purchasing manager can do is to suggest that this treatment be considered before the material is disposed of in other ways.

In some companies there is, within the manufacturing department, a separate salvage or "utilization" division to pass upon questions about possible reclamation. Indeed, the place of the "salvage engineer" is well established among many larger firms. This salvage division is primarily a manufacturing rather than a sales division and is concerned with such duties as the development of salvage processes, the actual reclamation of waste, scrap, or excess material, and the reduction of the volume of such material.

CATEGORIES OF MATERIAL FOR DISPOSAL

No matter how well a company may be managed, some excess, waste, scrap, surplus, and obsolete material is bound to develop. Every organization tries, of course, to keep such material at a minimum. But try as it may, this never will be wholly successful. The existence of this class of material is the result of a wide variety of causes, among which are overoptimism in the sales forecast; changes in design and specifications; errors in estimating mill usage; inevitable losses in processing; careless use of material by factory personnel; and overbuying resulting from attempts to avoid the threat of rising prices or to secure quantity discounts on large purchases.

We are not now concerned with the methods by which excess, waste, scrap, and obsolete material may be kept at a minimum, for these already have been discussed in connection with proper inventory and stores control, standardization, quality determination, and forward buying. The immediate problem has to do with the disposition of these materials when they do appear. We first need to distinguish among the five categories of material for disposal.

Excess or surplus material

Excess (or surplus) material is that stock which is in excess of a reasonable requirement of the organization. It arises because of errors in the amount bought or because anticipated production did not materialize. There are various ways in which such material may be handled. In some cases it may be desirable merely to store it until required, particularly if the material is of a nonperishable character, if storage costs are not excessive, and if there is a reasonable expectation that the material will be required in the future. Occasionally it may be substituted for more active material. Or, if the company operates a number of plants, it may be possible to transfer the excess to another plant. There are times, however, when these conditions do not exist and when fairly prompt sale is desirable. The chances for change in the style or design may be so great as to diminish considerably the probability that this particular material may be required. Or, it may be perishable. Factory requirements may be such as to postpone the demand for large amounts of this material so far into the future that the most economical action is to dispose of it and repurchase at a later date.

Many companies set some rough rule of thumb by which to determine when a stock item is to be classed as "surplus." Thus, according to one manufacturing organization:

> Generally speaking, the question of excess material should be decided on a six-month basis. Customarily, the excess would be that amount of material on hand which represents more than a six-months' supply. There are exceptions, however. Some material deteriorates so rapidly that any quantity on hand greater than two or three months' supply be treated as excess material. In other cases, where it takes six months or longer to buy new material, more-lengthy supply periods are frequently essential.

This rule suggests that all materials should be grouped into rough classifications, and normal requirement and supply periods established for each. Mere classification in itself is not sufficient. As with all classes of material, systematic, physical stock taking, continuous review of inventory records, and occasional "cleanup campaigns" are also necessary.

Another source of excess material usually appears upon the completion of a construction project. The company just referred to covers this situation as follows:

> All new material for a specific property on order and not used on the project in question constitutes an inventory and must be treated as such. As soon as the work is completed, all new, unused material should be transferred immediately to the custody of the stores department. The original cost of the material should be charged to "Reclamation Stores" which is an unclassified segment of the Stores Account and credited to the property order or authorization.

Provision is also made for the proper accounting of used material created or resulting from demolition work carried on in conjunction with construction projects.

In the case of one large manufacturing company, if the sales department has definitely obligated the company to make a certain quantity of an item, or has set up a sales budget for that quantity subsequently accepted by the management, and later finds itself unable to dispose of its quota, the losses sustained on the excess material are charged to that particular item or sales classification. The same practice is followed if the sales department, by virtue of recommending a change in design, creates an excess of material. This company feels that the loss should not be absorbed generally or distributed over other departments.

Obsolete material

Obsolete material differs from excess stock in that whereas the latter presumably could be consumed at some future date, the former is unlikely ever to be used inside the organization which purchased it. Material becomes obsolete as a result of a change in the production process or when some better material is substituted for that originally used. Once material has been declared obsolete, it is wise to dispose of it for the best price that can be obtained.

Although material may be obsolete to one user, this need not mean that it is obsolete for others. An airline may decide to discontinue using a certain type of airplane. This action makes not only the plane but also the repair and maintenance parts inventory obsolete. But both may have substantial value to other airlines or users of planes.

Rejected end products

Because of the uncertainties of the production process, or because of complex end-product quality specifications, a certain percentage of completed products may be rejected by outgoing quality control as unsatisfactory. In some instances these finished products can be repaired or reworked to bring them up to standard, but in other instances it is not economic to do so. The semiconductor industry is a good example, for because of the technological complexities of the process, the "yield" on a particular production line may be such that only 70 percent of the finished devices measure up to end-product specifications.

The rejected products may then be sold to users who do not require the normal quality in purchased items. These might be classified as "factory seconds." One problem is that if the end-product is identified with a name or trademark, unscrupulous buyers may then turn around and market the item as one which measures up to the stated quality requirements for the original item. To avoid this, the firm may find it necessary to destroy the rejected items (as is done in the pharmaceutical industry); or remove the distinguishing mark or identification; or melt the product down to recover any valuable metal content.

Scrap material

Scrap material differs from excess or obsolete stock since it cannot properly be classified as new or unused. "Scrap" is a term which may be applied to material or equipment which is no longer serviceable and has been discarded. It includes such items as worn machinery and old tools. In such cases, scrap arises because the company is replacing old machines with others which are more modern and more productive. A concern buying new machines, tools, and other equipment normally maintains a depreciation charge intended to cover the original cost of such items, so that the value of a machine has been written off by the time it is finally discarded. Such a depreciation charge normally covers an obsolescence factor as well as ordinary wear and tear. Actually, however, a discarded or scrapped machine may still have a value for some other manufacturer in the same type of business or in some other industry. It consequently may be disposed of at a price which will show a profit in many instances. This replacement of old or obsolete machines by others capable of larger production at the same or lower cost provides a real profit-making opportunity.

Another form of scrap is represented by the many byproducts of the production process, such as fly from cotton spinning, warp ends from weaving, and metal scrap from boring and planing machines. Start-up adjustment scrap is frequently significant, and in industries like paper making, paper converting, printing, polyethylene pellet manufacture, and many others it is one major reason for a significant price increase for small custom orders. The faster and the more automated the equipment, the higher the start-up scrap will be as a percentage of the total material used in small orders. Commonly, items of this class, which are a normal part of the production process, are considered a form of scrap; such material may frequently be salvaged. In the metal industries, the importance of scrap in this form has a definite bearing on costs and prices. For instance, a selection from among forgings, stampings, or castings may depend upon the waste weight. The waste weight to be removed in finishing plus labor costs of removing it may make a higher priced article the better value. In turning brass parts, the cost of the material (brass rod) may be greater than the price of the finished parts, because the recovered brass scrap is such an important element in the cost. Indeed, scrap is so valuable as an element in cost that it is not unusual for the purchase contract on nonferrous metals to include a price at which the scrap will be purchased by the supplier.

Scrap metals normally are separated into ferrous and nonferrous categories. Ferrous includes those products conceived from iron and generally are attracted by the scrap man's geiger counter (an ordinary magnet). The ferrous group consists of scrap steel, cast iron, white iron, etc. The nonferrous group includes two broad families: (1) red metals, which are copper based, and (2) white metals, which are aluminum tin, lead, or zinc based.

There are detailed, extensive specifications governing the grading and shipping of scrap materials. The Institute of Scrap Iron and Steel deals basically with ferrous materials, and The National Association of Recycling Industries is basically concerned with nonferrous materials.

Waste ◦

Waste has been defined as material or supplies which have been changed during the production process and which "through carelessness, faulty production methods, poor handling, or other causes have been spoiled, broken, or otherwise rendered unfit for further use." This definition is not entirely adequate. There is a form of waste not due to obsolescence and yet not a result of carelessness or poor handling. Waste, for example, may occur by the fact that the material is not up to specifications because of faulty machinery or breakdowns or because of chemical action not foreseen. In some instances, waste can be defined simply as the residue of materials which result from the normal manufacturing process and which have no economic (resale) value. An example is the smoke produced from burning fuel, or the cutting oil which becomes contaminated as a result of the normal manufacturing process. However, what is waste today and has no current economic value may change tomorrow. For example, years ago the natural gas produced in crude oil production was waste and was flared off in the oilfields because it had no sales value; today it has substantial economic value.

Theoretically, waste should not exist. However, there probably will never be a time when some waste will not exist in every plant. Every effort should be made to reduce the waste factor to the lowest possible point. Its reduction can be brought about in many ways, such as the installation of new processes and by improved production layout.

Some differences of opinion may exist as to the exact definitions of scrap, excess, and waste. From the standpoint of the purchasing manager who has to dispose of the material, these differences are secondary. The objective is to realize as large a return as possible from disposal of these items.

Should the purchasing department be responsible ◦ for material disposal?

The question of the responsibility for the management of material disposal in an organization is rather difficult to answer. In large companies where substantial amounts of scrap, obsolete, surplus, and waste materials are generated, a separate department may be justified. The manager of such a department may report to the general manager or the production manager. The limited surveys which have been made to determine the location of disposal responsibility have indicated that most of the companies depend on the purchasing department to handle disposal sales.

There are very legitimate reasons for assigning disposal of materials to the purchasing/materials management function. These include: (1) knowledge of probable price trends, (2) contact with salespeople is a good source of information as to possible users of the material, (3) familiarity with the company's own needs may suggest possible uses for, and transfer of, the material within the organization, and (4) unless a specific department is established within the firm to handle this function, purchasing is probably the only logical choice.

In conglomerate and highly diversified and decentralized types of organizations, there is great need for the coordination of salvage disposal if the best possible results are to be obtained. Where a corporate purchasing department is included in the home office organization structure, even if only in a consulting relationship with the various divisions of the company, available information and records and established channels of communication should help to ensure that salvage materials generated in any part of the company are considered for use in all parts of the company before being offered for sale outside the company.

The general conclusion is that except in the cases of companies with separate salvage departments, management has found the purchasing department, because of its knowledge of materials, markets, prices, and possible uses, in a better position other than departments of the company to salvage what can be used and to dispose of what cannot.

Keys to profitable disposal

Obviously, the optimum solution would be not to generate materials that need disposal. While this is not totally possible, every effort should be made, through good planning and taking advantage of modern technology, to *minimize* the quantity of material generated.

If scrap results as a normal, unavoidable part of the operation, it is essential that it be *segregated* by type. This should be done at the point where scrap is generated. If two types of scrap, for example steel and copper scrap, are mixed, the return per pound on sale likely will be less than the lowest priced scrap, since any buyer must go to the expense of separating the scrap before processing.

Also, every effort should be made to obtain *maximum competition* from sources available to buy scrap or surplus material. Unfortunately, the number of potential users and buyers of scrap in a particular area may be small, resulting in a non-competitive disposal situation. Purchasing should actively attempt to find new buyers and encourage them to compete in terms of price paid.

Disposal channels

There are several possible means of materials disposal. In general, the options are, in order of maximum return to the selling company:

1. *Use elsewhere within the firm on an "as is" basis:* An attempt should be made to use the material "as is," or with economical modification, for a purpose other than that for which it was purchased; e.g., substitution for similar grades and nearby sizes, and shearing or stripping sheet metals to obtain narrower widths.

2. *Reclaim for use within the plant:* For example, can the material be reclaimed or modified for use by welding? Welding has become a very important factor in disposing of materials to advantage. Defective and spoiled castings and fabricated metal parts can be reclaimed at little expense; short ends of bar stock, pipe, etc., can be welded into working lengths; and worn or broken jigs, fixtures, and machine parts can be built up or patched. Furthermore, castings and fabricated metal parts can be reduced in size by either the arc or acetylene cutting process. As a result of the materials shortages of the early 1970s, many firms have become interested in the possibilities of recycling of materials, such as paper, copper, zinc, tin, and precious metals. In addition to economic advantages, this may provide a partial solution to some of our environmental problems.[2]

3. *Sell to another firm for use on an "as is" basis:* Can any other manufacturer use the material either "as is," or with economical modifications? It should be noted that sales can often be made direct to other users who may be able to use a disposal item in lieu of a raw material they currently are buying. Or, one firm's surplus or obsolete equipment may solve another firm's equipment requirements nicely. A good example of this is the market which has existed for years for DC–3 aircraft which are obsolete for one air carrier and are bought for use by supplemental or commuter airlines.

4. *Return to the vendor:* Can it be returned to the manufacturer or supplier from whom it was purchased, either for cash or for credit on other later purchases? A great deal of steel scrap is sold by large-quantity purchasers directly back to the mills, who use it as a raw material in the steel production process. Normally, the firm using this disposal avenue must be a large consumer.

5. *Sale through a broker:* Brokers exist for the sale of both scrap and also for used equipment. Their role is to bring buyer and seller together, for which they take a commission. A great deal of metal scrap is disposed of through this channel.

6. *Sale to a local scrap or surplus dealer*: Every community of any size will have one or more scrap dealers. The return from sale through this channel likely will be low, for three reasons: (1) there may be only one dealer, a noncompetitive, sole buying source; (2) the dealer assumes the risk of investment, holding, and attempting to find a buyer. The profit margin for assuming this risk

---

[2]M. J. Mighdoll and Peter D. Weisse, "We Need a National Materials Policy," *Harvard Business Review* 54, no. 5 (September–October, 1976): 146–48.

may be quite high; and (3) extra movement and handling, which is costly, is involved.

7. *Discard or destroy the material or item:* If no buyer or user can be found for the item, the firm may have to destroy or bury the item. This can be quite costly and caution should be taken to protect the environment and to assure that disposal methods for dangerous materials do not create a safety hazard to the public.

Disposal procedures

When scrap is sold, careful attention should be given to the selection of a buyer and to the procedure for handling the sale. The yellow pages of the telephone directory provide lists of dealers who buy scrap and waste products. The *American Metal Market,* a daily paper, provides price information for most waste and scrap products for the major markets in the United States and *Iron Age* (weekly) also provides current price quotations.

In connection with the selling and delivery of material, a system should be set up which will be consistently followed and will afford the company protection against all possible loss through slipshod methods, dishonest employees, and irregular practice on the part of the purchaser. All sales should be approved by a department head and cash sales should be handled through the cashier and never by the individual whose duty it is to negotiate the sale. All delivery of byproducts sold should be effected through the issuing of an order form and sufficient number of copies made to provide a complete record for all departments involved in the transaction. The shipping department should determine the weight, count, etc., and this figure should go to the billing department without going through the hands of those who negotiate the sale.

Any department responsible for the performance of this function should maintain a list of reputable dealers in the particular line of material or equipment to be disposed of and should periodically review this list. At frequent intervals, the proper plant official should be instructed to clean up the stock and report on the weights and quantities of the different items or classes of items ready for disposal.

A common procedure is to send out invitations to four or five dealers to call and inspect the lots at the factory and quote their prices f.o.b. factory yard. Such transactions usually are subject to the accepted bidders' check of weights and quantities and are paid for in cash before removal. Not infrequently, acceptable and dependable purchasers with whom satisfactory connections have already been established are relied upon as desirable purchasers and no bids are called for from others.

If a firm generates large amounts of scrap materials consistently, the bidders may be asked to bid on the purchase of this scrap over a six-month or year time period. However, it is advisable to rebid or renegotiate such contracts at least annually, to encourage competition. Often the disposal agreement will have an escalator clause in it, tieing the price to changes in the overall market, as reported in a specifically-designated issue, e.g., the first Tuesday of each month, of the *American Metal Market*.

A disposal example

Disposal is still a managerial attitudinal problem, since most items can be disposed of profitably by use of imagination. The following examples are from a large forest products company which acquired a logging-lumber-veneer-flooring operation that was on the verge of bankruptcy. The new manager called a meeting of all salaried personnel, at which he stressed two major points:

1. "We don't have any problems—only opportunities to solve a few difficulties"; and
2. "There is no such thing as scrap, because there is a buyer for everything at the right price."

He concluded by telling the staff he expected them to provide him with the means of profitably disposing of all byproducts within two months. The following is a partial list of the accomplishments within three months of this meeting:

1.   Two years before the takeover, the state Department of Lands and Forests had insisted that some areas be "clean cut" and reseeded to birch. Balsam fir and spruce were just being cut and left to rot. A visit to a newsprint company resulted in an offer of $26 per cord for this pulpwood delivered to their plant. Contractors were hired to cut and deliver it for $22, resulting in a profit of $4 per cord to the company, plus a 100 percent saving of the former cost of cutting the spruce and balsam fir.

2.   A trucker had been hired to carry away veneer "cores." A gang saw was installed to cut them into boards which were automatically the right length for crating veneer, saving the veneer mill from having to buy crating material from the saw mill. Surplus cores were treated and sold as ornamental fence posts at $1.00 each.

3.   A plant visit to a fine paper manufacturer resulted in an offer of $28 per ton for hardwood chips from the veneer and flooring mills which had previously been dumped in the sawdust pit.

4.   Cut-offs from the flooring mill which had formerly been thrown into the sawdust pile were shipped some distance for $40 per ton (delivered) to a manufacturer of hardwood floor tiles.

5.   Slabs from the sawmill which had formerly been chipped and dumped in the sawdust pit were end-cut and sold to a distributor who stored them for a year (to air dry) and then resold them to campers for firewood over a radius of about 50 miles. He bought them for $4 per "estimated" cord (and made a killing by reselling them for about $32 per cord). This distributor initiated negotiations to cut up the "slash" in the bush at the same price for the same purpose. This would be pure windfall profit—and would leave less debris in the logging areas.

QUESTIONS FOR REVIEW AND DISCUSSION

1. Why is scrap disposal often a responsibility of the purchasing department?

2. How can the firm obtain maximum return from disposal of unneeded items?

3. What specific procedures should purchasing use to dispose of unneeded items?

4. What are the channels used in disposing of items, and what are the advantages of each?

5. What is the difference between surplus material, obsolete material, rejects, scrap, and waste?

CASE 11–1
GOODLAND PLASTICS CO., LTD.

When the new president decided suddenly to drop the line, Mr. Allan, manager of purchasing, Goodland Plastics Company, realized in November that he had some 75,000 pounds "PL" clear film left on his hands, normally about a three-month supply.

This biaxially oriented plastic was not made in North America. The Japanese manufacturer, eager to penetrate the North American market, had agreed to a price about 25 percent below European competition. Only this enabled the operation of fabricating and printing wrappers to customers' requirements, mainly in the food industry, viable. But after three years "PL" failed to realize the "miracles" predicted for it, and in the face of revitalized competition from long-established cellophane and the new polyesters it had lost ground.

Normal lead time had been eight-ten weeks from the Orient. Mr. Allan used to order every two months on the basis of firm production orders, in a variety of thicknesses and widths. The price varied by the thickness. The material was supplied in rolls of 2,000 and 4,000 meters, weighing approximately 125 kg. and 200 kg. gross.

The bulk of the stock consisted of 18 micron, 48", 4,000 meters. Mr. Allan estimated his average quoted price to be U.S. 70¢ a pound, f.o.b. delivered, duty (17 percent) paid. The material was in a heated warehouse, but the inventory carrying cost had not yet been calculated.

When examining the possibilities of finding a buyer for this now obsolete inventory, the purchasing manager was aware of several contraints:

a. Goodland also manufactured other film from resins but had no facilities for reworking extruded stock.

b. The company had publicly announced its intention to abandon "PL."

c. He could not guarantee the machinability or printability of the film to a third party less well-equipped and knowledgeable than the experienced Goodland Company. This put him at a disadvantage opposite original manufacturers of competitive plastics.

d. Goodland had a "quality house" reputation to protect.

CASE 11–2
FAIRWAY ELECTRONICS

Ted Abbott, manager of purchases at Fairway Electronics, was concerned about the forthcoming move to the new corporate head office. This would create a tremendous disposal problem as all office furnishings in former locations became surplus.

Fairway Electronics, a large, very fast growing organization, would in another three months complete its new head office building in downtown Atlanta, Georgia. The building had already drawn favorable reviews from the local community for its advanced architectural design, incorporating energy saving concepts as well as the open office format. Because of Fairway's rapid growth, its offices had been spread over eight different locations in Atlanta, mostly in rented quarters. It was hoped that the new 27-story tower would heighten the corporation's visibility and image while bringing all office employees under the same roof. The architect and the new building task force has decided to furnish all offices with new furniture and fixtures to complement the design of the building. As a consequence, all furnishings in the "old" locations would become surplus. Plans called for staged "moving in" of all departments over a four month period. Leases in the old locations were expiring accordingly.

Ted Abbott did not know how much furniture was involved. He guessed it might include over 2500 "bigger" items like desks, chairs, and filing cabinets. Some of these dated back to 1923 when the company was founded. Ted Abbott suspected that a large portion was not tagged properly, even though Fairway had an asset identification and tagging program. He also suspected most pieces would have been fully depreciated on the company's books.

According to corporate guidelines, purchasing was responsible for disposal of all capital assets subject to certain authorizations from budget unit heads and corporate officers depending on the asset's value. The vice-president of administration had requested Ted Abbott to pay special attention to the corporate manual clause: "Surplus items may be sold to Fairway employees at market or trade-in value. Notices of available items must be posted on all bulletin boards." Ted suspected this request might have something to do with the beautiful Early American cherry office set in the vice-president's office. Ted was also aware many Fairway employees had a sentimental attachment to their furnishings and that they might welcome a chance to purchase such items for their personal use.

Other relevant corporate instructions regarding disposal included:

> Surplus capital assets may be donated to charitable organizations. All such requests must be approved by the vice-president of administration.
>
> It is the responsibility of the corporate purchasing agent to obtain the highest possible return for all surplus items.

One of Ted's assistants suggested that all surplus furnishings be stored in a local warehouse until all moves were complete. At that point it would be clear what items and how many were available. Used furniture dealers could then be invited to bid on the whole lot. Warehouse space could probably be rented for about $1500 a month.

Ted had never before faced a disposal of this magnitude and wondered how he should proceed.

LEGAL ASPECTS OF PURCHASING

The competent professional purchaser does not require the training of a lawyer but should possess an understanding of the basic principles of commercial law. Such understanding should enable recognition of problems and situations which require professional counsel and also provide the knowledge to avoid legal pitfalls in day-to-day operations.

Legal authority of the purchasing officer •

What is the purchasing officer's legal status? Briefly, he or she has the authority to attend to the business of purchasing in accordance with the instructions given by his or her employer. These instructions are usually broad in character. In general, there should be, and in all progressive organizations there is, a clear understanding as to what the purchasing officer is expected to do. Attention already has been called to the necessity for a clear understanding of duties simply as a matter of good business policy. The reasons for this clear understanding, important as they are from other points of view, are strengthened by the fact that the law assumes an agreement between the agent and the employer as to the scope of the authority. Presumably, the purchasing officer performs these assigned duties to the full extent of his or her capacity. In other words, the purchasing officer has a right to expect from the employer a clear understanding as to duties and responsibilities; the purchasing officer, in turn, is expected to perform these duties in an honest, careful manner. So long as he or she does this, the obligations to the employer, from a legal point of view, are fulfilled. In agreeing to render service to an employer, there is no implied agreement that no errors will be made for some errors are incidental to all vocations.

By special stipulation, the purchasing manager may even assume responsibility to the principal for the risks from honest error but such arrangements are rare. Nevertheless, when a person accepts an appointment to serve as an agent for the principal, there does exist the implication that the person possesses the necessary skill to carry on the work. In some cases, a very high degree of skill is demanded and accepting an appointment under such circumstances implies the necessary skill. There are, of course, many possible modifications of this general statement. The purchasing officer becomes liable to the employer when damage occurs through active fault or through negligence. Many difficulties arise in an attempt to define what negligence is, although, in general, it may be said to constitute an "omission of due care under given circumstances."

Since the purchasing officer is acting as an agent for the company which he or she represents, it follows that he or she is in a position to bind the company within limits. Actually, of course, the power of an agent to bind the principal may greatly exceed the right to do so. This right is confined by the limits assigned, i.e., in accordance with the actual authorization; power to bind the principal, however, is defined by the *apparent* scope of authority, which in the case of most purchasing officers is rather broad. Furthermore, to avoid personal liability, it must be made clear to the person with whom the buyer deals that he or she is acting as an agent. In fact, the law requires even more if the buyer is not to be held personally liable; not only must the buyer indicate the fact that he or she is acting as an agent but also the person with whom he or she is dealing must agree to hold the principal responsible, even though the latter is at the moment unknown.

The actual authority delegated to an agent is not limited to those acts which, by words, the agent is expressly and directly authorized to perform. Every actual authorization, whether general or special, includes by implication all such authority as is necessary, usual, and proper to carry through to completion the main authority conferred. The extent of the agent's implied authority must be determined from the nature of the business to be transacted. These powers will be broad in the case of one acting as a general agent or manager. It is the duty of the third party dealing with the agent to ascertain the scope of the agent's authority. Statements of the agent as to the extent of powers cannot be relied on by the third party. Any limitation on the agent's power which is known to the third person is binding on the third person.

Personal liability of the purchasing officer •

There are certain conditions under which the purchasing officer may be held personally liable when signing contracts: (1) when he or she makes a false statement concerning authority *with intent to deceive* or when the misrepresentation has the natural and probable consequence of misleading; (2) when the agent performs without authority a damaging act, even though believing he or she has such authority; (3) when performing an act which is itself illegal, even on authority from the employer; (4) when willfully performing an act which results in damage to anyone; (5) when he or she performs damaging acts outside the scope of authority, even though the act is performed with the intention of rendering the employer a valuable service. In each of these cases, the vendor ordinarily has no recourse to the company employing the agent, since there existed no valid contract between the seller and the purchasing firm. Since such a contract does not exist, the only recourse which the vendor commonly has is to the agent personally.

Should the question arise as to who may be sued on contracts made within the apparent scope of the agent's authority but beyond the actual scope, because of the fact that there were limitations on the latter unknown to the seller, it may still follow that the principal can be held liable. Under these circumstances, the agent probably is in the wrong and is, of course, answerable to the principal. He or she may also be answerable to the seller, on the ground of deceit, on the charge that he or she is the real contracting party, or for breach of the warranty that he or she was authorized to make the precise contract he or she attempted to make for the principal.

Moreover, suits have been brought by sellers against purchasing managers when it was discovered that the latter's principal was for some reason unable to pay the account. For example, such conditions have arisen (1) when the employer became insolvent or bankrupt; (2) when the employer endeavored to avoid the legal obligations to accept and pay for merchandise purchased by the purchasing manager; or (3) when the employer became involved in litigation with the seller, whose lawyers decided that the contract price could be readily collected personally from the purchasing manager.

Although a purchasing officer should never attempt to replace the services of a competent lawyer, the alert buyer and purchasing manager should keep informed about court decisions and changes in laws which affect his or her actions. Purchasing trade publications normally report court decisions and major changes in laws which have an impact on the performance of the buying function.

The purchase order contract 🖊

There are many federal, state, and local statutes which govern purchasing practice but the Uniform Commercial Code covers most of the transactions involving purchase and sale of goods and services. The UCC resulted from the joint efforts of the American Law Institute and the National Conference of Commissioners on Uniform State Laws. Since the first publication of the Uniform Commercial Code in 1952, with subsequent revisions and refinements in 1958, 1962, 1966, and 1972, all of the states have enacted the code into law, except for the state of Louisiana.[1] Article 2, "Sales" governs purchase/sale transactions, and applies to transactions by "Merchants," defined as "a person who deals in goods of the kind or otherwise by his occupation holds himself out as having knowledge or skill peculiar to the practices or goods involved in the transaction or to whom such knowledge or skill may be attributed by his employment of an agent or broker or other intermediary who by his occupation holds himself out as having such knowledge or skill."[2]

A valid contract is based on four factors:

1. Competent parties—either principals or qualified agents.
2. Legal subject matter or purpose.

---

[1] The American Law Institute and National Conference of Commissioners on Uniform State Laws, *Uniform Commercial Code*, 1972 Official Text (Philadelphia, Penn.: The American Law Institute, 1972).

[2] Ibid, 2–104.

3. An offer and an acceptance.
4. Consideration.

The purchase order generally is regarded as containing the buyer's offer and becomes a legal contract when accepted by the vendor. Many purchase order forms have a copy that includes provision for acknowledgement or acceptance. There has never been universal agreement on how detailed the terms and conditions which are printed on the purchase order should be. Some companies' forms use the reverse side to spell out the complete terms and conditions which apply to any transaction. Some companies may include a separate printed sheet detailing terms and conditions applying to the order. Some companies provide only for the very basic items necessary for a valid offer and depend on the provisions of the UCC for proper legal coverage. The purchasing officer should depend on the legal counsel responsible for handling legal matters for the company in determining the policy to be followed.

An "offer" can be equally valid if made by a vendor, either in writing or verbally. Such an offer becomes a legal contract when accepted by the buyer.

Regardless of whether an offer is made by the buyer or the vendor, it can be modified or revoked before it is accepted. However, an offer in writing that includes an assurance that the price will remain firm for a specified period may not be revoked prior to the expiration of the period. Under the UCC, if a vendor makes a firm offer to sell, it generally must be held open for a "reasonable" time period. This reasonable time period generally has been held to be three months, unless a shorter period is stated by the vendor at the time the offer was made.[3]

The courts have generally held that advertisements and price lists do not constitute legal offers unless specifically directed to the buyer or unless an order placed on the basis of the advertisement or price list is specifically accepted by the vendor.

Acceptance of orders •

Since the purchase order form or the sales contract is intended to include all the essential conditions surrounding the transaction, it is customary to include in the agreement a statement such as, "Acceptance of this order implies the acceptance of conditions contained thereon." The purpose of such a provision is, of course, to make all the conditions legally binding upon the seller and to avoid cases in which the seller advances the defense that he or she was not aware of certain conditions. Statements similiar to that indicated are found in practically all purchase agreements, to give warning that there are conditions attached, either on the front or on the reverse side of the contract.

Having placed an order with a vendor, the purchasing officer wishes to assure that the order has been accepted. To obtain such assurance, it is customary to insist upon a definite vendor acknowledgement, usually in written form. It is not uncommon to incorporate as a part of the contract a clause requiring that the

---

[3]Ibid., 2–205.

acceptance be made in a particular manner, in which case a form is enclosed with the order, and the purchase order contains a clause which stipulates: ''This order must be acknowledged on the enclosed form.''

The question sometimes arises as to when an offer either of sale or of purchase has been accepted. As a matter of law, the person making an offer may demand, as one of the conditions, that acceptance be indicated in a specific manner. Ordinarily, however, when an offer is made, the offerer either expressly or by implication requires the offeree to send the answer by post or telegraph. When the answer is duly posted or telegraphed, the acceptance is communicated, the contract being complete from the moment the letter is mailed or the telegram is sent.

Sometimes the vendor may use an acknowledgement form of its own, which may conflict with some of the conditions stated in the purchase order. Often in such situations, a careful comparison is not made of *all* conditions stated in the offer with *all* conditions stated in the acceptance. If litigation subsequently occurs between buyer and seller, application of the UCC may resolve the question:

(1) A definite and seasonable expression of acceptance or a written confirmation which is sent within a reasonable time operates as an acceptance even though it states terms additional to or different from those offered or agreed upon unless acceptance is expressly made conditional on assent to the additional or different terms.

(2) The additional terms are to be construed as proposals for addition to the contract. Between merchants such terms become part of the contract unless:
   a. the offer expressly limits acceptance to the terms of the offer;
   b. they materially alter it; or
   c. notification of objection to them has already been given or is given within a reasonable time after notice of them is received.[4]

Thus, if the buyer does not wish to get into a dispute as to whether the vendor's acceptance ''materially'' alters any of the provisions of the original offer, on the face of the PO should be typed a statement that ''Absolutely no deviations from the terms and conditions as contained in this offer will be permitted.''

Purchases made orally

Most professional buyers have occasion to place orders over the telephone or orally in person. However, the UCC specifies that:

1. Normally there must be some written notation if the value of the order is $500.00 or more.
2. If the seller supplies a memorandum which is not in accordance with the buyer's understanding of the oral order, he or she must give a notice of objection to the supplier within ten days to preserve his legal rights.[5]

---

[4]Ibid., 2–207.
[5]Ibid., 2–201.

Authority of vendor's representatives

Another important consideration relates to the authority of the salesperson representing a company with which the purchasing officer is transacting business. Subject to the many exceptions arising out of varying circumstances, the courts have consistently held that although an employer is bound by all the acts of an agent acting within the scope of the employment, yet a salesperson's ordinary authority is simply to solicit orders and to send them to his or her employer for ratification and acceptance. It therefore behooves the purchasing officer to know definitely whether the salesperson has or does not have the authority to conclude a contract without referring it to the company which he or she represents.

Although a vendor does not authorize its salespeople to enter into binding contracts and although the company may do nothing to lead others to believe that its representative has such power, yet if the salesperson does enter into a contract with a buyer, that contract is likely to be held valid unless the seller notifies the buyer within a reasonable time that the salesperson has exceeded his or her authority. In other words, a contract results because the conduct of the employer is interpreted as acceptance. If the purchasing officer wishes assurance that the salesperson does have authority to sign the contract for the vendor, it is a simple matter to request a letter, signed by an officer of the vendor firm, specifying that the salesperson has the authority of a sales agent.

False statements on the part of the seller or its representative regarding the character of the merchandise being purchased cause the contract to become voidable at the option of the other party. It is true that his "undoubted right" to rely upon vendors' statements is at best a highly-qualified right, the value of which depends upon the circumstances surrounding the transaction. However, aside from any legal question which is involved under ordinary circumstances, the seller is likely to be sufficiently jealous of its reputation and goodwill to make substantial concessions.

One important right of the buyer is that of inspecting the goods before acceptance. The purpose of this rule is to give the buyer an opportunity to determine whether or not the goods tendered comply with the contract description. It is well established that a buyer who inspects goods before entering into a contract of sale is put on guard and is expected to use his or her own judgment with respect to quality, quantity, and other characteristics of the merchandise. The court is prone, however, to recognize circumstances which may affect the purchaser's ability to judge the accuracy of the vendor's statements. Thus, it has been held:

> In order to vitiate a contract of sale on the ground of fraudulent representations, such representations must relate to an existing fact, material to the contract, and upon which the other party has a right to rely and did rely to his injury. If the means of information as to the matters alleged to be misrepresented are equally accessible to both parties, they will be presumed to have informed themselves, and if they have not done so they must abide by the consequences of their own carelessness.

From this statement, it would seem to follow that where a purchaser accepts merchandise after inspection, either as to quality or quantity, the buyer ordinarily would be prevented from raising an issue with respect to these points. Also, a vendor cannot be held responsible for the failure of equipment to perform the work which the buyer expected of it, if the latter merely provides material specifications, without indicating to the seller the purpose to which the equipment or goods are to be put.

The courts generally have held that if a purchaser is not sufficiently experienced to be able to judge adequately the goods inspected, or if he or she relies upon a fraudulent statement made by a seller and purchases in consequence of that fraudulent statement, the buyer then may rescind the contract or hold the vendor liable for damages.

As previously stated, a purchasing officer is personally liable for the commission of any illegal act, and this liability holds even though he or she is unconscious of the illegality of the act and though it is done under the direction of the employer. A buyer is not likely to commit an illegal act consciously, but under stress of severe competition, in an effort to secure as favorable terms as possible for his company, the buyer may run afoul of the law unintentionally. It is well to remember that the antitrust acts apply to buyers quite as much as to sellers. The U.S. Supreme Court has held that these acts are applicable to all attempts to restrain trade, even though the restraint is exercised upon those not engaged in the same line of business and though based upon purchasing activities rather than selling activities, provided that the net result of the act is to restrain competition.

Cancellation of orders and breach of contract

Once a contract is made, it is expected that both parties will adhere to the agreement. Occasionally one or the other seeks to cancel the contract after it has been made. Ordinarily this is a more serious problem for the seller than it is for the buyer, although occasionally a seller may wish to avoid complying with the terms of an agreement, in which event he merely may refuse to manufacture the goods or he may delay the delivery beyond the period stipulated in the agreement. The rights of a purchaser under these circumstances depend upon the conditions surrounding the transaction. The seller is likely to be able, without liability, to delay delivering purchased goods when the buyer orders a change in the original agreement which may have the result of delaying the seller in making delivery; or if, after delayed shipment, the purchaser agrees to accept delivery.

If the seller fails to make delivery by the agreed time, the purchaser may without obligation refuse to accept delivery at a later date. However, the attempt to secure what the buyer might consider reasonable damages resulting from a breached sales contract is likely to be difficult, since the courts experience a good deal of trouble in laying down rules for the guidance of the jury in estimating the amount of damages justly allowed a buyer who sustains financial losses resulting from a seller's failure to fulfill a contract of sale. If there is a general rule, it is that the damages allowable to a purchaser if a seller fails to deliver goods according to contract are measured by the difference between the original contract price and the market value of the merchandise at the time when and at the place where the goods should have been delivered.

The seller is sometimes confronted by an attempted cancellation on the part of the buyer. It is not unusual, therefore, to find in the sales contract the following clause: "This contract is not subject to cancellation." As a matter of fact, the inclusion of such a clause has little practical effect, unless, indeed, it is intended merely to indicate to the purchaser that if he or she does attempt to cancel, a suit for breach of contract may be expected.

However, in a very strong seller's market, where the breach of contract by the seller is related to failure to deliver on a promised date or even to abide by the agreed price, the alternatives open to the buyer are almost nil. The latter still wants the goods, and may be unable to acquire them from any other suppliers any sooner or at any better price. Much the same restriction, in fact, exists even where the contract provides for the option of cancellation by the buyer. The purchaser wants goods, not damages or the right to cancel. Since the chances of getting them as promptly from any other supplier are slight, the buyer is likely to do the best he can with the original vendor provided, of course, that bad faith as to either price or delivery is not involved.

Warranties

Over time the rules governing warranty arrangements between buyer and seller have advanced from "caveat emptor" (let the buyer beware) to the legal provisions of the UCC which recognizes three types of warranties:[6]

a. Express warranty.
b. Implied warranty of merchantability.
c. Implied fitness for a particular purpose.

Essentially, express warranties include promises, specifications, samples, and descriptions pertaining to the goods which are the subject of the negotiation.

Implied warranty of merchantability has to do with the merchantable quality of goods, and the UCC statutes applying have developed out of mercantile practices. Accepted trade standards of quality, fitness for the intended uses, and conformance to promises or specified fact made on the container or label are all used as measures of marketable quality.

Implied warranty of fitness for a purpose usually results from a buyer's request for material or equipment to meet a particular need or accomplish a specific purpose. If the buyer provides detailed specification for the item requested, the seller is relieved of any warranty of fitness for a purpose.

Acceptance and rejection of goods

The acceptance of goods is an assent by the buyer to become the owner of the goods tendered by the seller. No unusual formalities are necessary to indicate

---

[6]Ibid., 2–313, 2–314, and 2–315.

that the buyer has accepted the goods. Any words or acts which indicate the buyer's intention to become the owner of the goods are sufficient. If the buyer keeps the goods and exercises rights of ownership over them, acceptance has taken place, even though he or she may have expressly stated that the goods are rejected. If the goods tendered do not comply with the sales contract,the buyer is under no duty to accept them; but if the buyer does accept the goods, he or she does not thereby waive the right to damages for the seller's breach of contract. If the buyer accepts goods which do not comply with the sales contract, the seller must be notified of the breach within a reasonable time.

The question of whether to reject goods delivered under a particular order may arise from various causes and may be dealt with in a variety of ways. For instance, the goods may be late; may have been delivered in the wrong amount; or may fail to meet the specifications. The problem for the purchasing officer is what to do under such circumstances. The important thing to keep in mind is that the purchaser wants the goods. A suit at law, therefore, is not desirable, even though the buyer is granted any one of the commonly-recognized judicial remedies for breach of contract, such as money damages, restitution, or insistence upon performance. Aside from the fact that it is goods the buyer wants, legal action is uncertain and the outcome costly; it may take a great deal of time; and it may cause the loss of a friendly supplier.

The purchasing officer therefore usually seeks other means of adjustment. Several courses are open. The first question is the seriousness of the breach. If not too serious, a simple warning to the vendor may be quite adequate. If somewhat more stringent action is called for and if the goods received are usable for some purpose, even though not quite up to specifications, a price adjustment frequently can be worked out to the mutual satisfaction of the buyer and the seller. Sometimes the goods, though not usable in the form received, may be reprocessed or otherwise made usable by the vendor, or by the purchaser at the vendor's expense. If the goods are component parts, they may be replaced by the supplier. If equipment is involved, or even processed material that is incapable of being efficiently used in its present form, the vendor may correct the defects at the user's plant. Or, as a last resort, the goods may be rejected and shipped back to the supplier, usually at the vendor's expense.

Protection against price fluctuations

Cancellations can be the direct result of action by the buyer. They arise in two ways, the first of which is not recommended. It comes about because the buyer, if compelled to live up to the agreement, would lose money. Conditions may have altered or sales may have fallen off. Therefore, the buyer no longer wants the goods. The market price may have dropped, and the buyer could now buy the goods for less money. Faced with these conditions, the buyer seeks some form of relief. He or she becomes extremely watchful of deliveries and rejects goods which arrive even a day late. Inspection is tightened up, and failure to meet any detail in the specifications is seized upon as an excuse for rejection. Such methods should never be followed by a good purchasing officer.

The second form of cancellation may arise in a perfectly legal and ethical manner, through evoking a clause—occasionally inserted in purchase contracts—which seeks to guarantee against price decline. In purchasing goods subject to price fluctuations, it is in the interests of the buyer to be protected against unreasonable prices. Occasionally a long-term contract is drawn up which leaves the determination of the exact price open until some deliveries are called for. To meet these conditions, a clause such as the following may be incorporated in purchase contracts:

> You warrant that the prices named herein are as low as any net prices now given by you to any customer for like materials, and you agree that if at any time during the life of this order you quote or sell at lower net prices similar materials under similar conditions, such lower net prices shall be substituted for the prices named herein.

These stipulations against price decline are not confined to purchase agreements; under some circumstances the buyer may receive price reductions upon the seller's initiative. An example of this type of clause is the following:

> Should the purchaser at the time of any delivery, on account of this contract, be offered a lower price on goods of equal quality and in like quantity by a reputable manufacturer, he will furnish the seller satisfactory proof of same, in which event the seller will either supply such shipment at the lower price or permit the buyer to purchase such quantity elsewhere, and the quantity so purchased elsewhere will be deducted from the total quantity of this contract. Should the seller reduce his prices during the terms of this contract, the buyer shall receive the benefit of such lower prices.

Such clauses are legally enforceable and frequently work to the buyer's advantage. However, the administrative problems in seeing to it that these clauses are lived up to are substantial. The moral effect doubtlessly is greater than the legal.

Title to purchased goods •   F.O.B.

The professional buyer should have a clear understanding of when the title of goods passes from the seller to the buyer. Normally, there will be an agreement on the f.o.b. (free on board) point, and the buyer receives title at that point. On capital goods it is particularly important for tax and depreciation reasons to establish title before the tax year ends.

In some instances, the buyer is given possession of the goods prior to the passing of a legal title. This is known as a "conditional sales contract." and the full title passes to the buyer only when final payment is made. This procedure permits a buyer to obtain needed material now and to pay at some future time.

Unless a buyer furnishes specifications which infringe on a patent, the seller has the basic responsibility for providing a guarantee that there is no patent infringement on the products sold.

Commercial arbitration

Regardless of the type of contract, disputes sooner or later will arise. These disagreements are annoying, and, for reasons that have been given, it usually is not advantageous to go to the court over them. In the majority of cases they are settled by some compromise. Occasions do arise when such compromises cannot be effected. To meet these situations and yet to avoid the necessity for resorting to a court of law, arbitration clauses frequently are included in commercial contracts. These provide that an impartial arbitrator, or panel of arbitrators, will listen to the evidence and then render a judgment, which both parties to the dispute have agreed in advance to accept, without appeal. This is much less costly and time consuming than court action.

However, merely because the contract includes a provision calling for arbitration, the purchasing officer may not be as fully covered as many have believed. There are prepared arbitration clauses which are valid, irrevocable, and enforceable under the arbitration laws[7] of certain states, notably: New York, New Jersey, Pennsylvania, Massachusetts, California, Louisiana, Connecticut, Rhode Island, New Hampshire, Arizona, Oregon, Ohio, and Wisconsin. For matters under jurisdiction of the federal courts, there is the Federal Arbitration Law. Even in states which do not have such laws, it is possible to demand arbitration if provision is made for the necessary procedure in the contract, and if there is a statute making "*future* disputes" the subject of binding arbitration agreements.

The use of arbitration clauses in contracts is a reasonable measure of protection against costly litigation. To ensure this protection, the following queries should be made with reference to arbitration clauses which are to be incorporated in commercial agreements:

1. Is your clause in proper form under the appropriate arbitration laws? Unless properly drawn it may not be legally valid, irrevocable, and enforceable.

2. Does your clause fully express the will of the parties or is it ambiguous? If it is uncertain in its terms, the time and expense involved in determining the scope of the clause and the powers of the arbitrators under it may destroy its value or increase costs.

3. Does your clause assure the appointment of impartial arbitrators? If a person serving as arbitrator is an agent, advocate, relative, or representative of a party, or has a personal interest in the matter being arbitrated, the award rendered may be vacated by the court on the ground of evident corruption or partiality on the part of an arbitrator.

4. Does your clause provide adequately, by reference to the rules of an Association or otherwise, for a method of naming arbitrators, thus safeguarding against deadlocks or defaults in the proceedings? If not, the actual hearing of the dispute may be unduly delayed, and the practical value of the arbitration may be defeated.

---

[7]The *Code of Arbitration Practice and Procedure* of the American Arbitration Association contains full information on the arbitration laws of the various states.

QUESTIONS FOR REVIEW AND DISCUSSION

1. Under what conditions is it realistic for a buyer to cancel a contract? For a seller to cancel a contract?

2. Does a vendor have to accept a PO exactly as offered by the buyer to create a legally-binding contract? Explain.

3. How much knowledge of the legal aspects of purchasing should a buyer have?

4. What is commercial arbitration? When and how should it be used?

5. Does a salesperson have basically the same legal authority as a buyer? If not, how do they differ?

6. What are the legal rights of the buyer if goods delivered by a vendor do not measure up to the specifications?

7. Under what conditions might a purchasing agent be held personally liable for contracts he or she enters into?

8. Is an oral contract legally enforceable? Under what conditions?

9. What authority does a purchasing agent have to make decisions which are binding on the principal?

CASE 12-1
THE CROSS ARMS

Suffolk Power Corporation was building three additional generating stations to serve the rapidly expanding energy market. To link these stations with the total area grid a new method of carrying the power lines using ornamental tubular poles instead of towers had been adopted. Suffolk was unfamiliar with poles and decided to subcontract the design engineering fabrication, and erection of the new line. [For company background, line project information, and the selection of engineering consultants see Suffolk Power Corporation (A). For selection of pole manufacturers see Suffolk Power Corporation (B). For selection of foundation and erection contractors see Suffolk Power Corporation (C).]

Work on the Addison-Smithfield section of the new power line was progressing well. All of the poles had been manufactured, tested, and received. Foundation work was 30 percent complete, and 10 percent of the poles had been erected. None of the wire had been strung yet. The engineering consultants had completed their assignment. The graceful new poles had already attracted favorable attention from Suffolk employees and the public.

On February 24, on a clear, crisp day, almost two years after the board of directors had approved the new line, the bad news hit like a thunderbolt. The cross arms on several of the newly installed poles were hanging limply along the pole for no apparent reason! Consternation struck Suffolk head-quarters. Weather conditions during the last month had been ideal. The previous night there had been only a slight breeze. Engineering tests of poles and cross arms showed that all specifications had been met. The installation contractor had followed proper procedures as far as anyone could tell.

A helicopter was used to inspect all poles, and no visible defects appeared on the cross arms which had not collapsed. Although speculation abounded, no one could assign a cause for the defects. Suffolk engineers dismantled the stricken poles and took sections into the laboratory. No one was sure how long it would be before an explanation could be found. Mr. Carter, director of purchases, wondered what action, if any, he should take with respect to the three subcontractors used on the project. The engineering consultants, the pole manufacturer, and the erector had all been involved at various stages. Whether all or any were to blame for the current mishaps was not clear. Within 24 hours of the first report of cross arm failure, three additional poles showed cross arms collapse.

CASE 12-2
THE CONTRACT

Mr. John Peters, president of Carlyn Corporation, returned from his visit to Blondin with a feeling of satisfaction. He had just finished negotiating what he considered a good price for the purchase of MS-7. He called Messrs. Harper, Grove, and Thomas into his office to tell them the good news. He finished his account by instructing Mr. Bill Thomas, purchasing manager, "to carry the ball from here on in." He also said: "Bill, Blondin asked us to stay away from them for awhile because they won't start up till later on anyway and because they are all busy on a new product introduction right now. So there is no hurry on this thing, but they want you to get in touch with them in October." Mr. Thomas replied: "That suits me just as well, anyway, with the holiday season coming up and everything else, I'll have things ready to roll in October for sure."

For the remainder of July and all of August the MS-7 file lay unattended, but early in September Mr. Thomas decided he had better start getting ready for his October meeting with Blondin. He knew that a formal contract should be drawn up, and on the basis of a friend's purchasing advice he felt it would be useful if Carlyn presented a contract at his first meeting with Blondin. This would mean some extra preparatory work for him now, but it could speed up final agreement on all terms later on. He was, therefore, wondering what type of initial contract to use.

Several years earlier Mr. Thomas had become concerned about his lack of knowledge in the design of formal purchase contracts. Through his membership in the National Association of Purchasing Management, he had become acquainted with Mr. Tom Shaw, director of purchases of Major Chemicals and generally known in the trade as a highly competent negotiator. He voiced his dissatisfaction to Mr. Shaw at a committee meeting they both attended, and Mr. Shaw invited Mr. Thomas to Philadelphia to see what Major Chemicals could do to help.

Mr. Thomas visited Major Chemical's purchasing department, and he was tremendously impressed. Mr. Shaw had arranged a number of appointments with various experts in contracts at Major, and Mr. Thomas spent a whole day learning from the "pros."

At the end of the day Mr. Shaw offered Mr. Thomas a sample blank contract which Major had found useful. Mr. Thomas had altered this contract slightly by substituting his own company's name on it (see Exhibit 1). He also had a few comments typed up resulting from his conversations during this Major visit (see Exhibit 2).

Exhibit 1
A general guide to negotiations and form of agreement for contracts of short duration and period price adjustment provision (Special provisions for individual cases to be added)

THIS AGREEMENT made and entered in this _____ day of _____ 19_____
by and between _____ (hereinafter referred to as "SELL-
ER") and CARLYN CORPORATION, INC., CHICAGO, ILLINOIS, (hereinafter

WITNESSETH:

The SELLER agrees to sell and deliver and the BUYER agrees to purchase and accept the material specified herein upon the following terms and conditions:

1. MATERIAL:
(Describe material in general terms, e.g., tubular containers, sulphuric acid, caustic soda, etc.) as specifically set forth in Schedule "A" attached hereto and made a part hereof.

2. SPECIFICATIONS:
The material(s) delivered by SELLER to BUYER hereunder shall meet the specifications set forth in Schedule "A" attached hereto and made a part hereof.

3. QUANTITY:
_____ percent of BUYER'S requirements for its _____
plant(s). SELLER to supply additional _____ percent of BUYER'S requirements if so requested by BUYER. Total annual requirements estimated at _____
_____.

4. PRICE:
In accordance with Schedule "B" attached hereto. The basic price (s) stated herein may be adjusted:

Yearly
Semiannually } by SELLER for subsequent periods
Quarterly

In accordance with Schedule "B" attached hereto. The basic price (s) stated herein may be adjusted:

Exhibit 1 *(continued)*

Quarter
Semiannual period
Annual period

Such price(s) shall be paid for all materials ordered hereunder on or after the date they become effective, unless subsequently again revised by the SELLER as provided herein. If any proposed increase is unacceptable to BUYER and SELLER is unwilling to offer the material at a price which is acceptable to BUYER, then BUYER shall have the right either to cancel from the agreement any portion of the material to be supplied hereunder so affected by the increase or to cancel this agreement in its entirety, providing BUYER gives SELLER written notice thereof on or before the effective date of the proposed price increase.

Notwithstanding the provisions of this clause 4 it is accepted by the parties that from time to time revisions may be made to the specifications on the request of either party. Any change in the specifications or the price arising out of such revisions is to be agreed upon mutually by the parties before such changes in specifications or price become effective.

5. TERM OF PAYMENT:

_____ % _____ days from date of monthly invoice.
Net _____ days from date of monthly invoice.

6. MEET OR RELEASE:
Should BUYER be offered any of the material specified hereunder of at least equal quality or material which BUYER considers equivalent at a lower delivered cost on a 100-percent contained basis to BUYER than the effective price hereunder and/or under more favorable terms or conditions, then SELLER shall either supply such quantities of material at the lower competitive price and/or under the improved terms or conditions offered to the BUYER or permit BUYER to purchase elsewhere such quantities, and this will result in a corresponding reduction of the BUYER'S obligations under this agreement.

7. MOST FAVORED NATIONS:
Should the SELLER during the term of this contract, sell or offer to sell any of the materials specified hereunder or materials which BUYER considers equivalent at a lower price than that in effect hereunder or under more favorable terms or conditions, the SELLER undertakes to notify the BUYER at once of the detail and timing of the sale or offer including the period for which either is effective, and the quantity involved and BUYER shall receive the benefit of such lower price or more favorable terms or conditions at BUYER'S option either for similar quantities or for the period they are effective or offered to be effective.

8. MEASUREMENT OF QUANTITY DELIVERED:
The amount of material deemed to have been delivered shall be determined by

_____ .

9. SHIPPING METHOD:
The above material shall be shipped in

SELLER'S   Tank cars
BUYER'S   Tank trucks
                   Other (specify)

Exhibit 1 *(continued)*

10. SUSPENSION:

If at any time the material delivered hereunder is not in accordance with the specifications set forth therefor or if delivery is not in accordance with BUYER'S instructions or if SELLER refuses or is unable to supply for any reason, BUYER reserves the right to purchase elsewhere until such time as SELLER demonstrates to BUYER'S satisfaction that said conditions have been corrected. Any quantities so purchased elsewhere will reduce BUYER'S obligations hereunder.

11. TERM OF CONTRACT:

_____ to _____

12. FORCE MAJEURE:

No liability hereunder shall result to either party from delay in performance or nonperformance caused by circumstances beyond the control of the party affected, including, but not limited to, act of God, fire, flood, war, government regulation, direction or request, accident, labor trouble or shortage of or inability to obtain material, equipment, or transportation. Deficiencies in deliveries hereunder due to such causes shall not be made up by the SELLER except by mutual agreement in writing. During periods of force majeure BUYER is entitled to receive a share of the available production in the proportion that BUYER'S contracted deliveries bear to the total contractual deliveries of the SELLER.

13. PATENTS:

SELLER warrants that the use or sale of the materials delivered hereunder will not infringe the claims of any AMERICAN patent.

14. ASSIGNMENT:

This agreement is not assignable or transferable by either party without the written consent of the other party.

15. ENTIRETY:

This agreement constitutes the entire contract of sale and purchase of the material(s) hereunder.

Failure on the part of either party in any one or more instances to insist upon the keeping, performance, or observance of any of the terms, conditions, or provisions of this contract shall not be construed or interpreted, and shall not operate, as a relinquishment of such party's rights to require the future keeping, performance, or observance of any such terms, conditions, or performance.

16. DEFAULT AND TERMINATION:

If either SELLER or BUYER shall fail to perform any of the convenants or obligations imposed upon it by the contract then in such event the other party may at its option terminate said contract by proceeding as follows: the party not in default stating specifically the default and requesting the defaulting party to remedy such default within thirty (30) days; if within said period of thirty (30) days the party in default does remedy the said default and fully indemnify the party not in default for any and all consequences of such breach, then the contract shall continue in full force and effect. In case the party in default does not so remedy the default or does not indemnify the party giving notice for any and all consequences of such breach, within said period of thirty (30) days, then at the option of the party giving notice, the contract shall terminate. Any termination of the contract pursuant to the provisions of this paragraph shall be without prejudice to the right of the SELLER to collect any

Exhibit 1 *(concluded)*

amounts then due to it for material delivered prior to the time of termination and shall be without prejudice to the right of the BUYER to receive any materials which it has not received but for which it has paid prior to the time of termination, and without waiver of any remedy to which the party not in default may be entitled for breach of the contract.

By _____

Title _____

CARLYN CORPORATION, INC.

By _____

Title _____

March, 1973

Exhibit 2
Some special comments concerning contracts by Major Chemical's purchasing staff

1. Never commit yourself to a major contract without legal opinion.
2. It is useful to draw up your own contract before the supplier has a chance to submit his own as a basis for discussion.
3. A contract is never a one-way street. Both parties have to live with it.
4. Usually draw up contracts for purchases one year and over in length.
5. Do not allow price adjustment on one-year contracts if you can help it, if supplier wants price adjustment only on that portion of cost subject to change. For example, if he argues his labor costs may go up and labor is 20 percent of total cost, keep him tied to this 20 percent of total cost as the only portion subject to change. Also find a reasonable index to tie price increases to. Historical review must be carried out, and supplier may offer alternatives.
6. Try to sign "requirements" contracts without a firm commitment to take or pay but may have to settle for as low as commitment as you can get. Sometimes it's useful to sign up for 90 percent of requirements and to leave 10 percent for competition. At the end of a contract ask for a period of time to evaluate other sources and allow for deliveries from other suppliers.
7. Sometimes it is useful to ask the seller for a price on his uncommitted plant capacity if he has any just in case you underestimated your requirements.
8. It may be useful in some cases to ask the supplier to carry a certain minimum amount of inventory as part of the overall agreement to assure a reasonable continuity of supply under other than force majeure situations.
9. Sellers occasionally want forecasts more than a year ahead. Make it clear that you are willing to give these only as the best indication you have to date but that you do not consider yourself bound in any way by them. Forecasts of this kind can be made in quarters for the following year and in annual amounts for succeeding years.
10. A contract is exactly what you make it. As long as you deal with a reputable supplier you may never have to pull it out. You can request his cost figures if this is what you agreed to, and on "requirements" contracts the seller can come and see that you are using the proper percentage of material. There must be mutual trust on each side.

Although Mr. Thomas had felt much better about his contract knowledge after his visit to Major, he did not have an opportunity to use the sample contract until the MS–7 deal, and he decided to try it out. As soon as he got started, however, he began to wonder what exactly to put down and what terms to insist on. He began to wonder if what applied to Major really applied to Carlyn. Yet, he was intrigued and decided he should give it a try. This meant he should decide whether price adjustments should be allowed, and, if so, what index to use. He also wondered if the meet or release and most favored nations clauses had any meaning in his case where only one buyer and one supplier existed. He saw these as some of his obvious problems, but he realized that others would crop up as he got involved more deeply.

CASE 12–3
JONES & BOND

Mr. Carter, director of purchases for Suffolk Power Corporation, had just received a legal opinion from Jones & Bond regarding the cross arm failure on a new power line. Suffolk had run into major problems during the erection phase of the new ornamental tubular poles, and Mr. Carter was anxious to assure early safe operation of the line. He was not sure on how to proceed with respect to repairs and recovery of additional costs since three different suppliers had participated in the project. [For company and power line background information and the selection of engineering consultants see Suffolk Power Corporation (A). For selection of pole manufacturers see Suffolk Power Corporation (B). For selection of foundation and erection contractors see Suffolk Power Corporation (C). For cross arm failure see The Cross Arms.

At the time of the cross arm failure it was not clear what caused the problem. Only after extensive engineering tests which lasted almost three months was the prime cause found. Had the conductors.been strung immediately or had the insulators been installed, as had been normal practice in all other tubular steel pole erections in this country, failure of the arms within a month of installation would not have occurred.

Mr. Carter had advised all three suppliers involved of the difficulties as soon as they arose. All three expressed concern and almost claimed their part of the job could not have been responsible and that all work had been done to specifications. All offered to be of any assistance they could and gave a number of suggestions throughout the research phase. All of the work on the line was halted until the reason for the failure was clear. Once the real cause was found, engineering was able to make recommendations for repair and strengthening which would prevent reoccurrence of the same difficulties (see Exhibit 1). Purchasing had obtained preliminary estimates showing an additional cost of about $1.8 million. Mr. Carter had written a letter to Suffolk Power's legal firm, Jones & Bond summarizing the situation to date (see Exhibit 2).

Jones & Bond had met with Mr. Carter five days later and confirmed their statements in this meeting by letter the following day (see Exhibit 3).

Twenty-six months had now passed since the beginning of the three-year project (see Exhibit 4). Suffolk Power Corporation was facing tremendous demand pressures for more power and simultaneously had not received particularly favorable treatment with rate increase requests. Mr. Carter was not sure where the extra funds to repair the cross arms would come from. The very high demand for capital in the corporation made it imperative that every avenue be explored to recover the extra costs to be incurred on the line. Workers had expressed fear about working near and with the poles. Since on time completion and safety were also both of the highest priority, Mr. Carter wondered what action to take next.

Exhibit 1
Suffolk Power Corporation
System Engineering Department

Memorandum: (Excerpt)

Re: Replacement of Henry Nelson Company—345KV Cross Arms—Addison-Smithfield-Mesa Valley

It is required that all the groundwire and conductor cross arms on the line be removed and replaced by modified or new cross arms. It is the purpose of this correspondence to review the problems that have occurred and to outline a specific specification for the handling of these damaged cross arms. We will also continue the procedures for the installation of new cross arms on poles already erected and on new poles which have not been erected.

Through an extensive engineering research program, it was determined that the existing Nelson Company cross arms have low fatigue properties. The existing cross arm will fail by low velocity wind induced (aeolian) vibration which can cause a fatigue failure in less than a month. Secondly, the cross arm can fail by fatigue over a period of approximately 15 years by the continuing reversal of stresses due to the galloping of the conductors.

The problem of aeolian vibration can be resolved by the use of dampening devices mounted on the ends of the cross arms. Examples would be the use of insulator strings on the conductor cross arms and stockbridge dampers on the groundwire cross arms. The problem of designing for galloping requires the reduction of the stress level at the weldment of the cross arm shaft to the cross arm baseplate. This can be accomplished by the use of stiffener bars on existing cross arms which have been fabricated but not erected. It can be accomplished on the damaged arms by the use of new thicker baseplates for the conductor cross arms. On new cross arms to be fabricated, there will be some of both of the types previously described.

Summary of estimates

Damaged arm repair	
1,310–Structures Canadian	$ 373,126.30
Nondamaged arm repair	
1,245–Structures Canadian	232,294.22
3,007–Henry Nelson	314,215.20
Contractor–remove and replace	820,000.00
Research costs	100,000.00
Total	$1,839,635.72

Exhibit 2
Suffolk Power Corporation
Director of Purchases

Memorandum to: Mr. T. R. Bond
Subject: Ornamental Poles and Arms

The company has experienced a most unfortunate failure of the eight arms of each of its first 345KV ornamental tubular steel pole transmission line. The failure results in our believing that we should try to recover our losses from two or all of the three contractors involved in (1) engineering, (2) designing and fabricating, and (3) erecting these poles and arms.

We purchased the engineering assistance from Pettigrew Associates of New York, N.Y. This contract issued two years ago covered the technical assistance we needed to: lay out the line circling our service area from Addison to Smithfield to Mesa Valley substations; the drawing up of specifications for our use in obtaining bids on the poles, arms and appurtenances; and their assistance to us in the evaluation of the bids on poles and arms when received.

Pettigrew Associates performed the services required by this contract according to the original schedule, and we had no idea that there was any difficulty with any of their performance until failure of the arms occurred. An analysis of the failure of the arms proved that failure was occasioned by what is known as the aeolian effect of wind on these free standing poles and arms. Had the insulators and cables been installed immediately as the poles and arms were constructed, there apparently would have been no failures; but our erection contractor chose to erect the poles and arms and then return months later to install the insulators and cables. It is well proven now that neither McTaggart Construction Company (our erector), the Nelson Company (the pole and arm fabricator), nor Pettigrew Associates (the engineer), or Suffolk knew of the possible low velocity wind induced vibration (aeolian) that could cause arm fatigue and failure. Pettigrew contends they did not draw up a detailed specification for poles and arms but rather a "performance" type specification.

Suffolk contends that the performance specifications should have included sufficient performance description to permit the poles to be erected without arm failure, and, if the aeolian effect existed and was a construction parameter that should have been avoided, they should have known it and so specified.

Suffolk awarded its contract for the designing, furnishing, and fabricating of poles and arms to the H. Nelson Company of Dallas, Texas. Our testing has proven that the poles and arms that Nelson Company designed and furnished to Suffolk would have withstood all of the performance requirements had we installed the insulators or some type of dampeners on the arms and not subjected them to the wind induced vibration in the freestanding condition. H. Nelson Company claims no knowledge of the aeolian effect. All arms need to be reworked and given more strength through the use of heavier materials; but this is not because of the aeolian effect but rather to strengthen the arms to withstand "galloping" conditions of the cables that develop in certain wind conditions. Perhaps Pettigrew Associates were derelict in not protecting us from this possible hazard also.

The McTaggart Construction Company in Indianapolis was awarded our contract for unloading of the poles and arms, installation of the foundations, erection of the poles and arms, and the stringing of the wire and cables. In our discussion of the arm failure with McTaggart, we attempted to point out their contributing to the failure by not installing insulators or dampeners and/or the cables and wires immediately upon

Exhibit 2 (continued)

erection of the poles and arms. They claimed they have erected lattice steel towers and ornamental poles and arms for many years without any concern or knowledge of the aeolian effect of wind-induced vibration and, therefore, could not know they had such an erection hazard to contend with. They have put insulators on while erecting on other tubular pole jobs, but they did it because of other erection problems—not the wind vibration.

We have attempted to have each of these companies assume obligation for our losses but to no avail yet. The costs likely to be incurred are as follows:

a. Rework of arms at Nelson Co. ....$ 314,215.20
b. Rework of a portion of the arms at
   Structures Canadian 605,420.52
c. Installation costs to be paid to
   McTaggart Construction 820,000.00
d. Suffolk's cost (study and processing) 100,000.00
   Total Cost $1,839,635.72

Your immediate attention to this matter would be very much appreciated.

John Carter

**Exhibit 3
Jones & Bond
Attorneys and Counselors
Chicago, Illinois**

Mr. John Carter,
Director of Purchases,
Suffolk Power Corporation.
Dear Mr. Carter:

Re: 345KV Transmission Pole Failures

This will confirm our opinion as expressed at the meeting held in your office on Monday. As you will recall, two basic legal matters were discussed, to wit: the possible bases of liability of the three parties involved and whether the Company would jeopardize its rights by proceeding to repair the poles without first consulting any of those parties.

Concerning the latter, if the Company is entitled to recover from anyone, it can reasonably expect to recover the cost of correcting the problem. The cost of doing so must be reasonable, and the repair must also be reasonably likely to correct the problem. In other words you cannot recover for a "gold plating" job, nor can you recover the cost of a repair which does not correct the problem. This right to recover is not affected by a failure to negotiate in advance with any party against which a claim might be made. If, however, any such party is consulted in advance of the commencement of a repair program and is given a chance to participate in determining the repair to be used, the chances of later being required to defend either the necessity of that repair or its cost would be greatly reduced.

With respect to the liabilities of each party, the contracts and related documents have been reviewed in detail on the basis of the Company's findings that the cause of the damage to the pole arms was wind vibration, which can be substantially avoided by dampening the arms with conductors, rather than letting the bare arms stand. As

Exhibit 3 *(continued)*
stated at the meeting, the bases for potential liability of each party can be set out, and
the Company can then assess the value of each on the basis of the known facts.

McTaggart Construction Company performed its services pursuant to a detailed
contract which covered the work to be done but which did not provide any specific
rights or remedies for a situation like the one now faced. In order to recover from
McTaggart, whether on a theory of breach of contract or of negligence, it will be
necessary to show that in erecting the poles, McTaggart did not exercise the degree of
care, skill, and diligence that a reasonably competent contractor, purporting to be
able to erect poles and lines, would have exercised. The McTaggart contract does
not, in our opinion, impose any burden upon McTaggart for engineering or design
adequacy.

As for Henry Nelson Company, their contract consists of a purchase order with
detailed specifications attached thereto. There are no commercial terms, such as
warranties, in the contract which relate directly to the arm failure problem. There are,
however, four (4) possible bases of liability, which are:

1. *Faulty design:* this would require that Nelson be shown to have had general design responsibility and that the current problem is a result of faulty design. The
   principal problem in this area is that the contract appears to give Nelson the
   burden of designing to Pettigrew Associates' specifications only.
2. *Breach of warranty:* if Nelson had reason to know the use to which the poles
   would be put and to know that Suffolk was relying on Nelson's skill and ability to
   produce a product fit for that purpose, then there would be in the contract an
   implied warranty that the poles would be fit for the purpose for which they were
   intended to be used. The primary weakness here is that the poles may well be fit
   for their ultimate intended use, and it would be necessary to show that Nelson
   knew or had reason to know that the poles would be erected and left standing
   without conductors.
3. *Failure to detail assembly procedures:* Section 14 of the Pettigrew Specification
   indicates in part that "the Vendor shall provide sketches indicating assembly procedures and the most desirable attachment points for raising the structures." With
   the benefit of hindsight, it can be argued that this includes the responsibility to
   direct that the arms be hung with conductors, although there seems to be general
   agreement that this is not necessarily what 14 was intended to cover.
4. *Failure to comply with the National Electrical Safety Code:* 24 of the Pettigrew
   specification requires compliance with the N.E.S.C., and it appears that there may
   be some basis for asserting that Nelson did not comply. This depends, as I understand it, largely upon whether the relevant section of the N.E.S.C. can be construed as covering poles erected without conductors.

Finally, as regards Pettigrew Associates, the Company has a contract pursuant to
which Pettigrew is selected ". . . to perform the Engineering and Design services in
connection with (the) Addison-Smithfield-Mesa Valley 345KV Transmission Line
Project." Article I provides that Pettigrew will ". . . furnish complete project administration for coordinating and expediting the Work" and is to perform services
". . . of the highest professional character . . ." with Pettigrew being ". . . fully responsible to Suffolk for the correctness of the engineering design and related data
. . .," which included pole design, In addition, Pettigrew evaluated all bids, including
designs offered, and recommended the award to H. Nelson. If it can be shown either

Exhibit 3 *(concluded)*

that the engineering design and related data were not correct or were not of the highest professional quality, then the Company should have a sound cause of action against Pettigrew. I might add that the term "incorrect" can readily be construed to include omissions. As for the professional quality ground, it would be necessary to introduce expert testimony or evidence, or both, to establish that a top-quality engineer would have at least considered the wind vibration problem.

Depending on the facts which you are able to establish, the Company may have a cause of action against one or more of the parties involved. We would be pleased to assist you further, should you so request, in progressing any claim the Company may wish to make.

Yours very truly,
T. R. Bond

Exhibit 4
Suffolk Power Corporation
Timetable for the new Addison-Smithfield-Mesa Valley power line

Year 1:	
March	Management approves use of ornamental tubular steel poles for the 140-mile line.
April–July	Preliminary work and search for engineering consultant.
August	Pettigrew Associates selected as consulting engineers to prepare pole specifications, line layout, and assist in selection of manufacturer and erection.
Year 2:	
March	Pettigrew Associates submits pole specifications and line layout.
April–July	Engineering and purchasing evaluation of manufacturing of poles for the first half of the line.
July	H. Nelson selected as the pole manufacturer.
June–September	Engineering and purchasing evaluation of foundation and erection contractors.
September	McTaggart Construction chosen for both foundation and erection of the new line.
October	Delivery of test poles by H. Nelson. Tests prove poles meet specifications.
January	Installation starts. New poles draw favorable employee and public attention.
February 20	H. Nelson completes manufacture of poles for Addison-Smithfield section.
February 24	First cross arm failure noted. Purchasing notifies all three suppliers. All deny blame.
February 26	All project work halted.
Year 3:	
March–April	Continuing pole cross arm failures. Engineering search for causes.
May 11	Engineering determines reason for failure.
May 25	Purchasing determines repair costs.
May 25	Mr. Carter sends memo to Jones & Bond for a legal opinion.
May 30	Jones & Bond representatives meet with Mr. Carter.
May 31	Letter from T. R. Bond confirming legal opinion.
Year 4:	
April 30	Project deadline.

PURCHASING TRANSPORTATION SERVICES 13

 Purchased goods must be transported from the point they are grown, mined, or manufactured to the place needed. The purchase of transportation services demands a high degree of skill and knowledge, if the costs of movement are to be minimized while at the same time meeting service needs. Due to the complexity of the transportation industry and the multitude of rules and regulations, getting best value for an organization's transportation dollar involves much more than simply "getting the best transportation rate."

The total transportation costs in the United States for movement of goods has been estimated to be well over $100 billion and a very large share of that total is for the movement of goods from the vendor's facility to the point where the industrial buyer needs them. Depending on the type of goods being moved, transportation may account for as much as 40 percent of the total cost of the item, particularly if it is of relatively low value and bulky, such as construction materials. But in the case of very high value, low weight and bulk electronics goods, transport costs may be less than one percent of total purchase costs.

If minimization of costs were the only objective in buying transportation services, the task would be easy. However, the transportation buyer must look not only at cost but also at service provided. For example, items are purchased to meet a production schedule, and the available modes of transport require different amounts of transport time. If items are shipped by a method requiring a long shipment time, inventory may be exhausted and a plant or process shut down before the items arrive. Also, reliability may differ substantially among various transportation companies and service levels, lost shipments, and damage may very greatly between two different carriers. The buyer should use the same skill and attention in selecting carriers as used in selecting vendors.

Organization for transportation decision

Due to the large number of dollars involved in the movement of goods into and out of an organization and the potential effect on profits, large firms have a separate traffic department with specialists in areas such as selection of carriers and routing, determination of freight classification and rates, tracing shipments, and handling claims in the case of loss or damage to goods during shipment. In the very large firm, the transportation function even may be specialized further, based on the purpose of shipment. For example, an automobile producer may

451

have three separate transportation departments, one concerned with incoming materials shipments, one making the decisions on in-plant and inter-plant materials movement, and the third concerned with the shipment of finished goods through the distribution channels to customers. In an organization operating under the materials management concept, the traffic manager typically will report to the director of materials and may have responsibility for all types of materials movement. This traffic manager must recognize that handling and shipping of raw materials and finished goods does not add value to the product itself. Instead, it is a key cost element in the operation of the firm and should be managed to minimize costs, within the parameters of needed service.

In the medium-size and smaller organization, the number of traffic decisions may not be large enough to warrant a full-time traffic specialist. Here the transport decisions are handled by the buyer or purchasing manager. This means that the buyer must have enough knowledge to make decisions on preferred f.o.b. terms, classification of freight, selection of carriers and routing, determination of freight rates, preparation of necessary documentation, expediting and tracing of freight shipments, filing and settlement of claims for loss or damage in transit, and payment procedures for transport services received. While some claim that the purchase of transportation services is simply another commodity or service and can be handled the same as other purchasing decisions, the complexity of this area makes it a very difficult area of decision making for the buyer.

Basic principles of the common carrier system

Over the past several decades, various laws, regulations, and interpretations have established the basic framework within which the common carrier system operates. While this umbrella is constantly changing, the buyer should be aware of the basic principles.

No discrimination. Common carriers enjoy the status of a public utility, in the sense that they are granted the right to service shippers at various geographical points and are protected against competition from new entrants into the market; in effect, they are in a monopoly position. Therefore, they may not discriminate among customers and are obligated to offer the same services to both small and large shippers, and at consistent rates. Of course, lower rates for volume shipments are permissible, much the same as quantity discounts may be justified for larger buyers. In addition, to begin service, a common carrier must make application to the appropriate regulatory agency and show that it is responsible and able to provide adequate service. It cannot begin service until approval has been granted, and it cannot discontinue serving an unprofitable route in order to concentrate on a more profitable one. The argument for this is that the volume of business on profitable routes will be balanced off against losses on marginal or unprofitable routes, and that the services to out-of-the-way locations are necessary for the public good.

Basically, when a carrier receives permission to engage in interstate transportation, it agrees to serve both large and small shippers, wherever they are located on the routes granted, and to give them equal treatment and at equal rates.

Inherent advantages of different transport modes. Each form of common carrier transportation, e.g., rail, truck, or air, has its own distinct advantages for shippers in respect to speed, available capacity, flexibility, and cost. By the same token, each mode has inherent disadvantages. For example, comparing air with truck transport, air has the advantage in terms of speed and time; truck transport can accommodate greater volume and has lower rates and greater flexibility in terms of delivery points. The astute buyer must recognize these advantages/ limitations and arrive at the best overall balance, considering the needs of the organization.

Regulation of carriers •

For the past 100 years, the transportation industry has been closely regulated under laws passed by Congress and regulations promulgated by various regulatory agencies. These laws generally were passed to assure that transport services are available in all geographic areas and without discrimination. Figure 13–1 presents a brief summary of the applicable transport laws.

Department of Transportation (DOT). This is an arm of the executive branch of government and is headed by a Secretary, who has cabinet status. It was established by Congress in 1966 with responsibilities of safety, systems, technology, and mass transit development. Operating under the DOT are three regulatory agencies:

1. Civil Aeronautics Board (CAB)
2. Federal Maritime Commission (FMC)
3. Interstate Commerce Commission (ICC)

The intent of Congress was "to concentrate and allocate federal resources in order to attain an integrated national transportation system, to identify significant transportation problems, to provide executive leadership in transportation, and to provide policy guidance . . ."[1]

Civil Aeronautics Board (CAB). The CAB, as it operates today, is an outgrowth of the Civil Aeronautics Act of 1938, the Presidential reorganization action of 1940, the Air Cargo Act of 1977, and the Airline Deregulation Act of 1978. The CAB has authority to regulate air carrier operations, including rates, routes, service levels, operating routes, and proposed mergers, consolidations, and abandonments; and it determines the necessity for and grants subsidies needed to provide specific service levels. It also monitors international air transportation and grants, subject to Presidential approval, international operating routes, and rights to both U.S. and foreign air carriers. The primary responsibility of the CAB is to assure reasonable and adequate service to the public, avoid undue discrimination among various classes of customers, and discourage unfair competitive practices.

---

[1] Grant Millar Davis, *The Department of Transportation* (Lexington, Mass: Heath Lexington Books, 1970), p. 2.

Federal Maritime Commission (FMC). The FMC was organized in 1961, although it has regulatory powers similar to those of its predecessor agencies. Three areas are of concern: (1) regulation of U.S. common carriers by water in foreign trade; (2) regulation of U.S water carriers in domestic, offshore service, such as between U.S. mainland ports and Alaska, Hawaii, or Puerto Rico; and (3) control of freight rates of common ocean carriers in domestic offshore service. The FMC has much less regulatory power over oceanborne foreign commerce, due to the freedom of the seas principle.

→ **Interstate Commerce Commission (ICC).** The ICC is the oldest of the regulatory agencies, dating from 1887. The original Act has been amended several times and now is known simply as the Interstate Commerce Act. The ICC regulates, in varying degrees, all surface carrier modes of transport, including (1) establishment of operating rights, routes, and freight rates; (2) mergers, expansions, and abandonments; (3) award of damages and administration of railroad bankruptcies; (4) development of uniform systems of accounts and records for carriers; (5) investigation and authorization of the issuance of securities or the assumption of financial obligations by railroads and certain motor vehicle common or contract carriers; and (6) development of emergency preparedness programs for rail, motor, and inland waterway transportation. The specific aspects of the ICC Act of interest to freight movers are: (1) Part I, which covers railroads and pipelines; (2) Part II, added in 1935, on motor carriers; (3) Part III, added in 1940, covering water carriers; and (4) Part IV, added in 1942, covering freight forwarders.

Under ICC jurisdiction, common carriers are required to:

1. furnish adequate freight transportation upon reasonable request.

2. cooperate with other carriers in establishing reasonable through rates so that adequate service is available over the entire transport system.

3. establish fair and reasonable freight classifications and rates.

To accomplish the above three objectives, the ICC is divided into three divisions: Division I handles operating rights; Division II handles rates, tariffs, and valuation; and Division III handles finance and service. In addition, there are five bureaus within the ICC which do most of the data gathering and analysis as needed by any of the three divisions. These bureaus also handle many of the matters which do not need the attention and review of the full Commission. These bureaus are:

1. *Bureau of Accounts:* does the necessary accounting and cost collection data so that financial data on specific carrier's operating results are complete, uniform, and accurate.

2. *Bureau of Economics:* generates statistical data, and analyzes results, to provide inputs for decisions necessary to assure the economic health of the nation's transport system.

3. *Bureau of Enforcement:* conducts investigations into cases where persons or carriers are charged with violating specific provisions of the ICC Act. Cooperates with U.S. Justice Department in prosecuting violators.

4. *Bureau of Operations:* monitors carriers' operations to assure they are in

Figure 13–1
Laws regulating transportation

Year enacted	Law	Purpose of law
1887	Interstate Commerce Act	Federal regulation of railroads
1903	Elkins Act	Prohibited RR from giving rebates or reductions from published rates
1906	Hepburn Act	ICC directives made binding without court action. RR can appeal, but burden of proof is on the RR
1910	Mann-Elkins Act	ICC given authority to act in rate matters in absence of a shipper complaint
1920	Transportation Act	ICC given authority to act on RR entry and abandonment of service
1926	Air Commerce Act	Air safety standards became responsibility of Commerce Department
1934	Air Mail Act	Competitive bidding required for air mail contracts. Prohibited airframe manufacturers from controlling airlines
1935	Motor Carrier Act	ICC given authority to regulate trucking industry
1938	Civil Aeronautics Act	Civil Aeronautics Authority established to regulate airlines
1940	Transportation Act	ICC must consider impact of rate regulations on all modes of transport
1940	Presidential Order	Civil Aeronautics Authority became Civil Aeronautics Board (CAB). Civil Aeronautics Administration (CAA) established within Commerce Department to promote air service and enforce safety standards
1948	Reed-Bulwinkle Act	Rate bureaus in railroad and trucking industry exempt from anti-trust laws
1956	Federal Highway Act	Established Federal Highway Trust Fund
1958	Transportation Act	ICC cannot increase rates of one mode to protect another ICC can order abandonment of passenger service
1966	Department of Transportation Act	Cabinet-level department (DOT) established
1970	Rail Passenger Service Act	National Railroad Passenger Corporation (Amtrak) set up
1973	Regional Rail Reorganization Act	U.S. Railway Association set up to reorganize bankrupt Northeast RRs
1976	Railroad Revitalization and Regulatory Reform Act	Gave RR greater freedom in setting rates
1977	Air Cargo Act	Air cargo industry deregulated
1978	Airline Deregulation Act	Began the deregulation of passenger air transportation

conformity with the Act. Informs carriers of violations in rates and other operating assets.

5. *Bureau of Traffic:* reviews the filing of tariffs, observance of tariffs, and renders opinions on the applicability of tariffs in specific situations.

The ICC has a field staff that makes period visits to carriers to check on observance of ICC regulations and investigates complaints which may be made by shippers, carriers, and the general public.

Transportation deregulation

Over the last five years or so, there has been much interest and discussion on the feasibility and advisability of removing all, or a significant amount, of the current regulation of the transportation industry. The proponents of deregulation argue that our present regulatory system is grossly inefficient; that it protects the inefficiently-operated carrier and encourages poor carrier management; that it discourages competition; that it denies shippers the frequent and efficient service needed from carriers; and that it results in shippers paying substantially higher prices for freight movement than would be the case with free competition. They argue that unnecessarily high transport rates have fueled the current inflationary trend and by raising a firm's cost of goods sold have made it more difficult for U.S. firms to compete in world markets.

The proponents of our current regulatory system argue that it is working well; that the U.S. has the lowest-cost and most efficient transport system in the world; and that, as a result, it is still the only major transport system that is privately, and not governmentally, owned. They further agree that regulation is needed to protect the public interest, and that, in its absence, large segments of the business community would not receive the transport service they need and at a price enabling them to compete with other firms.[2]

The air cargo industry was deregulated late in 1977, giving air cargo carriers the right to begin serving additional markets, revise schedules, and adjust rates. One large air cargo carrier, Tiger International, Inc., started service into seven new, domestic markets. Its air freight revenue grew 42 percent in 1978 over 1977, and its pretax profits rose by 86 percent. In addition, since deregulation eliminated barriers to air cargo carriers owning a motor carrier, Flying Tiger Line, a subsidiary of Tiger International, began to investigate the purchase of a trucking company that could feed its air cargo operation.[3]

The law deregulating the air passenger traffic industry was passed in 1978 (Public Law 95–504, the Airline Deregulation Act), culminating a four-year effort. Under this law, the Civil Aeronautics Board will be phased out by 1985, unless Congress decides later there is a need for such an agency. Basically, the

---

[2] Roger E. Jerman, Donald D. Anderson, and James A. Constantin, "Shipper/Carrier Perspectives on Transportation Regulation," *Journal of Purchasing and Materials Management* 13 (Spring 1977); 23–28.

[3] Roy J. Harris, Jr., "Tiger International, Following Gains in Air Cargo, Hunts A Trucking Prey," *The Wall Street Journal*, 4 April 1979, p. 10.

law allows existing airlines to pick one new, additional domestic or international route in each of the next three years. After that, any new firm can freely enter the airline business.

The possible deregulation of the trucking industry has attracted much interest, and Congress will be considering several bills directed at limited deregulation. Some changes certainly will be made, but it will be years before trucking will be totally deregulated. Adherents claim that deregulation will result in major benefits to the buyer through a wider variety of price/service options and greater competition in pricing.[4] Those opposing deregulation, which include many carriers, claim that it will not help shippers, stating that ". . . shippers have much to lose with deregulation . . . rates would go up, some routes would be dropped, decisions on plant locations would be affected—shippers would simply not be able to depend on the trucking industry as they now do.[5]

While future developments on the deregulation question are far from certain, it does seem likely that some movement in that direction will occur. And, depending on the extent of deregulation, buyers of transport services will be playing in a game with substantially altered rules, which they should recognize and adjust to. The potential effects are too great to do otherwise.

F.O.B. terms ✿

The term F.O.B. stands for "Free on Board," meaning that goods are delivered to a specified point with all transport charges paid. The selection of the F.O.B. point is important to the purchaser, for it determines three things:

1. who pays the carrier,
2. when legal title to goods being shipped passes to the buyer, and
3. who is responsible for preparing and pursuing claims with the carrier in the event goods are lost or damaged during shipment.

The claim that F.O.B. destination always is preferable, for the seller pays the transportation charges, is incorrect. While the seller may pay the transportation charges, in the final analysis the charges are borne by the buyer, since transportation costs will be included in the delivered price charged by the vendor. In effect, if the buyer lets the vendor make the transportation decisions, then the buyer is allowing the vendor to spend the buyer's money.

There are several variations in F.O.B. terms, as Figure 13–2 shows. In purchases from foreign suppliers, the ocean carrier typically does not provide any insurance on goods in transit; therefore, it is important when goods are bought F.O.B. Origin for the buyer to assure that adequate insurance coverage is provided. The two marine freight terms commonly used are C&F and C.I.F. C&F (cost and freight) is similar to F.O.B. origin, with freight charges paid by the seller. However, under C&F the buyer assumes all risk and should provide for insurance. C.I.F. (cost, insurance, and freight) means that the seller will pay the

[4]Thomas F. Dillon, "What Will Deregulation Mean to Purchasing?" *Purchasing,* 7 March 1979, pp. 48–52.

[5]"ACT Plans to Battle Deregulation of Trucking," *Purchasing* 11 April 1979, p. 13.

Figure 13–2
F.O.B. terms and responsibilities

F.O.B. term	Payment of freight charges	Bears freight charges	Owns goods in transit	Files claims (if any)	Explanation
F.O.B. origin, or F.O.B. freight collect . . . . .Buyer	Buyer	Buyer	Buyer	Buyer	Title and control of goods passes to buyer when carrier signs for goods at point of origin
F.O.B. origin, freight prepaid . . . . .Seller	Seller	Seller	Buyer	Buyer	
F.O.B. origin, freight prepaid and charged back . . . . . .Seller	Seller	Buyer	Buyer	Buyer	Seller pays freight charges and adds to invoice
F.O.B. destination, freight collect . . . . .Buyer	Buyer	Buyer	Seller	Seller	Title remains with seller until goods are delivered
F.O.B. destination, freight prepaid . . . . .Seller	Seller	Seller	Seller	Seller	
F.O.B. destination, freight collect and allowed . . . . .Buyer	Buyer	Seller	Seller	Seller	Buyer pays freight charges and deducts from seller's invoice

freight charges and provide appropriate insurance coverage. This is similar to F.O.B. destination, freight prepaid.

In some instances, the buyer may wish to provide equalization of freight charges with the nearest shipping point of the seller, or some competitive shipping point. In that case, the following clause can be used: "Freight charges to be equalized with those applicable from seller's shipping point producing lowest transportation cost to buyer's destination."

Freight classification *

Proper classification of freight shipments is of primary importance in the purchase of transportation services. Shippers are responsible for knowing the specific description of the merchandise being moved, and this "classification" determines the applicable tariff, or freight rate. For example, the gauge of steel being shipped determines the appropriate freight classification; if the wrong classification is indicated it literally can make a difference of thousands of dollars in freight charges on a large shipment. These commodity word descriptions must be used in shipping orders and bills of lading and must conform to those in the applicable tariff, including packing specifications where different rates are provided for the same article according to the manner in which it is packed for shipment. Failure to use the correct classification description will result in the carrier assessing an incorrect rate, and may possibly result in a charge that the shipper is fraudulently classifying shipments to get unwarranted low rates.

Classifications for rate-making purposes are based on many factors, such as weight per cubic foot, value per pound, and risk of damage or pilferage. Since shipments moving a long distance may move on several different railroads, the ICC has the responsibility of assuring that a uniform classification system is used. This is done through the Uniform Freight Classification, which became effective May 30, 1952, and is updated as needed. When motor carriers were brought under regulation in 1935, a National Motor Freight Classification was established and is in use today, although the New England states have their own classification system, the Coordinated Motor Freight Classification.

Most articles are shipped under a "class rating," which is the normal freight classification, which then determines the applicable freight rate. However, the ICC can authorize special "commodity rates," which normally are lower than the class rates and are granted to meet a particular competitive situation. A shipper and a carrier normally will work together in petitioning the ICC for this special commodity rate. For example, if a firm requires steel scrap as a principal raw material and an economic imbalance develops which causes a local shortage of steel scrap, the alternative is to transport scrap from some distance to meet production requirements. But the class rate on steel scrap may be so high that it is uneconomic to buy and transport the distant scrap. The buyer and carrier may decide to petition the ICC for a commodity rate on scrap, between these two points, on economic grounds of necessity to keep the industry in operation. The

ICC may grant this special lower rate on an economic necessity basis, either permanently or temporarily.

Selection of carrier and routing

Normally, the buyer will wish to specify how purchased items are to be shipped; this is the buyer's legal right if the purchase has been made under any of the F.O.B. Origin terms. If the purchaser has received superior past service from a particular carrier, it then becomes the preferable means of shipment. Or, a carrier may have been particularly helpful in assisting the shipper in petitioning the ICC for favorable rates on certain items of merchandise.

On the other hand, if the buyer has relatively little expertise in the traffic area and the vendor has a skilled traffic department, it might be wise to rely on the vendor's judgment in carrier selection and routing. Also, in a time of shortage of transport equipment (RR cars, or trucks), the vendor may have better information about the local situation and what arrangements will get best results. And, if the item to be shipped has special dimensional characteristics, requiring special rail cars, the vendor may be in a better position to know what's available and the clearances needed for proper shipment.

The first step is to determine the mode of transport, e.g., rail, truck, air, water, etc., which will best meet the transport requirement. Next, a decision must be made on specific carrier and the specific routing of the shipment. This information should be a part of the purchase order. The buyer then may wish to keep track of the freight movement to assure that it is going as planned.

The factors to be considered in selection of mode of shipment, carrier, and routing include:

1.   *Required delivery time:* The required date for material receipt may make the selection of mode of shipment quite simple. If two-day delivery from a distant point is needed, the only viable alternative probably is air shipment. If a longer time is available, other modes can be considered. Most carriers can supply estimates of normal delivery times and the purchasing department also can rely on past experience with particular modes and carriers.

2.   *Available services:* If the item to be shipped is large and bulky, this may dictate a particular mode of transportation. Special container requirements may indicate only certain carriers who have the unique equipment to handle the job.

3.   *Type of item being shipped:* Bulk liquids, for example, may indicate RR tank car, barge, or pipeline. Also, safety requirements in the case of potentially explosive items may make certain carriers and routings impractical.

4.   *Shipment size:* Items of small size and bulk can be moved by U.S. mail, United Parcel Service, or air freight forwarders. Larger shipments probably can be more economically moved by rail or truck.

5.   *Possibility of damage:* Certain items, such as fine china or electronics equipment, by their nature have a high risk of damage in shipment. In this case, the buyer may select a mode and carrier by which the shipment can come straight through to its destination, with no transfers at distribution points to another car-

rier. It is part of the buyer's responsibility to insure that the packaging of goods is appropriate for both the contents and mode of transport.

6. *Cost of the transport service:* The buyer should select the mode, carrier, and routing that will provide for the safe movement of goods, within the required time, at lowest total transport cost. This requires a thorough knowledge of freight classifications and published tariffs. Also, the buyer may make certain tradeoffs in purchasing transportation, just as are made in selection of vendors for other purchases.

7. *Carrier financial situation:* If any volume of freight is moved, some damages will be incurred, resulting in claims against the carrier. Should the carrier get into financial difficulty, or even become insolvent, collection on claims becomes a problem. Therefore, the buyer should avoid those carriers who are on the margin financially.

8. *Service quality:* While two carriers may offer freight service between the same points, the reliability and dependability may differ greatly. One carrier may be more attentive to customer needs; may be more dependable in living up to its commitments; may incur less damage, overall, to merchandise shipped; and in general may be the best freight vendor. The buyer's past experience is the best indicator of service quality.

9. *Handling of claims:* Inevitably, some damage claims will arise in the shipment of quantities of merchandise. Prompt and efficient investigation and settlement of claims is another key factor in carrier selection.

Private or leased carriers. One possibility is the use of private or leased equipment. A private carrier or a leased carrier does not offer service to the general public. Many companies have elected to contract for exclusive use of equipment, and some have established their own trucking fleet, through use of either company-owned or leased tractors and vans. One example of leasing to improve transport service is the case of the Salt River Project in Phoenix, Arizona which leased over 200 railroad petroleum tank cars in 1973 so that they could have greater assurance of availability as needed to move fuel oil to their generating stations.[6]

Leasing gives the firm much greater flexibility in scheduling freight services. It can be economically advantageous, but unless the equipment can be fully utilized, through planned back hauls of either semifinished or finished goods, it may turn out to be more costly than use of the common carrier system. Also, it is important that the firm recognize and provide adequate protection against the very substantial dollar liability that may result in the case of accident.

Freight rates

The charges for freight movement are determined by the classification of the item transported and the appropriate rate tariff. The tariffs of common carriers are publicly available to any interested party, although they are voluminous and dif-

---

[6]"Too Many Tank Cars," *Arizona Business/Industry* (July 1977), pp. 13–14.

ficult to read and interpret except by someone skilled in rate analysis. The basic charge is determined by the class rate, although lower commodity rates can be arranged for some items.

There are some additional variations available, providing the shipper is knowledgeable and innovative enough to obtain them.

→ **Quantity breaks.** As with other purchases, carriers (vendors) offer lower rates if the quantity of an individual shipment is large enough. Both rail and motor carriers offer discounts for full carload (CL) or truckload (TL) shipments. These will be substantially less per pound than less-than-carload (LCL) or less-than-truckload (LTL) quantities. If the shipper can consolidate smaller shipments to the same destination, a lower rate may be available (called a "pool car.") In some instances, shippers may band together through a shippers' association to get pool car transport rates.

The unit train is another innovation in which the shipper gets a quantity discount. By special arrangement with a railroad, a utility company is provided one or more complete trains, consisting of 100+ coal cars, which run shuttle between the coal mines and the utility's place of use. This speeds up the movement, and the materials are moved at an advantageous commodity rate.

Through rates. Basically, the longer the distance over which materials are transported, the lower is the per mile transport cost. Carriers may make provisions for payment of through rates under three variations:

1. *Diversion and reconsignment:* Here the shipper may change the destination of a rail car to a different location, or change the party to which the shipment is destined, and still pay the long-haul freight rate, providing the railroad is notified before the car passes a predetermined point. There is a charge for this service, but the freight bill still may be less than a combination of the two short-haul rates. For example, a shipper starts a carload of apples from the State of Washington, with Pittsburgh as the destination. Under the diversion privilege, the shipper can change the destination to another city, e.g., Atlanta or Miami, and still pay the long-haul rate to Atlanta or Miami, providing the railroad is notified of the new destination *before* the car passes an agreed-upon point, e.g., the Mississippi River. This privilege is particularly useful in movement of perishable items or items in which the allowable transit time is short and a determination of final destination has not yet been made.

2. *Stop-off privilege:* This permits a shipper to ship a full carload from point A to D, at the long-haul rate, but to stop the shipment at intermediate points B and C and drop off quantities. While the freight rate is calculated at the full carload weight even though the total shipment does not go to point D, it still may be cheaper than the LCL rates on shipments to points B, C, and D.

3. *Fabrication or storage-in-transit:* By special arrangement with a railroad, and approved by the ICC, a buyer of raw materials can ship from point A, stop the shipment at intermediate point B, fabricate the raw material, reload it within a specified number of days, e.g., 60 days, and ship it to final destination C, all at the long-haul rate from A to C. In general, the movement must be on a straight line, but this shouldn't be interpreted literally. For example, a buyer of steel can purchase it in Chicago, have it shipped to Milwaukee under the

fabrication-in-transit privilege, fabricate it, and reload it for rail shipment to Lansing, Michigan, all at the long haul, Chicago to Lansing rate. While an extra charge is paid for the in-transit privilege, it still is cheaper in total than paying two separate short-haul charges. Items can be unloaded for storage for several months under the same arrangement. The intransit privilege is available with motor freight also. The economic rationale for this privilege is that, without it, manufacture would be done at either the point of raw material production or at the final use point, and intermediate points (Milwaukee, in the above example) would not be able to compete for manufacturing or storage functions.

Intermodal shipments. To be competitive with other shipping modes, the railroads have developed special equipment and services. "Piggyback" service, where truck trailers are loaded on special rail cars for long distance shipment, and "containerization," where specially-designed containers are loaded, delivered by truck to a wharf, hoisted on board a ship, and then offloaded onto rail or truck carriers for shipment to their final destination, are examples of current innovations in shipping methods.

Documentation in freight shipments

The Bill of Lading (B/L) is the key document in the movement of goods. The Bill has been standardized by the ICC, and carriers are responsible to issue proper Bills, although in practice they normally are prepared by the shipper. Figure 13–3 shows a bill of lading.

While the Bill of Lading may be prepared in whatever number of copies is convenient, the following three copies are required:

1. *Copy 1, Original:* Describes shipment and is a receipt by the carrier for the goods. Signed by both shipper's and carrier's agents, it is proof that shipment was made and is evidence of ownership. It is a contract and fixes carrier liability; normally it will be kept by the party who has title to goods in transit, for it must be provided to support any damage claims.

2. *Copy 2, Shipping Order:* Retained by carrier; used as shipping instructions and as a basis for billing.

3. *Copy 3, Memorandum:* Simply acknowledges that B/L has been issued.

There are several variations on the B/L:

1. *Uniform Straight Bill of Lading:* This is the complete B/L, and contains the complete contract terms and conditions. Separate form is needed for motor and rail shipments.

2. *Straight Bill of Lading—Short Form:* Contains those provisions uniform to both motor and rail. Short bills are not furnished by carriers, but instead are preprinted by shippers.

3. *Unit Bill of Lading:* this is prepared in four copies; the extra copy is the railroad's waybill. This waybill moves with the shipment and may be of assistance in expediting freight movement.

4. *Uniform Order Bill of Lading:* Printed on yellow paper (the other B/Ls must be on white paper), this also is called a Sight Draft Bill of Lading. It is a negotiable instrument and must be surrendered to the carrier at destination before

Figure 13–3

SAMPLE ONLY

STRAIGHT BILL OF LADING—SHORT FORM

ORIGINAL — NOT NEGOTIABLE
(To be printed on white paper)

Shipper's No. 9523.

Carrier's No ....

Southern Pacific Transportation Co.
(Name of Carrier)

RECEIVED, subject to the classifications and tariffs in effect on the date of the issue of this Bill of Lading,

At ....Guadalupe, Calif.. February 23, , 1978

From...... DORFLER OIL CO OF CALIF ....

the property described below, in apparent good order, except as noted (contents and condition of contents of packages unknown), marked, consigned, and destined as indicated below, which said carrier (the word carrier being understood throughout this contract as meaning any person or corporation in possession of the property under the contract) agrees to carry to its usual place of delivery at said destination, if on its route, otherwise to deliver to another carrier on the route to said destination. It is mutually agreed, as to each carrier of all or any of said property over all or any portion of said route to destination, and as to each party at any time interested in all or any of said property, that every service to be performed hereunder shall be subject to all the terms and conditions of the Uniform Domestic Straight Bill of Lading set forth (1) in Uniform Freight Classification in effect on the date hereof, if this is a rail or a rail-water shipment, or (2) in the applicable motor carrier classification or tariff if this is a motor carrier shipment.

Shipper hereby certifies that he is familiar with all the terms and conditions of the said bill of lading, including those on the back thereof, set forth in the classification or tariff which governs the transportation of this shipment, and the said terms and conditions are hereby agreed to by the shipper and accepted for himself and his assigns.

Consigned to ...CLETRON ASPHALT ...... 1584 Parkway Road ....
(Mail or street address of consignee- For purposes of notification only.)

Destination . Phoenix .... State Ariz . County .... Delivery Address★ ...
(★To be filled in only when shipper desires and governing tariffs provide for delivery thereat.)

Route .. SP ....

Delivering Carrier .. ATSF Dlvy .... Car or Vehicle Initials. SP .. No. 726805

Trailer Initials Number . . . . Length . . . . Plan . . . .

. . . . Length . . . . Plan . . . .

Container Initials Number . . . . Length . . . . Plan . . . .

No. Packages	Kind of Package, Description of Articles, Special Marks, and Exceptions	*Weight (Subject to Correction)	Class or Rate	Check Column	Subject to Section 7 of Conditions of applicable bill of lading, if this shipment is to be delivered to the consignee without recourse on the consignor, the consignor shall sign the following statement:
20725	Gals.Liquid Asphalt AR16000	178234			The carrier shall not make delivery of this shipment without payment of freight and all other lawful charges.
	If delayed for any reason				
	notify Traffic Manager,				(Signature of consignor.)
	Dorfler Oil Co., PO Box 2900,				If charges are to be prepaid, write or stamp here, "To be Prepaid."
	Costa Mesa, CA 92626				To be Prepaid
	State cause of delay and				
	date car will go forward				Received $ .... to apply in prepayment of the charges on the property described hereon.
	TCFB Wt. Agmt. #2888				
					Agent or Cashier

*If the shipment moves between two ports by a carrier by water, the law requires that the bill of lading shall state whether it is carrier's or shipper's weight.

Note.—Where the rate is dependent on value, shippers are required to state specifically in writing the agreed or declared value of the property.

The agreed or declared value of the property is hereby specifically stated by the shipper to be not exceeding.............................per ....

Per .... (The signature here acknowledges only the amount prepaid.)

Charges advanced:

$..........................

DORFLER OIL CO. .... Shipper. .... John Smith .... Agent.

Per.. Jack Jones .... Per.......... 2/23/78 11. AM ......

Permanent postoffice address of shipper... PO Box 2900, Costa Mesa, CA 92626 ....

goods can be obtained. Its primary use is to prevent delivery until payment is made for the goods. To obtain payment, the shipper must provide a sight draft, along with the original copy of the B/L, to his bank; when the draft clears, the bank gives the B/L to the shipper, who then can obtain delivery of the merchandise.

Each shipment must have a Bill of Lading, which is the contract spelling out the legal liabilities of all parties. No changes to the original B/L can be made unless approved by the carrier's agent, in writing on the B/L.

Expediting and tracing shipments

As with the normal purchase of goods and services, expediting means applying pressure to the carrier (vendor) in an attempt to encourage faster-than-normal delivery service. The carrier often can and will provide faster service to assist the shipper in meeting an emergency requirement, provided such requests are made sparingly. Expediting should be done through the carrier's general agent and, if at all possible, the carrier should be notified of the need for speed as far in advance of the shipment as possible.

Tracing is similar to follow up, for it attempts to determine the status (location) of items that have been shipped, have not yet been received, and thus are somewhere within the transportation system. Tracing also is done through the carrier's agent, although the shipper may work right along with the carrier's agent in attempting to locate the shipment. If tracing locates a shipment and indicates it will not be delivered by the due date, then expediting is needed.

Getting results in tracing is a function of the kinds of movement records maintained by the carrier and the type of information available to the person doing the tracing. For example, in attempting to trace a CL rail shipment, the tracer should have (1) date material shipped, (2) description of material, (3) car number, (4) carrier, (5) origin, (6) destination, and (7) route.

While the ease with which various shipments can be traced will vary among carriers and various modes of transportation and may change from time to time as carriers and modes change their policies and record-keeping systems, the current traceability is:

1. *CL rail:* If one has the car initial and number, date of shipment, and routing, the railroad quickly can locate a car. Most have computerized locator systems.

2. *LCL rail:* Ability to locate a given shipment varies greatly among carriers. Some maintain detailed records; others maintain minimum records, making tracing almost impossible.

3. *TL motor:* If the shipper has the trailer number, most carriers can quickly tell the approximate current location, since it is kept track of through a series of movement points.

4. *LTL motor:* Normally, motor carriers can give complete and accurate information, since they account for LTL shipments as they move through the various checkpoints.

5. *Air shipment:* Information on exact location normally can be obtained with little difficulty.

6. *Parcel Post:* No records are maintained; tracing is impossible.

7. *United Parcel Service:* Shipment status can be supplied quickly and accurately.

8. *Freight Forwarders:* Since they use the service of common carriers, it is possible to trace these shipments in the same way that other shipments can be traced.

9. *Water Carriers:* Shipment can be located easily, for material is receipted for when put aboard, and it doesn't change carriers.

Loss or damage claims ♥

The carrier is responsible for the full, actual damage to or loss of merchandise while in its possession. To collect on proper claims, the owner of the merchandise must file properly-supported claims. If the merchandise is being shipped under any of the F.O.B. Origin terms, the buyer will have to pursue the claim. If shipment is F.O.B. Destination, the vendor must process the claim, but since the merchandise is in the buyer's hands, the buyer will have to supply much of the information to support the claim.

Section 20(1) of the Interstate Commerce Act specifies that shippers must have at least nine months to file claims in writing with a carrier and that if a claim is disallowed by a carrier, the shipper must have two years to bring court suit. The Straight Bill of Lading Condition 2(B) provides: ". . . Claims must be filed in writing with the receiving or delivering carrier, or carrier issuing this bill of lading; or carrier on whose line the loss, damage, injury or delay occurred, within nine months after delivery of the property or, in case of failure to make delivery, then within nine months after a reasonable time for delivery has elapsed; and suits shall be instituted against any carrier only within two years and one day from the day when notice in writing is given by the carrier to the claimant that the carrier has disallowed the claim . . .''

Under this provision, carriers generally have established nine months as the claim filing period, and two years and one day for the filing of court suits in the case of disallowed claims.

Unconcealed loss or damage. When it is evident on delivery that loss or damage has occurred, it is important that this be noted on the carrier's delivery receipt, and signed by the carrier's delivering agent. If this is not done, the carrier may maintain that he received a "clear receipt" and not admit any liability. It is a good idea for the receiving department to have an instant camera available, take one or more photos of the damaged items, and have them signed by the carrier's representative. Then, the local freight agent should be notified and an inspection report requested. This telephone request should be followed up in writing.

If it can be proven that the loss or damage occurred while the goods were in the carrier's possession, and if the cost of the damage can be established, prompt carrier payment can be expected.

Concealed loss or damage. Merchandise found short or damaged only after the container is opened is known as concealed loss or damage. The unpacking should be discontinued, photos taken, and the carrier's local agent should be requested to inspect the items and prepare an inspection report.

Concealed loss or damage claims often are difficult to collect, because it is hard to determine whether the loss or damage took place while the shipment was in the carrier's possession or whether it occurred before the shipment was delivered to the carrier.

Payment of freight bills

ICC rules provide that all common carrier freight bills must be paid within a set number of days—normally seven, but the ICC can change the allowable payment time as needed by carriers and to suit the current economic situation. If maximum payment period were not specified and standardized, some large shippers, by virtue of their volume, might insist on very long payment terms, which would discriminate against the smaller shippers.

If, due to the short payment terms, the shipper pays an overcharge as a result of (1) an error in classification, (2) an error in rate charged, (3) an error in weight, (4) duplicate payment of the same freight bill, or (5) calculation error(s), there is a three-year period to file an overcharge claim with the shipper. If the claim is substantiated by evidence, there will be no problem in recovering from the carrier. By the same token, the carrier has three years to bill shippers for any undercharges.

Demurrage charges often are incurred by shippers or receivers of merchandise. This simply is a daily rental charge for a rail car or a motor van that is tied up beyond the normal time for loading or unloading. Typically, the "free" period before the demurrage charge starts is 48 hours from the first 7 a.m. by which the carrier has spotted the car or van ready for unloading. The number of hours is set by the ICC and varies from time to time, as cars get in short or long supply. If demurrage were not charged, some firms would use the carrier's equipment as a free storage facility. The daily demurrage rate becomes progressively higher the longer the car or trailer is tied up, until it gets almost prohibitive. A shipper can enter into an averaging agreement with a carrier, whereby cars or vans unloaded one day early may be used to offset cars which are unloaded a day late. In an averaging agreement, settlement is made monthly. If the shipper owes the carrier, payment must be made; if the carrier owes the shipper, no payment is made, but instead the net car balance starts at zero in the new month. The purchasing department should be aware of the normal number of rail cars or vans which can be unloaded each day, and attempt to schedule shipments in so that they do not "back up" and result in payment of demurrage penalties.

Freight audits

Because of the complex regulations under which carriers operate, a careful audit of paid freight bills often will uncover instances of overpayment to the carrier. Since the shipper has three years to file claims for overpayment, this audit can be done on a yearly basis without jeopardizing the shipper's ability to collect.

In the larger firm, in-house freight bill audit capability often is available. In the smaller firm, the use of an outside freight audit consultant, referred to as a "traffic consultant" or "rate shark," should be used. The rate shark will examine all paid freight bills in an attempt to spot overpayment due to wrong classification, wrong rate, duplicate payment, or calculation errors. When overpayments are found, the rate shark will process a claim with the carrier. The agreement with the shipper typically is that the rate shark retains 50 percent of the dollars recovered, although occasionally the outside auditor will work for a smaller percentage. Due to the complexity of the freight purchase area, even a company with a sophisticated, well-trained traffic staff probably pays some overcharges, and with the advice of an outside auditor could generate substantial recoveries. And with the rate shark, if nothing is recovered, no payment is made.

QUESTIONS FOR REVIEW AND DISCUSSION

1. Discuss transportation deregulation, pro and con.
2. What factors should be considered in selecting a carrier?
3. How do firms organize to handle the traffic function?
4. To what extent are the various forms of common carrier transportation regulated; by whom?
5. What types of traffic damage might occur, and how should each be handled?
6. Why is classification so important in buying transportation services?
7. What is the use and significance of the Bill of Lading?
8. What are the basic principles under which the common carrier system operates?
9. What does F.O.B. stand for? What variations are there in F.O.B. terms?
10. When would a buyer want to use one of the "through rate" provisions?

CASE 13–1
JOHNSON FLIGHT SYSTEMS

Johnson Flight Systems, located in Phoenix, Arizona, produces precision equipment which it sells to all the airframe producers in the U.S., Canada, and Europe. Included in the components it purchases are small, precision forgings, weighing anywhere from two pounds to 30 pounds. Annually, Johnson buys approximately 7,000 of these forgings.

The primary supplier of these precision forgings is National Metals Company, located in Cleveland, Ohio. National Metals has a reputation for maintaining very high quality standards and has been a very reliable supplier to Johnson Flight Systems.

The buyer of castings at Johnson Flight estimates that their purchase of castings from National Metals over the next calendar year will total about 6,000, with an average weight of 15 pounds. Delivery requirements call for monthly shipments of approximately equal amounts. Since customer requirements often aren't known until shortly before these forgings must be put into production, Johnson can give National Metals its size requirements only about six weeks before the items are needed in the Phoenix plant. It typically takes National Metals about three weeks to make their production run and have the items ready to ship.

CASE 13–2
THE LAST NATIONAL BANK OF ST. LOUIS *

The Last National Bank of St. Louis, Missouri, placed an order for 12 special-purpose accounting machines with the Data-Max Corporation of Cincinnati, Ohio. Last National and Data-Max agreed to a firm-fixed price of $3,200 per unit, F.O.B. the shipping point (Cincinnati). In the purchase order, the bank's purchasing agent designated a particular carrier (Baltimore and Ohio Railroad) and Data-Max returned a signed acknowledgement copy without change in any of the terms and conditions.

On completion of the 12 units three months later, Data-Max shipped them via a common carrier truck line instead of the B&O Railroad. At time of shipment, an invoice was mailed to Last National. To take advantage of the 2 percent cash discount, Last National paid the invoice immediately, as was their custom. The machines had not yet arrived.

Unfortunately, as the truck was passing through Vincennes, Indiana, the driver lost control; the vehicle was involved in an accident, and the truck and contents were destroyed. The 12 machines were a total loss.

The buyer, on contacting Data-Max relative to the loss, was told: "Look, we sold these machines to you F.O.B. Cincinnati, and titled passed at the time they were loaded on the carrier. That's the law." At this point, the buyer pointed out that Data-Max had not shipped via the carrier specified on the purchase order. To this Data-Max replied: "Sure, that's true. But we saved you money by shipping via a less expensive transportation method." (This was, in fact, true.) "Futhermore, you acknowledged and accepted our action by paying our invoice, for the invoice clearly stated the date and method of shipment. It is your responsibility to work out any adjustment for the loss directly with the truck line."

CASE 13–3
WHO'S RESPONSIBLE?

The Johnson Company has been purchasing for use in its Dallas plant a costly machined part from the DeeMac Company in Des Moines, Iowa. The volume is large, and shipment normally is made weekly in LTL quantities via common carrier motor freight. Occasionally, a full truckload quantity is involved.

The purchase order specifies the method of packaging for shipment, which is a moulded plastic container, twenty of which fit into a standard corrugated shipping container. To the knowledge of the Johnson Company buyer, the packaging specifications have been consistently met by DeeMac Company, and there have been no quality problems on this part for the last 18 months, which is the time period over which this particular part has been purchased. Several motor freight common carriers have been used.

Approximately one month ago, at the request of the Johnson buyer, DeeMac Company made a slight change in the design of the part. When the LTL shipment of 180 cartons arrived last week, which was the first shipment of the newly-designed part, it was receipted for by the Johnson receiving clerk, and there was no notation of any visible damage to any of the containers.

Four days later, when the cartons were opened, it was found that 30 percent of the total shipment of 3,600 purchased parts had been damaged. While the damage was slight, the parts were not repairable and would not perform satisfactorily the function for which they had been designed.

The carrier was immediately contacted and its agent came to Johnson Company to examine the damaged parts. His response was that shipment had been made in the normal manner, and the damage must have resulted from improper packaging.

When the Johnson buyer contacted the vendor, their response was that the parts were checked following their standard statistical quality control system as usual and that no problems were evident. They also complied with the regular packaging specifications. Therefore, the damage must have taken place while the parts were in the motor carrier's possession.

CASE 13–4
AMATA MINING CORP.

Jack Patching, purchasing agent for foreign operations at Amata Mining Corporation, was concerned about complaints he had received from the Brazilian Mines purchasing manager. He complained about the quality of work being done by Arthur Dome Inc., the New York based freight forwarders who had handled Amata's Atlantic Shipping for many years.

Apparently, documentation errors were causing significant customs clearing problems in Brazil, often resulting in extensive delays in getting the needed items to the minesite. The errors apparently were of three types:

1. Omission of data meant that routine processing in customs was not possible.
2. Errors in data resulted in one or both of the following:
   a. Greatly increased costs because of improper evaluation for duty and special import restrictions. This had increased actual delivered total cost to the minesite by as much as 50 percent in some cases.
   b. Delays in processing until the errors could be corrected.
3. Missing forms or use of incorrect forms created severe delays.

The Brazilian government was attempting to promote local manufacture of many items formerly imported and Mr. Patching suspected that delays in customs were a partial reflection of this government stance. He knew that the intended use of the imported item could have a tremendous impact on the duties levied. For example, capital items imported so that Brazilian exports could be generated received favorable tariff treatment. Since Amata's Brazilian mine generated a substantial export volume, it was vital that all capital equipment imports be properly documented.

Arthur Dome normally received about a 7 percent commission from the shipping companies. Furthermore, they charged Amata for documentation preparation and extra charges for messenger services, telephone calls, stamps, etc. on a per shipment basis. For a typical shipment these costs would come close to $100. For the past 12 months Amata's direct payments for documentation and related charges had exceeded $30,000. Jack Patching estimated that Arthur Dome's total income from Amata shipments might well exceed $140,000.

Jack Patching wondered if Arthur Dome's management had become a little lax in its treatment of Amata's business because of the long time they had been associated together. He knew that the Brazilian managers were very upset and he was anxious to get the situation corrected as soon as possible.

CASE 13–5
SUPER K CANADA LIMITED*

Jim Hartley was the Manager of Research for Transportation, Distribution and Systems at Super K Canada's head office in Kitchener, Ontario, reporting to John McKenzie, the Transportation and Purchasing Manager. One day in September 1977, Mr. MacKenzie called Jim into his office. "Jim", he said, "I've heard that Customer Services are pretty happy with the first year of the

*Copyright 1979, The University of Western Ontario, School of Business Administration, and Queen's University, School of Business.

new computerized distribution system. As you know, it automatically processes each customer order as soon as it's received and triggers our warehouses to ship out the goods that very same day. But this is resulting in
numerous small deliveries a day to the same customer location. In turn, our
physical distribution costs have increased significantly, and I'm not even
sure that customer relations have improved as a result of the system. I want
you to investigate this problem and report back to me what you intend to do,
as soon as possible."

Company background

Super K Canada Limited was the Canadian subsidiary of a major North
American manufacturer and distributor of specialty hardware items. It had
been experiencing steady growth and maintaining its profitability for many
years. It sold consumer products nationwide to many retail and department
chains, and also sold industrial products directly to a number of firms. Super
K Canada's total number of customers was about 20,000, of which about
70 percent were retail, 25 percent department chains and 5 percent industrial. Its total sales were approximately 60 million dollars in 1976, of which
30 percent was retail, 55 percent department chains, and 15 percent industrial.

Physical distribution organization

The physical distribution function of Super K Canada was organized separately from the product divisions and was headed by William Bennett who
reported to the executive vice president of the company. Mr. MacKenzie
reported directly to Mr. Bennett. In 1976, Mr. Bennett's responsibilities were
expanded to include customer services, and in 1977 inventory control was
added.

The distribution system

The firm was characterized by a diverse line of products, having currently
5,000 catalogue items kept in stock and 15,000 items made to order or
imported from U.S. warehouses. The stock items were maintained in major
warehouses in Montreal, Toronto, Winnipeg, and Vancouver as well as in
branch warehouses in five smaller cities and the head office in Kitchener.
The "non-stock" items were manufactured in 12 plants located across
Canada and in the northeast and midwest of the United States of America,
where there were also numerous storage locations.

Transportation and storage

In total, Super K Canada made about 60,000 shipments from July 1976 to
June 1977. Of these, over 70 percent were for less than 200 pounds of mer-

chandise. Shipment was usually made by contract truck carrier. The trucks left at frequent intervals every day, at scheduled departure times depending on the destination region. Air freight was occasionally used for distant, specially expedited orders, and rail freight was customarily used for some major industrial shipments. Many of the retail customers did not order at regular intervals. However, most of the department chains had a long regular order cycle, different for each product, with average cycle time of about six weeks. Industrial users usually placed large orders infrequently, at irregular intervals.

Jim Hartly had studied the costs of transportation and warehousing and had developed curves relating unit costs to size of order, as illustrated in Exhibits 1 and 2.

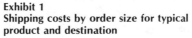

Exhibit 1
Shipping costs by order size for typical product and destination

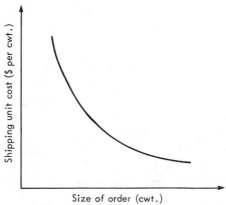

Exhibit 2
Warehousing costs by order size for typical product and location

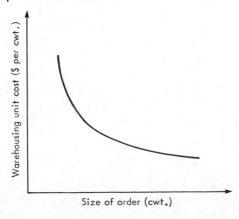

The order processing system

The order processing cycle had been fully automated since the introduction of a computerized system in the summer of 1976. Typically the cycle began with a customer order being received at one of the branch office or major warehouse centers. The order information was recorded and sent by telephone communications network to the large central computer at head office. An on-line file was already stored in the computer, showing the amount of each product available at each warehouse location. This file was searched and when the first available stock of the desired product was identified, a shipping waybill was automatically printed out at the corresponding warehouse for part or all of the order. The waybill was immediately sent to the shipping department at that location. Order processing to this point took at most half a day. Order picking and packing were then expedited to allow same-day shipment to the customer. This rapid service was intended to maintain the reputation of Super K Canada as a marketing-oriented organization where the customer's needs were paramount.

The order processing system had been running smoothly for over a year; however, various complaints had recently been received from some of the departmental chains regarding the frequency of truck visits to the receiving bays at their warehouses. This seemed to indicate that some modifications to the computer programs might be desirable. The programs were complex, which made them difficult to revise in any fundamental way; reprogramming costs were estimated to be in the order of $100,000.

Jim believed that his first priority was to think through the various strategies that could be followed to improve physical distribution performance. Once these strategies had been identified, he would then need to decide what information was required to evaluate and implement them.

PUBLIC PURCHASING

14

Any coverage of the purchasing area should give due attention to the unique problems of purchasing by governmental agencies (federal, state, provincial, county, municipal, public school systems, public libraries, public colleges and universities, and various governmental commissions). The funds spent by public purchasing managers deserve the same serious attention as dollars spent for industrial purchases, since the source of these funds is the taxpayer. If public purchasing funds are spent effectively and efficiently, benefits will accrue to all those people who pay for, and obtain the benefits from, the services provided by government.

If the total, annual tax-supported budget of a given governmental unit is two billion dollars, purchased supplies, materials, services, and construction probably account for approximately $500,000,000, which is much less than the purchase/sales ratio of the average industrial firm, since government operations are very labor intensive. Still, if an overall 10 percent reduction in purchase costs could be effected through better management of the purchasing function, that would result in a savings to the taxpayer of some $50,000,000—a significant amount, to say the least. This translates into a higher level of service, lower tax rates, or some combination of both. The events which started in California in 1978 with the passage of "Proposition 13", often referred to as the "taxpayers' revolt", show that the public is interested in greater governmental efficiency and is mandating this through the ballot box. Also, one of the significant contributing factors to the severe inflation rates experienced during the decade of the 70s has been the very high levels of government spending. Efficient and effective government purchasing can play a major role ·in combatting these inflationary pressures.

The figures in Table 14–1 indicate the magnitude of government spending. Government purchases, in total, have increased by about 30 percent over the four-year period of 1975 to 1978. The increase rate in state and local purchases (32 percent) has been greater than that of federal government purchases (27 percent). National defense expenditures of the federal government amount to about 65 percent of the total of federal government purchases of goods and services.[1] Government purchasing is big business, deserving a major amount of attention by government administrators!

The most important message of this chapter is that government buying *basically does not differ* from industrial purchasing. The same concepts of good

---

[1]*Survey of Current Business,* U.S. Department of Commerce, vol. 58 (August 1978), p. 5–19.

purchasing discussed in the previous chapters are applicable and should be followed to obtain maximum value for public dollars spent. The objectives of governmental purchasing are basically the same as for industrial purchasing, and include (1) assurance of continuity of supply to meet the service needs; (2) avoidance of duplication and waste through standardization; (3) maintenance of required quality standards in goods and services purchased; (4) development of a cooperative environment between purchasing and the agencies and departments served; (5) obtaining maximum savings through innovative buying and application of value analysis techniques; (6) administering the purchase function with internal efficiency; and (7) purchase at the lowest price, consistent with quality, performance, and delivery requirements (or as the military puts it, "obtain the most bang for the buck").

TABLE 14–1
Government purchases of goods and services, 1933 to 1978
($ millions)

| Year | Purchases | | |
	Federal	State and local	Total
1933	2.0	6.0	8.0
1941	16.9	7.9	24.8
1950	18.4	19.5	37.9
1970	96.2	123.3	219.5
1974	116.9	192.3	309.2
1975	123.1	215.4	338.4
1976	129.9	229.6	359.5
1977	145.1	248.9	394.0
1978*	156.1	285.2	441.3

*Estimated, based on first three quarters.
Source: *Federal Reserve Bulletin,* vol. 61 (December 1975), p. A54; and vol. 64 (November 1978), p. A52.

The major focus of this chapter will be to point out those areas, or practices, of governmental purchasing which may differ, at least in part, from those of industrial buying. The differences largely are a matter of degree, often caused by the specific legislation and statutes under which public purchasing operates, and are not in direct conflict with industry practice. The public purchasing manager, alert to these variations, will attempt to turn them into opportunities to maximize the utility obtained from public purchases. The major differences, or variations, between public and private purchasing practice apply to all types of public buying. The history, specific organization and practices of purchasing for the federal government, and state and local government then will be discussed.

Source of authority

The authority of the public buyer is established by law, regulation, or statute, such as federal and state constitutions and laws and municipal ordinances. The public buyer must observe the appropriate legal structure under which purchasing operates; ultimate responsibility is to some legislative body and the voters who elect that body. The industrial buyer, on the other hand, is responsible to an administrative superior and, ultimately, to the owner(s) of the firm.

When questions of authority or the interpretation of the legal requirements arise, these will be referred to the legal officer of the governmental agency (ultimately the attorney general's office in the case of federal or state purchasing, or the county or city attorney). This relationship is synonymous with that of the legal counsel of a private firm. If legislative changes are needed to permit the public buyer to do a more effective buying job, the cooperation of the agency's legal advisor should be sought. While changing the law is difficult and may take a long time to accomplish, the public buyer continually must assess the situation and press for needed modifications.

Budgetary restrictions/limitations

The use of budgets as planning and control devices is well known to buyers in both private industry and in government. As with any planning mechanism, when the environment or assumptions under which the budget was made undergo change, then the plan (budget) should be revised. Often the final budget for purchasing is approved by a legislative body on a line item basis, and changes in the budget for each line item must be approved by that legislative body in advance of expenditure. Obtaining such approval may be a very time-consuming process, due to the series of steps and public hearings required.

As a result, if the needed funds are not already in the budget, the public buyer may find it impossible to take advantage of spot buys of larger quantities of materials at particularly advantageous prices. In the private firm, funds normally can be made available in a very short time if the purchasing department can present a convincing case for spending those funds. This puts a real premium in public buying on the long-term planning and budgeting needed to anticipate requirements and opportunities; this planning often must be done at least 18 months in advance. Additionally, careful planning is necessary to assure that last-minute, often unwise purchases are not made just to obligate funds by an end-of-the-year budget expiration date.

Outside pressures

The public buyer realizes that the money spent comes from the taxpayer, and these taxpayers may become very vocal in their attempts to influence how this money is spent and with which vendors. It is not unusual for a given vendor firm to attempt to influence, through the political process, the placement of major dollar purchase contracts. In a sense, this is a type of reciprocity, with the taxpaying vendor firm feeling that since it is providing the tax dollars from which public purchases are made, it should be selected as the vendor from which government buys needed goods and services. It is the rare public buyer who does not, from time to time, receive a telephone call from a taxpayer who starts the conversation by saying, "You know, our firm pays a substantial amount of taxes, and we feel that we should receive better treatment, i.e., be able to sell more, from governmental purchasing."

When the industrial buyer receives such a request, it can be countered by the statement that "in our judgment, any supplier must be able to give us the best ultimate value for dollars spent." However, the public buyer knows that such a statement may not satisfy the caller, and that public purchasing may have to supply facts and figures to back up its decision to buy from a particular vendor.

Greater support of public service programs

In the last decade, there has been much interest on the part of the public in providing increased government support to certain special interest segments of society. There may be minority member segments which are assumed to have been the victims of past unfair, discriminatory actions. Thus, the general public has deemed that, in the interests of equity, these special interest segments should receive special consideration in future actions. Through the legislative process, laws have been passed to encourage the redress of these past injustices, and purchasing is one natural area through which funds can be channeled to these special interest segments. Examples are programs to favor small business firms in the award of purchase contracts, or the support of minority-owned vendors through special consideration in evaluating vendor capability and the placement of purchases.

While the long-term benefits to society may be worthwhile, in the short term, the governmental buyer may have to use a mix of vendors that meets the public's social demands but results in higher prices paid for items received. For example, a decision may be made that a specific percentage of total government purchasing dollars will be spent with minority-owned vendor firms. To meet that goal, a much greater amount of administrative time may be required to find and qualify vendors, and some purchases may be made from vendors which will not give maximum value for the purchase dollar. In the long run, this may be desirable to meet societal goals; in the short run, it's less than optimum purchasing. The public purchaser should make sure that the extra short-run costs from such actions are identified and agreed to by the legislative or administrative body setting such goals.

Absence of interest costs

One of the principal considerations in the industrial firm in determining inventory levels is the interest or opportunity cost of money tied up in inventory. An argument often is made that governmental agencies need not consider money costs in their decisions, since the funds are tax dollars that came into the governmental coffers at a specific date. This is spurious reasoning, for (1) government agencies today typically labor under a burden, large or small, of financial indebtedness, either short- or long-term, and interest cost is a very real cost of operation, and (2) when governmental funds are tied up in purchased inventories, these funds then are not available for employment in other productive uses. This effectively means that there is an opportunity cost of funds invested in inventory. The public buyer may have to take special care to educate other governmental administrators to the fact that inventory investment is expensive, and this cost should be considered in making inventory decisions.

Absence of inspection

Most industrial firms have a quality control or inspection department that handles decisions on both outgoing, finished products and incoming, raw materials or supplies. However, many governmental agencies (with the military as a notable exception) do not have any specialized inspection personnel. Yet, incoming inspection is needed in the case of many of the items bought.

Some steps need to be taken to assure that items delivered by vendors do meet the purchase specifications under which purchase order was written. Then, some specific arrangement should be made to accomplish needed inspection. This could take several forms, depending on the specific item being bought: (1) the user can be advised to check delivered items immediately and report any quality variance; (2) the vendor may be asked to supply notarized copies of inspection reports which show the specific tests conducted and the raw test data which resulted and formed the basis for a decision to ship the items; (3) the buyer may send materials, or samples, out to an independent testing laboratory; (4) the buyer may decide to peform certain simple tests on selected items; or (5) a separate incoming quality control department can be established within the public agency, if a persuasive case can be made that this is needed to assure that fair value is received for dollars spent.

Lack of traffic expertise

Most industrial firms of any size have a traffic specialist or group who handles both inbound and outbound shipments. However, it is rare for public purchasing departments to have a traffic expert or access to such an individual. Yet, materials movement often accounts for a significant part of the total cost of items bought. As a result, the public buyer normally specifies F.O.B. Destination as the shipping basis, which may not be most economical, since the buyer loses control over traffic decisions.

A trained traffic person might make a major contribution in such areas as classification and routing of shipments, selection of carriers, determination of freight charges, and filing damage claims generating savings that would be several times the salary received plus overhead.

Time required to modify the organization

Changes in the organization structure of public purchasing, e.g., the adding or deleting of positions, the changing of reporting relationships, or the redefinition of position duties and responsibilities, often take much longer to accomplish than would be required in an industrial firm. Frequently such changes require a public hearing and normally an investigation by someone from the personnel division. Also, the final approval may require action by some legislative body, such as a state legislature or a city council, and this may require several months. In one sense, this provides stability to public purchasing; on the other hand, the time required may be so long that managers get discouraged and don't bother pressing for needed change.

Procedures normally can be short circuited, when the need for speed is evident. And if the longer time to make organizational changes is recognized, this can be built into the planning horizon and action taken accordingly.

Salary levels

It is easier to make salary level adjustments in the private sector than in public purchasing. However, contrary to popular opinion, the salary levels of public buyers, at least at the lower to medium job assignment levels, are equal to or perhaps a bit higher than those in industrial purchasing. A study conducted in 1972 reported that, based on a sample of public and industrial buyers, salaries in the public/non-profit sector were approximately $1000 per year higher than for the industrial buyer.[2] Thus, the public purchasing department is normally not at any salary disadvantage in recruiting personnel and should be able to attract good people. But at the top levels, government pays salaries that are far below those of industrial firms. A vice president of purchasing for a large manufacturing firm may be paid an annual salary of $60,000 or substantially more, while it is unusual for the top manager or director in a public purchasing department to make over $40,000. Some of the heads of state purchasing departments are paid a salary in the $30,000 range, which is low in relation to the responsibilities of the job. Hopefully, the legislative bodies who set public purchasing salaries now are beginning to recognize the need to pay more realistic salaries to attract top quality managers to public purchasing.

Information cannot be kept confidential

The public buyer lives in a "fishbowl." All information on prices submitted by vendors, and the price finally paid, must be made available to any taxpayer requesting it. Any special arrangements between the buyer and the successful vendor and the final purchase contract are public knowledge. Since vendors realize that all data are available to competitors, they naturally are hesitant to offer the public buyer any special "deals" in an attempt to gain business, for this quickly would become known and would be demanded immediately by all other customers also. The net effect is that the public buyer probably will pay, on the average, higher prices than paid by the buyer in the private firm.

---

[2]I. V. Fine and J. H. Westing, "Organizational Characteristics of Purchasing Personnel in Public and Private Hierarchies," *Journal of Purchasing* 9 (August 1973): 10–11.

Admittedly, there is an advantage in the buyer being able to compare prices with those that others are paying, and this is perfectly legal in public buying, for the buyer is free to talk and exchange vendor information and prices paid with other public buyers. This assures that one public buyer will not be paying a higher price than paid by other agencies. Yet, in the final analysis, this practice operates to the long-term disadvantage of the public buyer, for no vendor will be anxious to give a public buyer a particularly attractive price when that price immediately will be divulged to a number of other public buyers, who will demand equal treatment.

This requirement that data obtained by the public buyer be made available to all is the factor which creates the greatest obstacle to good purchasing by public agencies. It is an understandable requirement, since the funds are obtained from the collective taxpayer who has a right to know how and why tax dollars are spent. Yet, it puts the public buyer at a real disadvantage.

Importance of specifications

Since a very large part of the purchasing actions of public buyers is based on the bidding process, it is vital that specifications for needed items be clear and accurate and written to assure that a maximum number of vendors can compete for the business. These specifications take the form of written descriptions, blueprints, drawings, performance requirements, industry standards, or commercial designation (trade or brand name). Unless all potential bidders can be furnished a complete and usable set of specifications, the bidding process will be imperfect and will not produce the competition necessary to provide best value. In addition, if a bidder can show that the specifications were not uniform, or were subject to varying interpretations, there is a good chance that legal action can be brought to overturn the purchasing department's contract award, which will result in lengthy and costly delays in contract performance.

The development of good, clean specifications requires considerable time and effort, and many governmental purchasing agencies have full-time personnel who work on the preparation and refinement of specifications. Considerable communication between the purchasing agency and the user is necessary to develop clear specifications, and the advantages of standardization between user agencies can be significant.

The public buyer can take advantage of the specification work done by other governmental agencies at the local, county, state, or federal level. The federal government, through the General Services Administration, has developed a multitude of specifications for use in federal purchasing, and these are readily available to anyone wishing to use them. The *Index of Federal Specifications and Standards* can be purchased from the Superintendent of Documents, U.S. Government Printing Office, Washington, D.C. 20402. The *Index* also is available at GSA regional offices, and the individual specifications may be purchased from the GSA in Washington, D.C.

Emphasis on the bid process

Because the public buyer spends funds generated through the tax system, governmental statutes normally provide that the award of purchase contracts should be made on the basis of open, competitive bidding. This provision is supposed to assure that all qualified vendors, who are taxpayers or who employ personnel who are taxpayers, have an equal opportunity to compete for the sale of products on services needed in the operation of government. Since the bids received are open to public inspection, it would be difficult for the public buyer to show favoritism to any one vendor. However, this system does tend to put a heavy weight on price as the basis for vendor selection, for it might be difficult for the buyer to defend selecting a vendor whose price is higher than that of the low bidder. Ideally, the buyer might choose to buy from other than the low bidder due to anticipated superior performance factors on the part of other than the low bidder, but this may be difficult to quantify and thus difficult to defend.

Competitive bidding is time consuming and requires administrative paperwork; for this reason, governmental statutes often will specify that informal bids may be used as the basis of award of purchase orders for requirements under a certain dollar amount, e.g., $1000. Also, in the case of items available from a sole source, purchase decisions may be made on the basis of formal negotiation; however, the sole source vendor situation should be avoided if at all possible, for this is a difficult situation and also costly, in terms of purchasing administrative costs.

When informal negotiations are used to buy requirements of relatively low value, all essential steps of formal bidding should be used, except that only a limited number of bids will be solicited, and this will be done by telephone requests to a limited number of vendors. The buyer needs accurate records of vendors requested to give a phone quote and the reason(s) why a particular vendor was selected, in the event that the decision later is challenged.

Use of bid lists. On the purchase of those items which probably will require repeated purchase actions, a master bid list is compiled. This requires the buyer to specify the characteristics that should be present in any qualified vendor firm, such as size (which relates to ability to provide the needed quantities), financial stability, quality control procedures, finished goods inventory levels (which may determine how quickly items can be obtained), warranty policy, spare parts availability and accessibility of maintenance/repair personnel, and transportation facilities available. Then, the purchasing department will conduct whatever type of vendor survey or investigation is required to assure that a given vendor can meet the minimum level of each important characteristic. If a given vendor is checked out and found to be unsatisfactory, this information should be communicated directly to that vendor so the vendor will know the types of changes which will be necessary if it is to compete for future business.

Deletions from the bid list will be made in the case of vendors who receive purchase awards and then do not perform according to the terms of the purchase agreement. This often is referred to as "blackballing" the vendor, and it is a perfectly legitimate practice, providing the decision to drop a vendor from the bid list can be substantiated with facts and figures from the purchasing department's vendor performance evaluation system. Obviously, a vendor who is being dropped from the bid list for cause should be notified of this action and the specific reasons for the action. One reason for deletion may be the unwillingness of a vendor to submit any bids over an extended period of time for specific requirements. If this is not done, the bid list may become too large and unwieldy, resulting in unneeded costs from sending out bid requests that will not be productive.

The public buyer generally must be willing to consider any vendor who requests to be put on the bid list, after, of course, an investigation of the vendor has been made. However, the competent public buyer is equally as aggressive as the private industry buyer in ferreting out new supply sources.

As part of the bidder qualification process, some type of vendor information form is used. However, even though this is a good initial starting point for the selection of qualified vendors, it will not contain enough information for a complete evaluation, and the public buyer probably will need to make an on-site vendor visit.

Advertising. The bid list, if properly developed and maintained, should provide a large enough group of qualified vendors to enable the public buyer to obtain competition in the bid process. However, many public purchasing agencies, as a matter of normal operating policy or because it specifically is required by statute or regulation, also advertise upcoming purchase needs in either the local newspaper or in the legal paper (normally a weekly). The advertisement says simply that if any given vendor firm wishes to receive a request for bid for a particular requirement, it should contact the purchasing department. The buyer then must determine whether the firm asking to bid meets the minimum vendor qualifications.

Advertising is simply a means of publicly announcing that a purchase will be made. In most instances, it will not produce any new vendors, but it might, and it assures that purchasing is not conducted under any veil of secrecy.

Bid procedures. In a formal bid system, the bidder typically will be sent (1) a complete list of specifications which the item being supplied must meet (in complicated procurements, the specification package may consist of several pages—several hundred pages, in some instances—and may detail the kinds of quality control procedures the buyer will use to assure that the goods delivered do, in fact, meet specifications; (2) a list of instructions to the bidder, spelling out how, when, where, and in what form bids must be submitted; (3) general and special legal conditions which must be met by the successful bidder; and (4) a bid form on which the vendor will submit price, discounts, and other required information.

The bidder typically must submit any bid on or before a specified date and hour, as for example, 1 p.m. on 15 March. No bids will be accepted after the bid closing and no changes will be permitted after the formal bid is received. The place where the bid must be delivered, usually the purchasing department, should be specified, and many public purchasing agencies use a locked container to maintain all sealed bids until the date and hour of the bid opening.

While these bid procedures may appear rather complicated, they do establish an environment in which the buying is conducted in such a way that all qualified vendors have an equal chance of consideration.

Use of bid bonds. Often the bid package requires that any bidder submit a performance bond at the time of the bid. In some states, this is a legal requirement, particularly in the case of purchased items or construction contracts for large dollar amounts. As an alternative, some public purchasing agencies require that the bid be accompanied by a certified check or money order in a fixed percentage amount of the bid. In the event the bidder selected does not agree to sign the final purchase contract award, or does not perform according to the terms of the bid, this amount is retained by the purchasing agency as liquidated damages for nonperformance. Obviously, the bid bond or bid deposit is an attempt to discourage irresponsible bidders from competing. In high risk situations the extra cost of the bid bond, which in some way will be passed back as an extra cost to the buyer, is warranted; in the purchase of standard, stock items available from several sources, the use of a bond is questionable.

Technically, there are three general types of bonds available. The bidder purchases each, for a dollar premium, from an insurance company, thus effectively transferring some of the risk to the insurance carrier:

1. The *bid bond* guarantees that if the order is awarded to a specific bidder, it will accept the purchase contract. If the vendor refuses, the extra costs to the buyer of going to an alternative source are borne by the insurer.

2. The *performance bond* guarantees that the work done will be done according to specifications and in the time specified. If the buyer has to go to another vendor for rework or to get the order completed, purchasing is indemnified for these extra costs.

3. The *payment bond* protects the buyer against liens which might be granted to suppliers of material and labor to the bidder, in the event the bidder does not make proper payment to its vendors.

Bid opening and evaluation. At the hour and date specified in the bid instructions, the buyer will open all bids and record the bids on some type of a bidder spread sheet. In some agencies, the buyer must call out the vendor name and bid, and a clerk records the information, checks the actual bid form for the amount, and then certifies that the information on the spread sheet is correct. Any citizen who wishes normally can attend the bid opening and examine any of the bids. Often vendors who have submitted bids, or ones who have chosen not to bid but who wish to see the bids of other vendors, will attend the opening. After the bids are recorded, the original bids should be retained for later inspection by any interested party for a specified time period (often 12 months).

The buyer than must make a selection of the successful bidder, based on the bid which will give the greatest value. Obviously, if all the specifications and conditions are met by a qualified vendor, the lowest bid will be selected. Otherwise, the bid process is destroyed. If other than the low bidder is selected, the buyer documents the decision very carefully, for it may be informally challenged later or in the courts.

In some public agencies, a purchase award cannot be made unless at least some minimum number of bids (often three) have been received. If the minimum number is not received, the requirement must be rebid, or the buyer must be able to justify that the nature of the requirement is such that it is impossible to obtain bids from any more vendors.

Bid errors. If the successful, low bidder notifies the buyer after the bid has been submitted, but before the award of the purchase order has been made, that an error has been made, the buyer normally will permit the bid to be withdrawn. However, the buyer makes some permanent note of this, since it reflects on the responsibility of the bidder.

A much more serious problem arises if the bidder, claiming a bid error, attempts to withdraw the bid *after* it has been awarded the purchase as the successful bidder. Of course, the use of a bid bond in the bid process is an attempt to protect the buyer if such a problem arises. If the bid bond wasn't used, the buyer must weigh the probability of having severe problems in court action to force performance or collect damages, against the problems and costs of now going to the closest other successful bidder (who now may not be interested) or going through the bid process again. Legal counsel is normally sought, but if the mistake was mechanical in nature, i.e., the figures were added up incorrectly, the courts probably will side with the vendor. However, if it was an error in judgment, e.g., the vendor misjudged the rate of escalation in material prices and used this figure in making the bid, then the courts generally will not permit relief to the vendor. Also, for the vendor to gain relief in the courts, the vendor must be able to show that once the error was discovered, the buying agency was notified promptly.

Obviously, if the buyer receives a bid which common sense and knowledge of the market would indicate is unrealistic, the bid should be rechecked and the bidder requested to reaffirm that it is a bona fide bid. In the long run, such action likely will be cheaper for the buying agency than if a long and involved legal action ensues, with an uncertain outcome.

Bid awards. As stated earlier, if two or more responsible bidders offer to meet the specifications and conditions, the low price bidder is selected. If other than the low bidder is selected, the buyer must be prepared to justify the decision with additional information. If identical low bids are received, and the buyer has no evidence or indication of any collusion or other bid irregularities, then a public "flip of the coin" is a satisfactory means of resolving the deadlock. If the buyer suspects collusion, all bids should be rejected and the requirement rebid. Additionally, this should be reported to the appropriate legal counsel, e.g., the attorney general or Federal Justice Department, for investigation and action.

The public buyer has no obligation to notify unsuccessful bidders of the award, since the bid opening was a public event and the bid and award documents are retained in the purchasing department and may be viewed, on request, by any interested individual. Courtesy suggests, however, that if an unsuccessful vendor makes a telephone or letter request for information, that information be provided promptly, and the requestor invited to come in and examine the file.

Federal government purchasing

There are some specific peculiarities in federal government purchasing, apart from those differences between public and private purchasing discussed earlier. While space does not permit an in depth discussion of these items, a brief discussion is in order.

History. Congress passed a law in 1792 which gave the Treasury and War Departments the authority and responsibility to make purchases for the government. The position of Purveyor of Public Supplies was established in the Treasury Department in 1795. Federal purchasing became more formalized with the Procurement Act of 1809, which required that formal advertising be used in purchasing to assure that all firms had a chance to bid on government requirements. Over the intervening years, federal legislation has been extended to require, in certain instances, such things as public bid openings and bid bonds, and has established extensive rules and procedures for military purchases.

In 1974 the Office of Federal Procurement Policy was set up to coordinate and improve the efficiency of government purchasing. Unfortunately, this agency has received much criticism for its failure to address major policy issues in federal purchasing; instead it is charged that it has dealt primarily with procedural matters and has made it difficult for the individual agencies, such as the Department of Defense, to meet their objectives. Since Congress did not extend its life, this office was discontinued in 1979.

Small business favoritism. Federal legislation in 1953 established the Small Business Administration (SBA), which was to provide aid, counsel, and assistance to small firms. In general, a small business is defined as one that is independently owned and operated, is not dominant in its field, and has dollar receipts below a certain number, depending on the particular industry. The SBA operates a Prime Contracts Program, which provides that on federal contracts above a certain dollar amount a percentage of the contract is set aside for small business firms. The SBA and the involved public buying agency then attempt to find and assist small firms in qualifying and obtaining the amount of purchases set aside.

In 1961, Congress passed Public Law 87–305 which provides that "a fair proportion" of purchases of items from public funds be awarded to small businesses. If a large firm obtains a government contract over a certain amount, it must make a "best effort" to locate and place orders with small subcontractors for a specific dollar amount of the total contract. In many instances, this results in the payment of premium prices to place business with small firms, and increases the administrative expense of purchasing, but Congress justifies this action by arguing that small business must be supported if it is to survive.

Labor surplus area favoritism. The Department of Labor classifies certain cities or areas as ones which have an unusually high unemployment rate or unusually high number of hard-core disadvantaged persons. Certain government purchasing requirements then are set aside for placement of a given percentage of the total buy to firms in those areas. A small business in a labor surplus area is in a particularly advantageous position to compete for these purchases, although the net effect may be that the government (taxpayer) pays a premium price for purchased requirements.

Buy American Act. Congress passed the Buy American Act ostensibly to make sure that the United States maintains its production capability in several "essential" areas, even though foreign firms are able to produce more efficiently and thus undersell domestic firms on requirements for delivery in the United States. It provides that on certain government requirements, the purchase order will be awarded to the domestic firm, providing that its price is not over a given percentage amount (normally 6 percent, or 12 percent if it is a labor surplus area) higher than that offered by the foreign vendor.

Renegotiation. Some of the items bought by the government, and particularly the military services, are so unique that only one supplier can be used; obviously competition cannot be depended upon to give the public buyer a realistic price. Couple this with the delivery time pressures under which military purchasing operates in wartime, and you have the reason for the Renegotiation Law, first passed by Congress in World War II and later superceded during the Korean War by the Renegotiation Act of 1951. It has been temporarily extended several times, but it expired in March 1979. Unless it is extended further, government buyers will have to rely on the Vinson-Trammell Act, passed in the 1930s, which sets allowable profit percentages which contractors can make on aircraft (12 percent) naval vessels (10 percent), and associated equipment. It is administered by the Internal Revenue Service.

Basically, these laws provide that if a firm has done over a certain total dollar annual amount of business with the government, its cost accounting records can be audited and any "excess profits" can be recovered by the government for deposit in the general treasury. Note that the renegotiation is done on a total business, and not on a contract-by-contract, basis, i.e., losses on one contract are used to offset excess profits on other contracts.

General Services Administration (GSA). As a result of a governmental committee (the Hoover Commission) report in 1949, Congress passed Public Law 152, the Federal Property and Administrative Services Act of 1949. The General Services Administration was set up under that Act. GSA is responsible for all federal purchasing, except that done by Department of Defense (DOD), the National Aeronautics and Space Administration (NASA), and the Energy Research and Development Agency (ERDA). In fact, these agencies, as well as certain state, county, and local agencies, also can buy against GSA contracts. GSA is organized under a central office in Washington, and ten regional offices. It sets standards for government purchases, buys and stores for later use, and issues long-term contracts at set prices. When an agency needs an item, it simply cites the appropriate GSA contract. In some instances, GSA actually operates retail-type stores, where any federal purchaser can go to obtain things such as office supplies and equipment.

GSA buying is, without question, big business. Total expenditures are approximately \$4.8 billion per year. Unfortunately, this governmental operation has not been free of scandal over the years, and allegations of fraud and theft have been made.[3]

Military purchasing. Following the experience of World War II, and after several studies to review past experience, Congress passed the Armed Services Procurement Act of 1947, which provides the authority for today's purchasing actions by the Department of Defense (DOD). In addition, it permits the use of negotiated procurements under certain conditions; it prohibits the use of cost plus profit-as-a-percentage-of-cost type contracts; and it establishes the policies under which purchasing for the Armed Forces is to be conducted. To meet the intent of the Armed Services Procurement Act, the Department of Defense has adopted the Armed Services Procurement Regulations (ASPR), which is the "Bible" for Armed Services procurement personnel. ASPR is a very lengthy, detailed volume, containing several thousand pages.

There are four types of contracts in common use by military buyers:

1.   *Firm-Fixed-Price (FFP) Contract:* The price set is not subject to change, under any circumstances. This is the preferable type of contract, but if the delivery date is some months or years away and if there is substantial chance of price escalation, a vendor may feel that there is far too much risk of loss to agree to sell under a FFP contract.

2.   *Cost-Plus-Fixed-Fee (CPFF) Contract:* In situations where it would be unreasonable to expect a vendor to agree to sell at a firm-fixed price the CPFF contract can be used. This situation might occur if the item is experimental and the specifications are not firm, or if costs in the future cannot be predicted. The buyer agrees to reimburse the vendor for all reasonable costs incurred (under a set of definite policies under which "reasonable" is to be determined) in doing the job or producing the required item, plus a specified dollar amount of profit. A maximum amount may be specified for the cost. This contract type is far superior to the old "cost-plus-percentage" type, which encouraged the vendor to run the costs up as high as possible to increase the base on which the profit is figured. While the vendor bears little risk under the CPFF, since costs will be reimbursed, the vendor's profit percentage declines as the costs increase, giving some incentive to the vendor to control costs.

3.   *Cost-No-Fee (CNF) Contract:* If the buyer can argue persuasively that there will be enough subsidiary benefits to the vendor from doing a particular job, then the vendor may be willing to do it provided only the costs are reimbursed. For example, the vendor may be willing to do the research and produce some new product if only the costs are returned, because doing the job may give the vendor some new technological or product knowledge, which then may be used to make large profits in some commercial market.

4.   *Cost-Plus-Incentive-Fee (CPIF) Contract:* In this type of contract, both

---

[3]James C. Hyatt and David Ignatius, "Fraud at GSA Stores is Only the Beginning of Agency's Troubles," *The Wall Street Journal,* (13 September 1978), p. 1.

buyer and seller agree on a target cost figure, a fixed fee, and a formula under which any cost over- or under-runs are to be shared. For example, assume the agreed-upon target cost is $100,000, the fixed fee is $10,000, and the incentive sharing formula is 50/50. If actual costs are $120,000, the $20,000 cost over run would be shared equally between buyer and seller, based on the 50/50 sharing formula, and the vendor's profit would be reduced by $10,000, or to zero in this example. On the other hand, if total costs are only $90,000, then the vendor's share of the $10,000 cost under run would be $5,000. Total profit then would be $10,000 + 5,000, or $15,000. This type of contract has the effect of motivating the vendor to be as efficient as possible, since the benefits of greater efficiency (or the penalties of inefficiency) accrue in part, based on the sharing formula, to the vendor.

State and local government purchasing

While purchasing done by state, country, municipal, and other public agencies tends to follow all the basic guidelines of public purchasing, there are some unique aspects which should be commented on briefly.

History: The state of Oklahoma was first to establish centralized purchasing, in 1910. With that start, in the 1920s, along with budget reform, many additional states adopted central purchasing. By 1967, all the states, with the exception of Delaware, had adopted central purchasing.[4] However, in many states there is not total centralization of purchasing, for many state agencies often handle their purchasing separately from the central purchasing office. One good example of this is the state universities, which often do all the purchasing needed by their institutions, using, where advantageous, existing state contracts.

Participation in GSA contracts: Those political subdivisions (cities, counties, and states) which are the recipients of some type of federal grant or funding are eligible to use the GSA contracts. In some instances this will allow the agency to buy items at a lower price, and with substantially lower administrative cost, than could be accomplished otherwise. Certainly the public buyer at least should check out the GSA prices before making a decision.

Prison-made goods: Some states require that if one of the state's penal institutions produces items required in the operation of state government, that penal institution must be given absolute preference in purchasing. The items produced might include foodstuffs, shoes, work clothing, and license plates. The public purchasing officer should know what kinds of items are available from the penal institutions and should communicate to the prison administrators the quality requirements which goods must meet.

Cooperative purchasing: In the last decade or so, the cooperative purchasing approach has received much attention, interest, and use in public purchasing. Basically, it is a system whereby two or more public, or not-for-profit, purchas-

---

[4] "Table 2: Estimated Volume of Purchases, Operating Costs, and Number of Employees, 1966–67," in George W. Jennings, *State Purchasing* (Lexington, Kentucky: The Council of State Governments, 1969), p. 11.

ing departments pool their requirements so that they can talk with vendors about substantially larger purchase quantities than would be required by any one buyer. It has been used successfully by local government units, public school districts, and hospitals, and it has its primary advantage for the smaller purchasing unit.

There are two basic variations used in cooperative purchasing: (1) joint buying, where two or more purchasing departments agree to pool their requirements for a particular item and let one of the purchasing departments commit the total purchase quantity to a specific vendor, at a specific price, and (2) a formal, contractual arrangement where several individual purchasing departments agree to establish and fund a separate cooperative buying agency and to use the purchasing services of that agency. For example, several hospitals in a particular area could agree to pool their requirements for basic items and then hire a full-time buyer (manager) of a cooperative hospital purchasing agency. The administrative costs of the cooperative agency would be shared by all hospital members on some basis such as size of hospital or total purchase dollars spent through the cooperative group. Such cooperative agencies do exist in the health-care field in several states and many universities are affiliated with the cooperative buying arm of the National Association of Educational Buyers.

In 1972, the Association of School Business Officials made a suvey of a large group of local school agencies and reported that about 61 percent of the 1,135 members reporting were participating in some type of cooperative purchasing arrangement. When asked to indicate the advantages of cooperative buying, some of the items they reported were (1) lower prices; (2) improved quality, through improved testing and vendor selection; (3) reduced administrative cost; (4) standardization; (5) better records; and (6) greater competition. Among the problems cited as arising from cooperative buying were: (1) inferior products; (2) longer lead times; (3) limited items available; (4) more paperwork; and (5) inability of small vendors to compete, due to larger quantities required.[5]

Local-bidder preference laws: In many governmental jurisdictions, the applicable law or statute states that, all other things being equal, local bidders must be granted a certain percentage price preference in bidding against non-local vendors. For example, if a local vendor submits a bid that is not over a given percent, e.g., 5 percent, higher than non-local vendors, then the local vendor must be awarded the purchase order, assuming all other factors are equal. This is a form of protectionism, similar to that of the Buy American Act. The argument for this is that local vendors have employees in the local area, and the award of orders to local vendors provides support for the local economy.

This practice is opposed by most purchasing professionals as being a non-competitive practice, which means that higher prices are paid for purchases than is necessary. It negates the advantages of economic specialization, and local vendors, knowing that such a preference is to be applied, will have a tendency to submit a bid that is higher than they otherwise would present. If we believe in

[5]Richard E. Munsterman, *Purchasing and Supply Management Handbook for School Business Officials,* Research Bulletin No. 22 (Chicago: Association of School Business Officials of the United States and Canada, 1978), pp. 176–77.

totally fair, open competition, then all vendors, regardless of location, should be permitted to compete solely on the basis of their ability to provide maximum value for the public funds expended. The National Association of State Purchasing Officials has gone on record as strongly opposing such a practice.

Proposed Model Procurement Code: Starting in the late 1960s a committee of the American Bar Association began discussing the need for a model procurement code for state and local purchasing activities. The Bar Association felt such a code was needed for two reasons: first, the substantial increase in and amounts of money spent in state and local purchasing, and second, since the federal government supplies funds to state and local governments, the spending of these funds should comply with sound purchasing practices.

In 1972 a Coordinating Committee on a Model Procurement Code for State and Local Governments was established to begin the work of drafting a model code. As of August 1978, the code had gone through two drafts. In addition, selected jurisdictions, states, and cities had been selected to serve as pilot jurisdictions to provide feedback on the workability of the proposed code. These included the states of Kentucky, Tennessee, New Mexico, Louisiana, and Utah, and the cities of Louisville, Kentucky; Knoxville, Tennessee; Baltimore, Maryland; and San Diego, California.[6]

The proposed Code itself is a 291 page document, divided into twelve parts or Articles, as follows:

Article 1: General provisions
Article 2: Purchasing organization
Article 3: Source selection and contract formation
Article 4: Specifications
Article 5: Procurement of construction and architect-engineer services
Article 6: Modification and termination of contracts for supplies and services
Article 7: Cost and pricing principles
Article 8: Supply management
Article 9: Legal and contractual remedies
Article 10: Intergovernmental relations
Article 11: Socioeconomic policies
Article 12: Ethics in public contracting[7]

QUESTIONS FOR REVIEW AND DISCUSSION

1. What changes should be made in public purchasing to make it more effective?
2. Are there any differences between Federal purchasing and state and local purchasing? Discuss.

---

[6]"Summary Background Statement" of the American Bar Association Coordinating Committee on a Model Procurement Code for State and Local Governments, dated October 1, 1978, 1700 K Street N.W., Washington, D.C. 20006.

[7]"A Model Procurement Code for State and Local Governments," Tentative Draft, July 10, 1978 by American Bar Association, Coordinating Committee on a Model Procurement Code for State and Local Governments, 1700 K Street N.W., Washington, D.C. 20006.

3. How do the objectives of public purchasing differ from those of industrial buying?
4. Discuss the advantages and problems arising from local bidder preference laws in state and local purchasing.
5. What are performance bonds, and why are they used?
6. How does the bid process in public buying differ from that in industrial buying?
7. What are the major differences between public buying and industrial buying? Which would be easiest to do?

CASE 14-1
GARDEN STATE

Ike Duncan, vehicle buyer at the Garden State central purchasing office, had just received the news that the new truck, ordered several months earlier, did not meet specifications.

It was standard practice in Garden State for local automobile dealers to submit quotations on invitations to bid which were both publicly advertised and sent to vendors on the approved dealers list. Ike knew that the dealers made their own arrangements with the manufacturers and suspected that, particularly on the high volume requirements, extensive consultation took place between dealers and manufacturers.

The engineering division of the department of public works had ordered a truck to replace an existing one. Specifications had been carefully worked out in consultation with the specification engineer. The truck had been part of an odd lot bid involving six vehicles. When the dealer advised that the truck had arrived, inspection by the engineering department revealed that on four counts the vehicle failed to meet the original specifications:

1. Gross Vehicle Weight (GVW) was supposed to be 27,500 pounds; 24,000 pounds was supplied. This reduced the maximum load which could be carried by 3,500 pounds.
2. The engine specifications called for 360 cubic inches; 351 were supplied.
3. The tires were supposed to be 12 ply; 10 ply was supplied.
4. The paint specification called for a particular number and make and a different shade and make was supplied.

Ike was disappointed with this news and was trying to determine what his best course of action would be.

CASE 14–2
FOLAN CITY

"I want you to know that I intend to fight this, and I am going to give the mayor a call right now!" shouted Bill Marsden as he hung up after talking with Andrea Sparton. They had been discussing the city's purchase of a compressor on which the Marsden firm had been low bidder but had not been awarded the contract. Andrea Sparton was director of purchases for Folan City, a west coast municipality with about 1,000,000 residents, well known for its natural attractions.

The compressor had been requested by the engineering shops and considerable care had been taken to draw up the appropriate specifications to reflect the variety of uses anticipated for this equipment. A Johnson, model TAR, was considered suitable, and bidders were invited to quote on this model or its equivalent.

Invitations to bid had been sent out and eight quotations were received, with Marsden Inc. as the low bidder by $2,300. Since Marsden's bid was based on a make and model different from the one referred to in the invitation to bid, Andrea had asked the city engineering department to assess the model proposed by Marsden to see if it was equivalent. According to the city engineer, the Marsden model was inferior to the one requested. On the basis of that assessment, another firm which had quoted on the Johnson TAR model had been recommended by purchasing for this contract. This recommendation had gone to the City's finance committee, which had accepted purchasing's recommendation at its regular Tuesday night meeting. The following morning, Bill Marsden, president of Marsden Inc., had telephoned Andrea to complain. Andrea realized that Bill Marsden was an influential local businessman whose aggressiveness was well known in local business and political circles. In his telephone call to Andrea, Bill maintained that the equipment he was offering was equivalent in quality and performance to the Johnson TAR model, and that, since he was the low bidder, he should receive the business. During his conversation with Andrea he also managed to raise the point: "We, local suppliers, seem to have a difficult time with this city's purchasing office. If we quote high, we don't receive the business, and if we quote low we aren't getting any business, either. What do we have to do to make an honest buck around here?"

CASE 14-3
MAYFAIR COUNTY BOARD OF EDUCATION

Mr. Fraser Lewis, supervisor of purchasing for the Mayfair County Board of Education (see Exhibit 1), listened thoughtfully to the supervisor of caretaking, Bob Oxford, outline his plans for the cleaning of ten new and near-new schools:

"As you know, Fraser, we are trying to find a flexible balance in the systems between the Caretakers' Association and outside contractors. We find no fault with the Association people but, naturally, they want an exclusive if they can get it, even though they are not actually a union. However, this depends on their doing a proper job, and there's nothing like a bit of competition to ensure keeping everyone on his toes. Even if we do contract for schools one to ten, we are large enough to be able to transfer existing staff to other schools without anyone suffering, especially at the rate we are expanding. As you remember, we don't need to employ our own caretaking staff for new schools, under our agreement."

"Fine," said Fraser Lewis. "This will run into quite a bit of money, so we'll have to advertise for tenders as well as approach firms we already know. We'll ask for bids on all or some of the schools and reserve the right to accept any combination. I think the board is still sticking to the policy of using our own forces, providing costs are pretty close?"

"That's right," replied the caretaking supervisor. "By the way, I'll send you the usual square footage specification information and work up costs for you when required. As it's nearly April now, perhaps you'll get this rolling quickly?"

"No problem, Bob. Send the material to Lin Godfrey who handles this buying for me."

Fraser Lewis smiled ruefully as he remembered this phone call which had been the starting point of the new cleaning contract. He had a high regard for Bob Oxford, who had formerly managed a national caretaking firm. It was now at the end of November, and the supervisor of caretaking was breathing down his neck. He would have to make a drastic decision soon. He phoned his caretaking buyer. "Lin, let's run through the caretaking file again to refresh my memory. Bob Oxford is furious about the Carlon situation."

"Well, here's the run-down, Fraser," said Godfrey, seating himself and opening a thick file. "On April 9, I advertised for bids. In addition, I sent it to about 15 firms we know. Some we had dealt with, including Carlon, and, of course, we asked for references and supplied complete specs. The prospective contractors had to examine the schools."

"What was Carlon's reputation?" interjected Lewis.

"Well, let's put it this way," said the buyer, "He's done a little for us in

Exhibit 1
General information

The board was one of the largest in the South and fast expanding. It controlled 143 schools with 78,000 pupils. The average cost of a school was $8 million. The operating budget was $125 million; the capital budget about $36 million for new buildings.

Exhibit 1 *(continued)*
Organization chart

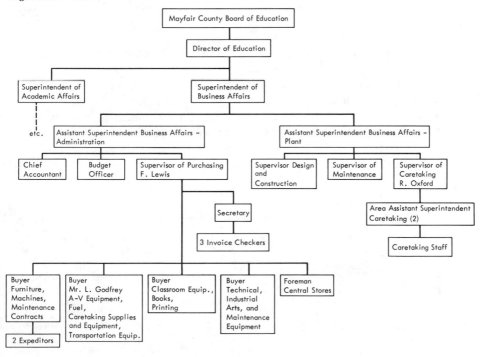

Purchasing information
Purchasing expenditures for supplies and equipment were $15 million annually.

The bid policy was:

$500 and under	Verbal quotation
$501 to $1,000	Verbal quotation plus written confirmation
$1,001 to $5,000	Formal quotation
Over $5,000	Publicly advertise for bids

Usually three quotations were required except when only small amounts were involved or there was too limited a number of suppliers. Public bids were opened by purchasing and the amounts read out to those contractors attending the opening. Mr. Lewis approved all bids and also signed all orders over $5,000. He reported this decision at regular reporting board of trustees meetings.

Unionization of contractors' labor was not demanded.

All things being equal, suppliers in or nearest the boards' territory were favored.

Abnormal bids were only drawn to suppliers' attention if there was an obvious error. Rebidding was permitted once in this event. However, a bidder could withdraw his tender up to the moment of opening.

the past reasonably well, but he's held some really important contracts for the federal government and quite an array of well-known industrial firms. I'd rate him adequate. Certainly not by any means low enough to exclude him from consideration, but not a leader like Smithers who walked off with the low bid on eight of the ten original schools. Smithers has done quite a bit of work for us before and always well."

"Did we get the usual bid bonds to ensure that the companies would go ahead if awarded a contract?"

"Yes, for 10 percent of the overall bid."

"And what about performance bonds for 10 percent of the contract value,"

"All O.K.," replied Godfrey, "as far as Smithers is concerned. Actually, Carlon's isn't in our file, but I have Surety's agreement to bond them for performance if they were successful. This was the situation," he continued. "I had all my figures from half a dozen people by April 24 (see Exhibit 2). Some of them go all over the shop. Smithers was lowest on schools 1, 3, 4, 5, 6, 7, 8 and 9 and Carlon on 2 and 10."

Exhibit 2
Janitorial service (bid summary in $000s)

			Bidder				Smithers	Carlon
School	Square feet	Present cost	A	B	C	D	E	F
1	180,550	74.8	74.2	72.2	—	69.9	58.7L	66.6
2	173,800	67.4	70.8	—	79.0	67.2	67.2	63.9L
3	169,644	67.6	69.2	72.3	76.7	78.3	58.4L	61.8
4	152,680	61.4	61.6	63.1	—	58.7	48.7L	58.4
5	180,384	69.5	74.6	76.7	82.0	69.4	59.7L	66.6
6	209,801	75.0	89.8	—	—	73.9	67.8L	76.4
7	77,015	31.2	39.2	30.8	—	31.1	30.1L	31.5
8	110,616	37.5	49.2	45.9	—	42.6	36.2L	43.0
9	130,897	—	59.3	—	—	46.7	42.6L	51.2
10	60,500	30.6	39.0	—	—	37.7	28.5	22.4L

Bids recorded April 24
L = Low bid.

"None of the bidders bothered to be present at the opening read-out on May 7, but somehow Carlon knew where he stood. That was obvious from subsequent conversations. It so happened that Carlon was about $3,300 below the next man on School No. 2 and $6,100 lower on School No. 10. In both cases Smithers was the competition." By June 6 we agreed internally to withdraw School No. 2—a large one—because Bob Oxford's cost estimates showed his own forces to be within 2 percent of outside bids. Actually, with your approval I issued the appropriate purchase orders on June 15. We told the board in our recommendation of June 20 that we had given eight schools to Smithers and only one to Carlon.

"When did Carlon react?" asked Mr. Lewis.

"Their sales manager phoned me at the end of June," said the buyer, "and confirmed it on July 6, asking leave to withdraw his quotation." (See Exhibit 3).

"And when did I write him about his obligations?" asked Mr. Lewis. "On July 13," said Mr. Godfrey. "Here it is." (See Exhibit 4).

"Then nothing further transpired until September when Bob Oxford's men noted sloppy work in School No. 10. He sent them a registered letter at the end of that month (see Exhibit 5) and received verbal assurances of improvement but complained again by letter a month later (see Exhibit 6) and got renewed assurance and a very temporary improvement. However, last week he was fed up and sent in one of his assistant superintendents with a team for a detailed inspection which proved the inefficiency of the cleaning. Some floors needed complete refinishing. Bob Oxford is mad. All he wants is to get these blank, blank people out."

"To tell you the truth, Fraser, this Carlon outfit has been around long enough to know what they are doing. I think they're trying to weasel and should be nailed. They know what a performance bond means. We always ask for a performance bond for ten percent of total contract price. Here is our chance to take 'vantage of it."

"Thank y   replied the purchasing supervisor, "I'll think it over."

Fraser L·   it was bad for a firm's reputation to have to call on surety to   .eficiency, yet to release the contractor from his responsi┤   .. affect the board's posture on future tendering. He wonde·   .easonable avenues of avoiding an unpleasant show-down had b.en explored.

Exhibit 3
Letter from Carlon

Exhibit 4
Reply to Carlon

Mayfair County Board of Education

July 13

Dear Mr. Inglis:

Your letter of July 6, to Mr. L. Godfrey requesting withdrawal of your tender covering Janitorial Services at Public School No. 10 has been referred to me.

I would like to draw to your attention the fact, included with your tender, was a bid bond which reads in part:

> Now, Therefore the condition of this obligation is such that if the aforesaid Principal shall have the tender accepted within sixty (60 days from the closing date of tender and the said Principal will, within the time required, enter into a formal contract and give a good and sufficient bond to secure the performance of the terms and conditions of the contract, then this obligation shall be null and void; otherwise the Principal and Surety will pay unto the Obligee the difference in money between the amount of the bid of the said Principal and the amount for which the Obligee legally contracts with another party to perform the work if the latter amount be in excess of the former.
>
> The Surety shall not be liable for a greater sum than the specified penalty of this Bond.

The difference between your tender and the next lowest is $6,100. If the services are not carried out by your company according to specifications, we shall have to refer the matter to your surety company for the extra cost to complete the work. This may not be in your best interest.

Please advise.

Yours truly,

F. Lewis,
Supervisor of Purchasing

Exhibit 5
Letter to Carlon

Mayfair County Board of Education

September 27

Re: Contract for Cleaning Services—Public School No. 10.

Dear Mr. Dale:

This letter will put on record our experience of the service your company has provided at School No. 10 since the beginning of your contract until the present time.

I personally inspected the interior of this school prior to the commencement of your contract and found it to be in a very clean condition. Since then, a steady deterioration in the general cleanliness of the school has been noted by the Principal and the Caretaker. Notes have been left daily for your staff to see regarding specific complaints. Your Mr. Johnson was called in by the Principal on September 21, and he agreed that the condition of the interior of the building had deteriorated since your company had assumed the cleaning contract and that some changes would have to be made.

At the Principal's request, Mr. Riddell, Assistant Supervisor of Caretaking, inspected the school this morning. His report to me read as follows:

1. None of the classroom floors had been swept.
2. Desk tops had not been cleaned.
3. Washroom floors had neither been swept or washed.
4. Toilet seats had not been washed.

Exhibit 5 (continued)

5. There was no indication that any "spray buffing" had been carried out on the floors the previous night.

This, Mr. Dale, is a very poor situation, and one which requires immediate attention by your company. I would expect an immediate drastic improvement in the quality of the service your company is providing and a firm assurance from yourself that this type of experience will not be repeated.

Yours very truly,

Mayfair County Board of Education.
R. Oxford, Supervisor of Caretaking.

Exhibit 6
Letter to Carlon

Mayfair County Board of Education

October 30

Re: Contract Cleaning Services—Public School No. 10

Dear Mr. Dale:

It has again become necessary to write to you regarding the condition of Public School No. 10, where cleaning services are presently being provided by your company. The school premises were inspected once more by my Assistant Supervisor on the morning of October 26. His report follows:

1. Room 29—floor dusty, desk tops dirty, corners dirty.
2. Music Room 28—risers not swept.
3. Large Gym—floor not swept.
4. Locker Rooms—toilets not cleaned, floors not swept.
5. Industrial Arts Room—floor not swept properly, bradley basin not cleaned.
6. Rooms 21–26 inclusive—floors poorly swept, desk tops dirty, chalk ledges dirty, corners of floor dirty.
7. Rooms 12–17 inclusive—desk tops sticky, floors not properly swept.
8. Art Room—floor needs refurbishing.
9. Rooms 3–9 inclusive—floors and desk tops in poor condition (the lunch room is particularly bad).
10. Library—table tops dirty, black base dirty.
11. Office—counter top dirty, dusting could improve.
12. Staff Room—there appeared to be a white film on the floor, tables dirty.
13. Corridors—dull, there is some kind of film all over.
14. The spray buffing program is not being carried out according to specifications.
15. Washrooms—urinals had been poorly cleaned.

As you can see, Mr. Dale, there has been no improvement since my letter of September 27. I would expect you to get in touch with me as soon as possible, as I do not feel that I can authorize payment for your October invoice.

I believe we should also talk about the future of your contract, as no apparent effort is being made by your company to live up to the specifications. You will remember that we offered to cooperate with you in rescheduling your help, receiving your assurance that this would enable you to do a satisfactory job. This has not been the case.

I will await your early reply.

Yours very truly,
Mayfair County Board of Education.
R. Oxford,
Supervisor of Caretaking.

CASE 14–4
THE EASTERN COUNTIES REGION

In early 1979 Hugh Carson joined the Eastern Counties Region Purchasing Department as senior buyer. Art Simpson, the purchasing agent who hired him, said: "Hugh, why don't you work with us for the next six months, become familiar with the work, and then we will sit down together and discuss your impressions. By August we will have to start work on our plans for 1980 and that will be an excellent time to incorporate any suggestions you may have. As you know, we are really just getting started here and you are likely to encounter all sorts of things that can stand improvement. I am interested in tackling the most important things first, so you will have to give some indication of your priorities."

As a busy first six months on the job neared their end in mid-July, Hugh received a reminder from Art who said: "Let's get together for half a day on the 3rd of August to discuss what's going on. Just so that we may have as useful a session as possible, please put your key ideas down in memo form and have these to me by the end of July. Then we will make your memo the starting point of our discussion."

The Eastern Counties Region

The Eastern Counties Region was established in 1978 to consolidate a number of counties, previously independently governed. One of the many objectives of the state in establishing regional government was to provide integrated region wide services. Regional responsibilities included planning, the production and distribution of water, bulk sewage collection and treatment, roads, traffic, police, social services including day care and senior citizen centers. The area encompassed about 800 square miles and employed approximately 1200 full-time employees.

Purchasing organization and responsibilities

The purchasing agent reported to the director of finance. The purchasing department was responsible for the procurement of all supplies and services for the counties with the exception of major construction contracts (roadways, bridges, new buildings, etc.). Annual purchases were estimated at $19–$25 million.

Personnel in the purchasing department included a purchasing agent, a senior buyer, a buyer/expediter and two clerk/stenos. Art Simpson believed that because of the large variety and types of products and services required, it was not practical to organize buyers' responsibilities by product type or classification. Therefore, buyers' responsibilities were divided among the different using departments which included: 19 water treatment plants, 14 pollution control plants, 5 senior citizen homes, 5 day care centers, 3 police detachments, totaling approximately 600 personnel, 3 roadyards, 10 administration departments, 1 fleet maintenance center, 1 traffic department, 1 in-plant print shop, and 3 social services departments.

Hugh Carson's impressions

Hugh Carson had previously worked as a buyer in the purchasing department of a large city in a nearby state. The regional job represented a promotion and an opportunity to help build a new department, a challenge he wished to experience. Several times during his first six months on the job he wondered why he had been so anxious to seek this new experience, because he found the present purchasing situation hectic. In his opinion, there were a large number of contributing factors. The more important of these follow.

1. The paper flow. The paper flow in purchasing was massive in Hugh's opinion and could best be illustrated by the following annual figures. The department:

a. Processed 12–14,000 purchase requisitions.

b. Issued 10–11,000 purchase orders and written releases against blanket orders and contracts.

c. Prepared written specifications and issued 250–300 formal requests for quotation. Each request was prepared individually starting with a blank sheet of paper. This required a great deal of typing, use of colored letterhead, collation, and assembly.

d. Summarized all appropriate quotations and prepared reports to the Regional Board with recommendation of awards.

e. Issued normal day-to-day correspondence.

In Hugh's opinion, this paperwork kept him chained to his desk, always behind, and made it difficult to do other necessary tasks.

2. Interdepartmental communication. Hugh quickly found out that there was no coordination of purchases between similar departments. For example, the 19 different water treatment plants did their own requisitioning of supplies with no communication between them, as was the case with the pollution control plants and other units. This resulted in multiple orders for identical or similar products.

3. The lack of standardization. Because of the poor communication between all departments, there was no standardization of materials. Every plant used different cleaning waxes, had preferences in tools different from the others, used different bearings for identical equipment, etc. Hugh understood this was logical, given the evolution of the current governmental structure, but he believed it created many problems for both purchasers and users.

4. Storage facilities. Hugh believed there was a general shortage of storage area in the system. There was no central warehouse for inventory of general supplies and materials and none of the using departments had sufficient storage space to stock large quantities of supplies. This hindered economical volume purchasing.

5. Delays in purchasing. To Hugh, the time period from issue of requisition to the placement of the purchase order was too long. Requisitions from all using departments had to go first to each using department's supervisor who approved them before forwarding them to purchasing. This in itself created a delay. Since all the regional mail was handled by the region's own delivery service, this created a further delay. Finally, the backlog of orders in the purchasing department meant that many requisitions were not acted upon for at least several weeks.

6. The annual budget rush. The annual budget created two peak loads for purchasing. Many department heads were anxious to spend their full budget before the expiry of the current year. This created a large number of last minute requests. Furthermore, once the new annual budget was approved this created a great rush of new requisitions. These activities increased the department workload substantially since they necessitated the issuing of formal quotations and bid requests and summaries and reports to the Board.

7. Departmental policies and guidelines. At present there was no legal provision which governed the policies and procedures of the purchasing department nor was there a purchasing manual or guidebook available for purchasing staff or using departments. As a result, Hugh was not sure whether all departments were using purchasing and whether the purchasing department left itself open to charges of violating the public trust.

8. Recommendations. Hugh Carson knew that Art Simpson was looking forward to his appraisal of the purchasing department. Even though he could see many areas for possible improvement, he was not sure where to begin. Since he had only several days left to prepare the memo Art Simpson had requested, he knew it was time to get his thoughts down on paper.

CASE 14–5
WAYFARER BOARD OF EDUCATION

Mr. G. Feltar, controller of purchasing for the Wayfarer Board of Education, was concerned about the impact of the four-year-old budget control system on his supply operations.

He was occasionally criticized by the schools for slow deliveries and red tape but considered that his department was being faulted, not by its own inefficiency, but rather by the intricate controls he had to enforce.

Decreasing enrollments had led to budget cuts, and the board deemed tight control over purchases to be a critical factor in its fight to conserve funds.

Although most educational expenditures were determined by the state, a large item over which the board exercised complete discretion was the $15 million purchasing budget. Approximately one third was spent on equipment and two thirds on general supplies.

The board was one of the largest in the state of Indiana, employing 3,000 teachers, 700 support staff, and operating 70 elementary and 15 secondary schools.

The budget year

The budget year ran from January 1 to December 31. However, the annual budget was not approved by the board until early March, causing a rush of orders in March. At that time most departments start ordering materials, especially equipment and supplies for elective programs such as a school's new camera club. Another rush occurred in November when the final purchases were requested to finish the budgets for that year. A third rush of orders was in June when teachers ordered everything to be ready for the next school year, September 1.

In January, Mr. Feltar received board approval to buy 75 percent of last year's annual budget for general supplies. This allowed him to purchase between then and March 1. This 75 percent, however, did not include equipment. Many items were once-only purchases which required the annual budget approval before they could be bought. The budget did vary substantially from year to year. Last year, for example, no equipment purchases were allowed. It was impossible under this system to buy on next year's budget before January 1 or carry over an unused budget amount into the following year. During these peak order times there was virtually no prompt delivery. If a principal telephoned and asked where his purchase order was in the process, or whether or not an order would be approved by the computer in time for him to switch it to another budget, Mr. Feltar often could not answer since he could not readily locate the order.

Purchasing at the board

Each school had numerous budgets, sometimes totaling fifty or more. Mr. Feltar came in contact primarily with the custodial, furniture, physical education, science, commercial, vocational and general supply budgets. His department (see Exhibit 1) handled all the actual purchases. All custodial, physical education, and some general supplies were shipped to the central warehouse. The remaining supplies were sent directly to the schools. The services which acted as courier for the schools' mail, delivering it to the post office or the administrative offices, would also distribute warehouse

Exhibit 1
Organization chart

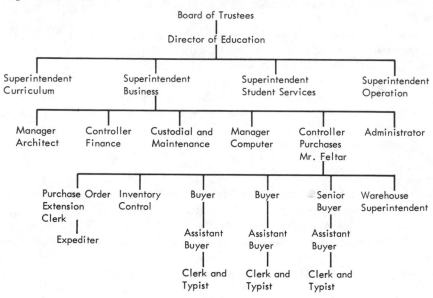

supplies. Most mail arrived every second day from secondary schools and twice a week from elementary schools, varying in some degree with the size of the school.

The warehouse, with an inventory of $140,000 made up primarily of standard school supplies, also handled special physical education and art equipment which schools could use on a loan basis. The warehouse provided prompt delivery on standard items and to some degree allowed purchasing to buy in economical quantities. Generally, delivery time from the warehouse was two weeks. Mr. Feltar thought ideally this should be one week.

The schools received weekly and at times daily printouts on how they stood in regard to their budgets, but still about two percent–five percent of the purchase orders were rejected due to lack of funds.

Sometimes it was necessary to make budget transfers. All budget transfers had to be approved at the Board of Trustees' meeting. If a transfer involved more than $1,000, approval had to be obtained before any action was initiated, but transfers under $1,000 were automatically approved at the next regular board meeting. A principal could resubmit a previously rejected requisition with a new budget number, noting the transfer status of the item.

The purchasing procedure

A budget committee of the Board of Trustees determined yearly the per student expenditure for supplies and allocated dollar appropriations for replacement and purchase of capital equipment. The resulting guidelines were then discussed and approved by the board's trustees.

When a principal or department head filled out a requisition form, he checked his budget for that category item to see whether funds were available.

Requisitions were then forwarded to the purchasing department. Here, the appropriate buyer recommended a supplier or checked the suggested supplier if the item was unique. He also added in or verified pice and quantity. Next the extension clerk checked sales tax, unencumbered budget amounts, and budget classification. The requisitions were then batched and punched on computer cards by the key-punch department. They were then forwarded to a technical school's computer center, and checked there against the master budget allocations. Batches of work had frequently been additionally delayed in this school because precedence was given to academic work which was handled on the same computer.

The requisitions were then returned to the finance department which sent the rejected forms back to the requisitioner. The approved requisitions were forwarded to the purchasing department which issued the purchase orders to suppliers or the warehouse as the case might be.

For supplies shipped directly to the school, the receiving slip, upon receipt of goods, was forwarded to the accounts payable department which verified the price and quantity and checked the budget approvals on the purchase order. Most invoices were paid promptly and all discounts taken. Mr. Feltar had, however, encountered situations where "When am I going to get my money?" arose. If he had helped a principal by ordering before budget approval was obtained and the service or goods had been delivered, the supplier had to wait until a budget transfer was completed.

Normally, the purchase cycle with suppliers took three weeks. At the end of the budget year this increased to five weeks. A tracer was sent out if an order was misplaced or the supplier did not ship. If a teacher complained about slow delivery, a tracer was also used.

Mr. Feltar explained that it was extremely difficult to locate orders. The purchasing department handled 33,000 purchase orders and 7,000 warehouse releases. The board had approximately 1,000 suppliers. Sixty percent of the dollar purchases were called on tender, taking the form of yearly contracts. In a recent computer survey of 10,000 purchase orders, 20 percent were under $10.00; 39 percent under $25.00; 56 percent under $50.00 and 72 percent under $100.00. Of these 10,000 orders, 2,200 were between $100.00 and $500.00 per order.

Areas of concern

Everyone in the purchasing department was under considerable pressure to live up to the "service department" expectation that the rest of the board held of purchasing. Mr. Feltar had to handle frequent "misunderstandings" between finance clerks, key-punch operators, and purchasing personnel, including the purchase order extension clerk. These "misunderstandings" were becoming more personal and created at times an unpleasant atmosphere. Mr. Feltar recognized that some of these difficulties were a direct result of the budgetary system and had introduced a number of ideas to alleviate the strain.

Mr. Feltar believed that the large number of purchase orders could be reduced, thereby decreasing the purchase order cycle time. He devised a mini-order system for school principals who would fill out the mini-order and send it directly to a supplier with a copy to the purchasing department. These were to be used only for small-dollar and low-quantity items which were not carried in the board's warehouse. Mr. Feltar had had little success from these mini-orders. Their usage was low and when they were used they were applied incorrectly. Mr. Feltar thought the users did not familiarize themselves enough with the orders. The users said they saw little advantage in using them.

In the past all requisition forms had the purchase order number printed upon them. If a principal phoned the purchasing department for approval he could use a requisition and subsequently quote its number to a supplier. If a budget problem occurred later, purchasing was stuck. Mr. Feltar now proposed to dispense with prenumbered requisition forms, forcing principals to phone him for a purchase order number and resulting approval.

Another area of concern was the increased use of petty cash. Under the prevailing system, a school had up to $150 in cash for small emergencies. A minimum dollar requirement per receipt was set at $10.00. Once the money was used up, the receipts were totaled and forwarded to the finance department. The petty cash would then be replenished. No fixed yearly amount was set as long as there were funds available in the user's budget. Mr. Feltar realized that if a school needed some supplies in a hurry it would resort to using petty cash. This resulted in paying the generally higher retail price. Sales tax was also paid on purchases which could have been avoided if handled on the board's purchase orders.

With the warehouse superintendent reporting directly to Mr. Feltar, a request for items that were in stock could be, if necessary, expedited quickly. Mr. Feltar, after receiving an urgent request, would telephone the order through and let the paper work "catch-up." This "special" expediting involved risks to Mr. Feltar. If it was early in the year, the paper work would certainly receive budget approval, but as the year progressed and the budgets approached their ceilings, the required approvals would become more uncertain. The time delays encountered in schools obtaining their supplies were generally lengthening. The paperwork was taking three to five weeks to complete its cycle. On the whole, the warehouse delivery could not be reduced from two weeks since all orders had to go through the computer system. Thus, depending upon the time of year and the delivery from suppliers, time estimates for receiving goods were unreliable. Moreover, supplies for school programs seemed always to be required "yesterday."

Cooperation and individual school priorities were ever-present hurdles to cross. Mr. Feltar would at times try to help a principal find a budget in some other school to cover an essential request. However, this was a difficult and delicate thing to carry out.

Mr. Feltar was convinced that the service image of his department was slipping in the schools (see Exhibit 2), but he could not easily define what actions to take or recommendations to make to remedy this.

Exhibit 2

High school teachers complained about a lack of trust and consultation by administration, expressing a desire to influence decisions regarding academic standards, examination policy, pupil-teacher ratios as well as curriculum matters.

They expressed harsh dissatisfaction with the business serices department of the board, particularly the purchasing system, contending that bureaucratic delays and tight budgeting procedures are often harmful to their programs.

They also charged the administration with encouraging too much permissiveness both in discipline and educational standards. Most would like to see schools offer a more structured approach to education than is found at present with regard both to discipline and standards.

The main thrust of school teachers' opinion, the report says, favors decentralizing administrative and decision-making processes, bringing them as far as possible to the individual school.

Administrators surveyed agreed that the school should be regarded as the key operational unit in the system, recognized tht up-dating of teachers should be part of the normal working day of the teacher, and proposed a continuous program in human relations for all personnel.

Source: Taken from the *Wayfarer Journal*.

PURCHASING RESEARCH, PLANNING, AND BUDGETING

15

The huge sums of money spent annually for all kinds of research by government, industry, and educational institutions during the last four decades have resulted in an explosion of knowledge and technology that has accelerated rates of change in all aspects of life.

Scientific research has produced new metals, new textiles, new plastics, new sources of energy, and new understanding of our universe. Research in mathematics and quantitative methods has developed new concepts and tools for the analysis of business problems. Research in the behavioral sciences has opened new areas of understanding why people behave the way they do. New concepts have been developed to aid in organizing and supervising human activity to encourage greater achievement.

In a rapidly changing environment, experience has taught us that change can be best managed if we plan for it. Most human achievement results from some kind of a plan. The plan may be in a person's head and be very informal, or it may be carefully developed step by step and formalized in writing and charts. Research and planning go hand in hand. Most research is preceded by careful planning, and the results obtained from research are best utilized through an appropriate plan.

PURCHASING RESEARCH

There has been a steady growth in the number of companies which have added research staffs to their purchasing departments since the early 1950s. A research study published in 1963 reported that approximately one-third of the 304 companies participating in the study had purchasing research staffs.[1]

Purchasing research is the systematic collection, classification, and analysis of data as the basis for better purchasing decisions. Figure 15–1 shows some of the data (information) which might be required for most effective buying decisions. The studies conducted in purchasing research include projects under the major research headings of

---

[1] Harold E. Fearon and John H. Hoagland, *Purchasing Research in American Industry*, Research Study 58 (New York: American Management Association, 1963).

1. Purchased materials, products or services (value analysis)
2. Commodities
3. Vendors
4. Purchasing system

Considerable attention has been given to a similar activity in the counterpart function of marketing research. Marketing research generally is well accepted in all medium- to large size firms as a necessary ingredient in decision making, and it has produced significant results for those firms that practice marketing research systematically.

Purchasing research, if approached in an organized manner, also has the potential for generating major improvements in purchasing decision making, although it has been overlooked by many firms in the past. However, the critical material shortages and delivery problems during the 1970s have emphasized to many firms the profit potential of effective purchasing decisions as well as their importance to the survival of a firm. Purchasing research is a key ingredient of these decisions.

Figure 15–1
Ingredients of effective buying

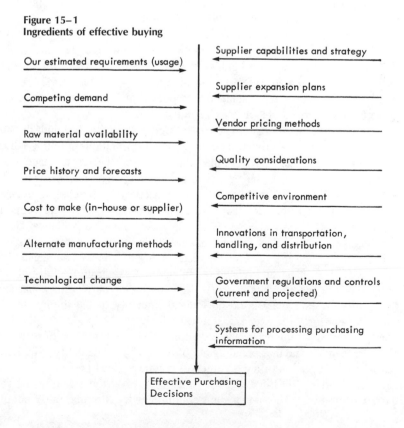

Organization for purchasing research

A firm could conduct purchasing research in one of two ways: (1) the assignment of full-time staff personnel to the task or (2) the use of regularly assigned buying and administrative personnel to conduct purchasing research as a secondary assignment.

As with its counterpart function, marketing research, there are some persuasive arguments for the establishment of full-time staff personnel to perform the purchasing research task. (These positions are typically called "purchase researcher," "purchase analyst," "value analyst," "purchase economist," or "commodity specialist.")

1. Time. A thorough job of collecting and analyzing data requires blocks of time and in many purchasing departments the buyers and administrators just do not have this time. They are fully occupied finding workable solutions to immediate problems.

2. Specialized skill. Many areas of purchasing research (for example, economic studies and system analysis) require in-depth knowledge of research techniques. These research techniques call for a level of skill not possessed by the typical buyer, primarily because research skill is not one of the criteria used in selecting persons for buying slots. Administrative assignments in purchasing also typically do not require this as a primary skill.

3. Perspective. The purchase researcher often must take a broad view of the overall effects of purchasing decisions on operating results. The buyer, on the other hand, may be so engrossed in his or her own narrow responsibility area that he or she may not be able to see the big picture.

There are arguments for placing the responsibility for purchasing research with the buyer and/or the purchasing administrator.

1. Immediate knowledge. The buyer is intimately familiar with the items he or she buys. A staff person does not have such information, initially, and may overlook important data. A system that requires a staff person to spend a good deal of time in going to the buyer or administrator for data may be inefficient.

2. Locus of decision making. In the final analysis, purchasing decisions are made by the buyer or administrator; the staff member merely presents data and advises. In some instances, conflict may develop between the staff person and the decision maker; thus the recommendations of the staff may not receive fair consideration and the value of the researcher's efforts will be negated.

3. Cost. The salary and related organizational expense of a full-time staff member adds to the administrative costs of operating the purchasing department. If the results of staff analysis do not add appreciably to the improvement of purchasing decisions, the expense is unwarranted.

One possibility—somewhat of a compromise between the use of a full-time purchase researcher and the spreading out of research responsibility to individual buyers—is the formation of a committee to pursue various projects. Such committees have various titles: for example, "task force," "tiger team," or "value analysis committee." The use of such committees has become fairly common over the past few years as firms have faced sudden materials-supply problems. Many companies have formed energy study committees in an attempt to generate data and guidance on their alternatives for coping with immediate and long-term problems.

The difficulty with such an approach is that it is hard to pinpoint responsibility for results when it is diffused over a number of individuals. However, the committee approach can work satisfactorily, provided that (1) committee members are carefully selected to ensure that each really has something to contribute; (2) the committee has strong leadership (from a functional point of view, it probably should be someone from the materials area); (3) a specific set of objectives and expectations of results is formulated and communicated to each member and the committee as a whole; and (4) each committee member's normal job responsibilities are rearranged to give the person the time and the resources necessary to ensure results. If any of these four conditions is not present, less than optimum outcomes are almost certain.

Current evidence indicates that in most instances research efforts will be most productive when persons are assigned to this activity on a full-time basis. Logic dictates that if a full-time researcher or analyst is the primary vehicle through which purchasing research is done, that individual will produce more and better research results. He or she has the primary assignment and time to do the research, and since the person presumably was selected, in part, on the basis of research ability and willingness and desire to do research, the results should be of higher quality. A study of purchasing research practices by the 500 largest U.S. industrial firms showed that, without exception, a larger percentage of those firms that had full-time purchase-research staff researched each of the 38 topics listed than was the case in those firms that had no staff.[2] Firms with staff researched from 1.6 to 1.9 times as many topics as was done by firms that relied on their buyers or purchasing administrators for such research.

Figure 15–2 presents an example of the organization structure for purchasing research in a large food producing company. A capsule view of how this purchase research effort fits into the overall purchasing organization and where this firm places its major emphasis follows:

Company A processes a wide variety of consumer food products and related lines of consumer goods. Annual sales are over a billion dollars.

Purchases, which account for over 70 percent of the sales dollar, are handled centrally; individual divisions and plants do, however, make the commitments for the raw agricultural materials, with guidance from the central office purchasing department. Packaging, equipment, and chemicals are purchased by the central office.

Four full-time purchase research personnel aid the director and assistant director of purchasing and the five purchasing managers by doing special purchasing projects and providing information and advice on purchase alternatives. Supervision of the researchers is handled primarily by the assistant director of purchasing. The work of the four analysts has been specialized, as follows:

---

[2]Ibid., pp. 31, 37, and 40.

Figure 15–2
Organization for purchasing research in a large food producer

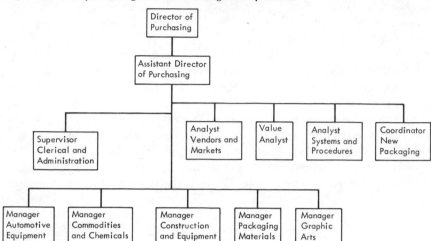

The analyst, vendors and markets, does work in (1) locating and assisting in the analysis of the capabilities and reliability of new and continuing vendors; (2) acting as the program coordinator to ensure that the individual plant purchasing departments each has its own purchase cost reduction program in place and operating; (3) assisting individual plants in coping with material shortages, by better planning of requirements, by assisting in expediting effort, and by locating alternate sources; and (4) monitoring the status of vendor labor agreements and problems to avoid unanticipated supply interruptions due to strikes.

The value analyst handles special projects relating to ways the purchase requirements could be met at lower cost. Included are make/lease/buy studies on specific items, standardization of purchases, substitution of materials, cost analysis of purchased items to establish negotiation targets, and price forecasting of key purchased items.

The analyst, systems and procedures, conducts continuing studies to improve the administrative methods used in processing purchase transactions. Utilization of computer services is a key activity area studied.

The coordinator, new packaging, works with the marketing and industrial engineering departments in determining the design and purchase of new packages. Interface with vendor personnel is a key element of the coordinator's assignment. After design decisions are reached, the actual purchase of production quantities is handled by the manager, packaging materials. Much of the work of the coordinator is in the value-engineering area (ensuring that the design selected will perform the function at the lowest cost possible).

Figure 15–3 presents a job description for a purchasing research manager in another large firm, in which the research staff consists of three professional research people.

Figure 15–3
Job description, manager of purchasing research

Objectives

1. Investigate and implement, and may initiate, programs and procedures involving the cost reduction of purchased goods and services and the storing, accounting, and disbursing of stores.

2. Develop, recommend, and implement cost reductions in operating the purchasing department.

3. Develop, recommend, and implement growth and educational programs for purchasing personnel.

4. Research and communicate trends and statistical data.

5. Direct special projects.

Method of Operation

This position conducts, coordinates, and administers work that by nature would be too expensive and specialized to be conducted by purchasing management, purchasing agents, or other officers who have primary responsibility. The purchasing research group's concerns and activities fall into five basic categories:

1. Commodity-review program.
2. Purchasing policies and procedures to implement the commodity-review program.
3. Preparation of reports and summaries of data.
4. Departmental training and orientation.
5. Special projects.

Work in these categories covers areas such as market analysis, price analysis, cost analysis, make-or-buy studies, methods of procurement, and the economic areas associated with standardization.

The total value of the purchased goods and services from which the manager may select or be assigned subjects for analysis is $300 million per year. The manager works closely with buying and administrative personnel to study, direct, coordinate, implement, and administer various studies, programs, systems, and procedures of purchasing activity.

The manager assists in the administration of short- and long-range planning programs of the purchasing department. He or she studies purchasing procedures and recommends, implements, and administers changes to improve administrative control of purchasing activity, to provide better control, more comprehensive information, simplified procurement procedures, more effective purchase agreements and contract negotiations, and to reduce costs associated with procurement, through data processing applications.

The principal challenge of the manager, purchasing research, is to research, initiate, develop, and coordinate procedures and programs for reducing the cost of purchased materials and services.

Principal Contacts

Internal: all levels of management throughout the company.

External: vendor personnel, government agencies, publishers of trade and technical papers, professional societies, economic consultants, government and private economists.

Since the types of data which bear on a major purchasing decision are numerous and since many different items are bought, the number of possible purchase-research projects is almost infinite. However, even if a company has full-time purchase analysts, it has limited resources and must use some method of deciding which purchase-research projects should have top priority.

Following is a list of criteria that are used by firms in deciding where they will direct their research effort. This is not intended to be in priority order (although by far the most used is the ''top dollar'' criterion).

A. *Value of product or service*
   Top dollar (current or projected).
B. *Product profitability*
   Red dollar (unprofitable end product).
C. *Price/cost characteristics*
   Infrequent price changes.
   Frequent or seasonal price fluctuations.
   End-product cost not competitive.
   Raw materials costs rising at a greater rate than selling price of product,
      resulting in reduced profit margin.
D. *Availability*
   Limited number of suppliers.
   New suppliers adding to available supply.
   Availability limited.
   Possibility of imports.
   Possibility of in-house manufacture.
E. *Quality*
   Have had quality or specification problem.
F. *Data Flows*
   Information for decisions often inaccurate, late, or unavailable.
   Cost of data is excessive.
   Buyer doesn't have time to do analysis work.

Research on purchased materials, products, or services (value analysis)

The research topics in this area are principally concerned with the specific products being purchased. Most of them fall under the generally understood category of value analysis, which historically is the area of purchasing research that first received attention, publicity, and acceptance.[3]

Value analysis compares the function performed by a purchased item with the cost, in an attempt to find a lower-cost alternative. Since purchasing decisions often are made under a good deal of time pressure, and since technology and manufacturing methods change fairly rapidly, in many instances a higher-priced item is purchased than is necessary. Some people make the distinction that value analysis is done on purchased items used in the ongoing production process, while value engineering looks at cost savings possibilities in the design stage, where items are being specified, and before production purchases actually are made. Obviously, value engineering at the design stage to arrive at the lowest cost material specification and design that will adequately perform the function is the most efficient way to do the job, but unfortunately this analysis, due to time

---

[3] The best, most comprehensive treatment of value analysis is by Lawrence D. Miles, *Techniques of Value Analysis and Engineering,* 2d ed. (New York: McGraw-Hill Book Company, 1972). 366 pages.

pressures, often is not done. Therefore, value analysis presents a fruitful area for purchase cost reduction. Detailed information on various aspects of the item to be purchased will enable a more intelligent choice from alternatives, thus providing better utilization of the purchasing dollar. Included as research topics are:

Lease or buy. Collection of data on the advantages and disadvantages of each alternative so that the most attractive decision can be identified.

Make or buy. Comparison of economic and managerial outcomes from each alternative in order than an informed choice can be made.

Method of production or manufacture. Investigation of the technology required as a basis of suggesting changes.

New product. Search to uncover new items that profitably might be purchased to meet an anticipated need or in lieu of an existing requirement.

Packaging. Investigation of processes and materials to determine the lowest cost method of meeting requirements.

Scrap disposal. Analysis of disposal methods, channels, and techniques to isolate those that will provide greatest net return to the firm.

Scrap recovery. Analysis of the factors causing the generation of scrap and of methods for handling scrap so that maximum potential return will be realized. One firm concluded that rather than sending precious metal scrap to a refiner for recovery, it would be more economical to build its own facility and recover its own metals.

Specification. Analysis of current specs to be sure they outline the required level of performance, do not result in purchases of unneeded attributes or unnecessarily high levels of performance, and enable competitive purchasing.

Standardization. Review of uses to which specific products are put and consideration of the possibility of using one item to fill the needs for which multiple items currently are purchased. For example, one large, multi-plant company reviewed its entire purchase of work gloves and found that its annual buy out amounted to over $1,000,000 and included some 400 different types and vendors. As a result of the value analysis, they were able to standardize on 46 different models, write blanket orders with vendors, negotiate lower prices, and save over $70,000 per year.

Substitution. Analysis of the technical and economic ramifications of using a different item in lieu of the one presently purchased.

Transportation. Investigation of movement requirements and alternative methods and costs. One firm found that by operating its own over-the-road vehicles, it not only would save in total transport cost but also would reduce congestion in and around its receiving area.

The standard approach to value analysis, which encompasses most of the above-listed topics, is to pose and provide detailed answers to a series of questions about the item currently being bought. Figure 15–4 details this approach and lists the standard value-analysis questions.

The emphasis on research on purchased materials, products, or services appears to have diminished over the past several years, probably because of the severe materials shortages and price increases, which caused scarce research re-

Figure 15–4
The value analysis approach: Comparison of function to cost

I. Select a relatively high cost or high volume purchased item to value analyze. This can be a part, material, or service. Select an item you suspect is costing more than it should.
II. Find out completely how the item is used and what is expected of it—its *function*.
III. Ask questions:
    1. Does its use contribute value?
    2. Is its cost proportionate to usefulness?
    3. Does it need all its features?
    4. Is there anything better, at a more favorable purchase price, for the intended use?
    5. Can the item be eliminated?
    6. If the item is not standard, can a standard item be used?
    7. If it is a standard item, does it completely fit your application or is it a misfit?
    8. Does the item have greater capacity than required?
    9. Is there a similar item in inventory that could be used?
    10. Can the weight be reduced?
    11. Are closer tolerances specified than are necessary?
    12. Is unnecessary machining performed on the item?
    13. Are unnecessarily fine finishes specified?
    14. Is commercial quality specified?
    15. Can you make the item cheaper yourself?
    16. If you are making it now, can you buy it for less?
    17. Is the item properly classified for shipping purposes to obtain lowest transporation rates?
    18. Can cost of packaging be reduced?
    19. Are your suppliers being asked by you for suggestions to reduce cost?
    20. Do material, reasonable labor, overhead, and profit total its cost?
    21. Will another dependable supplier provide it for less?
    22. Is anyone buying it for less?
IV. Now:
    1. Pursue those suggestions that appear practical.
    2. Get samples of the proposed item(s).
    3. Select the best possibilities and propose changes.

sources to be diverted away from value analysis and into the commodity-analysis area. Also, in many engineering departments, increased attention is being given to arriving at lowest-cost design initially (value engineering), which tends to reduce the dollar contribution that can be made through value analysis.

Commodity studies

These purchase research studies are directed at providing predictions, or answers to questions, about the short- and long-term future purchasing environment for a major purchased commodity or item. Such information should provide the basis for making sound decisions and presenting purchasing management and top management with relatively complete information concerning future supply and price of these items.

Typically, the focus of such research is on items that represent a major amount of purchase dollars, but it could be done on items of smaller dollar magnitude that are thought to be in critically short supply. Major raw materials, such as steel, copper, or zinc, normally would be studied, but manufactured items, such as motors or semiconductor devices, also might be researched. This area probably is the most sophisticated in terms of difficulty and skills needed to do a good job.

A comprehensive commodity study should include analyses of these major areas: (1) current status as a buyer, (2) production process alternatives, (3) uses of the item, (4) demand, (5) supply, (6) price, and (7) strategy to reduce cost and/or ensure supply. Figure 15–5 provides a set of guidelines that might be used to make a commodity study.

Over the period of 1972 to the present time there has been a decided increase in emphasis on the commodity study area. Some companies do very sophisticated commodity research, resulting in a well-documented strategic purchase plan. While a planning horizon of from five to ten years is the norm, some firms make a 15-year rolling forecast, updated each year. If a firm makes a 15-year strategic marketing plan, it makes sense to couple this with a strategic supply forecast and plan, for in the long-term the acquisition of an adequate supply of critical materials may be the crucial determinant in the organization's success in meeting its market goals.

The reasons for this increased emphasis are two-fold: (1) the increasing price trend, and (2) the increasing dependence on foreign (non U.S.) sources of supply. Prices for industrial commodities have escalated rapidly ever since the late 1960s and material costs likely will continue to increase rapidly at least through the mid-1980s. The extent of this escalation has been so pronounced that it casts doubt on the ability of some firms to operate profitably. The index of industrial raw material prices of the Bureau of Labor Statistics has moved up by almost 160 percent from January 1967 to January 1979, and it likely will triple by the mid-1980s.[4] Firms need to arrive at realistic estimates of price trends so that they can plan their strategy of adjusting material inputs to counter this trend. Second, the availability of supply of many items is questionable, due to dependence of U.S. firms on foreign supply sources, whose stability due to international politics and depletion of reserves is doubtful.[5] Table 15–1 presents some rough estimates of U.S. dependence on foreign supply sources.

The six specific research topics in this subject area are:

Demand forecast. Investigation of the firm's demand for the item, to include current and projected demand, inventory status, and lead times. Also considered are competing demands, current and projected, by industry and end-product use.

Supply forecast. Collection of data about current producers and suppliers, the aggregate current and projected supply situation, and technological and political trends that might affect supply.

Price forecast. Based on information gathered and analyzed about demand and supply, this forecast provides a prediction of short- and long-term prices and the underlying reasons for those trends.

Purchase of supply source. Consideration of the economic and legal ramifications of actually buying out a supply source to protect supply and/or costs. One

---

[4]This index is reported weekly on page 2 of *Business Week* magazine.

[5]"Now the squeeze on metals" *Business Week,* 2 July 1979, pp. 46–51.

Figure 15–5
Commodity study guidelines

The information resulting from a commodity study should:

1. Provide a basis for making sound procurement decisions.
2. Present purchasing management and top management with information concerning future supply and price of purchased items.

The completed commodity study should provide data and/or answers for each of the following points or questions. (The investigation should not be limited to these items; depending on the particular commodity under consideration, additional items may be very pertinent, and some of the listed items may not be important.)

   I. *Current Status*
     1. Description of commodity
     2. How and where commodity is used
     3. Requirements
     4. Suppliers
     5. How commodity is purchased
     6. How commodity is transported
     7. Current contracts and expiration dates
     8. Current price, terms, and annual expenditure
     9. Scheduling
    10. Receiving
    11. Inspection
    12. Expediting
    13. Packaging
    14. Storage capacity
  II. *Production Process*
     1. How is the item made?
     2. What materials are used in its manufacture?
      a. Supply/price status of these materials
     3. What labor is required?
      a. Current and future labor situation
     4. Are there alternative production processes?
     5. What changes are likely in the future?
     6. Possibility of making the item?
      a. Costs
      b. Time factor
      c. Problems
 III. *Uses of the Item*
     1. Primary use(s)
     2. Secondary use(s)
     3. Possible substitutes
      a. Economics of substitution
 IV. *Demand*
     1. Our requirements
      a. Current
      b. Projected into the future

Figure 15–5 *(continued)*

        c. Inventory status

        d. Sources of forecast information

        e. Lead times

    2. Competing demand, current and projected

        a. By industry

        b. By end-product use

        c. By individual firms

V. *Supply*

    1. Current producers

        a. Location

        b. Reliability as a source

        c. Quality levels

        d. Labor situation

        e. Ownership

        f. Capacity

        g. Distribution channels used

        h. Sales strategy

        i. Expansion plans

        j. Warranties and guarantees

        k. Strengths and weaknesses of such supplier

    2. Total (aggregate) supply situations

        a. Current

        b. Projected

    3. Import potential and problems

    4. Pertinent government regulations and controls

    5. Potential new suppliers

    6. Technological change forecast

    7. Political trends

    8. Ecological problems

    9. Weather

   10. Capital investment per unit of output

VI. *Price*

    1. Economic structure of producing industry

    2. Price history and explanation of significant changes

    3. Factors determining price

    4. Cost to produce and deliver

    5. Incremental costs

    6. Co-products or byproducts

    7. Effect of materials and labor cost changes on prices

    8. Transportation cost element

    9. Tariff and import regulations

   10. Effect of changes in the business cycle

   11. Effect of quantity on price

   12. Seasonal trends

   13. Estimated profit margins of various vendors

   14. Price objective(s) of vendors

   15. Potential rock-bottom price

   16. Do prices vary among various industries using the item?

Figure 15–5 *(concluded)*

17. Forecast of future price trend
18. Specific pricing system used by various vendors
19. Influence of actions of specific vendors on prices of others; that is, a price leader?
20. Relation to prices of other products
21. Foreign exchange problems

VII. *Strategy to Reduce Cost*

Considering forecast supply, usage, price, profitability, strengths and weakness of suppliers, and our position in the market, what is our plan to lower cost?

1. Make the item in our facility
2. Short-term contract
3. Long-term contract
4. Acquire a producer
5. Find a substitute
6. Develop a new producer
7. Import
8. Exploit all methods to make maximum use of our purchasing power
9. Detailed preplanning of negotiations
10. Use of agents
11. Hedging
12. Toll contract
13. Value engineering/analysis
14. Handling of scrap

VIII. *Appendix*

1. General information
   a. Specifications
   b. Quality control requirements and methods
   c. Freight rates and transportation costs
   d. Storage capacity
   e. Handling facilities
   f. Weather problems
   g. Raw material reserves
2. Statistics
   a. Price trends
   b. Production trends
   c. Purchase trends

---

firm, for example, decided to lease over 200 railroad tank cars so that it could better control the movement of potentially scarce petroleum products over the next several years. Another firm is investigating a joint venture with a petroleum company to drill gas wells as a source of supply for its plant energy requirements. A third firm is looking at metal mining and refining properties in the western part of the United States as a means of protecting its supply lines. Another firm just completed, on the basis of a rather complete commodity study, a several million dollar plant expansion loan to a steel producer with the proviso that it (the lender) is to have "first refusal" of the increased steel output from the newly-expanded mill. The steel-commodity study had given it a clear indication of severe shortages of particular types of steel before the end of this decade. In a sense, a loan of this type is a partial "purchase of a supply source" decision.

Foreign purchase alternatives. Search for and evaluation of the possibilities of making offshore purchases of major items, either raw materials or manufactured items. Many firms have not yet made major use of foreign suppliers, but as the supply base becomes more compact (and complex), in many cases this may provide a realistic alternative.

Tariff and import regulations. Analysis of barriers and regulations of the U.S. government and foreign governments as they affect foreign-purchase possibilities.

As a review of Figure 15–5 will show, a well done, comprehensive commodity study is a major undertaking, and if a thorough job of analysis is to be done, this requires the services of personnel who have both the technical expertise and the time. It would be the unusual situation where the buyer or purchasing administrator would have both; therefore, this tends to be a major activity area for the staff purchase researcher.

Table 15–1
U.S. dependence on foreign sources of materials

Commodity	Percent of need currently imported
Natural rubber	100
Manganese	100
Platinum	100
Sheet mica	100
Cobalt	99
Chromium	99
Aluminum (bauxite)	90
Nickel	90
Strontium	90
Asbestos	86
Bismuth	85
Tantalum	85
Titanium	78
Mercury	73
Gold	69
Silver	68
Tin	67
Cadmium	65
Zinc	64
Tungsten	60
Potassium	60
Crude oil	50
Iron ore	30

Sources: U.S. Bureau of Mines; U.S. Geological Survey; A.D. Little, Inc.

Vendor research

While the two research areas discussed earlier were directed primarily at the item being purchased, research in this category has its principal emphasis on the source of the purchase. In short, the previous two areas were the "what"; this one concerns "from whom." Obviously, the more knowledge a buyer has about present and potential vendors, their method of operation and market position, the better is his or her ability to select adquate, appropriate supply sources and to prepare for and successfully conduct vendor negotiations. The specific topic areas in this category are:

Analysis of financial capacity. Investigation of the financial health of present or potential vendors so that the risk of the vendor's running into financial trouble and its effects on the buying firm can be assessed. While this type of analysis often is done within the financial department of a firm, in some cases it has been pulled into purchasing and made a responsibility of purchasing research, to ensure that it is done with requisite thoroughness, considering the potential dollar value of the risk involved. For example, several purchasers of major computer systems from very substantial U.S. manufacturers have been surprised suddenly to find that their supplier "has gone bankrupt" in the computer business. With proper analysis, such a situation could have been anticipated well in advance.

Analysis of production facilities. Collection of data on the vendor's physical facilities, emphasizing capacities and limitations.

Finding new supply source. Search to uncover new vendors for a purchase need. During the supply shortages of 1973 and 1974, research on this topic consumed a great deal of the time of the purchase researcher, for many firms were totally unprepared. Through the information from the commodity studies currently under way, firms hope to avoid similar surprises down the road.

Estimate of distribution costs. Analysis of the steps performed in the process of moving items from their source to the point at which the firm takes possession, and calculation of the costs that the vendor should incur if the firm is reasonably efficient. This provides an input into what is a fair price and an evaluation of whether the most efficient distribution channels are being used.

Estimate of manufacturing costs. Analysis of what it should cost a vendor (direct material, direct labor, engineering, tooling, manufacturing overhead, general and administrative expense, and profit) to make an item, assuming reasonable efficiency. These data provide the basis for establishing a target price in negotiation planning. This is the most common research topic in this subject area, probably because it is productive of very large and immediate saving. Much cooperation between purchasing and the firm's industrial engineering personnel is needed for this research to produce maximum results. Many firms are experimenting with putting standard assumptions about the cost factors (for example, material prices and direct labor rates) into the computer and then writing a simple program that will permit the computer to produce a cost analysis for whatever set of specifications is fed into it. One company uses such a model to supply a cost analysis to its buyers on any purchase of corrugated. The computer is in the central office location, but it can be accessed through the telephone from any plant in the continental United States, thus giving the buyers immediate cost analysis capability.

Supplier attitude survey. Determination, through systematic survey techniques, of what vendors really think of the buying firm and its purchasing practices. This information is used in reviewing and modifying purchasing organization and policy. One firm developed a survey questionnaire through its purchase-research group and then had an independent public accounting firm administer the questionnaire and summarize the results. The firm found, to its surprise, general vendor sentiment to the effect that (1) it as a buyer was very unappreciative of superior vendor efforts, (2) buying decisions often were made on a personal-favoritism basis, and (3) if vendors could sell their output to someone else, no sales would be made to this firm. Such sentiments would have drastic effects on this firm's material supply situation in the event of another general shortage situation such as occurred in 1973 and 1974. Obviously, purchasing management in this firm made some major changes to remedy the situation.

Vendor performance evaluation. Collection and analysis of data as the basis for determining how good a job is being done by a given vendor so that decisions on sources for rebuys can be made more intelligently and present vendors can be advised where improvement is needed.

Vendor sales strategy. Development of a better understanding of a vendor's objectives and the means it is using to achieve these goals, so that the buyer can anticipate the vendor's actions and design a purchasing strategy to provide for the continued supply of needed items at lowest cost.

Countertrade. Locating vendors in foreign countries, analyzing their capabilities, and negotiating counterbalancing purchase agreements with them. Many foreign countries, and particularly the Peoples' Republic of China and those in the Communist bloc, are short of U.S. currency. Therefore, when they buy goods from a U.S. firm, they insist that all, or a specified part, of the purchase price be paid for in raw materials or finished products exported from their country. This essentially is a barter agreement, and in some companies purchase-research specialists are responsible for gathering and analyzing the data that form the basis for such agreements.

It might be assumed that the buyer, because of close, continuing relationships with vendors, is in the best position to do meaningful vendor research. However, since much of this research is technical in nature, it may be advisable to use staff personnel who have these requisite skills if maximum decision-making data are to be obtained.

Purchasing system research

Adequate knowledge about items to be purchased and the vendor from whom the purchase might be made, while important in attaining maximum value from the purchasing dollar, does not assure that the purchasing function will be discharged in the most efficient manner. Equally important is how the purchase is made. Efficient administrative procedures not only will reduce the expense of departmental operations but also will facilitate wise decisions on items purchased and their source. Research topics in the purchasing system area are directed at improving administration of the purchasing system. These might be described as systems and procedures studies with a special focus on materials administration. Specific topic areas usually researched include:

Blanket orders. Investigation of the ways in which umbrella-type contracts might be used to provide greater purchasing leverage and reduce administrative expense. With the prospect of recurring materials shortages, the use of long-term agreements as an inducement to ensure constant supply may be particularly attractive.

Forms design. Analysis of data requirements and flows so that forms used in purchasing are designed to facilitate the accurate, timely transmission of information.

Formulation of price index. Development of a procedure whereby an index or indexes can be prepared to show either the mix of prices actually paid for purchases or a mix of market prices against which actual prices paid can be compared, as one element in evaluating how well the purchasing department is performing.

Inventory control. Establishment of systems and procedures for the efficient and timely control of inventory so as to maximize inventory service levels for a given amount of dollar investment. Reorder points, reorder quantities, stock objectives, and safety stocks would be recommended.

Learning curve. Application of the time-reduction curve as a basis for establishing a target price in negotiation.

Payment or cash-discount procedures. Investigation and improvement of the system for making payment on vendor accounts and taking advantage of cash discounts, where advantageous. For example, some firms have investigated the use of vendor invoices as part of their payment system and decided to discontinue them, thus eliminating one piece of paper, and resultant handling costs, from their system. They simply close the purchase order by matching the PO file copy with the receiving report and the incoming inspection report. If they agree, a check for the previously-agreed upon amount is written to the vendor at the end of the cash discount period. The only major disadvantage is that purchases must be made f.o.b. destination, for there is no way to add in transport charges.

Receiving systems. Review of the methods currently used to verify quantities delivered by vendors, for payment purposes, in an attempt to simplify the system. Some firms have looked at the use of the receiving report on a cost/benefit basis and concluded that the cost of completing and processing the receiving paperwork is substantially greater than the value of the protection provided; they now simply pay based on a comparison of the PO file copy with the vendor invoice on all non-inventory purchases of under a certain dollar amount, e.g., $200 or under. In the event the item or material really never was received, they depend on the requisitioner to call that to their attention, and then they go back to the vendor and ask for either proof of shipment or a replacement. If the purchase has been made from a reliable vendor, there should be no problem.

Small or rush order procedures. Design of innovative methods for processing small or rush orders so that purchase needs are satisfied at lowest administrative cost. The blank-check buying system (also called the check-with-purchase-order system) is an example of the kind of innovation that can result when someone takes a thorough look at present practices in an attempt to effect improvement— and when the ''that's the way we've always done it'' syndrome is avoided.

Systems contracting. Investigation and establishment of arrangements with a single vendor, or a small group of vendors, for the supply of the buying firm's total annual requirement of a specific group of items.

Method for evaluating buyer performance. Establishment of a system by which the job performance of buyers can be measured.

Method for evaluating purchasing department performance. Establishment of a system by which the actual performance of the total purchasing effort can be compared against predetermined criteria. On the basis of this evaluation, action to correct deficiencies can be taken.

Method for evaluating supplier performance. Establishment of a system for rating how well vendors are meeting the requirements of the purchase orders and contracts they receive. Resultant data are essential for rebuy decisions and as a basis for providing feedback to the vendor on where improvement is needed.

Computer applications. Determination of areas in which computer usage could provide more accurate and timely manipulation of data and improved purchase decision making. The actual design of the computer software system could be an output of these studies, although purchasing research typically is applications-oriented and normally depends on the computer or management information systems people to come up with the software to support needed applications.

Unfortunately, purchasing has done the poorest job of all the major functional areas in exploiting the potential of the computer.[6] There are several reasons for this (including lack of aggressiveness on the part of purchasing personnel), but in many firms today, purchase research specialists are pursuing actively the development and refinement of computer-operating and management-reporting systems.

Study and development of computerized decision-making models also is under way by some purchase-research groups. Computer decision-assisting systems process data used to assist management in selecting among alternatives; these systems typically select an alternative, using techniques such as mathematical relationships, simulations, or other algorithms. The outcome is definitive in nature and presents the results in either a deterministic or probabilistic fashion. Computer decision models are being developed in the areas of price-discount analysis, factory simulation as it affects materials usage, materials budgeting,

[6]Harold E. Fearon and D. Larry Moore, ''Why Haven't Computers Been Used More Effectively in Purchasing?'' *Journal of Purchasing and Materials Management* 10, August 1974: 30–39.

quotation analysis, synthetic pricing, the negotiation process between opposing parties, and forward buying and futures trading.

While each of the 13 research topics in this subject area is in the systems and procedures area and could be handled by personnel from that department of the firm, the results probably will be more useful if the research is done by people in purchasing, who are aware of the problems and subtleties in day-to-day adminis-trative activities and who have to live with, and make work, the changes that are made. The potential saving from research in this area is great, particularly in a large firm with many thousands of transactions and complex data flows.

Data sources for purchasing research

Good purchasing decisions depend on the availability of adequate information—adequate in both quantity and quality. Purchasing research is the modern approach to obtaining and manipulating data so that new relationships and alternatives may be seen and acted upon.

Table 15–2 lists the information sources used by 30 large firms that completed a questionnaire in 1975 about purchasing research. The sources are listed in descending order of use by the total group of 30 firms; this is broken out by sources used by firms with staff and the group that had no research staff. The evaluation by the purchasing managers of which sources are most useful also is presented.

As would be expected, substantial reliance is placed on the more standard information sources. Some of the lesser known, but often most productive sources, such as trade association personnel, U.S. government personnel, and U.S. Department of Interior publications, received very little use.

It is doubtful whether the majority of firms are making the best use of avail-able information sources for research in purchasing, since many of the sources are being used by only a small percentage of the firms. And some of the more obscure data sources can provide much valuable information for a thorough job of research.

Another indication that less than optimum use is being made of available data sources is the fact that these firms were using, on the average, less than half (39 percent) of the available sources. There is some indication that the firms with full-time purchase-research staff were doing a more thorough job of using avail-able data, since the average usage percent of all data sources by firms with staff was 45 percent compared with only 38 percent in firms without staff. The con-clusion is that those with staff are more aware of the information sources that are available; this is only logical, of course, for staff personnel are more experienced in knowing where to look.

Evidently those firms with staff are doing a better job of using, or at least are more satisfied with, the data sources. Firms with staff indicated, on the average, that 37 percent of the sources employed were most useful compared with only 17 percent by the purchasing departments without staff. But again, we would ex-

Table 15–2
Data sources used for purchasing research

Source	Total 30 firms		6 with staff		24 without staff	
	Used	Most useful	Used	Most useful	Used	Most useful
Trade newspapers and magazines...............	83%	20%	67%	50%	88%	14%
Vendor sales personnel	80	33	100	50	75	28
Vendor technical personnel ...	73	18	83	20	71	18
Purchasing personnel in other companies	73	27	100	33	67	25
National Association of Purchasing Management publications	73	9	100	0	67	13
Vendor publications	70	5	100	17	63	0
Trade association publications	67	15	67	25	67	13
Books on purchasing	63	11	67	25	63	7
Other departments in the company	60	0	50	0	63	0
Corporate annual reports	57	0	50	0	58	0
U.S. Department of Labor publications.........	43	23	67	50	38	11
Consultants	37	18	33	50	38	11
U.S. Department of Commerce publications	27	25	33	50	25	17
Trade association personnel	20	0	17	0	21	0
Public libraries	20	0	17	0	21	0
University publications	10	33	0	0	13	33
U.S. government personnel ...	7	0	17	0	4	0
U.S. Department of Interior publications	3	0	17	0	0	0
Representatives of foreign governments..............	0	0	0	0	0	0
Foreign government publications	0	0	0	0	0	0
United Nations publications ..	0	0	0	0	0	0
U.S. Department of Agriculture publications	0	0	0	0	0	0
Average of the percents	39	20	45	37	38	17

pect firms with staff to be more experienced and skillful in getting the most out of the information sources available to them.

An assessment of purchase research results

Managers who use purchasing research are satisfied that it has paid off for their firm. Those with organized purchase research efforts feel it would be impossible for purchasing to continue making the current level of contribution to corporate success and profits without an aggressive program. Purchasing research has arrived on the corporate scene, but most managers contend that its potential really has been only partially tapped.

Purchasing research can contribute substantially to the ability of the purchasing department to cope successfully with future materials uncertainties and the demands for greater purchasing efficiency. Astute, aggressive purchasing executives will explore carefully the opportunities for maximizing purchasing profit potential through this approach.

PURCHASE PLANNING

The actual planning process starts with information derived from the annual sales forecast, production forecasts, and general economic forecasts. The sales forecast will provide a total measure of the requirements of materials, products, and services to be acquired by purchasing; production forecasts will provide information on the location at which the materials, products, and services will be required; and the economic forecast will provide information useful in estimating general trends for prices, wages, and other costs.

In most purchasing operations, less than 20 percent of the items purchased account for over 80 percent of the dollars spent. In breaking down the broad forecast into specific plans, the next step is to make price and supply availability forecasts for each of the major items (the 20 percent of all items which account for 80 percent of total purchase expenditures).

The estimates of material consumption are broken down into time periods, monthly and quarterly. These quantities are checked against inventory control procedures which take into account lead time and safety stocks. These estimates then are related to the price trend and availability forecasts for the material under consideration and a buying plan is developed. If the forecasts predict ample supplies of the material and a possible weakening in prices, a probable buying policy will be to reduce inventories to the lowest level which is economically feasible. On the other hand, if the forecasts predict a short supply and increasing price trend, prudence indicates a buying policy which will ensure that adequate stocks are on hand or are covered by contract, and the possibility of forward buying is considered.

The procedure outlined above is used for both raw materials and component parts. In forecasting trends which will affect the availability and price of component parts, consideration has to be given to the conditions expected to be present for the period being forecasted in the industries in which the parts' suppliers operate.

The 80 percent of the items purchased which account for 20 percent of the dollars spent in the average purchasing function can be classified into related product groups. The pattern of analysis followed in forecasting for the major items can be used for the related product groups.

After the monthly and quarterly unit quantities and estimated dollar costs for each item or related product group are tabulated and modifications made as a result of developing a buying plan, individual buyers make an analysis of the items for which they are responsible to determine if further modifications in prices should be made because of the objectives which they have established to guide their activities for the period of the forecast.

Special projects, such as the construction of new facilities or the planning for the manufacture of new major products not previously produced, may create uncertainty as to the time periods when new equipment or products will be needed, making planning difficult.

According to one purchasing executive, there is a tremendous value in preparing plans, not only in the aggregate but also for individual items.[7] Figure 15–6 presents his approach to developing a purchasing plan for raw materials.

PERT and CPM

Within the past 20 years, new planning techniques have been developed which are useful in complex situations in which many variables and interrelationships are present. The Critical Path Method (CPM) provides for determining the sequence of all tasks required from the start to the completion of a project. An arrow diagram is used to show graphically the interrelationship between tasks for any project and hence determine the longest or critical path required to complete a project. An estimated time requirement is assigned to each task.

The Program Evaluation Review Techniques (PERT) was developed by the U.S. Navy in cooperation with others for the purpose of reducing the development time for the Polaris Ballistic Missile System. PERT is similar to CPM in that each technique uses a network to diagram graphically the sequence of tasks, which in PERT terminology are called "events." Events are also defined as being "highly identifiable points in time." The network lines connecting events are known as "activities" and represent the elapsed time required to complete an event. Unless stated otherwise, activities are stated in seven-day calendar weeks with an assumed 40-hour work week. Figure 15–7 shows a simple PERT network diagram.

When the time interval "activity" to accomplish an event is uncertain, an estimate of the shortest time and the longest time expected is shown on the activity line by number, i.e., 5, 8, where five weeks is the shortest time and eight weeks the longest time that may be required to complete an event.

In Figure 15–7, phases 1 and 2 were related to internal data gathering for the purchasing plan, and phase 3 involved external information seeking from three different sources. This technique allows the purchasing manager to anticipate problems far enough in advance that there is an opportunity to do something about them.

---

[7] A.J. D'Arcy, "Planning for Buying," *Journal of Purchasing* 7, August 1971: 24–32.

Figure 15–6
Questions to be asked in developing a written plan for raw materials

1. What are the short- and long-term objectives of the business involved?
2. Quantity required at each using location—by months for the next one to two years?
3. What specification applies at each location? What alternative might be considered?
4. Storage capacity available at each location? What ideas do we have on how much inventory to carry? Is inventory limited by storage facilities, working capital, deterioration with age?
5. Method of delivery preferred at each location? What alternative methods of delivery can be considered without new investment or with new investment? What is the maximum quantity per delivery?
6. Consumption and price by location, by month, for previous one or two years?
7. Current suppliers at each location, price being paid, and quantity supplied for previous one or two years? Production department performance evaluation of current suppliers?
8. Prospective suppliers, their plant locations, capacities, and processes? Desirable features of prospective suppliers relative to current suppliers? Is supply regularly available or subject to seasonal or other factors?
9. Total industry capacity/demand ratio for the product for past one or two years, with estimate of expected demand in next few years, by end use?
10. Supplier labor review—renewal date on labor contract?
11. Process economic data, such as estimated production cost, raw material cost, co-product values, batch sizes, yields, make-versus-buy? Rank suppliers from lowest to highest cost producers. Relative profitability of suppliers?
12. Objectives for value improvements sought in new buying period?
13. Preferred quantity statement in new agreement, i.e., fixed quantity or percent of requirement, or fixed monthly minimum or fixed monthly maximum?
14. Specifications and methods of analysis to be described in contracts for use in receiving and accepting material?
15. Preferred length of contract period? What alternatives might be considered?
16. Is any option desired for contract extension?
17. Preferred terms of payment?
18. Method of invoicing?
19. What points of discussion must be explored between technical production personnel in buyer or seller organization?
20. What technical service might we require?
21. Who will provide transportation equipment? What alternatives should be considered?
22. Are suitable freight rates currently in effect? Do any new rates have to be established? Evaluate for each supplier.
23. Will all material move in bulk equipment or will some be required in containers? If so, how should it be packed?
24. Will purchases be negotiated or determined by bidding?
25. Distribution cost from the various suppliers' plants to each consuming location?
26. Do we want multiple suppliers for each consuming location?
27. How do we want to write our inquiry?

Input—output analysis

Input-output analysis may have substantial promise in the next few decades as a materials and market research concept.[8] The use of I–O tables, models, and

---

[8]M. F. Elliott-Jones, *Input-Output Analysis: A Nontechnical Description* (New York: The Conference Board, 1971).

Figure 15–7
Simple PERT network

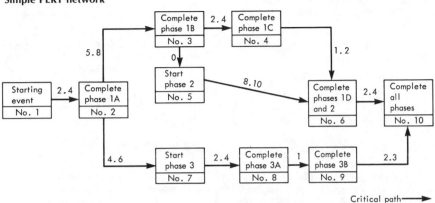

Critical path⟶

techniques permit the analyst to determine market shares and trends, develop forecasts, and provide an insight into material use and prices not easily accomplished by other means.

During recent years, one of Wassily Leontief's major contributions to economics—input-output analysis—has shown signs of finally becoming a practical tool of empirical economics. Availability of large capacity digital computers has allowed this development, and a growing inventory of statistics has furthered it. Presently, a number of economists anticipate development of input-output (I–O) during the next two decades comparable with development of aggregative econometric models since 1950.[9]

Industrial purchasing research becomes more complex as a finished product becomes farther removed from the product or material which a seller produces and also as the number of applications or uses of the seller's product increases. Input-output analysis helps identify the intermediate transactions which normally disappear in aggregate economic models. An example of a compressed input-output table is shown in Table 15–3.[10]

PURCHASING ADMINISTRATIVE BUDGETS

In addition to the purchase plan which is concerned with projecting the need for the acquisition of materials, products, and supplies required by the production facilities in manufacturing the products to be sold by the marketing department, as anticipated by the sales forecast, a budget should be prepared for all of the expenses incurred in the operation of the purchasing function. Such expenses include: salaries and wages; space costs, including heat and electricity; equipment costs for desks, office machines, files, and typewriters; data processing

---

[9]Ibid., p. 1.
[10]Ibid., p. 4.

Table 15–3
Sample of a compressed input-output table

		Purchases by						
		Manufacturing				Total	Final	Total
Sales by	Agriculture	I	II	Services	Imports	inter-mediates	demand	output
Agriculture	15	100	75	40	—	230	220	450
Manufacturing I		50	200	100	—	350	400	750
Manufacturing II ...	5	170	35	140	—	350	250	600
Services	20	30	40	20	—	110	390	500
Imports	10	100	50	20	—	180	−180	—
Value added	400	300	200	180	—			
Total inputs	450	750	600	500	—	1,220	1,080	2,300

Notes: The table may be read across rows: sales by the row sector to the sector named in the column. Or the table may be read in columns: purchases by the column sector from the row sector. Total sales to nonfinal users: the row sum of sales by a sector to every other using sector. Final demand consists of consumption, investment, exports, and government spending. Total output is the sum of sales by the row sector to all intermediate users, and final users. The column sum of final demands is equivalent to GNP, in this example 1080 units.

costs, including computer usage or time-sharing charges; travel and entertainment expense; educational expenditures for personnel who attend seminars and professional meetings; postage, telephone, and telegraph charges; office supplies; subscription to trade publications; and additions to the purchasing library.

A good starting point is to review the actual operating expenditures for the previous fiscal period. If a budget was in effect for the previous fiscal period, a comparison between budget and actual expenditures may point up problem areas. An attempt should be made to reconcile any substantial differences. Actually, expenditures should be compared with budget estimates on a monthly basis. This procedure is one means of controlling operating expenses and detecting problem areas promptly.

After reviewing the past department operating expense history, a budget should be prepared for the next fiscal period. The new estimates should include provision for salary increases and personnel additions or deletions as anticipated by the requirements of the purchasing plan. New estimates of all other expenses required in the efficient operation of the department should be made in keeping with the requirements of the purchasing plan. The final budget should be coordinated with the total budget for the organization.

QUESTIONS FOR REVIEW AND DISCUSSION

1. How does value analysis differ from value engineering? What are the steps in performing value analysis on a purchased item?
2. What are the various subject areas of purchasing research? Which area do you think would be most productive in (a) the short run, and (b) the long run?
3. In what ways might a firm organize to do purchasing research? What are the advantages and disadvantages of each? Which would you recommend in a (a)

small organization, (b) medium-size organization, and (c) a large organization?

4. What is countertrade, and how would it be used in purchasing?

5. Where in purchasing could the PERT/CPM techniques be used? How could PERT/CPM improve purchasing efficiency and effectiveness?

6. Will the U.S. dependence on foreign suppliers for raw materials likely increase or diminish in the decade of the 1980s? What factors will influence this dependence? What course of action in regard to foreign suppliers should purchasing departments in U.S. organizations be following?

7. On which basis would an organization decide where to direct its purchasing research efforts?

8. What questions would be asked in making a commodity study; where would you obtain the information?

9. What is the difference between a purchasing plan and a purchasing budget?

CASE 15–1
WILSON MANUFACTURING INC.

Peter Stone faced a difficult quality problem. As purchasing agent for Wilson Manufacturing he had been heavily involved during the past few years in the company's attempt to broaden its product line to include automotive springs. Recently, Wilson had landed its first contract which called for the supply of a range of springs varying from fairly small to large and heavy duty. Peter knew that the automotive customer was trying out Wilson as a supplier, and if this year's performance was satisfactory, significant increases in future volumes might be expected.

Wilson purchased steel bars cut to length from a nearby steel company and shaped and heat treated the springs in a new Wilson developed patented process. For a customer order for heavy duty springs, Peter Stone had issued a purchase order for 8,000 lengths of .756″ diameter steel bars. The mill rolled the steel at a nominal diameter of .750″, which was still within the standard mill tolerance of ± .008″. The inspection report of Wilson's quality control department showed that the actual diameter measured at .750″ ± .004″ with about 8 percent of the bars tested falling below .748″. On a small test production run of the bars it showed that almost all failed to meet the required load test rates specified by the automotive customer.

Peter Stone had contacted mill representatives when it had first become apparent that the steel bars did not meet specifications. They were noncommittal and had pointed out that .750″ was within the specified range. Peter was now wondering what action to take to resolve this matter.

CASE 15–2
ARDEN FOODS INC.

Bill Jones, purchase analyst in the corporate purchasing office at Arden Foods, was in the process of reviewing corrugated cartons purchases. He had gathered statistics on purchases from each plant and it was apparent that one supplier, Sartex Inc., had managed to increase its share of total carton business dramatically over the past 20 years.

Arden Foods Inc.

Primarily a meat packer and producer of quality foods, Arden Foods operated 13 major plants across the country, each of which was a profit center and autonomous within general corporate policy. Each plant had its own production, sales and administrative staff, and did almost all of its own purchasing. Total sales last year were close to $2½ billion.

Corporate purchasing

The corporate purchasing staff had traditionally been a very small one at Arden Foods, consisting of a manager, a buyer, and two secretaries. This staff was largely occupied with statistical work and did some contract purchasing, only of branded items common to all plants. The corporate manager of purchasing reported to the vice president of finance. When the former manager retired a year ago, the new manager who took over, believed a more aggressive stance for corporate purchasing was appropriate. One of his first moves was to visit all plant purchasing offices and this was followed by the first common meeting of all plant purchasing agents for a duration of two days. The plant purchasing agents pointed out that the statistics traditionally kept at head office were primarily of interest to the finance people, but were not particularly useful to them. As a result, Bill Jones, a recent college graduate who had specialized in purchasing and materials management, was "borrowed" by corporate purchasing from the largest plant's purchasing office. His job was to see if he could not only help develop more meaningful statistics, but also to investigate if corporate purchasing could not provide better other services to the plant locations.

Corrugated carton purchases

Bill Jones believed, and his manager agreed, that corrugated cartons represented a good sample area for him to start working on. Every plant purchased them and last year's total volume of purchases had been about $8½ million.

From the statistics and in talking with buyers and purchasing agents Bill Jones found out that historically a large share of the carton business had always gone to Sartex Inc. Sartex was a large, well-known packaging producer with plants from coast to coast. There was no obligation on the part of any plant purchasing agent to favor Sartex. Actually, most plants had at least two suppliers and in some cases three or four. It was simply that over the years Sartex had demonstrated they were tops in service, quality, and competitiveness.

The purchasing agent in Arden's largest plant who had hired Bill originally, explained the situation this way:

> As the Sartex share of Arden business grew, a special relationship between us developed. Increases in the cost of liner board, wages, or other expenses were not automatically passed on, but justifiable increases were negotiated between us on an annual basis. There is a very good reason why Sartex has so much of my business. They deserve it!

In the last four years Sartex's share had increased 5 percent each year and was about 80 percent of the total current corrugated business available from all Arden plants. Bill Jones forecast that if this trend continued, Sartex might become a sole source.

Bill Jones knew that each plant purchasing agent believed strongly in having full control over his corrugated purchases. As one explained:

> Corrugated is one product we have to have flexibility in and we must be able to deal directly with the local Sartex plant producing it. It is short notice business and sometimes they have to turn cartwheels to accommodate the last minute changes so common in our product line. Moreover, every plant has its own special products and requirements. The fact that all large corrugated producers are themselves decentralized with plants all over the country reinforces the need to be able to do corrugated business locally.

When Bill Jones had started this assignment he had hoped that something obvious would present itself, allowing him to make some useful suggestions for improvements. Now it appeared that all plant purchasing agents were quite satisfied with the status quo and that Arden Foods was lucky to have such a good source in Sartex. He, therefore, wondered how this information could be useful to corporate purchasing .in the plants. Was there an opportunity here for Arden Foods, or was his first assignment a bust and should he turn to something else?

CASE 15–3
MODEL ALUMINUM CORPORATION*
Function of a purchase research staff in a complex organization

In September, Mr. Brodie was assigned the position of manager of the purchase research department of the Model Aluminum Corporation, a large producer of ingots and finished aluminum shapes. Mr. Brodies' official job objective was to "formulate programs designed to increase efficiency and accomplish the maximum potential effect of each dollar expended for purchased goods and services." Annual expenditures for purchases by the Model Aluminum Corporation were $1 billion, going to 35,000 suppliers. Mr. Brodie decided to undertake whatever type of program seemed to offer a possibility of increasing purchasing efficiency or obtaining maximum values from purchasing expenditures. He believed that if possible it was essential not to limit the function of purchase research by strict definition, but rather to provide staff service wherever needed and allow the success of the programs to determine the ultimate size and objective of his department. Six months after becoming manager, Mr. Brodie was attempting to evaluate the development of the department so as to decide how long to wait before asking for personnel to assist him.

In addition to Mr. Brodie's special talents and interests, three factors helped to determine the function of the purchase research department during the first six months of its operation: (1) the size and complexity of the materials management function; (2) the type of materials purchased by the aluminum industry, and (3) the status of Mr. Brodie in the headquarters organization.

A. The great size of the Model Aluminum Corporation presented three types of problems to Mr. Brodie: (1) the difficulty of servicing a department of 50 buyers; (2) the need to consider the extent to which the company's purchasing power could influence a commodity market; and (3) the importance of coordinating purchase research with other staff and supervisory groups located in other departments of the central office.

1. The central purchasing department in Chicago consisted of: (a) a staff group which established corporationwide policies and (b) a department of 50 buyers which purchased all materials for the two major divisions consolidated with headquarters as well as common materials for the eight other divisions (see Exhibit 1). Mr. Brodie was thus located in the same office as the executives who determined corporation purchase policies for all the operating divisions and in the same department as the 50 buyers who purchased two thirds of the corporation's materials. The great number of buyers made it impossible for Mr. Brodie to work closely with each one without

Exhibit 1

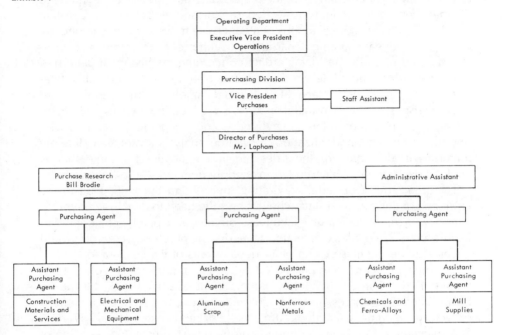

additional personnel in his department. He did not wish to develop a staff, however, until experience indicated what type of purchase research would be most effective. For this reason, his actual working contacts were with the six assistant purchasing agents and the three purchasing agents rather than the 50 buyers themselves.

2. The great purchasing power of the corporation in certain commodity markets such as scrap aluminum, steel, manganese, and coal made it essential to direct purchase research toward long-range pricing policies in addition to achieving the lowest immediate price. For example, corporation purchasing executives wished to keep prices as low as possible, but were aware of the danger of forcing certain prices excessively low with the resulting unstable markets and excessive pressure on suppliers. In many cases, pricing decisions had to be made too quickly to rely on the top economic policy advice of the senior executive committees. For this reason, purchase research was requested to undertake the evaluation of long-range price and supply conditions in the commodity markets.

3. Furthermore, due to the size of the central office, analysis and research staffs had already been developed in other departments of the headquarters group in Chicago, some of which undertook projects that could be considered to fall into the objectives of purchase research as broadly defined. Four staff groups in particular did work that was related to Mr. Brodie's assignment: (a) the staff assistant to the vice president of purchases accumulated

data relating to price changes of the major materials. He issued regularly to all management personnel in the department above the rank of assistant purchasing agent historical reports of recent price movements and economic changes; (b) the accounting department, which processed invoices for payment, could provide considerable data concerning the historical pattern of purchase orders, including the dollar value of different product classifications, the market percentage of individual suppliers, and certain other characteristics of the transactions; (c) the engineering department maintained a group of "consultant" metallurgists and mechanical engineers who undertook certain standardization and value analysis projects of different materials grades; and (d) the sales division maintained a large market analysis department, which undertook supply-demand studies of raw materials at the request of certain operating divisions in the field. Due to the existence of these related staff activities and the need to develop communication with many different executives, buyers, and plant personnel, Mr. Brodie considered that one major objective of purchase research would necessarily be the liaison with other departments of the corporation.

B. The type of materials purchased by the aluminum industry placed further restrictions on the type of research Mr. Brodie undertook. Of the $1 billion annual purchases, almost $600 million were for seven raw materials, refractory materials, scrap aluminum, steel, coal and coke, natural gas, zinc, and manganese. Although economic commodity studies could be made of these materials, Mr. Brodie considered it to be difficult to make cost savings in their purchase through ordinary value analysis methods. Savings through cost analysis were limited because the price of these materials was determined more by market pressures than by production costs. Savings through product analysis were difficult to achieve through a headquarters staff because of the specialized metallurgical knowledge required to change a grade of ore without making the aluminum-making process more difficult or influencing the physical and chemical characteristics of the finished aluminum. In addition to the seven major raw materials, $200 million was expended for new plant construction, electric power generating equipment, and for miscellaneous raw materials. Value analysis of capital equipment purchases was usually delegated to a field purchasing agent who could work closely with the design engineers at the location of the construction. Another $200 million was expended for maintenance, repair, and operating supplies such as valves, pumps, and hand tools, which presented opportunities for value analysis. Although they constituted a wide range of purchases and so lacked the possibility of great dollar savings from a single cost reduction that could be obtained in mass production industries, Mr. Brodie believed that considerable results could be obtained from effort devoted to this area.

C. A third characteristic that helped determine the function of the purchase research department was the status of Mr. Brodie in the organization. Three factors had placed Mr. Brodie in a position that tended to emphasize other purchase research activities rather than cost reductions through value analysis, which would require close contact with the buyers. First, the willingness of purchasing executives to support purchase research gave the function a status on the executive rather than the operating level of the organization (see Exhibit 1). Second, the desire of the vice president of purchases to have a highly placed staff man who was relieved of the pressure of day-to-day work resulted in some pressure on Mr. Brodie to devote time to advanced policy and requirements planning for the department. Third, the need to maintain the line authority of the assistant purchasing agents together with the large size of the buying department seemed to make direct contact inadvisable between Mr. Brodie and the buyers. Instead, it was decided that a description of any projects which the buyers were anxious to have investigated was to be submitted through channels to their purchasing agents and eventually to Mr. Lapham, the director of purchases. Under this plan, Mr. Lapham was then to select those projects he considered important and submit them to Mr. Brodie for investigation. Mr. Lapham thus acted as the program director for purchase research, using his key position in the department to assign problems he considered most essential to the organization. At the same time that projects were submitted to him from the buyers, Mr. Lapham also received notice of purchasing problems through his committee meetings with other executives in the company. For example, the manufacturing, the coal, and the appropriations committees met biweekly and the general superintendents' committee met bimonthly. Through these meetings and through the quarterly profit objective conferences, Mr. Lapham detected cost trends and materials management problems that could be investigated by Mr. Brodie.

Before coming to the purchasing department, Mr. Brodie had had considerable staff experience in the Model Aluminum Company. He had set up a sales evaluation system for the aluminum wire division and had spent two years in the finance department in the headquarters office. Mr. Lapham considered his broad staff experience throughout the company to be ideally suited for Mr. Brodie's new assignment and stated that it had taken almost two years to find the proper man for the job. Upon accepting the position, Mr. Brodie pointed out that he was new to purchasing and had no engineering training. For this reason, he preferred to work under the broadest possible definition of purchase research so that he could use his staff experience to advantage, rather than limiting his function to operating problems that might involve technical knowledge. "I'm not an operational man," he said, "I want the flexibility to develop anything that management feels should be developed to increase the control over purchases." Mr. Lapham agreed that it was best to let the new program undertake whatever projects seemed most promising during the first year without restricting the scope of its operations in advance. "This is a long-range project" said Mr. Lapham. "I don't expect results for more than a year. We'll let Brodie do whatever he wants and see by trial and error what the best kind of projects are. That way, he'll settle in through actual experience."

During the first six months in his new assignment and without the assistance of any personnel other than stenographic help, Mr. Brodie undertook five types of projects: (1) development of management systems and reports, (2) the establishment of a clearinghouse for purchasing information, (3) long-range economic commodity studies, (4) investigations into particular contract or product problems at the request of any of the 50 buyers, and (5) value analysis projects.

1. The development of management systems and reports required Mr. Brodie to determine what kinds of information useful to the supervision of the department could be assembled from the order processing system in current use. The general accounting division maintained a business machine department which processed invoices from IBM cards and submitted to Mr. Lapham summary reports of the dollar value of various purchase classifications. Mr. Brodie studied the code punched on the cards from the invoices and initiated two new reports using existing data: an inventory commitment report showing stocks on hand and on order for the six most important raw materials, together with price changes from the previous month; and a supplier's market report, showing the percentage of the company's business given to each supplier in the most important categories of purchases. In addition, Mr. Brodie decided that the use of five-digit code on the IBM cards was inadequate to give a sufficiently close breakdown of purchases by category and dollar value. He therefore studied the advisability of using a nine-digit code for the major purchases so that studies could be made of the costs of alternate shipping containers, means of transportation, or premium grades of material with different physical or chemical properties.

2. Since Mr. Brodie believed that one objective of the purchase research function should be to establish communication between the buyers and the people outside their department whose work related to theirs, he began to accumulate published data about sources of supply. By reading through the important supplier industry magazines and house organs, he believed he could come across useful information about new product developments, the plant expansions of suppliers, and the market conditions in supplier industries. This information was to be published in a bulletin called *Vendors' Notes* and distributed to buying and other interested personnel.

3. Shortly after Mr. Brodie became manager, the sales department of one of the operating divisions had requested that a commodity study of sulfur be made by the market analysis department of the headquarters sales division. When the study was completed, a copy was submitted to Mr. Lapham who then suggested to Mr. Brodie that he personally undertake a similar study on a larger scale to investigate the zinc situation. When Mr. Brodie accepted the request, he had in mind a full-scale investigation of the mining companies' cost of production, the pricing practice of the industry, the long-range supply-demand trends and research into all factors in the international market that affected the commodity price.

4. Since Mr. Brodie wished to make the buyers feel that he was available for help, he sometimes undertook investigations directly for them if circum-

stances indicated that the project was not a difficult one. The established procedure, however, required that the buyers refer their requests for purchases research service through their purchasing agents to Mr. Lapham, who would then assign the projects to Mr. Brodie. Despite the variety of his research projects, therefore, Mr. Brodie had little personal contact with the 50 buyers. His most direct contact with them was to review the cost savings reports which the buyers submitted so as to evaluate their claims for cost reductions.

5. Although the buyers' cost savings reports indicated a variety of methods of making cost reductions, their principal emphasis was on negotiations with suppliers. Mr. Brodie wished to originate cost reductions of his own through value analysis projects requiring changes in specifications and designs. Mr. Brodie had received reports of metallurgical studies made by company engineers to determine the cost and performance characteristics of the various grades of ore which accounted for almost 60 percent of the annual purchases. Since he was not an engineer, however, it was difficult for him to participate in value analysis projects in highly technical areas such as metallurgy. Mr. Brodie therefore decided that a cost reduction program through the standardization of maintenance, repairs, and operating supplies would be less difiicult to undertake without technical knowledge. For this reason, he selected as a test item the purchase of valves which accounted for $2 million of annual expenditures and began to evaluate the possibility of cost savings in a project that would eventually require supplier surveys and visits with requisitioning and using personnel throughout the corporation.

During his first seven months on the job, Mr. Brodie had spent a considerable amount of time in addition to working hours studying purchasing reports and developing the various projects he had started. He stated, "I can staff up eventually when I am sure what kind of assistance I need. What I've got to do now is to prove what the job can do by getting out some successful projects. When I've actually proved what can be done, it will be easy enough to get the help I need."

Mr. Brodie recognized that although the original objective of his job had been to make cost reductions in purchases, his value analyses were actually only a portion of the research projects. Part of this result, he believed was due to the difficulty of establishing effective contact between the buyers and the plant personnel who specified and used materials. He reasoned that value analysis could be effective only if cost and performance characteristics were investigated concurrently. The buyers, however, had little contact with the plant personnel. There were two groups in headquarters, however, who did have active contact with plant operations—the "consultant" engineers and the cost accountants.

Due to the highly technical nature of their work, it was difficult for Mr. Brodie to work closely with the engineers. The cost accountants, however, had effective access to the plants and could make the kind of analyses that Mr. Brodie wanted.

The accounting department of the Model Aluminum Corporation was the only one in which headquarters executives had both line authority over their field representatives in the plants and constant contact with them. As a management service group, the cost accountants often organized savings programs and evaluated the results of the projects. Many of the cost accountants were industrial engineers who could work directly with the operations problems facing plant personnel. In addition, the accounting headquarters maintained tabulating equipment with which to process complicated information from the field. For these reasons, the reports of the accounting department carried considerable weight with management executives and their evaluation of savings resulting from cost reduction programs were regarded as official.

Both Mr. Lampham and Mr. Brodie believed that the purchase research function would have to be defined more precisely as soon as the results of its initial programs could be evaluated. Mr. Brodie believed that the most important problem currently facing the development of value analysis was the need to establish close working relationships with the personnel who defined materials specifications and those who used the delivered supplies. Since his early attempt to make use of the facilities of the accounting department to establish contact with the plants had thus far met with indifferent success, he hoped to increase their interest in value analysis in the future. One possible solution, he believed, was to help organize a companywide cost reduction program under the supervision of the accounting department in which purchasing personnel could participate. On the other hand, a program of such magnitude might be difficult to organize without help from key executives in other departments. Mr. Brodie was not sure whether the relationship he needed could best be established by a companywide cost reduction program, by committee relationships through the senior executives, or through the slow development of informal contacts between himself and the accounting supervisors. As the scope of purchase research increased, Mr. Brodie felt the need to be more pressing to obtain personnel to assist him. On the other hand, he believed that until such problems were resolved as his relationship with the accounting department and a definition of the type and extent of value analysis projects that should be made, it was impossible to determine what kind of personnel should be hired to assist in the program.

PURCHASING DEPARTMENT REPORTS TO MANAGEMENT; EVALUATING PERFORMANCE; AND STRATEGY

16

The importance of good communications in achieving optimum results in the operations of a business is being given increasing recognition by top management. As the tempo of business activity has quickened and companies have become larger, more diversified, and more decentralized in operations, information and its proper communication have become essential in the development of managerial controls.

Chapter 3 explored many of the information flows which directly affect the decision-making activities of purchasing personnel. These information flows can be broadly classified as originating from the interface relationships with other functional areas within the firm and contacts with the outside worldwide marketplace. When the materials plan and the budget are submitted to top company management executives for approval, they provide the basic reports about expected activity for the forecast period. The accuracy of the projected plans and strategies is checked when reports on the actual performance of the materials task are made.

OPERATIONS REPORTS

We cannot give a detailed explanation of all the types of reports which might be useful under all circumstances. Emphasis on what information should be reported will vary with the type of industry. Too many purchasing executives limit their reports to a tabulation of the figures showing:

1. Total dollar volume of purchases.
2. Total dollars spent for department operating expenses.
3. Total number of purchase orders issued.

In some instances these figures are related to each other by calculating average figures and percentages to show:

1. Average dollar cost of the purchase orders written

$$\frac{\text{Dollar cost of operating department}}{\text{Number of P.O.s written}}$$

2. Operating costs as a percentage of total dollar volume of purchases.
3. Operating costs as a percentage of total dollar volume of sales.

Comparing the above figures and ratios with similar figures for previous time periods provides some perspective on what is happening in the purchasing function. However, these reports are of little use in providing a basis for the evaluation of how effectively the purchasing function is providing the materials and equipment needed at the lowest net cost, considering quality, service, and the needs of the user. Note that the lowest price is not necessarily the lowest net cost.

Data processing equipment, properly programmed, is capable of providing information promptly and in a form that facilitates analysis of most purchasing activities.

What to report, the frequency of reporting, and how to report are decisions which require careful analysis. In some situations top management specifies the type of report, the frequency, and whether the report is to be written or presented orally. The personality of major executives, the type of organization structure, and the nature of the industry have an influence on decisions affecting reporting procedures. Good reporting is important to the status and effective operation of the purchasing function because of the insights obtained from the analysis required in preparing reports, the information presented, and the opportunity to broaden the understanding of management of the results to be obtained by effective purchasing.

In general, purchasing operating reports which are prepared on a regular basis, monthly, quarterly, semiannually, or annually, can be classified under the following headings and include:

1. *Market and Economic Conditions and Price Performance*
   a. Price trends and changes for the major materials and commodities purchased. Comparisons with standard costs where such accounting methods are used.
   b. Changes in demand-supply conditions for the major items purchased. Effects of labor strikes or threatened strikes.
   c. Lead time expectations for major items.
2. *Inventory Investment Changes*
   a. Dollar investment in inventories, classified by major commodity and materials groups.
   b. Days' or months' supply, and on order, for major commodity and materials groups.
   c. Ratio of inventory dollar investment to sales dollar volume.
   d. Rates of inventory turnover for major items.
3. *Purchasing Operations and Effectiveness*
   a. Cost reductions resulting from purchase research and value analysis studies.

    b. Quality rejection rates for major items.

    c. Number of out-of-stock situations which caused interruption of scheduled production.

    d. Number of change orders issued, classified by cause.

    e. Number of requisitions received and processed.

    f. Number of purchase orders issued.

    g. Employee work load and productivity.

    h. Transportation costs analysis.

4. *Operations Affecting Administration and Financial Activities*

    a. Comparison of actual departmental operating costs to budget.

    b. Cash discounts earned and cash discounts lost.

    c. Commitments to purchase, classified by types of formal contracts and by purchase orders, aged by expected delivery dates.

    d. Changes in cash discounts allowed by suppliers.

Special project reports

From time to time, there is need to prepare special reports to bring to the attention of top management or to various functional managers matters which concern the interests of the firm. The alert purchasing executive who has an appreciation for the key position he or she occupies in the flow of information may have the opportunity to detect changes in trends of market practices or long-term supply situations. Purchasing departments having purchasing research staffs are in a good position to prepare such special reports.

Effective report presentation

Reports which are not read are a wasted effort. Reports consisting solely of a tabulation of figures often have little meaning to anyone except the compiler of the report.

A good starting point in preparing any report is for the writer to take the position of the person who is expected to read the report—what information is important in performing the job? Some of the fundamentals common to all reports are the need for clarity of presentation, simple and concise statements, and carefully-checked information to ensure accuracy. A title should be used which clearly describes the nature of the report.

Most busy executives prefer to see a brief summary of the important information, and, if appropriate, conclusions at the beginning of the report. This procedure alerts the reader to what follows in the main body of the report. Recommendations, when appropriate, appear at the end of the report. Short statistical tabulations are usually included in the body of the report or may be shown graphically by pie charts, bar charts, or graphs. Lengthy statistical tabulations should be provided in an appendix and identified and analyzed in the body of the report.

Provisions should be made in any system which issues regular reports to check from time to time to learn if the reports are useful to the recipients. All too frequently, reports continue to be issued because of habit rather than because they serve a useful purpose.

APPRAISING DEPARTMENT PERFORMANCE

Few organizations operate at full effectiveness. The company which is successful over time recognizes this fact of life and strives constantly to improve all aspects of its operation. In a highly-competitive environment, only the efficient survive.

An increasing number of managers have recognized that a properly organized purchasing function, staffed by competent employees, is capable of contributing significantly. Along with this recognition has come an awareness of the desirability of periodic appraisals of the performance of the function. Savings made flow directly to profit. In a free economy, profits are the lifeblood of business operation and a necessity for continued progress. Thus there is a continuing need for appraisal of purchasing performance with the purpose of improving effectiveness.

Problems in appraising efficiency

It is one thing to recognize the need for performance appraisal and quite a different situation to develop meaningful methods for measuring performance. For several years prior to 1950, various committees of the National Association of Purchasing Agents worked diligently to develop a uniform statistical method of evaluation which would apply generally to purchasing activities. It finally was concluded that no one method would fit all situations. Shortly after the end of World War II, the U.S. Air Force employed as consultants industrial purchasing executives who were acknowledged experts in their respective fields. These consultants were grouped in teams to make intensive performance evaluation surveys of the purchasing activities of the major prime contractors producing aircraft and other military equipment for the Air Force. These contracts involved billions of dollars in expenditures annually.

In the decade of the 1950s, increasing attention was given to developing new methods for the evaluation of the purchasing function. Many large corporations developed methods which met their specific needs. The accounting profession also expressed its interest and published results of research projects.[1]

Continued interest in the subject of evaluation into the 1960s is evidenced by the publication of a comprehensive report by the American Management Association.[2] Over 200 companies cooperated in the study, and 75 percent indicated that some method of evaluation was used.

Research in organization theory and human behavior in organizations has pro-

---

[1] Two of the best reports are: Institute of Internal Auditors, *The Internal Audit and Control of a Purchasing Department*, Research Report No. 2 (New York, 1955); and *Purchasing* (New York: Arthur Andersen and Company, 1960). The latter publication was revised in 1975.

[2] F. Albert Hayes, and George A. Renard, *Evaluating Purchasing Performance*, AMA Research Study 66 (New York: American Management Association, 1964).

duced greater understanding of how to organize for effective results. We have learned about the importance of clearly defining the purpose and the objectives or goals we expect a function and the employees in that function to achieve. A major problem in many organizations has been the lack of clearly defined objectives for the purchasing department and its personnel. Unless it can be determined what is to be evaluated, the question of how to make an evaluation has little meaning.

Purchasing objectives

Much has been written in recent years about "management by objectives." Companies which have used the concept to improve operations have learned that it usually requires a substantial period of time, often several years, to develop the climate of managerial philosophy which is essential to full implementation.

The chief purchasing executive or materials manager has the basic responsibility for determining general objectives for the function and the coordination of such objectives with the strategic objectives of the company as a whole. Once the overall objectives or targets are outlined, they are provided to subordinates not as a directive but as general guidelines for those who have decision-making authority to use in establishing the objectives which will govern their activities for some period of time. When properly administered, the individual's objectives act as a motivating force to give direction to work and subsequently a basis for appraising performance. The more responsibility the individual exercises in establishing and implementing objectives, the greater the opportunity for the motivation of employees and the individual's satisfaction which comes from a sense of accomplishment and achievement.

The establishment of objectives for a purchasing department is a procedure which is specific to a given organization at a particular period in time. The services of a competent purchasing research analyst or a purchasing research staff can be of great assistance in selecting objectives which will provide the greatest payback for the efforts expended.

Management by objectives

Careful research and planning will provide a better understanding of the job which has to be done. The use of the "management by objectives" concept should provide a means to implement the planning process, motivate the personnel responsible for operating any plan developed, and provide a mechanism for appraising results. In the final analysis a good plan should help personnel to do a better job, but it is the attitude and ability of the people on the job which will obtain maximum results. In recognition of this fact, permission has been obtained from Professor Alva F. Kindall to quote his five-step program for effective use of management by objectives to achieve company goals.[3]

---

[3] Alva F. Kindall, *Personnel Administration: Principles and Cases* (Homewood, Ill.: Richard D. Irwin, 1969), pp. 412–15. © 1969 by Richard D. Irwin, Inc. Reprinted by permission.

Step one: Position description areas of accountability responsibilities. In *step one,* the individual occupant of a position or job discusses his job description with his superior, and the occupant defines his areas of accountability—his responsibilities. He then outlines the *results* he is responsible for attaining in return for the pay he receives.

Since the occupant of a position or job knows more about what he does than anyone else, he should be given the opportunity to write his own position description. Obviously, the occupant should discuss this position description with his immediate superior to make certain that the two are in complete agreement on the responsibilities and duties of the occupant of the position.

Step two: Individual goals. In *step two,* having obtained complete agreement of his superior on the duties of a position or job, the occupant should then prepare a list of goals that he believes would represent reasonable performance in each of his areas of responsibility for, say, the next six months, or the next year. In other words, the occupant *plans* his activities for the forthcoming period, in accordance, of course, with the overall goals of his unit and his organization.

In establishing his own performance goals, the occupant must know the goals of the organization for which he works and the goals of his particular organizational unit. Every organization imposes certain constraints on individual activities, and these constraints must be communicated to the individual by the organization. Thus, an individual can set reasonable, manageable, and stretch goals for himself only when he knows the goals of his overall organization and the goals of his unit. This means that the organization must implement its program in the overall *planning* and must make its plans and objectives known to the individual.

Also included in an individual's goals for the forthcoming period should be his own personal goals for self-development.

No management, however, should attempt to introduce such a goal-setting program until it is firmly convinced that individuals will respond to this freedom and trust by establishing higher goals for themselves than those management would have imposed upon them from above. The fact that individuals will respond in this fashion has been proved over and over again in programs that are well conceived and administered.

Step three: Agreed-upon goals. In *step three,* the occupant discusses his goals with his immediate superior until they are in complete agreement on the goals. This third step is the most tricky and the most complicated in the entire procedure. For one thing, the moment a superior asks a subordinate to raise or lower a goal that he has set for himself, the goal then becomes the superior's, not the subordinate's. On the other hand, if some crisis exists that requires immediate action on the part of a subordinate, the superior obviously may have to change a subordinate's goal. But such action should be necessary only under emergency conditions.

In *step three,* the superior should act in the role of questioner, advisor, counselor, trainer, developer, and even "warner." The superior should not play the role of God or judge!

Step four: Standards, or checkpoints. In *step four,* the superior and the subordinate jointly establish the standards, or checkpoints, to be used by both parties during the course of the forthcoming period and at the end of the period to determine the subordinate's success in attaining objectives. Examples of such checkpoints are due dates; sales, financial and cost figures; statistical data; and comparisons.

Step five: Results.   In *step five,* the *results* of a person's performance become known; either he has attained or exceeded his goals or hc has failed to attain his goals. The mere attainment or failure to attain a goal is not of significance in itself. The important consideration here is: what has the person *accomplished?* Obviously, a man who establishes extremely high goals for himself and then almost attains them has accomplished more than a man who originally established low goals and then exceeded them. Judgment must be used in assessing *accomplishments.* The superior's task in *step five* is to eliminate negative accomplishments and to reward appropriately positive accomplishments.

Negative accomplishments are warning signals that something must be done. Perhaps the subordinate needs training or development. Maybe he needs additional help or new equipment. Or he could be misplaced in his position. After a superior has exhausted all means of help and guidance and the subordinate continues to produce negative accomplishments, he must make efforts promptly to transfer the subordinate into a position in which he can produce positive accomplishments. If the person fails this opportunity, he may have to be retired early or even discharged. For his own welfare and for the good of an organization, a person should not be continued in a position in which he cannot attain positive accomplishments.

On the other hand, the superior should appropriately reward a subordinate who has produced *positive accomplishments* by periodical salary increases and promotions.

In all of these five steps, no mention has been made of *personality traits.* No effort has been made to try to determine *why* a man produces certain results. The *cause* of a man's activities is not explored; he has not been put on the couch and psychoanalyzed. Instead, a person is judged on the basis of his *results*—his *accomplishments.* If a man has serious (not imagined) personality deficiencies, he will inevitably have negative accomplishments. The administrator, by eliminating negative accomplishments, automatically eliminates those with personality deficiencies. The task of identifying and improving serious personality deficiencies should be left to the professional when such advice is sought by the individual.

In the superior-subordinate relationship, judgmental statements on personality should *never* be communicated to the individual, and they should *never* be recorded on written forms or documents. Confine such statements to summaries of *actual results.* This principle applies to both positive and negative judgmental comments.

Procedures to be used in evaluation

There are essentially two approaches which can be taken in evaluating the performance of the purchasing function:

1.   The continuing evaluation which compares the operating results with the plan, budget, and objectives established for the department and personnel.

2.   The outside audit made by someone outside the department or the company.

While these two approaches are not mutually exclusive, in general practice in the company that has been progressive in its concepts of organization and has recognized the need to staff the purchasing department with highly competent people, there is less need to call on consultants from outside the company to participate in the evaluation process. Managements of organizations having well-established internal auditing departments obtain substantial help in evaluating various functional operations when internal auditors use a broader approach than just checking for integrity. Working cooperatively with the chief purchasing executive and staff, the auditors can help in making objective appraisals in areas such as:

1. Workload allocations.
2. Purchasing department relationships with other departments, and problem areas.
3. Relationships with vendors—vendors' attitudes toward the organization and toward the buyers.
4. Adherence to policies and procedures as detailed in policy statements and manuals.

Procedure to be used by an outside consultant

When an outside consultant is used for evaluation purposes, careful inquiry should be made to assure that the consultant has the specific expertise and breadth of experience needed for the job to be done. After a selection is made, a conference should be arranged between the consultant, the chief purchasing executive, and the executive to whom purchasing reports. A broad outline of the areas to be investigated should be agreed to by those attending the conference.

Contact with top management. Clearly, for an outside consultant, the place to begin is with whoever represents top management, presumably the chief operating executive, president, or in some cases the general manager. The consultant probably will want to talk to the other top executives sooner or later, but this is not the starting point. Quite aside from assuring the complete cooperation of the president, there are various things to be learned at the outset:

1.   What is the scope and responsibility of the department *as the president understands it?* This is important, because there are many instances in which confusion exists between the various levels of administration concerning just who is responsible for what. Often, too, it will be found that the authority is not in fact exercised by those who are thought to be exercising it.

2.   Who is responsible for the determination of purchasing policy concerning such important matters as inventory control and speculative buying? Are these policies set by the president or by some inner council of which the purchasing officer is not a member, or does the latter participate at all times?

3.   Does the purchasing officer hold his or her own on those occasions when called upon to sit in the top councils, or, on the contrary, does he or she contribute little? Does he or she have a broad understanding of business problems, exercise responsible judgment when called upon to do so, and command the respect of other top executives?

4.   If the purchasing officer is not rated a top executive, on what occasions is advice called for, and is the advice worthwhile when given?

5. Is there more than one purchasing department in the organization, and, if there are several, what are their respective responsibilities?

6. Does the president keep in touch with purchasing policy and its administration and, if so, to what extent?

What is learned from the president (and other top executives) will give an indication of the attitude toward the importance of purchasing and of the degree to which there is confidence in the purchasing organization and personnel. In addition to this information, partly in the form of facts and partly in the form of impressions, there will be some very useful clues to be followed as the investigation proceeds.

Interview with head of purchasing. The second step would be a preliminary interview with the head of the purchasing department. There are several obvious reasons for such an interview, including the desirability of explaining why the consultant has been called in at all and making it clear that the whole attitude is one of cooperation and constructive assistance rather than seeking to find fault.

The main purpose of the interview, of course, is to make at least a tentative evaluation of the character and ability of the person who is presumably responsible for the policy, personnel, organization, and procedures of the department. What sort of a person is this? (1) Thoroughly familiar with, and a student of, materials and manufacturing processes and business problems and practices beyond those directly related to materials? (2) Managing the department singlehandedly, or delegating authority wherever possible? (3) Tactful, yet able to come to a decision with firmness? (4) Of a receptive mind and an ability to gather information wherever it may be found and to screen out the useful from the worthless? (5) Belonging to what professional associations? (6) Reading what magazines of a trade, general business, and broad cultural nature, either regularly or occasionally? (7) Giving the impression of being honest, fair, vigorous, and pleasant?

It is inevitable that, as a result of such conversations, certain definite impressions will be formed. Although the final result will be a matter of judgment in any case, there is need to be most careful in crystallizing impressions too early and without adequate information. Preliminary opinions must be treated *as preliminary*—to be checked and rechecked later on. The importance of all this cannot be overestimated, for, with the possible exception of the size-up of the president of the company, the qualifications of the head of the department constitute the most important single element in the whole analysis.

Remaining steps in investigation. From this point on, the exact order of the investigation is not important. What the next step will be should depend upon what was learned at the previous step. The significant thing is that a wide range of points should be checked, and not the order in which this is done. Sooner or later, judgments must be formed on several points.

Points for judgment in appraisal

Is the organization of the department based on sound principles? Is the organization as it appears on paper the real, working organization? Are the lines of responsibility drawn with reasonable appreciation for the nature of the tasks and of the personnel available? Much of the required data on these points will be gained from the president or from the head of the department. But the information as to how well the organization works and whether it actually functions in the way that either the president or the head of the department *thinks* it does will be disclosed only by further study at the lower echelons within the department.

Is the physical layout of the department well planned? Is office space planned for the efficient performance of the work? Are there adequate reception room facilities to handle the salesmen and other callers? Do buyers have facilities where they can talk with salespeople without unnecessary interruptions? Proper office working facilities are not only important in building employee morale but also in obtaining the best possible attitude from the outsiders calling on the buyers and others in the department.

Is there a reasonably well defined purchasing policy? Is there a policy that is accepted by the president, as well as by other top executives, such as the sales, production, and engineering managers, and that actually is followed? Policies are often extremely hard to define, frequently still harder to follow, and bound to change from time to time. None of these facts provides an excuse for the department's not having established policies.

The statement of policy should be written and widely distributed, not only among the members of the department itself but throughout the entire company and even among the suppliers. All of these groups should actually have a permanent copy of the statement in their possession. They not only should know and understand it but also should have immediate access to it for reference purposes. In no other way can the best results of full cooperation be expected. Furthermore, such general familiarity with the policies makes close integration with the policies of other departments more probable and necessary modifications easier to effect. The mere writing of such statements helps to define policy in the minds of those responsible for carrying it out and keeps them "on their toes" in the observance thereof. Moreover, to reduce a company's policies and procedures to writing is one of the best means of ensuring that the department head has carefully, critically, and constructively thought out the objectives, policies, and administrative problems confronting the organization.

Are the procedures reasonable? There are two good reasons for checking the procedures in some detail. One is to be able to judge their adequacy. The other is that there is *no surer way of locating clues to departmental problems* than going over the procedures with the greatest of care. There, if anywhere, general weaknesses will be disclosed.

The number of small orders and the volume of rush orders, for instance, are revealing types of information. An analysis of the purchase orders and a comparison of them with the corresponding requisitions will indicate both the completeness of the latter and the independence exercised in placing the former. It will be revealing, too, to learn something of the extent of carload orders as against less-than-carload orders, of the distribution of suppliers as between local suppliers and those from out-of-town, of the degree of reliance on supply houses as against manufacturers, and of the total number of suppliers used. The very forms themselves are clues to the familiarity of the personnel with the "tools of the trade." So, too, is the filing system: how promptly can documents be located and inquiries, both those originating within and those originating from outside the department, be answered? What records—vendor, purchase order, contract, quotation, price, or other—are kept? To what extent are the records that are kept used?

Procedures and forms are, as a rule, very dull things; to most people they are, indeed, very elementary and routine. But for an evaluator of efficiency there is no greater source of "leads" than a study of procedures. Here, too, it would be well to find out whether the department has a formal written description or manual of procedure. The preparation of a manual leads to exactness in thinking, to certainty of responsibility, and to smoothness of operation, although, of course, it can also have undesirable effects if it becomes too much of a "Bible" and serves to cut down flexibility and initiative.

What is the record of the department with respect to prices paid and delivery? By a reasonable amount of the right kind of spot-checking, it is quite possible to determine whether the prices paid have been consistently at, below, or above the market. Particular attention should be devoted to the purchases of materials that are most important dollarwise. What has been the department's performance in getting deliveries on time? Has material arrived by the dates requested by the stores and production departments, or at least by the dates promised by the buyers to those departments? Have the buyers secured promised shipping dates from suppliers, and have the materials gone forward on those dates? Both of these—prices paid and deliveries—are obviously important points to check, and a reasonable effort should be made to learn whether or not all is being done that could be expected.

How is inventory controlled? Insofar as the department is responsible for inventory control, the following points must be looked into with great care: What evidences are there of "dead stock"? Have operating departments been handicapped by lack of material through the purchasing department's fault? Are there adequate controls on forward purchases? Are inventory policies and purchasing policies closely integrated administratively? An examination into these possibilities involves a study of the inventory policy itself, including the standards that are set, the devices for controlling the inventory, and the soundness of the judgment of those responsible.

What is the attitude of other departments? Another check point of great importance relates to the attitude of the other departments of the company toward the purchasing department and their feeling concerning its efficiency. Does the department have a reputation for being capable, alert to its opportunities, and helpful? Evidence on this score is one of the things which is often better obtained by an outside consultant than by an insider.

Attitude of suppliers. Related to this factor is the evidence of supplier goodwill. This, like intracompany goodwill, should be a factor of real concern. The fact that it is, of course, clearly one of the things that can least be reduced to any sort of a statistical measure is not important. Fortunately, considering its significance, it can be gauged by an intelligent person who is sensitive to the reactions of others.

By following checkpoints of the type outlined in the foregoing, by gaining clues from cost and other statistical data, and by the proper use of reports, an appraisal of the efficiency of a department can be made.

Quite obviously the department administrator also must continually appraise his or her own work as well as that of the organization. True, judgments on these matters may not coincide with those of the executive head of the company, and they may not be wholly unbiased. Yet, provided that the administrator is competent, much can be accomplished. If too busy with other matters (though evaluation is part of good administration), handicapped by inertia, deficient in the ability to judge these things, or lacking in knowledge of good management, then a new manager is needed.

There is much to be said, at the same time, in favor of an occasional outside check on the department. The much abused internal auditor and the outside consultant can bring a point of view which is very difficult for one who is continually "on the job" to get, and this is of value both to top management and to the department head. The latter gains because the independent critic can judge even better the degree of cooperation and the confidence in the department expressed by other departments of the business. Inefficient methods, otherwise easily overlooked, are spotted. The psychological effect of knowing an examination is to be made is excellent. The fact that the personnel in the department are forced to review and justify what they do helps considerably. At the same time, constructive and helpful suggestions should be forthcoming from the examiner and full credit should be given for what is commendable. And the consultant or internal auditor frequently makes it possible for the department head to secure the approval of the management group for desired changes, simply because of the fact that recommendations have the support of a representative of the management from "outside."

The performance of any department might be improved by such analysis. Yet management probably has the most to gain from the independent appraisal of a department like purchasing, whose efficiency is inherently difficult to evaluate and whose real function is not always well understood. Any assistance that management can get which will enable it to specify the contributions it has a right to expect from such a department, to segregate the particular function from the other major activities of the business, and to evaluate more adequately the company policies in that area should profoundly better the individual company concerned and, by and large, the complete structure of the economy as a whole.

Review of personnel policy

One of the keys to the success of any organization is the people who make it up and are responsible for making it "go." Investigation of the personnel program should start with an analysis of the work to be done, including the size of the total workload and the way in which various tasks with similar characteristics can be combined. From this analysis it should be possible to make estimates of how many people are required and the educational and experience qualifications such people should have. A comparison of these findings with the actual members of the department and their job assignments should provide a basis on which to begin an evaluation of personnel policy.

Selection of personnel. The next query is whether the people on the various jobs are personally qualified for the work they are doing. This, in turn, calls for several other lines of inquiry. One concerns the *manner of selection*. Is there a fairly definite understanding of the qualifications? What are the personal characteristics wanted? What academic training is expected? What experience background is called for? From what sources are new personnel recruited? The answers to each of these and similar questions will, of course, vary with the particular circumstances. Thus, if a potential buyer is being sought, most managers will look for a person with analytical ability and good judgment, honesty, and, of course, pleasing personality. Most likely the person will be a college graduate, specializing preferably, but not necessarily, in business.

Replacement program. Does the department have a regular *replacement program?* Too often there is a failure to have personnel distributed among the various age groups, with the result that all the buyers are older persons who will retire at about the same time and—to make the matter even worse—with no trained personnel coming along behind them.

In-house training. Another significant check point in the personnel program is the *training after employment*. Newcomers to the department have much to learn about purchasing, particularly since purchasing calls for specialized training. Under such circumstances, the new person is likely to have a good deal of difficulty in learning a new job in any office where no particular help is given, but information must be picked up by trial and error or from office mates, all of whom are busy with their own work. This means that the head of the department should actively encourage and take a continuing interest in the training of new people. In some sort of an evening class or by means of an in-house training program, assistance should be provided.

Is there an on-the-job training program? Many purchasing departments lack one. This is a most serious omission. Such a program may be built around the policy and procedure manuals. Study of the principal items purchased should be undertaken, perhaps with the aid of motion-pictures. Likewise, study of the products and processes of the particular company will fill in gaps. Reading assignments, films, regular written reports, group discussions, and even occasional outside lectures will all serve, in proper proportions, to keep up interest and provide learning opportunities.

Older members of the department also should be encouraged to remember that one's education is never completed, and that experience is by no means always the best teacher.

Compensation plan. A personnel program must cover more than selection and training. What is the *compensation plan?* Are people adequately paid? Is there a definite system for advancement, and, specifically, what are the young person's chances for advancement in rank and in responsibility? Does the department have enough people to do the work properly and still keep everyone reasonably busy? What is the general morale of the personnel, including the attitude of each toward the others, toward the head of the department, and, of course, toward the company itself?

Extent and areas of current performance measurement

A recent study was conducted among 18 U.S. organizations to determine how these firms actually attempted to measure purchasing performance. The size of the purchasing organizations ranged from 10 to 650 people, and annual dollar purchases ranged from $35 million to $4 billion. This study concluded, among other things, that (1) each organization should pick those measures that best fit its operating situation, (2) several measures, rather than just one, are needed to provide a valid indicator of overall accomplishment, (3) a good data base is needed for measurement, and (4) since measurement is very costly, management should be very selective in deciding what and how much measurement should be attempted.

This study found that 13 categories were used by these organizations for purchasing performance measurement (the first six measures appeared to be the key, most important ones): (1) price effectiveness, (2) workload, (3) cost savings, (4) administration and control, (5) vendor quality and delivery, (6) material flow control, (7) efficiency, (8) regulatory/societal, environmental, (9) procurement planning and research, (10) competition, (11) inventory, (12) transportation, and (13) purchasing procedure audits.[4]

PURCHASING STRATEGY

Over the past 80 years the purchasing function has slowly evolved from a clerical type function to one which requires complex processes to provide information for effective decision making by professional buyers. This change in turn has stimulated the development of strategies to maximize the effectiveness of the performance of the function.

A purchasing strategy is made up of substrategies, all of which are conceived by using all available information to project a plan which is directed to the achievement of a specific purpose. Some of the more common substrategies are:

1.   The strategy of supplier development, selection and evaluation.

2.   The strategy of buying: (a) the use of negotiation, (b) competitive bidding, (c) systems contracting, (d) national contracts, (e) foreign buying, (f) forward buying, (g) hand-to-mouth buying.

---

[4]Robert M. Monczka and Phillip L. Carter, "Purchasing Performance: Measurement and Control," Executive Summary, Graduate School of Business Administration, Michigan State University, E. Lansing, Michigan, January, 1978, 26 pp. The study was supported by the National Science Foundation.

3. The strategy of cost reduction through value analysis and purchasing research.

The careful development of a purchasing strategy is a difficult task but necessary if the full potential of the function is to be achieved.

QUESTIONS FOR REVIEW AND DISCUSSION

1. How can management by objectives (MBO) fit into the management of the purchasing and materials management functions?
2. What kinds of information on purchasing performance should be maintained in the purchasing department? How can this information be used?
3. What is meant by purchasing strategy? Is it important? Why?
4. Why isn't there a standard system for evaluating purchasing performance that could be used by all types of firms or not-for-profit organizations? How difficult would it be to develop such a standard system?
5. Set up a model personnel policy for a purchasing department. What advantages would your policy have in the operation of the department?
6. When should purchasing performance be evaluated by an outside evaluator? How would that person go about making the evaluation?

CASE 16–1
RIVIERA COSMETICS INC.

Evelyn Dobson had recently joined Riviera Cosmetics as a packaging buyer. At the time of her hiring, both the director of purchasing and her immediate supervisor, the purchasing agent in charge of packaging and printing, had impressed upon her that on time delivery was absolutely critical for Riviera. Production and promotion plans were carefully coordinated and Riviera's distinctive packaging was a hallmark of the corporation's success. Thus, it was with considerable dismay that Evelyn found out that her monthly delivery performance computer report showed her to have the worst record of all fifteen buyers in the office.

Riviera Cosmetics was a large, successful firm in the industry marketing a full line of male and female cosmetics. Purchasing was centralized and there were three purchasing agents who looked after raw materials and chemicals, packaging, and MRO and equipment purchases, respectively. Evelyn was one of the four packaging buyers and she had been assigned the fast growing Unisex line.

After her first nine weeks on the job, the purchasing agent had called Evelyn into his office and showed her a "delivery performance report," a computer printout which listed all fifteen buyers and their monthly on time deliveries as a percentage of their total expected deliveries. Almost all buyers fell into the 80–90 percent range. According to this report, of the 75 line item deliveries scheduled under Evelyn's name, 33 had arrived late, giving a 56 percent on time delivery result.

Evelyn found this news very strange, since she had been aware of only three delivery difficulties during her first two months, each of which she had managed to resolve satisfactorily between production and the supplier. Therefore, she could not give the purchasing agent any reasons why the report would show her performance to be so poor. She also asked why she had not received a copy of the report herself. The purchasing agent replied it was company policy to send it only to purchasing agents to minimize paperwork and to encourage face to face supervisor-subordinate discussion of report contents. He also explained he did not bother discussing the first month's report with her, since he figured that performance was largely due to Evelyn's predecessor.

Evelyn discussed her situation with the other packaging buyers and they shrugged it off. They told her that the computer system was often incorrect and that what really counted was keeping production happy.

One buyer explained: "Receiving is often late sending receiving input to data processing. They handle over 60,000 line item receipts a year and it can be a madhouse down there at times. What I do is phone them twice a day to find out which of my orders have come in. At the same time I ask them if they have already processed the data and when they say no, I say: 'Do me a favour, and punch it in now, or else my boss will get mad at me.' You see, even though they have their own terminals down there they often wait for slack moments to put their data in and when the paperwork pile gets too high after awhile, nobody down there wants to sit down at the terminals for a long time. And once I know what is going on, I phone production planning to let them know, because if I don't phone them, they will call me."

Evelyn decided she might give this approach a try. However, when she called the receiving department and asked for the status on her orders, the receiving supervisor angrily replied: "What do you buyers think we do around here . . . run an answering service? You will find out your status from the computer reports. That's the way the system was planned and that's the way I want to keep it."

CASE 16–2
M.E.C. CORPORATION

In early March, 1979, Mr. Jack Allison, assistant manager of purchasing and traffic department, was made responsible for administering the purchasing savings program for the following year by Mr. Robert Cockrane, the department manager, who was due to retire in the near future. The savings program had been in effect for a number of years without change, and Jack

Allison wondered if the 1978 savings of some $150,000 on an eligible out-lay of $12 million could not be considerably improved. Therefore, he insti-tuted a review of methods, procedures, and attitudes to determine what course to adopt for the coming year.

M.E.C. Corporation was part of a large conglomerate which had been formed in 1966. M.E.C. produced a wide range of electrical products for the measurement and control of industrial processes. M.E.C. had started in 1926 and had been privately owned until 1966. It had an excellent reputation for quality in the trade. M.E.C. operated with a high degree of autonomy. The conglomerate's corporate headquarters were primarily concerned with fi-nancial planning. M.E.C.'s sales totaled about $30 million in 1978 and were expected to reach $50 million by 1982. M.E.C. was divided into two sales divisions, industrial and utilities. Each accounted for about half of total sales.

Purchasing at M.E.C.

Total purchases at M.E.C. were about 40 percent of sales and were the responsibility of Mr. Cochrane, director of purchases, who had been in his post for 22 years. Mr. Cochrane planned to retire in July, 1980, and had recently brought in Jack Allison, an engineer, who had previously worked in quality control and design at M.E.C. There were two purchasing agents and six buyers. For production purchases the department was organized into the same divisions as corporate sales: industrial and utilities (see Exhibit 1 for

Exhibit 1
Organization chart

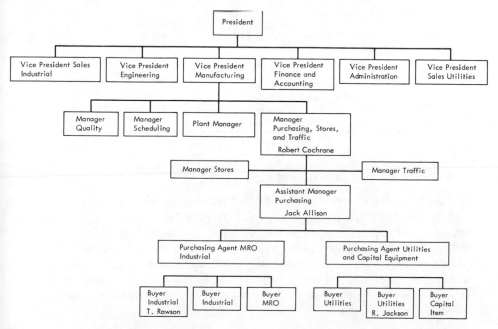

organization chart). Production purchases included raw materials like copper, steel, aluminum, and purchased parts like castings, stampings, and a wide variety of electrical and electronic items.

In April, 1978, the vice president of manufacturing took over responsibility for purchasing from the vice president administration who claimed that personnel and industrial relations matters prevented him from giving the purchasing function the necessary time.

Robert Cochrane told his assistant that before 1978 when he responded to the vice president administration, his reports of total savings realized used to elicit little interest.

"I think they do some cash flow projections up top," said the department manager casually, "but I guess our small savings are not that important. At any rate, they've never asked for savings forecasts. However, I think that the vice president of manufacturing will show more practical enthusiasm."

Savings in purchasing

Jack Allison had been given complete freedom to become acquainted with all facets of the purchasing operation. Robert Cochrane had thought it useful to give a few specific projects to Jack to work on during his familiarization phase, and the savings program was one area he asked Jack to take a good look at. Jack Allison went through the files to study past savings reports (see Exhibit 2) and talked to the buyers and purchasing agents about savings.

Exhibit 2

		1977 purchasing savings report	
From:	R. Cochrane		
To:	Vice President Administration		
	Total corporate purchases in 1977	$10.5 million	
	Total corporate savings in 1977	$120,000	
		1978 purchasing savings report	
From:	R. Cochrane		
To:	Vice President Manufacturing		
	Total corporate purchases in 1978	$12.0 million	
	Total corporate savings in 1978	$150,000	

Rules for reporting purchasing savings

Robert Cochrane had in September, 1968, established rules about how savings should be calculated (see Exhibit 3). Jack Allison found that while nearly all of the senior personnel had seen the rules some of the juniors had not, and Jack experienced some trouble in digging them out. One of the older men expressed some discontent at not being able to claim savings for more than one year ("They're still real enough after 12 months," he growled), but few held any strong opinions on them. One man said cynically

Exhibit 3
Rules for reporting purchasing savings

1. The material must have been purchased before.
2. Savings apply to orders placed within the calendar year under consideration.
3. Savings due to mixed contribution by purchasing and the personnel of other departments may not be claimed by the buying staff.
4. Savings are: a. The improvement over the old unit price multiplied by the projected annual usage at the time the first new order is placed, less tooling investment, if any.
   b. On indirect material where no forecast is available, utilize the one-time saving and any reorders in the same calendar year.
5. Savings may not be carried beyond one year. If a one-time, several-year commitment is made, credit may be claimed for the first year's estimated consumption.
6. Savings reports for the current calendar year must be submitted to me prior to January 31 of the next year.*

R. Cochrane,
Manager, Purchasing, Stores,
and Traffic

*M.E.C. Corporation's financial year-end was at the end of February.

that he doubted whether such reports were even read. "Has management heard of purchasing?" he inquired innocently. One of the purchasing agents thought that avoidance of cost increases through negotiation should also be included.

Savings report forms

Jack Allison studied the slender file of forms from previous years and discussed one of the cases (see Exhibit 4) with Mr. Cochrane. He mentioned that there were no supporting documents attached and wondered to what extent the claims were checked.

"Oh, the divisional buyers have a pretty good idea of what's what," said the manager, "so I never required them to clutter up their claims with a lot of documentation. However, as you know, all savings must be due to their efforts only. It's purchasing skills I'm demonstrating."

Jack Allison discussed the same savings report with T. Rawson, the buyer who had submitted it. "Would we work closely with production scheduling in such instances?" he asked. "For example, where did the consumption forecast come from?"

Rawson assured him that previous orders gave him a good idea of standard usage as it was a repetitive item, and that was how they usually derived their annual consumption for calculating claims. Of course, scheduling had cleared the requisition, but he never encouraged the operations people to pry into what he considered was purchasing's business. "It's just as well not to get these production guys involved in our commercial dealings with suppliers," he said seriously, "or before you know it you have back-door selling on your hands."

Exhibit 4
Buyer's savings report

```
Division _____SERVO_____                          Date: August 21/78

1. M.E.C. part number: 15723
2. Description: _____9V Nickel Battery Enclosure
3. Yearly usage: _____240,000
4. Purchase order no. (if applicable) S54754-1010
5. Savings Accomplished:
   Previous price: 93.6¢
   New unit price: 72.0¢
   Savings per unit: 21.6¢
   Saving this order: $51,840
   Savings per year: $51,840
6. How Was Saving Accomplished?
   Through the efforts of Ralph Jackson and myself placing orders simultaneously to earn
   the next price break and going a little long (with Division's agreement) on
   inventory.

7. Comments: It is my opinion that without interdivisional exchange of buying
   intelligence on common commodities this saving would not have come about.

                                        Submitted by: T. Rawson
                                        Approved: R. Cochrane
                                        Date: August, 1978
```

Motivation

Jack Allison found that the savings program played a relatively small part in the buyers' plans. It was something to be reported when the situation arose. Furthermore, he noted that higher in the buying echelon interest was desultory, as large orders were automatically handled by the seniors. Even Mr. Cochrane used to take a hand in the negotiation of equipment until the last year or so. The seniors skimmed the cream off. Relatively little attention was given to value analysis techniques.

Organization

Some cases of the two divisions buying the same material or components at different times without one buyer being conscious of the other's efforts had come to light. Separate savings reports dealing with the same commodity brought this to Jack Allison's attention.

Jack Allison had noted the buyers' reluctance to talk about their savings expertise outside of the department and wondered how necessary this secrecy was. It made him recall his own ignorance of what purchasing was done when he was a member of the design or quality groups at M.E.C. He also wondered what action, if any, he should take now that the savings program had become his responsibility.

BIBLIOGRAPHIES

GENERAL BIBLIOGRAPHY

Aljian, George W., ed. *Purchasing Handbook.* 3d ed. New York: McGraw-Hill Book Co., 1973.

Ammer, Dean S. *Materials Management.* 3d ed. Homewood, Ill.: Richard D. Irwin, Inc., 1974.

Baily, Peter, and Farmer, David. *Managing Materials in Industry.* London: Gower Press, 1972.

Ballou, Ronald H. *Business Logistics Management.* rev. ed. International Management Service. Englewood Cliffs, N.J.: Prentice-Hall, 1972.

Barlow, C. Wayne. *Purchasing for the Newly Appointed Buyer.* New York: American Management Association, 1970.

Buckner, Hugh. *How British Industry Buys.* London: Hutchinson, 1969.

Corey, E. Raymond. *Procurement Management: Strategy, Organization, and Decision-Making.* Boston: CBI Publishing Co., 1978.

Dand, R., and Farmer, D. *Purchasing in the Construction Industry,* London: Gower Press, 1970.

Daniel, Norman E., and Jones, J. Richard. *Readings in Business Logistics Concepts and Viewpoints.* Boston: Allyn and Bacon, Inc., 1969.

Dowst, Somerby H. *Basics for Buyers: A Practical Guide to Better Purchasing.* Boston: Cahners Books, 1971.

Fearon, Harold E. *Purchasing Economics.* New York: American Management Association, Purchasing Division. 1968.

Gravereau, Victor P., and Konopa, Leonard J., ed. *Purchasing Management: Selected Readings.* Columbus, O.: Grid, Inc., 1973.

Hedrick, Floyd D. *Purchasing Management in the Smaller Company.* New York: American Management Association, Inc., 1971.

Heinritz, Stuart F., and Farrell, Paul V. *Purchasing: Principles and Applications.* 5th ed. Englewood Cliffs, N.J.: Prentice-Hall, Inc., 1971.

International Federation of Purchasing: *Glossary of Purchasing and Supply Terms,* Brussels, Belgium: International Federation of Purchasing, 1972 (polyglot).

Lee, Lamar, Jr., and Dobler, Donald W. *Purchasing and Materials Management.* 3d ed. New York: McGraw-Hill Book Co., 1977.

McElhiney, Paul T., and Cook, Robert I. *The Logistics of Materials Management: Readings in Modern Purchasing.* New York: Houghton-Mifflin Co., Inc., 1969.

McMillan, Archibald Livingston. *Purchasing.* Scranton: International Correspondence Schools, 1969.

National Association of Purchasing Management, Inc. *Guide to Purchasing.* Vols. 1–3, New York; 1965, 1968, 1973.

Pegram, Roger M. *Purchasing Practices in the Smaller Company.* New York: Industrial Conference Board, 1972.

Scientific American. *How Industry Buys/1970.* New York: Scientific American, Inc., 1970.

Spinrad, P.   *Best in Purchasing,* New York: American Management Association, 1972.

Stelzer, W. R.   *Materials Management.* Englewood Cliffs, N.J.: Prentice-Hall, Inc., 1970.

Sussams, J. E.   *Industrial Logistics.* Boston: Cahners Books, 1972.

Tersine, R. J. and Campbell, J. H.   *Modern Materials Management.* New York: North-Holland, 1977.

Westing, J. H.; Fine, I. V.; and Zenz, Gary Joseph.   *Purchasing Management.* 4th ed. New York: John Wiley & Sons, Inc., 1976.

CHAPTER BIBLIOGRAPHIES

Chapter 1

Barath, Robert M., and Hagstad, Paul S.   "The Effects of Professionalism on Purchasing Managers," *Journal of Purchasing and Materials Management,* Spring 1979.

Bauer, Frank L.   "Better Purchasing: High Rewards at Low Risk," *Journal of Purchasing and Materials Management,* Summer 1976.

Bonfield, E. H., and Speh, Thomas W.   "Dimensions of Purchasing's Role in Industry." *Journal of Purchasing and Materials Management,* Summer 1977.

Spratlen, Thaddeus H.   "The Impact of Affirmative Action Purchasing." *Journal of Purchasing and Materials Management,* Spring 1978.

Chapter 2

American Management Association.   *Purchasing Department Organization and Authority.* Edited by George H. Haas et al. Research Study No. 45. New York: 1960.

Drucker, Peter F.   *Management: Tasks, Responsibilities, Practices.* New York: Harper & Row, 1973.

Ericson, Dag.   *Materials Administration.* Maidenhead: McGraw-Hill Book Company (UK) Limited, 1974.

Fearon, Harold E.   "Materials Management: A Synthesis and Current View." *Journal of Purchasing and Materials Management,* Summer 1975, pp. 37–43.

Toyne, Brian, and Rumpel, Charles H.   "Buying Authority in Multinational Corporation." *Journal of Purchasing and Materials Management,* Spring 1978.

Webster, Frederick E., and Wind, Yoram.   *Organizational Buying Behavior.* Englewood Cliffs, N.J.: Prentice-Hall, Inc. 1972.

Wind, Yoram.   "The Boundaries of Buying Decision Centres." *Journal of Purchasing and Materials Management,* Summer 1978.

Chapter 3

Blitz, Jack Francis.   *Policies and Techniques for Progressive Purchasing.* London: Industrial and Commercial Techniques, 1971.

Campanella, Joseph J., and Fearon, Harold E.   "An Integrated Computer Materials Management System." *Journal of Purchasing* 6 (August 1970): 5–27.

Cantor, Jeremiah.   *Evaluating Purchasing Systems.* New York: American Management Association, 1970.

Cone, R. J.   "Purchasing in the New Computer Environment." *Journal of Purchasing and Materials Management,* Summer 1978.

Elliott, Clifford. "Purchasing Attitudes toward EDP." *Journal of Purchasing and Materials Management,* Summer 1976.

Fearon, Harold E., and Moore, D. Larry. "Why Haven't Computers Been Used More Effectively in Purchasing." *Journal of Purchasing and Materials Management* 10 (August 1974): 30–39.

Moore, D. Larry, and Fearon, Harold E. "Computer-Assisted Decision-Making in Purchasing." *Journal of Purchasing* 9 (November 1973): 5–25.

Moore, D. Larry, and Fearon, Harold E. "Computer Operating and Management-Reporting Systems in Purchasing." *Journal of Purchasing* 9 (August 1973): 13–39.

Chapter 4

Brady, G. S. *Materials Handbook.* 10th ed. New York: McGraw-Hill Book Co., 1973.

Brown, Arthur W. "Technical Support for Procurement." *Journal of Purchasing and Materials Management,* Spring 1976.

Crosbie, Philip B. *Quality is Free.* New York: McGraw-Hill Book Co. 1979.

Desmond, David J. *Quality Control Workbook.* Boston: Cahners Books, 1971.

Lambert, David R. "Purchasing Confidence vis-a-vis Engineering." *Journal of Purchasing and Materials Management,* Spring 1976.

Springer, Robert M. Jr. "Risks and Benefits in Reliability Warranties." *Journal of Purchasing and Materials Management,* Spring 1977.

Chapter 5

Anthony, Ted F., and Buffa, Frank P. "Strategic Purchase Scheduling." *Journal of Purchasing and Materials Management,* Fall 1977.

Brooks, William A., and Alexander, Wayne Stephen. "Two Emerging Methods of Inventory Control." *Journal of Purchasing and Materials Management,* Summer 1977.

Carter, Phillip L., and Monczka, Robert M. "MRO Inventory Pooling." *Journal of Purchasing and Materials Management,* Fall 1978.

Chase, Richard B., and Aquilano, Nicholas J. *Production and Operations Management.* Rev. ed. Homewood, Ill.: Richard D. Irwin, Inc., 1977.

Clark, N. Les. "Closing the Planning-Operations Gap." *Journal of Purchasing and Materials Management,* Winter 1977.

Dewelt, Robert L. "Make Inventory a Working Asset." *Journal of Purchasing and Materials Management,* Spring 1977.

Fox, Harold W., and Rink, David R. "Coordination of Purchasing with Sales Trends." *Journal of Purchasing and Materials Management,* Winter 1977.

Fulbright, John E. "Advantages and Disadvantages of the EOQ Model." *Journal of Purchasing and Materials Management,* Spring 1979.

Johnson, Lynwood A., and Montgomery, Douglas C. *Operations Research in Production, Planning, Scheduling, and Inventory Control.* New York: John Wiley & Sons, Inc., 1974.

Monahan, James P., and Berger, Paul D. "Economically Sound Forecasts for EOQ Analysis." *Journal of Purchasing and Materials Management,* Winter 1976.

Orlicky, Joseph. *Material Requirements Planning*. New York: McGraw-Hill Book Co., 1975.

Phillips, Thomas E. "Management of Parts Inventories." *Journal of Purchasing and Materials Management,* Summer 1978.

Plossl, George W., and Welch, W. Evert. *The Role of Top Management in the Control of Inventory*. Reston: Reston Publishing Co., 1979.

Reuter, Vincent G. "The Big Gap in Inventory Management." *Journal of Purchasing and Materials Management,* Fall 1978.

Whybark, D. Clay. "Evaluating Alternative Quantity Discounts." *Journal of Purchasing and Materials Management,* Summer 1977.

Wiesner, Donald A. "Coordination of Purchasing with Sales Trends." *Journal of Purchasing and Materials Management,* Winter 1977.

Zimmerman, Steven M., and Glover, Douglas. "Combining EOQ and MRP to Optimize Savings." *Journal of Purchasing and Materials Management,* Winter 1977.

Chapter 6

Brokaw, Alan J., and Davisson, Charles N. "Positioning a Company as a Preferred Customer." *Journal of Purchasing and Materials Management,* Spring 1978.

Cavinato, Joseph L., and Perreault, William D. Jr. "Evaluating Vendors' Distribution Service." *Journal of Purchasing and Materials Management,* Summer 1976.

Cooley, James R.; Jackson, Donald W.; and Ostrom, Lonnie L. "Relative Power in Industrial Buying Decisions." *Journal of Purchasing and Materials Management,* Spring 1978.

Cooper, Steve D. "A Total System for Measuring Delivery Performance," *Journal of Purchasing and Materials Management,* Fall 1977.

Farmer, David H., and Macmillan, Keith. "Voluntary Collaboration vs. Disloyalty." *Journal of Purchasing and Materials Management,* Winter 1976.

Lamberson, L. R.; Diederich, J.; and Wuori, J. "Quantitative Vendor Evaluation." *Journal of Purchasing and Materials Management,* Spring 1976.

Roberts Barry J. "A Vendor Delivery Rating Model." *Journal of Purchasing and Materials Management,* Fall 1978.

Sibley, Stanley D. "How Interfacing Departments Rate Vendors." *Journal of Purchasing and Materials Management,* Summer 1978.

Wieters, C. David. "Influences on Vendor Rating Systems." *Journal of Purchasing and Materials Management,* Winter 1976.

Chapter 7

Bagot, J. Keith. *The Profit Potential of Purchasing Negotiations*. New York: American Management Association, Purchasing Division, 1968.

Browning, John M., and Andrews, M. A. "Target Purchasing: the Price-Volume Distinction." *Journal of Purchasing and Materials Management,* Summer 1978.

Dowst, Somerby R. "Better Bids Make Better Buys." In *Basics for Buyers*, pp. 13–17. Boston: Cahners Books, 1971.

Johnson, James C. "How Competitive is Delivered Pricing?" *Journal of Purchasing and Materials Management,* Summer 1976.

Jordon, R. B. "Learning How to Use the Learning Curve." *Bulletin of the National Association of Accountants,* January 1958, pp. 27–39; June 1958, pp. 77–78.

Karras, Chester L. *Give and Take: The Complete Guide to Negotiating Strategies and Tactics.* New York: Thomas Y. Crowell Company, 1974.

Karras, Chester L. *The Negotiating Game.* New York: World Publishing Co., 1970.

Long, Brian G., and Varble, Dale L. "Purchasing's Use of Flexible Price Contracts." *Journal of Purchasing and Materials Management,* Fall 1978.

Nierenberg, Gerald I. *Creative Business Negotiating: Skills and Successful Strategies.* New York: Hawthorn Books, Inc., 1971.

Pace, Dean Francis. *Negotiation and Management of Defense Contracts.* New York: John Wiley & Sons., Inc., 1970.

Chapter 8

Arthur, Henry B. *Commodity Futures as a Business Management Tool.* Boston: Harvard Business School, Division of Research, 1971.

Brown, C. P. *Primary Commodity Control.* New York: Oxford University Press, 1975.

de Keyser, ed. *Guide to World Commodity Markets.* New York: Nichols Publishing Company, 1977.

Dow Jones & Company. *The Dow Jones Commodities Handbood.* Princeton, N. J.: Dow Jones Books, 1976.

Giles, Harry Ed. *Forecasting Commodity Prices: How the Experts Analyze the Markets.* New York: Commodity Research Bureau, 1975.

Tersine, Richard J., and Grasso, Edward T. "Forward Buying in Response to Announced Price Increase." *Journal of Purchasing and Materials Management,* Summer 1978.

Zenz, G. S. *Futures Trading and the Purchasing Executive.* New York: Merrill Lynch. Pierce, Fenner, and Smith Co. and The National Association of Purchasing Management, 1971.

Chapter 9

Carmody, D. B., and O'Shaughnessy, John. "Interdepartmental Coordination in Buying Capital Equipment." *Journal of Purchasing and Materials Management,* Spring 1979.

Hamel, Henry G. *Leasing in Industry.* New York: National Industrial Conference Board, 1968.

Machinery and Allied Products Institute. *Leasing of Industrial Equipment.* Washington, D.C., 1965.

Robles, Herbert M. "Competitive Procurement of EDP Equipment." *Journal of Purchasing and Materials Management,* Winter 1976.

Chapter 10

Culliton, James W. *Make or Buy*. 4th reprint. Business Research Study No. 27. Boston: Harvard Business School, Division of Research, 1956.

Gross, Harry. *Make or Buy*. Englewood Cliffs, N.J.: Prentice-Hall, Inc., 1966.

Oxenfeldt, Alfred R. *Make or Buy: Factors Affecting Decisions*. New York: McGraw-Hill Book Co., 1965.

Chapter 11

Bird, Monroe Murphy, and Clopton, Stephen W. "A New Look at Scrap Management." *Journal of Purchasing and Materials Management*, Winter 1977.

Chapter 12

French, Warren; Henkel, Jan; and Cox, James, III. "When the Buyer is the Object of Price Discrimination." *Journal of Purchasing and Materials Management*, Spring 1979.

Murray, John E., Jr. *Purchasing and the Law*. Pittsburgh, Penn.: Purchasing Management Association of Pittsburgh, 1977.

Werner, Ray O. "Robinson-Patman: Purchasing's Responsibility Still Unclear." *Journal of Purchasing and Materials Management*, Spring 1978.

White, James J. "The Warranty Bill's Effect on Purchasing." *Journal of Purchasing and Materials Management*, Summer 1976.

Chapter 13

Jerman, Roger E.; Anderson, Ronald D.; and Constantin, James A. "Shipper/Carrier Perspectives on Transportation Regulation." *Journal of Purchasing and Materials Management*, Spring 1977.

Khan, M. A., and Neubauer, William C., Jr. "Bi-modal Movement of Air Cargo: Progress and Problems." *Journal of Purchasing and Materials Management*, Spring 1979.

Sampson, Roy J., and Farris, Martin T. *Domestic Transportation: Practice, Theory, and Policy*, 4th ed. Boston: Houghton Mifflin Co., 1979.

Stock, James R., and La Londe, Bernard J. "The Purchasing Approach to Transportation Mode Selection." *Journal of Purchasing and Materials Management*, Spring 1978.

Taff, Charles A. *Management of Physical Distribution and Transportation*. 6th ed. Homewood, Ill.: Richard D. Irwin, Inc., 1978.

Chapter 14

Blissett, Marlan. "Conservation of Energy in Public Procurement." *Journal of Purchasing and Materials Management*, Spring 1978.

Government Contracts Guide Chicago: Commerce Clearing House, Inc., 1972.

Jennings, George W.   *State Purchasing: The Essentials of a Modern Service for Modern Government*. Lexington, Ky.: The Council of State Governments, 1969.

Munsterman, Richard E.   *Purchasing and Supply Management Handbook for School Business Officials*, Research Bulletin No. 22 Chicago: Association of School Business Officials of the United States and Canada, 1978.

Ritterskamp, James J. Jr.; Abbott, Forrest L.; and Ahrens, Bert C.   *Purchasing for Educational Institutions*. New York: Bureau of Publications, Teachers College, Columbia University, 1961.

Steinhauer, Raleigh F.   "Intergovernmental Cooperative Purchasing." *Journal of Purchasing and Materials Management*, Spring 1976.

Chapter 15

Bauer, Frank L.   "Managerial Planning in Procurement." *Journal of Purchasing and Materials Management*, Fall 1977.

Clawson, Robert H.   *Value Engineering for Management*. New York: Auerbach Publishers, Inc., 1970.

Elliott-Jones, M. F.   *Input-Output Analysis: A Nontechnical Description*. New York: The Conference Board, 1971.

Fallon, Charles.   *Value Analysis to Improve Productivity*. New York: John Wiley & Sons, Inc., 1971.

Fearon, Harold.   *Purchasing Research: Concepts and Current Practice*. New York: AMACOM, A Division of American Management Association, 1976.

Fisk, John C.   "Procurement Planning and Control." *Journal of Purchasing and Materials Management*, Spring 1979.

Miles, L. D.   *Techniques of Value Analysis and Engineering*. 2d ed. New York: McGraw-Hill Book Co., 1972.

Monczka, Robert M., and Fearon, Harold E.   "Coping with Material Shortages." *Journal of Purchasing and Materials Management*, May 1974, pp. 5–19.

Mudge, Arthur E.   *Value Engineering: A Systematic Approach*. New York: McGraw-Hill Book Co., 1971.

"Now the Squeeze is on Metals." *Business Week, 2 July 1979, pp. 46–51*.

Paperman, Jacob B., and Shell, Richard L.   "The Accounting Approach to Performance." *Journal of Purchasing and Materials Management*, Summer 1977.

Valentine, Raymond F.   Value Analysis for Better Systems and Procedures. Englewood Cliffs, N. J.: Prentice-Hall, Inc., 1970.

Chapter 16

Cone, R. J.   "Dramatizing Purchasing Recognition." *Journal of Purchasing and Materials Management*, Summer 1976.

Croell, Richard C.   "Measuring Purchasing Effectiveness." *Journal of Purchasing and Materials Management*, Spring 1977.

Farmer, David H.   "Developing Purchasing Strategies." *Journal of Purchasing and Materials Management*, Fall 1978.

Kiser, G. E., and Rink, David. "Use of PLC Concept in Purchasing Strategies." *Journal of Purchasing and Materials Management,* Winter 1976.

Mendleson, Jack L. "Evaluating Purchasing Performance." *Journal of Purchasing,* August 1969, pp. 59–76.

Miller, J. Charles. "Supplier Turnover Rate as a Purchasing Measurement." *Journal of Purchasing and Materials Management,* Spring 1978.

Monczka, Robert M.; Carter, Phillip L.; and Hoagland, John H. *Purchasing Performance Measurement and Control.* East Lansing, Mich.: Division of Research, Graduate School of Business Administration, Michigan State University, 1979.

Pestel, Eduard. "The Long Range Outlook for Critical Materials." *Journal of Purchasing and Materials Management,* Fall 1977.

Rao, C. P. "Some Long Term Perspectives for Purchasing Management." *Journal of Purchasing and Materials Management,* Winter 1977.

Reck, Ross R. "Purchasing Effectiveness." *Journal of Purchasing and Materials Management,* Summer 1978.

INDEX TO CASES

571

SUBJECT INDEX

This book has been set VIP in 10 and 9 point Times Roman, leaded 2 points. Chapter numbers are 52 point Times Roman and chapter titles are 20 point Optima. The size of the type page is 27 by 47 picas.